# THE ARDEN SHAKESPEARE

## THIRD SERIES
General Editors: Richard Proudfoot, Ann Thompson
and David Scott Kastan

# TROILUS
# AND
# CRESSIDA

# THE ARDEN SHAKESPEARE

| | |
|---|---|
| ALL'S WELL THAT ENDS WELL | edited by G. K. Hunter |
| ANTONY AND CLEOPATRA | edited by John Wilders* |
| AS YOU LIKE IT | edited by Agnes Latham |
| THE COMEDY OF ERRORS | edited by R. A. Foakes |
| CORIOLANUS | edited by Philip Brockbank |
| CYMBELINE | edited by J. M. Nosworthy |
| HAMLET | edited by Harold Jenkins |
| JULIUS CAESAR | edited by David Daniell* |
| KING HENRY IV Parts 1 and 2 | edited by A. R. Humphreys |
| KING HENRY V | edited by T. W. Craik* |
| KING HENRY VI Parts 1, 2 and 3 | edited by A. S. Cairncross |
| KING HENRY VIII | edited by R. A. Foakes |
| KING JOHN | edited by E. A. J. Honigmann |
| KING LEAR | edited by R. A. Foakes* |
| KING RICHARD II | edited by Peter Ure |
| KING RICHARD III | edited by Antony Hammond |
| LOVE'S LABOUR'S LOST | edited by H. R. Woudhuysen* |
| MACBETH | edited by Kenneth Muir |
| MEASURE FOR MEASURE | edited by J. W. Lever |
| THE MERCHANT OF VENICE | edited by John Russell Brown |
| THE MERRY WIVES OF WINDSOR | edited by H. J. Oliver |
| A MIDSUMMER NIGHT'S DREAM | edited by Harold F. Brooks |
| MUCH ADO ABOUT NOTHING | edited by A. R. Humphreys |
| OTHELLO | edited by E. A. J. Honigmann* |
| PERICLES | edited by F. D. Hoeniger |
| THE POEMS | edited by F. T. Prince |
| ROMEO AND JULIET | edited by Brian Gibbons |
| SHAKESPEARE'S SONNETS | edited by Katherine Duncan-Jones* |
| THE TAMING OF THE SHREW | edited by Brian Morris |
| THE TEMPEST | edited by Frank Kermode |
| TIMON OF ATHENS | edited by H. J. Oliver |
| TITUS ANDRONICUS | edited by Jonathan Bate* |
| TROILUS AND CRESSIDA | edited by David Bevington* |
| TWELFTH NIGHT | edited by J. M. Lothian and T. W. Craik |
| THE TWO GENTLEMEN OF VERONA | edited by Clifford Leech |
| THE TWO NOBLE KINSMEN | edited by Lois Potter* |
| THE WINTER'S TALE | edited by J. H. P. Pafford |

\* Third series

THE ARDEN SHAKESPEARE

# TROILUS AND CRESSIDA

Edited by
DAVID BEVINGTON

The Arden website is at
http://www.ardenshakespeare.com/

The general editors of the Arden Shakespeare have been
W.J. Craig and R.H. Case (first series 1899–1944)
Una Ellis-Fermor, Harold F. Brooks, Harold Jenkins
and Brian Morris (second series 1946–82)

Present general editors (third series)
Richard Proudfoot, Ann Thompson and David Scott Kastan

This edition of *Troilus and Cressida*, by David Bevington,
first published 1998 by Thomas Nelson and Sons Ltd

Thomas Nelson and Sons Ltd
Nelson House  Mayfield Road
Walton-on-Thames  Surrey KT12 5PL  UK

I(T)P ® Thomas Nelson is an International
Thomson Publishing Company
I(T)P ® is used under licence

Editorial material © 1998 David Bevington

Typeset in Ehrhardt by Multiplex Techniques Ltd
Printed in Italy

*British Library Cataloguing in Publication Data*
A catalogue record for this book is available from the British Library

*Library of Congress Cataloging in Publication Data*
A catalogue record has been applied for

ISBN 0–17–443570-3 (hbk)
ISBN 0–17–443537-1 (pbk)

NPN   9  8  7  6  5  4  3  2  1

For
Janet Adelman
and
Richard Proudfoot

*The Editor*

David Bevington is Phyllis Fay Horton Professor in the Humanities at the University of Chicago. He has edited the Complete Works of Shakespeare in a single volume for HarperCollins (now Longman) and in individual paperbacks for the Bantam Shakespeare, as well as *King Henry IV Part I* (Oxford University Press) and *Antony and Cleopatra* (New Cambridge Shakespeare). He is the editor of *Medieval Drama* (Houghton Mifflin). His many other publications include *From 'Mankind' to Marlowe*, *Tudor Drama and Politics*, and *Action is Eloquence: Shakespeare's Language of Gesture*.

# CONTENTS

List of illustrations    ix

General editors' preface    xii

Preface    xvi

Introduction    1

*'A new play, never staled with the stage':*
*genre and the question of original*
*performance*    1

*'An envious fever of pale and bloodless emulation':*
*historical context in the last years of*
*Elizabeth's reign*    6

*'Wars and lechery':*
*demystification of the heroes of ancient Greece*    19

*''Tis but the chance of war':*
*sceptical deflation of Trojan honour and chivalry*    29

*'The gods have heard me swear':*
*tragic irony and the death of Hector*    33

*'As true as Troilus':*
*male obsessions about honour and sexuality*    37

*'As false as Cressid':*
*women as objects of desire*    47

*'Call them all panders':*
*voyeurism and male bonding*    59

*'What's aught but as 'tis valued?':*
*commercial and subjective valuation of*
*identity and worth*    67

*'Divides more wider than the sky and earth':*
    *the fragmentation of the divided self*         76
*'Stuff to make paradoxes':*
    *performance history of* Troilus and Cressida     87

## TROILUS AND CRESSIDA     119

Longer Notes                                  355

*'Instructed by the antiquary times':*
    *Shakespeare's sources*                      375
*'Words, words, mere words':*
    *The text of* Troilus and Cressida           398

Abbreviations and references
    *Abbreviations used in notes*                430
    *Shakespeare's works and works partly*
        *by Shakespeare*                         431
    *Editions of Shakespeare collated*           432
    *Ancient texts*                              435
    *Other works*                                436

Index                                         463

# LIST OF
# ILLUSTRATIONS

1   The first page of the publisher's advertisement added
    to the second 'state' of the 1609 Quarto (courtesy of the
    British Library, C34.k.61 P2)                                    2

2   Ben Jonson, in a nineteenth-century engraving after a
    contemporary portrait (courtesy of AKG, London)                 8

3   Robert Devereux, second Earl of Essex (1566–1601), by
    Marcus Gheeraerts the Younger (c. 1561–1635) (courtesy of
    the Bridgeman Art Library)                                      13

4   An Attic red-figure cup showing a fifth-century BC view
    of the struggle between Hector and Ajax, as depicted
    by Shakespeare in 4.5.95ff. The cup was made by Kaliades
    and painted by Douris, c. 490 BC (courtesy of Giraudon, Paris)  20

5   Alan Howard as Achilles and Richard Jones Barry as
    Patroclus in John Barton's production for the Royal
    Shakespeare Company, 1968 (courtesy of Zoe Dominic
    Photography)                                                    27

6   Detail from a fresco by Giulio Romano (1492–1546) and
    his workshop depicting Achilles in his chariot as he drags
    the body of the dead Hector; see 5.9–11. From the ceiling
    of the Sala di Troia, Palazzo Ducale, Mantua, c. 1538
    (courtesy of the Bridgeman Art Library)                         34

7   Clive Francis as a syphilitic drag-queen Pandarus, with
    Victoria Hamilton as Cressida, in Act 1, scene 2 of Ian Judge's
    production for the Royal Shakespeare Company, 1996
    (courtesy of Donald Cooper/Photostage)                          60

8 Oriel Ross as Helen and Max Adrian as Pandarus in
Michael Macowan's production for the London Mask
Theatre Company, 1938 (courtesy of the Manders &
Mitcheson Theatre Collection)                                    97

9 Tony Church as Pandarus, dead on barbed wire at the end of
Terry Hands's Royal Shakespeare Company production, 1981
(courtesy of Donald Cooper/Photostage)                          107

10 Juliet Stevenson as Cressida and Joseph O'Connor as
Agamemnon in Howard Davies's production for the Royal
Shakespeare Company, 1985 (courtesy of Joe Cocks Studio
Collection, Shakespeare Centre library)                         110

11 Alun Armstrong plays Thersites as a Geordie waiter
in Howard Davies's production for the Royal Shakespeare
Company, 1985 (courtesy of Chris Davies, Royal Shakespeare
Centre Library)                                                 112

12 Simon Russell Beale plays Thersites as a 'skid-row bum'
in Sam Mendes's 1990 production for the Royal
Shakespeare Company (courtesy of Donald Cooper/
Photostage)                                                     115

13 The title-page of the first 'state' of the 1609 Quarto
(courtesy of the British Library, 163.i.12)                     124

14 The title-page of the second 'state' of the 1609 Quarto       125
(courtesy of the British Library, C34.k.61)

15 The Folio cancel of the original setting of the first page of
*Troilus and Cressida*, backing the end of *Romeo and Juliet*
(courtesy of the Folger Shakespeare Library,
Washington, DC)                                                 403

16 The reset and enlarged version of the Folio first page of
*Troilus and Cressida*, backing a 'Prologue' to *Troilus and
Cressida* (courtesy of the Huntington, San Marino, CA)          404

17 4.5.97–109, as printed in the 1609 Quarto                     415
(courtesy of the British Library, C34.k.61, sig 12, r & v)

18  4.5.97–109, as printed in the 1623 Folio
(courtesy of the Huntington, San Marino, CA)                416

19  5.3.107ff. as printed in the 1609 Quarto, lacking the three
lines that appear in 5.3 of the Folio; both Q and F print
essentially the same lines at 5.11.32 4 (courtesy of the
British Library, C34.k.61, sig L2v)                417

20  5.3.107ff. as printed in the 1623 Folio, containing three
lines (the last three lines in this excerpt) that do not appear
in 5.3 of the Quarto (courtesy of the Huntington,
San Marino, CA)                418

# GENERAL EDITORS'
# PREFACE

The Arden Shakespeare is now nearly one hundred years old. The earliest volume in the first series, Edward Dowden's *Hamlet*, was published in 1899. Since then the Arden Shakespeare has become internationally recognized and respected. It is now widely acknowledged as the pre-eminent Shakespeare series, valued by scholars, students, actors, and 'the great variety of readers' alike for its readable and reliable texts, its full annotation and its richly informative introductions.

We have aimed in the third Arden edition to maintain the quality and general character of its predecessors, preserving the commitment to presenting the play as it has been shaped in history. While each individual volume will necessarily have its own emphasis in the light of the unique possibilities and problems posed by the play, the series as a whole, like the earlier Ardens, insists upon the highest standards of scholarship and upon attractive and accessible presentation.

Newly edited from the original quarto and folio editions, the texts are presented in fully modernized form, with a textual apparatus that records all substantial divergences from those early printings. The notes and introductions focus on the conditions and possibilities of meaning that editors, critics and performers (on stage and screen) have discovered in the play. While building upon the rich history of scholarly and theatrical activity that has long shaped our understanding of the texts of Shakespeare's plays, this third series of the Arden Shakespeare is made necessary and possible by a new generation's encounter with Shakespeare, engaging with the plays and their complex relation to the culture in which they were – and continue to be – produced.

## THE TEXT

On each page of the work itself, readers will find a passage of text followed by commentary and, finally, textual notes. Act and scene divisions (seldom present in the early editions and often the product of eighteenth-century or later scholarship) have been retained for ease of reference, but have been given less prominence than in the previous series. Editorial indications of location of the action have been removed to the textual notes or commentary.

In the text itself, unfamiliar typographic conventions have been avoided in order to minimize obstacles to the reader. Elided forms in the early texts are spelt out in full in verse lines wherever they indicate a usual late-twentieth-century pronunciation that requires no special indication and wherever they occur in prose (except when they indicate non-standard pronunciation). In verse speeches, marks of elision are retained where they are necessary guides to the scansion and pronunciation of the line. Final -ed in past tense and participial forms of verbs is always printed as -ed without accent, never as -'d, but wherever the required pronunciation diverges from modern usage a note in the commentary draws attention to the fact. Where the final -ed should be given syllabic value contrary to modern usage, e.g.

> Doth Silvia know that I am banished?
> (TGV 3.1.221)

the note will take the form

221 **banished** banishèd

Conventional lineation of divided verse lines shared by two or more speakers has been reconsidered and sometimes rearranged. Except for the familiar *Exit* and *Exeunt*, Latin forms in stage directions and speech prefixes have been translated into English and the original Latin forms recorded in the textual notes.

## COMMENTARY AND TEXTUAL NOTES

Notes in the commentary, for which a major source will be the *Oxford English Dictionary*, offer glossarial and other explication of verbal difficulties; they may also include discussion of points of theatrical interpretation and, in relevant cases, substantial extracts from Shakespeare's source material. Editors will not usually offer glossarial notes for words adequately defined in the *Concise Oxford Dictionary* or *Webster's Ninth New Collegiate Dictionary*, but in cases of doubt they will include notes. Attention, however, will be drawn to places where more than one likely interpretation can be proposed and to significant verbal and syntactic complexity. Notes preceded by * involve readings in which the rival textual claims of competing early editions (Quarto and Folio) are in dispute.

Headnotes to acts or scenes discuss, where appropriate, questions of scene location, Shakespeare's handling of his source materials, and major difficulties of staging. The list of roles (so headed to emphasize the play's status as a text for performance) is also considered in commentary notes. These may include comment on plausible patterns of casting with the resources of an Elizabethan or Jacobean acting company, and also on any variation in the description of roles in their speech prefixes in the early editions.

The textual notes are designed to let readers know when the edited text diverges from the early edition(s) on which it is based. Wherever this happens the note will record the rejected reading of the early edition(s), in original spelling, and the source of the reading adopted in this edition. Other forms from the early edition(s) recorded in these notes will include some spellings of particular interest or significance and original forms of translated stage directions. Where two early editions are involved, for instance with *Othello*, the notes will also record all important differences between them. The textual notes take a form that has been in use since the nineteenth century. This comprises, first: line reference, reading adopted in the text and closing square bracket; then: abbreviated reference, in italic, to the earliest edition to adopt the accepted reading, italic semicolon and noteworthy alternative reading(s), beginning with the rejected original reading, each with abbreviated italic reference to its source.

Conventions used in these textual notes include the following. The solidus / is used, in notes quoting verse or discussing verse lining, to indicate line endings. Distinctive spellings of the basic text (Q or F) follow the square bracket without indication of source and are enclosed in italic brackets. Names enclosed in italic brackets indicate originators of conjectural emendations when these did not originate in an edition of the text, or when this edition records a conjecture not accepted into its text. Stage directions (SDs) are referred to by the number of the line within or immediately after which they are placed. Line numbers with a decimal point relate to SDs not falling within a verse line and to SDs more than one line long, with the number after the point indicating the line within the SD: e.g. 78.4 refers to the fourth line of the SD following line 78. Lines of SDs at the start of a scene are numbered 0.1, 0.2, etc. Where only a line number and SD precede the square bracket, e.g. 128 SD], the note relates to the whole of a SD within or immediately following the line. Speech prefixes (SPs) follow similar conventions, 203 SP] referring to the speaker's name for line 203. Where a SP reference takes the form e.g. 38 + SP, it relates to all subsequent speeches assigned to that speaker in the scene in question.

Where, as with *King Henry V*, one of the early editions is a so-called 'bad quarto' (that is, a text either heavily adapted, or reconstructed from memory, or both), the divergences from the present edition are too great to be recorded in full in the notes. In these cases the editions will include a reduced photographic facsimile of the 'bad quarto' in an appendix.

# INTRODUCTION

Both the introduction and the commentary are designed to present the plays as texts for performance, and make appropriate reference to stage, film and television versions, as well as introducing the reader to the range of critical approaches to the plays. They discuss the history of the reception of the texts within the theatre and scholarship and beyond, investigating the interdependency of the literary text and the surrounding 'cultural text' both at the time of the original reproduction of Shakespeare's works and during their long and rich afterlife.

# PREFACE

'Editorially *Troilus and Cressida* presents, I think, more problems than any other play', wrote Alice Walker in her book about *Textual Problems of the First Folio*, 1953. I disagree with her conclusions about the kinds of texts that the Quarto of 1609 (Q) and the Folio of 1623 (F) represent, but can only nod my head in vigorous agreement when she laments that the variants between the two texts 'are indeed so numerous as to have suggested the possibility of revision and to have made it difficult for moderate responsible opinion to decide which is the better text' (68). And although most editors today would stress the strong likelihood or near certainty of revision rather than the 'possibility', that conviction has not made easier the task of ascertaining which early text is a revision of the other.

How then should an editor proceed? The uncertainties are comparable in some ways to those of other Shakespeare plays existing in two or more early and markedly differing texts, including *Hamlet*, *Othello*, *Henry V*, *The Merry Wives of Windsor*, *2 and 3 Henry VI*, *2 Henry IV* and, most famously, *King Lear*. Regarding the various proposed narratives about the origins of the early printed texts of *Lear*, Paul Werstine and Barbara Mowat have written eloquently: 'we discover that the evidence upon which they are based is questionable, and we become more skeptical about ever identifying with any certainty how the play assumed the forms in which it was printed' (New Folger Library edition, lxi). I share that pyrrhonistic scepticism as it applies to *Troilus and Cressida*, and have done my best to keep in mind the profound caution that it demands in editing such a difficult play.

One solution that recommends itself is to edit separately both the Q and F texts of *Troilus*, on facing pages or sequentially, as Eric Rasmussen and I have done with Marlowe's *Doctor Faustus* (Revels Plays edition, 1993). I seriously proposed this idea to the Arden editors, and hope that it will be done some day; but it goes against Arden policy generally (an exception being made for *Hamlet*), and there are reasons for making other choices. In favour of two-text editing are the myriad variants differentiating Q and F, and indeed differentiating the two 'states' of Q itself in 1609 – one representing the play as having been publicly acted at the Globe Theatre and the other addressed to a readerly audience eager to buy a play that had never been 'staled with the stage'. Many variants differentiating Q and F are essentially impossible to choose between when both are arguably authorial: 'broad' (Q) or 'loud' (F) at 1.3.27, 'forfend' (Q) or 'forbid' (F) at 1.3.302 and the like. If we could be certain which text came first and which second, we could decide to prefer the author's revision, but that certainty is hard to come by, and the distinct possibility of the involvement of other agencies (actors, censors, editors, copyists, compositors) is never absent. Hence the genuine appeal of a two-text edition. If the two texts represent different occasions, such as performance before different kinds of audiences, the case for regarding the two texts separately is strengthened still further. I am here arguing against the decision I have made to edit a single text.

Yet two-text situations are never wholly alike. In the case of *Doctor Faustus*, the so-called B-text of 1616 contains substantial scenes that very probably were added by other playwrights after the death of Marlowe. Here the two texts show us a glimpse of theatre history having to do with the exploitation of a very popular play about magic. *Troilus* is not like that. Nor is it like *Lear*, in which Q and F each contain substantial passages not found in the other. The texts of *Troilus* do not, as in *Henry V* or *A Midsummer Night's Dream*, reassign passages to different speakers and replace characters with others in certain scenes.

*Troilus*, in these respects, is closer to *Othello*, in that we have essentially the same play in Q and F when it comes to the length of the play, assignment of speeches throughout (with minor exceptions that may be the result of error in transmission), presence on stage of characters in any given scene, and the sequence and length of their individual speeches. A few instances of omission of three to five lines, chiefly in Q, are arguably the result of faulty transmission, although this point is still being argued. In any case, not much would happen to one's perception of the play and its characters if one were to read or see the play in a Q and then in an F text. There is nothing here approaching the reshaping of roles for Edgar and Albany that has been argued for the revision of *Lear* (Gary Taylor and Michael Warren, eds, *The Division of the Kingdoms*, Oxford, 1983).

The many differences in the Q and F texts of *Troilus* thus come down for the most part to individual word choice, and here it is possible to reason as carefully as one can with probabilities of authorial rewriting versus error in transmission. As a result, the textual notes in this edition are burdensomely numerous, and the commentary notes necessarily take up issues of competing readings on a case-by-case basis. With all the limitations of such a procedure, the method seems to me more useful in the last analysis than two-text editing, in which the variants would be presented in separate texts but without an easy way for the reader to find the significant variants and appraise their possible meanings. In any case, I hope that no one will suppose that this edition offers itself as having recovered 'the' single original of *Troilus*. The play certainly went through at least one process of revision, and if we could confidently sort out just how this went we could perhaps edit on that basis. I choose F as my basic text for this edition for reasons given in the essay on 'the text of *Troilus and Cressida*', pp. 422–6, but with (I hope) a healthy scepticism at all points and an awareness that Q offers many readings that are more persuasive on textual grounds. I have done all I could to stay away from subjective aesthetic judgements in such matters.

*Troilus* is no less controversial and experimental as a play about love and war, and as a script for theatrical performance. The play has enjoyed an explosive revival in recent years, both critically and theatrically. As much as any play Shakespeare ever wrote, *Troilus* demonstrates how brilliantly he questions our assumptions and challenges our new critical methods – feminist, Marxist, deconstructive, new historical – with endlessly new perspectives and insights. No play is better attuned to the temper (or distemper) of our times. I have tried to read everything written on the play, and to look at the entire history of production. I come away from the investigation with increased admiration both for the play and for the fruitfulness of modern-day critical and dramaturgic endeavours. This is an amazing play.

Paul Jorgenson wrote feelingly some years ago, at the close of his book about *Macbeth* (*Our Naked Frailties*, Berkeley, 1971), that he would not recommend to others that they devote years to the study of *Macbeth*. 'The gloom of the play, with the constant menace of the heresy of fatalism, closes in upon one' (219). My own experience with *Troilus*, for whatever reason, has been essentially different. I find I am exhilarated by the play's honesty in confronting the dismal and meaningless horrors of war. Shakespeare's wry exploration of the male psyche in his depiction of the men of this play, especially Troilus, has propelled me towards a critical self-examination that ought to be healthy. My reading of Cressida attempts to be deeply sympathetic in a way that is consistent, perhaps, with issues that gender studies have brought to our consciousness. If the approach seems critically anachronistic to some readers, I can only reply that the play seems to demand that kind of immediacy of engagement. To me the play is remarkably tender, sad and personal, in the midst of its unsparing depiction of brutality. For intellectual rigour, toughness of vision and compassionate honesty, this play is worthy, in my view, of comparison with Shakespeare's best-known masterpieces of the early seventeenth century – that period of extraordinary development and transition to which *Troilus* rightly belongs. As Janet Adelman says of *Antony and Cleopatra*, in her marvellous book about that play (*The Common Liar*, New Haven, 1973), quoting from Enobarbus: 'Kneel down, kneel down, and wonder' (171).

I offer this tribute to Janet Adelman as well as, of course, to Shakespeare, because I have dedicated this book in part to Janet. She and I have never been colleagues at the same institution, worse luck, but ever since 1973, when I first read *The Common Liar* in admiration and astonishment, she has been a crucial shaping influence on my reading of Shakespeare. The number of times her name appears in the citations will offer some rough index of the extent to which her seminal essays on *Troilus* have harmonized with and given needed eloquence to my ideas about the play. The other half of my dedication is to Richard Proudfoot, whom I have come to know chiefly as senior editor of the third Arden series. His role as a supervising editor for *Troilus* has taught me more than I can easily acknowledge. His pragmatic contributions are to be found everywhere in this edition; the language is his on numerous occasions. My choices between Q and F have had to stand the fearful and enlightening scrutiny of his masterful textual knowledge and good sense. I do a fair amount of supervisory editing myself, for Revels and for the Revels Student editions, and can only say that Richard has given me a wholly new perspective on how rigorously the assignment must be pursued. I am his student, and Janet's.

I am also happy to describe myself as a student of David Kastan, who studied with me at Chicago some years ago in the nominal sense of the term but who has gone on to become my teacher in ways that truly count. We have both found delightful comedy in the shifting of hierarchies that led to his drafting me, in his position as a senior editor of Arden 3, for this assignment, and then to his wonderfully helpful insights into every aspect of my manuscript. Ann Thompson, the third senior editor of Arden 3, though not assigned officially to this edition, has graciously read the Introduction and has given admirable advice. Others at Arden (Routledge, now Thomas Nelson) have helped greatly: Jane Armstrong, Jessica Hodge and (as copy editor) Judith Ravenscroft. I wish to acknowledge a special debt to Kenneth Palmer, whose previous edition (Arden 2) has helped me in many ways, as indicated in the notes. As Troilus puts it (5.2.196), 'Accept distracted thanks'.

*David Bevington*
*Chicago*

# INTRODUCTION

## 'A NEW PLAY, NEVER STALED
## WITH THE STAGE':
## GENRE AND THE QUESTION OF
## ORIGINAL PERFORMANCE

An enigmatic publicity blurb inserted in a revised Quarto edition of *Troilus and Cressida* in 1609, addressed to 'an ever reader' from 'a never writer', offers to the 'eternal reader' a 'new play, never staled with the stage, never clapper-clawed with the palms of the vulgar, and yet passing full of the palm comical'. In praising the dramatist as a writer of such 'dexterity and power of wit' that even those who are 'most displeased with plays' are sure to be 'pleased with his comedies', this publisher's preface goes out of its way to flatter a discriminating readership that prefers literature to stage performance. The appeal is neoclassical, learned, even academic in its insistence that the play deserves to be ranked 'as well as the best comedy in Terence or Plautus'. The potential buyer is urged to acquire a copy before the dramatist's comedies are 'out of sale'. The publisher represents himself as having made such a collectors' item available to his select reading public against considerable odds, 'since by the grand possessors' wills I believe you should have prayed for them rather than been prayed'. He does not say who these 'grand possessors' were who wished to keep back *Troilus and Cressida* from the *cognoscenti*, but his animus appears to be directed at the acting company. The dramatist is not named, although his name does appear on both versions or 'states' of the 1609 Quarto title-page: 'Written by William Shakespeare'.

Seldom has the publication of a book been surrounded with

1

# A neuer writer, to an euer reader. Newes.

Ternall reader, you haue heere a new play, neuer stal'd with the Stage, neuer clapper-clawd with the palmes of the vulger, and yet passing full of the palme comicall; for it is a birth of your braine, that neuer vnder-tooke any thing commicall, vainely: And were but the vaine names of commedies changde for the titles of Commodities, or of Playes for Pleas; you should see all those grand censors, that now stile them such vanities, flock to them for the maine grace of their grauities: especially this authors Commedies, that are so fram'd to the life, that they serue for the most common Commentaries, of all the actions of our liues. shewing such a dexteritie, and power of witte, that the most displeased with Playes, are pleas'd with his Commedies. And all such dull and heauy-witted worldlings, as were neuer capable of the witte of a Commedie, comming by report of them to his representations, haue found that witte there, that they neuer found in them-selues, and haue parted better wittied then they came: feeling an edge of witte set vpon them, more then euer they dreamd they had braine to grinde it on. So much and such sauored salt of witte is in his Commedies, that they seeme (for their height of pleasure) to be borne in that sea that brought forth Venus. Amongst all there is none more witty then this: And had I time I would comment vpon it, though I know it needs not, (for so

¶ 2

*much*

1 The first page of the publisher's advertisement added to the second 'state' of the 1609 Quarto

so many mysteries. We learn from this preface that Shakespeare was a name with which to sell books by 1609, and that some readers at least associated him with high culture. We do not learn, however, why publication was delayed some years after it was registered on 7 February 1603, or why a Quarto edition was finally published in 1609 in two states with two different title-pages and front matter, one advertising the play as having been acted by the King's Majesty's servants (Shakespeare's acting company) at their public theatre, the Globe, the other insisting that the play was never acted. Folio publication presents a puzzle as well. Why was the compositorial work on *Troilus and Cressida* evidently held up in the printing of the First Folio in 1622–3, leaving the play unlisted in the 'Catalogue' or table of contents, unpaginated for the most part and oddly placed between the histories and the tragedies?

Some details of textual history and bibliographical anomalies can be examined later on, but the puzzles themselves are essential to our understanding of the play's ambivalent status and genre. As many readers have observed,[1] the prefatory note 'to an ever reader' presents the play as a comedy, 'passing full of the palm comical', worthy of comparison with the best of Terence and Plautus. The two Quarto title-pages (see Figs 13 and 14, pp. 124–5) offer the play as 'The Historie of Troylus and Cresseida' and 'The Famous Historie of Troylus and Cresseid'. The first page in the Folio text calls it 'The Tragedie of Troylus and Cressida', and places it first among that volume's tragedies – or else last among the histories; the 'Catalogue' or table of contents for the Folio does not make clear to which category it belongs. The evidently last-minute decision to insert the play in an anomalous location between the histories and the tragedies appears to underscore the play's generic indeterminacy. Even the original publishers of Quarto and Folio seem not to have known what to call it.

---

1  For example, Alexander, '*TC*', 286; Morris, 481; Fiedler, 50–1; Snyder, 89; Muir, '*TC*', 28. Elton, 'Textual Transmission', proposes that the preface was written by John Marston, a friend of Henry Walley, who, with Richard Bonian, entered the play in the Stationers' Register in 1609; see also Finkelpearl.

*Troilus and Cressida* has struck many critics as in a genre, or *mélange* of genres, all to itself. To S. T. Coleridge, 'there is no one of Shakspere's plays harder to characterize'; one scarcely knows 'what to say of it'. Hazlitt finds *Troilus* 'the most loose and desultory of our author's plays'; Swinburne declares it to be a hybrid that 'at once defies and derides all definitive comment'.[1] Yeats and Jan Kott refer to it as a tragicomedy. Northrop Frye argues that the play is hard to fit into the usual Shakespearean categories – comedy, history, tragedy and romance – 'because it has so many elements of all four'. L. C. Knights argues a kinship to the morality play.[2]

Those who see the play as a tragedy of 'defeated potential' and 'tragic waste' readily concede that it lacks catharsis and does not invite deep sympathy for its characters.[3] Defenders of the play as a 'history' of the Trojan war emphasize its episodic structure and mixture of comedy with high seriousness, and point out that a number of history plays like *King John* and *Richard II* contain elements of tragedy,[4] but must also confront the fact that the so-called tragedies (such as *Julius Caesar* and *Coriolanus*) are often historical. 'Satirical comedy' or 'problem play' are useful terms in analysing the play's insistent mocking and raillery,[5] but are too easy or too nebulous for some observers; general agreement as to

1 Coleridge, 306; Hazlitt, *Characters of Shakespeare's Plays*, in *Works*, 1.221; Swinburne, 196–202, esp. 200. See also Heine, 3n. below.
2 Yeats, *Essays*, 240, and *Autobiography*, 286, cited by Mowat, 80 n. 1; Kott, 82; Frye, *Myth*, 62; Knights, '*TC*', cited by Tillyard, 49.
3 See A. Stein, 163–6; Chambers, 'Epilogue', 400; Bayley, *Tragedy*, 97; Coghill, 78, 125; Hargreaves, 58; Frye, *Fools*, 16, 59, 66, 69; Morris; Heine, '*Shakespeares Mädchen und Frauen*' (1839), trans. C. G. Leland (1891), also in *Heine on Shakespeare*, trans. Ida Benecke (1895), 42–5, reprinted in Var, 523, and in Martin, 44–5; Dollimore, 49; Rossiter, 147; Kott, 83; Danson, 75, 93; Oates, 142; Kaufmann, 'Ceremonies', 140; Stockholder, 539; Alexander, *Life*, 197, quoted in Coleman, 117; J. O. Smith, 167.
4 Dodd. Tatlock's contention (769n.) that 'There is absolutely no essential difference between *Troilus* and *Henry IV*' runs into a similar reductive difficulty. Cited and argued against by Lawrence, *Problem*, 169–70.
5 Michael Long, 104–5; Schlegel, 419, quoted in Martin, 34–5; Symons, quoted in Martin, 61–3; Brooks, 21, 24; Evans, esp. 169–70; Campbell, 185ff.; Jagendorf, 199; Everett, 125; Sacharoff; Kernan; Lawrence, *Problem*, 170–2; Lawrence, 'Troilus', 429–31; Boas, 375–8; Tillyard, 46; Bentley, 43–4. On Thersites as a satirist, see Bredbeck, 37–8; on Thersites as a railing fool, see Elliott, 137–9.

what constitutes a 'problem play' is hard to find.[1] If any consensus is to be found, it is that *Troilus and Cressida* is an experimental play, characterized throughout by an intermingling of mode, tone, genre and style. Such an open-ended play needs to be read inclusively, rather than being racked on some Procrustean bed of generic classification.[2]

The experimentalism of *Troilus* can be seen in context when we compare it with other works written during the pivotal years of Shakespeare's development, from about 1599 to 1603. *Hamlet* (c. 1599–1601), like *Troilus*, expresses disillusionment about human frailty and sexual inconstancy; so do the *Sonnets*, hard to date with any precision but at times close to *Troilus* in their exploration of the disabling consequences of female desertion. *Henry V*, in 1599, is an astonishing prelude to *Troilus*, as though seeming to measure the vast distance between the real if complex heroism of a charismatic English monarch and the fallen idols of the ancient classical world. *Julius Caesar*, also produced in 1599, gives a more sardonic anticipation of disillusionment with its ironic perception that republican efforts to forestall a dictatorship, however idealistically intended, lead ultimately to a collapse of the very senatorial freedoms that Brutus has conspired and fought for. *Measure for Measure* (1603–4) and *All's Well That Ends Well* (some time around 1601–5) are well matched with *Troilus* as 'problem' plays in their depiction of male inabilities to come to terms with sexual desire and, especially in *Measure for Measure*, a sense of social moral decline. In its experimentation and bleakness, *Troilus* anticipates *Timon of Athens*.[3] Whether performed (if it was performed) in public or possibly at one of the Inns of Court, or both, *Troilus* would presumably have found a receptive audience for its experimental dramaturgy and disillusioning

1  Lawrence, *Problem*; Tillyard; Toole; Rossiter; Ure; Schanzer. For a review of ideas about what constitutes the 'problem play', see Jamieson, 1–2.
2  Colie, 342–5; Helton, 120; Kernan, 192–8; Langman, 57, 67; Schwartz, 304–7; Foakes, '*TC*', 142–3; Marsh, 182; Seltzer, xxvi–xxxiv; Mowat, 88.
3  See Goddard, 2.21–8; Wheeler, *passim*; Kaufmann, 'Ceremonies', 141–2; Lawrence, *Problem*, 128ff.; Coghill, 78–127; Meyer, 51–2; Campbell, 191–3.

ambiance; we should not assume that public audiences would not have been fascinated by its mordant dramatization of hotly contemporary issues. At the same time, the play is manifestly difficult, controversial, even avant-garde.

## 'AN ENVIOUS FEVER OF PALE AND BLOODLESS EMULATION': HISTORICAL CONTEXT IN THE LAST YEARS OF ELIZABETH'S REIGN

Another aspect of *Troilus*'s generic instability and obscure early stage history can be seen when we look at the play in its immediate historical environment: the last years of the reign of Queen Elizabeth. *Troilus* takes on the dimensions of a *fin-de-siècle* work, exploring the disillusionment of troubled times. Two issues may be of particular relevance. The first is the play's putative role in the so-called 'War of the Theatres', to the extent that such a 'war' in fact existed among Ben Jonson, John Marston, Thomas Dekker and others about the competitive merits of 'public' and 'private' acting companies, popular morality versus the avant-garde and the like – the 'Rival Traditions' characterized by Alfred Harbage.[1] The second concerns the career of Robert Devereux, second Earl of Essex, and his catastrophic attempt at a coup d'état in 1601. Is *Troilus*'s depiction of insolent and divided leadership in time of war a reflection of contemporary disillusionment with some of England's governing elite? These questions depend upon, and can perhaps help determine, the dates of the play's composition and (if it was in fact performed) its performance(s).

The 'War of the Theatres', a major fascination in the 'old' historicism of the late nineteenth and earlier twentieth centuries, has been cut down to size more recently. At its height, the supposed 'stage quarrel' was imagined to have dominated the

1  Harbage, *Rival Traditions, passim.*

London scene in the years 1597–1603 or thereabouts and to have brought into the fray virtually every practising playwright.[1] The matter has been blown out of proportion. Still, the remark of an actor playing Will Kempe (in Part 2 of the anonymous *The Return from Parnassus*, acted at Cambridge University during the Christmas season of 1601–2), that 'our fellow Shakespeare puts them all down, ay, and Ben Jonson, too', has potential implications for *Troilus*. Did Shakespeare in fact 'put down' Jonson and others? 'O, that Ben Jonson is a pestilent fellow!' continues Kempe in his imagined conversation with Richard Burbage. 'And he brought up Horace giving the poets a pill, but our fellow Shakespeare hath given him a purge that made him beray his credit' (1809–13). The offensive 'Horace' who attacks other poets and playwrights is patently Jonson himself, whom Dekker and perhaps Marston had pilloried in *Satiromastix* (1601) by way of satirical riposte to Jonson's *Cynthia's Revels* (1600). In Act 5 of Jonson's *The Poetaster* (1601, written quickly by Jonson to anticipate *Satiromastix*), the poets Crispinus and Demetrius (thinly disguised lampoonings of Marston and Dekker) are arraigned for slandering Horace, whereupon Crispinus is administered emetic 'pills' by Horace and proceeds to vomit up scraps of Marston's recognizably eccentric dramatic language.[2] The 'pill' mentioned by Kempe is thus clearly identified, with its resulting purgative effect; but did Shakespeare then carry the attack further with his own 'purge'?

Jonson did take a swipe or two at Shakespeare in *Every Man Out of His Humour*, 1599. He parodied 'O judgement! Thou art fled to brutish beasts, / And men have lost their reason' (*JC* 3.2.106–7; compare 'Reason long since is fled to animals, you know', *Every Man Out* 3.4.33), and mockingly quoted '*Et tu, Brute*' in an absurd context (*JC* 3.1.78; *Every Man Out* 5.6.79),

1  Among the main proponents of a full-fledged War of the Theatres, see Fleay, 1.359–70, 2.68–72, Small, Penniman and Sharpe. On reducing the often extravagant claims of these earlier researchers, see Enck.

2  For a review of the literary exchanges among Jonson, Marston and Dekker, see Bednarz, 176–7, and Bevington, *Politics*, 279–88.

2  Ben Jonson, in a nineteenth-century engraving after a contemporary portrait

evidently in wry dismay at Shakespeare's amateurism as a neo-classicist. His chorus figures sardonically question how it comes about 'that in some one play we see so many seas, countries, and kingdoms passed over with such admirable dexterity?' (Induction, 281–6). The motto of the clown Sogliardo in *Every Man Out*, 'Not without mustard' (3.4.86), may glance at the motto *Non sans droict* on the coat of arms that Shakespeare had obtained for his father and himself in 1599.[1] Might this have elicited some response from Shakespeare? Jonson did at any rate append an 'apologetical dialogue' to *The Poetaster* in 1601, regretfully commenting that 'Some better natures' among the players had 'run in that vile line' of attack on him (ll. 141–52). Jonson, who elsewhere consistently views Shakespeare as of a gentle nature, seems to suggest that the latter was never the main target of his anger, and that Shakespeare's brief succumbing to the vituperative tactics of Marston and Dekker was much to be regretted.[2]

Could Jonson have taken the view, in 1601, that the portrait of Ajax in *Troilus* was modelled on him? The pun on Ajax and 'a jakes' or privy (see, for example, 3.3.247 and note), made notorious at this time by John Harington's scatological *The Metamorphosis of Ajax* (1596), might seem to be implicitly critical of 'the very basis of the cathartic theory of comedy that Jonson was currently proposing'.[3] Alexander's description of Ajax to Cressida as a man into whom Nature has discordantly 'crowded humours' of lion, bear, elephant, folly, discretion, and melancholy (1.2.19–30) might suggest a parody of the Jonsonian character sketch. The likening of Ajax to a bear could point to Jonson's shambling bulk, while 'slow as the elephant' might

1   See Bednarz, and Elton, 'Ajax'.
2   Chambers, *Shakespeare*, 1.71 and 2.202–11, is generally sceptical of personal identifications in the Poets' War and in *Every Man Out* in particular, but he does allow that 'Shakespeare may be one of the "better natures"' (2.204).
3   The pun, first proposed by Elton, 'Ajax', with citations from contemporary literature (745), is developed by Bednarz, 188–9. The linkage of Ajax to Jonson was first proposed by Fleay in an overstated case. In a similarly reductive vein, see Small, and Jonson, esp. 1.406–10, 418–27.

suggest Jonson's well-known laboriousness of style and slow pace of production. (Jonson berated Shakespeare for never blotting a line in his writing.) The virulent revilings of Ajax and Thersites against each other might conjure up the notorious quarrelling of Jonson and Marston. Thersites' 'gleeful morbidity' and his colourful ravings at the depraved sexuality he finds so fascinating have reminded several critics of Marston.[1]

Particular *roman-à-clef* identifications seem far-fetched and too reliant on analogies that can instead be explained by the play's internal dynamics.[2] Still, Jonson's apparent sensitivity and Kempe's allegation that Shakespeare had administered Jonson and others some kind of 'purge' could point to the way in which *Troilus* deliberately employs a consciously different kind of social critique from that of Jonsonian humours comedy. Beginning with a clear reference to the 'armed Prologue' of Jonson's *The Poetaster* (l. 2), the Prologue of *Troilus* insists that he comes as 'A Prologue armed, but not in confidence / Of author's pen or actor's voice' (23–4). He thus introduces a play that will not choose the Jonsonian path of authorial self-assertion and certitude. Shakespeare's play chooses instead to explore disillusionment and multiple perspectives in an experimental way that implicitly criticizes Jonson's more dogmatic approach. As James Bednarz argues, Shakespeare in effect negates 'the first principles on which Jonson had grounded his perspective – the self-confident conviction that he was capable of obtaining a knowledge of truth'.[3] Shakespeare may be addressing other satirists as well, like Marston, George Chapman and Joseph Hall, whose work had enjoyed so much notoriety in the late 1590s in non-dramatic publishing as well as on stage; venomed spleens like theirs had been subjected by Shakespeare to a

---

1   Bednarz, 203, citing Harbage, *Rival Traditions*, 116 and 118. See also Potts, Kimbrough, 9, 20 and Ramsey, 238–9.

2   Those who reject or criticize topical portraiture, of Jonson particularly, in *Troilus* include Tatlock, 726–34; Chambers, *Shakespeare*, 1.71–2 and 2.202–11; Ard², 19; Kimbrough, 21.

3   Bednarz, 206.

quizzical crossfire of debate about the merits and social dangers of formal satire by Jaques and Duke Senior in *As You Like It* (2.7.42–87).[1] If *Troilus* seems to lack the 'purge' that Kempe crows about in Part 2 of *The Return from Parnassus*, the forbearance is thoroughly in line with all that we know about Shakespeare, and might well have encouraged Shakespeare's company to take the view that Shakespeare had had the last word in this now ended Poets' War.

The circumstances of the debate tend, at any rate, to confirm a date for *Troilus*. *The Poetaster* and *Satiromastix* were performed in 1601; *Satiromastix* was registered for publication on 11 November 1601. The second part of *The Return from Parnassus*, announcing Shakespeare's 'purge' of Jonson, was acted at Cambridge in the Christmas season of 1601–2. 'The booke of Troilus and Cresseda as yt is acted by my lo: Chamberlens Men' was entered in the Stationers' Register on 7 February 1603. The Prologue's reference in *Troilus* to a 'Prologue armed ' (Folio text only) seemingly alludes to *The Poetaster*. This evidence points to a date of composition of some version of the play, including the Folio Prologue, in late 1601.[2]

*Troilus and Cressida*'s seeming comment on the Earl of Essex and his ill-fated rebellion of 1601 may also illuminate the play's experimental nature and the topical pertinence of its date of performance. Essex was often compared with Achilles in the last years of Elizabeth's reign. Both were controversial and notorious figures, at once mistrusted and admired. Achilles was suspect in Troy-sympathizing Elizabethan England simply because he was Greek; he was, moreover, truculent in refusing to fight alongside

1  Bevington, 'Satire', 120.
2  Earlier attempts to date the play in 1598 tend to be based on allegorical readings of the Essex affair, assuming that Shakespeare was urging him in 1598 to emerge from retirement and take action. See especially Harrison, 'Essex'. J. D. Wilson, 101–2, opts for late 1600. See also Honigmann, 'Shakespeare Suppressed', 112–14, opting for 1601. A date in late 1601 need not presuppose that it was written after the passage in 2.2.337–62 of *Hamlet* with seeming reference to the stage quarrel; that Folio-only passage may have been written later, and could refer, as Knutson argues, to more serious matters of offence to members of the Privy Council and other noblemen.

his fellow generals and treacherous in his slaying of Hector. On the other hand, he is, in the *Iliad*, an almost godlike figure whose mighty wrath is Homer's announced theme. George Chapman, whose translation of *Seven Books of the Iliads* in 1598 Shakespeare must have known, found in Achilles an admirable hero worthy of comparison with Essex, as though Homer, by 'sacred prophecy', did but 'prefigure' in Achilles the Earl of Essex as the 'now living instance of the Achillean virtues'. Nor was Chapman the first to laud Essex thus; Hugh Platt had done so in 1594, and Vincentio Saviolo had called him 'the English Achilles' in 1595.[1]

Chapman's comparison of Essex and Achilles, both known for arrogant dissension, was bound to be controversial. Even though Essex's star might still appear to be rising in 1598, his career as a politician had been turbulent. He had turned the Accession Day festivities of 1595, nominally intended to laud Queen Elizabeth on the anniversary of her coming to the English throne, into unabashed propaganda for himself in his candidacy to become leading adviser to the crown. Avidly anti-Spanish and interventionist in military affairs, he had led the successful attack on Cádiz in 1596 and the failed attack on the Azores in 1597, only to be passed over for supreme command in the aftermath of those raids. His surly withdrawal from court in 1597 for an extended period drew notices of disapproval. 'I have lately heard the different censures of many about thy absence in this high Court of Parliament', wrote a concerned follower to Essex; 'some, earnestly expecting the worthy advancement of thy most noble house and posterity, wish their service might ransom thy contentment; others, who make daily use of thy absence, confess thy worthiness, and in words only wish with the rest'. Essex's open impatience and 'discontentment' ended temporarily when the Queen relented in late 1597 by appointing him

---

1   Chapman, Dedication to *Seven Books of the Iliads* (1598), title and lines 60–1; see Briggs, 59. On Platt and *Vincentio Saviolo His Practice* (1595), see Honigmann, 'Shakespeare Suppressed', 115. See also J. A. K. Thomson, 211.

3  Robert Devereux, second Earl of Essex (1566–1601), by Marcus Gheeraerts the Younger (c.1561–1635)

Earl Marshal.[1] He quarrelled with Elizabeth over his personal right to ransom the prisoners he had taken, like Hotspur in *1 Henry IV*. Much as Achilles does with Queen Hecuba in *Troilus*, Essex secretly corresponded with Spain and Scotland over the question of the English succession.

Elizabeth's uncertainties and vacillations in dealing with Essex did not end with his appointment as Lord Marshal. Claiming to be an heir of Edward III, Essex offered himself as the saviour of English interests in Ireland against the rebel Tyrone in 1598, to the enthusiastic cheering of many hawkish Englishmen, including Edmund Spenser. Shakespeare seems to have joined in the praise. The chorus to Act 5 of *Henry V*, acted probably in 1599, applauds 'the General of our gracious Empress' who may in good time, 'from Ireland coming', bring 'rebellion broached on his sword'. The allusion is, for Shakespeare, unusually explicit in its topicality, and seemingly dates from the interval of time between March of 1599, when Essex hopefully set forth to Ireland, and late September of that same year, when he returned in utter failure to stand trial before a specially constituted court for abandoning his station and for contracting a dishonourable treaty with Tyrone.[2]

By the time Shakespeare had completed *Troilus and Cressida*, probably in late 1601, Essex had been arrested and executed for treason. Having persuaded Lord Mountjoy (who was to become Essex's more victorious successor as Lord Deputy of Ireland

1 *State Papers Domestic*, 265.10 (series 1, vol. 4, 532–4), loosely paraphrased by Harrison, *Elizabethan*, 2.235; see also 245 and 294. See Briggs, 60–2; Harrison, *Essex*, 183–210; Poel, 108ff., for a relevant document also quoted in Var, 377–8. On Essex and Accession Day, see McCoy; Strong, 141; Mallin, 166 and n. 68; Hammer. On Essex's communications with Spain and Scotland, see Honigmann, 'Shakespeare Suppressed', 116.

2 *DNB*, sv. Devereux, Robert. For a minority view arguing that the Prologue to Act 5 of *Henry V* may refer to Mountjoy rather than Essex, see W. Smith. Muir, Oxf[1], 7, is also sceptical that Essex is intended, but T. W. Craik, in his edition of *Henry V* (Ard[3]), offers a powerful argument for Essex (1–3). On Hotspur and Essex, see Harrison, 'Essex', and *Elizabethan*, 2.135.

later in 1601), the Earl of Southampton and others to join him in a conspiracy to rid the Queen of her pusillanimous advisers, Essex tried to raise the city of London on his behalf, failed to do so, was proclaimed traitor, and went to his death on 25 February 1601. The disillusionment was complete. All the emotional and military build-up of 1599–1600, as the English braced themselves for another possible Spanish invasion and pored over campaign bulletins from Ireland, collapsed into the dismal reality of a tarnished hero.

The case for Shakespeare's having written *Troilus and Cressida* with this unhappy saga at least partly in mind is circumstantial. It depends in part on Chapman's explicit linking of Achilles and Essex, on Shakespeare's likely acquaintance with Chapman's translation, and on Shakespeare's unusual tribute to Essex in *Henry V*. The case is strengthened by the thematizing of chivalry in *Troilus*. By 1599–1600, Essex was not only the 'now living instance of the Achillean virtues'; he was also the embodiment of a charismatic chivalry that posed a threat to the late Elizabethan regime. In its nostalgia for a rapidly disappearing social order in which aristocrats defended their nation and their ladies' honour, the idealizing of neofeudal chivalry naturally chose as its great image Sir Philip Sidney and the Protestant war party he had espoused, prominently including Essex in 1595 and the years following. The struggles between the Essex faction and the more cautious group gathered around Burghley and then (after Burghley's death in 1598) his son Robert Cecil became the central political story of *fin-de-siècle* England.[1] Essex was immensely

---

1 For the suggestion that Nestor and Ulysses can be taken as glancing at the Cecil faction, see Norbrook, 155; Honigmann, 'Date and Revision', and 'Shakespeare Suppressed', 115; Brooke, 76. Similarly, Campbell, 219–23, argues that any well-informed spectator in 1601 would have recognized in the comradeship of Achilles, Patroclus and Thersites an echo of the Essex group and especially of Essex's relationship with Southampton and with Essex's secretary, Henry Cuffe, a one-time professor of Greek at Oxford and reckless adviser of Essex who was executed for treason in 1601. J. D. Wilson argues that Shakespeare's intent in *Troilus* was to 'goad the earl into action', though not advocating rebellion (101).

popular with Londoners and theatre-goers, as *Henry V* attests. His campaign to brighten England's honour worked its appeal and then collapsed. Shakespeare's one-time patron, the Earl of Southampton, was caught up in the Essex débâcle and was condemned to death though reprieved and imprisoned 'during the Queen's pleasure'. Shakespeare's acting company was severely interrogated for its performance of *Richard II*, seemingly at the instigation of Essex's supporters, on 7 February 1601, the eve of the fateful rebellion. After the events of early 1601, the ideals of neofeudal heroism seemed no longer workable.

As Eric Mallin writes, 'the chivalric premise lay behind virtually every late Tudor court formality': its masques and pageants, its Accession Day celebrations, its ceremonial diplomatic missions. Yet this 'fashion of chivalry' was barely able to contain the contradictions of which it was composed. In its medieval form, 'chivalry masked savage and unregenerate self-interest'. Knighthood 'glorified bravery and martial prowess, but in so doing legitimated and rewarded rapacity'. These tensions were, moreover, exacerbated by conflicts of gender, in which the ideals of service on behalf of womanly honour ran into conflict with male anxieties at court about a woman ruler. Essex's notorious quarrels with Elizabeth – his insolent challenges and disrespectful references to her ageing person, her *volte-face* of bestowing special favours on him and then taking them away – gave visible definition to the paradoxes of chivalry as a 'forum for the visibility of masculine courtier power'.[1]

Whether or not we are meant to see a personal portrait of

---

1   Mallin, esp. 154 and 157; Montrose; McCoy, 313–20; Harrison, *Essex*, 42. J. Speed's *History* (1611) relates how the Earl of Essex, about to depart from Lisbon in May of 1589, 'in the courage of his martial blood, ran his spear and brake it against the gates of that city, demanding aloud if any Spaniard mewed therein durst adventure forth in favour of his mistress to break a staff with him' (Q. Eliz. Monarch 61, chap. 24, p. 865, cited by Palmer, Ard², 142 n. 274). In 1591, Essex wrote to the Marquis of Villars, Governor of Rouen, proclaiming 'that I am better than you, and that my Mistress is fairer than yours' (Harrison, *Essex*, 62, cited by Savage, 50, and by Mallin, 166). See Potter, 27–8. See also below, pp. 68–71.

Essex in Shakespeare's Achilles (Mallin in fact argues that the play gives us a bifurcated image of Essex in the opposed characters of Achilles and Hector) is less to the point than the similarities between the play and important social changes at work in late Elizabethan England. The nation was fascinated during these years with the story of the Trojan war, as though out of fear that if the great commercial city of Troy fell, so must London or 'Troynovant'.[1] The decline of feudal aristocracy in the late sixteenth century was synchronous with an increase in bourgeois mercantilism. Clinging to an outmoded feudal ideology and to the orthodoxies of an unchanging social order based on order and degree, those who had ruled medieval England found themselves displaced to an ever-increasing extent by new wealth. Their protest took rebellious forms of sexual licence and the practice of duelling, forbidden by the Tudor state.[2] Essex was the personification of this beleaguered chivalry. The insistent commercial metaphors of *Troilus*, as we will see, reflect unease in late Tudor England over social change. This is not to argue that Shakespeare takes sides in the conflict, but rather to suggest that he gives expression to many voices of anxiety and discontent in the England for which he wrote this play.

If Shakespeare wrote *Troilus and Cressida* in the wake of the Essex disaster, that event could explain a number of puzzling circumstances: the lapse of time between the Stationers' Register entry of February 1603 and eventual Quarto publication in 1609 after a change of ownership, the substitution of a second title-page and addition of a preface to the reader, and then still more delays to printing the play in the Folio of 1623. According to the hypothesis of Ernst Honigmann, Shakespeare's company may have found itself in a delicate position in the wake of Essex's abortive coup attempt. Whether Shakespeare and his acting associates had

1  Bruster. On the bifurcated image of Essex as both Achilles and Hector, see Mallin, 168. Savage, citing Merritt Clare Batchelder, 'The Elizabethan Elements in Shakespeare's *Troilus and Cressida*', unpublished University of Iowa dissertation, 1935, pursues overzealously the identification of Hector with Essex.
2  Clarke; Mead.

intended to make a political statement or not, their production of *Troilus* precipitated them into controversy. The connection between Essex and Achilles was a familiar one in England from 1594 onwards; so too were analogies of Burghley and then Cecil to Nestor and Ulysses. If the play Shakespeare had written proved too hot to handle in the upshot of a failed rebellion (and the company had been in trouble over their revival of *Richard II* in early 1601 on the eve of that attempted coup), the actors may have found it prudent to hold *Troilus* back. The players are to be identified, then, with the 'grand possessors' whom the publisher's preface in 1609 describes as having been reluctant to see the play in print. Other critics too have identified the 'grand possessors' as Shakespeare's company; and in any case the preface clearly refers to someone who tried to prevent 'the scape it hath made amongst you'. The proviso in the Stationers' Register entry of 1603 conferring rights of publication on James Roberts 'when he hath gotten sufficient aucthority for yt' should not be regarded as a 'blocking entry', since that romantic notion of a stratagem to forestall piracy has now been exploded as a fiction, but it does bespeak the need for authorization that may not have been granted.[1]

Might this scenario explain the substitute title-page and added preface in 1609 (see Figs 1, 13 and 14, pp. 2, 124–5), done in haste and at some expense and difficulty, removing all mention of performance from the first title-page, 'As it was acted by the King's Majesty's servants at the Globe', and speaking as though the play had never even been performed? The phrasing sounds more like an attempt at finding safe refuge than a reporting of the truth, in view of the conflicting evidence that the play was in fact acted. Cecil, now the Earl of Salisbury and more powerful than ever after the fall of Essex, was not a person to take lightly any lampoons that might seem slanderously aimed at him.[2]

Shakespeare and his colleagues seem to have found themselves with what was essentially a banned play on their hands. *Troilus*

---

1 Honigmann, 'Shakespeare Suppressed'. The 'blocking entry' scenario proposed by Pollard has been refuted by, among others, Blayney, 'Publication'.
2 Honigmann, 'Shakespeare Suppressed'.

*and Cressida* is, moreover, a sophisticated play, highly satirical at times, experimental in genre and attuned to an avant-garde idiom not unlike that of private-theatre plays performed with scandalous success by the boy actors. *Troilus* is rather like the play that Hamlet describes to the First Player as 'caviar to the general'; it 'pleased not the million' (*Ham* 2.2.436–7). *Hamlet* is such a play as well; both seem aimed at discriminating audiences whose judgements matter. In both *Hamlet* and *Troilus*, we seem to hear Shakespeare answering his critics with a defence of art that is experimentally difficult.

## 'WARS AND LECHERY': DEMYSTIFICATION OF THE HEROES OF ANCIENT GREECE

The experimentalism of *Troilus and Cressida* may well have contributed to a lack of stage success and belated publication in the 1600s, but that same quality has served the play well in the twentieth century. As the record of performance on stage can testify (see 'Performance history', pp. 87–117), *Troilus and Cressida* has come into its own in recent years. Critically, as well, the play has come to be appreciated for its major originality in achieving a balance between the war story and the love story in a way that no previous extant version does (see the essay on 'Shakespeare's sources', pp. 375–97 below). In good part, this is because the play is now perceived as speaking to our modern condition with vivid if dismaying relevance. Nowhere in Shakespeare can our present generation hope to find a more striking dramatization of the grim interconnectedness of war and the pursuit of eros.

We are constantly aware that Shakespeare, in metatheatrical fashion, is playing tricks with time.[1] He represents the action as

---

1  See Bayley, 'Time'; Berger, 135–6; and Charnes, 75–6, on the 'here and now' time sense of theatre, with everything taking place in and ending with the theatrical present. For an analysis of 5.2 in these terms, see Clifford Lyons, and Levine.

taking place at the time of the great Trojan war, far back in the mythical past, and yet he also expects us to listen and interpret with a modern awareness. The result, again and again, is that the characters in the play seem to anticipate their own destinies. Troilus, Cressida and Pandarus, in particular, appear to understand that history will hold them up as exemplars, even as stereotypes. 'Let all constant men be Troiluses, all false women Cressids, and all brokers-between panders', proposes Cressida's uncle, to which they all cry 'Amen' (3.2.197–9). Our knowledge that Pandarus' very name has passed into the language as a term for a pimp enriches the irony. Caught up in their hopes and excitement of the moment, these characters do not know what we know all too well, that nothing can save them from playing out the roles that history and legend have determined for them.

4  An Attic red-figure cup showing a fifth-century BC view of the struggle between Hector and Ajax, as depicted by Shakespeare in 4.5.95ff. The cup was made by Kaliades and painted by Douris, c. 490 BC

The war itself suffers perhaps the greatest demystification in this play about love and war. Shakespeare knew Homer's *Iliad* in George Chapman's translation (1598), at least in part, certainly enough to have savoured its tragic grandeur and its insistence on the war's great significance to the gods and to the human race. The *Iliad* has its share of disillusionment, to be sure, but finds greatness in its noble characters and denounces insubordination in Thersites. Shakespeare's depiction of war, contrastingly, focuses on the absurd.

Both sides in the conflict are aware of the ironies that link them to one another even as they long for slaughter. The rhetorical figure of oxymoron well expresses the paradox of friendly enemies who 'know each other well' and 'long to know each other worse'. Their exchanges of vaunts and loving invitations constitute 'the most despiteful'st gentle greeting, / The noblest hateful love, that e'er I heard of', concludes Paris (4.1.32–5). The two sides come increasingly to resemble each other as they compete for the same woman, and speak in metaphors that elide the difference between martial and erotic conflict. 'Better would it fit Achilles much / To throw down Hector than Polyxena' (3.3.209–10), Ulysses warns Achilles, using 'throw down' in a way that signifies both fighting and a sexual encounter laden with homo-erotic suggestion.[1] (Terry Hands's 1981 Royal Shakespeare Company production is only one of many in recent years that have made an erotic spectacle of the male body; see p. 104.) The bonds that link enemies are also heterosexual and familial, for men in this play 'traffic' in women and exploit family ties as a function of their homosocial interactions. Well-informed persons on both sides know that Achilles is secretly pledged to Priam's daughter Polyxena (194–204). All are aware that Ajax is half-Trojan, being the son of Priam's sister Hesione, which means

---

1   See Charnes, 83, 92–3; Sedgwick, 38; Lévi-Strauss, 29ff., esp. 42–51; and Rubin, on men's 'exogamous' trafficking in women. See also Bowen, *Gender*, 3–22; Cook, 42–3; French, 103; Jardine, 8; Patke, 16; B. Smith, *Desire* 59ff.; B. Smith, 'Rape'; and Spear, 409–12, on the homo-eroticizing aspects of warfare.

that he is a 'cousin-german' to the very Hector whom he is chosen to battle in the lists.[1] As Hector acknowledges his dilemma,
an 'obligation of our blood forbids / A gory emulation 'twixt us
twain' (4.5.123–4), and yet they fight.

Diomedes, plain soldier and artful seducer that he is, perceives with sardonic clarity the meaninglessness of a war fought
over Helen. When asked by Paris who is more deserving of
Helen, Paris himself as her current lover or Menelaus as the
estranged Greek husband, Diomedes has his ready assessment of
the rivals: they are 'Both alike'. Menelaus, 'like a puling cuckold,
would drink up / The lees and dregs of a flat 'tamed piece', that
is, would settle for the stale sediment of a broached wine keg,
while Paris must be content to breed his heirs out of 'whorish
loins'. Diomedes is bitter because 'She's bitter to her country',
indeed to both sides. 'For every false drop in her bawdy veins /
A Grecian's life hath sunk.' The toll is no less appalling on the
Trojan side (4.1.55–76). Diomedes' critique is all the more devastating because it is inspired by no moral idealism like that
appealed to by Troilus and Hector. Diomedes is a soldier who
sees this war as absurd in its cost. Women are to be enjoyed and
used, but not at such a fantastic price.

As Linda Charnes has observed, a 'notorious identity' hovers
over most of the characters in the play,[2] not simply Troilus,
Cressida and Pandarus in their prospective roles as archetypal
constant man, faithless woman and go-between, but also the
major contenders on both sides. Shakespeare's dramaturgical
techniques are those of disillusionment. Agamemnon, 'great
commander, nerve and bone of Greece' (1.3.55), is also presented as a figure of ridicule.[3] His noble insistence that the
Greeks' hardships are 'But the protractive trials of great Jove',
designed to test and thereby sort out those who are resolute from

---

1  Nass, 7.
2  Charnes, *passim.*
3  See Daniels, 286–7, Danson, 71, and Adamson, 36–9. For a more sympathetic reading of Agamemnon's rhetoric as 'close-woven' and 'virile', see Ellis-Fermor, 61, and
   Ard², 42–3.

those who, like chaff, deserve to be blown away by the 'wind and tempest' of Fortune's frown (20–6), must do battle with Thersites' reminder to us that Agamemnon 'loves quails' (5.1.50–51) – i.e. prostitutes – as do most men. Agamemnon does quarrel with Achilles over a woman in the *Iliad*, to be sure, but is not subjected in that poem to the satirical comedy of contradiction. In *Troilus and Cressida*, on the other hand, even his authoritarian bearing and 'topless deputation' or supreme power are the subject of mirthful parody when, as Ulysses reports to his fellow generals, Patroclus and Achilles amuse themselves in their tent with slanderous pageants (1.3.151–8). Recent stage productions have tended to see Agamemnon as dim-witted and obtuse (see pp. 105, 110). We do not necessarily assent to Patroclus' send-ups, but we find them diverting and informative because they represent a demystifying point of view.

Nestor is a figure of contradiction merely because he is old. Although Ulysses acknowledges a fit reverence for Nestor's 'stretched-out life', Ulysses is also unkind enough to relate to his fellow generals how the lampoons of Patroclus and Achilles use Nestor's 'faint defects of age' for their 'scene of mirth'. Ulysses obligingly imitates the way in which Nestor is perceived 'to cough and spit, / And with a palsy fumbling on his gorget / Shake in and out the rivet' as he prepares for military action (1.3.61, 172–5). Nestor's honourable career as a warrior reaches back further than anyone's, to the expedition against Troy headed by no less a hero than Hercules in reprisal for Laomedon's having defrauded Hercules over the building of the walls of Troy. Hector's grandfather Laomedon thus set in motion a war and lost his daughter Hesione to Telamon as a prize of war, prompting the Trojans to seize Helen in reprisal and thereby precipitate the present and most famous war of Greeks against Trojans. Nestor is a 'good old chronicle' that has 'walked hand in hand with time', known repeatedly as 'Most reverend Nestor' (4.5.203–5). Yet he is no less a tedious and senile old man, ready at a moment's notice to recall when 'I have seen the time' (210) and to ramble on through sententious truisms about shallow boats giving way before 'ruffian Boreas' and the like (1.3.31–54) as though he were actually adding something to what his fellow generals have already said.[1] Their polite condescension suits his role as one who never has an idea of his own and is all too willingly led by the nose by someone as clever as Ulysses. Recent stage productions have generally seen him as a wordy bore, slobbering over an orange (in Hands's 1981 production; see p. 105), ineffectual and weak.

Ajax is perhaps the figure whom the capricious memories of history and legend have treated most unmercifully.[2] He is no longer the mighty warrior of the *Iliad* but instead a fatuous, self-important gull, easily exploited as the tool of Ulysses' machinations aimed at goading Achilles into action. His dull-witted swapping of insults with Thersites, and his inevitable recourse to threats of physical violence when he is bested at the game of wits, make him a pathetic figure even in comparison with the play's most contemptible railer. To a modern producer like Hands (1981), he is a vacuous, gullible athlete, a 'roaring head-banger' out of Monty Python, practising karate chops on empty ammunition boxes (see p. 105).[3]

Broad parody thus offsets the play's more subtle demystifications of Homeric heroism. Ulysses is an interesting figure in this regard, because his character is in some ways close to the Odysseus of Homer. He is 'the sly Ulysses' celebrated in Homer's poem. Yet slyness or cunning is an asset in the Greek lexicon, an admired cultural trait, a way of dealing with dangerous enemies.[4] Shakespeare's Ulysses turns his cleverness and devious manipulations mainly against his own fellow officers like Achilles and Ajax, employing strategies of flattery, emulation

---

1  See Danson, 71–2, on Nestor's garrulity. Again, Ellis-Fermor (61) is more generous.
2  On the conflation of legends of two Ajaxes, Ajax Telamon and Ajax Oileus, see Edelman, 126–7; Cam[1], xxxiv; Oxf[1], 18; Dodd, 43; Bullough, *Sources*, 6.101; J. A. K. Thomson, 213.
3  See Girard, 201, and Hyland, *TC,* 73. On the use of music to underscore the ludicrousness of Ajax' situation, see Sternfeld, 203.
4  Those who support Ulysses as a valid commentator include Brower, 243, 253, Bethell, 99–101, and Tillyard, 75. More disillusioned appraisers include Burns, 124, A. Stein, 160, Adams, 91 n. 7, and Leech, 12. See 25 n. 2 and 54 n. 3 below.

and tantalizing.[1] Even his alliances are manipulative, as for example in his conspiratorial talk with Nestor. The wisdom of his speech in praise of order and degree (1.3.75–137), so often quoted out of context, takes on a more complex dimension when we hear Ulysses using his masterful rhetoric to encourage the very emulation he inveighs against.[2] On stage, the speech can be made to seem the vacuous locution of a pseudo-intellectual, as in Davies's 1985 production, when Ulysses' fellow officers rolled their eyes heavenwards in response to his pontificating (see p. 110). Ulysses is an old hand at gathering of intelligence and at deploying that information in a kind of elegant blackmail (3.3.198–210).

About women Ulysses is contemptuously wary. Cressida is for him only one more confirming instance of 'these encounterers, / So glib of tongue, / That give accosting welcome ere it comes, / And wide unclasp the tables of their thoughts / To every tickling reader' (4.5.59–62). Alone among the Greek generals who greet Cressida with sex-hungry leers and kisses, Ulysses refuses to beg a kiss. Never will be soon enough for him (53). He is appalled by the spectacle of grown men demeaning themselves before a woman; it puts him in mind of the root cause of the Trojan war. There they are, on Dardan plains, risking their very lives 'to gild his [Menelaus'] horns', that is, to put a specious appearance of decency on Menelaus' cuckoldry. This is the 'deadly gall and theme of all our scorns' (31–2). Perhaps it is not surprising that this most self-possessed and rational of all the Greek leaders, this apostle of self-control and control of others, should wish to rid himself of any indebtedness to 'the woman's part'.[3]

---

1   Girard, 205–6.
2   Those who view this speech as enacting its own loss of order and control through excessive use of accumulation, climax, neologisms and the like include Norbrook, 154–6; Grudin; Potter, 33; Elton, 'Ulysses', 98–100; Knights, 'Theme', 68–9; Roberts, 4–5 and 84; Goddard, 2.12–15. For more orthodox defences of the speech as an embodiment of noble ideas of order and degree, see, e.g., T. Spencer, 21–5, and Rossiter, 139–40; and see 24 n. 4 above.
3   The phrase, from *Cym* 2.5.20–2, also serves as the title of an influential collection of essays subtitled *Feminist Criticism of Shakespeare* (ed. Lenz *et al.*).

Achilles' decline in historical reputation, as dramatized in this play, is all the more dismaying in that it pertains to the tragic hero of the *Iliad*. Arrogant, sullen, envious, the Achilles of Homer's epic is notwithstanding a man whose choice not to fight and then to fight is of great consequence. The intensity of loyalties in conflict is for Homer a major theme. Shakespeare is not without sympathy, as theatrical performance can make clear, but he does allow his Achilles to luxuriate 'Upon a lazy bed, the livelong day' in indolent resentment, breaking 'scurril jests' and abetting insubordination (1.3.147–8). We seldom see him without Patroclus or Thersites, or both.[1]

Prurient whisperings about Achilles' relationship with Patroclus refuse to go away. Thersites may be partly mocking when he calls Patroclus 'boy' and reports saucily to him that 'Thou art thought to be Achilles' male varlet', or, in plainer terms, 'his masculine whore' (5.1.14–17), and Patroclus bridles at the charge as though denying its validity, but the assumption is inevitable and widespread. Achilles and Patroclus are virtually inseparable tent-mates. Achilles' refusal to fight is generally understood to be the consequence of his 'great love' for Patroclus, and Patroclus' 'little stomach to the war' (3.3.222–3). Achilles' love for Patroclus is of course central to the *Iliad*, but the unwillingness to fight is occasioned in the first instance by Achilles' quarrel with Agamemnon over a woman. By deleting this factor, Shakespeare focuses with special intensity on the friendship of Achilles and Patroclus. Achilles' being secretly in love with Priam's daughter Polyxena evinces a heterosexual desire that evidently accommodates bisexuality as well; such a desire, as Eve Kosofsky Sedgwick argues, often misogynistically eclipses women.[2] Male relations generally in this play 'work to the detriment of the females'.[3] Yet despite the subversively anti-authoritarian nature of his relationship to Achilles, Patroclus is

---

1    For a low estimate of Achilles as lazy, arrogant, etc., see, e.g., Chambers, *Survey*, 197–8, and Lawrence, 'Troilus', 435. On the other side, see Powell.

2    Sedgwick, 20–1, 33, 36.

3    Mallin, 159–65, esp. 163. See also G. Williams, *Sex*, 103.

5 Alan Howard as Achilles and Richard Jones Barry as Patroclus in John Barton's production for the Royal Shakespeare Company, 1968

treated as a hero in his death: the event is reported by Agamemnon in an epic catalogue of Greek casualties, and Patroclus' body is to be taken by soldiers to Achilles (5.5.13–17). As in Homer, he takes his place among the heroes of the war.[1]

The issue of bisexuality thus hovers ambiguously over this relationship, as it does also in Homer. Various voices give us contrasting surmises and interpretations. Theatre directors of late, ever since the pace-setting production of John Barton in 1968, have opted almost unanimously to flaunt a highly visible homosexuality of bared torsoes, shaved legs and drag costume (see pp. 102–3 and Fig. 5). We may take the view that Achilles' and Patroclus' sexual preferences are their own business into which we should not pry, but the play will not let us forget the question, perhaps because it bears so meaningfully on the issue of love and war. Troilus and Cressida struggle to find mutual comfort in a time of dislocation; so, in their various ways, do Paris and Helen, Hector and Andromache. The deep and eroticized friendship of Achilles and Patroclus is still another response to the need for human closeness in an anarchic world, all the more timely in that war brings men into such close and dependent relationship with one another. The friendship of Achilles and Patroclus is a counterpart to Ulysses' response to the sexual urge, which is to repress it and owe nothing to women – or men – in this sexual sense.

Achilles' brutal slaughter of Hector is the last definitive undoing of his reputation. Goaded by Ulysses into bestirring himself lest he fall victim to ungrateful Time, and then by thoughts of revenge for the death of Patroclus, Achilles takes the surest means possible of offending reputation by premeditated savagery that savours, in Bruce Smith's view, of a 'homosexual gang rape'.[2] Modern directors have transformed the scene into that of a firing squad (in Davies's 1985 production) or trench warfare (BBC,

---

1 Bredbeck, 27, 33–48, esp. 39; Mallin, 160–1; Skura, 23.
2 B. Smith, *Desire*, 61. See also Charles Lyons, 239–41. Shakespeare's account of the death of Hector is drawn in good part from Caxton's telling of the death of Troilus (638–9) and perhaps that of Lydgate (4.2647–779); see 'Sources', p. 390.

1981; see pp. 108, 110–1). Homer of course provides a precedent for the killing and the desecration of Hector's corpse, but Shakespeare has chosen to play up the worst aspects of post-Homeric legend (see p. 390). We see Achilles instruct his Myrmidons to fall upon Hector 'In fellest manner' and 'Empale him with your weapons round about' (5.7.5–6). To Hector's protest that 'I am unarmed. Forgo this vantage, Greek' (5.9.9), Achilles has no answer other than the fulfilment of what he has planned to do. Without remorse, he announces his intent to tie Hector's body to his horse's tail and drag him 'Along the field' (21–2). Achilles' exit line is his own epitaph as a man of any pretensions to honour in battle.

History has also dealt unkindly with Menelaus. He is a minor figure in Shakespeare's play, reduced to caricature. Virtually every mention of him refers to the inglorious fact of his being a cuckold, and he himself acknowledges the subject, albeit unwillingly (4.5.182). In a macho world of wars and lechery, where the men routinely challenge one another in the name of their mistresses, Menelaus is the emblem of what every man fears to be: an inadequate male. Modern directors like Davies (1985) generally find him a blockhead and despised nonentity (see pp. 110–1).[1] Reputation becomes the reality: to be known as a cuckold is to become subsumed by that identity.

## ''TIS BUT THE CHANCE OF WAR': SCEPTICAL DEFLATION OF TROJAN HONOUR AND CHIVALRY

The Trojans would appear at first glance to be treated more generously than the Greeks in Shakespeare's play, as historical scholarship used to argue; after all, pro-Trojan bias enjoyed a long-standing tradition in Western literature, as reflected in Chaucer and in Shakespeare's other medieval sources (see pp. 381ff.). English readers were familiar with the legends tracing

---

1  In Jacques Offenbach, *La Belle Hélène*, *morceau* 7B, Menelaus is derisively referred to as the ridiculous husband of Helen. Kott, 76, briefly pursues the comparison.

the genealogy of Brut, the supposed founder of the British Isles, back to his grandfather Aeneas.[1] To the extent that the Greeks are 'patriarchal, aggressive, masculine and grasping', as Emil Roy characterizes them, while the Trojans are fraternal, feminized in their willing submission to an idealized image of woman, bountiful and libidinal,[2] the Trojans are seen in an apparently attractive light. Theatre directors have generally been kind to the Trojans, dressing them handsomely as dashing cavaliers while the Greeks are made to appear moth-eaten and drab (see pp. 103, 105).

For these reasons, perhaps, the figure of Aeneas in this play is seen as an especially charismatic one. His appearance before the Greek tents in 1.3 is an arresting moment, one in which the demoralized Greek warriors are suddenly confronted by a chivalric idea, a challenge in the name of Hector. Aeneas speaks nobly if somewhat affectedly of his fellow Trojans: they are, in peace, 'Courtiers as free, as debonair . . . As bending angels', whereas in war, no one is so 'full of heart' (1.3.235–9). His challenge rouses the Greeks from their lethargy, and prepares for other interchanges between the two sides in which these enemies will confess a genuine admiration for one another. He is the perfect ambassador. Later, he deals with the delicate business of informing Troilus about the return of Cressida with all the considerable tact at his disposal. Aeneas is the impressive authority whom Ulysses cites for his admiring characterization of Troilus as 'a true knight' and the second hope of Troy (4.5.97–113) – an estimate of Troilus that should carry some weight, in view of its source.[3]

Yet Trojan chivalry is subjected to sceptical deflation in Shakespeare's play. The theme of Aeneas' challenge to the Greeks is disturbingly chauvinistic both in the jingoistic and in

---

1   See T. J. B. Spencer, Bruster, 99, and Kimbrough, 27–39. For a sceptical view of the Trojans, see Potter, 26–30, and 31 n. 1 below.

2   Roy, 109; B. Smith, *Desire*, 59; Aronson, 68.

3   For contrasting estimates of Aeneas and Ulysses as rhetorically authoritative or as untrustworthy here, see on the one hand Harrier, 144–6, and Flannery, 152; on the other hand, McAlindon, 32, Hyland, *TC*, 39, Meyer, 55–6, Haydn, 609, and Rossiter, 151.

the misogynistic sense.[1] If there is any Greek who dares avow the beauty of his mistress by declaring his willingness to fight, Aeneas proclaims, Hector will answer that dare one better: 'He hath a lady, wiser, fairer, truer, / Than ever Greek did compass in his arms' (1.3.265–76). My woman is more beautiful and chaste than your woman. This is the competitive and possessive male urge that also gets Posthumus Leonatus into such unnecessary trouble in *Cymbeline*, or Lucrece's husband Collatine in *The Rape of Lucrece*; it is the first step towards mistrust, emulation and jealousy.[2] The absence of any real woman to be fought over in Hector's challenge accentuates the sense in which this is essentially a competition among men.[3] It betrays an unease, a need to validate one's male sense of self-confidence through violence against other males. It is, in short, the impulse that gave rise to the Trojan war in the first place, reaching all the way back to Trojan resentment over the awarding of Laomedon's daughter Hesione to the father of Ajax. Aeneas, and Hector, too, are typically male when their competitive mating instincts are aroused. They can be brutal, as well. The first thing we learn of Hector is that this great and courteous warrior, 'whose patience / Is as a virtue fixed', is reported to have 'chid Andromache and struck his armourer' out of 'disdain and shame' that Ajax managed to strike him down in the previous day's fighting (1.2.4–34).[4] When Hector is angry, the women and servants suffer for it.

Hector's implicit endorsement of this code of male possessiveness is brought home in the play's most domestic scene, that of Hector with his wife, sister, brother Troilus and father as he prepares for battle and imminent death. His exchanges with his wife Andromache are brief to the point of being curt. When she attempts to chide him for stopping his ears against prophetic warnings of

---

1   See Walker, Cam[1], xv; Potter, 27; Colie, 335; and 30 n. 1 above. For a Lacanian interpretation, see Cook, 41–2, and Charnes, 92–3.
2   See Girard, 193, Garner, 140, and McAlindon, 36–7.
3   Mallin, 159–60.
4   Burns, 105; Hyland, *TC*, 63; Goddard, 2.22–3, who sees the episode as prophetic of Hector's end.

disaster, he cuts her off and orders her away from him: 'Andromache, I am offended with you. / Upon the love you bear me, get you in' (5.3.77–8). The 'love' she bears him means, in his terms, the unquestioned obedience that a wife owes to her husband. To such an unanswerable claim of authority Andromache can find no reply, and so she leaves without a further word, no doubt in tears.[1] Cassandra fares no better. Her prophetic vision of Hector's death in battle is met with contemptuous dismissal by Troilus: 'This foolish, dreaming, superstitious girl / Makes all these bodements' (79–80). Hecuba, who is such a defining emblem of the tragic destiny of Troy in Virgil and in Shakespeare's *Hamlet* and *The Rape of Lucrece*, is not present in this play, perhaps because such a powerful tragic vision would subvert the satiric tone. Perhaps, too, casting limitations are a factor, but in any case we know what Troilus at least thinks of motherly advice: 'Let's leave the hermit Pity with our mothers', he counsels Hector. (The Quarto version here at 45, 'Mother', brings the slighting remark even closer to the family constellation.)

Throughout, in the polarized world of love and war, the soft qualities of pity, compassion and gentleness are associated with women, and implacable, fierce protectiveness with men. Women are relegated to the margins of the male world, as they generally are in *Julius Caesar* and *Coriolanus*, for example, exhorting their men to be prudent and observant of prophecy. Andromache, like Calpurnia in *Julius Caesar*, has a limited role in a scene of futile pleading as immediate prelude to the disaster that women best foresee. Cassandra appears twice, once as a jarring intrusion upon the Trojan council of war, sounding 'high strains / Of divination' that move Hector to thoughtful reflection but prompt Troilus merely to reject out of hand the ravings of a 'mad' Cassandra. Her 'brain-sick raptures / Cannot distaste the goodness of a quarrel / Which hath our several honours all engaged / To make it gracious', insists Troilus (2.2.113–25). Cassandra's madness is indeed a token of a prophetic voice that men cannot

---

1 For comparisons with *Julius Caesar* and *Antony and Cleopatra*, and with Euripides' *The Trojan Women*, see Goddard, 2.31, Helms, and French, 335–6.

heed. Helen is isolated in a single scene (3.1), one that expresses the indolent infatuation that has consumed Paris as a fighter. Women are present in Troy as they are not in the Greek camp until Cressida, heretofore a resident of Troy, is paraded before the Greek officers. The Trojan women do indeed lend the softening perspective of wise utterance and domestic concern, but ultimately their presence serves merely to underscore the cultural differences of gender that drive men to be as they are because of their protective and commodifying fantasies about women. With brilliant insight, Shakespeare perceives that Hector's fateful decision to march off to his final rendezvous with death is made in a domestic context of the jousting relationship between men and women. Hector begs his father to bless his resolution to honour a commitment; he stands 'engaged to many Greeks', and no less to his fellow Trojans, to appear this morning in the battle. Priam reluctantly agrees (5.3.68–94). For all his arguing with Troilus about letting Helen go, Hector is too bound to the male honour of his family to follow his own best counsel.

## 'THE GODS HAVE HEARD ME SWEAR': TRAGIC IRONY AND THE DEATH OF HECTOR

Hector's role, as tragic hero in a play that is not a tragedy, calls attention to eternal paradoxes of prognostication and the fulfilment of destiny. Character is fate in Hector, as in the greatest of tragic heroes. He chooses what is destined. He chooses freely and yet is hemmed in by being who he is. Wise, mature, compassionate, more able than any other Trojan to see the moral complexity of the issue they all face, he nonetheless resolves to keep Helen, since it is 'a cause that hath no mean dependence / Upon our joint and several dignities' (2.2.192–3). His decision is distressing, and all too plainly related to the views of honour and of male dominance over women that he holds in common with Troilus and Paris, and yet we can see that he faces a genuine dilemma confronted by many a Renaissance gentleman anxious not to be suspected of cowardly behaviour.[1] As he later explains to his wife, 'Life every man holds dear, but the dear man / Holds honour far more precious-dear than life' (5.3.27–8).

'The gods have heard me swear', he says to Andromache, as he prepares to disavow her urgent pleadings and march away to his destiny (5.3.15). This is, in his view, a sufficient reply to her begging that he stay home. When his turn to die approaches, his very human decency and sense of fair play are used against him: he allows Achilles a pause in the fighting when Achilles is plainly on the defensive and losing, only to be disdained for this 'courtesy' and subsequently butchered (5.6.15–20). Troilus expresses the paradox well in one of the play's most telling oxymorons: 'Brother, you have a vice of mercy in you, / Which better fits a lion than a man' (5.3.37–8). Hector's greatest virtue is his

1 Gagen.

6 Detail from a fresco by Giulio Romano (1492–1546) and his workshop depicting Achilles in his chariot as he drags the body of the dead Hector; see 5.9–11. From the ceiling of the Sala di Troia, Palazzo Ducale, Mantua, c. 1538

greatest vulnerability. With cruel appropriateness, the practitioner of mercy towards those who are inadequately defended becomes the victim of an atrocity in which he is unarmed.[1]

Meaningless and horrible as it may seem at first, the death of Hector suggests a pattern of predetermined behaviour that manifests itself throughout the play. The debate in the Trojan camp about keeping Helen or letting her go is conducted largely in terms of will and 'election'. If 'I take today a wife', asks Troilus, by way of hypothetical example, 'and my election / Is led on in the conduct of my will . . . How may I avoid, / Although my will distaste what it elected, / The wife I chose?' (2.2.61–7). Nowhere is the lesson of 'As ye sow, so shall ye reap' more applicable than to the male pursuit and possession of women. Laomedon's cheating of Hercules led to the giving of Hesione to Telamon, which led to the 'rape' of Helen, which led to where things eventually finish up in this play, with Hector dead and the end of the war nowhere in sight. To the ancient Greeks, this kind of sequential destiny was usually the result of some curse, as in the case of the house of Atreus, extending through generations down to Clytemnestra's killing of her husband Agamemnon and Orestes' revenge. The gods' will must be fulfilled, through a human agency that seems inevitably to turn on itself.

This pattern of ironic inevitability, though decidedly more secular than in Greek myth,[2] is at the heart of *Troilus and Cressida*, first of all in Helen's relationship to Paris. She is, as Shakespeare characterizes her, an indolent and flirtatious beauty, interested chiefly in teasing Pandarus until he will admit what he knows about the budding affair of Troilus and Cressida. Helen's is a remarkably vapid role for some presumably handsome actress (originally for an Elizabethan boy actor gorgeously dressed).

---

1 For contrasting views of Hector as chivalrically betrayed or as overcome by his own greed and covetousness, see Colie, 348, Shalvi, 292, Edelman, 136–7, and Lynch, 'Hector'.
2 See Dusinberre, 88; Edwards, 106; Hunt; Fly, 'I Cannot', 150ff.; Knight, 67; Knowland, 361.

Modern directors have seen her as a Hollywood sex goddess in a low-cut dress (Michael Macowan, 1938), a mannequin in a display window (Anthony Quayle, 1948), a love object linked to Paris by a golden chain (Barton, 1976), a carefree woman suspended on a swing throughout the performance (Keith Hack, 1977), a gift package to be unwrapped like an expensive chocolate (Sam Mendes, 1990), a billboard poster reminiscent of Madonna (Wing-Davey, 1995) and a naked playmate emerging from a sunken steam bath (Ian Judge, 1996; see pp. 96–116). Yet Helen's place in the cosmic design of *Troilus and Cressida* is immense. She senses the nature of her own legend sufficiently to play up to the part as well as she can, speaking of herself in the royal plural (!) as she grandly consents to help unarm Hector on his return from battle (3.1.149–52). Helen's destiny is to be what she is, a projection of the erotic male imagination.[1]

Could Cressida become another Helen?[2] She and Troilus, at any rate, cannot hope to escape from a seemingly unavoidable destiny, one written in the history of the most famous war of antiquity. Because their love is so dwarfed by an all-engulfing conflagration, they are dominated by its vagaries in ways that they cannot control. No sooner does Troilus finally achieve Cressida than she is taken away from him, the very next day. The return of Cressida to the Greeks comes about through a sequence of unforeseen circumstances: the capture of the Trojan Antenor, the anxiety of the Trojan side to have him back, and most of all by the twists and turns of narrative in the story of Cressida's father Calchas – the Trojan seer who deserts to the Greeks, does favours for them and then wants his daughter back

---

1  Feminists who are critical of Helen, though holding the patriarchal social order to be chiefly responsible, include Cook, 39–40. To some, like Dusinberre, she is an ambivalent figure. Men often condemn Helen for duplicity and wanton seductive charm; see, e.g., Bethell, 102, and Coghill, 104. See also Oxf¹, 109, and Bache & Loggins, 221.
2  For comparisons of Helen and Cressida, see Rickey, 6 and 9–13; Bjelland, 'Cressida', 177; Helms, 30; Novy, 111; Frye, *Fools*, 67; Scott, 130–1; Dusinberre, 86–7; Rabkin, 35; G. Williams, *Sex*, 109.

in repayment. The cruelty of this turn of events is intensified by the fact that, in Shakespeare's play, Calchas' request is timed to coincide with the imagined consummation off stage of the love affair.[1] Calchas simply chooses this moment to ask for Cressida out of a sense of calculation and personal deserving; in Caxton (551), Calchas is bidden by Apollo to stay with the Greeks until they have won the war, and in Chaucer too (4.71–7) he knows that Troy will be burned to the ground (see pp. 242n., 383). The Greek generals who accede to Calchas' proposal have no inkling that Cressida might be unhappy about the swap, nor would they care if they knew. The Trojan generals are of course unaware of the irony that Antenor will betray Troy. The timing of it all seems arbitrary, but is meaningful nonetheless; Shakespeare shortens the interval between Cressida's surrender to Troilus and her return to her father in order to accentuate the perverse irony of fate, but we can readily see that it was an accident waiting to happen. Those who risk personal commitment in time of war had better be prepared for disappointments.

## 'AS TRUE AS TROILUS': MALE OBSESSIONS ABOUT HONOUR AND SEXUALITY

Yet the failures of Troilus and Cressida as lovers are not wholly, or even primarily, dependent on outward circumstances of war beyond their control. Their relationship is flawed by many of the same cultural expectations about gender that we see in the play's characters throughout.

Troilus, 'true knight' and 'second hope' of Troy (4.5.97–110), resembles his fellow warriors in his possessive and commodifying view of women.[2] His first question, in the Trojan council of war, is to ask rhetorically how Hector could consider weighing

---

1  Cf. *RJ* 3.3–5.
2  On commodifying women within the circuit of exchange, see Cook, 38, Lévi-Strauss, 29–145, Rubin, and Irigaray, 170–91.

'the worth and honour of a king' in something so base and commercially vulgar as 'a scale / Of common ounces', presuming with 'counters' or coin-shaped disks to sum up the immeasurable value ('past-proportion') of their king's 'infinite' worth (2.2.26–9); but when Troilus addresses the issue of returning or not returning Helen to the Greeks, his own metaphors are from the merchant's stall and the kitchen. 'We turn not back the silks upon the merchant / When we have soiled them; nor the remainder viands / We do not throw in unrespective sieve / Because we now are full', he argues (69–72). The images are not flattering: sexual union, by analogy, contaminates the woman. Marriage is, in Troilus' imagination, something from which one might 'blench' in 'evasion' because the will has learned to 'distaste' it (66–8).[1] Honour, conversely, is inestimably valuable, in relation to which a woman, even a wife, is a quantity of goods to be consumed and bargained for. A price can be put on a woman like Helen: 'she is a pearl / Whose price hath launched above a thousand ships / And turned crowned kings to merchants'. She was achieved in a trade: the Grecians keep aunt Hesione, and so the Trojans get to keep Helen, whom Paris brought home as a 'noble prize'. What is vitally at stake is not the woman herself so much as the honour of the men who all cried 'Go, go!' and thereby put their honour on the line for the possession of a 'prized' object that they have admittedly 'stol'n' (81–93). These commercial metaphors will return to haunt Troilus when he is called upon to assent to another trade for the honour of Troy, one in which Cressida will be turned over to the Greeks 'in right great exchange' for Antenor (3.3.21).[2]

In his wooing of Cressida, Troilus reveals his traits as a lover that help to spell his destiny. From the start, he describes the passion of love as an enervating 'battle' in his heart that renders him incapable of mastering himself (1.1.1–5). Love makes him

1 Adelman, 'Cressid', 135, and 'Union', 41.
2 See Engle, R. A. Yoder, 17, Adams, 82, and Kaula, 273–8.

'womanish' (103) in ways he does not admire: 'weaker than a woman's tear', 'Less valiant than the virgin in the night' (9–11). When asked by Aeneas why he is not afield in the fighting, Troilus replies, 'Because not there', and then goes on to characterize his own retort as a 'woman's answer' in that it chooses whim over rational discourse (101–3). These images, self-pitying in their purport, are also consistently condescending towards women. The latent fear hinted at in his talk of a 'wild and wand'ring flood' (98) may suggest that Troilus is sexually inexperienced;[1] stage productions, such as those of William Poel in 1912, Robert Atkins in 1946 and Barton in 1968, have often seen him as less urbane than Cressida, naive, confused, indecisive, easily disillusioned (see pp. 93, 99, 102).

On the brink of his success with Cressida, Troilus is a man possessed by dark and sensually indulgent images of the imminent sexual encounter. He likens himself to a 'strange soul' waiting 'upon the Stygian banks / Staying for waftage', as though Pandarus were the ferryman Charon and Cressida herself a kind of Hades to be achieved through the self-immolation of death (3.2.8–9). Sexual fulfilment and dying were often thought of in the Renaissance imagination, and in Shakespeare, as coterminous.[2] Troilus' hope is to 'wallow in the lily-beds / Proposed for the deserver' (11–12), picturing his reward as an exotic blend of the pagan abode of the blessed as described by Virgil (*Aeneid*, 6.637–59) and the lily-beds erotically depicted in the Bible's Song of Solomon. *Wallow* is a term that has not endeared him to many critics; it seems to bespeak an enervating softness that leaves little room for more tender emotions of mutual sympathy and commitment.[3] The idea that Troilus is a 'deserver', coming into his earned reward, is also not something that he should say of himself. In the religion of love it is blasphemy,

1  Sexual inexperience is also suggested at 3.2.18–20: 'What will it be, / When that the wat'ry palates taste indeed / Love's thrice-repured nectar?'
2  See Charles Lyons, 235.
3  See, e.g., Brower, 256, Southall, 228, and Farnham, 257–9.

like believing in one's own merit for salvation.[1] In his talk of love as a 'thrice-repured nectar' whose sweetness will cause him to 'lose distinction' in his 'joys' (3.2.16–25), he sounds too much like a connoisseur, anxious lest too much good wine render him unable to tell one excellent bottle from another.

Yet when the lady comes, escorted by Pandarus, Troilus is abased and paralysed, like some 'vassalage at unawares encount'ring / The eye of majesty' (36–7). He is speechless at first, then obsessed about 'performance' (81). The 'monstruosity in love' for him is that 'the will' – sexual desire – is infinite and boundless, but that the execution is 'confined' and the 'act' of sexual coupling 'a slave to limit' (78–80). All this, said before the lovemaking has actually begun, bespeaks a very male fascination with sex as performative and as a validation of male achievement, coupled with the painful reflection that this crowning deed of the male species must end in deflation. To achieve is to be spent. Orgasm is truly a kind of death for Troilus. When Cressida worries similarly that all lovers 'swear more performance than they are able, and yet reserve an ability that they never perform', having 'the voice of lions and the act of hares', to Troilus her statement amounts to a challenge that he will answer in deeds: 'Praise us as we are tasted, allow us as we prove' (81–8). Cressida, to be sure, encourages her lover to descend from his euphemistic dream of Petrarchan romance imagery into the sardonic realm of 'performance', in a sensual replay of the courtship of Romeo and Juliet (*RJ* 2.2); she and Troilus are separated by the barrier of a common tongue and do not fully understand each other's words or thoughts.

Troilus is the one who introduces into their love talk, even before they have slept together for the first and only time, an element of fearfulness about Cressida's constancy simply because she is a woman. 'O, that I thought it could be in a woman . . . To feed for aye her lamp and flames of love, / To keep her constancy

---

1   Cf. the Prince of Aragon in *MV* 2.9.51: 'I will assume desert'.

in plight and youth!', he exclaims, lamely inserting the proviso, 'As, if it can, I will presume in you' (153–6).[1] Cressida, he fervently hopes, may prove the exception to the widespread truth of women's inconstancy, but the case is yet to be tested, and the generalized arguments are heavily against it: the decay of beauty, the waning of passion and perhaps most of all Troilus' assumption that even Cressida cannot 'match' the 'weight' of the 'integrity and truth' and 'winnowed purity in love' that he is able to offer her (159–63). Troilus imagines Cressida's desertion of him even as he prepares to master her, blaming partly her natural condition as a woman and partly his own inability as a man to match desire with performance.

The oaths that the lovers swear, then, and the labels with which they caricature themselves for all of history – 'As true as Troilus', 'As false as Cressid' (177, 191) – are prompted partly by Troilus' sense of who he is as a male and by his fearfulness that the commodifying nature of his desire for Cressida might be answered in kind. His hyperbolic romanticizing of himself as outdistancing all the lovers of past or future generations, with their tired similes of undying affection – 'As true as steel', 'as turtle to her mate', etc. (171–4) – may be similarly prompted by a need to fend off and repudiate the banal urgency of his own physical craving and the prospect that once he has achieved Cressida he will no longer love her in quite the same way.

Early on the morning after the consummation of their love, Troilus must explain to Cressida his haste in leaving her. However much he agrees with her that the night has been too brief, day has come, and he has other things to do. He speaks to her patronizingly now, in the language of command, bidding her, 'Dear, trouble not yourself', and urging her 'To bed, to bed', where her 'pretty eyes' will be as untroubled 'As infants' empty of all thought' (4.2.1–6). The condescension is a clue that Cressida can now expect to find herself vulnerable in her new

---

1    See Helton, 124, and Adams, 81.

relationship to a man for whom men's business takes precedence.[1] His swift departure prompts Cressida to chide herself for having given in. 'You men will never tarry', she generalizes. 'O foolish Cressid, I might have still held off, / And then you would have tarried' (17–19).[2] We might be inclined to read this reaction simply as a manifestation of her seemingly ingrained cynicism, were it not that we have just learned that she is about to be returned to her father in the Greek camp. Troilus' light-hearted amusement at Pandarus' teasing of her over the loss of her maidenhead intensifies the dramatic irony of our knowledge that she and Troilus are about to lose each other.

The usual view of the matter is that Cressida deserts Troilus once she reaches her father's tent, and to an important extent that is true, but this interpretation overlooks too much in Troilus' own conduct in the separation. How will he take the news of the impending return of Cressida to her father? We know from the previous scene that Aeneas and Paris are knowledgeable about Troilus' new affair with Cressida and are regretful that the news of the exchange will upset him, but they see no alternative. 'The bitter disposition of the time / Will have it so', concludes Paris, perhaps unaware of the irony of his asking Troilus to do what he has been unwilling to do with Helen: give her up for the public good (4.1.50–1). No doubt Paris and Aeneas find the situation awkward and even embarrassing. Yet they both simply assume that Troilus will consent to the plan, and they are right. Troilus' public sense of honour does not even permit him to hesitate. Among men, with his brothers and fellow generals, Troilus knows his duty. His perspective is

1 See Adams, 83; Girard, 188; Adelman, 'Cressid', 125; Knights, 'Theme', 77; and Reid, 263–7, quoting Marcuse (*Eros and Civilization*) and Freud ('The Most Prevalent Form of Degradation in Erotic Life'). For classical and Renaissance expressions of the universality of postcoital triste, cf. Shakespeare's Sonnet 129 ('Th' expense of spirit in a waste of shame'), and Jonson's 'A Fragment of Petronius Arbiter': 'Doing a filthy pleasure is, and short' (8.294), based on Petronius, poem 28, *Foeda est in coitu et brevis voluptas*, LCL, 426–7. For a critique of Girard, see Hjort, 76–7 and 89–98.

2 Cf. the dialogue of Troilus and Pandarus in 1.1.16–20: 'Have I not tarried?', etc.

unremittingly male. He scarely bothers to consult Cressida's feelings or predicament. To be sure, he does expect to continue to visit Cressida in the Greek camp, much as Romeo hopes to be able to see Juliet, though once again the tonal differences between *Romeo and Juliet* and *Troilus and Cressida* manage to undercut every comparison.

When he learns from Aeneas that an exchange has been arranged and that 'We must give up to Diomedes' hand / The Lady Cressida', Troilus responds in two eloquently simple sentences: 'Is it concluded so?' and 'How my achievements mock me!' (4.2.68–71).[1] Much depends on how these lines are read, and the tone can vary from momentary disbelief and anger to sorrowful resignation, but in any case these words bespeak an immediate recognition on Troilus' part of the irony of his fate. His premise appears to be that the decision is irrevocable and that he must come to terms with it. He does not protest its injustice, or a lack of consultation. The men of Troy have made what he sees as a necessary if distasteful choice. He grasps at once that the opportunity to recover Antenor is too good to be missed: a valued warrior in exchange for a woman. And so he accepts, albeit with a sense of how he is mocked by his achievements: his having achieved Cressida on the previous night, and to no less extent his achievement as a young statesman arguing in the councils of the Trojan leadership that the honourable course is to keep Helen at any cost. That cost, he now realizes, is his giving up Cressida, but he does not flinch from that sacrifice. The greater the pain, the greater his public service. He is trapped, but not by his fellow officers, whom he never reproaches, even when Paris sanctimoniously protests that 'I know what 'tis to love' and wishes he could help (4.3.10–11). Troilus is trapped, in his view, by some larger cosmic perversity, some envy of the gods (see 4.4.27–8), that now tests him as a man. His definition of manhood requires that he assent to Cressida's return to her father. Perhaps the outcome

1 Adams, 84; Adelman, 'Cressid', 126; R. A. Yoder, 20–1.

even serves him well, in fact, for it allows him to be free of an ambivalently desired relationship without the burden of guilt, placing him in the position of the one who has behaved honourably.[1] This interpretation has made its way into some recent productions, such as that of BBC Television in 1981 and that of Howard Davies in 1985 (see pp. 105–9).

All that is required by the code of conduct to which Troilus subscribes is that he protect the lady's honour by keeping the affair secret, and this he proceeds to do by pledging Aeneas to secrecy (4.2.72–3). Aeneas assents, as he can well afford to do in any case, since news of the affair has been all over Troy before it even began (see 3.1.78–83). Then Troilus must say farewell to the lady. He firmly, if melodramatically, insists that she must go (4.4.29–47) – not, however, before she swears that she will be 'true of heart' to him. The iterated 'Be thou true', 'But yet, be true', 'Be not tempted', becomes such an insistent refrain of his admonitions to her that Cressida is prompted to fear that 'you love me not' (57–90). Clearly Troilus perceives that the gods have devised yet another test in this enforced separation, one in which he will simply be true to Cressida because 'it is my vice, my fault' (101), while Cressida's suspect integrity (suspect in part because she has already given herself to a man, to Troilus, and in part because he knows what men are like) will be shown for what it really is. Troilus' expectations of her are not really very different from those of Ulysses, who, in the next scene, greets her arrival at the Greek camp by setting her down as a slut (4.5.55–64).

Troilus' behaviour towards Diomedes as he turns Cressida over to the Greek betrays the extent to which he regards the possession of women as a matter to be settled among men. Troilus is obsessed with the presumed capacity of 'the Grecian youths' to woo artfully, assisted by their 'gifts of nature', their expertise in singing, conversation and dancing 'the high lavolt'; in all of

1   See Charnes, 80, Fineman, 103, and Girard, 194.

these accomplishments, he asserts, 'the Grecians are most prompt and pregnant' (4.4.75–87). Diomedes is the embodiment of his nightmare, but he is a man, and between men things must be straightened out about women. That is what the war is about, after all. Troilus proceeds to instruct Diomedes in the art of caring for Cressida before he delivers her 'to thy hand' (110), transferring her over to new ownership as a father might do in a wedding ceremony. Diomedes will of course have none of this tutoring. His own sense of manhood requires that he call Troilus' bluff, and we are left to wonder if his instantly conceived plan to take Cressida for himself is not motivated as much by male rivalry as by sexual desire.

Troilus has nothing to say during the epic assembly of the two sides for the contention of Hector and Ajax (4.5). Troilus' sole interest is in knowing what Diomedes and Cressida will be up to. At the scene's end, as the others leave to their feasting in the Greek camp, he takes Ulysses aside to ask the whereabouts of Calchas' tent. Ulysses is surprisingly solicitous towards a young man of the enemy army, sensing at once, with his instinct for prying into secrets and his inbred mistrust of women, that Troilus is in a fair way to becoming cuckolded by Diomedes – if one can be cuckolded when one is not even married.[1] Together, Troilus and Ulysses spy on Diomedes' brusque wooing, their whispered conversation punctuated by Thersites' obscene leering. Troilus' response is as to a nightmare turned reality. He is incredulous only in receiving such swift confirmation of what he so readily feared, outraged chiefly because of what may be implied about womanhood. 'Think, we had mothers', he urges Ulysses (5.2.136). His wish to assert that Cressida cannot have been there before his eyes[2] is a wish to protect 'the general sex' (138) against her example, and to cling to his own idealized view of sexual union as a desirable but also frightening fusion

---

1    See Gohlke, Kahn, 132, and A. Stein, 161–2.
2    Cf. *Oth* 4.1.173–205.

reminiscent of a child's blissful fusion with its mother. Like so many men, Troilus has bifurcated women into idealized mother figures and those who are sexual objects. Cressida herself becomes two women to satisfy his need for such a divided female nature: 'This is and is not Cressid' (153).[1]

Such a fracture seems to Troilus, in his personal agony, a sign and perhaps even a cause of the discord and 'mere oppugnancy' that follow in nature and the cosmos when humans foolishly 'Take but degree away' and untune the string that holds together social order (1.3.109–11): for him, the desertion of Cressida means that 'The bonds of heaven are slipped, dissolved and loosed' (5.2.163). As Robert Ornstein says, Troilus 'projects his inner confusion into a law of universal chaos and would have us believe that because *his* vanity is stricken the bonds of heaven are slipped'.[2] His response is one of rage. Unable to think long about Cressida directly, no longer willing to tolerate any association with 'mothers' in time of war (5.3.45),[3] he directs his rage against Diomedes, focusing all his newly achieved hypermasculine energy at recovering the sleeve he gave Cressida at their parting (4.4.69, 5.3.96) and on avenging the insult of Diomedes' having taken his horse (5.6.8). He is right in supposing that Diomedes values the horse more as a way of demonstrating to Cressida who is the better man of her two lovers than as a simple way of being generous to her: he is now 'her knight by proof' (5.5.1–5). Troilus' love for Cressida thus ends in a murderous rivalry between two men for whom the woman serves solely as the contested object of possession. Two frenzied opponents fight to establish, through brute strength, the superiority of one over his opposite number. In other words, the story ends where the war began.[4]

1 Adelman, 'Cressid', esp. 428–30; Adelman, 'Union', 41; Fineman, 99–100, Roy; Freud ('The Most Prevalent Form of Degradation in Erotic Life'); Greene, 'Cressida', 142.
2 Ornstein, 249. See also O'Rourke, 155.
3 See Adelman, 'Union', 61–2, on Q's 'Mother'. See also Roy, 111–12, and Rossiter, 146.
4 See Dollimore, 41, and Eagleton, 34–7.

# 'AS FALSE AS CRESSID':
## WOMEN AS OBJECTS OF DESIRE

Many critics find it hard to excuse Troilus' talk of wallowing on soft lily-beds. Many too are unhappy with the fact that Cressida's first words to Troilus, on the night of their assignation, are, 'Will you walk in, my lord?' (3.2.59).[1] She might have found something else to say first; the expression is too close to what one might expect from a prostitute inviting her client upstairs. Perhaps she means it innocently, or even sardonically, but it is not a well-chosen greeting. And indeed Cressida's manner of speaking can be daunting. She seems to enjoy putting men down, as it were.[2] She converses only with men in this play – lots of them. When we first see her, she is practising her wit on her servant Alexander, as though warming up for a few rounds of repartee with her uncle Pandarus. To Alexander's assertion that Ajax is reputed to be 'a very man *per se*, / And stands alone', she rallies with 'So do all men, unless they are drunk, sick, or have no legs' (1.2.15–18).[3] Alexander's witty disquisition on Ajax' mix of folly and valour makes her smile. Men are like that, in her view: a mass of contradictions, attractive sometimes but potentially dangerous, self-dramatizing, strong in weakness, part of the *comédie humaine*.

Pandarus amuses her too. A kind of Mardian to her Cleopatra, he is a plaything that she can endlessly abuse in the friendly guise of verbal volleying. Because he has also made plain his intention of delivering her to his friend Troilus, he poses a challenge to her sexual role that she finds both intriguing and fraught with peril. He complacently offers himself as the target

---

1 The less forgiving critics include Muir, '*TC*', 34; Rickey, 13; Rossiter, 132; Soellner, *Patterns*, 210; Van Doren, 174; Campbell, 109; Kendall, 136; Gérard, 147; Henderson, 140; Main, 172ff. See Greene, 'Cressida', 135. Some recent defenders of Cressida are Empson, *Pastoral*, 36; Eldridge, 38–41; R. A. Yoder; Tiffany; Greene, 'Cressida'; Adelman, 'Cressid'; Cook; Hale; D. Hooker; Lynch, 'Cressida'; Donaldson, 'Cressid'; Asp, 'Defense'; Bowen, *Gender*; Gaudet. For reviews of attitudes towards Cressida, see Voth & Evans; Harris; Asp, 'Defense'; D. Hooker.
2 On Cressida's defensive wit, see Roy, 112; Adelman, 'Cressid', 124–5; and 48 n. 1 below.
3 Discussed by Lynch, 'Cressida', 358, and McAlindon, 39–40.

of her wit, perhaps not always understanding the full force of her barbs. It is as though they have arrived at an implicit mutual understanding: her price for doing what he begs (though she will do so only on her own terms and in accord with her own wishes) is that he must allow himself to be teased.[1] Her sparring with Pandarus about Troilus' merits is a means both of keeping Pandarus and his importunities at arm's length and of assessing just who Troilus is. Cressida deflates in turn every proposed trait in Troilus that should make him lovable – his handsome complexion, his youth, his appeal to a woman like Helen, his need that only Cressida can satisfy – by pointing to the contradictions in Pandarus' arguments.[2] All the while, however, we sense her interest in Troilus.

That interest is confirmed at the end of her first scene in soliloquy, her only soliloquy in the play apart from her brief apostrophizing of Troilus in 5.2.113–18 that is overheard by Ulysses, Troilus and Thersites.[3] Perhaps the passage at the close of 1.2 functions as a soliloquy rather like Prince Hal's in *1 Henry IV* (also at the end of 1.2, his first scene): to afford us an insight into her sense of self, and to assure us that what we have just seen is not as threatening as it might otherwise appear. She has a plan, like Hal, and is self-possessed. We learn that she is indeed drawn to Troilus by qualities in him a 'thousandfold' more worthy than Pandarus' flattering praise can suggest (1.2.275–6). Yet she will hold off, for the simple and undeniable reason that men in love treat women as angels until they obtain what they want. In a series of sententious maxims, highlighted by the rhymed couplets in which they are uttered (273–86), she reiterates the truisms that 'Men prize the thing ungained more than it is' and

---

1  For contrasting views of Cressida's wit as a deceptive practice hiding her true self or as her authentic voice, see Tiffany, 55 n. 4; Hale; Lynch, 'Cressida'; D. Hooker; Voth & Evans. Everything hangs here on Shakespeare's mode of characterization and his use of the range of theatrical practice and possibility.
2  Cf. Beatrice's deflations of Benedick in *MA* 1.1.111–40 and elsewhere.
3  On the function of this soliloquy as compared with others in Shakespeare, and on the extent to which it reveals Cressida's private thoughts, see Loggins, 9–17, Tiffany, 45, and Gaudet, 131–2.

that 'Achievement is command; ungained, beseech'. To achieve a woman is to gain command over her, whereas when she is not yet won, the lover must beg. There is a strong element of calculation in this, as with Hal, but it is also sensible and self-knowing. She returns to this great truth immediately after her surrender. 'O foolish Cressid, I might have still held off, / And then you would have tarried' (4.2.18–19). The iteration of the language of tarrying and holding off (see 1.1.14–24 and 1.2.277, 'Yet hold I off') points to her basic stratagem.

Though Troilus is given a chance to speak in the ensuing dramatic action (during the Trojan council scene) and reveal who he is, Cressida remains silent and off stage until the eve of her giving herself to Troilus. She enters veiled – a stage gesture too easily overlooked by readers of the play. For all her candid soliloquizing at the end of 1.2, she is something of an unknown quantity. In the interim, men have argued hotly about a war fought over women and have somehow drifted on into a continuation of a senseless conflict. Helen and Paris, giggling, have attempted to pry out of Pandarus the secret of Troilus' looming affair with Cressida, though they seem to know all about it anyway (3.1.75–88). What has Cressida been thinking? Shakespeare leaves out much of what fascinates Chaucer during the period of negotiation (see pp. 382–5). The moment has somehow arrived.

Cressida's veil expresses a sense of shame, perhaps (or so Pandarus imagines), of mystery, and of the objectification of the woman as a sexual prize. 'Come, draw this curtain, and let's see your picture', Pandarus cackles, as she is unveiled like some portrait in a private collection (3.2.45–6).[1] Pandarus speaks of her also as a hawk who must be tamed (41–2), making a ribald joke about the fact that such a training method requires sleeplessness on the part of the animal or person being tamed. Hawk- or falcon-taming is a favourite metaphor of Petruchio (*TS*

---

1   Cf. *TN* 1.5.228–9 ('we will draw the curtain and show you the picture'), Sonnet 47 and *TGV* 4.2.116–28.

4.1.178–84), the key concept of which is to starve the bird into obedience. In still another erotic metaphor, Cressida is for Pandarus a beast of burden to be harnessed in the 'thills', the shafts of a cart, lest she 'draw backward' (43). Everything said to this point bespeaks male ownership and a transfer of the woman as property, with Pandarus acting as the close relative in the absence of a father. Perhaps Cressida's infamous first line, 'Will you walk in, my lord?', can be partly understood as a wry response to the situation in which she finds herself.

Cressida is candid with Troilus at this critical moment about her fears. They are not, like his, fears of failure in performance. They seem instead to be fears arising from the loss of autonomy in the act of giving oneself to a lover. To surrender thus is to lose control, to make oneself vulnerable both to events and to the wavering inclinations of another person. Whether Cressida has had other lovers before Troilus is something on which the play gives mixed signals,[1] but in any case the present decision is momentous for her. She faces the logic of this immense hazard with admirable intelligence. She knows that men vow more than they are able to 'perform' (83), not in the performative sense that Troilus nurtures but in the sense of holding to their vows. She knows that Troilus is a man. What sort of man he is remains the decisive question, one she has been debating with Pandarus and herself since 1.2.

Why then does she give in? Why does she go on to confess to Troilus her whole strategy of playing at 'Hard to seem won' (3.2.113), especially when she knows that this admission will give him tyrannical power over her? Her confessing all her tricks and devices is as crucial a surrender as the giving of her body in love, and prompts from her at once a rueful sense of regret: 'Why have I blabbed? Who shall be true to us / When we are so unsecret to ourselves?' (120–1). It is as though her capitulation

---

1 For divided views as to whether Cressida has had previous sexual experience, see Fluchère, 214, R. A. Yoder, 22, and Adelman, 'Cressid', 136 n. 21. Cressida is evidently not, like Chaucer's Criseyde, a widow.

is already complete and irrevocable; the joining of two bodies will but confirm the man's victory. She is ready to 'repent' (127), as though experiencing on a spiritual level a kind of post-coital *triste*. She sees herself as two persons, one a 'kind of self' that clings longingly to Troilus and another 'unkind self' (143–5) that wishes to get away from her more clinging self lest she lose her personal autonomy – a dividing of her personality that anticipates Troilus' cry of despair in her desertion of him: 'This is and is not Cressid' (5.2.153).[1]

Despite these inner conflicts, the giving of herself is genuine and as intellectually calculated as such an emotional act can be. She has evidently decided that she can trust Troilus, or at least that he is worth the taking of a great chance. She knows, far more than Troilus, that 'to be wise and love / Exceeds man's might' (3.2.151–2); only the gods can hope for such wisdom, and (she might have added) even the Olympians do not fare very well on that score. Armed with that insight, she plunges into surrender for what she hopes it can give her in return for the loss of autonomy: the unspeakable comforts of trust and mutuality.[2] The need for such comforts is all too visible in a war-torn world, with her father dwelling in the enemy camp.

Nowhere, despite what men will say of her, does Cressida reveal herself as driven by promiscuous sexual desire. That interpretation is of course open to directors (and was exploited as such by Barton and Hall in 1960 and Hands in 1981, among others; see pp. 101–2, 104), but it is not unambiguously called for in the script. When she speaks to Pandarus earlier, she does employ what is for her an uncharacteristic image of explicit sexuality, insisting that she will lie 'Upon my back to defend my belly' (1.2.251), but even here she speaks of resisting. When she asks Troilus on the morning after their consummation if he would like to 'come you again

---

1   See Adelman, 'Cressid' 123; Rossiter, 134–5; Asp, 'Defense', 411; Charnes, 78.
2   See Wheeler, 202, 207, 211. Though Wheeler does not discuss *Troilus* in detail, his thesis about 'trust and autonomy in Shakespeare's development' (154–221) is highly applicable to this play.

into my chamber', she perceives from his smiling laughter that Troilus has read erotic meaning into her invitation, reminiscent as it is of 'Will you walk in, my lord?', but she is probably to be believed when she insists that 'I think of no such thing' (4.2.37–40). She meant only that someone has knocked at the door and that it behoves them to retire decorously from view. This is not to say that Cressida fails to be sexually attracted to Troilus; to the contrary, she confesses to him that she 'was won . . . With the first glance that ever . . .', whereupon she breaks off in blushing confusion (3.2.113–14). The point rather is that the longing for trust and the opposite fear of loss of autonomy appear to dominate her thinking and her emotions as she moves with some deliberation towards her affair with Troilus.

The unbearably painful sequel is something she might have predicted; indeed, she has foreseen something like it as all too probable: Troilus consents to her return to her father. Unlike Chaucer's Troilus, who begs Criseyde to steal away with him and considers asking Priam to let him keep her (4.554–5), Shakespeare's young hero informs Cressida that she has no choice other than to obey. Four times she asks if she must indeed leave, and four times he tells her that she must. Where are the trust and the mutuality in this? Her response is as opposite to Troilus' as could be: 'O you immortal gods! I will not go' (4.2.95).[1] For her to leave Troilus would be to desert him, just when he has taken the place of father, kindred, all consanguinity (97–9). Whereas Troilus inveighs against the envious gods for having taken her from him, Cressida's question is still the practical one, expressed in monosyllabically simple language: 'And is it true that I must go from Troy?' 'What, and from Troilus too?' 'Is't possible?' 'I must, then, to the Grecians?' (4.4.29–54). These iterated questions punctuate Troilus' flights of imagination about the 'injury of chance' that 'Puts back leave-taking' and 'forcibly prevents / Our locked embrasures' (32–6). Troilus' self-pitying scenario finds fault in the envious gods and in 'injury

1 See Adams, 84–5, Schwartz, 316, and Donaldson, 'Cressid', 78.

of chance', blaming everyone and everything but himself, while her thoughts are of the stunning lack of inevitability in what he proposes. Seizing on what few practical options are left, she repeatedly asks, 'When shall we see again?', 'When shall I see you?', though (like Juliet) she worries about Troilus' personal safety if he comes to find her in the enemy camp (56–70). She says little; Troilus leads the conversation.[1] The last thing she ever says to him is, 'My lord, will you be true?' (100). It is a question prompted by his insistent interrogation of her, though he puts the matter not as a query but as a refrain of command: 'Be thou but true of heart', 'Be thou true', 'But yet, be true' (57–73). Troilus has introduced the element of doubt into their relationship; he has shown her how to consider the infidelity that her whole being has rejected until now.

Cressida's arrival at the Greek camp is another major mark against her in criticism about the play, and it does indeed show her in an unattractive light. She herself has nothing to say in defence of her conduct once she has left Troy. We witness a return to the brittle, combative wit that characterized her earlier encounters with Pandarus. She is now among sex-hungry men who are accustomed to fight over women as prizes of war. Whatever the scene may reveal about Cressida, it is a replay of the competitive male rutting rituals that have brought the Greeks to Troy in the first place. The chief generals go first in kissing Cressida, as though the 'order' and 'degree' that Ulysses so highly values were instituted among men to make possible this prioritizing of desire. The others line up like customers at a prostitute's doorway. Patroclus cannot resist the opportunity of turning the occasion into one more tired jest at the expense of Menelaus' horns, by 'popping' in when it comes to be Menelaus' turn as Paris has already done (4.5.29–30). Cressida joins in the cruel fun, making points with the assembled males by scorning Menelaus and putting him down as an 'odd' man with whom

1  See Tiffany, 45; Adelman, 'Cressid', 127; Donaldson, 'Cressid', 74; Garber, 143–4.

Paris has got 'even' (36–46). She is perhaps trying to 'exercise some control over the game of homosocial rivalry by showing that she can play it'.[1] She learns quickly enough how to get the men to beg, as Juliet Stevenson discovered in her portrayal of Cressida in 1985 (see pp. 108–110). Cressida acts out Helen's role in this encounter, as she is expected to do; the men see these women as two of a kind.[2] Cressida is wielding once again the only weapons available to her as an unattached, attractive woman: denial and 'tarrying'.

When Ulysses' turn arrives, he begs a kiss and then refuses it, in a gesture that has become the subject of varying interpretation in criticism and in the theatre.[3] His choice can be seen as the right-minded and wholesome decision of a man who speaks so 'wisely' elsewhere (1.3.75–137) in the view of some critics, or it can sound puritanical and repressed. Or, Ulysses may be overreacting to Cressida's putting him in the humiliating position of begging for what the others, except Menelaus, have been freely given. Davies's 1985 production interpreted Ulysses' reaction to Cressida's witty ploys as a misogynistic outburst of hurt male pride (see p. 109). Dramaturgically, at any rate, Ulysses provides a valuable counterweight to his fellow officers, establishing a debate about how men should judge and relate to Cressida. The text does not make clear whether the actress (or boy actor) acting the part of Cressida is to play the slattern in this scene for all she is worth, or whether Ulysses' bitter denunciation of her as one of those 'sluttish spoils of opportunity / And daughters of the game' (4.5.63–4) grows out of some sort of premonition based on his own cynical nature; the director and actor get to choose.[4] Ulysses' fierce sermon does at any rate spell out the issues in relation to which Cressida must now define herself, and delineates the coquettish role that she is now expected to play.

---

1    Engle, 162. See also Gaudet, 138.
2    See 36 n. 2 above and Bayley, 'Time', 68.
3    See Hjort, 101–2; Adamson, 120–3; and 24 n. 4 and 25 n. 2 above.
4    See Adamson, 121.

Cressida gets the message. Whether it is Ulysses denouncing her as a whore or Diomedes insisting upon having her as his whore, Cressida hears one set of instructions from the men with whom she must now live.[1] Even her father, Calchas, regards her more as a possession, and as a means of testing the Greek generals' willingness to keep their promises to him, than as a person in her own right. We do not see Calchas greet her solicitously (as Shakespeare could easily have shown, out of Chaucer and Lydgate). His sole function in the play, once she has arrived, is to answer (off stage, as though from his tent) Diomedes' importunate question, 'Where's your daughter?' with the compliant answer: 'She comes to you' (5.2.3–5). He too has apparently assumed that once she arrives among the Greeks she will take up with some Greek officer.

What is a woman to do when the men are so unanimous in their judgements of her and their plans for her? Ulysses accompanies Troilus to a place where they can witness her assignation with Diomedes, partly perhaps out of solicitude, partly to confirm his own low estimate of her. Thersites, also a secret witness, knows before she has spoken more than a few words that 'She will sing any man at first sight' and that her 'juggling trick' is 'to be secretly open' (10–26). But Diomedes is her 'guardian' (a term she uses twice, at 8 and 50), appointed by the Greek officials to escort her back to the Greek camp. Even Troilus understands that she is now placed under Diomedes' protection and tutelage (4.4.108–36). To whom else is she to turn? She appears now to be confined to what Lars Engle describes as 'an unappealing choice between being promiscuously used or accepting the protection of a predatory male'.[2] How is she to resist being what all these importunate men expect her to be?

Arguably, Cressida yields to Diomedes not so much through

---

1   See Ornstein, 245; de Beauvoir, 155; Greene, 'Cressida', 133–6; Styan, *Comedy*, 21–2; Lynch, 'Cressida', 363.
2   Engle, 162. See also Lynch, 'Cressida', 365.

*goût pour l'homme* (despite Thersites' choric slavering about 'the
devil Luxury', with 'his fat rump and potato finger', tickling
these two together, 5.2.57–8) as through fear, susceptibility to
male authority, and hopelessness.[1] She acquiesces, as women are
taught to do in her culture – just as Andromache bends to
Hector's will in the next scene, sensing that she is right and that
Hector will die as a consequence of his refusal to listen to her
(5.3.80–7). Cressida even tries to resist Diomedes, snatching
back the sleeve that Troilus gave her (only to have Diomedes
retrieve it again), insisting that she will not keep her word to
Diomedes since the deed is not yet done (5.2.72–87). She tries to
tell Diomedes that she is promised to another, and loyally
declines to name that man lest he be put in danger.

Whatever sympathies we are encouraged to feel, Cressida
makes no attempt to defend her actions.[2] Her sense of inevitability about her surrender to Diomedes robs her of what little
courage she might attempt to muster in resisting such an importunate man. Diomedes' threat to leave her to her own
indecisiveness – 'Why then, farewell. / Thou never shalt mock
Diomed again' – attacks her where she is most vulnerable, facing
the prospect of being without a man to protect her. (Her father
is no help.) Diomedes may well not be bluffing; he has better
things to do than wait around for a tease to make up her mind.
He cynically regards this shilly-shallying on her part as 'fooling'
(105–8), and some critics agree that she is merely playing hard to
get,[3] but her anguish of uncertainty ('Ay, come. – O Jove! – Do,
come. – I shall be plagued', 111) points to genuine histrionic
imagination.

Once the die has been cast, she is miserable and self-accusing,
putting all the blame not on circumstance or on Diomedes, or for
that matter on Troilus, but on the sad, sad way in which her
heart and mind have been swayed by her corrupted will. 'Ah,

1  See Kott, 82, for a comparison to the Lady Anne in *R3*.
2  See Tiffany, 44–5.
3  See Rossiter, 133, and 47 n. 1 above.

poor our sex!'[1] She sees herself as hopelessly divided against herself, one eye looking on Troilus and the other prompted by her 'heart' (113–15), as she herself feared earlier (3.2.143–6) and as Troilus soon laments in his cry that 'This is and is not Cressid' (5.2.153).[2] Too ready to use general propositions to justify particular moral choices, she concludes that her destiny must be that of other women: 'The error of our eye directs our mind' (116). Apart from this appeal to a generalized condition over which she had no control at birth, that of being female, she seeks no consolation in the idea that she has been victimized. Most devastatingly, she has acquiesced in the male view of women that so suffuses this play and the culture in which she lives: women are led by their appetites and are appropriately considered to be objects of desire.[3] Her own conduct may or may not reinforce that low estimate; was she really led by her eye, or by her fears? Whatever the case, she now accepts and internalizes the male verdict about her as being undeniable simply because she is a woman.

Richard Wheeler argues well that in the *Sonnets* and in the so-called 'problem' plays, notably *Troilus and Cressida*, Shakespeare unveils the terrifying spectre that has menacingly threatened his earlier plays in the shape of a male nightmare: the woman who is in fact untrue to her vows as a lover. The Dark Lady and Cressida do betray and cheat their men. In earlier plays, an assortment of men, like Claudio in *Much Ado About Nothing* and Bassanio in *The Merchant of Venice*, are hoodwinked – usually by their own penchant for thinking the worst of women and of themselves – into imagining that they have been two-timed. Seldom, however, has the supposition been true, though Margaret of Anjou in *2*

---

1 Among those who readily agree with Cressida in putting the blame on her are Lawrence, *Problem*, 141–2; Foakes, '*TC*', 143; Marsh, 189; Kimbrough, 86–8; Presson, 132. See also 47 n. 1 and 56 n. 3 above. Conversely, those who compassionately view her at this point as a victim of a patriarchal social order include Voth & Evans, 236, O'Rourke, 140, and Clifford Lyons, 111.
2 See Adelman, 'Cressid', 129.
3 See Greene, 'Cressida', 135–42, and Dollimore, 48.

*Henry VI* offers an exception; the problem has instead been with the diseased imagination of males, too prone to see themselves as cuckolds and to see women as monsters of betrayal. The comedies especially have steered a wide berth around actual female sexual infidelity; Titania's exceptional behaviour in this regard (in *A Midsummer Night's Dream*) can be attributed to the strange ways of fairydom. The pattern of near-tragedy leading to reconciliation and forgiveness in earlier Shakespearean comedy often turns upon the plot of a suspected infidelity that turns out to be chimerical, thus enabling the comedy to end happily in reclamation of the wrongly suspected woman and forgiveness of the wrongly suspecting male.[1]

What if the nightmare turns out to be true? The revelations of Pandora's box in the *Sonnets* are indeed bitter. The Dark Lady is darkly beautiful but promiscuous and heartless, leaving the poet in self-abasement, fury and disgust directed as much at himself and the unfaithful young male friend as against the lady herself. A director like Mendes in 1990 (see p. 113) could choose to present Cressida as the Dark Lady indeed, of whom the spectators were invited to ask not why she betrayed Troilus but why, in the fallen world of this play, she even entertained for a brief time the possibility of faithfulness. Yet the script compassionately offers us a woman who accepts fully the blame for what she regards as her quick failure, even if we see that she is partly driven to it by compelling circumstances.[2]

Not the least of these circumstances is that, in her terms, Troilus has deserted her. She was ready to give up everything for him. The male system of values that has led him to choose 'honour' over keeping her is deeply flawed. It exhorts men to fight over women as possessions while refusing to trust them or heed their counsel. To examine the love of Troilus and Cressida in a time of war is not simply to become aware of how love is vulnerable to

---

1  Wheeler, 57–75 and *passim*. See also R. G. Hunter, *passim*.
2  See, e.g., R. A. Yoder, 23–5.

social conflicts, as in *Romeo and Juliet*; it is to realize that Troilus fails Cressida because he is so much like the other men in his culture, and that her failure too epitomizes the dilemmas of female dependence and vulnerability in a world controlled by anxious men. War intensifies the conflict and indeed is produced by it, but the problem is inherent in the uneasy and needful relations of the sexes.

## 'CALL THEM ALL PANDERS': VOYEURISM AND MALE BONDING

Pandarus, among the three major figures of the love plot, is the one whose decline from Chaucer's sympathetic portrayal is the most precipitous (see pp. 382–5). Pandarus is a sort of counterpart to Thersites: both are leering, choric figures whose estimates of human sexuality are about as disillusioning as can be imagined.[1] Both speak customarily in colloquial prose that is discordantly juxtaposed with the more poetically impassioned speech of other characters.[2] Pandarus gets to end the play with an epilogue; Thersites is often on the scene, with a satirical phrase for nearly everyone in sight.[3]

Ever since the play was first revived in the early twentieth century, directors have seen Pandarus as a vapid social butterfly (Macowan, 1938), a pathological nanny (Shaw, 1954), a diseased wretch (Barton and Hall, 1960), a syphilitic, mincing drag queen (Judge, 1996). He has been fitted out in top hat and Ascot attire (Guthrie, 1956), a blazer (Mendes, 1990) and a giant dildo (Wing-Davey, 1995). In his epilogue, he has been seen draped lifelessly over a barbed-wire fence (Hands, 1981) or picking out a tune on a piano that, when he rises, continues to play by itself (Davies, 1985).

---

1   Those who compare Pandarus and Thersites include Hyland, *TC*, 75–80; Foakes, *Dark Comedies*, 57–8; Kott, 82; Lawrence, *Problem*, 140–1; Schwartz, 318; Brooks, 18–19; Ard², 92. See also Findlay, 151, and Elliott, 137–8.
2   McAlindon, 39–40.
3   For instances of this colourful invective, see 5.1.6–7, 29–33 and 52–5, and 5.4.2–13.

7 Clive Francis as a syphilitic drag-queen Pandarus, with Victoria Hamilton as Cressida, in Act 1, scene 2 of Ian Judge's production for the Royal Shakespeare Company, 1996

Pandarus is not a satirical railer like Thersites, but he is no less effective in pulling down the tone of any scene in which he appears. His prosy interruptions of Troilus' sad eloquence in the play's opening scene direct our attention away from the 'cruel battle' raging in Troilus' heart to the fussy complaints of his older companion who protests that he will 'meddle' no longer in Troilus' hoped-for affair (1.1.1–14). The repeated word 'meddle' (see 63 and 79) is more appropriate for Pandarus than he perhaps realizes: his enjoyment is derived from being officious in the lives of his friends and relatives. He torments Troilus with his talk of Cressida's beauty and his own unappreciated efforts, lamenting that he has had 'small thanks for my labour' (69). His advice is sententious, his observations self-important and self-pitying. He is also a vastly entertaining and even sympathetic character.

Pandarus' scene with Helen and Paris is the chief time in the play that we see him apart from both Troilus and Cressida, though even here he is trying his best to promote their affair. His ministrations turn out to be much ado about nothing, like all that he undertakes: he requests that Paris discreetly 'cover' for Troilus at supper that evening. If King Priam asks for Troilus, Paris is to 'make his excuse' (3.1.73–4). Nothing could be more pointless, since all Ilium appears to be buzzing with the news. Still, Pandarus' visit gives Shakespeare a chance to look at him in the company of the 'pearl / Whose price hath launched above a thousand ships', i.e. Helen of Troy, the woman who is in Troilus' eyes 'a theme of honour and renown' (2.2.81–2, 199) but who is conversely for Menelaus 'a deadly theme' (4.5.182). Pandarus' scene with Helen and Paris tends to confirm Menelaus' view and to show us the jaded world in which Pandarus would like his niece Cressida to shine.

Why Pandarus wants to solicit his own niece for Troilus we perhaps never quite understand,[1] but we do perceive that he is a

---

1 See Berger, 133, Girard, 208, and Fly, 'I Cannot', 153.

voyeur who takes pleasure vicariously in promoting and watching what others do. He scarcely ever leaves the two lovers alone on stage. He unnecessarily pumps Troilus up for her imminent arrival, describing how she blushes and pants, encourages Troilus to kiss her and seems preoccupied with what is to follow: 'Have you not done talking yet?' (3.2.96–7). He offers to be guardian and patron of the child that will result from their union – provided it is a boy (100–1). Like a connoisseur, he gives appreciative ratings of their kisses: 'Pretty, i'faith' (131).

Pandarus is destined to be what he has become, a dirty old man. His last words in this scene confirm the least attractive side of him: he talks of the bed he has arranged for the lovers, bidding them 'press it to death', and, in a concluding moment on stage alone that anticipates his epilogue of the entire play, promiscuously extends his role as pander to embrace anyone as customer for his services, including 'all tongue-tied maidens here' in the playhouse (203–5). The theatrical gesture of direct address to the audience, used only by Pandarus and Thersites, accentuates the collapsing of time and theatrical space through which the ancient classical past is made present; the 'there' of Troy becomes the 'here' of the theatre. His invitation to the spectators to imagine themselves in Troilus' and Cressida's situation has the effect of making randy voyeurs of them all – of us all.

It should not surprise us that Pandarus is complicit in Troilus' desertion of Cressida, that is, his sad but firm resolve to send her back to her father.[1] Even before the distressing news of the exchange with Antenor arrives, Pandarus' gloating over the night's events is obtrusively male. As Cressida expects, he will not let go. He professes not to be able to recognize Cressida, since she was a virgin. 'How now, how now, how go maidenheads?' When Cressida upbraids him for bringing her 'to do' and then flouting her for it, he wants her to be explicit: 'To do what, to do what? – Let her say what. – What have I brought you to

---

1   See Adelman, 'Cressid', 126; Kaufmann, 'Ceremonies', 149; Fly, 'I Cannot', 154.

do?' (4.2.24–9). As in Chaucer, but with less delicacy, he mockingly pities her for having spent a sleepless night: 'Would he not – ah, naughty man – let it sleep?' (33–4). The 'it' demotes Cressida to the status of child. Pandarus has no words of raillery for Troilus. His comic fascination is with the piercing of the maidenhead and with the performative feats of 'doing' all night long, like an infantilized child contemplating the primal scene. Troilus is vicariously his hero, having sexually conquered Pandarus' own niece. The displacement of desire from Troilus himself to a near relative may legitimate the gloating humour, though with incestuous overtones that make for an uncomfortable moment in the theatre.

When he learns the bad news that Cressida must return to her father, Pandarus has thoughts only of pity for himself and for Troilus. 'Oh, poor gentleman!' He seems ready to blame Cressida for the whole thing: 'I knew thou wouldst be his death'. He is much more concerned with his own suffering ('Would I were as deep under the earth as I am above!') than with his niece's plight. Indeed, Pandarus never acknowledges that she is herself in difficulty; what matters is Troilus. ''Twill be his death, 'twill be his bane; he cannot bear it.' And when at length he tells her what has been decreed, he speaks in the form of an imperative: 'Thou must to thy father and be gone from Troilus'. To her insistence that she will not go, he answers 'Thou must' (4.2.83–96). He has had no time to consult with Troilus about this; instead, he simply understands the order of priorities as Troilus understands them. The demands of honour are not to be resisted with silly talk of an elopement. And, of course, marriage has never been discussed in any case.

The impression is inescapable that both Troilus and Pandarus are ready to give up Cressida. For all their wringing of hands at the enforced separation, she has been conquered, and to that major extent the excitement is over for both chief performer and voyeur. Certainly the loss of Cressida means little to Pandarus personally; he dismisses any thought of her other than to reflect bitterly on 'the foolish fortune of this girl' and to attempt to bring a letter from her to Troilus (5.3.99–102), for she is, after all, his avenue of approach to Troilus.

Indeed, the serious fall-out of this unhappy affair for Pandarus is the loss of Troilus' friendship.[1] In a disillusioning replay of *Romeo and Juliet*, the romantic hero of this play is separated from the irreverent companion of his youth and must face the ending of his story alone.[2] In their penultimate appearance together (5.3.97–111),[3] Troilus reads a letter that Pandarus has brought him from Cressida in a final attempt to act as go-between, and tears the letter into shreds. That gesture effectively ends his connection with Pandarus as well, and repudiates the bonding between the two men that the letter was intended to effect. 'I cannot come to Cressid but by Pandar' (1.1.91), Troilus has earlier complained, using a shortened form of Pandarus' name that, in retrospect, seems prognosticatory.[4] Has Pandarus ever been much more for Troilus than a pander, as a means of achieving Cressida? Certainly the ending of the relationship with Cressida means for Troilus the ending of a need for Pandarus, and perhaps instead a scapegoating of Pandarus for having set up such unhappiness. Autonomously on his own, unwilling to engage in commitment with friend or lover, Troilus becomes in Act 5 an almost inhuman warrior bent on a vengeance that is now both personal and xenophobic.

Alone on stage in the play's epilogue after a final brief encounter with an angry Troilus, Pandarus complains mockingly of the ill-treatment afforded panders, wonders at the hypocrisy of those who use go-betweens and then scorn them, thoroughly

1  See Cook, 42, and Irigaray, 171–2.
2  See *RJ* 3.5.22–39; also 4.3.19. For comparisons of Pandarus with Enobarbus, Mercutio and Falstaff, see Frye, *Fools*, 59.
3  See pp. 416–22 for an analysis of the differences between the Q and F endings of *TC*, the second of which includes at the end of 5.3 a dismissal by Troilus of Pandarus (duplicating lines found at 5.11.32–4) as though for a version of the play in which Pandarus would disappear at that point.
4  Fly, 'I Cannot', 153–4. The shortened form, 'Pandare', appears frequently in Chaucer's poem.

implicates the audience and the entire patriarchal social order in his chortling reflections on venereal disease, gestures topically at the houses of prostitution standing in the jurisdiction of the Bishop of Winchester (where plays were publicly performed), and seems to promise a sequel to the play of which he is the closing master of ceremonies.[1] The separation between Pandarus and the young man he has so intensely befriended is complete. Pandarus has nowhere to go other than into history and imaginative art as a soiled prototype of one who abets and procures.

As a kind of replacement for Pandarus in most of the fifth act we are given Thersites. He is the first to come on stage after Troilus' tearing of Cressida's letter at the end of 5.3. His role, especially in Act 5, is greatly expanded over what we find in Homer and Caxton (see p. 378, 390). His crabbed commentary reduces the friendship of Achilles and Patroclus into an affair of erotic dimensions only, with Patroclus as Achilles' 'masculine whore' (5.1.17). Thersites' vocabulary is insistently one of surgical wounds and of every imaginable disease. His slanderous epithets for those he rails against rely considerably on demeaning animal analogies: camel, elephant, ass, ox, dog, fox, quail, parrot, finch egg.

Given far more soliloquies than any other character,[2] especially in Act 5, Thersites is provided with an opportunity to editorialize on all aspects of human folly in the Greek camp: on Agamemnon as a petticoat-chaser, Menelaus as a cuckoldy yes-man, Nestor as a senile bore, Ulysses as a machiavel, and so on. He never says anything against Hector, Aeneas or the other Trojans, other than one passing disparagement of Troilus (5.4.3–4), thus reflecting the bias of the play as a whole towards the Trojan cause; even Paris, who would seem an inevitable

---

1  The likelihood of a sequel seems severely diminished by the lack of material from the legend of Troy that Shakespeare might include in another play. The situation is not like that of *1H4*, which ends with Falstaff not yet banished.

2  Findlay, 233, notes that Thersites 'has nine out of the play's fourteen soliloquies and addresses over half his lines to the audience'.

target for satirical venom, is spared.[1] We are thus inclined to accord Thersites a warped kind of choric voice, even if it is distastefully vitriolic. The pyrotechnic versatility of his abusive language is captivating, like that of Falstaff. He shares too with Falstaff a mordantly philosophical outlook on the absurdities of human conduct in wartime. His cowardice, when he comes face to face with the redoubtable Hector (5.4.25–34), gives him material for comic reflection that seems coupled, as in Falstaff, with a lack of genuinely craven fear. As a bastard, he is a person of hybrid and marginal status well suited to act as commentator for a notoriously hybrid play.[2] For these and other reasons he is, in the absence of any more decent and temperate spokesman, the degenerate *raisonneur* of the play. Theatre directors have depicted him as a communist intellectual (Macowan, 1938), a war correspondent (Guthrie, 1956), a Geordie waiter (Davies, 1985), a skid-row bum in filthy pinstriped trousers and Gay Lib button (Mendes, 1990), and much more. In Barton's 1968 production, Thersites' codpiece flaunted a versatile and obscene phallus (see pp. 96, 100, 102, 111, 114–15).

Thersites' presence in the scene of Diomedes' pursuit of Cressida gives him extensive occasion to comment on the love plot of this play. His observations are all deflationary and obscene. Any man can 'sing' Cressida, he proposes, if he can 'take her clef' (5.2.12–13). The fascination with Cressida's 'clef', or 'cleft', reminds us that Thersites is no less a voyeur than Pandarus, and in a way that uncomfortably urges us to adopt a similarly obsessive curiosity. Thersites' meditation on a woman who is 'secretly open' (26) is no less pornographic in its pictorial imagining. He habitually combines a show of moral dismay with a dwelling on anatomical particulars and erotic gestures, as when he exclaims, *sotto voce*: 'How the devil Luxury, with his fat rump and potato finger, tickles these together! Fry,

1 See Lawrence, 'Troilus', 433, and Coghill, 99.
2 Parker, 227; Findlay, 67–9, 150–2, 234–5.

lechery, fry!' (57–9). We are invited to disapprove, but in a prurient way that uses moral condemnation as an excuse for graphic
description. Thersites paces the erotic action, urging it on with
'Now she sharpens. Well said, whetstone!' (78–9), only to sub-
side into a sententious rhymed couplet that is all the more
marked for being his sole utterance in verse: 'A proof of strength
she could not publish more, / Unless she said, "My mind is now
turned whore"' (119–20). His couplet mocks those of Cressida
(113–18), who has concluded her presence in the scene with
heartfelt self-reproach. Left to soliloquize once more at the
scene's end, Thersites reiterates the theme that connects the sad
love story of this play to its surrounding environment: 'Lechery,
lechery, still wars and lechery; nothing else holds fashion'
(201–2).

## 'WHAT'S AUGHT BUT AS 'TIS VALUED?': COMMERCIAL AND SUBJECTIVE VALUATION OF IDENTITY AND WORTH

'What's aught but as 'tis valued?' asks Troilus in the debate of the
Trojan leaders (2.2.52), thus posing a question that is central to the
play's concern with valuation. Commercial images abound in
Troilus' speech and throughout the text. 'We turn not back the
silks upon the merchant / When we have soiled them' (69–70), he
argues, by way of demonstrating why Helen must not be returned
to the Greeks, thus implying that she is an object of trade whose
value is diminished by her having been used. Yet the contest for
Helen remains keenly mercantile. 'Is she worth keeeping?' he asks.
'Why, she is a pearl / Whose price hath launched above a thousand
ships / And turned crowned kings to merchants' (81–3). Earlier,
Troilus has cast himself in the role of merchant adventurer in his
quest for Cressida: 'Her bed is India; there she lies, a pearl . . .
Ourself the merchant, and this sailing Pandar / Our doubtful
hope, our convoy and our bark' (1.1.96–100). Cressida, for her
part, knows that her value depends on her astute management of

the male acquisitive instinct. 'Men prize the thing ungained more than it is', she confides in her chief soliloquy (1.2.280). As Janet Adelman observes, Cressida 'seems to have internalized the principle of valuation that rules this society, the principle implied in Troilus' question "What's aught but as 'tis valued?" '[1]

Hector has an answer to Troilus' question and its implied premise that value resides subjectively in the eye of the beholder. 'But value dwells not in particular will', insists Hector. Value derives also from the extent to which the desired thing is 'precious of itself' (2.2.53–5), that is, possesses intrinsic worth. Hector thus finds validity in both intrinsic and conferred value, as Terry Eagleton observes, though tragically Hector abandons the potentially rich and complex fusion of the two under the pressure of loyalty to his culture's outmoded chivalric ideals. The danger of unalloyed relativism, argues Eagleton, is that 'reality', distorted by the subjectivity of personal vision, becomes humanly created and sterile; self-praise and even love are caught up in endless circularity. To know oneself becomes difficult when, as Ulysses advises Achilles, no one can know anything of himself until he beholds his best qualities 'formed in th'applause / Where they're extended' – that is, given substance by the applause of those by whom they are valued and assessed (3.3.120–1). The relativity of such a position challenges the notion that such qualities have any reality at all.[2]

All values become suspect; in Una Ellis-Fermor's words, 'emotional, intellectual, and moral values resolve alike into futility'.[3] The crisis is so acute that, in the view of some critics, it elicits from Ulysses a theory of political and social order anticipating that of Thomas Hobbes.[4] William Elton, for example, explores

1  Adelman, 'Cressid', esp. 122. See also James, 85–118. Other critical studies not cited in the following notes that discuss the relativity of value in *Troilus* include Bentley; Fly, 'I Cannot'; Fischer; Gérard; D. Wilson. The topic of value surfaces in Renaissance drama as early as Henry Medwall's *Fulgens and Lucrece* (c. 1490–1501).
2  Eagleton, 13–38. See also Dusinberre on failures of self-knowing.
3  Ellis-Fermor, esp. 57. On the importance of the print revolution, see G. Williams, *Sex*, 99ff.
4  Nowottny. See Kermode for a reply, stressing the dangers of bringing on Hobbes before his time.

conflict in this play as an expression of a change in ideas of value philosophy from Aquinas to Hobbes, from fixed and divinely sanctioned concepts of value to those of a kind of marketplace in which (to quote Hobbes) 'the value or worth of a man is, as of all other things, his price'. Hobbes means that a man's value is determined by 'so much as would be given for the use of his power'. When humans fight for honour, in Hobbes as in Ulysses' speech on order and degree, value is quantified into power: '*Honourable* is whatsoever possession, action, or quality, is an argument and sign of power . . . Dominion and victory is [sic] honourable because acquired by power'. Elton also cites Montaigne and Machiavelli as writers for whom 'value is not only relative: it is quantified'.[1] Achilles reflects a similar estimate of the human struggle for honour and power when he argues that no man is honoured for himself, but rather for 'those honours / That are without him', i.e. external to him, 'as place, riches and favour' (3.3.81–2). And the general whose power Achilles so much resents, Agamemnon, shares a comparable view of how self-worth should be valued: 'If he [Achilles] overhold his price so much, / We'll none of him' (2.3.131–2).

Transitions in Renaissance thinking towards subjective valuation of identity and worth are a manifestation of the philosophical scepticism that, as Rolf Soellner shows, was current and controversial in Shakespeare's day. Philosophically, says Soellner, Ulysses is a sceptic in his insistence that knowledge of the true nature of things is unattainable in view of the contradictory evidence presented by the senses and interpreted by the mind. So, too, is Troilus up to a point, though he is also a hedonist and confused by the passions of his youth. Thersites, the play's greatest sceptic, has none of Troilus' inconsistencies, though he is also presented as reprehensible, so that it is difficult to say which of the sceptical statements of various characters are to be trusted. Nonetheless, the play as a whole, and especially the battle scenes

1 Elton, 'Ulysses', esp. 96–101 and 105, citing Hobbes, 3.76 and 3.79–80.

at the end, 'use the skeptics' favorite method of negating man's illusionary ideals by pragmatic and brutal realities'.[1]

Shifts in valuation correlate also with historical changes in the Renaissance from an idealized feudalism to early modern capitalism. The social life of Renaissance London was beginning to take on some bourgeois characteristics, as Raymond Southall observes. Changes in social behaviour 'expressed a new ethic', that of the marketplace. The decay of feudal and medieval values brought with it a decline in chivalry and the courtly love ethic, substituting for those values a coarsening of life that manifests itself throughout the play, as in Calchas' talk of ransom that will 'buy my daughter' (3.3.28), or in Troilus' lament for the thousand sighs with which he and Cressida 'Did buy each other' and must now 'poorly sell ourselves' (4.4.39), or in Paris' wry observation that by denouncing Helen, Diomedes is only doing what 'chapmen' or merchants do, 'Dispraise the thing that you desire to buy' (4.1.77–8). The ethic of the play, for all its nominally historical setting, is 'neither ancient (Greek or Trojan) nor medieval (romantic or chivalrous) but Elizabethan-Jacobean . . . in short, the spirit of capitalism'.[2] The play can be seen, in Larry Clarke's words, as an 'allegory of the conflict between late feudal aristocracy and the rising bourgeoisie that played so great a part in [Shakespeare's] own time'. The aristocracy's social function and feudal base had been shifting since the early Tudor era from military service and ownership of land to a more centralized structure in which the lords of the realm became a 'service aristocracy', still clinging to mythologies of feudal greatness but in fact reduced to dependence on taxation and the granting of monopolies by the monarchy.[3] A world of rank and royalty

---

1    Soellner, *Patterns*, esp. 207 and 214. See also Soellner, 'Prudence', and Levine, on radical doubt and Pyrrhonism.
2    Southall, esp. 218–20 and 224. For refinements of the arguments, see 3 n. below and 71 nn. 1–2. See also Empson, *Pastoral*, 34–43, and Bruster. The phrase used in this paragraph, 'from idealized feudalism to early modern capitalism', is Engle's (155).
3    Clarke, esp. 209–11.

that Shakespeare found in his medieval sources gives way, as Lars Engle observes, to one of competition, emulation, a business-like insistence on a reasonable return for one's investment, and the social mobility that Ulysses so vehemently mistrusts.[1]

To this picture of economic and social conflict can be added valuable background information on changing attitudes towards money as a way of assessing value. A large increase of metals brought back from the New World, and other aspects of mercantilist enterprise, gave impetus to changing attitudes towards money, as Stephen Mead shows. Formerly held to be of intrinsic worth, specie was seen increasingly as a form of 'representational signification'. Bills of exchange, use of long-term credit, and manipulation of rates of exchange came to dominate the marketplace, bringing with them a sense that all systems of exchange are cold and ruthless and that the value of money is 'a matter of opinion'.[2] Hence, perhaps, Troilus' derisive outcry at the prospect of weighing 'the worth and honour of a king . . . in a scale / Of common ounces', or of trying to sum up the infinite value of that honour 'with counters', that is, with disks used in computation (2.2.26–9).

Similarly, the economic inflation that manifested itself during the late 1590s and early 1600s, not only in market prices but in honours at court, can provide a context for the play's fascination with the language of increase and dilation, spending, swelling, dearness, usury and husbandry. This dilation manifests itself, as Patricia Parker observes, in mocking references to Ajax' 'spacious and dilated parts' (2.3.244), in the allusions to Achilles' 'great bulk' (4.4.127), and in many other word choices. The play throughout is 'bloated, forced/farced, or stuffed' with hyperbolic language, from the Prologue's metaphors of cramming to Ulysses' 'rhetorically swollen' manner of speaking in the *gravis*

---

1   Engle, esp. 155.
2   Mead, esp. 237–9 and 243. On the meaning and value of coins, see Fischer, *passim.*

style of Cicero's *Rhetorica ad Herennium*.[1] The inflation of hon-
orifics in the play manifests itself, as C. C. Barfoot demonstrates,
in such words as *fair*, *true*, *brave*, *valiant*, *gallant*, *great*, *good*,
*worthy*, *heroic* and *sweet*, with a particular focus on the linguisti-
cally interrelated terms *praise*, *prize* and *price*.[2] In the Marxist
terms employed by Gayle Greene, the marketplace provides a
'cash nexus' where supply and demand operate in the exploitative
fashion that Marx deplored.[3]

Greene's main point is that Cressida's valuation of herself,
and, more broadly, women's tendency to see themselves as
objects of desire, come to be associated in this play with
economic competitiveness. Certainly the play employs commercial metaphors to evoke a sense of what women are worth in
men's eyes. 'To her own worth / She shall be prized', says
Diomedes in response to Troilus' rapturous praising of Cressida
(4.4.132–3), prompting Jill Mann to argue that Shakespeare
'denies us access to Cressida's inner life' as a means of stressing
the oppressive extent to which her value is imposed by male sensibilities 'from outside, without reference to her inner being'.[4]
Claire Tylee similarly argues that Cressida is 'unable to maintain
a sense of her own integrity'; in a world where 'a person's nature
or identity is determined by the value set on that person by others', especially males, Cressida 'seems to have had no
opportunity to act autonomously, according to her own emotions, and so she seems never to have been allowed to develop her
own sense of self'.[5] Women in the Troy story, as Carol Cook
points out, are the victims of a whole series of exchanges involving Hesione, Helen and Cressida in what threatens to become
'an endless cycle of repetition'. Helen, though merely a cipher,
generates desire and violence; her value is thus 'produced by the

1  Parker, esp. 185, 214, 220 and 222–3.
2  Barfoot, esp. 48–9.
3  Greene, 'Cressida', esp. 136.
4  Mann, esp. 117 and 125, who sees this externalizing of evaluation as a major change
   in Shakespeare as compared with Chaucer's *TC*.
5  Tylee, esp. 63 and 65.

economy which she also activates'.[1] The mystique of a system of gift exchange governs male appropriations of women and helps demythologize a story that was once transcendent and aristocratic to one that is now couched in the mordantly pragmatic terms of economic transition.[2]

Closely related to the motif of relative value is that of reflected images seen in a mirror or in the eye of some observer. As Howard Adams argues, this image pattern expresses a fascination in the play with wanting to know who another person really is, and conversely with the way in which the play's chief figures go about fashioning their personal identities in response to others' perceptions of them. Troilus asks Apollo to tell him 'What Cressid is' (1.1.95). He also craves to know 'what Pandar is', and what 'we' are, meaning himself. He finds that he must continually readjust his notion of Cressida until he wonders at last whether her identity is single or double (5.2.131–67). Cressida, for her part, confesses in soliloquy that she sees a thousandfold more worth in Troilus 'Than in the glass of Pandar's praise may be' (1.2.276). Ajax, blind to his own qualities, must be reminded by Agamemnon that 'Pride is his own glass, his own trumpet, his own chronicle' (2.3.153–4). Ulysses employs a similar image in reference to Achilles: 'Pride hath no other glass / To show itself but pride' (3.3.47–8), and goes on to expound, in conversation with Achilles, the notion that the eye cannot behold itself; 'speculation', the power of sight, 'turns not to itself / Till it hath travelled and is mirrored there' – i.e. in another's eyes or some other reflective means – 'Where it may see itself' (106–12). Thus, as Adams puts it, the 'internalizing of social signals is woven into the fabric of the play by Shakespeare's repeated use of images of reflection'.[3]

1 Cook, esp. 38–9.
2 Engle, esp. 159. His book title, *Shakespeare and Pragmatism*, nicely captures the flavour of his discussion in chap. 7 on *TC*.
3 Adams, esp. 75–6. Critics who discuss specular imagery, in addition to those mentioned below, include Charnes; Cook; Cox; Elton, 'Ulysses', 103–4; Garner; Greene, 'Cressida'. See also Stamm on what he calls 'mirror passages'.

For Harry Berger, as well, optical imagery in the play is a sign of relativity in perspective. Ulysses' famous speech on order and degree in 1.3, if read in a straightforward way, seems to refer to a 'natural system' in which 'self and value, rights and duties, depend on one's fixed position relative to others, in a hierarchical universe'. Yet his unsettling talk of 'the ill aspects of planets evil' (92), reminding us that the heavenly bodies themselves owe their sense of position to the observer's eye, whence they beam down on earth their terrible 'influence' (the Quarto reading of 'aspects'), suggests all too plainly that 'appetite, the universal wolf, is the true nature of things', and that 'degree is a lid shakily imposed on nature, an artificial system of distinctions and constraints which rubs against the grain of reality'. Ulysses' second meaning thus 'stresses the subjective agency of seers as they influence their objects by the way they see'. Throughout, the nature, value and rewards of performance 'are too little in the power of agents and too much under the control of observers' who are not up to their responsibility.[1]

The play's specular images evince troublesome symptoms of narcissistic self-regard, as Juliet Dusinberre perceives. 'Pride is his own glass', Agamemnon warningly reminds Ajax (2.3.153). The danger everywhere is a failure of self-knowing. Achilles is perceptive enough to be aware that his mind 'is troubled, like a fountain stirred', and that he cannot himself 'see the bottom of it' (3.3.309–10), and yet his attempts at self-reflection lead ultimately to a terrible act of brutality that will forever darken his image as reflected in others' opinion of him.[2] These images are symptomatic of frustrating and self-defeating reflexiveness: 'The raven chides blackness' (2.3.208), 'He that is proud eats up himself' (2.3.152), 'lechery eats itself' (5.4.34) and 'Pride hath no other glass / To show itself but pride' (3.3.47–8). The specular imagery can take on metatheatrical resonances, especially

1 Berger, esp. 125–8. See also O'Rourke, esp. 143–5; Lacan, *passim*; Kristeva (see, e.g., 209–25 on *RJ*); Hegel, 6; Willbern, 240–3; Freedman, 252.
2 Dusinberre, esp. 92–3. See also Kopper.

when Patroclus' 'imitation' of Agamemnon and Nestor becomes the subject of Ulysses' irate rhetoric (1.3.149–84).[1]

Specular themes and imagery thus sharpen our awareness of our presence in the theatre. The play turns its speculative eye on itself, holding up for examination its double plot structure and its telling of the twice-told tale of Troy. Both war and gender become the stuff of theatre performance, as Barbara Bowen and Laura Levine point out. Parodic metatheatre, especially as reported in Ulysses' diatribe against Patroclus' play-acting in 1.3 and in Thersites' marvellous impersonation of Ajax (3.3.253–300), encourages us to be aware of, and mistrustful of, all forms of representation. Pandarus' epilogue has the uncomfortable effect of eroticizing spectatorship and of refusing us the comfort of closure that a dramatic performance might lead us to expect. Theatre becomes an instrument of radical scepticism.[2]

Such metatheatricality suggests a comparison of *Troilus* with its near contemporary, *Hamlet*. As Peter Hyland points out, no other plays in the Shakespeare canon are so insistently conscious of theatre and role-playing.[3] One striking similarity is that of Ulysses' critical account of Patroclus as 'like a strutting player, whose conceit / Lies in his hamstring' (1.3.153–4), and Hamlet's ire at 'a robustious periwig-pated fellow' who can do nothing but 'tear a passion to tatters, to very rags' (*Ham* 3.2.9–10).[4] Contemporary links are discernible also in Shakespeare's use of prostitution and self-abasement as predominant metaphors for the practice of the theatre, as in Sonnet 111 and in Pandarus' consciously theatrical epilogue: 'Why should our endeavour be so desired and the performance so loathed?' (5.11.38–9). Pandarus thus closes the play by linking together the motifs we have been discussing thus far: specular metaphors, metatheatrical images of performance, a

---

1  Fineman, esp. 95.
2  Bowen, *Gender*, esp. xxii and chap.1; Levine, 26ff.
3  Hyland, *TC*, 91–2.
4  Cf. *R3* 3.5.5–11 and Skura, 154.

problematic view of the nature of theatrical representation, and a jest about the unstable nature of value.[1]

## 'DIVIDES MORE WIDER THAN THE SKY AND EARTH': THE FRAGMENTATION OF THE DIVIDED SELF

A sense of an unbridgeable gap between expectation and performance haunts this play. The gap is perceivable in war, where all hopes and designs fail 'in the promised largeness' (1.3.2–5), in sexual experience, where even the merry humble-bee 'doth sing / Till he hath lost his honey and his sting' (5.11.41–2), and in our frustrated experiencing of a play whose heroes turn out not to be heroic after all. 'The monstruosity in love', Troilus confesses to Cressida just as they are about to consummate their relationship, is that 'the will is infinite and the execution confined'; 'the desire is boundless and the act a slave to limit' (3.2.78–80). Cressida needs no such instruction; she knows only too well what people say, that 'lovers swear more performance than they are able'. Her concern is that lovers, male lovers especially, 'reserve an ability that they never perform', vowing great perfections and yet 'discharging less than the tenth part of one' (81–4). Her version of 'monstruosity' thus expresses a woman's concern about lack of commitment, while Troilus' anxiety is about male performance.[2]

A major cause of Troilus' bitter disillusionment, as David Kaula explains, is that he longs for both honour and love in ways that the world cannot provide. Defending an idealized Helen and seeking the love of a Cressida existing only in his ardent imagination, Troilus sets himself up for fury and despair when he cannot find the something beyond, the Agape (in Denis de Rougement's

---

1 See J. Lenz, esp. 833–6 and 850. Skura, cited in the previous note, has many perceptive things to say about the self-abasement of the actor in Shakespeare that is perhaps hinted at in Pandarus' jesting about a loathed performance.

2 See Adelman, 'Cressid', notes 4 and 19. Also discussing the gap between expectation and performance are Kaufmann, 'Ceremonies'; Farnham; Belsey, 93; Kendall.

terms), that his idealism craves. 'Men prize the thing ungained more than it is', as Cressida has known from the start (1.2.280). A radical disjunction between willing and acting is at the centre of Troilus' sensibility. He seems unable to differentiate the two wills that motivate his longing, one sexual in nature and thus resistant to rational control, the other holding out the promise of deliberate choice. The latter directs his aspiration to a disembodied, generalized image of womanly perfection that collapses into incomprehension when 'the real Cressida' has 'been absorbed into the realm of constant flux'. A similar futility mocks the dreams of most of the male characters in the play.[1]

The gap between expectation and performance is part of a larger disjunction that afflicts all identities and relationships in the play. It takes the forms of various dualisms, as G. Wilson Knight points out: love and war, heroism and pride, deep mutual attachment and romantic infatuation, intellect and intuition, reason and emotion, individualism and social order.[2] For L. C. Knights, the play's many disjunctions, especially those of public life and reason as espoused by the Greeks versus intuition and feeling as espoused by the Trojans, are gathered under the comprehensive rubric of appearance versus reality.[3]

The fragmentation is at all events universal, often manifesting itself in divided selves. Thersites is called a 'fragment' (5.1.8), Troilus 'a minced man' (1.2.247), Ajax a 'gouty Briareus' with 'the joints of everything' (1.2.27–8).[4] Such barbs are often in jest, but the motif of dissecting and anatomizing is nonetheless insistent. 'Instead of creating and organizing the assurances of selfhood', says John Bayley, 'Shakespeare divides and dissolves them'.[5] Ajax, we learn, is 'half made of Hector's blood' (4.5.84). Hector, for his part, is at a loss to know how to separate Ajax' Greek limbs from

---

1 Kaula, esp. 272 and 275–9, citing de Rougemont (67ff.).
2 Knight, esp. 51–2.
3 Knights, 'Theme'.
4 Adelman, 'Cressid', 15n.
5 Bayley, 'Time', 70. For a Jungian analysis, see Aronson.

his Trojan limbs so that Hector might kill the one and spare the other (125–33). Achilles' response on seeing Hector for the first time is to ask rhetorically 'in which part of his body / Shall I destroy him?' (242–3).[1] The result, says Arnold Stein, is a 'disjunctive imagination' that finds dichotomies not simply between Greeks and Trojans but crossing over that hostile barrier through divided loyalties (Achilles' love for the Trojan Polyxena, Hector's kinship with Ajax) and invading the inner self.[2]

This universal disjunction may arise, in part at least, out of the sense of nostalgic longing for an imagined medieval, orthodox and chivalric past. We have seen how the shift from feudalism to early modern capitalism brought with it an unsettling new ethic of subjective and commercial valuation that is reflected widely in Shakespeare's play. In the present context, as A. M. Potter observes, *Troilus and Cressida* appears to question those medieval orthodoxies and accept the fact that the age of chivalry is dead, while at the same time anatomizing the unravelling of the social fabric that results from change. Elizabethan culture, still broadly medieval, clung to a world-view that offered the illusion at least of God-given wholeness and immutability. Shakespeare chose sources (Caxton and Lydgate in particular) that enshrined the myths of courtly love and knights in shining armour. His play, conversely, shows us Trojans and Greeks alike who break all the rules of chivalry in which they profess to believe.[3] For A. P. Rossiter, as well, the play questions medieval universals under the pressure of the Jacobean *Zeitgeist*, much as John Donne explores the anxieties of the new astronomy with his lament that 'new philosophy calls all in doubt', leaving 'all in pieces, all coherence gone'.[4] Hiram Haydn attributes this fragmentation to a new,

---

1  Burns, esp. 126–7.
2  A. Stein, esp. 145–6. Other writers, not cited here, who discuss fragmentation include Stiller, 57–72, Soellner, 'Prudence', Charnes, Dollimore, Glasser, LaBranche, Powell, A. J. Smith, esp. 14, and R. A. Yoder.
3  Potter, *passim*.
4  Rossiter, 148–9, citing John Donne's 'An Anatomy of the World', 1612, 'The first Anniversary', ll. 205 and 213.

fanatical, 'counter-Renaissance' pursuit of reputation and honour among the aristocracy in revolt against the principles of
classical humanism; Paul Siegel calls this 'the neo-chivalric cult
of honor'.[1] Hamish F. G. Swanston proposes that in its pursuit
of antitheses, images of mutability, dialectical ontology, contrasts of state and 'a whirl of being', and in its seeking for unity
in diversity, *Troilus and Cressida* shows itself to be akin to the
Baroque.[2]

The consequences of disintegration for the play's formal
structure are momentous. The chaotic splintering of the final
act, so distressing to many critics in the past, has found an eloquent defender in Una Ellis-Fermor, who asks what better
ending could be devised for a play with discord as its central
theme.[3] Richard Fly's essay on 'Imitative Form' in *Troilus and
Cressida* argues similarly that the 'disjunctive and nonsequential'
shape of the play is there to jolt the audience out of its complacent expectation of conventional design, and thus to invite the
spectators to 'participate in disorientation'.[4] As Barbara Everett
observes, the play appears to lack a 'story', or narrative organi-
zation that conventionally signals purposiveness and coherence;
it does so in order that it may instead depict 'The Way We Live
Now'.[5] In Philip Edwards's words, it is as though Shakespeare
chose to confront how to 'organize the disorganized' and 'give
meaning to the absurd', daring to invoke a spirit of anti-art that
makes the play so astonishingly contemporary and Brechtian
for us.[6]

Stylistically and verbally, *Troilus and Cressida* revels in linguistic demystification and discontinuity. Latinate vocabulary

---

1  Haydn, 555–618, and Siegel, esp. 40, cited and discussed in Gagen. See also Watson,
   *passim*, and Shalvi.
2  Swanston, *passim*, and Glasser. On Mannerism, see G. Williams, *Sex*, 101.
3  Ellis-Fermor, esp. 58, 61 and 63. See also Rabkin, 33, Taylor, 'Attitude', and
   Traversi, 27. For instances of critical disapproval of the play's 'chaotic' ending, see
   Lawrence, *Problem*, 165–6; Kimbrough, 61–74; Evans.
4  Fly, 'Suited', esp. 277–8, 282.
5  Everett, esp. 129, 132.
6  Edwards, esp. 95. See also Slights, and Evans.

and new coinages, especially heavy in scenes of public debate, seem calculated to produce anticlimax and dissonant effect, as T. McAlindon argues. Self-referentially, the play calls attention to failures in communication, as when Ajax 'raves in saying nothing' (3.3.251), or Ulysses notes the trouble a person has to 'communicate his parts to others' (118), or Pandarus prompts Troilus with 'Words pay no debts; give her deeds' (3.2.54). Prominent among the play's rhetorical figures are inflation of speech (which Puttenham calls 'surplusage' and, more pointedly, 'bombophilogia', the vice of the *miles gloriosus*) and, at the opposite extreme, deflation or 'diminishing'. The first manifests itself as bombast and repetition, the second as abasement and name-calling.[1]

Those who admire the play's styles do so because of its multiple perspectives in the dialogue, its Bakhtinian 'heteroglossia'.[2] Shakespeare is fascinated with 'self-negating forms' of words created by adding prefixes or suffixes, like 'disorbed', 'distaste', 'unfamed', 'uncomprehensive', 'bragless', 'languageless', that 'take away with one hand what they give with the other'.[3] Vivian Thomas looks at the 'fractured universe' of the play in terms of its hyperbole of numbers – 'many thousand dismes' lost in the war, 'above a thousand ships' launched by Helen's great price, 'ten thousand eyes' with which to weep for Troy, the 'thousand sons' of emulation, 'a thousand complete courses of the sun' used to calculate length of life, 'a thousand Hectors in the field'. In the same vein, the fragmentation of the human body is noted in vivid particularity: heels, hand, leg, arms, cheek, blood, member and the like. The anatomizing of language is symptomatic of the

---

1  McAlindon, esp. 35–9, citing Puttenham, 3.22 (259-60). See also P. Thomson, esp. 37, 40 and 53. For critical disagreement as to what is or is not bombastic, see also Schmidt di Simoni, 71–3, 146–9; Vickers, *Artistry*, 253; J. O. Smith; Van Doren, 172–3.

2  See Bakhtin. Among the many admirers in recent days of the play for its diversity of speech and discordant viewpoint are Berger, 134, Adamson, 29–30, Danson, Cole, Engle, 161, Flannery, and Schwartz. LaBranche discusses the disjunctions of the play in terms of visual patterns on stage.

3  Adamson, 25, 30.

anatomizing of the self.[1] Language is severed from its referent. Paradox, as Rosalie Colie notes, is essential to an 'imagery of fragmentation' that calls received opinion into question in a shattered vision of 'fractions', 'orts', 'fragments' and 'greasy relics' (5.2.165–6).[2] William Empson shows how the language of the play is a gloss on its own structure.[3]

The very nature of language itself 'strains against the rule of unity and the laws of non-contradiction to which the language of logic aspires', observes Elizabeth Freund as she explores the contradictions and paradoxes of 'Ariachne's broken woof'.[4] This image (5.2.159), with its seemingly deliberate amalgam of the stories of Arachne and Ariadne, typifies for several deconstructive critics the heightened language consciousness of the play as it seeks to problematize the paradoxical truth of Troilus' bitter observation: 'This is and is not Cressid' (153). J. Hillis Miller sees vast consequences in the disjunction: 'when one *logos* becomes two, the circle an ellipse, all the gatherings or bindings of Western logocentrism are untied or cut'. Miller, like I. A. Richards before him, is captivated by the play of meanings in 'Ariachne' and in various key phrases upon which the certitudes of logocentric metaphysics were once thought to rest, such as 'unity', 'discourse', 'cause', 'authority', 'reason' and 'instance'.[5]

One major source of imagery in the play as a means of expressing the disjunctions of the human psyche is the animal kingdom. Hybrid metaphors of man-as-animal introduce us to a terrifying collapse of boundaries between species, and look forward to the apocalypticism of *King Lear*. To Jeanne Addison Roberts, the superficially static metaphorical language of many of

---

1  Thomas, esp. 81–7. For passages cited in the references to 'a thousand ships', etc., see 2.2.19, 82 and 101, 3.3.157, 4.1.29, 4.5.121–39 and 5.1.17–23.
2  Colie, esp. 340, 342 and 347.
3  Empson, *Pastoral*, 33.
4  Freund, 20–1.
5  J. H. Miller, 44 and 47; Richards, 367–76. Vickers, *Appropriating*, 189–98, replies to Miller. See also Freund, esp. 20–1, Belsey, 92, Scott, 130ff., Kopper, esp. 159–60, and Bjelland, 'Cressida'.

the male characters 'represents a society engaged in shoring up
its collapsing world, a male Culture in danger of disintegration
through the threatening forces of females and foreigners'. Hence
the metaphors of monstrosity: lion, bear, elephant, camel, crow,
daw, dog, fox and so on. The metaphors of ass and ox, cat, fitchew
(skunk), toad, lizard, owl, puttock (kite) and herring (5.1.57–60)
begin conventionally only to be distorted into images of prodigious deformity, like the Sagittary or centaur (5.5.14). Appetite,
in Ulysses' metaphor, is 'an universal wolf' that eventually eats
up itself (1.3.121–4). The Amazon or masculinized woman
presents a hybrid image of male/female.[1] The hybrid of
Ariadne/Arachne conjures up a legend of the betrayed woman
and juxtaposes it with a legend of poisonous woman-as-spider.[2]

Images of appetite, cooking and the spoiling of food, noted by
Caroline Spurgeon and others as especially dominant in *Troilus
and Cressida* (as also in *Hamlet*), are expressive of the disillusion
and despair, the 'sick revolt and disgust on finding on one's
tongue only "greasy relics" or rotting fruit' that is so essential to
the play's tortured vision of disjunction.[3] Troilus grieves to see
how the 'fractions' of Cressida's faith, the 'orts of her love', the
'fragments, scraps, the bits and greasy relics / Of her o'ereaten
faith, are bound to Diomed' (5.2.165–7). Such is the dismal but
appropriate end of Troilus' 'imaginary relish' of tasting 'Love's
thrice-repured nectar' (3.2.17–20); his sensory nature is satiated
and then disgusted by what he had longed to feed on. He is self-
mocked for his earlier impatience at the slow process of
grinding, bolting, leavening, baking and cooling (1.1.15–24), and
for his own argument in the Trojan council that a gentleman
does not throw 'in unrespective sieve' the 'remainder viands' of
a feast simply because he now is full (2.2.70–1). A self-consum-
ing flaw linking Troilus to Achilles, Ajax, Diomedes and other

---

1  Roberts, esp. 93; Thomas, 130. On animal characterization as a vehicle for satire
   especially of Achilles, Ajax, Patroclus, Cressida, Menelaus and Thersites, see
   A. Yoder, 41–3.
2  Adelman, 'Cressid', 139.
3  Spurgeon, esp. 320–4. See also Aronson on appetite.

men expresses itself in metaphors of arrogance basted with its own 'seam' or lard, of pride enlarged when it is 'fat-already' (2.3.182, 192), and of a lechery that eats up itself. Value is measured in terms of comestibles: common soldiers are, to Pandarus, 'chaff and bran, chaff and bran; porridge after meat' (1.2.233–4), like Falstaff's 'food for powder, food for powder' (*1H4* 4.2.64–5). Eating is an image of destructive rivalry: 'one man eats into another's pride' (3.3.137).

Achilles is especially linked to images of appetite, feeding and decay. Even his virtues are too likely to 'rot untasted' like 'fair fruit in an unwholesome dish' (2.3.118–19). He has 'a woman's longing, / An appetite that I am sick withal', to behold Hector (3.3.239–41). Later, when the moment comes to dismember Hector, Achilles' craving is only partially sated by the bloodshed: 'My half-supped sword, that frankly would have fed, / Pleased with this dainty bait, thus goes to bed' (5.9.19–20). Achilles has failed to come to terms with the galling truth that a person's worthy deeds are merely 'scraps' which are 'Devoured' by oblivion 'as fast as they are made' (3.3.149–50).

Thersites, who speaks of Achilles as a 'full dish of fool' (5.1.8) and is himself called a 'fragment' and a 'crusty batch of nature' (5–8), is both the crabbed observer and grotesque embodiment of appetite disjoined from temperate use. That he is also, for Achilles, 'my cheese, my digestion' (2.3.39) suggests how intemperate Achilles has become in his self-indulgence. Imagery of appetite in this play is often linked to sexuality, as when Ulysses speaks of 'a young conception' that Nestor must help bring to some 'shape' to deal with the 'seeded pride' that is 'blown up' to maturity in 'rank' Achilles and must be 'cropped' lest it 'breed a nursery' of evils (1.3.312–19), and the like. As Raymond Southall puts it, the whole play 'is busily reducing life to the demands of the belly'.[1]

---

1 Southall, 226. Others who look at culinary and digestive imagery include Muir, '*TC*', 33–4; Kaufmann, 'Ceremonies', 153–7; Fluchère, 214; Traversi, 33; Thomas, 127–31; and D. Hillman, *SQ*, 48 (1997), 295–313.

Images of disease, important in *Hamlet*, are also vividly at work in this play, especially in the wry observations of Thersites and Pandarus. The list of diseases that Thersites wishes on Patroclus – colic, hernia, kidney stones, stroke, paralysis, asthma, bladder infection, sciatica and much more (see 5.1.17–23 and LN) – is a regular medical dictionary of afflictions. He also wishes 'the Neapolitan bone-ache', or syphilis, on the entire Greek camp (2.3.17–18). He jests about surgical probing of wounds (5.1.11) and boils with 'botchy' cores that 'run' (2.1.2–6), and compares himself to 'the louse of a lazar' (5.1.63). He curses both sides in the war by consigning them to 'A burning devil' (5.2.202–3), thereby suggesting the fires of eternal punishment, the fire that will destroy Troy, and the burning symptoms of venereal disease. Pandarus, too, points to sexual malaise in his imagery of the diseased body. In his sardonic farewell at the end of the play he bequeathes us his diseases (5.11.56). His doing so reminds us that the entire war was bred out of the 'whorish loins' of Helen, who is, in Diomedes' devastating phrase, 'contaminated carrion' (4.1.65, 73). The men are all infected: Paris is a 'firebrand brother' who 'burns us all' (2.2.110); Troilus, 'mad / In Cressid's love', complains of 'the open ulcer of my heart' (1.1.48–50) that 'beats thicker than a feverous pulse' (3.2.34); Achilles is 'lion-sick' (2.3.84) and 'batters down himself' in raging 'commotion' (172–3); Hector's sumptuously dressed victim in battle is a 'putrefied core' (5.9.1). Every Greek, in Ulysses' view, is 'sick / Of his superior' and 'grows to an envious fever / Of pale and bloodless emulation' (1.3.132–4). Both war and love are thus conceived of as conditions of disease.[1]

The irreparable differences dividing the lovers in this play echo the mythological strife afflicting Mars, Venus and her lame husband, Vulcan. Helen is, to one observer at least, 'the

1   Among various critics who study imagery of disease in the play are Kaufmann, 'Ceremonies', 150–3; Spurgeon, 320; Traversi, 39; T. Spencer, 114; Adelman, 'Union', 43–4; Bentley.

mortal Venus, the heart-blood of beauty, love's visible soul' (3.1.31–2). Troilus, deserted by Cressida, vows that his passionate anger will be divulged 'In characters as red as Mars his heart / Inflamed with Venus', and with such deadly force that not even a 'casque composed by Vulcan's skill' can hope to save Diomedes (5.2.170–8). Such references are common; with minor exceptions, the names of Venus, Mars and Vulcan appear more often in this play than any other by Shakespeare. As in *Antony and Cleopatra*, but here with more dispiriting implications, these images reflect ambivalent and contradictory traditions. To classical writers like Plutarch and Renaissance neoplatonists like Pico della Mirandola, Mars and Venus potentially betokened male heroism and female beauty harmoniously complementing one another in a *discordia concors* of loving strife. The beautiful female fostered male achievement with her admiration, while the male protected and adored the woman. At the same time, the myth was also seen as one of infatuation and inversion of sexual roles, with the woman emasculating her man like Omphale with Hercules, leading him besottedly into extremes of self-destructive behaviour.[1] Shakespeare's *Venus and Adonis* and *Antony and Cleopatra* show his long-standing fascination with the contradictions of the story. In *Troilus*, the devastating consequences of male infatuation and rivalry are everywhere apparent. The beautiful but destructive image of Venus as love goddess applies with equal bitterness to Helen and to Cressida.

One last overarching motif in *Troilus* is subject to a similarly double interpretation: Time as renewer but also as destroyer. Renaissance neoplatonism found in Time an eternal

---

1  Pico della Mirandola, *Commento*, Book 2, chaps 8–24, pp. 494–517; Wind, 86–96; G. Williams, *Sex*, 102; Jones-Davies; Panofsky, 163–4. On *Antony and Cleopatra* and *Venus and Adonis* in relation to Mars and Venus, see Bevington, *AC*, 8–9, 106, 127, 255; Houser, 124; Waddington; R. Miller. See also LaBranche, 443–5, on stage images of the 'unsoldierly soldier'. The classical authorities for the myth of Mars and Venus include Homer's *Odyssey*, 8.266–366 (LCL, 1.290–9), Ovid's *Ars Amatoria*, 2.561–600 (LCL, 104–7), and Ovid's *Metamorphoses*, 4.171–89 (LCL, 1.190–1).

principle emerging out of the flux of mutability, establishing through decay and renewal the enduring and stable forms that give meaning to existence. Repeatedly, characters in the play give voice to comforting truisms about Time: 'The end crowns all' (4.5.224), 'time must friend or end' (1.2.75–6). Nestor is a 'good old chronicle' who has 'long walked hand in hand with time' (4.5.203–4). At the same time, Nestor's 'palsy fumbling' and other 'faint defects of age' (1.3.172–5) are the subject of unseemly mirth. Time is a negligent and even malicious presence who, 'like a fashionable host', 'slightly shakes his parting guest by th' hand, / And, with his arms outstretched as he would fly, / Grasps in the comer' (3.3.166–9). Ulysses counsels Achilles to grab Time by the forelock, taking 'the instant way' (154), but when Achilles does so by murdering Hector he manages to murder his own honour and reputation as well.

Time is, as Kenneth Palmer puts it, 'the most powerful of Shakespeare's dramatis personae', a 'bloody tyrant' as portrayed also in Sonnet 16, remorseless, implacable.[1] Troilus, confronting the prospect of losing Cressida so soon after winning her, laments that 'Injurious Time now with a robber's haste / Crams his rich thiev'ry up, he knows not how' (4.4.41–2). To Ulysses, Time is a 'great-sized monster of ingratitudes' with 'a wallet at his back' containing the pitiable 'alms for oblivion' that men attempt to save up for an eternity of honourable memory but which Time totally ignores because they are over his shoulder where he cannot see them (3.3.146–8). All that humanity can seem to know about Time, in Agamemnon's estimate, is that 'What's past and what's to come is strewed with husks / And formless ruin of oblivion' (4.5.167–8). Time thus deals solely in oblivion; the past gives no meaning to human destiny. In such a lack of caring for the logic of past and future in relation to the

---

1   The play's fascination with Time is discussed by Danson, 86; Frye, *Fools*, 66; Ard²,
    68; A. & J. Thompson, 13–46; Stříbrný; Knight, 72–4; Bayley, 'Time'; Knowland;
    Muir, '*TC*', 28–33; Hyland, *TC*, 89–94; Thomas, 132–4; J. O. Smith, 178.

present, Shakespeare's characters deny and dissolve history, with the dispiriting result that history itself is made into an illusion.[1]

## 'STUFF TO MAKE PARADOXES': PERFORMANCE HISTORY OF TROILUS AND CRESSIDA

*Troilus and Cressida* self-reflexively casts gloom on its own medium of theatre, as on everything else. Ulysses expresses quiet fury at the 'ridiculous and awkward action' with which Patroclus slanders the Greek generalship in what he calls his 'imitation'. Patroclus 'pageants' his superiors like a 'strutting player, whose conceit / Lies in his hamstring', like an actor who is besotted with the inert dialogue he utters and the sound of his own tread on the 'scaffoldage'. His 'seeming' is 'to-be-pitied' and 'o'erwrested', like 'a chime a-mending'; it makes 'paradoxes', or wise-seeming folly, out of the deeply serious political material that it chooses to parody (1.3.149–84). Patroclus is not representative of all acting, to be sure, but the indictment does encompass, by implication, a lot of bad acting in Shakespeare's day, on the public stage and also in the productions of the boys' companies for whom Marston and others wrote their libellous lampoons. The manifesto against inept performance is all the more telling for its resemblance to Hamlet's irritation at actors who saw the air with their hands and improvise lame jests not set down for them in their parts (*Ham* 3.2.1–45).

Hamlet's wariness of the 'groundlings' and the 'unskillful' who encourage this sort of thing in the public theatres by being for the most part 'capable of nothing but inexplicable dumb shows and noise', and his marked preference for the good opinion of 'judicious' auditors whose 'censure' or judgement must 'o'erweigh a whole theater of others', seem attuned to a number of puzzling factors in the early production history of *Troilus and*

---

1 Bayley, 'Time', 59; Hyland, *TC*, 94. Foakes, '*TC*', makes the point that the play's inconclusive sense of time explains the fitness of the double ending, neither simply comic nor tragic.

*Cressida*: the assertion in a prefatory note added to the second 'state' of the 1609 Quarto that the play was 'never staled with the stage' or 'clapper-clawed with the palms of the vulgar', the revised title-page no longer claiming that the play had been 'acted by the King's Majesty's servants at the Globe', the lack of any record of performance at the Inns of Court or Whitehall or anywhere else, the limit of publication to one Quarto, the evident difficulties of including the play in the Folio of 1623, and the play's highly experimental sense of genre. Yet *Hamlet*, despite its flouting of plebeian taste, was immensely popular in the theatre and in print, whereas its near contemporary, *Troilus*, virtually disappeared from sight.

Might such a play as *Troilus* have been performed at the Inns of Court? Could such a circumstance explain its anomalous and uncertain history of performance? The idea has appealed to many critics since it was first proposed by Peter Alexander in 1929.[1] (Earlier critics, beginning with Edmond Malone, had suggested performance at court.) W. W. Lawrence imagines that the intellectual rather than emotional treatment of love and war in *Troilus* and its lengthy philosophical speeches, along with 'the disillusioned treatment of romantic love, the ribald jesting, the direct allusions to the sexual looseness of the time, and the familiar tone' all 'might be supposed to appeal to such an audience', since the Inns of Court 'had a reputation for indecorum'.[2] Philip Finkelpearl notes that one of the play's publishers in 1609, Henry Walley, was a close friend of John Marston, a dramatist of the private stage; William Elton speculates that Marston may have written the preface included in the second state of the 1609 Quarto.[3] Yet no compelling historical evidence exists to connect *Troilus* with the Inns of Court, and Shakespeare is not known ever to have written a play on commission for a

---

1   Alexander, '*TC*'. The position is supported by 'most critics', according to Oxf[1], 8, and Ramsey, 224.
2   Lawrence, *Problem*, 128.
3   Finkelpearl, and Elton, 'Textual Transmission', 65–9.

private audience; his plays were taken to court and elsewhere, but his source of income was the public stage. The staging requirements for *Troilus* are not exacting; it could have been presented without special difficulty on the Globe stage or at court or at one of the Inns of Court, although T. J. King sees the larger than average number of actors needed to perform the play (fourteen men and four boys, by his count, plus eight mute extras) as suggestive of private performance.[1] Conceivably, as Nevill Coghill proposes, *Troilus* was originally acted at the Globe and then taken to the Inns of Court, with its unusual Epilogue tacked on as a bit of smut for the lawyers who congregated there;[2] *The Comedy of Errors* had been acted at Gray's Inn in 1594 on a night of tumultuous revelling, presumably after it had been performed in public. Still, no evidence exists to show that such a command performance took place, and the hypothesis is unprovable. *Hamlet* too is a play confessedly written for discriminating audiences,[3] and yet it succeeded in public. Even if *Troilus and Cressida* was perceived as experimental, its disappearance may have come about because it proved itself to be a political liability for the acting company. As a bitter commentary on the decline of civilization, it may have succeeded all too well.

We have already considered the possibility (Introduction, pp. 15–18) that the play was so politically controversial that Shakespeare's acting company prudently withheld it (after, perhaps, a very few performances) and dissociated themselves from it on the revised title-page of the 1609 Quarto. Another possible answer is that *Troilus* may have been too far ahead of its time. Indeed, today it is acclaimed for its experimental brilliance and is

---

1 King, 89–90. Among those who profess scepticism at the notion that *Troilus* was performed at the Inns of Court are Harbage, *Rival Traditions*, 116; Baldwin, *Var*, 356–7; Kimbrough, 21–2; and Ramsey, 225ff. See also Reynolds.

2 Coghill, 78–97. See also Nosworthy, esp. 84.

3 Attesting to *Hamlet*'s intellectual appeal are the assertion on the title page of Q1 that the play was acted in London 'as also in the two universities of Cambridge and Oxford', and Gabriel Harvey's pointing to *Hamlet* and *The Rape of Lucrece* as works that 'have it in them to please the wiser sort' (MS notes in a copy of Speght's *Chaucer*, 1598), reprinted in Chambers, *Shakespeare*, 2.197–8).

enjoying a renaissance in the theatre. We have no testimonial as to its worth in Shakespeare's day, but that very silence is deafening. In fact, the only significant production of *Troilus* known to have been mounted between the decade of the 1600s and the very end of the nineteenth century[1] was an undertaking on John Dryden's part to refashion the play to such an extent that its presumed defects would be unrecognizable, or at least forgivable.

Dryden's *Troilus and Cressida, or Truth Found Too Late*, staged at the theatre in Dorset Garden in 1679, was of course not the only Shakespeare play to be recast wholesale in such a way as to render it acceptable to Restoration audiences. Convinced that he had discovered how to 'reduce nature into method' by maintaining 'that probability of fiction' which is 'the soul of poetry', Dryden undertook to rescue *Troilus* from what seemed to him its manifest deficiencies. Perhaps, he speculated, Shakespeare 'grew weary of his task' in the midst of composition. Dryden especially deplored the inconclusive ending and the lack of poetic justice: 'the latter part of the tragedy is nothing but a confusion of drums and trumpets, excursions and alarms. The chief persons, who give name to the tragedy, are left alive; Cressida is false, and is not punished.' Dryden insisted on classifying it as a tragedy, and a failed tragedy at that. 'Yet, after all, because the play was Shakespeare's, and that there appeared in it the admirable genius of the author, I undertook to remove that heap of rubbish under which many excellent thoughts lay wholly buried.' As redactor, Dryden could bring to bear certain rules of dramatic composition based on 'good sense, and sound reason'.[2]

---

1   A minor exception to the otherwise total lack of other productions during the period from the 1600s to 1898 seems to have been one at Smock Alley, Dublin, at some time prior to 1700. Nothing is known, however, of this production. See Bald, 378. An unproduced adaptation by the actor T. H. Lacy was published as part of 'Cumberland's British Theatre' some time around 1852 by G. H. Davidson (rpt Cornmarket Press, 1970). Also, a text altered for acting and provisionally cast by John Philip Kemble in the late 1790s, though never actually produced by him, survives as a prompt book in the Folger Library; see Shattuck, 467, Newlin, 'Darkened Stage', and Bowen, 'Stage History', 270–1.

2   Dryden, *Works*, 130–1; *Essays*, 1.203–4, quoted in Danson, 95; and Odell, 2.49. See Muir, 'Adaptations', 223–8. The passages are reprinted in Var, 489.

The result is a play in which the diction is 'refined' of its 'obsolete' figurative meanings, while the characters are simplified into an heroic mould. Structurally the play aims at 'coherence' and 'dependence' of its individual scenes 'on the main design'. In order to provide poetic justice and a more 'tragic' ending, Dryden arranges matters so that Cressida remains true to Troilus even when she is transferred to the Greek camp; she reluctantly entertains Diomede as her wooer only to please her father and divert suspicion from Calchas' plan for their escape back to Troy. The crucial scene in which Troilus eavesdrops on Diomede's importunity (5.2 in Shakespeare) proves her undoing, for Troilus is misled into supposing her false. When he confronts her with her presumed infidelity, she protests her innocence but is confuted by Diomede, who, with the villainy of an Iago or Iachimo, produces the ring that she has unwillingly given him as evidence of his having possessed her. Thus having lost her true lover and having been betrayed by Diomede, Cressida dies a suicide. Troilus finds out the truth too late (hence Dryden's subtitle), slays the despicable Diomede in battle and is felled in turn by the Greeks, falling dead on Diomede's body.

Dryden does not need to rearrange substantially the handling of time and place in accordance with classical precept, as in his redaction of *Antony and Cleopatra* entitled *All for Love* (1678), since Shakespeare's *Troilus* begins 'in the middle' with 'what may be digested in a play' (Prologue 28–9). To be sure, Dryden does avoid 'leaping from Troy to the Grecian tents and thence back again in the same act', in order that 'a due proportion of time' may be 'allowed for every motion', providing in all only six shifts between the opposing camps. Throughout, Dryden curtails the war plot of Shakespeare's play (including the councils of war in the Greek and Trojan camps) in order to focus on the tragic story of the lovers and to urge a politically orthodox view that subjects must 'learn obedience to their kings' (the play's final line). He augments the love interest by playing up the lasciviousness of the love scenes involving Troilus, Cressida and Pandarus, and by inserting a quarrel between Hector and Troilus over the exchange of Cressida for Antenor. Andromache is given a more significant role than in the original in order to heighten the heroic dilemma in which Hector finds himself. The death of Hector is described but not presented on stage. Even though the rivalry of Ajax and Achilles is intensified, the war generally becomes 'a panoramic backdrop for the presentation of a more personal tragedy'.[1]

Dryden's version enjoyed an initial success in 1679, with Thomas Betterton as Troilus and as Prologue 'representing the ghost of Shakespeare' and with Mrs Betterton as Andromache; Mary Lee played Cressida. For a 1709 revival at the Theatre Royal in Drury Lane, Betterton took the part of Thersites. Four more revivals ended in 1734 at the Theatre Royal in Covent Garden,[2] after which the play disappeared from the English stage until the twentieth century. The neglect was not casual; it bespoke a puzzlement over the play's 'unfinished' structure and a moral revulsion over its dilemmas of sexuality that extended as well to *Measure for Measure* and *All's Well That Ends Well*.

Revival of interest began with George Bernard Shaw, who, as champion of Ibsenism and other heterodoxies, welcomed the experimentalism of this maligned play. Having joined the New Shakespere Society, he prepared a paper on *Troilus and Cressida* in 1884.[3] Other rediscoveries of the play soon followed, at first on the Continent rather than in England. A production at Munich's Theater am Gärtenplatz, in April 1898, that authentically eschewed scenery on stage and used male actors in the women's parts, was followed by productions in Berlin in 1899 and 1904, Hungary in 1900, Vienna in 1902, Prague in 1921 and

---

1 Bernhardt, 135; Odell, 1.48–51. See also H. Spencer, 231–2, and Kaufmann, 'Poetics', 86.
2 Var, 504, and Hogan, 1.451–4.
3 Cohn, 322–5.

still others in middle Europe that were attuned to current political crises.[1] It was as though *Troilus* had found at last a world in chaos to which the play's bleakness and generic indeterminacy seemed refreshingly true. Charles Fry brought the play back onto the English stage in 1907 with a production at London's Great Queen Street Theatre, Fry himself taking the part of Thersites as though to emphasize what was subversive and satirical in the play.

As he had done with some other Shakespeare plays like *The Comedy of Errors* (1895) and *Romeo and Juliet* (1905), William Poel illuminated *Troilus*'s experimentalism by staging it in Elizabethan (not Roman classical) costuming on a bare stage. The Greeks, as Robert Speaight reports, were outfitted as Elizabethan soldiers, 'smoking the tobacco which Raleigh had brought back from Virginia, the long pipes rising and falling with the argument at Agamemnon's GHQ'. The Trojans were sophisticated courtly figures dressed for a Renaissance masque.[2] Poel directed this production for the Elizabethan Stage Society in 1912 at King's Hall, Covent Garden, acting the part of Pandarus in cockney, with Edith Evans in her stage debut as Cressida and Hermione Gingold as Cassandra. Older and more experienced than Troilus, Cressida was soon bored with the self-pitying hyperboles of her lover; when the time came for their separation, she pinned on her hat as though resolved to look smart for her arrival in the Greek camp. Her existential approach to a life that must be carved out of wartime uncertainties mirrored the production's view of the war itself as absurd.

Poel, who had been cautioned by his tutor in 1870 never even to read *Troilus* or *Measure for Measure* as plays too indelicate for Victorian sensibilities, was ready by 1912 to assert that *Troilus* was not only readable but performable in public. His antiwar sentiments and dislike of military pomposity manifested themselves

---

1 Var, 512–17; Muir, '*TC*', 28; Bowen, 'Stage History', 273.
2 Speaight, *Shakespeare on Stage*, 139.

in the cutting of Ulysses' speech on order and degree (1.3) and Troilus' bloodthirsty rantings in the fifth act. Clearly alluding to the storm clouds of war that were gathering in Europe, Poel invited his audiences to ponder a similar set of topical resonances in 1599–1601 when the Earl of Essex had embarked on a self-wounding campaign of truculence akin to that of Achilles in the play. Poel dressed Thersites as an Elizabethan clown to highlight the tragicomic absurdity of a love affair and a war that had doomed it to failure. The production's reviewers spoke of 'disillusion, misanthropy, and despair', seeing the play as 'a sort of dark seance' that was 'decadent', strangely disquieting and ugly. Audiences were sufficiently taken with its pertinent cynicism for the production to be invited to Stratford-upon-Avon for two performances on a single day in 1913 (partly, to be sure, because F. R. Benson entertained qualms about directing the play himself), where an actress took the part of Thersites as a jester with a Scots accent. Poel's production subsequently exerted a considerable influence on those of B. Iden Payne, W. Bridges-Adams and others. *Troilus* was on its way to a very belated theatrical recognition.[1]

By the time the Marlowe Society of Cambridge University staged *Troilus* in 1922, World War I was over. The play's depiction of war-weariness and disenchantment struck all observers, perhaps especially because it was performed by college-age men like those who had sacrificed their lives in such numbers in the trenches of France. Frank Birch's production was such a success that it was taken to London, with professional actresses in the female roles. In the following year, to celebrate the 300th anniversary of the publication of the First Folio, Robert Atkins produced *Troilus* at the Old Vic Theatre as the last in a ten-year project of performing all of Shakespeare's Folio plays by Miss

1    Newlin, 'Modernity', 359–62, quoting the *Daily Telegraph*, 11 December 1912; and Speaight, *Poel*, 192–201. See also Edward Garnett, '*Troilus and Cressida* and the Critics', *Contemporary Review*, 103 (February 1913), 184–90; *Poel*, 108–12; and Jamieson, 1.

Baylis's company. Ion Swinley was Troilus. The year 1928 saw a production at the intimate Maddermarket Theatre in Norwich by Nugent Monck, who had been William Poel's stage manager. Clearly, the play's time had arrived, most of all because of its striking relevance to an era of world war and class revolution.

B. Iden Payne's staging of the play in Elizabethan dress at the Shakespeare Memorial Theatre in Stratford-upon-Avon, 1936, was an avowed homage to William Poel, who had proudly declared his version to be 'the first significant production in the stage history of *Troilus and Cressida*' (playbill, December 1912). Payne dressed Cressida and Helen in panniered farthingales and feathered hats, and brought on other characters to add to the colourful effect; in scene 2, for example, he gave concreteness to Alexander's observation (in response to Cressida's opening question) on the passing-by of Hecuba and Helen by introducing both of those women on stage. As the Trojan warriors returned from battle in the same scene, Payne provided a cheering section of citizens and three 'girls' who, in the fashion of groupies, flocked especially to Troilus. The entrance onto the scene of Troilus was markedly different from that of the older battle-scarred veterans: he peeped through a lancet window in the upper stage of the set, caught sight of Cressida and Pandarus, saluted them and received in return a meaningful curtsy from Cressida. Her lines were substantially cut, leaving her to practice her dissimulations with coy glances and a giddy insincerity that, in the eyes of one reviewer at least, prognosticated her 'coming demoralization'. More a creature of body language than of voice, attracted to a Troilus who was adored by other women, the Cressida of this production became the object of a male gaze that contemporary audiences were invited to see as disarmingly contemporary. A production in 1934 directed by Payne for the Carnegie Institute's theatre department, one of the earliest recorded in the United States, seems to have made similar choices, with a lisping Cressida suggesting by her manner of talk her 'infantile fickleness': 'A woeful Cwessida 'mongst the mewwy Gweeks'.[1]

Michael Macowan's antiwar production by the London Mask Theatre Company, Westminster Theatre, in September 1938 took full cognizance of its appearance on the eve of another war. In its languid scenes of amorous encounter, this modern-dress version presented its actors as the *bon vivants* of a 1930s clubbish set. In Pandarus' scene with Helen and Paris (3.1), for example, Max Adrian as Pandarus accompanied himself in a Gershwin cocktail-piano fashion as he sang his 'Love, love, nothing but love'. Helen (Oriel Ross), looking like a Hollywood goddess in a low-cut evening dress, grabbed the spotlight while a slickly groomed Paris (Michael Denison) beamed with self-congratulatory appraisal. The court set, in formal attire, sat on stylish settees or stood at the bar sipping their aperitifs, in the cool ambience of a tastefully lighted room. Reviewers saw Adrian's Pandarus as an 'affected, elderly roué and society butterfly', a 'chattering and repulsive fribble of the glassily squalid night-club type'. The military scene was another matter, with the Trojans in khaki drill dress and the Greeks in uniforms of pale blue. Ulysses (Robert Speaight), as Jeanne Newlin describes him, was at once 'a diplomat with gold eyeglasses on broad black ribbon' and 'a world traveler who arrives for battle in tennis trousers'. Thersites (Stephen Murray) was 'a Communist intellectual, a left-wing, railing journalist in a bright red tie'. Nestor was a wordy bore; Cassandra burst strikingly upon the Trojan council of war in 2.2 in a black velvet cocktail dress.[2] *Troilus* had shown that it was capable of being vividly topical at a moment when Neville Chamberlain was caving in to the Nazis at Munich (September 1938).

---

1   Hodgdon, 266–7; D. Hooker, 899, citing Harold Geoghegan, ' "The Play's the Thing" ', *Carnegie Magazine*, 8 (1934), 249–51.

2   Newlin, 'Modernity', 363–5. See Desmond McCarthy, *New Statesman and Nation*, 16 (1938), 491; Ivor Brown, *Observer*, 25 Sepember 1938, 18; and, for photographs, *Theatre Arts Monthly*, 22.12 (December 1938), 867–9.

8  Oriel Ross as Helen and Max Adrian as Pandarus in Michael Macowan's production for the London Mask Theatre Company, 1938

Even during the early years of the war, in March 1940, a production by the Marlowe Society under the direction of George Rylands did all that it could to deglamorize its Homeric pseudo-heroes: Ajax was a 'gullible athlete', Achilles 'wildly neurotic', Pandarus mincing and Achilles' murder of Hector the climax of the show.[1] Later in the war, patriotic feeling may have made such disillusionment with war unacceptable in the theatre, but in early 1940 the British were still facing, in May, the disaster of Dunkirk.

Robert Atkins's postwar production at the Open Air Theatre in Regent's Park, June 1946, was cut in such a way as to magnify the degradation of once-noble aspirations, with Ajax (Hugh Manning) caricatured as a spoilsport, Pandarus (Russell Thorndike) as a 'perverted Punch' (in the words of a *Times* reviewer), Ulysses (David Read) as a 'cold and austere' though quick-minded intellect and Thersites (Ivan Staff) as an envenomed and tormented embodiment of all that is bitter in this play.[2] At Stratford-upon-Avon, two years later, Paul Scofield starred as Troilus in an interpretation that markedly contrasted the splendour of the Trojans with the shabbiness of the Greeks. Anthony Quayle, the director, ended his production with Troilus' announcement of the death of Hector (5.11.2), dispensing with Pandarus' smarmy epilogue that may also have been cut in some versions of the play in Shakespeare's day (see 'The text of *TC*', pp. 419–21). The effect was to insist on mordant tragedy. An austere set, spare classical costuming and contrastive lighting methods emphasized the disillusionment of Troilus as, accompanied by Ulysses (William Squire), down stage and to one side, he witnessed the capitulation of Cressida to Diomedes (Heather Stannard and Michael Godfrey) at a removed location up stage (5.2). The effect was voyeuristic,

---

1   Var, 507. According to Bowen, 'Stage History', 276, Rylands, who had acted Diomedes in Birch's 1922 production, went on to produce the play again in 1948, in 1954 (the first television version), and in 1956 with John Barton as his co-director.

2   Var, 507–8, quotes *The Times*, 29 June 1946, 6.

distancing, painfully conscious of illusion, as in Othello's witnessing with Iago the supposed evidence of Desdemona's unfaithfulness.[1]

Quayle, the director in 1948, played Pandarus in Glen Byam Shaw's 1954 production at the Shakespeare Memorial Theatre, Stratford-upon-Avon. Shaw's vision of the play was a deeply cynical one, attuned to the nihilistic spirit of many intellectuals confronted with raw consumerism on the one hand and atomic cold-war menacings on the other. Quayle's Pandarus became, in the eyes of various reviewers, a 'lisping, giggling, intriguing old fribble', a 'very carefully managed study of senile blethering and fussing', a 'pathological nanny'. Achilles (Keith Michell) was a mindless brute, hard-pressed to know how to find 'the meanest possible motives' for any action he chose to take, a 'vehement essay in the unheroic'. The despondent and egotistical lovers, Troilus (Laurence Harvey) and Cressida (Muriel Pavlov), were stripped of any illusions of poetic or romantic idealism.[2] Classical period costuming narcissistically accentuated the bodies of both men and women. In scene 2, for example, the haughty gestures of the returning warriors, as they nodded condescendingly to sentinels or handed helmets or gloves to their lackeys, re-enacted what Barbara Hodgdon describes as 'a communal sense of an exclusively upper-class wartime community' engaged in 'a serious male ritual' with the display of the male body at its centre. Similarly, Cressida's shimmering Attic robes and nightgowns hinted at the contours of her body.[3] Pandarus unveiled her for Troilus in 3.2 as though unwrapping a mannequin

1 Var, 508, records a production of the Marlowe Society and the A.D.C. in March 1948 at Cambridge, directed (as in 1940) by George Rylands, as a 'grimly humorous exercise in denigration'. See Newlin, 'Modernity', 370–3, on a production in Cambridge, Mass., in late 1948 and January 1950.
2 Newlin, 'Modernity', 366–8, citing (in order of quotation) Ivor Brown, *The Shakespeare Memorial Theatre, 1954–1956* (1956), 5; Eric Keown, *Punch*, 21 July 1954, 130–1; *The Times*, 14 July 1954; and Ivor Brown, *Observer*, 18 July 1954, 11. For pictures of this production, see Ivor Brown and Anthony Quayle, *The Shakespeare Memorial Theatre, 1948–1950: A Photographic Record* (New York, 1951).
3 Hodgdon, 267–8.

in a display window. Eric Keown summed up his response with a shudder: 'One can scarcely wait to have a bath after *Troilus and Cressida*'s black glimpses of the human zoo'.[1]

Tyrone Guthrie was perhaps the first important modern director to choose a period setting that was neither classical Greek, Elizabethan, nor contemporary twentieth-century (as Michael Macowan had chosen in 1938). For his production at the Old Vic in 1956, Guthrie adopted the Edwardian fashion of the German and Austrian empires in the late nineteenth and early twentieth centuries (centring in fact on 1913, just before World War I), an epoch that has proved irresistible to a number of directors since then for all manner of Shakespeare. The period setting gave the audience a world of decorously selfish elegance and unbridgeable class divisions gaily diverting itself on the brink of momentous and revolutionary change. Pandarus (Paul Rogers) wore a grey top hat and field glasses as if dressed for Ascot, Cressida (Rosemary Harris) a riding-costume, Achilles a chic dressing-gown; Helen (Wendy Hiller) lounged decorously on a grand piano and smoked a cigarette as Pandarus played her a love song. Thersites (Clifford Williams) was a cynical war correspondent with sketchbook and camera. Affectation and folly were effectively exposed in contrasts between the rigours of military life and the languid creature comforts of Troy. Guthrie's satire of war resonated in 1956 with the news about Suez and Hungary.[2]

The fad of period costuming displayed its new currency at the American Shakespeare Theatre in Stratford, Connecticut, in 1961, celebrating the centennial of the American Civil War in a

1  Eric Keown, *Punch*, 21 July 1954, 130–1, cited in Newlin, 'Modernity', 368. Leiter (751–2) gives an account of a production by Luchino Visconti in Florence in 1949, with a set design by Franco Zeffirelli that was shockingly lavish for postwar Italy: an entire Troy of winding staircases and rooftop patios, setting off the rich multi-coloured costumes of its inhabitants and surrounded by the camp of the Greeks.
2  W. A. Darlington, *Daily Telegraph and Morning Post*, 4 April 1956, 8; T. C. Worsley, *New Statesman*, 14 April 1956, 370; Brian Inglis, *Spectator*, 13 April 1956, 490; Berry, 53–6; Bowen, 'Stage History', 278–9; Styan, *Revolution*, 203–5; Leiter, 752–3.

production that featured Priam as Robert E. Lee, Agamemnon as Ulysses S. Grant, Cressida (Jessica Tandy) as a flirtatious southern belle and Troilus (Ted van Griethuysen) as a naively idealistic Confederate officer. Pandarus entertained the lovers on the mandolin as they met in the wisteria draped garden of his home, visibly a mansion of the Old South.[1]

Co-directors John Barton and Peter Hall, at Stratford-upon-Avon in 1960, chose to play their disillusioning *Troilus* against a social context of sexual revolution, growing controversy about deteriorating family values and unease about superpower confrontations after some fifteen years of cold war. The show was, with deliberate ambiguity, presented as part of a season of comedies. Dorothy Tutin, dressed in a classical robe slit in front to the hip, played Cressida for sensual allure. As she crossed barefoot a large octagonal circle of sand set in front of a blood-red backdrop, she was, in Bernard Levin's phrase, 'a wisp of rippling carnality'. Her suggestive glances at Troilus left little to the imagination as to what she had in mind, and her embracings of Diomedes in 5.2 were no less erotic. Leslie Hurry's set was a major presence throughout, a wasteland whose whiteness of sand, in Robert Speaight's view, 'answered the redness of the backcloth, as the satire of the play answers its violence'. The Prologue, according to Eric Keown, spoke 'in a series of hammerblows that are a warning that this production will pull no punches'. Pandarus, interpreted by an obviously older Max Adrian than in the 1938 production, was a diseased wretch who urged on the mating of Cressida and Troilus (Denholm Elliot) 'with horrid zest that turns in the end to hollow disgust'. Thersites, as played by Peter O'Toole, seemed 'to retch at the very thought of the human race'. The fighting in Act 5 was a

1  Newlin, 'Modernity', 369; Judith Crist, *New York Herald Tribune*, 25 July 1961; Claire McGlinchee, 'Stratford, Connecticut, Shakespeare Festival, 1961', *SQ*, 12 (1961), 419–23; Leiter, 754–5. For a more recent production in a Civil War mode by the Georgia Shakespeare Festival at Oglethorpe University, Atlanta, June–August 1996, see Nanette Jaynes, *Shakespeare Bulletin*, 15.2 (1997), 23–4; also 117 n. 1 below.

nightmare of violence and death, 'all smoke and brilliantly lighted armour', culminating in the slaughter of Hector (Derek Godfrey). That terrible event, and the furrow left in the sand pit by the dragging of Hector's body through it, became the play's final statement on the disjunctions of chivalry and human degradation. All reviewers were struck by the play's unsparingly modern resonance at a time when England had recently gone through the humiliation of its tainting involvement in the Suez crisis.[1]

Barton returned to *Troilus* in 1968 and 1976, both at Stratford-upon-Avon, with no less reason certainly for cynicism about contemporary world affairs. The war in Vietnam was a burning issue in 1968, along with uprisings in France and Czechoslovakia. Alan Howard as Achilles and Richard Jones Barry as Patroclus were lovers in this year's production, as they have tended to be in staged interpretations since then. Howard, blond-haired in tight gold braids and with shaved legs, flaunted Achilles' homosexuality and danced in full drag costume with his intended victim, Hector. Hector and Ajax stripped for their combat to loin-cloths reminiscent of figures on Attic vases, with their 'friezes of bare-torsoed warriors in tiny kilts and huge, bird-like helmets' (in the words of Ronald Bryden). As Carol Rutter dryly reports of this production, 'The bodies it was interested in were male . . . Combat was voluptuous, and both sides desired it'. The lovers were marginalized, deprived entirely of the scene (4.4) in which they exchange love tokens. Cressida (Helen Mirren), powerfully sensual, was a coarse tease who took pleasure in torturing a confused and indecisive Troilus (Michael Williams). Norman Rodway, cast as Thersites, 'was made up to suggest tertiary syphilis and wore a codpiece representing a war mask, with a huge rope phallus for a tongue', with which the actor 'could do some pretty indecent things'. His sneering

---

1   Bernard Levin, *Daily Express*, 27 July 1960, 4; Speaight, '1960', 451; Eric Keown, *Punch*, 10 August 1960, 208; Hodgdon, 268; Newlin, 'Modernity', 368–9; Speaight, *Shakespeare on Stage*, 281; Berry, 56–7; Styan, *Revolution*, 209–10; Leiter, 753–4.

appraisal of human folly set the tone for a production in which nobility had been trampled under foot.[1]

Barton co-directed the Royal Shakespeare Company production in 1976 with Barry Kyle, as a pointless and bitter struggle between antipathetic enemies who were alike fatally out of touch with their truest selves. The Greeks, drably costumed in grey wool and brown leather, were seen as ageing and dispirited. Achilles (Robin Ellis) and Patroclus 'strolled through the Greek camp holding hands', and the male anatomy was persistently on display. The Trojans were sensual and youthful in their pastel silks and gold jewellery, lacking restraint or wise judgement in their hedonism. Helen was linked to Paris and led about the stage by a golden chain. When Cressida (Francesca Annis) was 'symbolically disrobed' by Diomedes on her arrival in the Greek camp (4.5), she was discovered to be a 'metamorphosed Greek courtesan', her laced bodice cupping her breasts and covering her nipples with gauze, thus confirming what Ulysses (Tony Church) says of her. As she left with Diomedes, a courtesan's mask worn at the back of her head was revealed to the audience for the first time. Pandarus, as Barbara Bowen reports, 'donned a death mask for his final scene

---

1   Rutter, 'Cressida's Glove', 115–16; Ronald Bryden, *Observer*, 11 August 1968, 21; Rodway, 2.50; Irving Wardle, *The Times*, 9 August 1968, 10; Harold Hobson, *Sunday Times*, 11 August 1968, 41; Benedict Nightingale, *New Statesman*, 16 August 1968, 208; Berry, 57–60; Leiter, 757–8. Bowen, 'Stage History', 280–1, and Leiter, 749 and 755–61, describe some other anti-imperialist and antiwar productions of these same years: Michael Langham's production in 1963 (when the Civil Rights movement was at its height) with Achilles' Myrmidons as Ku Klux Klansmen; Roger Planchon's unabridged French version at the Odéon in Paris in 1964; Alf Sjöberg's version in 1967 with 'the Trojans as a dark-skinned people beset by French and American colonists in parachute gear'; Adrian Hall's use in 1971 (Trinity Square Repertory Company, Providence) of military uniforms of many different periods (Napoleonic, Russian Cossack, Rommel in North Africa, guerrilla fighters), with visible relevance to the war in Vietnam; Romanian director David Esrig's production in Munich, 1972, emphasizing farce and satire through visual spectacle; Jerry Turner's accentuation of the blindness of the generals on both sides (Ashland, Oregon, 1973) by giving Agamemnon an eyepatch and making Priam helplessly sightless; Edward Payson Call's production at the 1976 San Diego National Shakespeare Festival, showing the Trojan Council gathered together in a steam bath in 2.2; Keith Hack's use in 1977 of a carefree Helen suspended throughout on a swing; and Marek Grezesinski's Warsaw production of 1978 with its revolving set displaying the Greek and Trojan camps as two sides of the same world.

and descended into a gravelike vault which revealed, when closed, Thersites clutching a life-sized female doll'.[1]

A notable lack in most of the productions surveyed thus far is any sympathy for Cressida as victim of war and of male importunity. Joseph Papp is an exception. His responsiveness to the feminist movement in his 1965 New York production was such that it 'created an unfortunate conflict' between the director and his actor playing Troilus; Papp saw Cressida as a victim 'of men, their wars, their desires, and their double standards'.[2] Even as late as 1981, however, Terry Hands's Royal Shakespeare Company production at the Aldwych featured a Cressida (Carol Royle) who, in Robert Cushman's account, 'establishes herself from the start as that most dangerous commodity, a knowing and flirtatious virgin'. Barefoot and wearing an ankle-length orange chiffon shift, she languidly observed the parade of returning warriors in 1.2 from her well-cushioned vantage on a siege machine. Hands's emphasis was on male spectacle, as (in Barbara Hodgdon's words) 'the heroes wittingly and witlessly showcase[d] themselves as comic-opera buffoons, each displaying a quirky stereotype of male attributes'. Even Hector (Bruce Purchase) was 'King Kong-like', 'an about-to-go-to-seed footballer who draws audience laughter'. Paris took from his servant a mirror with which to do his hair; Helenus limped in on a crutch. David Suchet as Achilles and Chris Hunter as Patroclus were so intensely enamoured of each other that, in David

1 Rutter, 'Cressida's Glove', 116–17; Irving Wardle, *The Times*, 19 August 1976, 5; Michael Billington, *Guardian*, 18 August 1976, 6; Robert Cushman, *Observer*, 22 August 1976, 20; Bowen, 'Stage History', 283; Berry, 60–1. The *Sunday Times*, 15 April 1976, 29, features a photograph of Mike Gwilym as Troilus, Francesca Annis as Cressida and David Waller as Pandarus. For an account of a production by the absurdist and surrealistic Swiss director Werner Düggelin in Zürich in 1979, see Leiter, 762–3.

2 Joseph Papp, 'Directing *Troilus and Cressida*', in *The Festival Shakespeare 'Troilus and Cressida'* (New York, 1967); Bowen, 'Stage History', 272; Tiffany, 52. According to Michael Billington, Meg Davies similarly mustered a sense of 'mutinous defiance when she was passed from hand to hand, and mouth to mouth, in the Greek camp', in Richard Cottrell's austere Bristol Old Vic production at the Edinburgh Assembly Hall in August 1979 (Billington, *Guardian*, 23 August 1979, 8). On Keith Hack's production for the Oxford University Dramatic Society in 1977, see Berry, 61–2.

Nokes's view, theirs was 'the only physically convincing relationship in the whole play'. Suchet, sporting a red skirt and
carmined nipples, 'danced lubriciously, fingers clicking, to hyp-
notised Hector'. Eroticism, says Rutter, 'was (homo)sexualized,
literalized, symbolized, spectacularized', as in Barton's productions of 1968 and 1976, even if Hands chose to emphasize
decadence and disfigurement rather than gorgeous male naked-
ness. Helen's sole appearance, in 3.1, was an orgy of groping,
with her 'curly-headed, cockney attendants all joining in the fun
with Paris' (as G. M. Pearce reports).[1]

As in many earlier productions, women were degraded in a
comprehensive diatribe against carnality and opportunism. The
sense of time was eclectic, with the Trojans in a kind of medieval-
classical getup (Raymond Llewellyn as Priam was a bearded guru,
sitting cross-legged among his sons), the Greeks as trench warriors of World War I (Tony Church as Pandarus was thrown over
a fence of barbed wire at the play's end). Shakespeare's language
was often sacrificed to stage business calculated to deconstruct the
rhetorical seriousness of any lofty speech: during Ulysses' long
speech in 1.3, Agamemnon popped pills, Nestor slobbered over an
orange, and Ajax (Terry Wood), a 'roaring head-banger' out of
Monty Python, practised karate chops on empty ammunition
boxes. Terry Hands's dislike of coherence and linear development
prompted him, in Irving Wardle's view, to release the actors 'from
any binding directorial concept and give them the chance to live to
the full on their own terms — apparently in the hope that if a pattern does emerge it will be Shakespeare's'.[2]

Suzanne Burden, the Cressida of Jonathan Miller's production of the play for BBC Television in 1981, wrestled with the

---

1   Hodgdon, 269; Robert Cushman, 'War Games', *Observer*, 12 July 1981, 33; B.
    Smith, *Desire*, 307 n. 15, citing David Nokes, *TLS*, 17 July 1981, 810; Rutter,
    'Cressida's Glove', 117; G. M. Pearce, *CahiersE*, 20 (October 1981), 114–15;
    Benedict Nightingale, *New Statesman*, 10 July 1981, 24–5; Mark Amory, *Spectator*,
    18 July 1981, 26; and Sheridan Morley, *Punch*, 15 July 1981, 104. Hands had guest-
    directed a production at the Burgtheater, Vienna, in 1977 (Leiter, 761–2).
2   Irving Wardle, *The Times*, 8 July 1981, 11; Michael Billington, *Guardian*, 8 July
    1981, 10; and David Nokes, *TLS*, 17 July 1981, 810.

issue of feminine dignity and with her male cohorts in a way that accentuated a crossfire of rival interpretations on the issue of gender. Anton Lesser, cast as Troilus, reported in an interview that the 'triumvirate' of Troilus, Cressida and Pandarus turned out for him to be an 'amazing' collaboration, in which the actors found together a 'mutual dependence' that was then shattered traumatically 'when one of them is ejected and the triple relationship breaks up'. The director, though not conceiving of Cressida as 'a corrupt and sexually titillating girl', nonetheless pictured her as one 'whose innocence is too inexperienced to handle the shock and the overwhelming stimulus of these rough attractive Greek warriors she comes across'. He therefore directed her to play Cressida 'as sexually excited by being kissed, as thoroughly enjoying the game and her own power of arousal'. Miller was encouraged in this view by John Wilders, who, as consultant to the BBC/PBS Shakespeare productions, saw Cressida's behaviour in the Greek camp as 'entirely understandable' in view of her 'shallowness' and her being 'a vulnerable girl alone in an enemy camp'. Flattered by Diomedes' attentions, she is 'instinctively responsive to his sexual advances'.[1]

Burden, for her part, felt herself estranged from what Lesser and Miller had in mind. Her view of Cressida's relationship to her uncle, as she later explained, ran as follows: 'Taught by Pandarus, she's just about learned the ropes and she's quite aware that to him she's a puppet, a plaything he enjoys, but as soon as he's through playing that game he'll forget her . . . I felt she was a victim of states and men and rulers'. Burden complained angrily of hearing her character, in the scene of arrival in the Greek camp, dismissed in rehearsal as merely 'a tart and a sexual tease', whereas she saw Cressida as a witty and intelligent young woman who is just discovering herself, enormously unprotected by her supposed guardian. Burden perceived

1  Tylee, 72, citing an interview for Henry Fenwick, 'The Production', *The BBC Television Shakespeare 'Troilus and Cressida'* (1981); and Sheppard, 136–7, citing John Wilders (1988), 179–80.

9  Tony Church as Pandarus, dead on barbed wire at the end of Terry Hands's
Royal Shakespeare Company production, 1981

Cressida as so terrified that her survival instincts come into play: 'There's got to be a way out of this and if I have to use my sex I will'.[1] Whatever the results of the production (and it proved to be better than many in the BBC Television series), the experience on the set was clearly one in which men and women were having trouble understanding one another. The text meant very different things to the director and his actors, depending on who was reading the lines. The play was produced in Renaissance costuming, though a number of the visual and sound effects were more modern; the battle scenes especially, including the death of Hector, evoked a sense of trench warfare in World War I, making effective use of the camera to juxtapose Thersites' sardonic speeches in Act 5 with pictures of marching troops and muddy devastation. The tone of the production was, in Stanley Wells's view, dispassionate, minimizing directorial interpretation in favour of a kind of bland realism that missed the play's oppressive sense of the futility of war and the collapse of human pretensions to heroism.[2]

Juliet Stevenson's sympathetic portrayal of Cressida in Howard Davies's 1985 production by the Royal Shakespeare Company was thus something of an event – one that was sure to be controversial. Irving Wardle warmly welcomed Stevenson's reclamation of a role 'for which some actresses apologize', and found the interpretation impressively anchored 'in the facts of human behaviour'. Michael Coveney, on the other hand, irately saw political correctness in Stevenson's New Woman: 'It may be hard cheese on the RSC feminist puritans, but Shakespeare is writing about falsity and sexual wantonness, not rape'. Even though some fifteen years had passed since Estelle Kohler, as Isabella in John Barton's *Measure for Measure* at Stratford-upon-Avon, had elected to decline the Duke's sudden offer of

1  Tylee, 72–3; see previous note.
2  G. M. Pearce, *CahiersE*, 21 (April 1982), 59–60; and Stanley Wells, 'Speaking for Themselves', *TLS*, 20 November 1981, 1366. The part of Thersites was played by the actor known as The Incredible Orlando (Jack Birkett), with shaved head. See John J. O'Connor, *New York Times*, 17 May 1982, Section C, 16.

marriage, the issue of feminist interpretation was still far from resolved.[1]

Stevenson's Cressida was a victim of war and male violence. Grief-stricken at the prospect of being forcibly separated from Troilus, she was, as Claire Tylee puts it, 'bundled off in her nightie, her vulnerability never more clear'. Manhandled by the leering Greek officers among whom she suddenly found herself in 4.5, she nevertheless learned quickly enough how she could get them to beg; by the time Ulysses had his turn to ask for a kiss, she humiliated him with a snap of her fingers indicating that he was to kneel. The result was an outburst of misogyny from Ulysses that reflected his hurt male pride much more than a reasoned indictment of opportunistic women. For Robert Wilcher, the scene was a 'brutal paradigm of how women are reduced to objects'. Faced with such bleak prospects, Cressida was sure to lose; the brazen manner she had adopted from the start as (in Roger Warren's phrase) 'a cover to protect herself from becoming a love object like Helen' collapsed as she began to play the Greek soldiers' game. She was left no choice but to become 'a love-object after all'. This Cressida finally succumbed, in Claire Tylee's description, to 'being a toy in a boys' game', acting out her scene of flirtation with Diomedes as if she had been 'emotionally cauterized'.[2]

Howard Davies appears to have been at odds with Juliet Stevenson; he wanted to create a threesome of Pandarus, Troilus and Cressida, whereas Stevenson understood Cressida to be wary of her uncle and of her prospective lover from the start. Quite possibly, these tensions enriched the production by emphasizing the disjunctions of gender that were apparent also in the directorial

1 Irving Wardle, *The Times*, 27 June 1985, 8; Michael Coveney, *Financial Times*, 27 June 1985, 25; Michael Billington, *Guardian*, 27 June 1985, 22; Ros Asquith, *Observer*, 30 June 1985, 19; Hodgdon, 270–2. On Estelle Kohler as Isabella in John Barton's *Measure for Measure*, see Speaight, '1970', 444.

2 Tylee, 68 and 73, also citing, on 68, Robert Wilcher, 'Value and Opinion in *Troilus and Cressida*', an unpublished lecture delivered at the Royal Shakespeare Summer School, Stratford-upon-Avon, 1985. See also Warren, 114–18; Nicholas Shrimpton, *TES*, 5 July 1985; Shrimpton, '1984–5', 203–5; and Rutter, 'Cressida's Glove', 118–20.

10 Juliet Stevenson as Cressida and Joseph O'Connor as Agamemnon in
Howard Davies's production for the Royal Shakespeare Company, 1985

work of Hands and others. Certainly Davies was interested in fragmentation and disunion. Like Guthrie in 1956, Davies updated
the play to the era of England's last decades as a world power,
choosing in this case the Crimean war or some later time. 'The
decaying mansion which constituted the set', reports Vivian
Thomas, 'epitomised the decadence that characterised the play'.
Anachronisms exploited the huge gap of time between ancient
Greece and modern Europe: a flash photographer captured the
moment of Achilles' handshake with Hector, Achilles'
Myrmidons carried machine guns, and Agamemnon used a field
telephone to report the death of Patroclus. Ulysses (Peter Jeffrey)
was a loquacious pseudo-intellectual whose pontificating on order
and degree prompted even the dim-witted Agamemnon to raise his
eyes heavenwards. Paris (Sean Baker) emerged as 'the most distasteful and self-indulgent character in the play, egotistic and
self-important'. Menelaus turned out to be a 'blockhead', a

'despised nonentity'. Thersites (Alun Armstrong) was a brilliantly amusing 'Geordie waiter' who, as servant at the officers' mess table, undertook at one point to re-enact the whole 'order' argument of Ulysses and the rest (1.3) by first tidying and arranging everything on the mess table and then pulling the tablecloth, precipitating it all onto the floor. Achilles (Alan Rickman) was an 'unkempt and surly' degenerate 'to whom murder came naturally'. The massacre of Hector (David Burke) in Act 5 'took the form of a firing squad, emphasising both his helplessness and naïvety'.[1]

Whatever might be said for Cressida as a victim of men and war, the devotees of eros in Davies's production generally found themselves trapped by their own hedonism. Helen (Lindsay Duncan), for all the vapid giddiness and her seeming high on drugs, gave way to moments of anguish and desolation, fracturing the 'coarse gaiety' of her garishly luxurious existence with ' "This love will undo us all." / O Cupid, Cupid, Cupid!' (3.1.104–5). Pandarus (Clive Merrison) was central to Davies's conception of the play as a monument to the collapse of civilization. Suavely hatted, Pandarus opened the play 'by sitting at a table sipping wine and reading his paper'; by the end of it all, he was to be seen (as Michael Billington describes the moment) 'picking out a wistful tune on the piano as the lights of battle blaze[d] and as structured society disintegrate[d]'. He then rose from the piano, 'pale, gaunt and half-blind', to discover that the piano was playing by itself. This 'jaunty voyeur', and the play surrounding him, went out on a wry joke about self-annihilation.[2]

By the mid-1980s, *Troilus and Cressida* had become a parable of our postmodern era. Gary Taylor demonstrates how eloquently the Berliner Ensemble's 1986 production, directed by

---

1 Tylee, 72–3, citing an unpublished talk given by Juliet Stevenson at the Royal Shakespeare Theatre Summer School in Stratford-upon-Avon, 1985; Thomas, 135–6; and Juliet Stevenson's observations quoted in Rutter, *Voices*, xviii. See also Irving Wardle, *The Times*, 27 June 1985, 8; John Peter, *Sunday Times*, 30 June 1985, 41; Christopher Edwards, *Spectator*, 17 May 1986, 37; and Jill Pearce, *CahiersE*, 31 (April 1987), 65–6.

2 Thomas, 135–6, citing Michael Billington, *Guardian*, 27 June 1985, 22.

Manfred Wekwerth, seems to have spoken to the people of that divided city caught in the toils of a seemingly endless military stalemate. The production's feminist interpretation of male brutality was no less insistently contemporary. Cressida (Corinna Harfouch) was stunned by Troilus' betrayal of her in agreeing to send her back to her father. Her surrender to Diomedes, and her transformation into the woman that men insisted on her becoming, were signalled by her taking a red ribbon (Troilus' parting gift to her) out of her hair and fashioning it into a garter for her thigh. Until that moment her gestures had been modest and discreet. Her arrival in the Greek camp earlier that day was subjected to comic deflation by the fatuous appearance of Ajax, repeatedly jogging past at the back of the stage, never stopping to beg for a kiss, as he warmed up for his encounter with Hector. Throughout, as Taylor shows, the production was Brechtian in its collaborative ensemble playing, its readiness to disengage the

11 Alun Armstrong plays Thersites as a Geordie waiter in Howard Davies's production for the Royal Shakespeare Company, 1985

audience from stage illusion, and above all its embracement of performance as a social and political act.[1]

Sam Mendes's production of *Troilus and Cressida* at the Royal Shakespeare Company's Swan Theatre (Stratford-upon-Avon) in 1990 has been aptly described by Carol Rutter as an eclectic affair well attuned to the new radicalism of the 1990s, in which authority is utterly abandoned in favour of impassivity, pluralism, internal contradiction and a kind of egotistic nihilism. Theatrical signs were open to multiple readings, and stage images incorporated their own subversion, as for example when Paris unwrapped a gold-draped package in 3.1 to reveal, teasingly, Helen of Troy (Sally Dexter), beautiful enough but absurdly artificial in her heavy makeup and tight red dress, a tasty dish not impressive enough to justify the waste of war in her behalf. She was 'woman as icon', a 'bizarre visual complication of Golden Calf and expensively wrapped chocolate'; a 'sultry, regal barmaid'. Achilles (Ciaran Hinds), a 'lethal, black-leather-clad gang-leader', 'sat propped against his "tent"', his hair greased to outshine his leather trousers, wearing a black string vest, munching popcorn'. Agamemnon (Sylvester Morand) wore a shapeless, moth-eaten cardigan over his breastplate. Norman Rodway as both Prologue and, later, Pandarus was a natty chap in a blazer whose wheezing and giggling established the squalidness of the cause for which the Trojan war was fought. Cressida (Amanda Root) was, in Irving Wardle's description, 'an emotionally damaged refugee whose sexual and comic strategies form[ed] a protective shell which she sheds in full knowledge of the likely penalty'. The question turned out to be not why she betrayed Troilus 'but why she ever entertained the possibility of faithfulness'.

Thersites (Simon Russell Beale), more than any other character perhaps, embodied the production's visual concept of disjunction, with his filthy pinstriped trousers of Etonian origin having metamorphosed themselves into the outfit of a skid-row

---

1  Taylor, *Reinventing*, 298–304.

bum, complete with Gay Lib button, a flasher's overcoat and a leather skull cap that put one reviewer (Martin Hoyle) in mind of a 'leering Brueghel face carved out of a potato'. The disillusioning eclecticism of the whole suggested to some viewers a reading of the play especially well suited to Shakespeare's mordant scepticism, and clarified once again how this strange play has come into its own for late-twentieth-century audiences.[1]

The Royal Shakespeare Company's most recent production, directed by Ian Judge at Stratford-upon-Avon in July 1996, suggests the extent to which the postmodern reading of this play as a thorough debunking of history and myth may have become the orthodoxy of our age. The battleground of this production, wrote Steve Grant, turned out to be 'a homo-erotic playground of laddish boasting, bursting thongs, shining pectorals, wobbling buttocks, rock-star leather, all-male snogging and (if you're Helen) instant orgasm'. Sex and death provided the 'chilling link' between our own age and that of the Renaissance: 'sex is easy, but love and faith are out of the question'. The Prologue, assigned to Thersites (Richard McCabe), sent up the whole business of the war as if he were a 'TV warm-up man'. Helen and Paris (Katia Caballero and Ray Fearon) emerged naked from a sunken steam bath 'for some determined foreplay'. Cressida (Victoria Hamilton), as Nicholas de Jongh viewed her, changed from a 'serious, self-possessed girl, delighted by first love' into a 'fatal casualty of war', one who yielded only from 'sheer, pressured desperation' to the advances of a 'surly, beach-boy hunk' in the person of Diomedes (Richard Dillane).

The final battle scenes were staged under a blood-red sun. Pandarus (Clive Francis), mincing, queenly, wasted and diseased, spat out his final curses as a syphilitic voyeur; what had begun as

---

1 Rutter, 'Cressida's Glove', 120–2; Irving Wardle, *Independent*, 6 May 1990, 27; Martin Hoyle, *Financial Times*, 28 April 1990, Weekend FT XI; Nicholas de Jongh, *Guardian*, 28 April 1990, 21; Michael Coveney, *Observer*, 29 April 1990, 54; John Peter, *Sunday Times*, 29 April 1990; Paul Taylor, *Independent*, 30 April 1990, 15; Peter J. Smith, *CahiersE*, 38 (October 1990), 83–6; Elizabeth Beroud, *CahiersE*, 39 (April 1991), 57–70; Iska Alter and William B. Long, *Shakespeare Bulletin*, 9.1 (1991), 18. When the production moved to the Pit, it was reviewed by Michael Coveney, *Observer*, 23 June 1991, 48, and John Peter, *Drama*, 6.9 (29 September 1991).

a 'jaunty comedy' ended, in Michael Billington's opinion, as 'a soured, dispirited view of the devouring tyranny of time'. The eloquent humanity shown in this production by Philip Voss's Ulysses appeared lost in a dreary world of cheap jokes and posturing, and even he proved capable of pique in his unjust condemnation of Cressida. The overall effect was, for some critics, overly entertaining, slick, 'operatic', 'stagey', 'choreographed' in the bad sense of supplying artifice in place of gravitas.[1]

*Troilus*, it seems, has so thoroughly established itself as

1  Steve Grant, *Time Out*, 31 July 1996; Michael Billington, *Guardian*, 25 July 1996; John Gross, *Sunday Telegraph*, 28 July 1996; Nicholas de Jongh, *Evening Standard*, 25 July 1996; Carole Woddis, *What's On*, 31 July 1996; Paul Taylor, *Independent*, 26 July 1996; Alastair Macaulay, *Financial Times*, 26 July 1996; Robert Hewison, *Sunday Times*, 28 July 1996; Jack Tinker, *Daily Mail*, 25 July 1996; Benedict Nightingale, *The Times*, 26 July 1996; Robert Butler, *Independent on Sunday*, 28 July 1996; Robert Gore-Langton, *Daily Telegraph*, 26 July 1996; reprinted in *Theatre Record*, issue 15 (15–28 July 1996), 964–9. See also Dorothy and Wayne Cook, *Shakespeare Bulletin*, 15.1 (1997), 13–14.

12  Simon Russell Beale plays Thersites as a 'skid-row bum' in Sam Mendes's 1990 production for the Royal Shakespeare Company

Shakespeare's play of disillusionment about 'war as a kind of lechery and lechery as a sort of war' (Benedict Nightingale) that our current *fin-de-siècle* impulse has been to celebrate that insight as theatrical camp. Mark Wing-Davey's production at the Delacorte Theater in Central Park, New York, in the summer of 1995, revelled in what one critic called 'almost everything you hate about modern life': sordid and petty motivations at every hand, a kind of charming repulsiveness, sulky mood, nasty art. Ulysses (Stephen Skybell) delivered his oration on order and degree to the accompaniment of channel surfing by his fellow officers, bringing in fragments of news on CNN about Bosnia. The love scene of Paris and Helen (Bill Camp and Tamara Tunie) yielded 'a little anthology of everything congressional opponents of the NEA think subsidized art is all about', with Pandarus (Stephen Spinella) sporting a giant prop dildo that responded on cue to his song about the 'dying' and 'groans' of love. Cassandra (Catherine Kellner) was a 'shrilly amateurish yuppie' with a vacuum cleaner; Achilles (Paul Calderon) was a street-smart 'wacked-out druggie'. Cressida (Elizabeth Marvel) resembled, on her first appearance, 'a cocktail waitress from Caesar's Palace'. Troilus (Neal Huff) had a lap-top computer for his penultimate scene. Helen's ubiquitous presence was suggested by a billboard-sized poster. Thersites (Tim Blake Nelson) festooned his scabrous commentary with updated obscenities. The costuming and set, bringing together soldiers in camouflage with Greek togas, Japanese kimonos and medieval armour, gave the postmodern effect of 'one gigantic heap of cultural compost'. The effect was not essentially different, in some reviewers' eyes, from what one might get from reading tomorrow's headlines on the subway at 3 a.m.[1]

---

1  Benedict Nightingale, *The Times*, 26 July 1996; Michael Feingold, *Village Voice*, 29 August 1995, 77; Ben Brantley, *New York Times*, 18 August 1995, C3; David Sterritt, *Christian Science Monitor*, 24 August 1995, 14; Donald Lyons, *Wall Street Journal*, 23 August 1995, A10. Feingold recalls 'with a certain sickly fondness' the previous New York Shakespeare Festival production of the play, staged by David Schweizer at the Newhouse in 1973, featuring a dead horse down stage right which, when kicked by Pandarus (William Hickey) in his scene with Paris and Helen, provided a kind of musical accompaniment for Pandarus' song by means of a speaker in the horse's rear end.

Contemporary interpretations such as these, for all their immediacy and cleverness of analogy, should warn us how dangerous it is to suppose that (as Barbara Bowen puts it) 'we alone see the play as it is', and that, given the short and recent performance history of *Troilus*, 'our performances are definitive'. As Bowen says, no performance can escape 'its own time and culture'; and her observation may apply especially to a play like this, since we are too readily prone to imagine that *Troilus* 'really *is* about Vietnam'. To the extent that the stage, and especially the Shakespearean stage, 'tells us more about history than it does about the play itself', the remarkable brief history of *Troilus* 'points to and participates in a much larger history of cultural politics'.[1] Now assured of its place in today's theatre, *Troilus* will undoubtedly form a part of our cultural history as it is being written and will be written in the years to come.

1  Bowen, 'Stage History', esp. 265–6.
    Some recent productions in North America should be mentioned: one by the Folger Theatre company in Washington, D.C., in the autumn of 1983 that was negatively reviewed by Gary Jay Williams, *SQ*, 35 (1984), 225–6; one at Cedar City, Utah, in 1984; one the same year at Ashland, Oregon, directed by Richard E. T. White; one at the Stratford Festival in Stratford, Canada, in 1987, directed by David William in an antiheroic vein with visual memories of the war in Vietnam, featuring Achilles as a homosexual punk who also appears in a flaming-red version of a Nazi officer's uniform, and Paris as a transvestite (see Owen E. Brady, *Theatre Review*, 40 [1988], 110–14); one at Shakespeare Repertory, Chicago, in the autumn of 1987, directed by Barbara Gaines; one presented by the Yale Repertory Theatre in early 1990 under the direction of Andrei Belgrader (see Dorothy and Wayne Cook, *Shakespeare Bulletin*, 8.2 [1990], 16–17); one at Stratford, Connecticut, in 1991, staged by Jack Landau, setting the play in the American Civil War era with Agamemnon an embodiment of Ulysses S. Grant, Priam an echo of Robert E. Lee, and Cressida (Carrie Nye) a blonde southern belle (see Judith Crist, *New York Herald Tribune*, 24 July 1991, 6); one directed by Bill Alexander for the Shakespeare Theatre, Washington, D.C., in the autumn of 1992 (see Miranda Johnson-Haddad, *SQ*, 45 [1994], 98–108, and Edwin Wilson, *Wall Street Journal*, 6 October 1992); one presented at the Mount in Lenox, Mass., in the summer of 1993, directed by Dennis Krausnick (see Joan Mento, *Shakespeare Bulletin*, 12.2 [1994], 12–13); and a second production by Shakespeare Repertory, Chicago, in early 1995, again directed by Barbara Gaines (see Justin Shaltz, *Shakespeare Bulletin*, 13.2 [1995], 13–14). Productions have also taken place in Oklahoma (1992), Houston (1990), New Haven (1990), Berkeley (1988), Los Angeles (1984–5) and elsewhere.
    William Walton composed an opera on *Troilus and Cressida* with libretto by Christopher Hassall, based loosely on Chaucer's poem and on Dryden's play and first performed at the Royal Opera House in Covent Garden in 1954.

# TROILUS
# AND
# CRESSIDA

*A Never Writer to an Ever Reader. News.*

Eternal reader, you have here a new play, never staled with the stage, never clapper-clawed with the palms of the vulgar, and yet passing full of the palm comical; for it is a birth of your brain, that never undertook anything comical vainly. And were but the vain names of comedies changed 5 for the titles of commodities, or of plays for pleas, you should see all those grand censors, that now style them such vanities, flock to them for the main grace of their gravities – especially this author's comedies, that are so framed to the life that they serve for the most common commentaries of 10 all the actions of our lives, showing such a dexterity and power of wit that the most displeased with plays are pleased with his comedies. And all such dull and heavy-witted worldlings as were never capable of the wit of a comedy,

*A Never Writer* On the importance of this publisher's preface of 1609 to an understanding of the play's publishing history and record of early performance, see Introduction, pp. 1–3, 17–18, 88 and 400.

1–3 **never staled . . . vulgar** never rendered flat, insipid and unpalatable through performance, and never applauded by popular audiences of vulgar tastes. See LN.

3 **passing . . . comical** exceedingly well endowed with a comic genius worthy of the palm of excellence

4 **your brain** i.e. the brain or talent that people talk about. On the colloquial use of *your*, cf. *RJ* 1.2.51: 'Your plaintain leaf is excellent for that'. The brain of Shakespeare, the writer suggests, never gives birth to a comical idea that is not brilliant.

5–6 **were . . . commodities** 'if only what we disparagingly call "comedies"

were given a name signifying commercial value'. *Titles* plays on the sense of 'legal rights to' (Foakes, *TC*), anticipating the wordplay on *plays* and *pleas* or lawsuits.

7 **grand censors** i.e. the London authorities, both in trade and in the Church, which were generally hostile to dramatic performances as ungodly and subversive

7–8 **style . . . vanities** call them idle and worthless

8 **for . . . gravities** in appreciation of the way in which they present weighty matters with pleasing graciousness

9–10 **framed . . . life** lifelike, verisimilar

10 **common** universal

12 **the most . . . plays** those *grand censors* (7) who are most vehement in denouncing plays, or, more generally, any who do not like theatre

14 **capable of** able to understand

coming by report of them to his representations, have       15
found that wit there that they never found in themselves
and have parted better witted than they came, feeling an
edge of wit set upon them more than ever they dreamed
they had brain to grind it on. So much and such savoured
salt of wit is in his comedies that they seem, for their height   20
of pleasure, to be born in that sea that brought forth Venus.
Amongst all there is none more witty than this; and had I
time I would comment upon it, though I know it needs not,
for so much as will make you think your testern well
bestowed, but for so much worth as even poor I know to be   25
stuffed in it. It deserves such a labour as well as the best
comedy in Terence or Plautus. And believe this, that when
he is gone and his comedies out of sale, you will scramble
for them and set up a new English Inquisition. Take this for
a warning, and, at the peril of your pleasure's loss, and   30
judgement's, refuse not, nor like this the less for not being
sullied with the smoky breath of the multitude; but thank
fortune for the scape it hath made amongst you, since by the
grand possessors' wills I believe you should have prayed for

---

15 **by . . . them** in response to gossip
about the plays
**representations** stage performances
(*OED* 3)
18 **edge** sharpness
21 **in . . . Venus** Venus, goddess of love
and hence especially appropriate to
romantic comedy, was associated with
the Greek goddess Aphrodite, whose
name (from *aphros*) means 'born from
the foam' of the sea.
23 **needs not** is not necessary
24–6 **for so much . . . in it** The publisher
is self-deprecatingly aware of how little
his own comment on the play could add
to the value that the purchaser will
receive for his *testern* or sixpence.
27 **Terence or Plautus** Shakespeare is
similarly compared with these writers
of Roman 'new comedy' by Ben

Jonson in his commemorative poem in
the First Folio of 1623, and with
Plautus by Francis Meres in his
*Palladis Tamia*, 1598.
28 **out of sale** out of print
29 **Inquisition** (1) assiduous search; (2) a
jesting allusion to the ecclesiastical tri-
bunal or Holy Office established by
the Catholic Church for the suppres-
sion of heresy, begun in the thirteenth
century and notoriously severe in
Renaissance Spain. See LN.
33 **scape . . . you** i.e. publication, thereby escaping oblivion
34 **grand possessors' wills** i.e. the
intentions (presumably) of the acting
company that owned the play. See
Introduction, pp. 17–18.
34–5 **you . . . been prayed** you would
have importuned in vain for that

them rather than been prayed. And so I leave all such to be    35
prayed for, for the states of their wits' healths, that will not
praise it. *Vale*.

acting company to release the play for
publication, rather than being begged
to buy the play (as you are being
begged now in this letter of advertisement). *Them* refers to the comedies as
a whole (Oxf[1]).

35–7 **I . . . praise it** The publisher, with
tongue in cheek, suggests that those

who do not like the play are heading
for a state of damnation, not in the
normal Christian sense but in the
sense of damning their intelligences to
the secular hellfire of stupidity.

37 *Vale* farewell (Lat.), but continuing
the jest about damnation, since *Vale*
literally means 'Be strong and healthy'

# THE
# Historie of Troylus
## and Cresseida.

*As it was acted by the Kings Maiesties*
seruants at the Globe.

*Written by* William Shakespeare.

*George Steevens.*

## LONDON
Imprinted by *G. Eld* for *R Bonian* and *H. Walley*, and
are to be sold at the spred Eagle in Paules
Church-yeard, ouer against the
great North doore.
1609.

13   The title-page of the first 'state' of the 1609 Quarto

# THE
# Famous Historie of
## Troylus *and* Cresseid.

*Excellently expressing the beginning*
of their loues, with the conceited wooing
of *Pandarus* Prince of *Licia*.

*Written by* William Shakespeare.

LONDON
Imprinted by *G.Eld* for *R. Bonian* and *H. Walley*, and
are to be fold at the fpred Eagle in Paules
Church-yeard, ouer againft the
great North doore.
*1609*.

14  The title-page of the second 'state' of the 1609 Quarto

# LIST OF ROLES

PROLOGUE

## THE TROJANS

| | |
|---|---|
| PRIAM | *King of Troy* |
| HECTOR | |
| PARIS | |
| DEIPHOBUS | |
| HELENUS | *his sons* |
| TROILUS | |
| MARGARETON | |
| AENEAS | *Trojan commanders* |
| ANTENOR | |
| CASSANDRA | *Priam's daughter, a prophetess* |
| ANDROMACHE | *Hector's wife* |
| CRESSIDA | *Calchas' daughter* |
| CALCHAS | *Cressida's father, a Trojan priest,* |
| | *a defector to the Greeks* |
| PANDARUS | *a lord, Cressida's uncle* |
| ALEXANDER | *Cressida's servant* |
| A BOY | *Troilus' servant* |
| SERVANT | *attending on Paris* |
| OTHER TROJANS | *including Soldiers and Attendants* |

## THE GREEKS

| | |
|---|---|
| AGAMEMNON | *general commander of the Greeks* |
| MENELAUS | *King of Sparta, his brother* |
| HELEN | *Menelaus' wife, living with Paris in Troy* |
| ACHILLES | |
| AJAX | |
| ULYSSES | *Greek commanders* |
| NESTOR | |
| DIOMEDES | |
| PATROCLUS | *Achilles' companion* |
| THERSITES | *a deformed and scurrilous Greek* |
| SERVANT | *attending on Diomedes* |
| OTHER GREEKS | *including Soldiers, Myrmidons* |
| | *and Attendants* |

126

LIST OF ROLES Rowe was the first editor to provide a list of *dramatis personae*, somewhat incomplete, grouping the men as either Trojan or Greek, with the women listed below the men, and the unnamed extras last. Foakes adopted a plan, as here, of including all Trojans in one group and all Greeks in another, with the Speaker of the Prologue as the one speaking role not thus grouped. For historical information on the characters of this play and their roles in Shakespeare's sources, see pp. 375–97.

T.J. King (89–90) calculates that 'the fourteen men required in fifteen principal parts are significantly more than the average of ten men required in principal parts for other Shakespeare plays, and this lends support to the argument that the play was written for private performance. The fourteen men and four boys in principal parts speak 98% of the lines . . . Six men can play ten small speaking parts and eight mutes . . . The casting requirements for Q and F differ only in that F includes a Prologue . . . and the direction "*Enter common Souldiers*"' (1.2.231.1). King's characterization of the Prologue as containing '3 lines' (90) is presumably a typographical error for '31'. See King's Tables 64 and 80 (215–16, 255) for a detailed and feasible hypothesis of how the doubling might have worked. This unusually large number of the roles does not allow for much doubling – another characteristic of private performance (see Bevington, *Mankind*, 26–47 and *passim*.)

PRIAM also called *Priamus*, at 2.2.207 and 5.3.54

HELENUS a priest; see 2.2.37

TROILUS a son of Priam mentioned late and briefly in the *Iliad* as having been killed before Hector (24.257, LCL, 2.580–1). For his expanded role in medieval accounts, see Sources, pp. 381ff. The name can be pronounced in two or three syllables as 'Troy-lus' or 'Tro-i-lus'; see, e.g., 4.4.30 and 31.

MARGARETON Priam's bastard son is thus named in Benoît's *Roman de Troie*, 15768 (see pp. 381–2). He is called 'Margarelon' on the one occasion that his name is mentioned in Shakespeare's play ('bastard *Margarelon*', 5.5.7), in both Q and F, but that spelling is probably a common error due to misreading (Cam¹, 138).

CASSANDRA daughter of Priam and Hecuba who resisted the love of Apollo and in consequence was given the gift of prophecy, but was condemned never to be believed; see 2.2.98 and n. After the fall of Troy she fell to the lot of Agamemnon and was taken home to Mycenae by him, where she was killed by Clytemnestra; see Aeschylus, *Agamemnon*, 1203–1330 (LCL, 2.102ff.), and Euripides, *The Daughters of Troy*, 353–461 (LCL, 1.384–93).

CRESSIDA more often called 'Cressid' (37 times in the Concordance as compared with 9 for 'Cressida'). The longer form is used here since it appears in the play's title and in Chaucer's poem (Criseyde). Cressida is not mentioned in the *Iliad*, though that epic begins with a quarrel over Agamemnon's mistress, Chryseis, daughter of Chryses, priest of Apollo. For Cressida's development in medieval accounts, see pp. 381ff.

PANDARUS also called 'Pandar', with generic suggestion that appears to be recognized by a shift of spelling in F to 'Pander'; see esp. 3.2.197–206 and 5.11.47–8. A Trojan warrior called Pandarus figures in the *Iliad*, especially in his treacherous wounding of Menelaus and in his fighting with Diomedes (4.85–140, 5.95–105, 280–96; LCL, 1.158–63, 200–1, 214–17), but for the development of the essentially non-Homeric uncle of Cressida in medieval accounts of the Troy story, see pp. 382–5.

A BOY Troilus' servant is called 'Boy' in QF at 1.2.262ff. and 'Man' at 3.2.0.1ff.; Troilus addresses him as 'Sirrah' at 3.2.5. These two brief appearances are almost certainly parts of a single minor role.

SERVANT *attending on Paris* called 'Man' in Q and 'Seruant' in F (3.1). Cf. the casual inconsistencies about 'Boy' and 'Man' in the previous note, and cf. SERVANT *attending on Diomedes*, below.

HELEN also called 'Helena' once in F, at 3.1.41.1, and 'Nell' twice in QF, at 3.1.51 and 131. *MND* and *AW* similarly use both 'Helen' and 'Helena', *AW* strongly preferring 'Helen', *MND* somewhat preferring 'Helena'. Cf. CRESSIDA and DIOMEDES.

AJAX In Greek mythology, the so-called 'greater' Ajax was a son of Telamon, King of Salamis in Greece, and Periboea or Eriboea (daughter of Alcathous, a son of Pelops). It was his half-brother Teucer who was the son of Telamon and Hesione, sister of King Priam of Troy. In Shakespeare's sources (Lydgate, 3.2046–8, Caxton, 589) and in this play (see 4.5.84 and 121), Ajax is the son of Telamon and Hesione. Hercules' giving of Hesione to Telamon, as a reward for their assault on Troy in reprisal against the treachery of Laomedon, Hesione's father, is an early incident leading up to the Trojan war. See 2.1.12, 2.2.77 and n., and 4.5.121–35.

DIOMEDES more often called 'Diomed'; the longer form appears only twice in the Concordance (once a possessive) as compared with 33 for 'Diomed'. The longer form is used in this edition by analogy with CRESSIDA (see above) and because the form *Diomedes* does appear in SDs in QF at 1.3.0.2 and 4.3.0.2 and in F alone at 2.3.65.2 and 3.3.0.1, where metre is not under consideration (though it is *Diomed* in five SDs). In *AC*, similarly, the F spelling is *Diomedes* for the SD at 4.14.117.1, though 'Diomed' thrice in the ensuing dialogue.

*SERVANT *attending on Diomedes* called '*Seruant*' at 5.5.0.1 in Q but '*Seruants*' in F; addressed as 'my servant' at 5.5.1 in QF, so that F's SD is perhaps a misreading. The SP for the single speech of this character at 5.5.5 is *Man.* in Q and *Ser.* in F; see A BOY *and* SERVANT *attending on Paris*, above.

# TROILUS AND CRESSIDA

## [THE PROLOGUE]

[*Enter* Speaker of the Prologue, *in armour.*]

PROLOGUE

In Troy there lies the scene. From isles of Greece
The princes orgulous, their high blood chafed,
Have to the port of Athens sent their ships
Fraught with the ministers and instruments
Of cruel war. Sixty and nine, that wore          5

PROLOGUE 1 *In . . . scene The F punctuation, preserved here, suggests that
the speaker of the Prologue gestures
towards his stage: 'Troy is right there,
before your eyes; the stage is where
Troy is imagined to be'. Editors often
add a comma after 'Troy', implying,
'In Troy, that is where the action
occurs'. Such a reading stresses the
metaphorical sense of *scene* at the
expense of theatrical immediacy.
**isles of Greece** Shakespeare's sense
of Greek geography is imprecise.
Ulysses (Odysseus) is from the isle of
Ithaka, but Menelaus' Sparta and
Agamemnon's Mycenae are on the
Peloponnesian mainland; Achilles and
his Myrmidons are associated with the
island of Aegina but also with
Thessaly in the north of Greece, etc.

2 **orgulous** proud, haughty. A fairly
common word in the Middle Ages and
in Caxton, Bk 3, derived from
Romance languages (cf. Fr. *orgueilleux*,
proud, and Spenser's Italianate
*Orgoglio* in Bk 1 of *The Faerie Queene*),
but archaic by the early seventeenth
century. Shakespeare uses it only here,
as part of the consciously elevated
style of this Prologue.

**their . . . chafed** their aristocratic blood
warmed to valour; their high-strung
temperaments or humours irritated

3 **port of Athens** Shakespeare took this
detail, of the mustering of the Greek
ships at Athens, from his more immediate sources: see Caxton, 545–6, and
Lydgate, 2.5066.3, 5096, 5155, 5208,
etc. In Homer (*Iliad*, 2.303, LCL,
1.72–3), Aeschylus (*Agamemnon*, 190,
LCL, 2.20–1), Euripides (*Iphigeneia at
Aulis*) and other classical authors, the
assembling takes place at Aulis, in
Boeotia, north of Athens, on the
Euboic Gulf.

4 **Fraught** freighted, laden; suggesting
also 'big with menace', as in the phrase,
'fraught with peril' (*OED ppl.e. & ppl.a.*
3)
**ministers** agents, soldiers who will
prosecute the war

5 **Sixty and nine** Shakespeare follows
Caxton's report (545–6) that 'The
some of kynges and dukes' who
'assemblid them to gyder at the porte
of athenes' (see 3) 'were sixty and
nyne'. From Chapman's translation of
Homer's *Iliad*, Bk 2, Shakespeare
would have known the catalogue of
Greek ships.

PROLOGUE] 1–31] *F; not in Q* 0.1] *Cam¹, subst.; not in F; Spoken by one in armour / Singer*

Their crownets regal, from th'Athenian bay
Put forth toward Phrygia, and their vow is made
To ransack Troy, within whose strong immures
The ravished Helen, Menelaus' queen,
With wanton Paris sleeps; and that's the quarrel.　　　　10
To Tenedos they come,
And the deep-drawing barks do there disgorge
Their warlike freightage. Now on Dardan plains
The fresh and yet unbruised Greeks do pitch
Their brave pavilions. Priam's six-gated city –　　　　15
Dardan and Timbria, Helias, Chetas, Troien
And Antenorides – with massy staples
And corresponsive and fulfilling bolts,
Spar up the sons of Troy.

6　**crownets** crowns worn by nobles. The term, a variant of 'coronet', is a diminutive of 'crown', indicating a lesser dignity than that assigned to the sovereign.

7　**Phrygia** a region in western Asia Minor or modern-day Turkey; used as a poetic equivalent for Troy in Roman and Renaissance poetry

8　**immures** walls

9　**ravished** abducted, seized and carried off. Like the word 'raped', which originally meant 'taken away by force', *ravished* takes on the sense of sexual assault. The ambivalence is sustained in the famous story of the 'rape' of Helen.

10　**quarrel** complaint, accusation, charge; but with strong overtones of petty and spiteful bickering over nothing (*OED sb.*[3] 1, 4)

11　**Tenedos** small island off the coast near Troy

12　**deep-drawing barks** heavily laden vessels lying low in the water

13　**freightage** freight (of armed men); the word ('frautage', F) is itself fraught with ominous suggestion, as in *Fraught*, 4

**Dardan** Trojan. Dardanus, the son of Zeus and the Pleiad Electra, was founder

of Troy and mythical ancestor of its ruling family, five generations before Priam.

14　**unbruised** unbruisèd

15　**brave pavilions** splendid tents; suggesting also a showy bravado

16–17　The names of the six gates are from Caxton (507) and Lydgate (2.596–605), in spellings closer to Caxton's.

17　**Antenorides** pronounced in five syllables, accented on the first, third and fifth

17–18　**with . . . bolts** 'each gate being equipped with massive U-shaped rods driven into posts [*OED* staple *sb.*[1] 2] into which are fitted huge corresponding bolts'. *Fulfilling* suggests both 'complementary' and 'fill[ed] to the full' (Cam[1]).

19　*Spar up F's reading, 'Stirre vp', is perhaps defensible, if we read 15–19 in inverted construction as follows: 'The men of Troy rouse to action the city of King Priam, with its six impregnable gates'. But Theobald's emendation ('Sperre') allows for a more plausible construction: 'the massive bolted gates defensively shut in the Trojans'. The plural form of *Spar* is allowable following the itemization of the six gates.

8 immures] *F (emures)*　12 barks] *F2; Barke F*　13 freightage] *F (frautage)*　17 Antenorides] *Theobald; Antenonidus F; Anteroridas Pope*　19 Spar] *Singer (Coleridge); Stirre F; Sperre Pope (Theobald); Sperrs Capell*

Now expectation, tickling skittish spirits 20
On one and other side, Trojan and Greek,
Sets all on hazard. And hither am I come,
A Prologue armed, but not in confidence
Of author's pen or actor's voice, but suited
In like conditions as our argument, 25
To tell you, fair beholders, that our play
Leaps o'er the vaunt and firstlings of those broils,
Beginning in the middle, starting thence away
To what may be digested in a play.
Like or find fault; do as your pleasures are; 30
Now good or bad, 'tis but the chance of war. [*Exit.*]

**1.1** *Enter* PANDARUS *and* TROILUS.

TROILUS

Call here my varlet; I'll unarm again.

---

20 **skittish** lively; with overtones also of 'restively playful, fickle, given to shying' (*OED a.* 1–3). Expectation is allegorized as wanton; *tickling* anticipates a repeatedly erotic use of the word in its various forms at 1.2.131, 3.1.114, 4.5.62, and 5.2.58 and 184.

22 **Sets . . . hazard** turns it all into a roll of the dice, or a tennis match (*OED* hazard *sb.* 1, 6). Expectation, rather like Fortune, doesn't care who wins. With this proverbial phrase (Dent, A208.1), cf. also 'The chance of war is uncertain' (Dent, C222).

23 **armed** in armour; armed with weapons; prepared. See LN.

23–4 **not . . . Of** not as though having any overweening confidence in. Cf. Rosalind's epilogue to *AYL*: 'What a case am I in then, that am neither a good epilogue nor cannot insinuate with you in the behalf of a good play!' (7–9).

24–5 **suited . . . argument** costumed to suit the plot of our play. *Argument*

suggests both 'plot' and 'quarrel'; cf. 10 and n. *Suited* also suggests 'fitted'.

27 **vaunt and firstlings** beginning. *Vaunt* is an independent use of the prefix *vant-* or *vaunt-*, meaning first part of something (*OED*).

28 **Beginning . . . middle** See LN.

29 **digested** disposed of, assimilated, comprehended

31 'whatever your verdict, we take it as the chance of war' (Ard¹). The uncertain chance of war is proverbial (Dent, C223).

1.1 The setting is understood to be King Priam's royal palace called Ilium (see 1.1.97 and n.). In the general absence of scenic effects on the Elizabethan stage, the actors establish the sense of locale by dialogue, gesture and costume (Foakes, *TC*).

1 **varlet** page, attendant on a knight (without pejorative connotation); presumably the 'Boy' who enters at 1.2.262.1 and at 3.2.0.1 (where he is called '*Troylus Man*' in QF)

---

25 conditions] *F*; condition *Cam¹* 28 Beginning in the] *F*; 'Ginning i'th' *Theobald* thence away] *F*; thence *Pope* 31 SD] *Cam¹*, subst.; not in *F* 1.1] *F (Actus Primus. Scoena Prima.); not in Q*

Why should I war without the walls of Troy,
That find such cruel battle here within?
Each Trojan that is master of his heart,
Let him to field; Troilus, alas, hath none.                              5

PANDARUS   Will this gear ne'er be mended?

TROILUS

The Greeks are strong, and skilful to their strength,
Fierce to their skill, and to their fierceness valiant;
But I am weaker than a woman's tear,
Tamer than sleep, fonder than ignorance,                              10
Less valiant than the virgin in the night,
And skilless as unpractised infancy.

PANDARUS   Well, I have told you enough of this; for my
part, I'll not meddle nor make no farther. He that will
have a cake out of the wheat must tarry the grinding.        15

TROILUS   Have I not tarried?

PANDARUS   Ay, the grinding; but you must tarry the bolting.

TROILUS   Have I not tarried?

PANDARUS   Ay, the bolting; but you must tarry the leavening.

---

2   **without** outside of
2–3 On the allegory of war among the
   body's members, see LN.
5   **to field** go to the field of battle
   **none** i.e. no heart for fighting
6   **gear** business. See 14n.
   **mended** rectified, cured
7–8 **to . . . to . . . to** in proportion to, in
   addition to
10  **Tamer** more docile
   **fonder** more foolishly doting
11  **the virgin** i.e. any innocent and easily
   frightened young woman
12  **unpractised** (1) inexperienced, inex-
   pert, untried; (2) guileless
14  **meddle nor make** i.e. 'have anything
   more to do with it'. A common expression (Dent, M852), often suggestive of
   sexual activity, and possibly continuing
   here a smarmy metaphor beginning
   with the mending of *gear* (i.e. sexual

organs) in 6. *Grinding, bolting, making,
heating, oven* and *cooling* in 15–24 all
lend themselves to the same wordplay.
See G. Williams, *Dictionary*, 126–7,
303–4, 587–8, 624–5, 846–7 and 870.
The idea of *meddling* is dear to
Pandarus; see 63 and 79.
15  *****must** The F reading, 'must needes',
   is probably a sophistication rather than
   an authorial change. The three pages
   of the precancellation F text make
   clear that 'the original intention was to
   produce a simple reprint of the extant
   Quarto' (*TxC*, 425).
   **tarry** wait for (*OED v.* 6), not 'delay'
   (*OED* 1–2)
17  **bolting** sifting (of flour)
19  **leavening** producing fermentation in
   dough by means of 'leaven', the fer-
   menting agent (often a small quantity
   of dough from a previous batch)

3 within?] *F*; within, *Q*   4 Trojan] *QF* (*Troyan, Troian*); *and so throughout*   15 must] *Q*; must needes *F*

TROILUS    Still have I tarried.    20

PANDARUS    Ay, to the leavening; but here's yet in the word
hereafter the kneading, the making of the cake, the
heating the oven, and the baking. Nay, you must stay
the cooling too, or ye may chance burn your lips.

TROILUS

Patience herself, what goddess e'er she be,    25
Doth lesser blench at suff'rance than I do.
At Priam's royal table do I sit,
And when fair Cressid comes into my thoughts –
So, traitor! 'When she comes'! When is she thence?

PANDARUS    Well, she looked yesternight fairer than ever I    30
saw her look, or any woman else.

TROILUS

I was about to tell thee – when my heart,
As wedged with a sigh, would rive in twain,
Lest Hector or my father should perceive me,

---

21–2 **but . . . kneading** 'but the word
"tarry" still has to cover the kneading',
etc. Some editors put *hereafter* in
inverted commas to suggest that it is
the operative term, but *tarry* is more
plausibly the word that Pandarus
means.

23 **stay** wait for

24 **chance** happen to
**burn your lips** with a suggestion of
venereal infection. See G. Williams,
*Dictionary*, 175–7, and 14n. above.

25–6 'Not even Patience herself, of whatever nature such a goddess might be,
flinches less at suffering than I do.' To
*blench* is to flinch, quail, turn pale
(*OED* v.¹ 6 and v.²). *Suff'rance* can
mean 'patient endurance', but here
seemingly also extends to 'suffering'

(*OED* sufferance 1, 4).

29 **traitor** i.e. traitor to Love, for even
imagining that Cressida might be out
of his thoughts for a moment
'**When she . . . thence?** The QF reading, 'So (Traitor) then she comes,
when she is thence', can be defended
as a declarative statement meaning that
Cressida is bodily absent but remains
constantly in Troilus' thoughts,
tormenting him with an unfulfilled
love; but the interrogative form seems
more idiomatic and makes better sense
of *traitor*.

32 **was about to** was preparing to

33 **As wedged** wedgèd; as if split by a
wedge
**would rive** (1) seemed about to split;
(2) wanted to split

---

21 here's] *QF, subst.;* there's *Cam*¹    23 heating] *Q , Fa;* heating of *Fb*    24 ye] *Q (*yea*);* you *F*
burn] *Q;* to burne *F*    26 suff'rance] *Q (*suffrance*);* sufferance *F*    29 When she . . . thence?] *Pope,
subst.;* then she comes when she is thence. *Q;* then she comes, when she is thence. *F; inverted commas,
Dyce*³    30–1] *Q; F lines* Well: / looke, / else. /    32 thee – when] *Capell, subst.;* thee when *Q;* thee,
when *F*

I have, as when the sun doth light a-scorn,                    35
Buried this sigh in wrinkle of a smile;
But sorrow that is couched in seeming gladness
Is like that mirth fate turns to sudden sadness.

PANDARUS    An her hair were not somewhat darker than
Helen's – well, go to – there were no more comparison            40
between the women. But, for my part, she is my
kinswoman; I would not, as they term it, praise her. But
I would somebody had heard her talk yesterday, as I did.
I will not dispraise your sister Cassandra's wit, but –

TROILUS

O Pandarus! I tell thee, Pandarus –                    45
When I do tell thee there my hopes lie drowned,
Reply not in how many fathoms deep
They lie indrenched. I tell thee I am mad
In Cressid's love. Thou answer'st 'She is fair',
Pour'st in the open ulcer of my heart                    50
Her eyes, her hair, her cheek, her gait, her voice;
Handlest in thy discourse, O, that her hand,

35 ***doth light a-scorn** shines in scorn.
Troilus compares his hiding of his
lovesickness to the sun glaring in a pretended smile. The image is difficult, and
some editors, following Rowe, emend to
'doth light a storm', meaning 'lightens
up his stormy mood with a smile'.
36 'forced myself to hide my grief by
fashioning my looks into a smile'
(Ard¹)
37–8 To Troilus, any attempt to mask
sorrow in a pretence of happiness is as
unstable and easily defeated as mirth
that is vulnerable to a sudden reverse
of fortune. *Couched* means 'concealed',
with implicit metaphors of (1) laid
abed; (2) lying in ambush.
39 **An** if
   **somewhat darker** Fairness of complexion and hair was widely consid-

ered more beautiful than a darker complexion, as in Shakespeare's 'Dark
Lady' Sonnets; see, e.g., Sonnets 127
and 130. Pandarus concedes a point in
Helen's favour.
40 **go to** an expression of impatience
   **were** would be
41–2 **But . . . praise her** i.e. 'But I don't
want to sound prejudiced in her
favour, being her kinsman'.
43 **somebody** viz. Troilus
44 **wit** intelligence (possibly with a resonance of our modern sense, since
Cressida is at any rate witty even if
Cassandra is not)
48 **indrenched** drowned
49 **In Cressid's love** for love of Cressida
   **fair** beautiful
52 'you discourse upon that wondrous
hand of hers'

35 a-scorn] *F*; a scorne *Q*; a Storm *Rowe*; askance *Oxf*    42 her. But] *Q* (her, but*)*; it, but *F*
49] *inverted commas*, *Hanmer*, *subst.*    50 Pour'st] *F* (Powr'st*)*; Powrest *Q*    52 discourse, O, that]
*Capell, subst.*; discourse: O that *Q*; discourse. O that *F*

In whose comparison all whites are ink
Writing their own reproach; to whose soft seizure
The cygnet's down is harsh, and spirit of sense          55
Hard as the palm of ploughman. This thou tell'st me –
As true thou tell'st me – when I say I love her;
But, saying thus, instead of oil and balm,
Thou lay'st in every gash that love hath given me
The knife that made it.          60

PANDARUS    I speak no more than truth.

TROILUS    Thou dost not speak so much.

PANDARUS    Faith, I'll not meddle in it. Let her be as she
is. If she be fair, 'tis the better for her; an she be not, she
has the mends in her own hands.          65

TROILUS    Good Pandarus – how now, Pandarus?

PANDARUS    I have had my labour for my travail, ill
thought on of her, and ill thought on of you; gone
between and between, but small thanks for my labour.

---

53 **In whose comparison** in comparison
with which

53–4 **all . . . reproach** Troilus' hyperbole
is that even the hands of all pale-
complexioned and beautiful women, in
comparison with Cressida's lovely
white hand, indict themselves as black
and ugly, like the ink used in writing.
On Elizabethan preference for pale
complexion in women, see 39n. and
*LLL* 4.3.243–73.

54 **to whose soft seizure** in comparison
with the clasp of which

55 **cygnet's** young swan's
**spirit of sense** a supposed essence or
invisible animating vital principle that
was thought to transmit sense impressions to the mind and soul, and was
thus the most delicate of material sub-
stances

57 **As true . . . me** and in saying so you
say true

58 **oil and balm** soothing and healing

ointments

62 'What you say does not come up to the
complete truth (about the incompa-
rable Cressida).'

64–5 **she has . . . hands** i.e. 'she can
find her own remedy'; 'she can always
use cosmetics'. Or, 'she can provide
her own pleasure'. A proverbial phrase
(Dent, M872). *Mends* means 'amends',
'remedy', a collective singular.

66 Troilus expresses consternation at
Pandarus' apparent determination to
have done with the business.

67 **I have . . . travail** To have nothing but
labour for one's pains is a proverbial
complaint (Dent, L1). *Travail* puns on
'labour' and on the sense of 'journey-
ing' in 'gone between and between',
68–9 (Seltzer). The QF spelling,
'trauell', nicely catches the common
Elizabethan double sense of journey-
ing and labouring.

68 **on of** by

63 in it] *Q;* in't *F*     67 travail] *QF (*trauell*)*     68 on of you] *F;* of you *Q*

TROILUS    What, art thou angry, Pandarus? What, with me?    70

PANDARUS    Because she's kin to me, therefore she's not so
fair as Helen; an she were not kin to me, she would be
as fair o' Friday as Helen is on Sunday. But what care
I? I care not an she were a blackamoor; 'tis all one to me.

TROILUS    Say I she is not fair?    75

PANDARUS    I do not care whether you do or no. She's a
fool to stay behind her father; let her to the Greeks, and
so I'll tell her the next time I see her. For my part, I'll
meddle nor make no more i'th' matter.

TROILUS    Pandarus –    80

PANDARUS    Not I.

TROILUS    Sweet Pandarus –

PANDARUS    Pray you, speak no more to me; I will leave all
as I found it, and there an end.                    *Exit.*

*Sound alarum.*

TROILUS

Peace, you ungracious clamours! Peace, rude sounds!    85
Fools on both sides! Helen must needs be fair,
When with your blood you daily paint her thus.

---

72–3 **an . . . Sunday** i.e. 'if she were not
my kinswoman, I would say she is as
beautiful on a fasting day in her
plainest attire as Helen in her Sunday
best'. A charming anachronism.

77 **her father** Calchas, the Trojan priest
whose foreknowledge (through the
oracle of Apollo) of the fall of Troy
prompted him to defect to the Greek
side. (Shakespeare could have learned
this from Caxton, 551–2, or from
Chaucer, *TC*, 1.66ff., though Shakespeare mentions nothing about
Calchas' motives for leaving Troy in
that character's appearance on stage in
3.3.) With unintended irony, Pandarus
anticipates what will become of

Cressida.

84 **there an end** a proverbial and colloquial way of ending a conversation
(Dent, E113.1)

84.1 *Sound alarum* sound (off stage) the
trumpet or drum signal to arms.
Troilus hears the sounds of battle in
the distance.

85 **ungracious**    rude,    unmannerly;
unfavourable; graceless, unattractive
**rude** harsh, ungentle, boisterous
(*OED* 5–6)

86 **must needs be** must be

87 Troilus speaks of blood as though it
were a red cosmetic to rouge Helen's
lips and heighten the colour of her
complexion.

---

72 were not] *Fc;* were *Q , Fu*    73 o' Friday] *Q (* a Friday*);* on Friday *F*    what care] *F;* what *Q*
76 SP] *Q , Fu (Pan.); Troy. Fc*    78 her. For] *F (* her: for*);* her for *Q*    84 SD *Exit*] *Q; Exit Pand. F*

I cannot fight upon this argument;
It is too starved a subject for my sword.
But Pandarus – O gods, how do you plague me!                    90
I cannot come to Cressid but by Pandar,
And he's as tetchy to be wooed to woo
As she is stubborn-chaste against all suit.
Tell me, Apollo, for thy Daphne's love,
What Cressid is, what Pandar, and what we?                    95
Her bed is India; there she lies, a pearl.
Between our Ilium and where she resides,
Let it be called the wild and wand'ring flood,
Ourself the merchant, and this sailing Pandar
Our doubtful hope, our convoy and our bark.                    100

*Alarum. Enter* AENEAS.

AENEAS
How now, Prince Troilus, wherefore not afield?

88 **upon this argument** for this cause or theme, this quarrel; suggesting also the idea of not fighting on an empty stomach (Ard¹). See next note.
89 **starved** meagre, poverty-stricken (*OED* 2–3)
92 'and Pandarus is as peevish at being solicited to act as go-between'
94 Ovid (*Met.*, 1.452–567, LCL, 1.34–43; 1.545–700 in Golding's translation) tells of Apollo's ardent pursuit of the nymph Daphne and of her being transformed at her own entreaty, as a way of preserving her chastity, into a bay tree or laurel bush, which became sacred to Apollo. As Ard² notes, Apollo pleads with Daphne in terms that are like those that Troilus also uses, and laments the wound in his heart that even he, the great musician and healer, cannot cure.
95 **we** I
96 **India** either the West or the East Indies, far overseas and fabled to be luxurious in wealth

**pearl** a symbol of virginity and of that which is precious in a woman (G. Williams, *Dictionary*, 1005–6)
97 **Ilium** the royal palace of Troy, but originally a name for Troy after the name of the city's founder, Ilus; sometimes spelled 'Ilion' in Q and F (cf. Chapman's *Seven Books*, 1.412 and 2.64). Shakespeare tends to follow Caxton in using the name ('Ilyion') to refer to the palace, the citadel of the city, though some instances are ambiguous.
98 **flood** open sea
99 **sailing** with meaning that shades into 'selling', attracted by 'merchant' (Barfoot, 47).
100 i.e. 'my uncertain hope, protector and means of access'. A *bark* is a sailing vessel, here serving metaphorically as naval escort for Troilus' uncertain voyage to Cressida.
101 **wherefore not afield?** why aren't you at the field of battle?

92 woo] *QF (*woe*)* 93 stubborn-chaste] *Theobald (*stubborn-chast*);* stubborne, chast *QF* 97 resides] *F (*recides*);* reides *Q* 101] *Q; F lines Troylus? / field? /*

137

*[handwritten note in left margin: answers in a feminine way]*

TROILUS

Because not there. This woman's answer sorts,

For womanish it is to be from thence.

What news, Aeneas, from the field today?

AENEAS

That Paris is returned home, and hurt.          105

TROILUS

By whom, Aeneas?

AENEAS                    Troilus, by Menelaus.

TROILUS

Let Paris bleed. 'Tis but a scar to scorn;

Paris is gored with Menelaus' horn.          *Alarum.*

AENEAS

Hark, what good sport is out of town today!

TROILUS

Better at home, if 'would I might' were 'may'.          110

But to the sport abroad. Are you bound thither?

AENEAS

In all swift haste.

TROILUS                    Come, go we then together.          *Exeunt.*

---

102 Troilus applies the misogynistic proverb, '*Because* is woman's reason' (Dent, B179).
  **sorts** is fitting
105 **returned** returnèd
106 **by Menelaus** If Shakespeare consulted the violent encounter of Paris (Alexander) and Menelaus in the *Iliad*, 3.329–83 (LCL, 1.140–5), he deliberately demythologizes it. Troilus sees the wound as little more than occasion for a jest about cuckold's horns (108). As worn by Menelaus the notorious cuckold, they are only metaphorical ones, able to inflict minor damage at best; at 1.2.206–7 Pandarus makes light of the wound, if wound it is at all. Paris, besotted and indulgent, never mentions it.
107 **a scar to scorn** 'a scar deserving of scorn' (because the scar is so slight; see

previous note); or, 'a scar in return for Paris' insulting and scornful behaviour towards Menelaus'; or, 'a scar to be proud of' (cf. Pistol's 'cudgeled scars', *H5* 5.1.87)
109 **out of town** outside the walls, on the field of battle. (The fighting is imagined in terms of a city under siege, the kind of warfare Shakespeare normally portrays in his history plays.)
110 'If I had my wish, it would be to seek amorous "sport" at home.'
111 **abroad** on the battlefield, outside the walls
111–12 Troilus' complete swing in attitude and intention may be the result of Aeneas' news that 'good sport' is to be had this day on the field of battle (109). The young lover is mercurial of mood.

110] *inverted commas, Theobald, subst.*

138

**[1.2]**     *Enter* CRESSIDA *and her man* [ALEXANDER].

CRESSIDA

Who were those went by?

ALEXANDER                                Queen Hecuba and Helen.

CRESSIDA

And whither go they?

ALEXANDER                    Up to the eastern tower,

Whose height commands as subject all the vale,

To see the battle. Hector, whose patience

Is as a virtue fixed, today was moved.                                5

He chid Andromache and struck his armourer;

And, like as there were husbandry in war,

Before the sun rose he was harnessed light,

And to the field goes he, where every flower

Did as a prophet weep what it foresaw                              10

In Hector's wrath.

CRESSIDA                    What was his cause of anger?

ALEXANDER

The noise goes, this: there is among the Greeks

---

1.2 Location: see LN.

3   **as subject** 'as being under its dominion' (Ard¹); and see next note. Ilium
*commands* the surrounding countryside
by virtue of its superior strategic position (*OED v.* 14).
**the vale** i.e. the low-lying ground
adjacent to the hilltop fortifications of
Ilium

5   Alexander plays with a paradox: even
Hector's patience, *fixed* (steadfast) as a
virtue should be, was *moved* (angry).
Patience was one of the cardinal
virtues and the pre-eminent stoic
virtue (Cam¹).

7   **like as** as if
**husbandry** careful management.
Hector, by rising early to his work,

shows that he is a good 'husband' in
war as in family matters. Cf. *Mac*
2.1.4–5: 'There's husbandry in heaven;
/ Their candles are all out'.

8   **harnessed light** outfitted in light
armour; in armour quickly

9   **the field** the battlefield; with suggestion of the husbandman's or farmer's
field, developing the image of 7 (Cam¹)

10–11 **weep . . . wrath** To anyone at all
familiar with the story of the *Iliad* and
with the phrase 'the wrath of Achilles',
this weeping of the flowers (wet with
dew, and anticipating that they will be
mown down) foretells both the carnage
Hector will inflict and his own death.

12 **noise** rumour

---

1.2] *Capell, subst.*   0.1 CRESSIDA] *QF (Cressid)*   0.1 ALEXANDER] *Theobald, subst.*   1 SP ALEXAN-
DER] *Malone; Man. / QF (+2, 12, 15, 19, 33, 37, 39)*   6 chid] *Q;* chides *F*   struck] *QF (strooke)*

139

A lord of Trojan blood, nephew to Hector;
They call him Ajax.

CRESSIDA                    Good, and what of him?

ALEXANDER

They say he is a very man *per se*,                    15
And stands alone.

CRESSIDA   So do all men, unless they are drunk, sick, or
have no legs.

ALEXANDER   This man, lady, hath robbed many beasts of
their particular additions. He is as valiant as the lion,        20
churlish as the bear, slow as the elephant; a man into
whom nature hath so crowded humours that his valour
is crushed into folly, his folly sauced with discretion.
There is no man hath a virtue that he hath not a
glimpse of, nor any man an attaint but he carries some        25
stain of it. He is melancholy without cause, and merry
against the hair; he hath the joints of everything, but
everything so out of joint that he is a gouty Briareus,
many hands and no use, or purblind Argus, all eyes

13 **nephew** At 4.5.121 Hector greets Ajax as 'my father's sister's son'– what we would call a first cousin (Foakes, *TC*).
14 **Good** all right
15–16 **per se . . . alone** all to himself, without peer. (A proverbial phrase; Dent, A275.) But Cressida deflates the heroic image into a matter-of-fact observation: any reasonably sober, healthy man can stand on his own two legs. (She may imply a sexual meaning as well; 'stand' is often bawdy.)
19–21 **many beasts . . . elephant** On beast lore, see LN.
20 **particular additions** essential characteristics, marks of distinction (Onions, 'additions'), titles added to one's surname. Cf. 4.5.142.
21 **churlish** violent, rough, surly (not stingy or boorish)

**slow** ponderous, slow-moving (not obtuse, lazy or dilatory)
22 **humours** temperamental characteristics; literally, the four bodily fluids thought to cause anger, melancholy, etc., through the predominance of one 'humour' or another
22–3 *****his valour . . . discretion** See LN.
25 **glimpse** trace, tinge (*OED* 2)
**attaint** stain, blemish (*OED sb.* 6)
25–6 **but he . . . of it** of which Ajax has not some trace
27 **against the hair** a proverbial phrase (Dent, H18) for something that goes against the natural order of things; equivalent to our 'against the grain'. *Hair* could mean 'sort, kind, nature; stamp, character' (*OED sb.* 6, now obsolete).
27–30 **he hath . . . sight** See LN.

13 Trojan] *QF (* Troian*)*   15–16] *Capell; one line, QF*   17 they] *F; the Q*   23 sauced] *QF;* farced *Oxf (Theobald);* forced *Cam¹*   29 purblind] *Q;* purblinded *F*

and no sight.                                                        30

CRESSIDA   But how should this man, that makes me
smile, make Hector angry?

ALEXANDER   They say he yesterday coped Hector in the
battle and struck him down, the disdain and shame
whereof hath ever since kept Hector fasting and waking.   35

*Enter* PANDARUS.

CRESSIDA   Who comes here?

ALEXANDER   Madam, your uncle Pandarus.

CRESSIDA   Hector's a gallant man.

ALEXANDER   As may be in the world, lady. *gossipy character*

PANDARUS   What's that? What's that? - *gossipy*          40

CRESSIDA   Good morrow, uncle Pandarus.

PANDARUS   Good morrow, cousin Cressid. What do you
talk of? – Good morrow, Alexander. – How do you,
cousin? When were you at Ilium?

CRESSIDA   This morning, uncle.                           45

PANDARUS   What were you talking of when I came? Was
Hector armed and gone ere ye came to Ilium? Helen
was not up, was she?

CRESSIDA   Hector was gone, but Helen was not up?

PANDARUS   E'en so. Hector was stirring early.           50

CRESSIDA   That were we talking of, and of his anger.

PANDARUS   Was he angry?

---

31 **should** could possibly (Abbott, 325)
33 **coped** encountered, came to blows
with (Fr. *couper*, to strike). The verb is
often used of a sexual encounter (G.
Williams, *Dictionary*, 304–5).
34 **disdain** vexation, anger (*OED* 2);
ignominy, wounded pride (Schmidt)
35 **waking** sleepless
42 **cousin** kinswoman, here niece
49 Cressida mockingly repeats her uncle's

fussy questions as much ado about
nothing, with risqué possibilities.
Some editors end the sentence with a
full stop, as though Cressida answers
Pandarus' inquiries.
50 **stirring early** a suggestive phrase, in
view of the eroticism that runs
through the dialogue (see 33n., 63n.,
81n., etc.)

34 struck] *QF* (stroke*)*   disdain *Q (*disdaine*);* disdaind *F*   35.1] *F; not in Q*   47 ye] *QF* (yea*);* you
*Theobald*[2]   49 up?] *QF;* up. *F2*

CRESSIDA   So he says here.

PANDARUS   True, he was so. I know the cause too. He'll
  lay about him today, I can tell them that; and there's        55
  Troilus will not come far behind him; let them take
  heed of Troilus, I can tell them that too.

CRESSIDA   What, is he angry too?

PANDARUS   Who, Troilus? Troilus is the better man of the
  two.                                                          60

CRESSIDA   O Jupiter, there's no comparison.

PANDARUS   What, not between Troilus and Hector? Do
  you know a man if you see him?

CRESSIDA   Ay, if I ever saw him before and knew him.

PANDARUS   Well, I say Troilus is Troilus.                      65

CRESSIDA   Then you say as I say, for I am sure he is not
  Hector.

PANDARUS   No, nor Hector is not Troilus in some degrees.

CRESSIDA   'Tis just to each of them; he is himself.

PANDARUS   Himself? Alas, poor Troilus, I would he were.        70

CRESSIDA   So he is.

PANDARUS   Condition I had gone barefoot to India!

---

53 **he** Alexander. This is the last time
Alexander has any part to play in the
scene; see LN.

55 **lay about him** fight fiercely, strike
with vigour (*OED* lay *v.*[1] 44c)

63 **know a man** recognize a complete
man. But Cressida may choose to understand the phrase in its more mundane
sense of 'recognize a man's identity',
and perhaps hints at a sexual meaning as
well; *knew him* (64) can mean 'had sex
with him'. The degree of her sexual
knowingness in this scene can be adjusted
in performance by the extent to which
she exploits available innuendoes.

65 **is Troilus** is himself, i.e. that remarkable warrior we've been talking about.
Again, Cressida deflates to the literal.

68 **in some degrees** in some respects; by
a long shot

69 **he is himself** each is who he is.
Cressida offers sardonic praise: 'with
your usual precision of intellect,
you've established that Hector is
Hector and Troilus is Troilus'.

70 **Himself** To the serious idea of what it
means to be oneself, Pandarus counters
with a trite colloquialism: *he's not himself*
(74), i.e. he's out of sorts, not up to par.

72 **Condition** on the condition that; even
if (Cam[1]). Pandarus laments that
Troilus will recover his true self about
as soon as Pandarus might undertake a
barefoot pilgrimage to India; Pandarus
hyperbolically suggests that he would
walk that far to restore Troilus' peace

---

55–6 there's Troilus] *QF*; there's [*Exit Alexander.*] Troilus *Ard*[2]   59–60] *Q one line; F lines Troylus?*
/ *two.* /   66–7] *Q one line; F lines* say, / *Hector.* /   68 nor] *Q;* not *F*   69 just to . . . them; he] *Rowe,*
*subst.;* iust, to each of them he *QF*

CRESSIDA   He is not Hector.

PANDARUS   Himself? No, he's not himself, would 'a were
    himself! Well, the gods are above; time must friend or   75
    end. Well, Troilus, well, I would my heart were in her
    body. No, Hector is not a better man than Troilus.

CRESSIDA   Excuse me.

PANDARUS   He is elder.

CRESSIDA   Pardon me, pardon me.   80

PANDARUS   Th'other's not come to't; you shall tell me
    another tale when th'other's come to't. Hector shall not
    have his wit this year.

CRESSIDA   He shall not need it, if he have his own.

PANDARUS   Nor his qualities.   85

CRESSIDA   No matter.

PANDARUS   Nor his beauty.

CRESSIDA   'Twould not become him; his own's better.

PANDARUS   You have no judgement, niece. Helen herself
    swore th'other day that Troilus, for a brown favour –   90
    for so 'tis, I must confess – not brown neither –

CRESSIDA   No, but brown.

of mind. Cf. Emilia in *Oth*: 'I know a
lady in Venice would have walked
barefoot to Palestine for a touch of his
nether lip' (4.3.41–2, cited by Ard²).

74 **'a** he

75–6 **the gods . . . end** As he often does,
Pandarus parries with a medley of
proverbial clichés (Dent, H348, M874,
T308.2, Tilley, T338). As Ard²
observes, Chaucer's Pandarus is given
to proverbs; see *TC*, 1.624–721, and
Troilus' reply at 1.752–60.

75 **friend** befriend

78 **Excuse me** i.e. I beg to differ. *Pardon
me* in 80 has much the same meaning.

81 **Th'other's . . . to't** 'Troilus has not
yet come to full maturity, like Hector.'
*Come to't* may well have the same sexual undertone as *go to it*. Especially in
82, the phrase suggests, 'when Troilus

has become sexually active'.

81–2 **you . . . tale** more proverbial colloquialism (Dent, T49): 'you'll change
your tune'

82–3 *****Hector . . . year** 'Hector cannot
possibly compete with Troilus in intelligence any time soon.' QF's 'will' is an
easy error for 'witt', and Rowe's emendation has been generally accepted,
though Hulme (96) sees 'will' as appropriate in the sense of 'sexual energy' or
'carnal appetite'; see 81n. above.

86 **No matter** i.e. Why would Hector
need Troilus' qualities (his capacities
and nature)?

90 **for a brown favour** considering he
has a dark or sunburnt complexion

92 Cressida mocks her uncle's fussy
attempts at making distinctions: 'No,
not brown, merely brown'.

74 Himself? No, he's] *Pope;* Himselfe? no? hee's *QF*   76 end. well] *F, subst.;* end well *Q*   83 wit]
*Rowe;* will *QF*

PANDARUS  Faith, to say truth, brown and not brown.

CRESSIDA  To say the truth, true and not true.

PANDARUS  She praised his complexion above Paris'.          95

CRESSIDA  Why, Paris hath colour enough.

PANDARUS  So he has.

CRESSIDA  Then Troilus should have too much. If she praised him above, his complexion is higher than his; he having colour enough, and the other higher, is too flaming          100 a praise for a good complexion. I had as lief Helen's golden tongue had commended Troilus for a copper nose.

PANDARUS  I swear to you, I think Helen loves him better than Paris.

CRESSIDA  Then she's a merry Greek indeed.          105

PANDARUS  Nay, I am sure she does. She came to him th'other day into the compassed window – and you know he has not past three or four hairs on his chin –

CRESSIDA  Indeed, a tapster's arithmetic may soon bring

---

98 **should** must logically

99 *\*above** above Paris. Cressida mockingly tosses back to her uncle the phrase he used in 95. The Q compositor may have dropped out 'Paris'; the prose of this speech is widely and irregularly spaced, perhaps the result of press correction without consulting copy (Ard², quoting Philip Williams's Ph.D. dissertation on the printing of the texts of *TC*).

100 **flaming** high-flown, vivid, highly coloured (*OED* 4), but probably with the risible suggestion also that Troilus' excessively 'high' colour of complexion is inflamed, like Bardolph's, with drink. This idea then leads to the joke about the *copper nose* (102) – a nose made red by too much drink, though *copper* may also suggest the false metal nose of an advanced sufferer from syphilis.

101 **I had as lief** I would have been just as glad if

105 **a merry Greek** a merry person, roisterer, boon companion, person of loose habits (*OED* Greek *sb.* 5). Shakespeare uses this proverbial phrase (Dent, M901) later at 4.4.55; cf. *TN* 4.1.17. Cressida jestingly hints that Helen already has enough of a reputation for being 'fast' without dallying with Troilus. Cf. *Greek* in another pejorative sense at 1.3.246 and n.

107 **compassed window** window with a semicircular bay, regular in proportion (*OED ppl. a.* 3b and compass *sb.*¹ 1) as though drawn with a pair of compasses (Oxf¹)

109 **a tapster's arithmetic** limited to the simplest kind of tavern reckoning, the sort that a drawer like Francis in *1H4* can manage. Cressida continues the metaphor in her witticism about totalling up Troilus' *particulars* or individual items, as on a tavern bill (*OED* particular *sb.* B 2–3). Cf. 3.3.254–5 and n., and *LLL* 1.2.40–1: 'I am ill at reckoning; it fitteth the spirit of a tapster'.

93 say] *QF;* say the *Cam¹*  94 say the] *QF;* say *Ard²*  103–4] *Q; F lines* you, / Paris. /

his particulars therein to a total. 110

PANDARUS   Why, he is very young, and yet will he within
three pound lift as much as his brother Hector.

CRESSIDA   Is he so young a man, and so old a lifter?

PANDARUS   But to prove to you that Helen loves him: she
came and puts me her white hand to his cloven chin – 115

CRESSIDA   Juno have mercy, how came it cloven?

PANDARUS   Why, you know 'tis dimpled. I think his smiling
becomes him better than any man in all Phrygia.

CRESSIDA   O, he smiles valiantly.

PANDARUS   Does he not? 120

CRESSIDA   O, yes, an 'twere a cloud in autumn.

PANDARUS   Why, go to, then. But to prove to you that
Helen loves Troilus –

CRESSIDA   Troilus will stand to the proof, if you'll prove
it so. 125

PANDARUS   Troilus? Why, he esteems her no more than I

---

113 **young . . . so old a lifter** callow,
green . . . so experienced a thief. (Cf.
the modern expression, 'shop-lifter'.)
Cressida practises her wit on
Pandarus' words of praise, *young* and
*lift*. A *limb-lifter* is a fornicator (*OED*
limb *sb.*[1] 5, citing Gosson's *School of
Abuse*, 33), suggesting a sexual joke
here (Cam[1]). See G. Williams,
*Dictionary*, 'lift', 810–11.

115 **puts me** puts. *Me* is an archaic dative
used as a kind of emphatic marker
(Abbott, 220).

115–16 **cloven . . . cloven** Cressida's
mock alarm turns Pandarus' innocent
term for a dimpled chin into a suggestion that Troilus has suffered a nasty
cut (*OED* cloven *ppl.a.*: 'split into
pieces, cleft asunder'), or perhaps that
there is something sinister in a sign
widely associated with the devil's feet.
As Hulme (96) points out, *cloven* anticipates the sexual joking about the

*forked* hair at 159 (see n.) suggesting
cuckoldry. Cressida thus continues the
erotic banter of *lifter* in 113.

121 i.e. 'Oh, sure, his smile is as valiant as
the sun attempting to shine through
rain clouds'. Pandarus appears not to
hear the raillery in this. Cressida's
metaphor of elemental conflict
between sun and cloud echoes that of
Troilus at 1.1.32–8, perhaps suggesting an attentiveness to his manner of
speaking (though she is not actually
present at 1.1.32–8) that is like that of
Beatrice's dwelling on Benedick in 1.1
of *MA*.

124 **stand to the proof** stand up to the
test; with a bawdy quibble on *stand
to*, meaning 'be erect'. Cf. the reflections
of *Macbeth*'s Porter on how excessive
drink makes a man 'stand to and not
stand to' (2.3.33), and G. Williams,
*Dictionary*, 1305–9.
**if you'll** if you want to

---

112 lift] *F;* liste *Q*   124 the] *F2;* thee *QF*   124–5] *Q one line; F lines* to thee / so. /

esteem an addle egg.

CRESSIDA  If you love an addle egg as well as you love an idle head, you would eat chickens i'th' shell.

PANDARUS  I cannot choose but laugh, to think how she    130
tickled his chin. Indeed, she has a marvellous white hand, I must needs confess –

CRESSIDA  Without the rack.

PANDARUS  And she takes upon her to spy a white hair on his chin.    135

CRESSIDA  Alas, poor chin! Many a wart is richer.

PANDARUS  But there was such laughing! Queen Hecuba laughed that her eyes ran o'er –

CRESSIDA  With millstones.

PANDARUS  And Cassandra laughed –    140

CRESSIDA  But there was a more temperate fire under the pot of her eyes. Did her eyes run o'er too?

PANDARUS  And Hector laughed.

CRESSIDA  At what was all this laughing?

127 **addle** rotten, putrid
128–9 Cressida's joke hinges on the fact that an *addled* egg is sometimes one that is partly hatched and hence no longer fit for food. The wordplay on the like-sounding *addle* and *idle* is a common one that may derive from the shared idea of abortiveness (*OED* addle *sb.* and *a.*, 2.B.1). Cf. the proverbs, 'As good be an addled egg as an idle bird' (Dent, E71.1) and 'to eat a chicken (chickens) in the shell' (Dent, C290.1).
131 **marvellous** (QF: 'maruel's') marvellously
133 Cressida sardonically applies the idea of physical torture to Pandarus' *confess*, by which he meant simply 'declare, acknowledge'. Her point is that it takes little to get him to talk.
136 Cressida again denigrates and deflates by contrasting the hairlessness of Troilus' chin (to its disadvantage)

with a disfiguring and diminutive wart – one perhaps supplied with its own tuft of hairs, like that on the nose of Chaucer's Miller (*CT*, General Prologue, 554–5).
138 **that** so much that
139 To 'weep millstones' is to be utterly hard-hearted (Dent, M967), as in *R3*, when Richard congratulates the appointed murderers of Clarence: 'Your eyes drop millstones when fools' eyes fall tears' (1.3.353). Cressida's joke is that nothing funny enough has been said to produce any tears of laughter on this present occasion.
141 **a more temperate fire** Cressida points out wryly that Pandarus has said nothing about Cassandra's eyes running over; didn't she think this hair was funny too? (Cassandra, being an unhappy and ignored prophetess of doom, seldom laughed.)

131 marvellous] *QF* (maruel's)    141 was a] *Q*; was *F*

PANDARUS   Marry, at the white hair that Helen spied on   145
Troilus' chin.

CRESSIDA   An 't had been a green hair I should have
laughed too.

PANDARUS   They laughed not so much at the hair as at his
pretty answer.   150

CRESSIDA   What was his answer?

PANDARUS   Quoth she, 'Here's but two-and-fifty hairs on
your chin, and one of them is white'.

CRESSIDA   This is her question.

PANDARUS   That's true, make no question of that. 'Two-   155
and-fifty hairs', quoth he, 'and one white: that white
hair is my father, and all the rest are his sons.' 'Jupiter!',
quoth she, 'which of these hairs is Paris, my husband?'
'The forked one', quoth he; 'pluck't out, and give it
him.' But there was such laughing, and Helen so   160
blushed, and Paris so chafed, and all the rest so

---

145 **Marry** an interjection; from the oath,
'by the Virgin Mary'

147 **green** The incongruity of the colour
would be funny in itself; it might also
suggest the 'greenness' of youth and
the 'greensickness' of lovers. Cf. *LLL*
1.2.79–86 and *RJ* 3.5.156.

150 **pretty** cute

152 **two-and-fifty** Priam traditionally
had fifty sons; perhaps, as Thiselton
suggests, the forked hair (159) is
meant to stand for two. The Q
spelling of 'heare' for *hair* at 134–49
shifts to 'heire' and 'heires' at 152–8,
suggesting wordplay on 'heir' and
'heirs'. The difference between
'heare' and 'heire' is so visual that it
could reflect an essentially visual pun
in the copy-text, but in any event a
theatrical audience ought to be able to
catch the double meaning as part of
what Pandarus thinks is so funny

about Troilus' joke.

154 Cressida quibbles: 'You said you
would give Troilus' answer but
instead you are garrulously repeating
Helen's question'. Cf. Hamlet's jibe at
Osric about Laertes: 'HAMLET
What's his weapon? OSRIC Rapier and
dagger. HAMLET That's two of his
weapons – but well' (*Ham* 5.2.143–5).
Pandarus attempts to parry in 155 by
employing *question* in a conventional
phrase.

159 **The forked one** Paris was of course
the cuckolder of Menelaus, not the
cuckold with imaginary branched
horns on his head, but Troilus may
hint that being cuckolded is the common lot of men who are married to
coquettish beauties. See 115–16n. on
the linking of *cloven* and *forked*.

161 **so chafed** was so angry

---

152 two] *QF;* one *Theobald*   hairs] *QF (*heires, haires*); +* *156, 158*   152–60] *inverted commas,*
*Capell, subst.*

laughed, that it passed.

CRESSIDA   So let it now, for it has been a great while
going by.

PANDARUS   Well, cousin, I told you a thing yesterday.   165
Think on't.

CRESSIDA   So I do.

PANDARUS   I'll be sworn 'tis true. He will weep you an
'twere a man born in April.

CRESSIDA   And I'll spring up in his tears, an 'twere a   170
nettle against May.                          *Sound a retreat.*

PANDARUS   Hark, they are coming from the field. Shall
we stand up here and see them as they pass toward
Ilium? Good niece, do, sweet niece Cressida.

CRESSIDA   At your pleasure.                       175

PANDARUS   Here, here, here's an excellent place; here we
may see most bravely. I'll tell you them all by their
names as they pass by, but mark Troilus above the rest.

*Enter* AENEAS [*and passes over the stage*].

162 **it passed** it surpassed all description
(as in *MW* 1.1.277). But Cressida
(163–4) reduces the phrase to the
banality it deserves: 'let it pass, for it's
been a tedious long time passing by'.
Perhaps she also means, 'let it die and
go to its reward' (*OED* pass *v.* 11, with
citations from 1300 onwards).

165 **a thing** a certain thing (Abbott, 81).
Often erotically suggestive; see G.
Williams, *Dictionary*, 1379–81.

168–9 **weep . . . April** weep like one born
in the month of showers. (*You* is an
archaic dative – see 115n. – but also
suggesting that Cressida is the cause of
Troilus' weeping.) April's showers are
proverbial; the month is also appropriate to youth and love (Dent, A310;
Chaucer, *CT*, General Prologue, 1).

170–1 **an . . . May** as if I were a nettle at
the coming on of May, watered by the
shower (of tears). With her sardonic
misapplication of a proverbial cliché
('April showers bring May flowers',
Dent, S411), Cressida proposes to
*nettle* Troilus. *Against* means 'in anticipation of'.

171 SD *retreat* trumpet signal for forces
to withdraw from military action, not
in this case a falling back under pressure. The troops are coming in for the
night.

173 **stand up here** For staging, see LN.

177 **bravely** excellently

178 **mark** pay attention to, note

178.1, 182.1 According to medieval tradition, Aeneas and Antenor, the first to
enter here, were the traitors who

163–6] *Q; F lines* now, / by. / Cozen, / on't. /
*after 169, QF*   174 Ilium] *F (*Illium*);* Ilion *Q*   178.1 *and passes over the stage*] *Rowe, subst. (+ 182.1,
191.1, 204.1, 209.1, 218.1)*   167 do] *Q (*doe*);* does *F*   171 SD] *Capell, subst.;*

CRESSIDA   Speak not so loud.

PANDARUS   That's Aeneas; is not that a brave man? He's   180
one of the flowers of Troy, I can tell you, but mark
Troilus; you shall see anon.

*Enter* ANTENOR [*and passes over the stage*].

CRESSIDA   Who's that?

PANDARUS   That's Antenor. He has a shrewd wit, I can
tell you, and he's a man good enough; he's one o'th'   185
soundest judgements in Troy whosoever, and a proper
man of person. When comes Troilus? I'll show you
Troilus anon; if he see me, you shall see him nod at me.

CRESSIDA   Will he give you the nod?

PANDARUS   You shall see.   190

CRESSIDA   If he do, the rich shall have more.

*Enter* HECTOR [*and passes over the stage*].

PANDARUS   That's Hector, that, that, look you, that;

betrayed Troy (Proudfoot). See
Caxton, 650–77.
*passes over the stage* The editorially
added language here and in the following entry directions uses a standard
Elizabethan theatrical locution for an
entry through one door, across the
stage, and out of another door. In
Marlowe's *Faustus*, A-text, Helen
'*passeth over the stage*' for the delec-
tation of Faustus (5.1.25.3). Allardyce
Nicoll's theory that actors entered and
left through the yard is probably unnecessarily elaborate.
180 **brave** excellent
182 **anon** right away
186 **judgements** persons having good
judgement, competent critics (*OED* 8c,
giving this passage as its first citation)

**whosoever** of anyone at all, whosoever
the others may be
186–7 **a proper man of person** a fine
specimen of a man
189 **give you the nod** (1) recognize you
and convey his salutation through a
proverbially universal signal (Dent,
N198.1); (2) call you a simpleton. *Nod*
can mean 'noddy', fool (*OED* nod *sb.²*,
citing two Renaissance instances,
though not this one). Cf. *TGV*
1.1.111–24.
191 **the rich . . . more** i.e. you as a fool
will thereby increase in folly. Cressida
gives a profane turn to Christ's parable
of the talents, Matthew, 25.29: 'For
unto every man that hath, it shall be
given, and he shall have abundance'
(Ard²).

181 can tell] *Q;* can *F*   182.1 *Enter* ANTENOR] *Capell; after 183, QF*   185 a man] *F;* man *Q*
186 judgements] *Q;* iudgement *F*   192–3 you, that; there's] *Q, subst.;* you, that there's *F*

there's a fellow! Go thy way, Hector! There's a brave
man, niece. O brave Hector! Look how he looks! There's
a countenance! Is't not a brave man?                    195
CRESSIDA    O, a brave man!
PANDARUS    Is 'a not? It does a man's heart good. Look you
what hacks are on his helmet, look you yonder, do you
see? Look you there, there's no jesting; there's laying
on, take't off who will, as they say; there be hacks.   200
CRESSIDA    Be those with swords?
PANDARUS    Swords, anything, he cares not; an the devil
come to him, it's all one. By God's lid, it does one's
heart good. Yonder comes Paris, yonder comes Paris!

*Enter* PARIS [*and passes over the stage*].

Look ye yonder, niece, is't not a gallant man too, is't   205
not? Why, this is brave now. Who said he came hurt
home today? He's not hurt. Why, this will do Helen's
heart good now, ha? Would I could see Troilus now. You
shall see Troilus anon.

*Enter* HELENUS [*and passes over the stage*].

193 **Go thy way** The phrase often has a
lachrymose and sentimental imprecision
about it, as when the Nurse goes natter-
ing on to Juliet, 'Go thy ways, wench.
Serve God' (*RJ* 2.5.44). Pandarus is not
urging Hector to move on. Cf. 227.
198 **hacks** gashes, dents
199–200 **there's laying . . . say** there's
proof of vigorous blows, there's no
denying that, as the saying goes.
(*Laying on* and *taking off* are played
against each other in a verbal antithesis
to which Pandarus coyly calls attention
with his *as they say*, conceding at the
same time that the witticism is proverbial and clichéd; Dent, L131.) *Take't*

*off who will* can also mean, literally,
'notches such as no smith or armourer
could obliterate' (Cam¹).
201 **Be** often used in questions (Abbott,
299, 300)
203 **all one** all the same
**By God's lid** by God's eyelid (a common oath)
203–4 **it . . . good** a proverbial truism
(Dent, G320.1), used again by
Pandarus at 207–8
206–7 **Who . . . not hurt** Pandarus makes
light of Paris' reported wound (see
1.1.106 and n.), which indeed appears
not to be serious.
208 **ha?** i.e. won't it? (Oxf¹)

196 a brave] *Q;* braue *F*    197 man's] *F (*mans*);* man *Q*    199 there's laying] *Q;* laying *F*    200 off]
*F;* off, *Q*    will] *Q;* ill *F*    204.1 *Enter* PARIS] *Capell; after 201, QF*    209 shall see] *Q;* shall *F*    209.1
*Enter* HELENUS] *Capell; after 210, QF*

CRESSIDA   Who's that?                                                    210

PANDARUS   That's Helenus. I marvel where Troilus is.
That's Helenus. I think he went not forth today. That's
Helenus.

CRESSIDA   Can Helenus fight, uncle?

PANDARUS   Helenus? No – yes, he'll fight indifferent well.    215
I marvel where Troilus is. Hark, do you not hear the
people cry 'Troilus'? Helenus is a priest.

CRESSIDA   What sneaking fellow comes yonder?

*Enter* TROILUS [*and passes over the stage*].

PANDARUS   Where? Yonder? That's Deiphobus. – 'Tis
Troilus! There's a man, niece! Hem! Brave Troilus, the    220
prince of chivalry!

CRESSIDA   Peace, for shame, peace!

PANDARUS   Mark him, note him. O brave Troilus! Look
well upon him, niece, look you how his sword is
bloodied, and his helm more hacked than Hector's, and    225
how he looks, and how he goes! O admirable youth! He
ne'er saw three-and-twenty. Go thy way, Troilus, go thy
way! Had I a sister were a grace, or a daughter a
goddess, he should take his choice. O admirable man!
Paris? Paris is dirt to him, and I warrant Helen, to    230
change, would give money to boot.

212 **he** Troilus
215 **indifferent** moderately, tolerably
220 **Hem!** Pandarus acknowledges his
error (Foakes, *TC*), or tries to get
Troilus' attention, or asks for Cressida's
assent to his praise (Oxf[1]). Cressida's
response tends to support the second
of these possibilities.
225 **helm** helmet
226 **goes** walks
227 **Go thy way** Cf. 193 and n.
228 **a grace** one of the three goddesses in

Greek mythology personifying loveli-
ness or grace. Chaucer's Pandarus similarly professes willingness to have
even his sister be Troilus' lover, if he
so chooses (1.860–1).
230–1 **to change** in exchange
231 ***money** The unpleasantness of the
F text here is thoroughly in character
for Pandarus; Q's 'an eye' is a plausible
reading, but the F version may not be
a simple misreading of Q, *pace TxC*.
**to boot** into the bargain

210 Who's] *Rowe*; Whose *QF*   215 indifferent well] *F2*; indifferent, well *QF*   217] *inverted commas,*
*Dyce[1]*   223 note] *Q*; not *F*   227 ne'er] *F*; neuer *Q*   231 money] *F*; an eye *Q*

*Enter Common Soldiers [and pass over the stage].*

CRESSIDA  Here comes more.

PANDARUS  Asses, fools, dolts; chaff and bran, chaff and
bran; porridge after meat. I could live and die i'th' eyes
of Troilus. Ne'er look, ne'er look, the eagles are gone;     235
crows and daws, crows and daws! I had rather be such
a man as Troilus than Agamemnon and all Greece.

CRESSIDA  There is among the Greeks Achilles, a better
man than Troilus.

PANDARUS  Achilles? A drayman, a porter, a very camel.     240

CRESSIDA  Well, well.

PANDARUS  'Well, well'! Why, have you any discretion?
Have you any eyes? Do you know what a man is? Is not
birth, beauty, good shape, discourse, manhood,
learning, gentleness, virtue, youth, liberality and so     245
forth the spice and salt that season a man?

CRESSIDA  Ay, a minced man; and then to be baked with
no date in the pie, for then the man's date is out.

233–4 **chaff and bran, chaff and bran**
Cf. Falstaff's 'food for powder, food
for powder', *1H4* 4.2.64–5.

234 **porridge** soup, usually eaten before the
main course; served afterwards, it would
seem out of place and anticlimactic

234–5 **i'th' eyes of Troilus** 'looking at
Troilus', or, perhaps, 'when he is there
looking upon me' (Ard¹)

236 **daws** jackdaws, small crowlike birds;
figuratively, simpletons, fools (*OED* 2);
diminutive and drab in contrast with
eagles

237 **Agamemnon . . . Greece** An audience might hear 'grease', hinting that
the 'greatness' of Agamemnon is all
gone into corpulence.

240 **drayman** one who drives a dray or
wheel-less sled
**camel** See 2.1.52 and n.

245 **gentleness** good breeding

247 **minced** cut up into tiny pieces (as in
the itemized culinary description
Pandarus has just given) as though being
readied to be baked in a pie; made dainty
or mincing, affected in mannerism;
diminished, deprived of some essential
part, like a pie with no date in it (*OED* 1,
2, 3). The lack of some essential part may
suggest sexual impotency; hence the sudden erotic drift of the conversation.
*Dates*, like figs, medlars, poppering pears
and prunes, could be erotically suggestive, and were often used in pies; cf. *RJ*
2.1.39 and 4.4.2, and *WT* 4.3.45–8. See
G. Williams, *Dictionary*, 369.

248 **the man's . . . out** the man is past his
prime, his sell-by date (proverbial;
Dent, D42.1). The lack of dates, an
ingredient much used for flavouring
and sweetening, would leave the pie
sour and shrivelled. *Out* also can mean

231.1 *Enter Common Soldiers*] F; *not in Q    and pass over the stage*] Rowe, *subst.*    232 comes] Q; come
F    234 i'th'] F; in the Q    238 among] F; amongst Q    242] *inverted commas, Staunton, subst.*
245–6 so forth] F; such like Q    246 season] Q; seasons F    248 date is] Q; dates F

PANDARUS    You are such another woman! One knows not
at what ward you lie.

CRESSIDA    Upon my back to defend my belly, upon my    250
wit to defend my wiles, upon my secrecy to defend
mine honesty, my mask to defend my beauty, and you
to defend all these; and at all these wards I lie, at a
thousand watches.                                                                255

PANDARUS    Say one of your watches.

CRESSIDA    Nay, I'll watch you for that; and that's one of
the chiefest of them too. If I cannot ward what I would
not have hit, I can watch you for telling how I took the
blow – unless it swell past hiding, and then it's past    260

'not in', perhaps reinforcing the bawdy
implications of a shrivelled bodily part
(see previous note). In *1H4*, Falstaff
speaks of a true face and a good conscience as qualities he has once had,
'but their date is out' (2.4.498).
249 *You . . . woman 'What a woman
you are! *i.e.* how full of japes and jests!'
(Ard¹), or, 'You are no different from
other women' (Foakes, *TC*). F's reading, followed here, tends to support
Ard¹. See 262 and n.
250 at what . . . lie what posture of
defence you employ. Pandarus uses
technical terms from fencing to
express his frustration at Cressida's
continual parry and thrust.
251 **Upon my back** See LN.
252 **secrecy** (1) practice of keeping
things secret; (2) the secret and sexual
part of me (*OED* 1, 3b)
253 **honesty** (1) chastity; (2) reputation
for chastity. Cressida is enigmatic as to
which means more to her.
**mask** a barrier against the sun to preserve the whiteness of complexion that
was considered more beautiful than a
dark complexion; it also protected a lady
from public gaze (Linthicum, 272)
253–4 **and you . . . these** you as my uncle
and legal guardian; but also suggesting

'you as my bawd'; see 272 and LN 251
254 **wards** defensive, parrying postures
in fencing, as at 250; guarded entrances
to a fortress; appointed stations, posts
(*OED sb.²* 8, 14, 15)
255 **watches** periods of the night; actions
of keeping vigilant guard (*OED* watch
*sb.* 4, 8). Both *watch* and *ward* trigger a
series of word games in the following
lines, playing also on 'watch and ward',
to keep watch and ward, guard against
attack (*OED* watch *v.* 6b, 10).
256 **watches** Pandarus' innuendo suggests
'night vigils', 'devotional exercises',
'wakes or revels', anything that involves
keeping awake at night (*OED sb.* 2–4).
257 **watch you** keep an eye on you
257–8 **that's . . . too** 'keeping an eye on
you is one of the main *watches* or
actions of keeping guard that I have to
worry about'
258–9 **ward . . . hit** i.e. shield my virginity. For erotic wordplay on the word *hit*,
Ard² cites the extended archery conceit
in *LLL* 4.1.118–37, and Donne's 'On
Black Hair and Eyes', *Poems*, 1.460–1.
259 **watch . . . telling** 'take steps to prevent you from telling'
260 **swell** (1) swell up with trauma and
infection from the hit; (2) swell in
pregnancy

249 such another] *F;* such a *Q*    One] *F;* a man *Q*    252 wiles] *QF;* will *(Johnson)*    254 lie, at] *Q;* lye
at, at *F*    258 too] *F;* two *Q*

153

    watching.

PANDARUS   You are such another!

             *Enter [Troilus'] Boy.*

BOY   Sir, my lord would instantly speak with you.

PANDARUS   Where?

BOY   At your own house. There he unarms him.      265

PANDARUS   Good boy, tell him I come.      *[Exit Boy.]*

    I doubt he be hurt. Fare ye well, good niece.

CRESSIDA   Adieu, uncle.

PANDARUS   I'll be with you, niece, by and by.

CRESSIDA   To bring, uncle?      270

PANDARUS   Ay, a token from Troilus.

CRESSIDA   By the same token, you are a bawd.   *Exit Pandarus.*

    Words, vows, gifts, tears and love's full sacrifice

    He offers in another's enterprise;

    But more in Troilus thousandfold I see      275

    Than in the glass of Pandar's praise may be.

---

260–1 **past watching** too late to do anything about

262 'What a woman you are!' Cf. 249 and n. (Proverbial; Dent, A250.)

267 **doubt** fear

269 **by and by** very soon, straightaway

270 i.e. 'Are you coming to bring something or someone?' But Cressida also completes Pandarus' phrase in such a way as to turn it into a colloquialism: 'be with you to bring', meaning 'I'll be even with you' (Onions, 'bring'), 'Indeed', 'With a vengeance'. She may imply that the saying has an obscene suggestion when addressed to women (Schmidt, 'bring'). Hieronimo, in Kyd's *The Spanish Tragedy*, expresses vengeful purpose when he says, *sotto voce*, 'And, Balthazar, I'll be with thee to bring' (3.12.22). Ard[1] cites other parallel usages.

271 **token** love token, keepsake (*OED sb.* 9)

272 **By . . . token** Cressida plays with a worn catch phrase, meaning 'by this same corroborating evidence' or 'by this fact' (*OED sb.* 15), but also here with particular signification: 'as demonstrated by this same love token or keepsake that you promise to bring'.

273 **love's full sacrifice** everything that the lover can offer to his mistress in the way of selfless devotion. *Sacrifice* suggests worshipful offerings, self-sacrifice, an act of propitiation and homage.

274 **in . . . enterprise** in managing affairs for another person (i.e. Troilus)

276 **glass** mirror

---

262.1] *Q; after 261, F    Troilus*'] *Capell*    265 There he unarms him] *Q; not in F*    266 SD] *Capell*
269 I'll be] *F;* I wilbe *Q*    270 bring, uncle?] *Hudson;* bring vncle: *Q;* bring Vnkle. *F;* bring, Uncle.
*F4;* bring, uncle – *Pope*    272 SD] *F (Exit Pand.); not in Q*

Yet hold I off. Women are angels, wooing;
Things won are done; joy's soul lies in the doing.
That she beloved knows naught that knows not this:
Men prize the thing ungained more than it is.          280
That she was never yet that ever knew
Love got so sweet as when desire did sue.
Therefore this maxim out of love I teach:
'Achievement is command; ungained, beseech'.
Then, though my heart's contents firm love doth bear,     285
Nothing of that shall from mine eyes appear.

*Exit [with Alexander].*

[1.3]   *Sennet. Enter* AGAMEMNON, NESTOR, ULYSSES,
      DIOMEDES, MENELAUS, *with others.*

AGAMEMNON   Princes,

---

277  **wooing** being wooed
278  *\*'Things achieved lose their interest;
the essence of delight is in the achieving.' Lines 278, 280, 284 and 5.2.118 in
Q, and 1.2.284 in F, are marked by
inverted commas to indicate sententious meaning; 284 is italicized for a
similar reason in Q and F; 1.3.117 is
italicized in Q alone (Ard²). The
rhymed couplets from 273 onwards
underscore the wryly sententious character of Cressida's maxims (especially
284) about wooing.
279  **That she beloved** any woman who is
loved
280  **than it is** than its intrinsic worth. Cf.
2.2.51–96.
281–2  'Never was there a woman who
experienced so sweet a love when
the man obtained his desire as when
unfulfilled desire prompted him to
beseech that she grant his request.'
283  **out of love** as from love's book (Ard²)
284  'To achieve a woman's love is to gain

command over her; when she is not yet
won, the lover must entreat.'
285–6  *\*'Then, though the contents of my
heart sustain a firm love, nothing of
that will be evident in my glance or
expression.' Q's 'content' and F's
'Contents' are probably indifferent
variants of the same word (Ard²),
though some editors (such as Ard¹,
Oxf¹ and Foakes) take *content* to mean
'satisfaction', 'contentment', 'wish'
and 'capacity'. *TxC* speculates that
'Contents' 'may have been deliberately
altered to remove the ambiguity'.
286.1  [*with Alexander*] See LN 53. Shakespeare possibly overlooked Alexander
as a distinctly minor character (Oxf¹),
or assumed that the matter could be
easily taken care of in rehearsal.
1.3  The location is the Greek camp.
0.1  *Sennet* trumpet call signalling a pro-
cessional entrance or exit
0.2  *others* i.e. soldiers and attendants

---

280 prize] *F;* price *Q*    284] *inverted commas, QF*    285 Then] *Q;* That *F*    contents] *F;* content *Q*
286.1 *with Alexander*] *Capell, subst. (Exeunt)*    **1.3**] *Capell, subst.*    0.1 *Sennet*] *F; not in Q*    1–2] *F;*
*one line, Q*

What grief hath set the jaundice on your cheeks?
The ample proposition that hope makes
In all designs begun on earth below
Fails in the promised largeness. Checks and disasters          5
Grow in the veins of actions highest reared,
As knots, by the conflux of meeting sap,
Infects the sound pine and diverts his grain
Tortive and errant from his course of growth.
Nor, princes, is it matter new to us                           10
That we come short of our suppose so far
That after seven years' siege yet Troy walls stand,
Sith every action that hath gone before,
Whereof we have record, trial did draw
Bias and thwart, not answering the aim                         15

---

2 **grief** trouble, displeasure, mental distress
**the jaundice** i.e. sallowness or yellowness of complexion – appropriate to a mood of envy and jealous rivalry. The disease, caused by a blockage of the bile, leads to a yellowness of skin, loss of appetite and weakness. Agamemnon's metaphor addresses a lack of morale in the army resulting in lassitude and bickering. Q's 'these Iaundies' is indicative of a tendency in the Renaissance to treat the word as a plural, as in other plural names of diseases like measles, mumps and glanders (*OED*).

3 **proposition** action of putting forward or offering for acceptance; proposal (*OED* 2, 6). *Hope*, a heavenly attribute, gives to human designs conceived here on earth *below* the heavens an amplitude of conception, but those designs then fail to achieve their promise – the *promised largeness* of 5.

5–9 **Checks . . . growth** 'Stalemates and disasters thwart the success of actions conceived on a grand scale, just as knots, at the conjunction of moving

streams of sap, adversely affect the healthy pine by twisting the arrangement of its fibres, diverting the tree from its proper course of growth.' See LN.

8 *\*Infects affect adversely by the introduction of an extraneous element (*OED* 9). See LN.

11 **suppose** expectation; purpose (*OED sb.* 3, 4)

12 **seven years' siege** According to Lefèvre, whose work Caxton translated, Hector dies in the seventh year of the war (Var). In the *Iliad*, the Greek expedition to Troy is in its tenth year (2.134 and 295, LCL, 1.60–1, 72–3).

13–15 **Sith . . . thwart** 'since experience (*trial*) has turned awry (*Bias and thwart*) every past military enterprise of which we have any record'. History shows that frustrations and setbacks are to be expected in enterprises of this sort. See LN.

15–17 **not answering . . . shape** 'not following the conception and abstract idea that gave the planned action imagined shape'

---

2 the] *F;* these *Q*   jaundice] *QF (*Iaundies*)*   on] *F;* ore *Q*   8 Infects] *Q;* Infect *F*   13 every] *F;* euer *Q*   15 aim] *Q (*ayme,*);* ayme: *F*

And that unbodied figure of the thought
That gave't surmisèd shape. Why then, you princes,
Do you with cheeks abashed behold our works
And think them shames, which are indeed naught else
But the protractive trials of great Jove                    20
To find persistive constancy in men?
The fineness of which metal is not found
In Fortune's love; for then the bold and coward,
The wise and fool, the artist and unread,
The hard and soft, seem all affined and kin.              25
But in the wind and tempest of her frown,
Distinction, with a broad and powerful fan,
Puffing at all, winnows the light away,
And what hath mass or matter by itself
Lies rich in virtue and unmingled.                        30

17 **surmised** surmisèd
18 **works** undertakings
19 ***shames** F's 'shame' may be a simple misreading.
20 **protractive** long, drawn-out. On the trials imposed by Jehovah in the Bible, see, e.g., Hebrews, 12.6, Job, 23.10, and Zachariah, 13.9 (Var, citing Carter).
21 **persistive** steadfast, persistent. Both this word and *protractive* appear to be Shakespearean coinages used by him only once, characterizing Agamemnon as a user of Latinate neologisms.
22 **metal** QF's 'Mettall' catches a common duality of meaning: (1) strong substance; (2) mettle, the 'stuff' of which a person's character is made. The *fineness* of the metal here suggests both superior quality and the ability to be drawn out in thin filaments or sheets, like gold. See LN.
23 **In Fortune's love** when Fortune smiles. Prosperity does not bring out the best in people; they must be tested to show what stuff they are made of.
**then** in a time of prosperity
24 **artist** learned person skilled in the lib-

eral arts (as in 'Master of Arts')
25 **affined** related, connected
26 **her** the goddess Fortune's
27 ***broad** F's 'lowd' is defensible as conjuring up the image of a destructive, noisy wind; but misreading between Q's 'broad' and F's 'lowd' is quite feasible in either direction, and the Q reading is more intelligible in a biblical image of separating wheat from chaff and fool from wise (see next note).
**fan** any kind of fanning contrivance used to winnow chaff from grain. The figurative use can refer to Matthew, 3.12, where John the Baptist prophesies that Christ will come with a fan in his hand to gather up the wheat and burn the chaff. See also Luke, 22.31.
29 **mass or matter** The image of heavy grain remaining in place is mingled with that of metal in 22.
30 **virtue** excellence, value
**unmingled** pronounced in four syllables: 'un-ming-el-ed'

19 think] *F;* call *Q*    shames] *Q;* shame *F*    27 broad] *Q;* lowd *F*

NESTOR

With due observance of thy godly seat,
Great Agamemnon, Nestor shall apply
Thy latest words. In the reproof of chance
Lies the true proof of men. The sea being smooth,
How many shallow bauble boats dare sail      35
Upon her patient breast, making their way
With those of nobler bulk!
But let the ruffian Boreas once enrage
The gentle Thetis, and anon behold
The strong-ribbed bark through liquid mountains cut,    40
Bounding between the two moist elements
Like Perseus' horse. Where's then the saucy boat

31 **observance of** respect for. The actor may bow.
    **seat** throne; figuratively, regal authority. A throne need not be brought on stage. 'Seat' is commonly used to denote God's throne in the Bishops' Bible; see Matthew, 5.34 and 23.22 (Noble, 213, Shaheen, 115–16).

32 **apply** give to a theoretical idea a specific reference (*OED* 9); gloss, expound (as with a learned text) (Ard²). In fact, what Nestor does is to elaborate further on the sententious truisms that Agamemnon has advanced.

33 **In . . . chance** either (1) in the patient rebuffing or confutation of misfortune, or (2) when Fortune chides. With wordplay on *reproof*, and *proof* (test, demonstration) in the next line. Cf. the proverb, 'Great courage is in greatest dangers tried' (Dent, C715).

34–6 **The sea . . . breast** more sententious proverbialism; cf. 'In a calm sea every man may be a pilot' (Dent, S174), and Erasmus, *Tranquillo quilibet gubernator est*, *Adagia*, 2.1047E

(chil. 4, cent. 4, prov. 96), from Seneca, *Epistulae Morales*, 85.34, *tranquillo enim, ut aiunt, quilibet gubernataor est*, 'for anyone, in the words of the proverb, is a pilot in a calm sea' (LCL, 306–7). Stoical truisms like these of Nestor are often Senecan in origin.

35 **bauble** toylike. A bauble is a child's plaything.

37 **bulk** size, volume; but with more specific nautical meaning of 'cargo, heap, hull into which cargo is loaded'; also 'bodily frame'

38 **Boreas** the north wind. Shakespeare's only use.

39 **Thetis** i.e. the sea; in Greek mythology, a Nereid or sea-maiden, daughter of Nereus (the old man of the sea) and mother of Achilles. Perhaps (as often in the period) confused with Tethys, the wife of Oceanus.

41 **the two . . . elements** air (hot and wet) and water (cold and wet). The other two elements are fire (hot and dry) and earth (cold and dry).

42 **Perseus' horse** For the mythological account, see LN.

31 thy godly] *F*; the godlike *Q*    33] *Q; F lines* words. / Chance, /    36 patient] *F*; ancient *Q*

Whose weak untimbered sides but even now
Co-rivalled greatness? Either to harbour fled
Or made a toast for Neptune. Even so                    45
Doth valour's show and valour's worth divide
In storms of fortune. For in her ray and brightness
The herd hath more annoyance by the breese
Than by the tiger; but when the splitting wind
Makes flexible the knees of knotted oaks                50
And flies flee under shade, why then the thing of
      courage,
As roused with rage, with rage doth sympathize,
And with an accent tuned in selfsame key
Retorts to chiding fortune.

ULYSSES                     Agamemnon,
Thou great commander, nerve and bone of Greece,        55

---

43 **untimbered** frail, without a strong wooden frame or cross-timbering

43–4 **but . . . greatness** 'only a moment earlier kept company with, and vied with, larger and stronger vessels'. *Co-rivalled* need not imply competitiveness (cf. *Ham* 1.1.14, where 'The rivals of my watch' signifies 'partners'), but the image here of saucy boats alongside greater vessels implies the kind of insubordination that Nestor and his fellow senior officers are concerned about.

45 **toast** sop, toasted bread floating in wine; a tasty morsel for Neptune

45–7 **Even . . . fortune** 'Similarly, the mere appearance of valour becomes distinguishable from true valour itself in crises of fortune.'

47 **For . . . brightness** 'for in the radiance and brightness of good fortune'

48 **breese** gadfly; with a pun on 'breeze', light wind, in contrast to the *splitting wind* in 49. *Breese* and 'breeze' are really the same word with different meanings; the archaic form *breese* is

often used, as here, to distinguish it from the more familiar form.

50 **knees** See LN.

51 **And flies . . . shade** The image picks up on *breese*, gadfly, in 48; under the pressure of adversity, the annoying tormentor retreats and hides.
*flee Capell's emendation corrects an easy misreading in Secretary hand of final -*e* as -*d*. The QF reading is intelligible as meaning 'are fled, have fled', but as worded the construction seems elliptical. The image is more compatible with oak trees on land than with oaken ships at sea.
**shade** shelter from wind and weather (*OED sb.* 11a). The image contrasts with the 'ray and brightness' of 47.
**the thing of courage** any brave heart

52 **As** being
**sympathize** correspond (in a sympathy of boisterous mood)

54 *Retorts For textual choices, see LN.

55 **nerve** sinew

47] *Q; F lines* Fortune. / brightnesse, /    48 breese] *QF (*Bryze, Brieze*)    51] *Q; F lines* then / Courage, /    flee] *Capell;* fled *QF; get Pope    54 Retorts] *Hudson (Dyce);* Retires *QF, subst.;* Returns *Pope;* Replies *Hanmer    55 nerve] *F;* nerues *Q*

Heart of our numbers, soul and only spirit,
In whom the tempers and the minds of all
Should be shut up: hear what Ulysses speaks.
Besides th'applause and approbation
The which, [*to Agamemnon*] most mighty for thy
  place and sway,                                                    60
[*to Nestor*] And thou most reverend for thy
  stretched-out life,
I give to both your speeches, which were such
As, Agamemnon, every hand of Greece
Should hold up high in brass; and such again
As venerable Nestor, hatched in silver,                             65
Should with a bond of air, strong as the axletree
On which the heavens ride, knit all Greeks' ears

56 Agamemnon is heart and soul *of our numbers*, i.e. of our army (*OED* number *sb*. 9). *Spirit* means 'animating or vital principle, essential character, mettle' (*OED* 1, 8, 13a). Q's spelling, 'spright', may point to pronunciation in one syllable, but the modern form is 'spirit'.

57 **tempers** dispositions, temperaments

58 **Should . . . up** are embodied in ideal form; 'should be contented to find themselves absorbed' (Ard[1])

60 **The which** which
**place and sway** office and sovereign authority

63 **\*As, Agamemnon, every** Oxf's reading, originally proposed by Proudfoot, is considerably less awkward than the QF original (see t.n.), which is easily accounted for by supposing that the printer's copy read 'eu⁰ye', with a superscript loop for '*er*', and that this was mistaken by the compositor for 'd', leaving 'eu' to be misread as 'an' and 'ye' as the equivalent of 'the'.

64 **hold . . . brass** i.e. 'hold up as models of eloquence, immortalized in brass

inscription'

64–8 **and such again . . . tongue** i.e. 'and such a speech – made of air, but paradoxically as strong as the axis of the universe – as Nestor should use to unite all Greeks in listening to his experienced voice'

65 **hatched in silver** i.e. with hair looking as though inlaid with strips of silver. Cf. the portrait of Nestor as orator in *RL*, 1401ff., 'encouraging the Greeks to fight', with 'his beard, all silver white', wagging up and down (Malone). *Hatched* can also mean 'engraved' (*OED v*.[2] 1, 2) in silver. Hulme (171) cites the Latin adage, *In magno pretio ruga senilis erat*: 'The wrinkles of old men shall be in great account'.

66 **a bond of air** Nestor's speech, though invisible and intangible, knits or binds his listeners' ears to the utterance of his tongue. The power of speech to act thus is a Renaissance commonplace; cf. Alciati's *Emblems* (180), where the bonds are made visible (Var).

66–7 **the axletree . . . ride** See LN.

56 spirit] *F;* spright *Q*    59 th'applause] *Q;* the applause *F*    60, 61 SD] *Rowe*    61 thy] *F;* the *Q*    63] As, Agamemnon, every] *Oxf (Proudfoot);* As *Agamemnon* and the *QF*    67 On] *Q;* In *F*    the heavens ride] *F;* heauen rides *Q*    Greeks'] *F (*Greekes*);* the Greekish *Q*

To his experienced tongue, yet let it please both,
Thou great, and wise, to hear Ulysses speak.

AGAMEMNON

Speak, Prince of Ithaca; and be't of less expect          70
That matter needless, of importless burden,
Divide thy lips, than we are confident,
When rank Thersites opes his mastic jaws,
We shall hear music, wit and oracle.

ULYSSES

Troy, yet upon his basis, had been down,                  75
And the great Hector's sword had lacked a master,
But for these instances:
The specialty of rule hath been neglected;
And look how many Grecian tents do stand
Hollow upon this plain, so many hollow factions.         80

---

69 **great, and wise** i.e. Agamemnon as great, Nestor as wise

70–4 ***be't . . . oracle** i.e. 'let no one any more expect you to speak irrelevantly than we should expect foul-mouthed Thersites to speak eloquently'. (These lines, omitted in Q, seem necessary as a signal for Ulysses to begin his long oration.)

70 **expect** expectation. Shakespeare's only use as a noun.

71 **importless burden** trivial content and meaning

73 **rank** haughty; reckless, violent; offensively smelly; lecherous; gross; festering. On Chapman's *Seven Books*, see LN.
**mastic** resinous, gummy. *Mastic*, as a noun, signifies a gum used in the East as a chewing gum and by Elizabethans to stop decaying teeth; to 'masticate' is to chew. The image is of drooling. Perhaps there is a suggestion too of 'mastix', a common suffix (as in *Histriomastix*

and *Satiromastix*) meaning 'scourge', 'satirist'. Thersites is known in the Greek camp for his railing.

75 ***yet upon his basis** still standing on its foundations. The line has no internal punctuation in QF and could possibly mean 'Troy would have been reduced to its foundations in spite of everything' (*OED* yet III.9).

77 **instances** causes; illustrative examples, particulars

78 **The specialty of rule** prerogatives and contractual obligations of wise government; 'the particular rights of supreme authority' (Johnson)

78–108 For possible sources, see LN.

79–80 **look how many . . . so many** however many . . . there are just as many. (Cf. the Latin construction, *toties . . . quoties*.)

80 **Hollow . . . hollow** empty, unsubstantial, all cover and no substance . . . insincere, false, deceiving

---

70–4] *F; not in Q*   75 SP] *F; not in Q*   75 basis] *F;* bases *Q*

When that the general is not like the hive
To whom the foragers shall all repair,　*marked*
What honey is expected? Degree being <u>vizarded,</u>
Th'unworthiest shows as fairly in the mask.
The heavens themselves, the planets and this centre　　　85
Observe degree, priority and place,
Insisture, course, proportion, season, form,
Office and custom, <u>in all line of order.</u>
And therefore is the glorious planet Sol *Sun*
In noble eminence enthroned and sphered　　　90
Amidst the other, whose med'cinable eye

81 **When that** when
　**the general** (1) Agamemnon; (2) the state, the general good (Empson, *Pastoral*, 40–1)
　**like the hive** i.e. serving as the nucleus of productive activity, the command centre. Ulysses' comparison is elliptical: 'when the general is not to the army like the hive to the bees, the repository of the stock of every individual' (Johnson). See LN.

82 **shall** must
　**repair** return. For the image of soldiers as beelike foragers, cf. the Archbishop of Canterbury's beehive metaphor in *H5* 1.2.193–6: 'Others, like soldiers, armed in their stings, / Make boot upon the summer's velvet buds, / Which pillage they with merry march bring home / To the tent royal of their emperor'; see LN 81.

83–4 **Degree . . . mask** 'When rank and hierarchy are masked or obscured, the person of lowest rank looks as handsome in his mask as the most noble.' (This lack of visual differentiation would also apply to a masque. The QF spelling here, 'maske / Maske', could apply to these various meanings.) Cf. Sophocles' *Ajax*, 669–83 (LCL, 92–3).

85–8 Cf. the homily 'On Order and Obedience': 'Almighty God hath created and appointed all things, in heaven, earth and waters, in a most excellent and perfect order . . . And man himself also hath all his parts both within and without . . . in a profitable, necessary and pleasant order. Every degree of people, in their vocation, calling and office, hath appointed to them their duty and order' (quoted in Milward, 119; see LN 78–108).

85 **this centre** the earth, centre of the Ptolemaic universe (see LN 66–7)

87 **Insisture** (the sole recorded use of the word) 'persistency, constancy' (Schmidt), 'regularity, or perhaps station' (Nares); 'steady continuance' in their path (*OED*). See LN.

88 **line** station, rank (as in *1H4* 1.3.168), rule, principle (Schmidt)

89 **glorious planet Sol** the brilliant sun, regarded as a planet because of its apparent rotation around the earth and motion through the fixed stars; a Ptolemaic conception

90 **sphered** placed in its heavenly sphere, the transparent concentric globe in which it was thought to move about the earth

91 **other** others. A common uninflected plural form (Abbott, 12).
　**med'cinable** healing

87 Insisture] *F; * In sisture *Q; * Infixture *Oxf*

Corrects the ill aspects of planets evil
And posts, like the commandmeut of a king,
Sans check, to good and bad. But when the planets
In evil mixture to disorder wander,                                    95
What plagues and what portents, what mutiny,
What raging of the sea, shaking of earth,
Commotion in the winds, frights, changes, horrors,
Divert and crack, rend and deracinate
The unity and married calm of states                                  100
Quite from their fixure! O, when degree is shaked,
Which is the ladder to all high designs,
The enterprise is sick. How could communities,
Degrees in schools and brotherhoods in cities,
Peaceful commerce from dividable shores,                              105
The primogeneity and due of birth,

92 *aspects the relative positions of the heavenly bodies as seen from an observer on earth at any given time; see LN.
93 posts speeds
94 Sans check without pause
  to good and bad The sun's curative warmth encourages the good and corrects the bad.
95 mixture conjunction. When two or more planets appear to occupy the same location in the heavens and are thus in a single *aspect*, their combined 'influence' (Q's term) can be disastrous. See LN 92.
  to disorder wander As the planets move into harmful conjunctions, they produce disorder on earth. 'Planet' originally meant 'wandering star', as opposed to the fixed stars (from the Greek *planetes*, 'wanderer'). Both *mixture* (*OED* 1e) and 'conjunction' (2b) can connote sexual intercourse (Ard²).
98 changes alterations in climate, etc., but suggesting also political changes,

'innovations'. *Mutiny*, 96, has a similar political resonance.
99 Divert deflect from their proper course
  deracinate pluck up by the roots, eradicate. Shakespeare appears to have been the first to use this term, here and in *H5* 5.2.47.
100 states rulers, the common weal – all that rank and degree imply
101 fixure fixedness, stability
102 ladder The earliest meaning of *degree* is 'a step or rung of a ladder', from Lat. *de-*, down, + *gradus*, step (*OED* 1). Cf. Dent, S848.
104 Degrees in schools academic ranks in universities
  brotherhoods guilds, societies
105 from dividable shores i.e. between countries that are separated by the sea
106 *primogeneity i.e. primogeniture (the usual form), the right of the eldest-born son to inherit (the *due of birth*). See LN.

92 ill . . . evil] *F;* influence of euill Planets *Q*   101 fixure] *QF;* fixture *Oxf*   102 to] *F;* of *Q*   106 The primogeneity] *Q (*The primogenitie*);* The primogenitiue *F;* The Primogeniture *Rowe;* Primogeneity *(Proudfoot)*

163

Prerogative of age, crowns, sceptres, laurels,
But by degree stand in authentic place?
Take but degree away, untune that string,
And hark what discord follows. Each thing meets          110
In mere oppugnancy. The bounded waters
Should lift their bosoms higher than the shores
And make a sop of all this solid globe;
Strength should be lord of imbecility,
And the rude son should strike his father dead;          115
Force should be right; or rather, right and wrong,
Between whose endless jar justice resides,
Should lose their names, and so should justice too.
Then everything includes itself in power,
Power into will, will into appetite;                     120
And appetite, an universal wolf,
So doubly seconded with will and power,

108 **authentic** authoritative; legally valid (*OED* 1–2).
109ff. For possible sources and analogues for this passage, see LN.
110 **Each** every
110–11 *****meets . . . oppugnancy** would dissolve in total conflict. See LN.
111 **bounded** ordinarily (but no longer) held back by the shore. The image of war between sea and land is a commonplace of the chaos of elemental strife when order is not present, as in Boethius' fifth-century treatise, *The Consolation of Philosophy*, Bk 1, mets 5 and 7, Bk 2, met. 8, etc. (pp. 17–19, 24, 54–5).
112 **Should** must inevitably, would (also in 114–18)
113 **sop** piece of bread or toast floating in wine, recalling Nestor's *toast for Neptune* at 45. The solid earth is here soaked and then devoured by the sea.

114 'the strong would rule the weak and impotent'
115 **rude** brutal, wild, violent
116 Cf. the proverb 'Might overcomes (makes) right' (Dent, M922).
117 i.e. Justice resides somewhere between competing claims and is arrived at through a prolonged *jar* or discord of opposing viewpoints. See LN.
119–20 i.e. 'Then all virtuous qualities like right, wrong and justice become simply a question of who is most powerful; power in turn grows self-willed and self-indulgent, leading to limitless debauchery and greed.' To *include* is to terminate (everything terminates in power) or to enclose (*OED v.* 1, 4). Cf. R. Hooker, *Ecclesiastical Polity*, Bk I, 7.7, on how 'the hastiness of our wills' prevents 'the more considerate advice of sound reason' (p. 81).

110 meets] *F; melts Q*   117] *F, subst., placing the line in round brackets but in roman type; in round brackets and italic, Q*   resides] *QF (recides, recides); presides Hanmer*   118 lose] *QF (loose)*   their] *Q; her F*   too.] *F; to? Q*   119 includes] *F; include Q*

Must make perforce an universal prey
And last eat up himself. Great Agamemnon,
This chaos, when degree is suffocate,                      125
Follows the choking.
And this neglection of degree it is
That by a pace goes backward in a purpose
It hath to climb. The general's disdained
By him one step below, he by the next,                    130
That next by him beneath; so every step,
Exampled by the first pace that is sick
Of his superior, grows to an envious fever
Of pale and bloodless emulation.
And 'tis this fever that keeps Troy on foot,              135
Not her own sinews. To end a tale of length,
Troy in our weakness lives, not in her strength.

*splitting up & ignoring degree*

NESTOR
Most wisely hath Ulysses here discovered
The fever whereof all our power is sick.

AGAMEMNON
The nature of the sickness found, Ulysses,                140
What is the remedy?

ULYSSES
The great Achilles, whom opinion crowns

---

123 **prey** the action of preying, of pillag-
ing and devouring
125–6 i.e. 'After the choking that accompanies the suffocation of rank and order
comes the chaos of death, the dissolution of ordered life'. *Suffocate* means
'suffocated' (Abbott, 342). *Choking* may
suggest that appetite chokes itself
through greedy devouring and thereby
consumes or *eats up* itself (124).
127–9 *And . . . climb* 'And this neglect
of order and degree means that everything goes backward, step by step, when

the intention was to advance.' See LN.
132–3 **Exampled . . . superior** 'given
precedent by the insubordinate stepping up of the lesser person towards his
superior', or 'justified by the precedent
of the sick (i.e. morally corrupt, envious) step that his superior takes first'
134 **emulation** grudge against the superiority of others (*OED* 3). See LN.
137 *lives For textual choices, see LN.
138 **discovered** revealed
139 **power** army
142 **opinion** reputation, public opinion

124] *Rowe¹; QF line* himselfe. / *Agamemnon,* /    127 it is] *Q;* is it *F*    128 in] *F;* with *Q*    137 lives]
*F;* stands *Q*

The sinew and the forehand of our host,
Having his ear full of his airy fame,
Grows dainty of his worth and in his tent                    145
Lies mocking our designs. With him Patroclus,
Upon a lazy bed, the livelong day
Breaks scurril jests,
And with ridiculous and awkward action –
Which, slanderer, he imitation calls –                       150
He pageants us. Sometime, great Agamemnon,
Thy topless deputation he puts on,
And, like a strutting player, whose conceit
Lies in his hamstring, and doth think it rich
To hear the wooden dialogue and sound                        155
'Twixt his stretched footing and the scaffoldage,
Such to-be-pitied and o'erwrested seeming
He acts thy greatness in; and when he speaks,
'Tis like a chime a-mending, with terms unsquared,

143 i.e. 'the strength and mainstay of our
army'. *Sinew* and *forehand* both connote the vanguard and supporting
force.
144 **airy fame** reputation, on everyone's
lips but inherently insubstantial
145 **dainty** fastidious, oversolicitous;
chary, sparing
147 **Upon a lazy bed** lazily upon his bed
(Abbott, 419a)
148 **scurril** scurrilous. Shakespeare uses
the term only one other time, in *TNK*
5.1.147.
149 **awkward** The *OED*'s oldest and now
obsolete meaning, 'turned the wrong
way', 'back foremost' (see also *OED*
awk, *a.* 1), has the same potentially
sodomitical suggestion as 'preposterous' (5.1.23 and n.). See Puttenham,
3.13 and 3.22 (170, 255), and Parker,
20ff.
151 **pageants** mimics, as in a pageant or

play; a nonce word in this sense
152 'he assumes your supreme dignity of
office'. *Deputation* may suggest both a
deputed office and a vicegerency as
Jove's substitute (Ard²).
153–4 **whose . . . hamstring** whose wits
are in his thighs
155–6 'to hear the inert, lifeless inter-
action of mere noise that takes place
between his long strides and the stage
scaffolding on which he walks'. See
LN.
157 **o'erwrested** overstrained, wound up
too high (see *OED* over- 28c, and
'wrested'). A *wrest* is used to tune a
stringed instrument; see next note.
159 **a chime a-mending** a chime of
bells being tuned or in need of tuning
**unsquared** not properly fitted, like
lumber or stone not cut at right
angles

143 sinew] *QF* (sinnow, sinew)   149 awkward] *F;* sillie *Q*   156 scaffoldage] *QF* (scoaffollage, Scaffolage)
157 o'erwrested] *QF* (ore-rested)   159 unsquared] *F;* vnsquare *Q*

Which from the tongue of roaring Typhon dropped     160
Would seem hyperboles. At this fusty stuff
The large Achilles, on his pressed bed lolling,
From his deep chest laughs out a loud applause,
Cries 'Excellent! 'Tis Agamemnon just.
Now play me Nestor; hem, and stroke thy beard,     165
As he being dressed to some oration.'
That's done, as near as the extremest ends
Of parallels, as like as Vulcan and his wife;
Yet god Achilles still cries, 'Excellent!
'Tis Nestor right. Now play him me, Patroclus,     170
Arming to answer in a night-alarm.'
And then, forsooth, the faint defects of age

160 **Typhon** or Typhoeus, one of the monsters of Greek mythology, associated particularly with earthquakes and volcanos; Ovid describes him as buried beneath Mount Etna in Sicily (*Met.*, 5.321, LCL, 1.260–1; 5.408ff. in Golding's translation). Patroclus' ranting imitation of Agamemnon outdoes the roar of an earthquake. See also Ovid, *Fasti*, 2.451 (LCL, 88–9).

161 **fusty** stale, high-sounding, as at 2.1.99

162 **large** (1) physically huge; (2) prodigal, lax, indulgent; and see next note
**pressed** weighted down by the *large* (i.e. heavy and self-important) Achilles

164 ***just** exactly. Q's 'right' has the same meaning; the words seem more or less interchangeable for Shakespeare. Since the substitution in F is unlikely to be compositorial, authorial revision seems probable.

165 **me** i.e. for my benefit (Abbott, 220). Cf. *play him me* at 170.
***hem** clear the throat, cough. F's 'hum' may be a non-substantive variant introduced in transmission or printing.

166 **dressed to** prepared for

167–8 **as near . . . parallels** Parallel lines in the same plane never meet – a truism of Euclidian geometry.

168 **Vulcan . . . wife** The marriage of the Roman fire god and smith, Vulcan (identified with Hephaestus), with Venus (or Aphrodite), the goddess of love, is the archetype in Homer (*Odyssey*, 8.266–366, LCL, 1.290–9) and elsewhere of a comic mismatch involving an older, misshapen male who is being cuckolded by his sexy younger wife.

169 **god** a sardonic salute to Achilles' lofty contempt for his fellow commanders, and a wry acknowledgement of his attribute in Homer: *dios Achilleus*. As the son of King Peleus and the goddess Thetis, one of the Nereids, Achilles was made invulnerable by his mother except for his heel (the Achilles' tendon) and thus nearly immortal.

170 **me** i.e. for me. See 165n.

171 **answer . . . night-alarm** respond to a military alert at night

172 **faint . . . age** defects of age causing feebleness. Shakespeare often uses adjectives signifying effect to signify cause; Abbott, 4.

161 seem] *Q;* seemes *F*   164–78] *inverted commas, Hanmer, subst.*   164 just] *F;* right *Q*   165 hem] *Q;* hum *F*   169 god] *QF;* good *F2*

Must be the scene of mirth; to cough and spit,
And with a palsy fumbling on his gorget
Shake in and out the rivet. And at this sport          175
Sir Valour dies; cries, 'O, enough, Patroclus,
Or give me ribs of steel! I shall split all
In pleasure of my spleen.' And in this fashion,
All our abilities, gifts, natures, shapes,
Severals and generals of grace exact,                 180
Achievements, plots, orders, preventions,
Excitements to the field, or speech for truce,
Success or loss, what is or is not, serves
As stuff for these two to make paradoxes.

NESTOR

And in the imitation of these twain,                  185
Who, as Ulysses says, opinion crowns
With an imperial voice, many are infect.
Ajax is grown self-willed and bears his head
In such a rein, in full as proud a place
As broad Achilles; keeps his tent like him,           190

---

173 **scene of mirth** subject of mirthful
dramatic representation
174 **palsy** palsied, tremulous (*OED*
*sb.(a.)*, B, *adj.*)
**gorget** armour for the throat. Cf. *rivet*
(175), *beaver* and *vambrace* (296–7) as
terms describing the armour of
medieval warfare.
176–7 **dies . . . steel** To die or be ready to
burst with laughing, and to crave ribs
of steel, are proverbial expressions
here conveying the hyperbole suggested also in the sardonic *Sir Valour*
(Dent, L.94 and 94.1, S844.1).
177 **all** all my ribs and sides; altogether
178 **spleen** This ductless abdominal
organ was regarded as the seat of
melancholy and of laughter. Achilles'
laughter is spleenful, i.e. mirthful but
whimsical, hot-tempered, ill-natured.
180 'the individual and group excellences
that truly adorn us and are of consum-

mate merit'
181 **plots** strategies
**preventions** defensive precautions
182 **Excitements** exhortations
184 **paradoxes** statements contrary to
received opinion; absurdities that
declare wisdom to be folly and the like
186–7 **crowns . . . voice** raises to the dignity of absolute authority
187 **infect** infected. Cf. *suffocate* at 125.
188–9 **bears . . . rein** bridles as a proud
horse does when reined in, throwing
up the head and drawing in the chin in
resentment or offended dignity; or,
refuses to rein himself in
189 **in . . . place** just as vain of his own
dignity and status
190 **broad** broad-shouldered; but suggesting also outspoken, puffed up,
coarse (*OED a*. 1, 6 a and b)
**keeps** keeps to

188 self-willed] *QF (*selfe-wild, selfe-will'd*)*   189 place] *QF;* pace *Pope*   190 keeps] *Q;* and keepes *F*

Makes factious feasts, rails on our state of war,
Bold as an oracle, and sets Thersites –
A slave whose gall coins slanders like a mint –
To match us in comparisons with dirt,
To weaken and discredit our exposure,                                    195
How rank soever rounded in with danger.

ULYSSES

They tax our policy and call it cowardice,
Count wisdom as no member of the war,
Forestall prescience, and esteem no act
But that of hand. The still and mental parts,                            200
That do contrive how many hands shall strike,
When fitness calls them on, and know by measure
Of their observant toil the enemy's weight –
Why, this hath not a finger's dignity.
They call this bed-work, mapp'ry, closet war;                            205

---

191 **factious** seditious, quarrelsome; for his faction
  **our state of war** our preparedness for war; our army in a state of readiness; our council of war
192 **oracle** the mouthpiece of a deity, such as a priest, who could tell unwelcome tidings even to kings
193 **slave** servile wretch
  **gall** secretion of the liver known also as bile, thought to induce rancour and asperity; one of the four humours, equated with choler
  **like a mint** 'i.e. as fast as a mint coins money' (Malone)
195–6 **our . . . danger** 'us in our vulnerable situation, thickly hemmed in as we are with dangers'
197 **tax our policy** 'censure our sagacious conduct of affairs'. Cf. this speech with Ulysses' address to the Greek generals in Ovid, *Met.*, 13, esp. 360–9 (LCL, 2.254–5; Cam¹).
198 **member** part of the body. The metaphor of the body politic continues

in *hand* and *mental parts* in 200–1 (Ard²). The *war* is seen as a body of soldiers and as a war effort, as in 191.
199 **Forestall prescience** obstruct and depreciate careful planning
200 **of hand** of immediate physical response
  **The . . . parts** See LN.
202 **fitness** fit time and readiness
202–3 **know . . . weight** determine by hard-won observation the enemy's might
204 **hath . . . dignity** is not worth a snap of the fingers, is of small worth. (In terms of body imagery, a finger is primarily a small member; cf. *Oth* 3.4.148–50.)
205 'They call this armchair strategy, mere map-making, war planned in the study.' *Mapp'ry* is a Shakespearean coinage, used only this once by him. Cf. *Oth* 1.1.19–28, where Iago complains of Cassio as one who has 'bookish theoric' only.

---

195 and] *F;* our *Q*    202 calls] *Q;* call *F*    203 enemy's] *QF* (enemies)

So that the ram that batters down the wall,
For the great swinge and rudeness of his poise,
They place before his hand that made the engine
Or those that with the fineness of their souls
By reason guide his execution.                                    210

NESTOR

Let this be granted, and Achilles' horse
Makes many Thetis' sons.                                  *Tucket.*

AGAMEMNON     What trumpet? Look, Menelaus.

MENELAUS    From Troy.

                    *Enter* AENEAS [*with a Trumpeter*].

AGAMEMNON    What would you 'fore our tent?        215

AENEAS

Is this great Agamemnon's tent, I pray you?

AGAMEMNON    Even this.

AENEAS

May one that is a herald and a prince
Do a fair message to his kingly ears?

207 *'because of the massive driving power and violence of the battering ram's forcible impact'. Q's 'swinge' and F's 'swing' essentially mean the same thing; F may represent simply a variant spelling.

208 'they value (the battering ram) more highly than the engineer who devised it'

209 the . . . souls their superior intellectual abilities. Q's 'finesse' and F's 'finenesse' are probably only spelling variants. Modern spelling requires an arbitrary choice.

210 By reason using powers of reasoning; reasonably, sensibly; with proper authority

his execution the carrying out of the battering ram's function

211–12 'If we grant the argument that the mere instruments of war outvalue the military planners, then Achilles' horse is worth many an Achilles' (the son of Thetis, as in 169n.). Lexically, as Seltzer proposes, *horse* here could mean 'horsemen', referring to Achilles' Myrmidons; but the animal gives a stronger and more convincing sense of contrast.

212 SD *Tucket* (F only) a trumpet flourish, perhaps also with drum, signalling the march (here, arrival) of troops

219 fair courteous, pleasing, peaceable

207 swinge] *Q;* swing *F*   209 fineness] *F;* finesse *Q;* finesse *Oxf*   212 SD] *F; not in Q*   214.1 *Enter*
AENEAS] *F; not in Q   with a Trumpeter*] *Sisson, subst.*   219 ears] *F;* eyes *Q*

AGAMEMNON

    With surety stronger than Achilles' arm        220
    'Fore all the Greekish lords, which with one voice
    Call Agamemnon head and general.

AENEAS

    Fair leave and large security. How may
    A stranger to those most imperial looks
    Know them from eyes of other mortals?

AGAMEMNON                   How?    225

AENEAS   Ay.

    I ask, that I might waken reverence,
    And bid the cheek be ready with a blush
    Modest as morning when she coldly eyes
    The youthful Phoebus.                  230
    Which is that god in office, guiding men?

---

220 **surety** certainty of obtaining a result; security. Agamemnon understands that Aeneas is asking for safeguard in the enemy camp, the *large security* he acknowledges in 223.

221 **'Fore** leading into battle; preeminent among. Agamemnon capitalizes on Achilles' great reputation as a way of impressing a Trojan visitor, but goes on quickly to assert his own supreme authority. The *arma Achillea* or arms of Achilles had become proverbial in the Renaissance as affording the best in protection; but since *arm* (220) does not means 'arms', the resonance is to be questioned here. *lords QF's 'heads' is probably an anticipation of *head* in the next line. Both 'host' and *lords* (the latter adopted here) have been plausibly proposed as emendations; see t.n.

223 **Fair leave** courteous permission
**large** broad, comprehensive. See 220n.

224 **A stranger** By seeming not to recognize Agamemnon, despite the imperial

manner in which that lord has addressed him, Aeneas has as his nominal excuse the fact that the warriors on both sides are understood to fight in complete armour with covered face and head (see 4.5.196–7) and that the two of them have not been formally introduced, but the slight is still discernible in Agamemnon's response at 233–4 to what appears to be mock politeness (Ard²).

227 **waken reverence** 'call up in myself a reverent demeanour' (Ard¹); with perhaps a sly suggestion of 'give the wake-up call to some senior military officers'. See previous note.

228 *bid F's 'on' is hard to explain as an error, but it is also hard to account for as an authorial choice. The idiom is unusual, and *bid* is the stronger reading.

229–30 The morning sun is personified as leaving the bed of the goddess Aurora, or Eos, the dawn, whose modest blushes are the soft pinks of daybreak.

---

221 lords] *Ard²*; heads *QF*; host *Oxf¹ (Kinnear)*   222 head] *QF*; heart *Oxf*   226–7] *Malone; one line, QF*
228 bid] *Q*; on *F*   229–30] *F; one line, Q*   231 god in office,] *F, subst.* (God in office*)*; god, in office *Q*

Which is the high and mighty Agamemnon?

AGAMEMNON [*to the Greeks*]

This Trojan scorns us, or the men of Troy

Are ceremonious courtiers.

AENEAS

Courtiers as free, as debonair, unarmed,                    235

As bending angels – that's their fame in peace.

But when they would seem soldiers, they have galls,

Good arms, strong joints, true swords, and – Jove's

   accord –

Nothing so full of heart. But peace, Aeneas,

Peace, Trojan; lay thy finger on thy lips!                    240

The worthiness of praise distains his worth

If that the praised himself bring the praise forth.

But what the repining enemy commends,

That breath Fame blows; that praise, sole pure,

   transcends.

AGAMEMNON

Sir, you of Troy, call you yourself Aeneas?                    245

---

235 **free** generous, noble
   **debonair** gracious in manner (Fr. *de bonne aire*). Shakespeare's only use.
236 **bending** bowing in courteous reverence
   **fame** reputation
237 **galls** i.e. 'spirit to resent injury or insult' (*OED sb.*¹ 3b). See 193 and n.
238 **Jove's accord** Jove being in full accord, God willing
239 **Nothing . . . heart** of unequalled courage
240 **Trojan** Modern spelling misses something of the import of QF's 'Troyan', meaning 'inhabitant of Troy', and is ambiguous as to whether the *j* is a vowel equivalent of *i* (*i/y*) or

a consonant (*i/j*).
   **lay . . . lips** shut up, stop talking
241–4 'Worthy praise sullies its own worth if the subject of praise speaks in his own behalf; but Fame itself trumpets the report when an enemy grudgingly admits excellence. Praise of that sort, unmixed with unworthy motives, is transcendent and pure.' *Repining* means 'mortified by defeat'. The sentiment is proverbial, as is the gesture of laying one's fingers on one's lips in 240; see Dent, F239, M476 and P547, and *Proverbs*, 27.2.
245 *****Sir, you** For textual choices, see LN.

233 SD] *Oxf*  233 Trojan] *QF* (*Troyan*); + *240, 255, 273, 338 and generally throughout play; also 'Troian'*  236 fame] *F*; fame *Q*, *but with an* f *that looks as though it were an* ∫ *in some copies; it is faintly but clearly identifiable as an* f *in the Huntington quarto*  238 Jove's] *F*; great *Ioues / Q*  241 worth] *Q, subst.* (worth,); worth: *F*  242 that the] *Q*; that he *F*  244 Fame] *F*; fame *Q*  245 Sir, you] *F*; Sir you *Q*

AENEAS   Ay, Greek, that is my name.

AGAMEMNON   What's your affair, I pray you?

AENEAS

Sir, pardon, 'tis for Agamemnon's ears.

AGAMEMNON

He hears naught privately that comes from Troy.

AENEAS

Nor I from Troy come not to whisper him.                    250

I bring a trumpet to awake his ear,

To set his sense on the attentive bent,

And then to speak.

AGAMEMNON                  Speak frankly as the wind;

It is not Agamemnon's sleeping hour.

That thou shalt know, Trojan, he is awake,                  255

He tells thee so himself.

AENEAS                        Trumpet, blow loud!

Send thy brass voice through all these lazy tents;

And every Greek of mettle, let him know

What Troy means fairly shall be spoke aloud.

                                        *The trumpet sounds.*

We have, great Agamemnon, here in Troy                      260

A prince called Hector – Priam is his father –

---

246 **Greek** The implications of 'cunning or wily person' and 'one who cheats at cards' (*OED sb.* 4) that hover about this term (cf. Cressida's reference to Helen as 'a merry Greek indeed' at 1.2.105, *OED sb.* 5) are perhaps excused, in Aeneas' view, by his having been addressed as 'Sir, you of Troy'; see LN 245. The language of both men is close to belligerence.

250 *\*whisper often transitive, as here. This F reading, omitting the 'with' of Q, may be authorial. On the double negative, *Nor . . . not*, see Abbott, 406. The metre recommends full stress on *him*.

251, 263, 277 **trumpet** trumpeter

252 'to rouse him to attention' (Ard¹)

253 **frankly** freely

258 **mettle** spirit, courage; substance. The Q and F spellings, 'mettell' and 'mettle', suggest the commonly combined sense of 'metal' and 'mettle', as in 22. *Brass* in 257 anticipates the sense of metal.

259.1 *\*F's word order may reflect authorial revision, but the plural in F (see t.n.) is probably a simple misreading. Aeneas addresses a single trumpeter in 256–9.

---

247 affair] *F; affaires Q*   249] *Q; F lines* priuatly / Troy. /   250 whisper] *F; whisper with Q*
252 sense on the] *F; seat on that Q*   256 loud] *F; alowd Q*   259.1] *Capell, subst.; Sound trumpet. Q; The Trumpets sound. F*

Who in this dull and long-continued truce
Is resty grown. He bade me take a trumpet,
And to this purpose speak: 'Kings, princes, lords,
If there be one among the fair'st of Greece            265
That holds his honour higher than his ease,
That seeks his praise more than he fears his peril,
That knows his valour and knows not his fear,
That loves his mistress more than in confession
With truant vows to her own lips he loves,             270
And dare avow her beauty and her worth
In other arms than hers; to him this challenge:
Hector, in view of Trojans and of Greeks,
Shall make it good, or do his best to do it,
He hath a lady, wiser, fairer, truer,                  275
Than ever Greek did compass in his arms;
And will tomorrow with his trumpet call,
Midway between your tents and walls of Troy,

262 **long-continued truce** The inconsistency between this characterization and the reports of fighting in 1.2.33ff. (see also 2.3.223 and 256, 3.1.142–3, 4.1.13 and notes), not likely to be noticed in the theatre, is the result of Shakespeare's having compressed his source accounts in Caxton and Lydgate. See Stříbrný, 107.

263 ***resty** restive; sluggish, indolent (*OED a.*[1] 1, 2). F's 'rusty' is intelligible but could easily be a scribal or compositorial sophistication of the more unusual word in Q, one that provides a better incentive for action in this present context.

265 **fair'st** noblest as warriors

269–70 'who shows his love for his beloved more in deeds of arms than in the idle vows he confesses or professes to her, paying lip service'. (*Truant* suggests neglect of duty, both to the mistress and to war.)

272 **In . . . hers** 'in the arms of warfare rather than in the arms of the woman he loves'

275–6 Aeneas uses the language of the tiltyard and of medieval romance. Cam[1] points to examples in Chambers, *Lee*, 269, and in Thomas Lodge's *Euphues' Shadow: The Battle of the Senses* (1592), vol. 2, sig. E1, p. 33.

276 ***compass** encompass, embrace. Q's 'couple' makes fine sense, and carries the added meaning of 'link heraldically in his coat of arms' (see Cam[1], citing *OED* coupled *ppl.a.* 1), but the F reading may be an authorial choice in revision.

277 **trumpet** See 251n.

262 this] *F;* his *Q*   263 resty] *Q (restie);* rusty *F*   264–83] *inverted commas, Oxf[1]*   265 among] *Q;* among'st *F*   267 That seeks] *F;* And feeds *Q*   276 compass] *F;* couple *Q*

To rouse a Grecian that is true in love.
If any come, Hector shall honour him;                    280
If none, he'll say in Troy when he retires,
The Grecian dames are sunburnt, and not worth
The splinter of a lance.' Even so much.

AGAMEMNON

This shall be told our lovers, Lord Aeneas.
If none of them have soul in such a kind,              285
We left them all at home; but we are soldiers,
And may that soldier a mere recreant prove
That means not, hath not, or is not in love.
If then one is, or hath, or means to be,
That one meets Hector; if none else, I'll be he.       290

NESTOR [*to Aeneas*]

Tell him of Nestor, one that was a man
When Hector's grandsire sucked. He is old now;
But if there be not in our Grecian mould
One noble man that hath one spark of fire
To answer for his love, tell him from me,              295
I'll hide my silver beard in a gold beaver
And in my vambrace put this withered brawn;

---

279 **rouse** with erotic potential, as in 272,
   carried forward to 'The splinter of a
   lance',   283;   see   G.   Williams,
   *Dictionary*, 'lance', 780–2
280 **honour him** i.e. do him the honour
   of taking up his challenge
281 **retires** leaves the field, returns to Troy
282 **sunburnt** Sun-darkened complexion
   was reckoned unbeautiful by Elizabethan standards. See 1.1.39 and 53–4
   and notes.
283 **Even so much** a formulaic close, signifying: 'This concludes my message'
285 **soul . . . kind** 'a spirit ready to take
   up the challenge' (Ard¹)
286 **We left** i.e. 'you may say that we left'
   (Ard¹)

287 **mere recreant** utter coward
288 **means not, hath not** means not to
   be, has not been. (The next line is similarly elliptical.)
293 ***in our Grecian mould** 'from our
   Grecian land, made out of the earth of
   our native Greece and out of our mortal condition and bodily form' (*OED
   sb.*¹ 4–6). For textual choices, see LN.
296 **beaver** lower portion of the face-
   guard of a helmet (*OED*). Cf. next note
   and 174n. for terms used in medieval
   warfare.
297 **vambrace** 'avant-bras. A vambrace;
   armour for the arm' (Cotgrave). F's
   'Vantbrace' is a variant form.
   **brawn** muscle, i.e. arm

---

289 hath, or means] *F*; hath a meanes *Q*   291 SD] *Oxf*   293 mould] *F*; hoste *Q*   294 One . . . one]
*F*; A . . . no *Q*   297 vambrace] *Q*; Vantbrace *F*   this withered brawn] *F*; my withered braunes *Q*

And, meeting him, will tell him that my lady
Was fairer than his grandam and as chaste
As may be in the world. His youth in flood, 300
I'll prove this truth with my three drops of blood.

AENEAS

Now heavens forfend such scarcity of youth!

ULYSSES   Amen.

AGAMEMNON

Fair Lord Aeneas, let me touch your hand;
To our pavilion shall I lead you first. 305
Achilles shall have word of this intent;
So shall each lord of Greece, from tent to tent.
Yourself shall feast with us before you go
And find the welcome of a noble foe.

[*As all are leaving, Ulysses detains Nestor.*]

ULYSSES   Nestor! 310

NESTOR   What says Ulysses?

ULYSSES

I have a young conception in my brain;
Be you my time to bring it to some shape.

NESTOR   What is't?

ULYSSES   This 'tis: 315

299 **Was** Nestor will defend the honour
of some lady of long ago rather than
allow the Greeks to suffer humiliation.

300–1 ***His . . . blood** 'Even if Hector is
in the prime of youth, I'll stake what
little blood I have to prove true my
boast of my lady's chaste beauty.' F's
'pawne' is possible but requires an
elliptical reading.

300 **in flood** being at the full (an absolute
construction with implied participle;
Abbott, 381)

302 ***forfend** Proudfoot conjectures that

the fullness of the line of type in F
may have tempted the compositor to
substitute 'forbid' for the slightly
longer *forfend*. *Forfend* is also attractive
as the more difficult reading, though
F's 'forbid' is common in Shakespeare
and could be authorial.
***youth** Q's 'men' is acceptable, but the
F reading is plausibly authorial.

313 **my time** my period of gestation. Old
Nestor is to play the part of Time in
bringing Ulysses' conception to maturity (Rolfe).

298 will tell] *F; tell Q*   301 prove] *Q; pawne F*   truth] *F;* troth *Q*   302 forfend] *Q;* forbid *F*
youth] *F;* men *Q*   303] *F; at start of 304, Q*   304 SP] *F; not in Q*   304] *Pope; F lines Aeneas, / hand: /*
305 first] *F;* sir *Q*   309.1] *F, subst. (Exeunt. Manet Vlysses, and Nestor); not in Q*   315 This 'tis] *F;*
*not in Q*

Blunt wedges rive hard knots; the seeded pride
That hath to this maturity blown up
In rank Achilles must or now be cropped
Or, shedding, breed a nursery of like evil
To overbulk us all.                                              320
NESTOR   Well, and how?
ULYSSES
This challenge that the gallant Hector sends,
However it is spread in general name,
Relates in purpose only to Achilles.
NESTOR
The purpose is perspicuous even as substance     325
Whose grossness little characters sum up;
And in the publication make no strain
But that Achilles, were his brain as barren
As banks of Libya – though, Apollo knows,
'Tis dry enough – will with great speed of judgement,   330

316 **Blunt . . . knots** a proverbial idea found in Erasmus's *Adagia*, 2.70F (chil. 1, cent. 2, prov. 5), *Malo nodo malus quaerendus cuneus*, though *blunt* seems unexpected; proverbially, knotty wood requires sharp wedges of iron (Dent, P289). Ulysses' point may be that Achilles' insolence must be stopped by whatever means, and that hard knots will blunt even wedges of steel. *Rive* = split. **seeded** planted (in Achilles) and allowed to grow, but now gone to seed, threatening an explosive new growth of pride
317 **blown up** sprouted to full growth, puffed up, erupted (suggesting also 'swarming with larvae, fly-blown')
318 **rank** haughty; overripe, too luxuriant; swollen; festering (*OED a., adv.* 1, 5, 6, 14). The adjective is applied to Thersites at 73.
**or now** either now
319 **shedding** scattering seed

**nursery** plot of ground used to nurture young plants, a school; also a crop of offspring; and continuing the metaphor of midwifery from 312–13
320 **overbulk** outgrow, tower over
325–6 **perspicuous . . . up** 'as plain as a large amount expressed in little numbers'. (Nestor expresses through metaphor the idea that the character of an enterprise is revealed in small details.)
326 **grossness** massive size; obviousness
327 'and in the public announcement will leave no doubt'; or, *And . . . / But that* (327–8) may mean 'and, when this is publicly announced, you may be sure that'. *Make* may ambiguously represent (1) a present indicative verb, 'makes', whose subject is *purpose*; (2) an imperative addressed to Ulysses.
329 **banks of Libya** sandbanks or shores of the Libyan desert
330 **dry** barren

325 The] *F;* True the *Q*   even as] *F;* as *Q*   328 Achilles, were] *F; Achilles* weare *Q*

Ay, with celerity, find Hector's purpose
Pointing on him.
ULYSSES     And wake him to the answer, think you?
NESTOR
Yes, 'tis most meet. Who may you else oppose,
That can from Hector bring his honour off,                    335
If not Achilles? Though't be a sportful combat,
Yet in this trial much opinion dwells;
For here the Trojans taste our dear'st repute
With their fin'st palate. And trust to me, Ulysses,
Our imputation shall be oddly poised                         340
In this wild action; for the success,
Although particular, shall give a scantling
Of good or bad unto the general,
And in such indexes, although small pricks

---

333 **wake . . . answer** rouse him out of
his lethargy to respond to the challenge
334 ***Yes** Q's 'Why' is plausibly emphatic,
but the alteration is most easily
explained as authorial.
   **meet** fitting (that we adopt this course
of action)
   **else oppose** otherwise put forward as
an opponent
335 **from . . . off** acquit himself honourably in opposing Hector
336 **a sportful combat** a combat not
pursued 'to the edge of all extremity'
(4.5.69)
337 **opinion dwells** reputation is at stake
338–9 **taste . . . palate** 'put our reputation to its most severe test, sample
our reputation at its most precious, as
in tasting food with their most refined
palate'
340 'our reputation will be unequally balanced', i.e. will be subjected to no ordinary risk
341 ***wild** rash. Q's 'vilde' is also possible
in the sense of 'paltry, trivial', and F's

'wilde' could be interpreted as 'willed'.
The F reading in any case is plausibly
authorial.
   **success** outcome
342 **particular** specific (to Achilles)
   **scantling** measure or sample of a person's quality or ability (*OED sb.* 2c);
small specimen, sample (*OED* 6).
Nestor's point is that a victory in this
contest will be seen as a promise of
success for the Greeks generally.
Shakespeare's only use of the term.
343 **the general** (1) the army in general;
(2) the public, the general view
344 **indexes** table of contents; pointers;
signs, tokens (*OED sb.* 1, 2, 4b, 5). The
more usual modern spelling is
'indices', but *indexes* is still current and
is perhaps intentionally echoed in
*pricks* in the same line.
344–5 **small . . . volumes** small markers
in comparison with the volume that
follows. *Pricks* are small marks or ticks.
An erotic *double entendre* seems to run
through the sentence, from *small pricks*
to *baby figure* and *at large*, responding

---

331–2] F; one line, Q   334 Yes] F; Why Q   335 his honour] F; those honours Q   337 this] F;
the Q   341 wild] F; vilde Q

To their subsequent volumes, there is seen          345
The baby figure of the giant mass
Of things to come at large. It is supposed
He that meets Hector issues from our choice;
And choice, being mutual act of all our souls,
Makes merit her election and doth boil,             350
As 'twere from forth us all, a man distilled
Out of our virtues; who miscarrying,
What heart from hence receives the conqu'ring part,
To steel a strong opinion to themselves!
Which entertained, limbs are his instruments,       355
In no less working than are swords and bows
Directive by the limbs.
ULYSSES     Give pardon to my speech:
Therefore 'tis meet Achilles meet not Hector.
Let us, like merchants, show our foulest wares,     360
And think perchance they'll sell; if not,
The lustre of the better yet to show
Shall show the better. Do not consent

perhaps to Ulysses' earlier suggestion
that Nestor serve as the midwife to
Ulysses' *young conception* (312).
*Subsequent*, used only this once in
Shakespeare, is accented on the second
syllable.
350 **election** basis of choice – a definition not in *OED*, but seemingly
required by context. The Greeks will
exercise their preference by choosing
to promote merit.
352–4 *****who miscarrying . . . themselves!** 'and if our champion
should fail, what cheer will the
conquering side (i.e. the Trojans)
feel in this, to strengthen their good
opinion of themselves!' For textual

choices, see LN.
355–7 *****i.e. 'To entertain such a good
opinion of oneself is to arm oneself
with the strength of self-esteem and
high morale, much as our swords and
bows derive their efficacy from the
management that our limbs provide'.
*His* in 355 means 'its', referring to
'opinion'; *Directive* in 357 means
'capable of being directed'; it is used
only this once by Shakespeare (Rolfe).
For textual choices, see LN.
362 *****'the lustre of the better goods which
yet remain to be shown'. Lines 358–63
are substantively different in Q and F
(see t.n.), apparently representing two
authorial versions.

353 from hence receives the] *F; receiues from hence a Q*   355–7] *F; not in Q*   355 his] *F2; in his F;*
e'en his *Oxf*   358–63] *F; Q lines* meete, / Marchants / sell; / exceed, / consent, /   360 show our
foulest wares] *F;* First shew foule wares *Q*   362–3 yet . . . better.] *F;* shall exceed, / By shewing the
worse first: *Q*

That ever Hector and Achilles meet,
For both our honour and our shame in this                     365
Are dogged with two strange followers.

NESTOR

I see them not with my old eyes. What are they?

ULYSSES

What glory our Achilles shares from Hector,
Were he not proud, we all should wear with him.
But he already is too insolent;                               370
And we were better parch in Afric sun
Than in the pride and salt scorn of his eyes
Should he scape Hector fair. If he were foiled,
Why then we did our main opinion crush
In taint of our best man. No, make a lott'ry,                 375
And by device let blockish Ajax draw
The sort to fight with Hector; among ourselves
Give him allowance as the worthier man,
For that will physic the great Myrmidon,
Who broils in loud applause, and make him fall               380

---

366 **two strange followers** i.e. one dishonourable result if Achilles loses and
another if he wins; a lose/lose situation
368 **shares from** gains at the expense of
(*OED v.*² 4d, citing this passage);
shears away from (*OED v.*¹). In the
theatre and in Elizabethan speech,
*shares* and 'shears' would sound alike.
369 ***wear** Q's 'share' could involve a pun
with the word *shares* in 368, as Ard²
argues, but the image of wearing
Hector's honour as a badge of victory
seems like authorial choice.
371 **Afric** African
372 **salt** bitter, stinging (*OED a.*¹ 4, 5)
373 **scape** escape
  **fair** prosperously, successfully
  **foiled** defeated

374 **we . . . crush** we would destroy the
mainstay of our reputation. *Main* suggests 'mighty, of highest consequence,
chief, pertaining to all'.
375 **In taint** in the disgrace
377 **sort** lot, to be used in the *lott'ry* of
375. A lottery occurs in the *Iliad*,
3.315–16 (LCL, 1.140–1).
378 **allowance** praise, acnowledgement
379 **physic** dose with a purgative, or
bleeding, to cleanse the body of an
excess humour
  **Myrmidon** According to the *Iliad*,
2.684 (LCL, 1.100–1), Achilles led to
the siege of Troy a band of warlike
Myrmidons from Thessaly. Zeus had
created them out of ants or *murmekes*.
380 **broils** basks, warms himself
  **fall** let fall, bow down

365–6] *F; prose, Q*   369 wear] *F;* share *Q*   371 we] *F;* it *Q*   374 did] *F;* do *Q*   378 as the worthier]
*F;* for the better *Q*

His crest that prouder than blue Iris bends.
If the dull brainless Ajax come safe off,
We'll dress him up in voices; if he fail,
Yet go we under our opinion still
That we have better men. But, hit or miss,                385
Our project's life this shape of sense assumes:
Ajax employed plucks down Achilles' plumes.

NESTOR

Now, Ulysses, I begin to relish thy advice,
And I will give a taste of it forthwith
To Agamemnon. Go we to him straight.                     390
Two curs shall tame each other; pride alone
Must tar the mastiffs on, as 'twere their bone.     *Exeunt.*

**[2.1]** *Enter* THERSITES, *[followed by]* AJAX. [*Ajax is having trouble getting the attention of Thersites, who is no doubt pretending not to hear.*]

AJAX    Thersites!

THERSITES    Agamemnon — how if he had boils, full, all

---

381 **crest** plumes on helmet, or the helmet itself
   **Iris** Juno's messenger, the rainbow; and the blue flower
   **bends** arches. Ulysses' purgative medicine will cause Achilles to bow down the plumed crest that now arches and waves more proudly than the rainbow. *Bends* thus ironically continues the metaphor of *fall* in 380.
383 **dress . . . voices** attire him in our applause, 'in a manner appropriate to . . . a part which one aspires to play' (*OED* dress *v.* 7d; Ard²)
384 'we can still continue to maintain our opinion'

385 **hit or miss** i.e. whether Ajax win or lose (Dent, H475)
386 'the success of our project comes down to this'
388 \*Now . . . **advice** Var '73's emendation (see t.n.) is attractive. Shakespeare makes frequent use of the licence of the extrametrical vocative, as in the first line of this present scene, and an inversion of 'Now, Ulysses' for 'Ulysses, now' would be an easy misreading.
390 **straight** straightaway, at once
391 **Two . . . other** proverbial (Tilley, C918)
392 **tar** incite, provoke (*OED* tar, tarre *v.²* 1)
2.1 Location: see LN.

388] *QF; Ulysses, now I relish thy advice Pope;* Now I begin to relish thy advice *Capell;* Ulysses, / Now I begin to relish thy advice *Var '73*    389 of it] *F;* thereof *Q*    392 tar] *F (*tarre*);* arre *Q*    their] *F;* a *Q*    2.1] *Rowe, subst.*    0.1–3] *this edn; Enter Aiax and Thersites QF*

over, generally?

AJAX　Thersites!

THERSITES　And those boils did run (say so), did not the　　5
general run, then? Were not that a botchy core?

AJAX　Dog!

THERSITES　Then there would come some matter from
him. I see none now.

AJAX　Thou bitch-wolf's son, canst thou not hear? Feel, then.　10
*Strikes him.*

THERSITES　The plague of Greece upon thee, thou
mongrel beef-witted lord!

AJAX　Speak, then, thou vinewed'st leaven, speak. I will
beat thee into handsomeness.

THERSITES　I shall sooner rail thee into wit and holiness;　15

---

3　**generally** anticipating a pun on *general* in 6. Agamemnon is a general who should rule, but 'the general is a mob' (Empson, *Pastoral*, 39).

5–6　**And . . . then?** 'Let's say these boils were to run, would not Agamemnon run, then?' *The general* may also punningly suggest 'the whole army'; see 3n. *Run* plays on two senses: (1) ooze like a running sore; (2) run from the battle. QF's *And* can mean 'and', or 'an', 'if'.

6　**botchy core** (1) tumour with a central hard core (a 'botch' is a tumour); (2) badly patched up heart or body (lacking courage)

8　**matter** (1) good sense; (2) pus

11　**The plague of Greece** Apollo strikes the Greek forces with plague in Bk 1 of the *Iliad*. Lydgate too reports plague (3.4876–83), and Caxton (610), but Thersites' curse may simply reflect his view that the Greeks are plagued in all they do.

12　**mongrel** See notes on LIST OF ROLES (AJAX), LN 2.2.77, and 4.5.84 and 121–2, for Shakespeare's assumption

that Ajax' parents were the Greek Telamon and Hesione, sister of King Priam of Troy.

**beef-witted** beef-brained, thick-witted, stupid (*OED* beef *sb.* 5), and perhaps referring also to the notion that a diet of beef dulls the wits, as in *H5* 3.7.149–52 and *TN* 1.3.84–5. A proverbial idea; Dent, B215.1.

13　***vinewed'st leaven** mouldiest substance added to dough to cause fermentation, often a batch of the old dough added to new dough for this purpose, as in sour dough. Ajax accuses Thersites of being one who spreads contamination. See LN.

14　**handsomeness** decency, graciousness; pleasantness of appearance (*OED* 2–4). Part of Ajax' oxymoron is that beating cannot make Thersites look any worse than he normally does.

15　**rail . . . holiness** bring you into a condition of intelligence and piety by abusing you with jests (*OED* rail *v.*[4] 3). Cf. *MV* 4.1.139: 'Till thou canst rail the seal from off my bond'.

---

6　then] *Q; not in F*　8　there] *F; not in Q*　10.1] *F; not in Q*　13　thou] *Q; you F*　vinewed'st] *Knight;* vnsalted *Q;* whinid'st *F;* unwinnow'd'st *Theobald;* windyest *Warburton;* vinew'd *Johnson;* unsifted *Oxf*

but I think thy horse will sooner con an oration than
thou learn a prayer without book. Thou canst strike,
canst thou? A red murrain o'thy jade's tricks!

AJAX    Toadstool, learn me the proclamation.

THERSITES    Dost thou think I have no sense, thou strik'st        20
me thus?

AJAX    The proclamation!

THERSITES    Thou art proclaimed a fool, I think.

AJAX    Do not, porcupine, do not. My fingers itch.

THERSITES    I would thou didst itch from head to foot. An        25
I had the scratching of thee, I would make thee the
loathsomest scab in Greece. When thou art forth in the

---

16 **con** memorize

17 **without book** by heart (Dent, B532)

18 **A red murrain** a plague. *Red* is
'applied to various diseases marked by
evacuation of blood or cutaneous
eruptions' (*OED* 16b, cited by Var).
Cf. *Tem* 1.2.367: 'The red plague rid
you', and *Cor* 4.1.13: 'the red pestilence' (Rolfe).
**jade's tricks** ill-tempered behaviour
of a worthless horse, or of a woman. A
proverbial comparison (Dent, J29.1).

19 **Toadstool** poisonous mushroom; suggesting also the stool or excrement of a
toad (Oxf[1])
**learn me** ascertain for me (Ard[1]), or
tell me. On *me*, see 1.3.165 and 170 and
notes.

20 **sense** faculty of sensation; perhaps
with a suggestion also of 'perception,
intelligence', since the conversation
hinges to such an extent on *beef-witted*,
*matter* and the like

22 **The proclamation!** Ajax' iteration of
this phrase (see 19, 29) is like Othello's
'the handkerchief!' in *Oth* 3.4.92–8.

24 **porcupine** a small, ungainly, prickly

animal that, like Thersites, is able to
afflict its attackers with scratches and
itchings 'from head to foot' (25). In
Bk 5, Satire 3 of Joseph Hall's
*Virgidemiarum*, 1598 (1–2), the porcupine is the emblem of Satire, shooting
'sharp quills out in each angry line'
(Ard[2], citing Harold Brooks). QF's
'Porpentin' and 'Porpentine' are common spelling variants, always used by
Shakespeare.
**My fingers itch** i.e. 'I am itching to
give you a good thrashing'. A commonplace expression (Dent, F237), as
is 'from head to foot' in 25 (Dent,
T436, 436.1). Cf. *RJ* 3.5.164.

25 **An** if

27 **scab** (1) crust forming over a wound;
(2) 'scurvy' fellow, scoundrel (*OED sb*.
3, 4)

27–8 *When . . . another Conceivably
Shakespeare meant to cut these lines,
as suggested by their absence from F,
or they may have been cut in production, but an error in transmission
could also account for the omission.
The sentence might seem a *non*

---

16 oration] *F;* oration without booke *Q*    17 learn a] *F;* learne *Q*    18 o'thy] *F3;* ath thy *Q;* o'th thy
*F*    19 Toadstool] *Q (*Tode-stoole*);* Toads stoole *F*    20 strik'st] *F;* strikest *Q*    23 a fool] *F;* foole *Q*
24 porcupine] *QF (*Porpentin, Porpentine*)*    25 foot. An] *Sisson, subst. (anon. in Cam);* foote, and
*QF, subst.*    26 thee, I] *F;* the, I *Q*    27 loathsomest] *Q (*lothsomest*);* lothsom'st *F*    27–8 When . . .
another] *Q; not in F*

incursions, thou strikest as slow as another.

AJAX    I say, the proclamation!

THERSITES    Thou grumblest and railest every hour on    30
Achilles, and thou art as full of envy at his greatness as
Cerberus is at Proserpina's beauty, ay, that thou bark'st
at him.

AJAX    Mistress Thersites!

THERSITES    Thou shouldst strike him –    35

AJAX    Cobloaf!

THERSITES    He would pun thee into shivers with his fist,
as a sailor breaks a biscuit.

AJAX [*Beats him*]    You whoreson cur!

THERSITES    Do, do.    40

AJAX    Thou stool for a witch!

THERSITES    Ay, do, do! Thou sodden-witted lord, thou

---

*sequitur* in this particular speech of
Thersites, but it picks up on Ajax'
striking of Thersites at 10 and on the
subsequent banter about beatings.
28 **incursions** sudden attacks (on the
Trojans)
32 **Cerberus** the monstrous many-
headed dog guarding the entrance to
Hades. Snarling dogs are emblematic
of envy and railing, such as might well
be directed at the beautiful *Proserpina*
(32), Queen of Hades. Baldwin, Var,
has found an erudite tradition recorded in Natale Conti's *Mythologiae* (204)
that all who wished to wed Proserpina
had to do battle with Cerberus, who,
perhaps out of envy, tore them apart.
34 Ajax' jeering insult suggests effeminacy, shrewishness and pusillanimity.
35 **Thou shouldst** if you were to. But
perhaps Shakespeare wrote 'Shouldst
thou' (see t.n.); an easy verbal transpo-
sition.
36 **Cobloaf** small roundish or lumpy loaf

(*OED* cob *sb.*¹ 7), 'a little loaf made
with a round head' (Minsheu, 79, cited
by Malone, Var '21)
37 **pun** pound (dialectical)
   **shivers** fragments, splinters
38 **as . . . biscuit** Biscuits would become
extremely dry and brittle over a period
of time at sea. Jacques compares
Touchstone's exceedingly dry brain to
'the remainder biscuit / After a voyage' (*AYL* 2.7.39–40).
39 **whoreson** lit., 'bastard'; used as a general term of contempt and abuse, here
adjectivally
40 i.e. go ahead, I dare you; or, go on with
your jokes (cf. Trinculo in *Tem*
4.1.240)
41 *****stool** (1) privy; (2) low, contemptible
thing; cf. *Toadstool*, in 19. See LN.
42 **sodden-witted** rendered dull and stupid, 'soaked', intoxicated. (On *sodden*
as a strong participle of 'seethe', boil,
see 3.1.40n.)

---

35 Thou shouldst] *QF;* Shouldst thou *(Nares in Cam)*    36 AJAX Cobloaf!] *F; Aiax Coblofe, / Q,
printed as continuation of 35*    37, 39, 40 SP] *F; not in Q*    39, 51 SD] *Rowe, subst.*

hast no more brain than I have in mine elbows; an
asinico may tutor thee. Thou scurvy-valiant ass, thou
art here but to thrash Trojans, and thou art bought and     45
sold among those of any wit, like a barbarian slave. If
thou use to beat me, I will begin at thy heel and tell
what thou art by inches, thou thing of no bowels, thou!

AJAX    You dog!

THERSITES    You scurvy lord!     50

AJAX [*Beats him*]    You cur!

THERSITES    Mars his idiot! Do, rudeness, do, camel; do, do!

*Enter* ACHILLES *and* PATROCLUS.

ACHILLES
Why, how now, Ajax, wherefore do ye thus? –
How now, Thersites, what's the matter, man?

THERSITES    You see him there, do you?     55

ACHILLES    Ay, what's the matter?

44 *asinico little ass, fool, dolt. From Sp.
*asnico*, a little ass (*asno* = ass). *TxC*
proposes that Shakespeare intended to
reproduce the Spanish word, and that
the text should read 'asnico'.
**scurvy-valiant** being valiant in a contemptible manner and a shabby cause
(*OED* scurvy *a*. 2)
45 *thrash The variant spellings of
'thrash' in Q and 'thresh' in F may or
may not point to intended semantic
difference, but in any event suggest
wordplay on (1) beat severely and (2)
harvest, as in the grim reaping of war.
Cf. 5.5.24–6 and notes, where Hector
is described as a mower with a scythe.
45–6 **bought and sold** i.e. sold down the
river, treated like merchandise,
exploited (Dent, B787)
46 **barbarian** foreign, non-Greek; barbarous. Cf. *Oth* 1.3.358 and *Cor*
3.1.243.

47 **use** continue, make it a practice
**tell** count, itemize, catalogue; declare
48 **by inches** methodically, inch by inch
**bowels** sensitivity, human feeling; but
Thersites also uses the word ironically,
calling attention to Ajax' girth and
beefy build (see 1.2.21, 2.3.2, 3.3.127
and 140, 4.5.137), and to the linking of
his name to the 'jakes' or privy, as at 62
52 **Mars his** Mars' (Abbott, 217)
**camel** perhaps a riposte to *porcupine*
and *Cobloaf*, 24 and 36 above. Camels
can also be regarded as misshapen and
lumpy beasts of burden, of ungainly
proportions and with small brains for
their huge bodies. Cf. 1.2.240.
55–64 Thersites' comic insistence that
Achilles carefully scrutinize Ajax
resembles Pompey's urging that
Escalus mark well the face of Master
Froth in *MM* 2.1.148–60.

43 hast no] *QF;* hast in thy skull no *Oxf*    brain] *QF;* brain in thy head *(Capell)*    44 Thou] *F;* you
*Q*    45 thrash] *Q;* thresh *F*    52.1] *F; not in Q*    53 ye thus] *Q;* you this *F*

185

THERSITES   Nay, look upon him.

ACHILLES   So I do. What's the matter?

THERSITES   Nay, but regard him well.

ACHILLES   Well, why, I do so.                                    60

THERSITES   But yet you look not well upon him; for, whosomever you take him to be, he is Ajax.

ACHILLES   I know that, fool.

THERSITES   Ay, but that fool knows not himself.

AJAX   Therefore I beat thee.                                     65

THERSITES   Lo, lo, lo, lo, what modicums of wit he utters! His evasions have ears thus long. I have bobbed his brain more than he has beat my bones. I will buy nine sparrows for a penny, and his pia mater is not worth the ninth part of a sparrow. This lord, Achilles – Ajax, who   70 wears his wit in his belly and his guts in his head – I'll tell you what I say of him.

ACHILLES   What?

60 **Well** (1) all right, okay; (2) 'Well?', repeating Thersites' word in 59

62 **whosomever** whomsoever; a common variant form in Shakespeare. See Abbott, 274, on vagaries in the inflection of 'who' and 'whom'.
   **Ajax** probably with a pun on *a jakes*, a latrine, reflecting English pronunciation of classical names in the period

64 Thersites responds as though Achilles had said, 'I know that fool' in 63. *Nosce teipsum*, know thyself, was a commonplace wisdom in Renaissance culture derived from the ancient Greeks (Dent, K175).

65 Ajax replies, in effect, 'If I had known myself better, if I had not forgotten myself, I would not have beaten you'. This attempt at wit in giving 'know thyself' a new definition meets with Thersites' sarcasm, 'Lo, lo', etc. (66ff.).

66 **modicums** small amounts. Shakespeare's only use of the term,

here italic in Q and F as though a foreign term, like *pia mater* at 69.

67 **His . . . long** His evasions have ears as long as those of an ass; i.e. his dodgings and sallies of attempted wit are asinine. (The actor gestures.)
   **bobbed** pummelled

68–9 **nine . . . penny** The price for a sparrow here is halfway between that of Matthew, 10.29: 'Are not two sparrows sold for a farthing?' (i.e. a quarter of one penny), and Luke, 12.6: 'Are not five sparrows bought for two farthings?' (Baldwin).

69 **pia mater** brain (lit. a delicate membrane enveloping the brain and spinal cord)

70–1 **who . . . head** The phrase, *Quorum cerebrum est in ventre, ingenium in patinis*, 'whose brain is in his belly, whose inclinations are in the stewpan', occurs in Robert Burton's 'Democritus Junior to the Reader', *The Anatomy of Melancholy*, 1.53, citing Cornelius Agrippa.

60 I do so] *F*; so I do *Q*   62 whomsoever] *QF (who some euer)*   66 modicums] *QF (modicums)*
68 I] *F*; It *Q*   69 pia mater] *Q (pia mater); Piameter F*   71 I'll] *F*; I *Q*

THERSITES   I say, this Ajax –

[*Ajax threatens to beat him; Achilles intervenes.*]

ACHILLES   Nay, good Ajax.                                                    75

THERSITES   Has not so much wit –

ACHILLES   [*to Ajax*]   Nay, I must hold you.

THERSITES   As will stop the eye of Helen's needle, for
    whom he comes to fight.

ACHILLES   Peace, fool!                                                        80

THERSITES   I would have peace and quietness, but the
    fool will not – he there, that he. Look you there.

AJAX   O thou damned cur, I shall –

ACHILLES   [*to Ajax*]   Will you set your wit to a fool's?

THERSITES   No, I warrant you, for a fool's will shame it.    85

PATROCLUS   Good words, Thersites.

ACHILLES   What's the quarrel?

AJAX   I bade the vile owl go learn me the tenor of the
    proclamation, and he rails upon me.

THERSITES   I serve thee not.                                                 90

AJAX   Well, go to, go to.

THERSITES   I serve here voluntary.

ACHILLES   Your last service was sufferance, 'twas not

---

78  **stop** stop up, fill, as in the biblical image
of the eye of a needle (Matthew, 19.24;
cf. *R2* 5.5.17); probably also with bawdy
suggestion, given Helen's loose reputation. Ard[2] cites Mistress Quickly's complaint in *H5* 2.1.32–5: 'we cannot lodge
and board a dozen or fourteen gentle-
women that live honestly by the prick of
their needles, but it will be thought we
keep a bawdy-house straight'. See G.
Williams, *Dictionary*, 'needle', 943–4.

84  proverbial: 'Do not set your wit against
a fool's' (Dent, W547), derived from
Proverbs, 26.4: 'Answer not a fool
according to his foolishness, lest thou
also be like him' (Baldwin, Var)

86  **Good words** i.e. speak reasonably,

restrain your speech. From Terence's
*Andria*, 204 (LCL, 1.22–3): *Bona
verba, quaeso*, a familiar schoolboy text
(Baldwin, *Small Latine*, 1.747–8). Cf.
*MW* 1.1.114–15: '*Pauca verba*'.

87  Cf. Prologue 10: 'and that's the quarrel'.

88  **owl** 'applied to a person in allusion to
. . . repugnance to light, to appearance
of gravity and wisdom (often with
implication of underlying stupidity),
etc. Hence = wiseacre, solemn dullard'
(*OED sb.* 2).

93  **Your . . . sufferance** 'The beating you
just underwent was pure suffering,
something you had to endure'; with a
pun on *sufferance* (1) suffering; (2)
barely tolerated compulsion

---

74.1] *Rowe, subst., at 73*   77, 84 SD] *Oxf*   85 for a] *F; the Q*   88 the vile owl] *Q; thee vile Owle, F*
tenor] *Q; tenure F*   93 sufferance] *F; suffrance Q*

voluntary; no man is beaten voluntary. Ajax was here
the voluntary, and you as under an impress. 95

THERSITES  E'en so. A great deal of your wit, too, lies in
your sinews, or else there be liars. Hector shall have a
great catch an 'a knock out either of your brains. 'A
were as good crack a fusty nut with no kernel.

ACHILLES  What, with me too, Thersites? 100

THERSITES  There's Ulysses and old Nestor – whose wit
was mouldy ere your grandsires had nails on their toes
– yoke you like draught-oxen and make you plough up
the war.

ACHILLES  What? What? 105

THERSITES  Yes, good sooth. To, Achilles! To, Ajax, to!

AJAX  I shall cut out your tongue.

THERSITES  'Tis no matter. I shall speak as much as thou
afterwards.

PATROCLUS  No more words, Thersites. Peace! 110

THERSITES  I will hold my peace when Achilles' brach
bids me, shall I?

---

94–5 **Ajax . . . impress** 'Ajax was the vol-
unteer, you were conscripted.' (A pun
on *impress* suggests also that Thersites
was stamped on, marked, subjected to
the imprint of blows; *OED* impress *sb.*[1]
1 and 2.) *Voluntary* means 'voluntarily'.
96 **E'en so** exactly
**your wit** emphatic: you too, Achilles
97 **or . . . liars** unless report is a liar
97–8 **Hector . . . brains** said ironically:
Hector won't find much to repay his
efforts if he knocks out the brains of
Achilles or Ajax.
98 ***an 'a** if he. (F's changing of the more
colloquial 'and a' to 'if he' could well
be a sophistication of transmission; see
pp. 424–5.)
98–9 **'A were as good** he might as well

99 **fusty** mouldy
103 **draught-oxen** animals used for
pulling a cart or plough
106 **To . . . to** Thersites imitates drivers
urging on their teams of oxen.
108 ***much** For textual choices, see LN.
111 ***brach** i.e. bitch hound, fawning
hanger-on; prostitute, catamite. QF's
'brooch', in the sense of 'jewel, ornament, bauble, plaything', is possible,
since jewels appear in a pejorative context in Shakespeare (see *AW* 1.1.158,
*R2* 5.5.66 and *KL* 1.1.272), but the
reading seems more strained, and is
easily explained as an error in transmission if the compositor or copyist
read 'broch'.

---

98 an 'a knock out] *Kittredge;* and knocke at *Q;* if he knocke out *F*   98–9 'A were] *Q (*a were*);* he
were *F*   102 your] *Theobald;* their *QF*   on their toes] *F; not in Q*   104 war] *F;* wars *Q*   108 much]
*QF;* much wit *Capell*   110 Peace!] *Q; not in F*   111 brach] *Rowe;* brooch *QF*

ACHILLES    There's for you, Patroclus.

THERSITES    I will see you hanged like clotpolls ere I come
    any more to your tents. I will keep where there is wit          115
    stirring and leave the faction of fools.                    *Exit.*

PATROCLUS    A good riddance.

ACHILLES [*to Ajax*]

    Marry, this, sir, is proclaimed through all our host:
    That Hector, by the fifth hour of the sun,
    Will with a trumpet 'twixt our tents and Troy          120
    Tomorrow morning call some knight to arms
    That hath a stomach, and such a one that dare
    Maintain – I know not what; 'tis trash. Farewell.

AJAX    Farewell. Who shall answer him?

ACHILLES

    I know not. 'Tis put to lottery. Otherwise          125
    He knew his man.

AJAX    O, meaning you? I will go learn more of it.          *Exeunt.*

113 i.e. 'Thersites got you that time,
Patroclus', or, 'That's what you get for
trying to interfere'.
114 **clotpolls** blockheads. *OED* lists
'clodpoll' and 'clotpoll' as separate
entries with similar meanings. A 'clod'
is a lump of clay or earth; a 'clot' is a
congealed mass or lump. 'Poll' means
'head'.
115–16 **I will . . . fools** Thersites echoes
biblical passages about wise men and
fools (see Proverbs, 13.20, and
Ecclesiastes, 9.16–17, cited by Carter,
384) in a mocking tone of sancti-
monious superiority.
115 **keep** dwell, live
118 **Marry** lit. 'by the Virgin Mary'; a
mild oath

119 *\*fifth hour* eleven o'clock. Cf.
3.3.296–7, where Thersites, mimick-
ing Ajax, declares that 'by eleven
o'clock it will go one way or other',
thus confirming the F reading and
suggesting that Q may be in error (see
t.n.).
122 **stomach** (1) appetite (for fighting);
(2) courage. Cf. *H5* 4.3.35–6: 'he
which hath no stomach to this fight, /
Let him depart'.
124 **answer him** accept the challenge;
oppose him
126 **knew** would know
127 SD *Exeunt* Probably Achilles and
Patroclus have already started to leave,
so that Ajax' last speech is spoken not
to Achilles but in scornful apostrophe.

114 clotpolls] *QF (Clatpoles,* Clotpoles*)*    118 SD] *Oxf*    119 fifth] *F (*fift*);* first *Q*    123 Maintain
– I] *Hanmer;* Maintaine I *QF*    127 SD] *Pope; Exit. F; not in Q*

**[2.2]**               *Enter* PRIAM, HECTOR, TROILUS,
                        PARIS *and* HELENUS.

PRIAM

After so many hours, lives, speeches spent,
Thus once again says Nestor from the Greeks:
'Deliver Helen, and all damage else –
As honour, loss of time, travail, expense,
Wounds, friends, and what else dear that is consumed          5
In hot digestion of this cormorant war –
Shall be struck off'. Hector, what say you to't?

HECTOR

Though no man lesser fears the Greeks than I
As far as toucheth my particular,
Yet, dread Priam,                                             10
There is no lady of more softer bowels,
More spongy to suck in the sense of fear,
More ready to cry out 'Who knows what follows?'
Than Hector is. The wound of peace is surety,

---

**2.2** Location: Troy. The palace.

3 **Deliver** release; hand over (*OED v.*[1] 1, 8)

4 **travail** exertion, hardship; with a suggestion also that the Greeks have come a long distance. The QF spellings ('trauell', 'trauaile') catch the multiple meaning. Cf. 1.1.67.

5 **dear** cherished, esteemed; precious, valuable, costly

6 **cormorant** a large and voracious seabird; hence, 'insatiably greedy'

7 **struck off** cancelled, as by a stroke of a pen (*OED* strike *v.* 82a)

9 *****toucheth** F's 'touches' is suspect as a possible sophistication; it might also be an attempt to make 9–10 read as a single line of verse, as printed in QF.
**particular** personal concern (*OED*

B.6)

11 **more softer bowels** Shakespeare often uses the double comparative (Abbott, 11), as at 5.2.156 and 5.6.21. The *bowels* are the abdomen, considered as the seat of pity and compassion, as at 2.1.48; cf. 1 John, 3.17 (A.V.), 'bowels of compassion', and elsewhere in the Bible.

12 **fear** i.e. fear for the general safety of Troy

14–15 **The wound . . . secure** 'The greatest threat to peace is the overconfidence and feeling of safety it breeds.' Cf. Dent, W152: 'He that is secure is not safe'. *Secure* here means 'free from apprehension, careless, overconfident' (*OED, a.* 1).

---

2.2] *Rowe, subst.* 3–7] *inverted commas, Capell, subst.* 3 damage] *F;* domage *Q* 4 travail] *F* *(*trauaile*);* trauell *Q* 7 struck] *QF (*stroke*)* 9 toucheth] *Q;* touches *F* 9–10] *Collier; one line, QF; Capell lines* yet, / Priam 13] *inverted commas, Pope, subst.* 14–15 surety, / Surety] *F;* surely / Surely *Q*

Surety secure; but modest doubt is called                    15
The beacon of the wise, the tent that searches
To th' bottom of the worst. Let Helen go.
Since the first sword was drawn about this question,
Every tithe soul 'mongst many thousand dismes
Hath been as dear as Helen – I mean, of ours.                    20
If we have lost so many tenths of ours
To guard a thing not ours, nor worth to us
(Had it our name) the value of one ten,
What merit's in that reason which denies
The yielding of her up?
TROILUS                         Fie, fie, my brother!                    25
Weigh you the worth and honour of a king
So great as our dread father in a scale
Of common ounces? Will you with counters sum
The past-proportion of his infinite
And buckle in a waist most fathomless                    30
With spans and inches so diminutive

15 **modest doubt** prudent caution
16 **tent** surgical probe, roll of absorbent
material for cleaning a wound
17 **Let Helen go** See LN.
19 'every human life exacted by the war as
a tithe – and there have been many
thousand such exactions'. '*Dismes*
(Decimae) is made of the French
*Decimes*, and signifieth *tithe*, or the
tenth part of . . . our labour due unto
God' (Minsheu, 148, cited in Var).
21 **tenths** i.e. lives thus claimed by war.
Hector does not mean literally to mul-
tiply one-tenth by many thousands.
23 **Had . . . name** even if Helen were
Trojan
**one ten** one tenth, one Trojan life, one
tithe exacted by the war
24 **reason** reasoning, argument
26–8 **Weigh . . . ounces?** i.e. 'Are the
worth and honour of the Trojan king,

and his cause in this war, to be weighed
in a scale designed for petty exchanges
involving small units?'
28–9 **with counters . . . infinite** 'use
coin-shaped tokens of no intrinsic
value to sum up the immeasurable
value of his infinite worth'. *Counters*
are used in performing arithmetical
calculations. *Past-proportion of his infinite* means 'that greatness to which no
measure bears any proportion'
(Johnson).
30 **waist** In the theatre, the sense of
'waste' is plainly audible, though contrary to Troilus' meaning.
**fathomless** i.e. immeasurable; lit. too
deep to measure
31 **spans** measures of nine inches or so,
spanning the hand from thumb to little
finger; a short space

17 worst. Let] *F;* worst let *Q*    27 father] *F;* fathers *Q*    29 past-proportion] *Johnson, Var '73;* past
proportion *QF*    30 waist] *QF (*waste*)*

As fears and reasons? Fie, for godly shame!
HELENUS
   No marvel though you bite so sharp at reasons,
   You are so empty of them. Should not our father
   Bear the great sway of his affairs with reason,                    35
   Because your speech hath none that tell him so?
TROILUS
   You are for dreams and slumbers, brother priest;
   You fur your gloves with reason. Here are your
      reasons:
   You know an enemy intends you harm;
   You know a sword employed is perilous,                             40
   And reason flies the object of all harm.
   Who marvels, then, when Helenus beholds
   A Grecian and his sword, if he do set
   The very wings of reason to his heels,
   And fly like chidden Mercury from Jove,                            45

---

33 **reasons** Helenus mocks Troilus' *reasons*
   (32) by punning on 'raisins', similarly
   pronounced, thus giving bite to the culinary image of biting and being *empty*;
   see next note. Cf. *AYL* 2.7.98–100, and
   *1H4* 2.4.237: 'If reasons were as plentiful as blackberries', etc.
34 **empty** (1) empty-headed; (2) hungry;
   (3) unfurnished (see previous note)
   **not our father** our father not
35 **sway . . . affairs** royal authority in dealing with issues of concern to the state
36 *\*'simply because you, in your un-
   reasonable speech, urge him to govern
   unreasonably?' Q's 'tell' implies 'you
   that tell him so'; F's 'tels' might imply
   that the subject of the verb is *speech*.
   Either is possible, but F may be an
   error or sophistication.
38 **fur . . . reason** i.e. make yourself
   warm and comfortable with arguments
   of prudence, rationalize the case for

appeasement. (*Fur* and *gloves* may be a
dig at priestly garb, which was often
trimmed and lined with fur.)
41 'and "reason" in this prudent sense
   avoids the sight of anything harmful'.
   *Object* means 'the presentation (of
   something) to the eye or perception'
   (*OED sb.* 9).
45 **chidden Mercury** The fourth Homeric
   hymn, 'The Hymn to Hermes', tells
   how Hermes ('Mercury' in the Roman
   pantheon), while still in his cradle,
   stole fifty cattle belonging to Apollo,
   for which he was arraigned before
   Zeus and ordered to restore the lost
   property (LCL, 362–405). Shakespeare
   could have known the story in Ovid,
   *Met.*, 2.685–875 (LCL, 1.108–21), and
   in Horace, *Odes*, 1.10 (LCL, 30–1;
   Ard²). More generally, as messenger of
   the gods, Mercury was subject to
   Jove's chiding and impatient bidding.

---

33 at] *F*; of *Q*   34 them. Should . . . father] *F, subst.*; them should . . . father; *Q*   35 reason] *Q*;
reasons *F*   36 tell] *Q*; tels *F*   38 reason] *QF*; Reasons *Rowe*³   45–6] *Q*; *F reverses lines*

Or like a star disorbed? Nay, if we talk of reason,
Let's shut our gates and sleep. Manhood and honour
Should have hare hearts, would they but fat their
    thoughts
With this crammed reason; reason and respect
Make livers pale and lustihood deject.                              50

HECTOR
Brother, she is not worth what she doth cost
The holding.

TROILUS                    What's aught but as 'tis valued?

HECTOR
But value dwells not in particular will;
It holds his estimate and dignity
As well wherein 'tis precious of itself                            55
As in the prizer. 'Tis mad idolatry
To make the service greater than the god;
And the will dotes that is inclinable

---

46 **disorbed** dislocated from its sphere –
the usual Elizabethan explanation of
'shooting stars'. (The metre of this
line is irregular, seemingly with six
stresses, but not even Pope has wished
to emend it.)

47 ***Let's** Q's 'Sets' might signify 'Set's',
'set we', 'let us set', but F is clearly easier, and Q's initial 'S' could well be an
anticipation of the next word.

48 **Should . . . hearts** would have the
timorous spirit of hares (Dent, H147)
**fat** fatten, feed, nourish

49 **crammed** fatted, overfed
**respect** caution, deliberation

50 ***Make livers pale** See LN.
**and lustihood deject** and cause bodily vigour to be thrown down

52 ***The holding** Q's 'the keeping' is also
attractive, and the reason for the variant reading is unclear. This edition follows F in such marginal cases.

**What's . . . valued?** proverbial (Dent,
W923). See Introduction, pp. 67ff.

53 **particular** of any one person

54 **his** its (Abbott, 217, 228)
**dignity** worth, excellence

55–6 **As well . . . As** both . . . and

55 **of itself** intrinsically

56 **in the prizer** in the opinion of the
person who prizes or appraises it

56–7 **'Tis . . . god** Cf. Matthew, 23.19:
'Ye fools and blind, whether is greater,
the offering, or the altar which sancti-
fieth the offering?' Protestant theolo-
gians regarded this biblical passage as
condemning the Catholic church for
idolatry in making the altar more
important than the offering (translated
as 'gift' in the Bishops' and Rheims
bibles and in the A.V.; Noble, 214).

58–60 ***And any will is besotted that
attaches itself in a mutually contagious
way to the object it desires without any

---

47 Let's] *F*; Sets *Q*    48 hare] *Q*; hard *F*    50 Make] *Q*; Makes *F*    51–2 Brother . . . holding.]
*Theobald; prose, Q; F lines* worth / holding. / *; Proudfoot lines* Brother, / holding. /    52 holding] *F*;
keeping *Q*    56 mad] *Q (*madde*);* made *F*    58 inclinable] *F*; attributiue *Q*

To what infectiously itself affects,
Without some image of th'affected merit.                    60
TROILUS
I take today a wife, and my election
Is led on in the conduct of my will,
My will enkindled by mine eyes and ears,
Two traded pilots 'twixt the dangerous shores
Of will and judgement. How may I avoid,                    65
Although my will distaste what it elected,
The wife I chose? There can be no evasion
To blench from this, and to stand firm by honour.
We turn not back the silks upon the merchant
When we have soiled them; nor the remainder viands        70
We do not throw in unrespective sieve
Because we now are full. It was thought meet
Paris should do some vengeance on the Greeks.

appearance of demonstrable merit in that object.' For textual choices, see LN.

61 **I . . . a wife** Troilus' hypothetical case, applied to Paris, hints at Troilus' own personal feelings about love; it could hardly be more inept here, given that Helen is wife to Menelaus.
**election** choice

62 **in the conduct of** under the supervision of

64 **traded** conversant, skilful in their trade; trafficking back and forth. Consistent with his abjuring reason (46–7), Troilus characterizes the senses, rather than reason, as mediating between will and judgement (Knight, 58–9).

65 **avoid** rid myself of (*OED v.* 5)

66 **distaste** come to dislike, have no taste for

67–8 **There . . . honour** either (1) 'There's no subterfuge that could

enable me to evade this commitment without loss of honour'; or (2) 'There can be no possible way of wavering in constancy (to my wife) while remaining constant to my honour'.

70 *soiled For textual choices, See LN.
**remainder viands** leftovers. Cf. 5.2.165–7 and Introduction, pp. 82–3.

71 **unrespective sieve** receptacle in which to throw leftover food (*the remainder viands*, 70) indiscriminately. A sieve can be any basket for market produce (*OED sb.* 3). This one is *unrespective* or undiscriminating in that it does not sift or separate as sieves in the more familiar sense normally do. The image of 'throwing' suggests vomiting (Southall, 229). Cf. *AW* 1.3.199: 'captious and intenible sieve'.

73 **vengeance** i.e. in return for the abduction of Hesione, as Troilus goes on to explain

64 shores] *F;* shore *Q* 67 chose?] *Rowe;* chose, *F;* choose, *Q* 70 soiled] *Q* (soild); spoyl'd *F*
71 sieve] *Q* (siue); same *F;* place *F2;* sink *Delius;* sewer *Oxf (Walter)*

Your breath of full consent bellied his sails;
The seas and winds, old wranglers, took a truce,                          75
And did him service; he touched the ports desired;
And for an old aunt whom the Greeks held captive
He brought a Grecian queen, whose youth and
      freshness
Wrinkles Apollo's, and makes stale the morning.
Why keep we her? The Grecians keep our aunt.                             80
Is she worth keeping? Why, she is a pearl
Whose price hath launched above a thousand ships
And turned crowned kings to merchants.
If you'll avouch 'twas wisdom Paris went –
As you must needs, for you all cried 'Go, go!';                          85
If you'll confess he brought home noble prize –
As you must needs, for you all clapped your hands
And cried 'Inestimable!' – why do you now
The issue of your proper wisdoms rate
And do a deed that never Fortune did,                                    90
Beggar the estimation which you prized
Richer than sea and land? O theft most base,
That we have stol'n what we do fear to keep!

---

74 *breath . . . consent* 'vote of consent
freely given'; or (in the Q text, which
reads 'with' in place of F's 'of'), the
phrase could mean 'encouragement
with full consent'
   *bellied* swelled, as though in pregnancy as well as in sailing. Cf. *MND*
2.1.128–9: 'to see the sails conceive /
And grow big-bellied with the wanton
wind'.
75 *old wranglers* traditional opponents
76 *touched* landed at
77 *an old aunt* Hesione, sister of Priam.
See LN.
79 'makes the handsome Apollo look old

and wrinkled by comparison, and similarly makes Eos or Aurora, rosy-
cheeked goddess of dawn, seem stale'.
*Stale* is the opposite of *freshness* in 78.
81–3 *a pearl . . . merchants* For sources,
see LN.
85 *must needs* must perforce
88–92 *why . . . land?* 'why do you now
criticize the result (or offspring) of
your own wise deliberation, and do
something that even the goddess
Fortune, in all her caprice, never did:
devalue what you claimed to prize
above all the world?' (*Estimation* means
something which one values; *OED* 1b.)

---

74 of] *F;* with *Q*    79 stale] *F;* pale *Q*    82 launched] *F; Q* (lansh't)    85] *inverted commas, Pope, subst.*
86 he] *F;* be *Q*    noble] *F;* worthy *Q*    88] *inverted commas, Hanmer, subst.*    90 never Fortune] *Q;*
Fortune neuer *F*

But thieves unworthy of a thing so stol'n,
That in their country did them that disgrace          95
We fear to warrant in our native place!

*Enter* CASSANDRA, *with her hair about her ears.*

CASSANDRA
  Cry, Trojans, cry!
PRIAM                    What noise? What shriek is this?
TROILUS
  'Tis our mad sister. I do know her voice.
CASSANDRA   Cry, Trojans!
HECTOR   It is Cassandra.                             100
CASSANDRA
  Cry, Trojans, cry! Lend me ten thousand eyes,
  And I will fill them with prophetic tears.
HECTOR   Peace, sister, peace!
CASSANDRA
  Virgins and boys, mid-age and wrinkled old,
  Soft infancy, that nothing canst but cry,          105
  Add to my clamour! Let us pay betimes
  A moiety of that mass of moan to come.

94 **But thieves** either: 'we are no better
than thieves', or 'even worse, we are
thieves'. Ard², preferring the latter,
sees Troilus as arguing *a fortiori*: it is
reprehensible to keep a stolen thing
fearfully, but still more heinous to be
fearful about justifying the theft even
to ourselves. See next note.
95–6 'we who in Sparta gave an affront
(i.e. the abduction of Helen) that we
are too craven to justify even here at
home'. See Abbott, 244, on the omission of the understood 'that' or
'which' after *disgrace*.
96.1 On placing this SD, see LN.

98 **our mad sister** When this daughter
of Priam and Hecuba resisted the
advances of Apollo, the god vitiated
the gift of prophecy he had bestowed
upon her by seeing to it that her
prophecies would never be believed.
See Aeschylus, *Agamemnon*, 1203–14
(LCL, 2.102–5).
104 **old** old persons (*OED sb.*¹ C1).
Equivalent in meaning to Q's 'elders'.
105 **that nothing canst** who can do
nothing
106 **betimes** early; in advance
107 **moiety** part

96.1] *F; Enter Cassandra rauing. Q; after 100, Theobald*   97, 99 SP CASSANDRA] *QF, subst.;*
CASSANDRA *[within] / Theobald*   97 shriek] *QF (shrike, shreeke)*   104 old] *F; elders Q; eld Collier
(conj. Theobald in Warburton correspondence)*   105 canst] *Q; can F*   106 clamour] *F; clamours Q*

Cry, Trojans, cry! Practise your eyes with tears!
Troy must not be, nor goodly Ilium stand;
Our firebrand brother Paris burns us all.                    110
Cry, Trojans, cry! A Helen and a woe!
Cry, cry! Troy burns, or else let Helen go.          *Exit.*

HECTOR

Now, youthful Troilus, do not these high strains
Of divination in our sister work
Some touches of remorse? Or is your blood ·              115
So madly hot that no discourse of reason,
Nor fear of bad success in a bad cause,
Can qualify the same?

TROILUS                        Why, brother Hector,
We may not think the justness of each act
Such and no other than th'event doth form it,           120
Nor once deject the courage of our minds
Because Cassandra's mad. Her brain-sick raptures
Cannot distaste the goodness of a quarrel
Which hath our several honours all engaged

---

108 **Practise** make use of (*OED v.* 7)
109 Cf. Virgil's *Aeneid*, 2.56: *Troiaque nunc staret, Priamque arx alta maneres*, 'and Troy might now be standing, and thou, lofty citadel of Priam, might still remain' (LCL, 1.298–9; cited by Steevens, Var '93).
110 **firebrand** When Priam's wife, Queen Hecuba, was pregnant with Paris, she dreamed that she would be delivered of a firebrand destined to burn down Troy. The infant was left to die in an exposed place but was brought up by shepherds (alluded to in Virgil, *Aeneid*, 7.319–20 and 10.704–5, LCL, 2.24–5 and 2.218–19).
113 **high strains** exalted rhapsodies
115 **remorse** (1) regret for wrongs com-

mitted; (2) hesitation, scruple; (3) compassion (*OED*, 1, 2c, 3)
116 **discourse of reason** rational argument
117 **success** outcome, as at 1.3.341; with a sense also, in *bad success*, of 'succeeding all too well'
118 **qualify** moderate
119–20 'We must not judge the justice of our proceedings solely by the way things turn out.' Cassandra's 'brain-sick raptures' (122) are no proof that the Trojan cause is wrong.
121 **deject** cast away, lower, depress
123 **distaste** render distasteful and repugnant (*OED v.* 5; first occurrence)
124 **our ... engaged** committed the honour of each of us

---

109 Ilium] *Oxf¹*; Ilion *Q;* Illion *F*   120 th'event] *Oxf¹*; euent *QF*   121–2 minds / Because Cassandra's mad.] *Pope, subst.;* mindes, / Because *Cassandra's* madde, *Q;* mindes; / Because *Cassandra's* mad, *F*

To make it gracious. For my private part,                    125
I am no more touched than all Priam's sons;
And Jove forbid there should be done amongst us
Such things as might offend the weakest spleen
To fight for and maintain.

PARIS

Else might the world convince of levity                      130
As well my undertakings as your counsels.
But I attest the gods, your full consent
Gave wings to my propension, and cut off
All fears attending on so dire a project.
For what, alas, can these my single arms?                    135
What propugnation is in one man's valour
To stand the push and enmity of those
This quarrel would excite? Yet I protest,
Were I alone to pass the difficulties
And had as ample power as I have will,                       140
Paris should ne'er retract what he hath done

125 **To . . . gracious** to make it righteous
(*OED a.* 6); to grace it, set it off (Rolfe)
126 **touched** affected; implicated. The
metre of the line is unsure. QF's
spellings ('toucht', 'touch'd') may
imply a stress on *more*; an alternative
possibility is 'I'm no more touchèd . . .'.
127–9 'and Jove forbid that any of us
should do something that would
offend the least courageous (the dullest
and coldest of heart) to fight for and
support'. (*Spleen* can connote melancholy, mirth, caprice and impetuous-
ness as well as courage.) Troilus rejects
Hector's implication that Paris has
behaved dishonourably and that they
all must therefore fear 'bad success in a
bad cause' (117).
130 **convince** convict. Shakespeare's
only use of the term in this sense, as
also with *attest* in 132.

131 **As well . . . as** both . . . and (as in
55–6)
132 **attest** call to witness
133 **propension** inclination (Shakespeare's only use, as with *propend* at
190)
135 'For what, alas, can these arms of
mine (i.e. both limbs and weapons)
accomplish alone?' The excessive
reliance of this speech on abstract gen-
eralities is symptomatic of a kind of
insincerity manifested also by Angelo
and by Bertram in the final scenes of
*AW* and *MM*, where they are wrig-
gling to escape exposure.
136 **propugnation** defence, protection
(Shakespeare's only use)
137 **stand the push** withstand the attack
139 **pass** experience, undergo
141 Paris grandly speaks of himself in the
third person.

139 the] *QF;* these *Cam (anon.)*

Nor faint in the pursuit.
PRIAM                                 Paris, you speak
Like one besotted on your sweet delights.
You have the honey still, but these the gall;
So to be valiant is no praise at all.                          145
PARIS
Sir, I propose not merely to myself
The pleasures such a beauty brings with it;
But I would have the soil of her fair rape
Wiped off in honourable keeping her.
What treason were it to the ransacked queen,                   150
Disgrace to your great worths, and shame to me,
Now to deliver her possession up
On terms of base compulsion! Can it be
That so degenerate a strain as this
Should once set footing in your generous bosoms?              155
There's not the meanest spirit on our party
Without a heart to dare, or sword to draw,
When Helen is defended, nor none so noble
Whose life were ill bestowed, or death unfamed,
Where Helen is the subject. Then, I say,                      160

---

142 **faint** flag, lose heart
144 proverbial; cf. Dent, H551.1 and 561, Tilley, H556
145 **So** thus, under these circumstances
   **praise** merit, value, virtue (*OED sb.* 3)
146 **propose** put forward for considera-tion, call before the eye of the mind (Schmidt)
148 **soil** stain
   **her fair rape** the abduction of her in all her beauty (transferred epithet); perhaps also with the oxymoronic sug-gestion that Paris' abduction of Helen was 'fair', honest
149 **honourable keeping her** either 'honourably keeping her' (Abbott, 1), or, 'the honourable keeping of her'. The latter balances grammatically with *fair rape* (148).

150 **ransacked** carried off as plunder (*OED* ransack *v.* 4b)
152 **her possession** possession of her
153 **base** ignoble, dishonourable
154 **strain** 'admixture in a character of some quality somewhat contrasting with the rest' (*OED sb.*[1] 8b); laboured thought; tenor, drift, impulse (*OED sb.*[2] 8c and 14)
155 **generous** noble
156–7 **There's . . . dare** 'not even the most ignobly born soul on our Trojan side lacks the heart to be daring'
158–60 **nor . . . subject** 'nor is there any Trojan nobleman whose life would be unworthily given, or whose death would not be celebrated eternally, where Helen is the occasion of arms'

Well may we fight for her whom, we know well,
The world's large spaces cannot parallel.

HECTOR

Paris and Troilus, you have both said well
And on the cause and question now in hand
Have glozed – but superficially, not much                    165
Unlike young men, whom Aristotle thought
Unfit to hear moral philosophy.
The reasons you allege do more conduce
To the hot passion of distempered blood
Than to make up a free determination                         170
'Twixt right and wrong; for pleasure and revenge
Have ears more deaf than adders to the voice
Of any true decision. Nature craves
All dues be rendered to their owners. Now,
What nearer debt in all humanity                             175
Than wife is to the husband? If this law
Of nature be corrupted through affection,
And that great minds, of partial indulgence
To their benumbed wills, resist the same,
There is a law in each well-ordered nation                   180
To curb those raging appetites that are

---

162 **The . . . spaces** all the world
165 **glozed** commented, glossed, spe-
ciously expounded
166–7 **Aristotle . . . philosophy** For the
intellectual background, see LN.
168 **conduce** lead, tend
169 **distempered blood** one of the four
bodily humours, disordered through
excess (or deficiency), leading to a diseased condition of body and mind,
especially anger or 'hot passion' (*OED*
blood *sb*. 5)
170 **free determination** unbiased
judgement
172 Cf. Psalms, 58.4: 'Their poison is
even like the poison of a serpent: like
the deaf adder that stoppeth his ear',

and Dent, A32.
174 Cf. the proverbial wisdom: 'Give
everyone his due' (Dent, D634), and
Romans, 13.7: 'Give to all men therefore their duty . . . custom to whom
custom'.
177 **affection** passion, appetite
178 **And that** and if; so that (Abbott,
285)
**of partial indulgence** out of self-
interested overlenience. *Indulgence*
may carry here the Roman Catholic
sense of 'remission of the punishment
which is still due to sin after sacramental absolution' (Ard², *OED sb*. 3).
179 **benumbed** benumbèd; morally
paralysed

Most disobedient and refractory.
If Helen then be wife to Sparta's king,
As it is known she is, these moral laws
Of nature and of nations speak aloud                         185
To have her back returned. Thus to persist
In doing wrong extenuates not wrong,
But makes it much more heavy. Hector's opinion
Is this in way of truth; yet, ne'ertheless,
My sprightly brethren, I propend to you                      190
In resolution to keep Helen still;
For 'tis a cause that hath no mean dependence
Upon our joint and several dignities.

TROILUS

Why, there you touched the life of our design!
Were it not glory that we more affected                      195
Than the performance of our heaving spleens,
I would not wish a drop of Trojan blood
Spent more in her defence. But, worthy Hector,
She is a theme of honour and renown,
A spur to valiant and magnanimous deeds,                     200

---

182 **refractory** obstinate (*OED* 1b's first citation), with a moral and spiritual stubbornness harking back to *indulgence* and *benumbed mills*

184–5 **laws . . . nations** i.e. divine or 'natural' law and man-made law; the latter was thought to be derived from the higher law of God. See R. Hooker, *Ecclesiastical Polity*, Bk I, chaps 3–10 (pp. 63–110), and Aristotle, *Nicomachean Ethics*, 5.7.1–7 (LCL, 294–7; Ard²).

188 **heavy** serious

189 **truth** abstract principle, absolute truth

190 **sprightly** full of spirit, animated
**propend** incline, am disposed (*OED* 2's first citation in this sense, and Shakespeare's only use)

191 **still** (1) notwithstanding (reinforcing

'yet, ne'ertheless' in 189); (2) in continuation of the present state of affairs; (3) always, never to give her up. The weight of Hector's determination among these competing scenarios is left unstated.

192–3 **that hath . . . dignities** 'that depends to no small degree upon our collective and individual honours – and in turn has consequences for our honours'. *Dependence* can suggest a relation or connection in this wide sense (*OED* depend *v.* 2b).

195–6 **more . . . spleens** 'aspired to more than the working out of our aroused anger and spite'. On *spleens*, see 127–9n.

199 **theme** cause of or for specific action; matter, subject (*OED sb.* 1b)

182 refractory] *QF* (refracturie)    185 nations] *Q;* Nation *F*

Whose present courage may beat down our foes
And fame in time to come canonize us.
For I presume brave Hector would not lose
So rich advantage of a promised glory
As smiles upon the forehead of this action          205
For the wide world's revenue.
HECTOR                                   I am yours,
You valiant offspring of great Priamus.
I have a roisting challenge sent amongst
The dull and factious nobles of the Greeks
Will strike amazement to their drowsy spirits.       210
I was advertised their great general slept,
Whilst emulation in the army crept.
This, I presume, will wake him.                  *Exeunt.*

201–2 'the bold and ready spirit of which will enable us to defeat our foes today, and the fame of which may come in time to enshrine us in the roster of famous heroes'. Helen's cause is a spur that will goad the Trojans to fight bravely. *Whose* may also suggest that, in Troilus' view, Helen herself embodies some of these attributes of bold spirit and everlasting renown. The beautiful woman inspires men to fight bravely and honourably. *Present* courage is paired antithetically with fame *in time to come*; *present* also suggests 'at hand'. (*Canonize* is accented on the second syllable.)

205 **smiles . . . forehead** 'looks auspiciously upon the forefront or beginning'; and with a more pictorial suggestion of a halo or crown of laurels planted upon the imagined forehead of 'this action'

206 **revenue** revènue

208 **roisting** boisterous, vaunting, clamorous. Shakespeare's only use.

210 **Will** that will. Hector presumably has not heard back yet from Aeneas' embassy in 1.3. He does appear, however, to have dispatched Aeneas with his personal challenge before the present debate began, thus having resolved to continue fighting the Greeks.
  *strike Q's 'shrike' is entirely plausible in the sense of 'shriek', and F's 'strike' could then be a sophistication, but the idiom *strike amazement* is well attested and could represent here the correction of an easy error in Q.

211 **advertised** (accented on second syllable) informed
  **their great general** either Agamemnon, seen here as inattentive to discipline, or Achilles

212 **emulation** ambitious rivalry for power or honours, factious contention, envy or disparagement of one's superiors (*OED* 2, 3). Cf. 1.3.134, 'pale and bloodless emulation', 3.3.157 and 4.5.124.

203 lose] *QF (*loose*)    210 strike] *F*; shrike *Q*

**[2.3]**                    *Enter* THERSITES, *alone.*

THERSITES  How now, Thersites? What, lost in the
labyrinth of thy fury? Shall the elephant Ajax carry it
thus? He beats me, and I rail at him. O worthy
satisfaction! Would it were otherwise – that I could beat
him whilst he railed at me. 'Sfoot, I'll learn to conjure and          5
raise devils but I'll see some issue of my spiteful
execrations. Then there's Achilles – a rare engineer! If
Troy be not taken till these two undermine it, the walls will
stand till they fall of themselves. O thou great thunder-
darter of Olympus, forget that thou art Jove, the king of          10
gods; and Mercury, lose all the serpentine craft of thy
caduceus, if ye take not that little, little, less than little wit
from them that they have! – which short-armed ignorance
itself knows is so abundant scarce it will not in
circumvention deliver a fly from a spider without drawing          15
their massy irons and cutting the web. After this, the

**2.3** Location: the Greek camp. Before
Achilles' tent, as in 2.1.

2  **elephant** 'i.e. thick skinned and clumsy' (Oxf[1]). Cf. 1.2.21, where Alexander
describes Ajax as 'slow as the elephant'
(Ard[2]).
   **carry it** carry off the honours, have
the better of it

3  **rail at** abuse verbally, revile, scold. See
2.1.15.

5  **'Sfoot** by His (God's) foot. A common
oath.

6  **but I'll see** i.e. 'if it takes doing that to
see'; 'or whatever it takes to see';
'rather than not see'
   **issue** result

7  **execrations** curses
   **engineer** one who digs countermines
or tunnels underneath the enemy's
battlements; deviser, plotter

11–12  **the serpentine . . . caduceus** 'the

magical power of your wand, twined
about with two serpents'. Thersites
mockingly suggests that if Jove and
Mercury (god of thievery) cannot pun-
ish Ajax and Achilles by depriving them
of the little intelligence they possess,
then the gods have little power indeed.

13  **short-armed** finding everything
beyond its grasp. Ignorance itself can
see what is stupid about Ajax and
Achilles.

14  **abundant scarce** an oxymoron: Ajax'
and Achilles' scarcity of intelligence is
to be seen on all sides. On adjectives
used as adverbs, see Abbott, 1.

15  **circumvention** craft, artifice, outwit-
ting. Thersites lampoons Ajax' and
Achilles' stratagem against the enemy as
overreaching itself by the mindless use of
brute force, like using *massy irons* (16) or
hefty swords to cut a mere spider's web.

**2.3**] *Capell, subst.*   0.1 *alone*] *QF (solus)*   1 SP] *Hanmer; not in QF*   11 lose] *QF (*loose*)*   12 ye]
*Q;* thou *F*   16 their] *Q;* the *F*

vengeance on the whole camp! Or rather, the Neapolitan
bone-ache! For that, methinks, is the curse dependent on
those that war for a placket. I have said my prayers, and
devil Envy say 'Amen'. – What ho! My Lord Achilles!                    20

*Enter* PATROCLUS [*at the entrance of Achilles' tent*].

PATROCLUS   Who's there? Thersites? Good Thersites,
    come in and rail.                          [*Patroclus disappears briefly.*]
THERSITES   If I could ha' remembered a gilt counterfeit,
    thou wouldst not have slipped out of my contemplation;
    but it is no matter. Thyself upon thyself! The common       25
    curse of mankind, folly and ignorance, be thine in great
    revenue! Heaven bless thee from a tutor, and discipline
    come not near thee! Let thy blood be thy direction till
    thy death; then if she that lays thee out says thou art a
    fair corpse, I'll be sworn and sworn upon't she never       30

17–18 ***Neapolitan bone-ache** syphilis
or other venereal disease. F's omission
of Q's 'Neapolitan' lessens the venereal specificity, and could be an oversight of transmission.
18 **dependent on** hanging over; appertaining to (*OED* dependent *a.* 1, 2b)
19 **a placket** a petticoat, or slit at the top
of a petticoat, and hence, indecently, a
woman's vagina and the woman herself
(G. Williams, *Dictionary*, 1048–51)
22 SD  Patroclus need not exit in the usual
sense; he is understood to be in
Achilles' tent, perhaps visible at the
entrance from time to time. He hears
enough of Thersites' mutterings to ask
what 'Amen' is all about; see 32–5.
23 **ha'** have (Q: 'a'). See t.n. and essay on
text, pp. 424–5.
    **gilt counterfeit** counterfeit coin
(often called a 'slip'; hence the quibble

on *slipped* in 24)
25 **Thyself upon thyself!** Professing
that he simply forgot to include
Patroclus in his cursing of Ajax and
Achilles because Patroclus is such a
sham and easily overlooked, Thersites
now wishes on Patroclus the worst
curse imaginable: may Patroclus simply be the fool that he is!
26–7 **in great revenue** in plentiful
amounts (as Patroclus' inheritance)
27 **bless thee from** protect you from (so
as to preserve your native folly and
ignorance). *OED* bless *v.*[1] 3.
    **discipline** instruction (*OED*, 1)
28 **Let . . . direction** may you be gov-
erned by your passions
29 **lays thee out** prepares your body for
burial (*OED* lay *v.*[1] 56b)
30 **fair** sound, not diseased (*OED a.* and
*sb.*[2] 7)

17 Neapolitan] *Q; not in F*   18 dependent] *F; depending Q*   20] *inverted commas, Hanmer, subst.*
20.1 *Enter* PATROCLUS] *F; not in Q; Patr.* [*within*] / *Cam*[1] *(anon. in Cam)   at . . . tent*] *Oxf, subst.*
22 SD] *this edn; Exit / Oxf*   23 ha'] *Q (a); haue F*   gilt] *QF (guilt)*   24 wouldst] *F; couldst Q*
29 art] *F; art not Q*   30 corpse] *QF (course, coarse)*

shrouded any but lazars.

[PATROCLUS *reappears.*]

Amen. – Where's Achilles?

PATROCLUS   What, art thou devout? Wast thou in prayer?

THERSITES   Ay. The heavens hear me!

PATROCLUS   Amen.                                              35

*Enter* ACHILLES.

ACHILLES   Who's there?

PATROCLUS   Thersites, my lord.

ACHILLES   Where? Where? O, where? – Art thou come?
    Why, my cheese, my digestion, why hast thou not served
    thyself in to my table so many meals? Come, what's       40
    Agamemnon?

THERSITES   Thy commander, Achilles. Then tell me,
    Patroclus, what's Achilles?

PATROCLUS   Thy lord, Thersites. Then tell me, I pray
    thee, what's thyself?                                     45

THERSITES   Thy knower, Patroclus. Then tell me,
    Patroclus, what art thou?

PATROCLUS   Thou mayst tell that knowest.

ACHILLES   O, tell, tell.

THERSITES   I'll decline the whole question. Agamemnon       50
    commands Achilles, Achilles is my lord, I am Patroclus'
    knower, and Patroclus is a fool.

---

31 **shrouded** wrapped in a winding sheet
   **lazars** lepers
39 **cheese** thought to be an aid to digestion
40 **so many meals** for so many meals, in
   so long a time (Abbott, 202)
50 **decline** go through the various

permutations of (as when declining or
inflecting the grammatical forms of a
noun). What Thersites in fact does is
more like a comic syllogism, somewhat
in the spirit of Feste's undertaking to
'catechize' Olivia in order to 'prove'
her a fool (*TN* 1.5.54–69).

31.1] *this edn;* Enter PATROCLUS *Cam¹ (anon. in Cam)*   33 in] *Q;* in a *F*   35] *Q; not in F*   38 O,
where?] *Q; not in F*   40 in to] *Capell;* into *QF*   45 thyself] *F; Thersites Q*   48 mayst] *F; must Q*
knowest] *Q;* know'st *F*

PATROCLUS    You rascal!

THERSITES    Peace, fool, I have not done.

ACHILLES    He is a privileged man. – Proceed, Thersites.          55

THERSITES    Agamemnon is a fool, Achilles is a fool,
Thersites is a fool, and, as aforesaid, Patroclus is a fool.

ACHILLES    Derive this. Come.

THERSITES    Agamemnon is a fool to offer to command
Achilles, Achilles is a fool to be commanded of          60
Agamemnon, Thersites is a fool to serve such a fool,
and Patroclus is a fool positive.

PATROCLUS    Why am I a fool?

THERSITES    Make that demand to the creator; it suffices
me thou art. Look you, who comes here?          65

*Enter [at a distance]* AGAMEMNON, ULYSSES, NESTOR,
DIOMEDES, AJAX *and* CALCHAS.

ACHILLES    Patroclus, I'll speak with nobody. – Come in

---

53–7 *Q's omission of these lines could
have been the result of eyeskip, since
52 and 57 end in 'Patroclus is a fool'.
But Q is coherent as it stands.

55 **a privileged man** Professional fools
were allowed to speak without
restraint. A proverbial phrase (Dent,
P595.2).

58 **Derive** explain, deduce, trace the
derivation of (continuing the grammatical metaphor of *decline* in 50 and
anticipating *positive* in 62; see 62n.)

59 **offer** attempt

62 **positive** absolute, unconditional. The
rest are fools under given circumstances; Patroclus is a fool without
qualification or comparison. The word
*positive* is applied grammatically 'to
the primary form of an adjective or
adverb which expresses simple quality,

without qualification, comparison, or
relation to increase or diminution'
(*OED a.* and *sb.* 4).

63 Patroclus asks, 'What reasons can you
give for calling me a fool?', but
Thersites answers in 64–5 as though
the question were, 'What explanation
is there in the scheme of things for my
being a fool?'

64 **Make that demand to** ask that question of, pose that question to
*to the creator i.e. to Zeus. Q's 'of
the Prouer' could mean 'of anyone
who may think it necessary to prove'
(Baldwin, Var), but in the absence of
support from the *OED* for such a reading, Q remains enigmatic and perhaps
corrupt. At the same time, Q's 'of' is
arguably more idiomatic than F's 'to'.

---

53–7] *F; not in Q*    60–1 of Agamemnon] *F; not in Q*    62 Patroclus] *F; this Patroclus Q*    64 to the
creator] *F; of the Prouer Q*    65.1–2] *Q; after 63, F; after 72, Dyce¹*    65.1 *at a distance] Bevington³*
65.2 *and* CALCHAS] *QF; om. Capell*    66 Patroclus] *F; Come Patroclus Q*

with me, Thersites.                                      *Exit.*

THERSITES   Here is such patchery, such juggling and
    such knavery! All the argument is a whore and a
    cuckold; a good quarrel to draw emulous factions and     70
    bleed to death upon. Now the dry serpigo on the
    subject, and war and lechery confound all!           [*Exit.*]

AGAMEMNON [*to Patroclus*]   Where is Achilles?

PATROCLUS
    Within his tent, but ill-disposed, my lord.

AGAMEMNON
    Let it be known to him that we are here.                75
    He shent our messengers, and we lay by
    Our appertainments, visiting of him.
    Let him be told so, lest perchance he think
    We dare not move the question of our place
    Or know not what we are.                               80

PATROCLUS   I shall so say to him.                       [*Exit.*]

ULYSSES
    We saw him at the opening of his tent.

---

68 **patchery** knavery (such as one would
expect from a 'patch' or fool, and hence
a logical conclusion to Thersites' roll
call of fools); or, perhaps, bungled work
that is patched together (Schmidt)
**juggling** cheating, playing tricks.
Jugglers, like 'patches', were entertaining buffoons associated with knavery.
69–70 **All . . . cuckold** The whole war is
only about Helen and her cuckolded
husband, Menelaus. *Argument* suggests quarrel, matter of dispute,
debate, theme, subject. Cf. the speeches of Paris and Troilus at 2.2.146–62
and 194–206.
70 **draw emulous factions** bring into

conflict envious rival factions
71 **serpigo** skin eruption. 'A general term
for creeping or spreading skin diseases'
(*OED*). Here used as a curse.
71–2 **the subject** (1) the whole topic; (2)
the subject of the quarrel, Helen (Rolfe)
72 **confound** destroy, defeat; throw into
confusion
76 *****shent** insulted, disgraced. A difficult
crux. For textual choices, see LN.
77 **appertainments** appurtenances, the
gear and prerogatives appertaining to
our (my) high dignity
**visiting of** visiting (Abbott, 178)
79 **move . . . place** assert or raise the
question of our (my) authority

---

67 SD] *F; not in Q*   69–70 a whore and a cuckold] *Q;* a Cuckold and a Whore *F*   70 emulous
factions] *Q;* emulations, factions *F*   71–2 Now . . . all!] *F; not in Q*   71 serpigo] *F (*Suppeago*)*
72 SD] *Theobald*   73 SD] *Oxf*   76 shent our messengers] *Theobald;* sate our messengers *Q;* sent our
Messengers *F;* fobbed our messengers *Sisson;* faced our messengers *Oxf;* sent our messenger back
*(Proudfoot)*   77 appertainments] *F;* appertainings *Q*   78 so, lest] *Q (*so, least*);* of, so *F*   81 so say]
*F;* say so *Q*   SD] *Rowe³*

He is not sick.

AJAX   Yes, lion-sick, sick of proud heart. You may call it
melancholy, if you will favour the man, but, by my   85
head, 'tis pride. But why, why? Let him show us the
cause. – A word, my lord. [*He takes Agamemnon aside.*]

NESTOR   What moves Ajax thus to bay at him?

ULYSSES   Achilles hath inveigled his fool from him.

NESTOR   Who? Thersites?   90

ULYSSES   He.

NESTOR   Then will Ajax lack matter, if he have lost his
argument.

ULYSSES   No. You see, he is his argument that has his
argument: Achilles.   95

NESTOR   All the better; their fraction is more our wish
than their faction. But it was a strong composure a fool
could disunite.

ULYSSES   The amity that wisdom knits not, folly may
easily untie.   100

---

84 **lion-sick** a sickness of pride, appropriate to the king of beasts

86–7 ***the cause** Q's 'a cause' is defensible and amusing in suggesting that
Achilles might not be able to show *any*
cause, but F is idiomatic and plausible.

88 **bay at him** bark at Achilles, much as a
hunting hound might bark at a lion
(see *lion-sick*, 84), aggressive and yet
cowed

92 **matter** material for expression; something to say (*OED sb.*[1] 9)

92–3 **his argument** the subject of his
railing, Thersites; but Ulysses punningly replies in a way that defines *his
argument* as also meaning 'his quarrel
with Achilles'. See next note.

94–5 'No, Ajax hasn't lost his argument,
since he can now quarrel with Achilles

– the man who now has Thersites, the
subject of Ajax' railing.' An Achillean
argument is proverbially endless and
insoluble (Erasmus, *Adagia*, 2.278E,
chil. 1, cent. 7, prov. 41, as noted by
Grey, 2.240), much as this one will be.

96–8 ***their fraction . . . disunite** i.e.
'this fracture or discord between
Achilles and Ajax is more to be desired
than any faction they might form
against us. But the bond uniting them
was hardly a strong one if a mere fool
could pull it apart.' (Q's 'composure',
meaning 'combination, bond', is a
stronger and more precise reading than
F's 'counsell'; the Q reading seems
authentic, whereas the F substitution
might stem from a corrupt transmission or editorial sophistication.)

---

85 if you] *Q;* if *F*   86 'tis] *Q;* it is *F*   86–7 the cause] *F;* a cause *Q*   87 A . . . lord] *F; not in Q*   SD]
*Capell, subst.; To Agamemnon / Rowe*   95 argument:] *F2 (*argument,*); argument QF*   97 composure]
*Q;* counsell that *F*   99 knits not,] *Q;* knits, not *F*

*Enter* PATROCLUS.

Here comes Patroclus.

NESTOR    No Achilles with him.

ULYSSES

The elephant hath joints, but none for courtesy;
His legs are legs for necessity, not for flexure.

PATROCLUS

Achilles bids me say he is much sorry                              105
If anything more than your sport and pleasure
Did move your greatness, and this noble state,
To call upon him; he hopes it is no other
But for your health and your digestion sake,
An after-dinner's breath.

AGAMEMNON                          Hear you, Patroclus:            110
We are too well acquainted with these answers;
But his evasion, winged thus swift with scorn,
Cannot outfly our apprehensions.
Much attribute he hath, and much the reason
Why we ascribe it to him; yet all his virtues,             115
Not virtuously on his own part beheld,
Do in our eyes begin to lose their gloss,
Yea, like fair fruit in an unwholesome dish,
Are like to rot untasted. Go and tell him
We come to speak with him. And you shall not sin          120

---

103  See LN.
104  **flexure** kneeling as a sign of respect to a superior
107  **noble state** assemblage of nobles (*OED* state *sb.* 26)
109  **digestion sake** Shakespeare often uses the uninflected form, as in 'for fashion sake' (*AYL* 3.2.252).
110  **breath** breath of fresh air, stroll, time for breathing or exercise (*OED* 8)
113  **apprehensions** (1) arrest; (2) understanding (*OED* 4, 8)
114  **attribute** credit, reputation, honour
116  'when they are not virtuously observed or kept to by him' (*OED* behold *v.* 1)
118  **unwholesome** dirty, contaminated
119  **like** likely
120  **sin** i.e. tell a lie; or, be at fault

100.1] *F; not in Q*   102  him.] *Q;* him? *F*   104  His legs] *Q;* His legge *F*   legs for] *QF;* for *(this edn)* flexure] *Q;* flight *F*   109  digestion] *QF;* digestion's *Cam¹*   110  Hear] *F;* Heere *Q*   116  on] *Q;* of *F* 117  lose] *Q;* loose *F*   118  Yea] *Q;* Yea, and *F*   unwholesome] *Q;* vnholdsome *F*   120  come] *Q;* came *F*

If you do say we think him over-proud
And under-honest, in self-assumption greater
Than in the note of judgement; and worthier than
    himself
Here tend the savage strangeness he puts on,
Disguise the holy strength of their command,                    125
And underwrite in an observing kind
His humorous predominance – yea, watch
His pettish lunes, his ebbs, his flows, as if
The passage and whole carriage of this action
Rode on his tide. Go tell him this, and add              130
That if he overhold his price so much,
We'll none of him, but let him, like an engine
Not portable, lie under this report:
'Bring action hither; this cannot go to war'.

122 **under-honest** 'lacking in straight-forward courtesy' (Ard[1])

122–3 **in self-assumption . . . judgement** 'greater in his own estimation than in what true judgement notes of him'; or, 'more assured of himself than showing the mark of good judgement'

123–4 **worthier . . . puts on** 'worthier persons than himself here stand in attendance while he assumes a rude and barbarous aloofness'

125 'veil that authority which in all righteousness they might well assert' (Ard[1])

126–7 **And . . . predominance** 'and deferentially submit to the humour now dominant in him – i.e. blood, engendering pride – and subscribe docilely to his capricious ascendancy'. *OED* (b) notes that *predominance* in early use is frequently applied to the humours; the idea of 'dominance' has astrological implications.

128 *****pettish lunes** ill-humoured tantrums. F's 'lines' could mean 'course of

action, procedure, life, thought, or conduct' (*OED* line *sb.*[2] 27), but Hanmer's emendation supposes an easy error and introduces the strong metaphor of the tide in 128–30 (*TxC*), along with suggesting a kind of 'lunacy' that was thought to be influenced by the changes of the moon.

128–30 **as if . . . tide** 'as if the progress of events and entire carrying out of the Trojan expedition had to wait on him'. The sense depends upon a metaphor of commerce by sea: 'as if the voyage and whole conveyance from one place to another of this enterprise depended on the tide being at the flood'. *Passage* may also suggest 'channel'.

131 **overhold** overvalue, overestimate

132 **engine** machine or instrument used in warfare, such as a battering ram, catapult or cannon

133 **lie under** be subject to, at some disadvantage (*OED* lie *v.*[1] 3b)

124 tend] *Q;* tends *F*   on,] *F;* on *Q*   128 pettish lunes] *Hanmer;* pettish lines *F;* course, and time *Q*
his flows, as] *F;* and flowes, and *Q*   129 carriage of this action] *F;* streame of his commencement *Q*
134 Bring] *Q, Fc;* ring *Fu*   *inverted commas, Theobald*

A stirring dwarf we do allowance give 135
Before a sleeping giant. Tell him so.

PATROCLUS
I shall, and bring his answer presently.

AGAMEMNON
In second voice we'll not be satisfied;
We come to speak with him. – Ulysses, enter you.

*Exit Ulysses [following Patroclus].*

AJAX    What is he more than another? 140

AGAMEMNON    No more than what he thinks he is.

AJAX    Is he so much? Do you not think he thinks himself
a better man than I am?

AGAMEMNON    No question.

AJAX    Will you subscribe his thought, and say he is? 145

AGAMEMNON    No, noble Ajax. You are as strong, as
valiant, as wise, no less noble, much more gentle, and
altogether more tractable.

AJAX    Why should a man be proud? How doth pride grow?
I know not what pride is. 150

AGAMEMNON    Your mind is the clearer, Ajax, and your
virtues the fairer. He that is proud eats up himself.
Pride is his own glass, his own trumpet, his own

---

135 **stirring** active
    **allowance** approbation, praise
137 **presently** immediately
138 **In second voice** with a reply
    through a deputy (i.e. Patroclus)
139.1 Patroclus could exit as he finishes
    speaking in 137, or Agamemnon in
    138–9 may still be addressing to
    Patroclus his pointed observation that
    the Greek generals will not tolerate a
    reply sent only through Achilles'
    companion. Hence, Agamemnon dis-
    patches Ulysses to go also.
145 **subscribe** sign your name to,

endorse
147 **gentle** well bred, honourable, courte-
    ous, mild in disposition
150 *****pride** This Q reading is attractive
    for the way in which it underscores the
    joke, and is certainly authentic, where-
    as F's weaker 'it' might be the result of
    editorial tinkering.
153 **his own glass** its own mirror. Pride
    proverbially reflects its own true
    nature, blows its own trumpet (cf.
    Dent, T546), and serves as its own
    chronicle (Dent, C375.1).

137 presently.] *QF;* presently. *[Exit. / Rowe*   139 enter you] *F;* entertaine *Q*   139.1 *Exit Ulysses*] *F;*
*not in Q    following Patroclus*] *this edn; with Patroclus / Oxf; see 137n.*   150 pride] *Q;* it *F*   151 Ajax]
*F; not in Q*

chronicle; and whatever praises itself but in the deed
devours the deed in the praise.                                    155

*Enter* ULYSSES.

AJAX    I do hate a proud man as I hate the engendering of
toads.
NESTOR [*aside*]    Yet he loves himself. Is't not strange?
ULYSSES
Achilles will not to the field tomorrow.
AGAMEMNON
What's his excuse?
ULYSSES                         He doth rely on none,                160
But carries on the stream of his dispose,
Without observance or respect of any,
In will peculiar and in self-admission.
AGAMEMNON
Why, will he not, upon our fair request,
Untent his person and share the air with us?                       165
ULYSSES
Things small as nothing, for request's sake only,
He makes important. Possessed he is with greatness
And speaks not to himself but with a pride

---

154 **but in the deed** other than in performing praiseworthy deeds. Cf. the
proverb: 'A man's praise in his own
mouth does stink' (Dent, M476); cf.
also Dent, P547, and Aeneas' statement of a similar idea at 1.3.241–2.
156 **engendering** (1) copulation; (2)
spawn (Rolfe)
159 **will not to** See Abbott, 405, on the
ellipsis of verbs of motion after *will* or
*will not.*
161 'but continues the bent of his disposition'
162 **observance** notice, heed (*OED* 4)

**respect** (1) heed; (2) consideration; (3)
deferential regard (*OED sb*. 13, 14, 16)
163 'guided by his own wilfulness and self-
approbation, heeding only his own fancy'
166 **for . . . only** merely because they are
requested
167 **Possessed** i.e. as though possessed
by demons
168–9 **And . . . self-breath** 'and can
scarcely speak even to himself, or find
adequate terms to praise himself, being
almost too proud to do so'; 'speaks with
a pride that makes him blame or scorn
himself for speaking' (Hudson²)

---

156 I hate] *F*; I do hate *Q*    158 Yet] *F*; And yet *Q*    SD] *Capell, subst.*    164 Why, will] *F*; Why will
*Q*    165 the air] *F*; th'ayre *Q*

That quarrels at self-breath. Imagined worth
Holds in his blood such swoll'n and hot discourse          170
That 'twixt his mental and his active parts
Kingdomed Achilles in commotion rages
And batters down himself. What should I say?
He is so plaguy proud that the death-tokens of it
Cry 'No recovery'.

AGAMEMNON                    Let Ajax go to him. –          175
Dear lord, go you and greet him in his tent.
'Tis said he holds you well and will be led,
At your request, a little from himself.

ULYSSES
O Agamemnon, let it not be so!
We'll consecrate the steps that Ajax makes          180
When they go from Achilles. Shall the proud lord
That bastes his arrogance with his own seam
And never suffers matter of the world
Enter his thoughts, save such as doth revolve
And ruminate himself – shall he be worshipped          185

169–73 **Imagined . . . himself** For the intellectual background, see LN.
172 **Kingdomed** Achilles is like a kingdom at war with itself. For the intellectual background, see LN.
173 **batters . . . himself** as if in siege warfare, employing a battering ram against the walls
174 **death-tokens** fatal symptoms, usually the angry pustules symptomatic of the plague. *Plaguy* has thus both a literal pestilential meaning and a colloquial sense of 'confoundedly, exceedingly' (*OED* plaguy B. and plaguily). Cf. *LLL* 5.2.420–4.
177 **holds** regards
178 **from himself** i.e. away from his usual haughty behaviour
180–1 **We'll . . . Achilles** i.e. 'Let us rather venerate Ajax for having noth-

ing to do with Achilles'.
182 **seam** fat, grease. In this grotesque culinary image, Achilles' arrogance nourishes its own ardour and is basted in the hot pleasure of self-regard. Sweat was commonly thought to be fat or grease exuded by the body. Cf. 'In the rank sweat of an enseamed bed' (*Ham* 3.4.94). See 192 and n. below.
183 **suffers** allows
184 ***doth** This Q reading seems authentic, following *matter* as its subject. F's 'doe' ('do') is understandable as referring to *matter of the world* and *thoughts* as a plural idea, but could be a sophistication.
184–5 **revolve . . . himself** meditate upon and consider or concern himself (*OED* revolve *v.* 4b and ruminate *v.* 1c, citing this passage as its sole instance)

169 worth] *Q;* wroth *F*    173 down himself] *Q;* gainst it selfe *F*    175] *inverted commas, Hanmer, subst.*    184 doth] *Q;* doe *F*

213

Of that we hold an idol more than he?
No; this thrice-worthy and right valiant lord
Must not so stale his palm, nobly acquired,
Nor, by my will, assubjugate his merit,
As amply titled as Achilles' is,                                    190
By going to Achilles.
That were to enlard his fat-already pride,
And add more coals to Cancer when he burns
With entertaining great Hyperion.
This lord go to him? Jupiter forbid,                               195
And say in thunder: 'Achilles, go to him'.

NESTOR [*aside to Diomedes*]

O, this is well. He rubs the vein of him.

DIOMEDES [*aside to Nestor*]

And how his silence drinks up this applause!

AJAX

If I go to him, with my armed fist
I'll pash him o'er the face.                                       200

---

186 'by one (Ajax) whom we venerate
more than we do Achilles?'
188 *stale his palm cheapen his laurels,
lower the dignity of his nobly acquired
fame through excessive familiarity
(*OED* stale *v.*² 2b, citing this passage).
The palm leaf is a symbol of triumph.
The QF spelling, 'staule', could conceivably be a variant spelling of 'stall',
'bring to a standstill', but the idiom
seems to require *stale*. Cf. *Ham* 1.3.64:
'do not dull thy palm'.
189 **assubjugate** debase, reduce to sub-
jugation (*OED*'s earliest citation and
Shakespeare's only use)
190 *"a merit that is as dignified as is
Achilles". If *Achilles* is read without
the possessive form – QF's 'Achilles'
can signify either possessive or nominative – the line might mean: 'granted
that Achilles is rich in title also'.

192 **enlard** smear with fat, baste. The
image continues the vivid cooking
metaphor of fatty pride basting and
nourishing its own fire in 182.
193–4 'and add more fire to the heat of
summer'. The sun (*Hyperion*) enters
the zodiacal sign of *Cancer* at the beginning of summer. Adding fuel to fire is a
proverbial idea (Dent, F785); here it is
wittily applied to the image of Cancer
cooking in a hot kitchen to entertain his
guest. In some Greek mythological
accounts, the charioteer Helios (the
sun) is son of the Titans Hyperion and
Thea; in others, Hyperion is identified
directly with the sun.
197 **rubs . . . him** soothes his humour,
encourages his inclination, as if applying an ointment
199 **armed** armèd
200 **pash** smash, strike violently

188 Must] *F;* Shall *Q* stale] *Rowe;* staule *QF* 190–1] *Capell; one line, QF* 190 titled] *F;* liked *Q*
Achilles'] *QF (Achilles)* 196] *inverted commas, Hanmer, subst.* 197, 198 SD] *Capell, subst.*
198 this] *F;* his *Q* 199–200] *Rowe³; prose, QF* 200 pash] *F;* push *Q*

AGAMEMNON   O, no, you shall not go.

AJAX

An 'a be proud with me, I'll feeze his pride.

Let me go to him.

ULYSSES

Not for the worth that hangs upon our quarrel.

AJAX   A paltry, insolent fellow!                                205

NESTOR [*aside*]   How he describes himself!

AJAX   Can he not be sociable?

ULYSSES [*aside*]   The raven chides blackness.

AJAX   I'll let his humorous blood.

AGAMEMNON [*aside*]   He will be the physician that should      210
be the patient.

AJAX   An all men were o' my mind –

ULYSSES [*aside*]   Wit would be out of fashion.

AJAX   – 'a should not bear it so. 'A should eat swords first.
Shall pride carry it?                                         215

NESTOR [*aside*]   An 'twould, you'd carry half.

ULYSSES [*aside*]   'A would have ten shares.

---

202 **An 'a** if he
  **feeze** 'do for', 'settle the business of'.
  A slang expression, as in Christopher
  Sly's 'I'll feeze you', i.e. I'll fix you, get
  even with you (*TS* Induction 1).
204 i.e. 'Not for all that we have spent on
  this Trojan expedition'. *Worth* also
  suggests the honour that is at stake in
  the war. On *quarrel*, see Prologue 10,
  2.2.138 and 2.3.70.
208 proverbial; Dent, R34, and cf. 'the
  pot calls the kettle black'
209 \*i.e. 'I'll bleed him – as though he
  were a patient needing medical treatment for an excess of irascible humour'.
  F's 'humours' may simply be an
  idiomatic contraction ('humour's') of
  Q's 'humorous'; cf. QF's 'maruel's' for
  *marvellous* at 1.2.131. Or F's 'humours'

may represent a possessive singular or
plural, yielding the meaning, 'I'll let out
the blood of his humour or humours'.
214 **eat swords** 'swallow my sword, be
  stabbed'; perhaps with an attempt at
  wit by varying the proverb, 'to eat
  one's words' (Dent, W825)
215 **carry it** carry all before it, prevail.
  (But Nestor puns on the more literal
  meaning; see 216 n.)
216 'If pride would carry the day, you'd
  bear half the load of pride on your
  shoulders' (punning on *carry*, 215).
217 \***ten shares** i.e. ten tenths, all of it. Q
  assigns 217–19, '*A would . . . warm*, to
  Ajax. F's reassignment (see t.n.) is
  much more satisfactory, except that
  'He's not yet through warm' makes better
  sense given to Nestor in his next aside.

---

202–3] *Q; prose, F*   202 'a] *F (*a*);* he *Q*   206 SD] *Capell, subst. (+ 208, 210, 213, 216, 217, 219)*
209 let] *F;* tell *Q*   humorous] *Q;* humours *F;* humour's *Hudson;* humours' *Staunton*   212 o' my] *F (*a
my*);* of my *Q*   216 An 'twould] *QF (*And two'od, And 'twould*)*   217 SP] *F; Aiax Q*

AJAX    I will knead him; I'll make him supple.

NESTOR [*aside*]    He's not yet through warm. Farce him
    with praises. Pour in, pour in! His ambition is dry.                220

ULYSSES [*to Agamemnon*]
    My lord, you feed too much on this dislike.

NESTOR [*to Agamemnon*]
    Our noble general, do not do so.

DIOMEDES [*to Agamemnon*]
    You must prepare to fight without Achilles.

ULYSSES
    Why, 'tis this naming of him does him harm.
    Here is a man – but 'tis before his face;                            225
    I will be silent.

NESTOR                  Wherefore should you so?
    He is not emulous, as Achilles is.

ULYSSES
    Know the whole world, he is as valiant –

AJAX    A whoreson dog, that shall palter thus with us!

Plausibly, the F compositor followed his
corrected copy generally but misread the
point at which Nestor was to begin.

218 **knead him** i.e. 'twist him into new
shapes like dough'. Nestor jocosely
continues the culinary metaphor in his
aside comments (216–20), with *farce*
and *pour in.*

219 **through** thoroughly
    *****Farce** stuff. QF's 'Force' is an obso-
lete form (*OED* force *v.*³).

221 i.e. 'My lord, you are brooding more
than you should on Achilles' truculence;
you're letting it get to you'. The remark
might seem at first to be addressed to
Ajax, but the subsequent conversation,
addressed in 222 to 'Our noble general',
suggests that the Greek officers, who
have been laughing at Ajax behind his

back, are here setting Ajax up by seeming to plead with Agamemnon to rely on
Ajax as their best hope.

223 **to fight** i.e. in general battle with the
Trojans (see 253–6 and esp. 256n.).
Diomedes does not refer to Hector's
challenge; the matter of naming
Hector's opponent has been put to lottery. On the inconsistency between this
report of fighting and the reference to a
long-continuing truce, see 1.3.262 and n.

224 'It is this continual citing of Achilles
that causes the mischief.'

227 **emulous** envious, greedy for praise
and power (*OED* 3a, citing this line)

228 **Know . . . world** let the whole world
know

229 **that shall palter** who thinks he can
play fast and loose

218 SP] *F; not in Q*   219 SP] *Theobald; after* warm. *QF*   Farce] *QF (Force)*   220 praises] *F;*
praiers *Q*   pour in! His] *F, subst.;* poure, his *Q*   221 SD] *Capell*   222, 223 SD] *Oxf*   223 You] *F;*
Yon *Q*   224 does] *Q;* doth *F*   225–6 Here . . . silent] *F; one line, Q*   229 thus with us] *F;* with vs
thus *Q*

Would he were a Trojan!                                      230
NESTOR

What a vice were it in Ajax now –
ULYSSES

If he were proud –
DIOMEDES                    Or covetous of praise –
ULYSSES

Ay, or surly borne –
DIOMEDES                    Or strange, or self-affected.
ULYSSES [*to Ajax*]

Thank the heavens, lord, thou art of sweet composure.
Praise him that got thee, she that gave thee suck;        235
Famed be thy tutor, and thy parts of nature
Thrice-famed beyond, beyond all erudition!
But he that disciplined thine arms to fight,
Let Mars divide eternity in twain
And give him half; and for thy vigour,                     240
Bull-bearing Milo his addition yield
To sinewy Ajax! I will not praise thy wisdom,

---

233 **surly borne** bearing himself in a
surly manner
**strange** haughty, distant (*OED* 11)
**self-affected** conceited
234 **composure** temperament, constitu-
tion (*OED* 6c)
235ff. For the intellectual background,
see LN.
235 **got** begot. Q's 'gat' is a common
archaic form.
**she** her (Abbott, 211)
236–7 **thy parts . . . erudition!** i.e.
'praise be to your natural gifts, thrice-
famous beyond what your tutor taught
you, and indeed beyond all learning!'
(with an ironic subtext, not intended
to be heard by Ajax, that erudition can
have added little to his 'parts of nature'
since he is 'beyond all erudition',

where it can't reach him)
238 **disciplined . . . fight** taught you the
discipline of arms
239 **eternity** i.e. eternal fame
240 **for** as for
241 'may bull-bearing Milo yield up his
title'. See LN.
242 **sinewy** muscular
**I will not** In the rhetorical figure of
*occupatio*, 'I will not' has the effect of
meaning 'I will': 'I will praise your wisdom, etc., even though I say I won't'.
The figure further implies, 'I forbear
to, because the task is too great' (but
here with a sardonic subtext, not for
Ajax' ears: 'I won't'). Cf. Job, 41.3 on
Leviathan: 'I will not keep silence concerning his parts, nor his power, nor his
comely proportion' (cited by Cam¹).

---

234 SD] *Oxf*   235 got] *F*; gat *Q*   236 Famed] *Q*; Fame *F*   237 beyond, beyond all] *F*; beyond all
thy *Q*   238 thine] *Q*; thy *F*

Which, like a bourn, a pale, a shore, confines
Thy spacious and dilated parts. Here's Nestor,
Instructed by the antiquary times;                                      245
He must, he is, he cannot but be wise.
But pardon, father Nestor, were your days
As green as Ajax' and your brain so tempered,
You should not have the eminence of him,
But be as Ajax.

AJAX                    Shall I call you father?                        250

ULYSSES

Ay, my good son.

DIOMEDES                Be ruled by him, Lord Ajax.

ULYSSES

There is no tarrying here; the hart Achilles
Keeps thicket. Please it our great general
To call together all his state of war.
Fresh kings are come to Troy; tomorrow                                  255
We must with all our main of power stand fast.
And here's a lord – come knights from east to west,
And cull their flower, Ajax shall cope the best.

AGAMEMNON

Go we to council. Let Achilles sleep.

243–4 **Which . . . parts** 'which, like a
  boundary, a fence, a shoreline, defines
  the huge perimeter of your ample
  gifts' (but with a sardonic suggestion
  that Ajax is a man of extended girth
  and of inflated rhetoric; see Parker,
  220ff.)
245 **antiquary** ancient (*OED*, citing this
  line as its first instance in adjectival
  use; Shakespeare's only use)
248 **green** youthful, immature (*OED* 7)
  **tempered** composed, constituted
249 **have the eminence of** have eminence over (Abbott, 165)

250–1 *For textual choices, see LN.
253 **Keeps thicket** i.e. stays hidden in
  the underbrush. (A metaphor from
  hunting.)
254 **state** council
256 **main of power** full force. See notes
  at 1.3.262 and 2.3.223.
257 **from east to west** a common phrase
  meaning 'from everywhere' (Dent,
  E43.1)
258 **cull their flower** pick their flower of
  chivalry
  **cope** match, encounter with (*OED v.*² 7)

243 bourn] *F;* boord *Q*   244 Thy] *F;* This *Q*   248 Ajax'] *QF (Aiax)*   251 SP ULYSSES] *F; Nest.
Q*   253 our great] *Q;* our *F*   255 to Troy] *QF;* to Troy to-day *Hudson² (Lettsom);* today to Troy *Oxf*
258 cull] *F;* call *Q*

Light boats sail swift, though greater hulks draw deep.     260
                                                        *Exeunt.*

**[3.1]**     *Music sounds within. Enter* PANDARUS *and a* Servant.

PANDARUS     Friend, you, pray you, a word. Do not you
follow the young Lord Paris?
SERVANT     Ay, sir, when he goes before me.
PANDARUS     You depend upon him, I mean.
SERVANT     Sir, I do depend upon the Lord.                  5
PANDARUS     You depend upon a notable gentleman; I must
needs praise him.
SERVANT     The Lord be praised!
PANDARUS     You know me, do you not?
SERVANT     Faith, sir, superficially.                        10
PANDARUS     Friend, know me better: I am the Lord Pandarus.
SERVANT     I hope I shall know your honour better.

260 **\*greater . . . deep** 'large and
unwieldy sea vessels have deep
draughts, require deep water'. A
proverbial idea (Dent, S346). The
depth of water which a vessel *draws* is
the depth required to float the vessel
(*OED* draught *sb*. 19, draw *v*. 13). *Draw*
may also suggest pulling something
along by traction, in laboured movement as opposed to 'sail swift'. For textual choices, see LN.
**3.1** Location: Troy. The palace.
3 **goes before** By *follow*, in 2, Pandarus
meant 'serve', but the Servant, with sly
insolence, pretends to have understood
the word to mean 'follow after'. On the
figure of hysteron proteron in this
quibble, see Parker, 28.
5 Another cheeky pun. The Servant
twists Pandarus' *depend upon*, 'serve as
a dependent to', in 4, to a spiritual
sense of being wholly dependent upon

the Lord, playing on 'Lord Paris' and
'Lord God'. The joking continues in
6–8 on the theme of praise.
6 **\*notable** F's 'noble' is also perfectly
possible, but could be a sophistication
or misreading of the somewhat less
expected 'notable'.
6–7 **must needs** must
10 **superficially** by sight, slightly; but
with a jesting suggestion that the relationship is shallow, not genuine, and
that it might be 'deepened' by
Pandarus' reaching into his pocket. In
the next line, Pandarus probably fails
to take the hint.
12 'I hope to be better acquainted with
Your Honour'; but suggesting 'I hope I
can find something honourable in you
to be acquainted with', with a hint too
of hoping still to receive a handsome
gratuity. Cf. *TN* 3.1.49ff.

260 sail] *Q;* may saile *F*  hulks] *Q;* bulkes *F*  **3.1**] *Rowe, subst.*  0.1 *Music sounds within.*] *F, after*
*'Exeunt' at the end of 2.3; not in Q  and a* Servant] *F; not in Q*  1 not you] *F;* you not *Q*  3–40 SP
SERVANT] *F (Ser.); Man. Q*  6 notable] *Q;* noble *F*

PANDARUS    I do desire it.

SERVANT    You are in the state of grace?

PANDARUS    Grace? Not so, friend. 'Honour' and 'lordship'        15
are my titles. What music is this?

SERVANT    I do but partly know, sir: it is music in parts.

PANDARUS    Know you the musicians?

SERVANT    Wholly, sir.

PANDARUS    Who play they to?                                     20

SERVANT    To the hearers, sir.

PANDARUS    At whose pleasure, friend?

SERVANT    At mine, sir, and theirs that love music.

PANDARUS    'Command', I mean, friend.

SERVANT    Who shall I command, sir?                              25

PANDARUS    Friend, we understand not one another: I am
too courtly and thou too cunning. At whose request do
these men play?

SERVANT    That's to't indeed, sir. Marry, sir, at the request
of Paris my lord, who is there in person; with him, the    30
mortal Venus, the heart-blood of beauty, love's visible
soul –

---

14 For biblical parallels, see LN.

17 **partly** (1) partially; (2) *in parts*, as in part-music

19 **Wholly** more cheekiness: the antithesis of *in parts* (17)

20 **Who** whom (Abbott, 274), as also at 4.5.177

22 **pleasure** Pandarus means 'command', as he explains in 24, but the Servant wilfully takes the word to mean 'enjoyment'.

24 *****friend** F's supplying of this word missing from Q might be an editorial attempt to regularize the pattern of Pandarus' address to the servant in 22–6, but is also plausibly authoritative.

27 *****thou too** F's 'thou art too' is acceptable, but likely to be a sophistication;

cf. 6 and n. So also at 36–7.

29 **to't** to the point

31 **heart-blood** life-blood, vital energy, life

31–2 *****visible soul** embodiment, quintessence (stated as an oxymoron, like *mortal Venus*; the soul is normally invisible). QF's 'inuisible' has been defended as suggesting that love's 'celestial essence' is made manifest in Helen (Cowden Clarke, 1868 ed., cited in Var), but the idea runs against the Servant's emphasis on *mortal Venus* and *heart-blood*. Cam[1] emends plausibly to 'indivisible', which could easily have been miscopied as 'inuisible', but 'indivisible' seems a more strained way than *visible* of conveying Helen's embodiment of all love and beauty.

---

15] *inverted commas, Oxf*[1]    16 titles] *Q;* title *F*    24] *inverted commas, Oxf*    friend] *F; not in Q*
27 thou too] *Q (*thou to*);* thou art too *F*    30 who is] *Q;* who's *F*    31 visible] *Hanmer;* inuisible *QF;*
indivisible *Cam*[1] *(Daniel, Notes, and in Cam);* invincible *(Becket)*

PANDARUS   Who, my cousin Cressida?

SERVANT   No, sir, Helen. Could not you find out that by
    her attributes?                                                    35

PANDARUS   It should seem, fellow, thou hast not seen the
    Lady Cressid. I come to speak with Paris from the
    Prince Troilus. I will make a complimental assault upon
    him, for my business seethes.

SERVANT   Sodden business! There's a stewed phrase      40
    indeed.

*Enter* PARIS *and* HELEN [*attended by Musicians*].

PANDARUS   Fair be to you, my lord, and to all this fair
    company! Fair desires, in all fair measure, fairly guide
    them! – especially to you, fair queen. Fair thoughts be
    your fair pillow!                                                  45

HELEN   Dear lord, you are full of fair words.

PANDARUS   You speak your fair pleasure, sweet queen.
    [*to Paris*] Fair prince, here is good broken music.

---

36–7 *\*thou . . . Cressid* F's 'that thou . . .
*Cressida*' might be the result of sophistication, as at 6 and 27.

38–9 **I . . . upon him** I will besiege him
with courteous compliments.

39 **seethes** boils with urgency, as when a
person seethes with agitation or excitement

40 **Sodden** overcooked; dull, insipid,
soaked, heavy; pale from intoxication
(*OED* sodden *pa. pple.* 1–3). As the
strong past participle of *seethe*, boil,
*sodden* suggests that Pandarus' business is *stewed* indeed – with a quibble
on the 'stews' or brothels and on the
sweating treatment for venereal disease. Cf. 2.1.42, and see G. Williams,
*Dictionary*, 'sodden', 1268.

42 **Fair** fair wishes

43 **fairly** favourably. Pandarus' overuse of
*fair* in his *complimental assault* (38) on
Paris and Helen plays imprecisely on
meanings of 'pleasing', 'graceful',
'desirable', 'equitable', 'beautiful',
'blonde', 'agreeable', 'unblemished',
'kind' and the like, but chiefly conveys
(as does the repeated word *sweet* also)
the enervation of this courtly scene.
Helen's reply in 46 hints at a more
negative value of 'specious, plausible,
flattering' (*OED* fair *a.* 5).

47 **You . . . pleasure** i.e. 'Whatever you
say'.

48 **broken** arranged for different families
of instruments, such as strings and
woodwinds, or for different voices
(*OED ppl. a.* 16)

---

34 not you] *Q;* you not *F*   36 thou] *Q;* that thou *F*   37 Cressid] *Q; Cressida F*   38 complimental]
*QF (*complementall*)*   40 There's] *F;* theirs *Q*   41.1 HELEN] *Q (Hellen); Helena F   attended by
Musicians*] *Oxf; attended / Theobald*   48 SD] *Oxf*

PARIS   You have broke it, cousin, and, by my life, you shall
   make it whole again; you shall piece it out with a piece   50
   of your performance. – Nell, he is full of harmony.

PANDARUS   Truly, lady, no.

HELEN   O, sir!

PANDARUS   Rude, in sooth; in good sooth, very rude.

PARIS   Well said, my lord. Well, you say so in fits.   55

PANDARUS   I have business to my lord, dear queen. – My
   lord, will you vouchsafe me a word?

HELEN   Nay, this shall not hedge us out. We'll hear you
   sing, certainly.

PANDARUS   Well, sweet queen, you are pleasant with me.   60
   – But, marry, thus, my lord: my dear lord and most
   esteemed friend, your brother Troilus –

HELEN   My Lord Pandarus, honey-sweet lord –

PANDARUS   Go to, sweet queen, go to – commends
   himself most affectionately to you.   65

HELEN   You shall not bob us out of our melody. If you do,
   our melancholy upon your head!

PANDARUS   Sweet queen, sweet queen, that's a sweet

---

49 **broke** interrupted (with wordplay on
   *broke*). On the dropping of the
   inflected *-n* ending in *broken*, see
   Abbott, 343.
   **cousin** a term of intimacy in courtly
   address
50 **piece it out** mend or enlarge it (*OED*
   *v.* 1, 7); with wordplay on *a piece of
   your performance* (50–1), 'a sample of
   your own singing'. *Harmony* (51) continues the wordplay: (1) tuneful,
   melodic music; (2) agreeable and
   peaceable sentiments.
54 **Rude** i.e. 'I fear I am unpolished,
   unskilful'. (A conventional apology
   when asked to sing.)

55 **in fits** by fits and starts (*OED* fit *sb.*²
   4c); but with wordplay on *fits* as short
   strains of music or cantos of a poem
   (*OED* fit *sb.*¹). Paris may suggest that
   Pandarus is inconsistent, that he does
   not always try to beg off with apologies.
58 **hedge us out** shut us out, fob us off
   (*OED v.* 6b, Cam¹)
60 **pleasant** jocular
63 **honey-sweet** a conventional metaphor, as again at 135 and in *H5* 2.3.1
   (Dent, H544.1).
64 **Go to** an expression of mild exaspera-
   tion at being interrupted
66 **bob** cheat

---

51 performance. – Nell, he] *F, subst.* (performance. *Nel,* he); performance. *Nel.* he *Q;*
performance. / HELEN He *Alexander (anon. in Cam)*   55 lord. Well, you . . . fits.] *QF, subst.;* lord.
Will you . . . fits! *Oxf*   61 my lord: my] *Theobald, subst.;* my Lord my *Q;* my Lord, my *F*
64–5] *Capell; QF line* Queene, go to? / you. /   66–7] *Hanmer; QF line* melody, / head. /

queen, i'faith –

HELEN   And to make a sweet lady sad is a sour offence.        70

PANDARUS   Nay, that shall not serve your turn, that shall
   it not, in truth, la. Nay, I care not for such words, no,
   no. – And, my lord, he desires you that if the King call
   for him at supper, you will make his excuse.

HELEN   My Lord Pandarus –                                     75

PANDARUS   What says my sweet queen, my very very
   sweet queen?

PARIS   What exploit's in hand? Where sups he tonight?

HELEN   Nay, but, my lord –

PANDARUS   What says my sweet queen? My cousin will        80
   fall out with you.

HELEN [*to Paris*]   You must not know where he sups.

PARIS   I'll lay my life, with my disposer Cressida.

PANDARUS   No, no, no such matter, you are wide. Come,
   your disposer is sick.                                      85

PARIS   Well, I'll make 's excuse.

PANDARUS   Ay, good my lord. Why should you say

---

70 Helen plays mockingly on Pandarus'
   *sweet queen* (68–9) with the conventional antithesis of *sweet* and *sour*.
72 **la** an expression calling attention to an
   emphatic statement
73–4 **he desires . . . excuse** The reason
   for Pandarus' effusive embassy is at
   last apparent: he must ask Paris to
   'cover' for Troilus, excusing his non-
   appearance that evening at Priam's
   dinner table, where he would normally
   be expected. Pandarus has arranged an
   assignation between Troilus and
   Cressida at her father's house. His
   fussy secretiveness and wish to speak
   out of Helen's hearing amuse Paris and
   Helen, both of whom know well
   enough what is going on; see 82 and n.

80–1 **My cousin . . . you** i.e. 'My good
   friend Paris will be angry with you for
   flirtatiously interrupting so'.
82 i.e. (amusedly) 'You see how Pandarus
   is trying to conceal from you Troilus'
   plans for this evening'.
83 *Paris pretends surprise at an idea that
   suddenly comes to him: Troilus will be
   with Cressida! On the word *disposer*,
   see LN.
84 **no such matter** a common set phrase
   (Dent, M754.1)
   **wide** wide of the mark
84–5 **Come . . . sick** i.e. 'How could
   Cressida be receiving Troilus this
   evening? She's sick.' An unpersuasive
   fib.
86 **make 's** make his

---

69 queen, i'faith] *F4 (*I'faith*);* Queene Ifaith *QF;* queen. ay, faith *Oxf*   74 supper, you] *F;* super. You
*Q*   82 SP] *QF (Hel.); om. Hanmer*   SD] *Oxf¹*   83 I'll . . . life] *Q; not in F*   disposer] *QF;* dispenser
*Oxf (+ 85)*   86 make 's excuse.] *Alexander (Capell);* makes excuse? *Q;* make excuse. *F*

Cressida? No, your poor disposer's sick.

PARIS  I spy.

PANDARUS  You spy? What do you spy? – Come, give me     90
an instrument. [*He is handed a musical instrument.*]
Now, sweet queen.

HELEN  Why, this is kindly done.

PANDARUS  My niece is horribly in love with a thing you
have, sweet queen.     95

HELEN  She shall have it, my lord, if it be not my Lord Paris.

PANDARUS  He? No, she'll none of him. They two are twain.

HELEN  Falling in after falling out may make them three.

PANDARUS  Come, come, I'll hear no more of this. I'll sing
you a song now.     100

HELEN  Ay, ay, prithee. Now by my troth, sweet lord, thou
hast a fine forehead.

PANDARUS  Ay, you may, you may.

---

89 Paris uses this singsong phrase from a children's game of hide-and-seek to suggest in mockery that he sees what's going on. In the game, one child covers his eyes as the others scatter and hide; the one who is 'it' must then find the others before they touch home base. In a more sedate version, the child who is 'it' announces that 'I spy' an object in plain view which the others are to guess.

90–1 **Come . . . instrument** Dropping his pretended reluctance earlier to sing, Pandarus finds singing an apt way to change a conversation that is getting out of hand. He is still hoping for secrecy. Pandarus will accompany himself, perhaps on the lute or cittern, as he sings; cf. *TS* 2.1.38–159.

93 Helen thanks Pandarus for agreeing to sing.

94–5  **a thing you have** The erotic possibilities of this phrase set up the sexual joking that follows. Cf. *Oth* 3.3.317: 'I have a thing for you'. In 96, Helen interprets Pandarus to have said

that Cressida wants a man in her bed – Paris, or some other sexual partner such as Paris is to Helen. Cf. 1.2.165n. and G. Williams, *Dictionary*, 'thing', 1379–81.

97 **are twain** are not in accord, have nothing in common. Cf. Jesus' characterization of man and wife in Matthew, 19.5–6: 'And they twain shall be one flesh. Wherefore they are no more twain, but one flesh' (Shaheen, 120).

98 Helen plays on a proverb, about lovers who fall out with each other only to fall in again (Dent, F38.1), to make the risible suggestion that 'The reconciliation and wanton dalliance of two lovers after a quarrel, may produce a child, and so make three of two' (Tollet, Var '78, 9.74, cited in Var).

103 **you may** i.e. 'Get along with you', 'have your joke'. Helen cajoles Pandarus by referring to his *fine forehead* (102) as a sign of handsomeness and intellectual prowess; perhaps she strokes him there.

---

88 poor disposer's] *F;* disposers *Q;* poor dispenser's *Oxf*   91 SD] *Bevington[1]*   94 horribly] *Q;* horrible *F*   101 prithee. Now] *Q (*prethee, now*);* prethee now: *F*   lord] *F;* lad *Q*   102 hast] *F;* haste *Q*

HELEN    Let thy song be love. 'This love will undo us all.'
    O Cupid, Cupid, Cupid!                                           105
PANDARUS    Love? Ay, that it shall, i'faith.
PARIS    Ay, good now, 'Love, love, nothing but love'.
PANDARUS    In good truth, it begins so.
    [*He sings.*]
            Love, love, nothing but love, still love, still more!
                For, O, love's bow                                  110
                Shoots buck and doe.
            The shaft confounds
            Not that it wounds,
            But tickles still the sore.

            These lovers cry, 'O! O!', they die!                    115
                Yet that which seems the wound to kill
            Doth turn 'O! O!' to 'Ha, ha, he!'
                So dying love lives still.
            'O! O!' a while, but 'Ha, ha, ha!'

104 **'This love'. . . all'** perhaps a snatch of a song, or a title. The phrase turns up later in Nathan Field's *A Woman is a Weathercock* (1609–10), 3.3 (*Nero and Other Plays*, ed. Herbert P. Horne *et al.*, Mermaid Series, 1888, p. 384).
107 **good now** please (Abbott, 13)
    **\*Love . . . but love** For textual choices, see LN.
111 **buck and doe** i.e. male and female
112–13 'The shaft of Love's arrow pierces and overwhelms without inflicting a physical wound'; as in sex, the shaft penetrates and tickles. *Not that* can mean 'not that which' or 'not because' or 'not so much that'. See G. Williams, *Dictionary*, 'shaft', 1223.
114 **still** continually (reiterating the word in 109)

**the sore** the wound, the 'cut' or pudenda (G. Williams, *Dictionary*, 1273–4); with a play on *sore* as meaning a buck in its fourth year (*OED sb.*²), echoing 111. The adjectival forms *sorrel* and *sore* (*OED adj.* 2), used to describe bucks of the third and fourth years (and also hawks), both mean 'reddish-brown'.
115–18 **die, dying** terms often used to describe sexual orgasm
116 **the wound to kill** 'the fatal wound'. Lines 116–17 can also be read erotically: 'But what seems like a deadly assault on the "wound" or pudenda turns a cry of alarm into an expression of ecstasy'.
117 i.e. turns groans to laughter
118 This oxymoron of dying and living celebrates the torture and the joy of sexual euphoria.

104] *inverted commas, Oxf* ¹    107] *inverted commas, Oxf* ¹ *(Delius)*    108 SP] *Fc; not in Fu*    In . . . so] *F; not in Q*    truth] *F (*troth*)*    108.1 SD] *Dyce, subst.*    109 Love,] *Fc; Pan. Loue. / Fu;* Pand. *Loue Qc, Qu*    still love, still more] *Q, subst.; still more / F*    110–11] *F; one line, Q*    112–13] *Pope; one line, QF*    112 shaft confounds] *F; shafts confound / Q*    115, 117 'O! O!'] *Pope, subst.;* oh ho *QF, subst.* 119–20 'O! O!'] *Capell, subst.;* O ho *QF*

'O! O!' groans out for 'Ha, ha, ha!' –                    120
Heigh-ho!

HELEN    In love, i'faith, to the very tip of the nose.

PARIS    He eats nothing but doves, love, and that breeds
hot blood, and hot blood begets hot thoughts, and hot
thoughts beget hot deeds, and hot deeds is love.            125

PANDARUS    Is this the generation of love? Hot blood, hot
thoughts and hot deeds? Why, they are vipers. Is love a
generation of vipers? – Sweet lord, who's afield today?

PARIS    Hector, Deiphobus, Helenus, Antenor and all the
gallantry of Troy. I would fain have armed today, but      130
my Nell would not have it so. How chance my brother
Troilus went not?

HELEN    He hangs the lip at something. – You know all,
Lord Pandarus.

PANDARUS    Not I, honey-sweet queen. I long to hear how    135
they sped today. – You'll remember your brother's
excuse?

PARIS    To a hair.

---

120 **groans** suggesting the pain and
ecstasy not only of sexual penetration
but of subsequent childbirth (G.
Williams, *Dictionary*, 626)

121 **Heigh-ho!** Cf. *MA* 2.1.305: 'Heigh-
ho for a husband!'

123 **doves** often associated with Venus
and Cupid, and as drawing Venus'
chariot; hence, in Paris' jocose speech,
a source of meat that would heat the
blood and produce erotic desire. Of
the four bodily humours, the blood is
most directly the seat of passion.

126 **generation** genealogy (*OED* 1c)

128 **generation of vipers** Both John the
Baptist and Christ castigate the
Pharisees and other non-believers as a
'generation of vipers' (Matthew, 3.7,

12.34, 23.33, Luke, 3.7, thus phrased
in the Bishops' Bible except at 12.34,
and in the Geneva Bible at 23.33),
meaning 'offspring of vipers'.

130 **gallantry** gallants collectively (cited
by *OED* as its earliest instance)
**fain** gladly

131 **How chance** how chances it that

133 **He . . . lip** 'Pandarus pouts, sulks,
looks vexed' (see *OED* hang *v.* 4b).
Apparently said to Paris. Helen could
conceivably mean that Troilus must be
sulking.

136 **sped** succeeded, fared

138 to the last detail (Dent, H26).
Perhaps Paris' answer amusedly recalls
the jesting about the forked hair on
Troilus' chin at 1.2.145–62 (Seltzer).

---

121 Heigh-ho!] *Var '85 (Ritson); as conclusion of song, QF (hey ho)*    122 i'faith] *F (yfaith); I faith Q; ay,
faith Oxf (see 69)*    128 Sweet . . . today?] *Pope; one verse line, QF*    who's] *QF (whose)*    129 Deiphobus]
*QF (Deiphobus, Deiphoebus)*    Antenor] *QF (Anthenor)*    131–2 How . . . not?] *Pope; one verse line, QF*
134 Pandarus.] *Q; Pandarus? F*    136–7 You'll . . . excuse?] *Pope; one verse line, QF*

PANDARUS    Farewell, sweet queen.

HELEN    Commend me to your niece.                    140

PANDARUS    I will, sweet queen.                    [*Exit.*]

*Sound a retreat.*

PARIS

They're come from field. Let us to Priam's hall
To greet the warriors. Sweet Helen, I must woo you
To help unarm our Hector. His stubborn buckles,
With these your white enchanting fingers touched,        145
Shall more obey than to the edge of steel
Or force of Greekish sinews. You shall do more
Than all the island kings: disarm great Hector.

HELEN

'Twill make us proud to be his servant, Paris.
Yea, what he shall receive of us in duty            150
Gives us more palm in beauty than we have,
Yea, overshines ourself.

PARIS    Sweet, above thought I love thee.            *Exeunt.*

[**3.2**]    *Enter* PANDARUS *and Troilus'* Boy[, *meeting*].

PANDARUS    How now, where's thy master? At my cousin
Cressida's?

---

148 **the island kings** the Greek lords,
come 'From isles of Greece' (Prologue
1)

151 'bestows more honour upon me than
is derived from my beauty'. Helen
speaks of herself in the royal plural;
Pandarus addresses her repeatedly as
'queen' (to which Elizabethan audiences might well add the sense of

'quean' or whore), and she is well
aware of the regal role she plays in history. Her husband Menelaus is, after
all, a prince.

3.2.0.1 *Boy Troilus' servant is called
'Man' at this point in QF, but is almost
surely the same servant as appears
briefly at 1.2.263–6. See n. on LIST OF
ROLES.

---

141 SD *Exit*] *Rowe*    142 They're] *F;* Their *Q*    field] *F;* the field *Q*    143 woo] *F2* (wooe); woe
*QF*    145 these] *F;* this *Q*    153 SP] *Q; not in F*    Sweet, above *Rowe;* Sweete aboue *QF*    thee.]
*F;* her? *Q*    **3.2**] *Capell, subst.*    0.1 *and*] *F; not in Q*    Boy] *Dyce; man QF;* Servant *Capell*    *meeting*]
*Capell*

BOY    No, sir, he stays for you to conduct him thither.

*Enter* TROILUS.

PANDARUS    O, here he comes. – How now, how now?          4
TROILUS [*to his Boy*]    Sirrah, walk off.                [*Exit Boy.*]
PANDARUS    Have you seen my cousin?
TROILUS

    No, Pandarus. I stalk about her door
    Like a strange soul upon the Stygian banks
    Staying for waftage. O, be thou my Charon,
    And give me swift transportance to those fields          10
    Where I may wallow in the lily-beds
    Proposed for the deserver! O gentle Pandar,
    From Cupid's shoulder pluck his painted wings
    And fly with me to Cressid!
PANDARUS    Walk here i'th' orchard. I'll bring her straight.    15
                                  *Exit Pandarus.*

3    **thither** The phrase suggests that the scene begins in a location – perhaps Pandarus' house – that is separate from Cressida's father's house, where she apparently resides (see 4.1.39 and n.). By a common theatrical sleight of hand, Pandarus' undertaking to *conduct* (Troilus) *thither* requires only a few steps and a change of imagined location to the garden of her house (the *orchard* of 15), where the lovers meet. For similar 'journeys' on the Elizabethan stage, see the transition from 1.4 to 1.5 in *RJ*, and from 2.1 to 2.2 in Lyly's *Sappho and Phao*.
5    **Sirrah** a term of address used in speaking to servants, social inferiors and boys
6    **cousin** relative, i.e. niece
8–9 **Stygian . . . Charon** For classical precedents, see LN.
9    **waftage** passage

10    **transportance** conveyance. *OED*'s earliest two citations are this line and the translation in Chapman's *Iliads* (1611), commentary to Bk 16 (1.347).
11    **wallow** See LN.
12    **Proposed for** promised to
    *\*Pandar** Even if this shortened form of the name (the Q reading) might seem painfully ironic in its anticipation of Pandarus' role in arranging a chamber and bed at the end of this scene, Troilus has repeatedly called him by this name already (1.1.91, 95, 99) as well as by the fuller form, suggesting that metre is a factor in the dramatist's choice. It may be so in this present instance. F's '*Pandarus*' might well be a sophistication.
13    **painted** highly coloured, variegated; illusory; as rendered in a painting
15    **orchard** garden. See 3n.

3 SP] *Dyce; Man. QF* he stays] *F; not in Q* 3.1] *F; not in Q* 5 SD *to his Boy*] *this edn; To the Servant / Hanmer Exit Boy*] *Dyce; Exit* Servant *Capell* 8 Like a] *F;* Like to a *Q* 10 those] *F;* these *Q* 12 Pandar] *Q; Pandarus F* 15.1] *F; not in Q*

TROILUS

    I am giddy; expectation whirls me round.
    Th'imaginary relish is so sweet
    That it enchants my sense. What will it be,
    When that thc wat'ry palates taste indeed
    Love's thrice-repured nectar? Death, I fear me,    20
    Swooning destruction, or some joy too fine,
    Too subtle-potent, tuned too sharp in sweetness,
    For the capacity of my ruder powers.
    I fear it much; and I do fear besides
    That I shall lose distinction in my joys,    25
    As doth a battle, when they charge on heaps
    The enemy flying.

*Enter* PANDARUS.

PANDARUS   She's making her ready; she'll come straight.
    You must be witty now. She does so blush, and fetches

---

17 **relish** taste, flavour; with suggestion also of 'sample, specimen' (*OED sb.*[1] 1a, 1c)

19–20 \***When that . . . nectar** 'when our poor, starved palates taste in reality the thrice-purified nectar of love'. *Wat'ry* can variously suggest a thin or humble diet (cf. *KL* 1.1.262, 'waterish Burgundy'), a watery and colourless appearance, the watering down of wine, and perhaps mouth-watering in anticipation. The plural construction in QF is sometimes emended to 'palate tastes', but could refer to any hopeful lovers.

20 **thrice-repured** thrice-repurèd, thrice-purified

21 **Swooning destruction** 'utter loss of senses in fits of fainting' (Ard[1]). QF's

'Sounding' is a normal spelling for *swooning*, but may also hint at sinking and plumbing the depths as with a nautical line and lead.

23 **ruder** 'not sufficiently refined' (Ard[1])

25 'that I shall lose the ability to distinguish one pleasure from another'. Cf. Sappho's 'Epistle to Phaon' in Ovid's *Heroides*, 15.49 (LCL, 184–5): *et quod, ubi amborum fuerat confusa voluptas,* 'and when the joys of both had mingled into one' (Baldwin, Var).

26 **battle** army
   **on heaps** in a mass, together (*OED* heap *sb.* 5c). The image may also suggest, through a transferred epithet, the heaping up of enemy bodies.

29 **witty** in full possession of your wits; sparkling, amusing (*OED a.* 3b, 7)

---

19 palates taste] *QF (*pallats taste*);* palate tasts *Hanmer*  20 thrice-repured] *Q (*thrice repured*);* thrice reputed *F*  21 Swooning] *QF (*Sounding*)*  destruction] *QF (*distruction*);* distraction *Cam[1] (Orger in Cam)*  22 subtle-potent] *Theobald;* subtill, potent *QF, subst.*  tuned] *Q;* and *F*  too] *F;* to *Q*  25 lose] *QF (*loose*)*  27.1] *F; not in Q*

her wind so short, as if she were frayed with a sprite. I'll    30
fetch her. It is the prettiest villain! She fetches her
breath as short as a new-ta'en sparrow.        *Exit Pandarus.*

TROILUS

Even such a passion doth embrace my bosom.
My heart beats thicker than a feverous pulse,
And all my powers do their bestowing lose,              35
Like vassalage at unawares encount'ring
The eye of majesty.

*Enter* PANDARUS, *and* CRESSIDA [*veiled*].

PANDARUS    Come, come, what need you blush? Shame's a
baby. [*to Troilus*] Here she is now. Swear the oaths now
to her that you have sworn to me. [*Cressida draws back.*]    40
What, are you gone again? You must be watched ere you
be made tame, must you? Come your ways, come your
ways; an you draw backward, we'll put you i'th' thills.

---

29–30 **fetches . . . short** is short of
breath, pants
30 **frayed . . . sprite** frightened
('affrayed') by a ghost. *Frayed* is an
aphetic form of 'affrayed', alarmed.
31 **villain** wretch (said endearingly, play-
fully). See also 41–2n.
32 **new-ta'en** just captured. Sparrows were
often taken in nets to be sold as food.
34 **thicker** faster (*OED* thick *a*. 5b), and
suggesting also a pounding heart
35 **bestowing** employment, function, use
36–7 'like humble subjects unexpectedly
finding themselves in the king's
observant and awe-inspiring presence'
38–9 **Shame's a baby** This proverbial-
sounding phrase chides Cressida for
being babyish in her shamefaced reluctance.

41–2 **You . . . tame** i.e. 'you must be kept
awake like a hawk that is being tamed
and made obedient so that it can hunt
game', like the *falcon* and the *tercel*
mentioned in 51. A recurring image in
this scene: Cam¹ points out that *villain*,
31, can mean a hawk (*OED sb.* 2). *You
. . . watched* also suggests 'I must keep
an eye on you'.
42 **Come your ways** come along
43 **an** if
   **thills** shafts of a cart or wagon.
Another image, like hawking, of
'domesticating' the woman as though
she were a work animal. QF ('filles',
'fils') give obsolete dialectal forms
(which may point to a pronunciation
more speakable in the theatre than *i'th'
thills*).

---

30 frayed] *Capell* (fray'd); fraid *QF*; 'fraid *Hanmer*   sprite] *F*; spirite *Q*   32 as short] *Q*; so short *F*
SD] *F*; *not in Q*   35 lose] *F3*; loose *QF*   36 unawares] *Fc*; vnwares *Q, Fu*   37.1 PANDARUS, *and*
CRESSIDA] *F, subst.*; *pandar and Cressid. Q   veiled*] *Bevington³*   38 Come . . . blush] *Pope; one verse line,
QF*   39, 44, 47 SD *to Troilus] Capell, subst., Oxf¹*   40 SD] *Bevington³*   43 thills] *QF* (filles, fils)

[*to Troilus*] Why do you not speak to her? [*to Cressida*]
Come, draw this curtain, and let's see your picture. [*She* 45
*is unveiled*.] Alas the day, how loath you are to offend
daylight! An 'twere dark, you'd close sooner. [*to Troilus*]
So, so, rub on, and kiss the mistress. [*They kiss*.] How
now, a kiss in fee-farm? Build there, carpenter, the air is
sweet. Nay, you shall fight your hearts out ere I part you. 50
The falcon as the tercel, for all the ducks i'the river.
Go to, go to.

TROILUS    You have bereft me of all words, lady.

PANDARUS    Words pay no debts; give her deeds. But she'll
bereave you o'the deeds too, if she call your activity in 55

45 **curtain** i.e. veil. Curtains were hung
in front of pictures when they were
not being viewed. Olivia, in *TN*
1.5.228–9, uses the same metaphor as
she unveils to 'Cesario'.

45–6 SD Although editors generally
assume that Pandarus unveils his
niece, she may do so herself.

47 **close** come close together, unite; join
together two close-fitting connections;
conclude, bring matters to a close;
come to close quarters or to grips, as in
hand-to-hand fighting; come to terms
of agreement (*OED v*. 8–14)

48 **rub . . . mistress** terms from the
game of bowls, given erotic meaning.
To *rub* in bowls is to encounter some
impediment which retards or diverts
the course of the bowl or ball (*OED v*.[1]
14b); to *kiss the mistress* is to touch with
your bowl the jack or target bowl, a
small bowl used for the players to aim
at and here called *mistress* for the
word's erotic potential (*OED* master
*sb*. 9).

49 **in fee-farm** prolonged and with
unending rights, as in the holding of
property in return for a perpetual
fixed rent

49–50 **the air is sweet** (1) the air is fresh
and unpolluted; (2) Cressida's breath
is sweet (*OED* air *sb*.[1] 9). Cf. *AYL*
Epilogue 19–20.

51 **The falcon . . . river** i.e. The female
will be as keen as the male in pursuing
this sport of love, like female and male
hawks flying after ducks. Pandarus is
willing to bet any amount that the
female and male will be well matched;
'all the ducks i'the river' is his stake in
the bet. (The male is called the *tercel*
because it is roughly one-third the
weight of the female.) Chaucer's reference to 'Both heroner and faucoun for
ryvere' (*TC*, 4.413) depicts a similar
pairing; a 'heroner' is a falcon trained
to fly at the heron (Ard²). Cf. 'duck' as
a term of affection, as in *WT* 4.4.317:
'My dainty duck, my dear-a'.

54 **Words . . . debts** proverbial (Dent,
W840.1 and 820), here playing on the
euphemism of 'doing' and 'deeds' as
sexual activity

55 **bereave you o'the deeds** i.e. undo
your manhood (playing in *bereave* on
Troilus' *bereft* in 53)
   **activity** virility

44 SD *to Cressida*] Capell, subst., *Oxf*    45–6 SD] *This edn; not in QF; Snatching her mask / Johnson*
48 SD] *Bevington*³

question. [*They kiss.*] What, billing again? Here's 'In witness whereof the parties interchangeably'. Come in, come in. I'll go get a fire. [*Exit.*]

CRESSIDA Will you walk in, my lord?

TROILUS O Cressida, how often have I wished me thus! 60

CRESSIDA Wished, my lord? The gods grant – O my lord!

TROILUS What should they grant? What makes this pretty abruption? What too-curious dreg espies my sweet lady in the fountain of our love?

CRESSIDA More dregs than water, if my fears have eyes. 65

TROILUS Fears make devils of cherubims; they never see truly.

CRESSIDA Blind fear, that seeing reason leads, finds safer

56 **billing** caressing, kissing (*OED* bill *v.*[2] 3; earliest citation); with a possible double meaning of 'enter something in an account book or reckoning' (*OED v.*[3]), since Pandarus proceeds to quote a standard legal formula (Ard[2])

56–7 **In witness . . . interchangeably** a legal formula used in indentures, to which the two parties to the contract set their hand and seals on each half of the document, after it had been divided in two along a jagged edge so that the fit of the two halves could not be reproduced by any other document. Pandarus may hint at a sexual coupling of two halves thus uniquely complementary to each other (Ard[2]). The phrasing also imperfectly recalls the betrothal ceremony in the Book of Common Prayer (Oxf[1]). *Interchangeably* means 'reciprocally'.

58 **fire** In Chaucer (*TC*, 3.978), Pandarus provides for the lovers a bedroom with a fire in the fireplace. QF's 'fire?' probably represents 'fire!'

63 **abruption** breaking off (*OED*'s earliest citation, and Shakespeare's only use)

**too-curious** finicky, oversubtle, hidden, imperceptible

66 **Fears . . . cherubims** 'our fears make even angels look like devils'. Proverbial sounding, and analogous to 'He thinks every bush a bugbear' (Dent, B738), as in *MND* 5.1.21–2 (Ard[2]). The QF spelling of 'cherubins' is a native plural of *cherub* dating from the early sixteenth century; the more usual form of the plural is 'cherubim'.

68–9 **Blind . . . without fear** 'Fear that allows itself to be guided by clear-sighted reason is on surer ground than irrational thinking that is oblivious to dangers.' A fine example of antimetabole, or the symmetrical repetition of words in inverted order (Puttenham, 3.19, 208–9). Cf. *VA* 995: 'She clepes him king of graves and grave for kings'. Cressida is 'crossing' Troilus' proverbial-sounding sentiment in 66–7 with a proverb of her own, playing on *fear* in two senses: (1) wise precaution; (2) fright or dread. She also plays on *blind*: (1) physically destitute of sight; (2) heedless, reckless.

56 SD] *Oxf* 56–7] *inverted commas, Hanmer, subst.* 58 fire.] *F2;* fire? *QF* SD] *F2* 60 Cressida] *F; Cressed Q* 65 fears] *Pope;* teares *QF* 66 cherubims] *QF (*Cherubins*)* 68 safer] *Q;* safe *F*

footing than blind reason, stumbling without fear. To
fear the worst oft cures the worse.                                      70
TROILUS    O, let my lady apprehend no fear. In all Cupid's
pageant there is presented no monster.
CRESSIDA    Nor nothing monstrous neither?
TROILUS    Nothing but our undertakings, when we vow to
weep seas, live in fire, eat rocks, tame tigers, thinking it      75
harder for our mistress to devise imposition enough
than for us to undergo any difficulty imposed. This is
the monstruosity in love, lady, that the will is infinite
and the execution confined; that the desire is boundless
and the act a slave to limit.                                            80
CRESSIDA    They say all lovers swear more performance
than they are able, and yet reserve an ability that they
never perform, vowing more than the perfection of ten
and discharging less than the tenth part of one. They
that have the voice of lions and the act of hares, are they       85
not monsters?

69–70 **To fear . . . worse** 'To be intelli-
gently wary of the worst that may
befall can often enable us to avoid lesser dangers.' *Worse* as a comparative is
less than *worst*, the superlative form. A
common proverbial formulation
(Dent, W912).

72 **pageant** allegorical stage tableau, as
in a street procession or courtly
masque

76 **devise . . . enough** think up tasks
sufficiently rigorous to impose upon
us

78 **monstruosity** a distinct form derived
from Fr. *monstruosité*, whereas, according to the *OED*, 'monstrosity' is
derived from late Lat. *monstrositas*. In
practice the two overlapped in
Renaissance usage, where spelling is
never very precise, and are in any case
synonymous.

**will** desire, longing, volition; with a
strong suggestion of sexual appetite.
Cf. the punning on *Will* in Sonnet
135.

80 **the act** human striving generally; the
sexual act (Oxf[1])

83 **the perfection of ten** 'the accomplishments of ten worthy lovers'
(Onions, 'perfection'). Or the phrase
may be a hyperbole, sardonically
mocking lovers that swear more than
ten on a scale of ten.

84 **discharging** fulfilling

85 **lions . . . hares** proverbial types of
bravery and timidity. Cf. Erasmus's
*Adagia*, 'Inconstantia (*Leo prius, nunc
leporem agit*)', and *Cor* 1.1.170, 'Where
he should find you lions, finds you
hares' (Var, and Cam[1]). *Act* also suggests the sexual act. Cf. 80n.

70 worse] *QF;* worst *Hanmer*  71–2] *Pope; QF line* feare, / monster. /  73 Nor] *Q;* Not *F*
neither?] *F;* neither. *Q*    77 This is] *F;* This *Q*   78 monstruosity] *QF, subst.;* monstrositie *F3*

TROILUS    Are there such? Such are not we. Praise us as we
are tasted, allow us as we prove. Our head shall go bare
till merit crown it. No perfection in reversion shall have
a praise in present. We will not name desert before his          90
birth, and, being born, his addition shall be humble.
Few words to fair faith. Troilus shall be such to Cressid
as what envy can say worst shall be a mock for his truth,
and what truth can speak truest not truer than Troilus.
CRESSIDA    Will you walk in, my lord?                            95

*Enter* PANDARUS.

PANDARUS    What, blushing still? Have you not done
talking yet?
CRESSIDA    Well, uncle, what folly I commit, I dedicate

---

87 **we** Troilus' plural pronouns in this
speech point forwards to his role as the
archetype of oath-swearing lovers in
169–78.

87–8 **Praise . . . prove** Cf. the proverbs
'Praise at the end' (Dent, E124.1),
'Praise at parting' (Tilley, P83) and
'Prove ere you praise' (Dent, P614.2).
*Praise* is etymologically related to *prize*
and *price*, words used often in this play.
*Allow* means 'praise', as well as 'approve
of, accept, admit as valid, permit,
bestow' (*OED v.*). *Tasted* plays on the
near-homonym, 'tested' (Barfoot, 53).

89–90 **No . . . present** 'No promise of
some future achievement should be
celebrated now; don't count chickens
before they are hatched.' A *reversion* is
'a thing or possession which one
expects to obtain', such as an estate
that one has a legal right to reclaim
after another has done with it and the
term of the grant has expired (*OED* 1,
2); here, metaphorically, the hoped-for
thing is excellence, achievement.

90–1 **We . . . humble** Desert, or the quality of being worthy of proper reward,

is here personified as a frail child that
one should hesitate to name at all lest it
die at birth or in early infancy, and that
even then should be named with all
due modesty, since (in a truism of
Senecan philosophy) to predict success
is to set oneself up for disappointment.
An *addition* is a title, as at 2.3.241 and
4.5.142.

92 **Few . . . faith** still another proverb: cf.
'Where many words are, the truth goes
by' (Tilley, W828) and 'Few words
among friends are best' (Dent, W796).

93–4 **as what . . . Troilus** 'that malice
itself can do nothing more hurtful than
to mock Troilus for being so constant a
lover (or, malice at its worst will be
nothing more than a mock or trifle
which his constancy can easily rise
above), while truth itself cannot speak
more truly than the truth embodied in
Troilus'. The wit of this antithetical
hyperbole plays in part on *true* as meaning 'veracious, truthful' and 'loyal, honourable, upright' (*OED a.* 1–3).

98 **folly** (1) foolishness; (2) wantonness
(*OED sb.*[1] 1, 3)

89 crown it. No perfection] *F, subst.;* louer part no affection *Q;* cover it: no perfection *Ard*[2]    92 to
fair] *Qc, F;* to to faire *Qu*    95.1] *F; not in Q*

to you.

PANDARUS  I thank you for that. If my lord get a boy of     100
you, you'll give him me. Be true to my lord. If he
flinch, chide me for it.

TROILUS [*to Cressida*]  You know now your hostages: your
uncle's word and my firm faith.

PANDARUS  Nay, I'll give my word for her too. Our     105
kindred, though they be long ere they be wooed, they
are constant being won. They are burs, I can tell you;
they'll stick where they are thrown.

CRESSIDA

Boldness comes to me now, and brings me heart.
Prince Troilus, I have loved you night and day     110
For many weary months.

TROILUS

Why was my Cressid then so hard to win?

CRESSIDA

Hard to seem won; but I was won, my lord,
With the first glance that ever – pardon me;
If I confess much, you will play the tyrant.     115
I love you now, but till now not so much
But I might master it. In faith, I lie;
My thoughts were like unbridled children, grown

---

98–9 **dedicate to you** 'assign or ascribe
to your role in this'; but Pandarus parries by taking the verb to mean 'bestow
as a gift, as a token of affection'. He
will accept the child as having been
'dedicated' to him.

106 ***be wooed** F's 'are' could be a
sophistication; Q's 'bee' is arguably
hypothetical and general and thus renders *are* in 107–8 as more affirmative.

107–8 **burs . . . stick** proverbial: 'to stick
like burs' (Dent, B724)

108 **thrown** with a possible sexual double
meaning, 'thrown down and seduced'.

Cf. 3.3.209–10: 'And better would it fit
Achilles much / To throw down
Hector than Polyxena' (Ard²). See G.
Williams, *Dictionary*, 'throw', 1384–5.

118 **unbridled** i.e. not restrained or held
in check
***grown** F's 'grow' is defensible, in the
sense '[who] grow', with the relative
understood, and Q's 'grone' could be a
misprint for 'groue'; but F's 'children
grow' also might be a transmission
error in attempting to improve on Q's
'children grone'.

103 SD] *Oxf*   106 be wooed] *Q;* are wooed *F*   109–11] *Rowe; prose, QF*   114 glance that ever –
pardon me;] *F2, subst.;* glance; that euer pardon me *Q;* glance; that euer pardon me, *F*   116 till now
not] *Q;* not till now *F*   118 children, grown] *F2;* children grone *Q;* children grow *F*

Too headstrong for their mother. See, we fools!
Why have I blabbed? Who shall be true to us                    120
When we are so unsecret to ourselves?
But though I loved you well, I wooed you not;
And yet, good faith, I wished myself a man,
Or that we women had men's privilege
Of speaking first. Sweet, bid me hold my tongue,              125
For in this rapture I shall surely speak
The thing I shall repent. See, see, your silence,
Cunning in dumbness, in my weakness draws
My soul of counsel from me! Stop my mouth.                     129

TROILUS

And shall, albeit sweet music issues thence. [*He kisses her.*]

PANDARUS   Pretty, i'faith.

CRESSIDA [*to Troilus*]

My lord, I do beseech you, pardon me;
'Twas not my purpose thus to beg a kiss.
I am ashamed. O heavens, what have I done?
For this time will I take my leave, my lord.                   135

TROILUS   Your leave, sweet Cressid?

PANDARUS   Leave? An you take leave till tomorrow
morning –

---

126 **rapture** transport, ecstatic joy. *OED*
(5) gives no instance prior to Milton's
*On the Morning of Christs's Nativity* in
1629, but the definition seems
required here. The fact of its being
such a recent definition may suggest
that the older meaning of 'carrying off
a woman' resonates here also.
Shakespeare uses the word in *TC*
2.2.122 and *Cor* 2.1.206 to mean 'fit' or
'paroxysm'.

127–9 *****your . . . from me** 'your silence,
cunningly designed to encourage me

to talk too much, draws forth my
inmost thoughts'. QF's 'Comming'
can be defended as meaning 'forward,
apt', but one word could easily be mistaken for the other in manuscript, and
Pope's emendation gives us a forceful
oxymoron that seems more fitted to
what Cressida is saying.

129 **Stop my mouth** i.e. 'Stop me from
blabbing'; but Troilus replies in the
more ordinary sense of this expression, 'stop one's mouth with a kiss'. Cf.
*MA* 2.1.296–7 and Dent, M1264.1.

---

121 ourselves?] *F* (our selues?*)*; our selues. *Q*    128 Cunning] *Pope;* Comming *QF* in my] *Oxf;*
from my *QF*    129 My soul of counsel from me] *F;* My very soule of councell *Q*    130 SD] *Rowe,
subst.*    132 SD] *Oxf*    137 Leave? An] *F2, subst. (*Leave! and*);* Leaue: and *QF*    138 morning –] *F3;*
morning. *Q;* morning.: *F*

CRESSIDA

   Pray you, content you.

TROILUS                  What offends you, lady?

CRESSIDA   Sir, mine own company.                 140

TROILUS   You cannot shun yourself.

CRESSIDA   Let me go and try.

   I have a kind of self resides with you,

   But an unkind self that itself will leave

   To be another's fool. Where is my wit?           145

   I would be gone. I speak I know not what.

TROILUS

   Well know they what they speak that speak so wisely.

CRESSIDA

   Perchance, my lord, I show more craft than love

   And fell so roundly to a large confession

   To angle for your thoughts. But you are wise,      150

   Or else you love not, for to be wise and love

   Exceeds man's might; that dwells with gods above.

TROILUS

   O, that I thought it could be in a woman –

---

139 **content you** i.e. don't get upset, take it easy

143–5 **I have . . . fool** 'Part of me longs to cling to you, but another part of me rebelliously feels it unnatural for me to desert my true self and lose my personal autonomy by becoming the plaything or dupe of another person like yourself.'

144 **unkind** unnatural (with a play of antithesis on *kind of* in 143)

145 **Where . . . wit?** i.e. What am I saying?

147 'Anyone who can speak so wisely must know what he or she is saying.'

148 **Perchance** i.e. 'perhaps you will think that'
   **craft** cunning

149–50 **And . . . thoughts** 'and began confessing to you so outspokenly and freely just to draw from you a similar frankness'

150–2 **But . . . above** i.e. 'But you are not easily taken in, because you're wise, or – to put it another way – because you don't really love me, since it is impossible to be wise and be in love at the same time'. Cressida wryly ends with a proverb found in Publilius Syrus' *Sententiae* 22 (*Amare et sapere vix deo conceditur*, 'to love and be wise is scarcely granted to a god', LCL, 16–17), in Erasmus's *Adagia*, 2.476E (chil. 2, cent. 2, prov. 81), and often cited; see Dent, L558.

145–6 Where . . . what.] *F*; I would be gone. / Where is my wit? I know not what I speake, *Q*
147 that speak] *Q*; that speakes *F*    152 might; that] *F* (might, that); might that *Q*

As, if it can, I will presume in you –
To feed for aye her lamp and flames of love,　　　　155
To keep her constancy in plight and youth,
Outliving beauty's outward, with a mind
That doth renew swifter than blood decays!
Or that persuasion could but thus convince me
That my integrity and truth to you　　　　160
Might be affronted with the match and weight
Of such a winnowed purity in love;
How were I then uplifted! But alas,
I am as true as truth's simplicity,
And simpler than the infancy of truth.　　　　165

CRESSIDA

　In that I'll war with you.

TROILUS　　　　　　　　O virtuous fight,
When right with right wars who shall be most right!
True swains in love shall in the world to come

---

154 **presume** i.e. 'presume that it is, indeed'
155 'to keep lighted for ever a lamp dedicated to constancy in love' (like a lamp kept illuminated in a sepulchre or before a monument). *Lamp and flames* is an instance of hendiadys, a figure of speech (called 'twins' by Puttenham, 3.16, 177–8) that 'will seem to make two of one not thereunto constrained', as when a poet writes 'with venom and with darts', meaning 'venomous darts'.
156 'to keep the constancy of her affection ever vigorous as when it was plighted, and as fresh' (*OED* plight *sb.*[2] 5b, youth *sb.* 3)
157 **beauty's outward** beauty's outward appearance (which inevitably decays). If read as 'beauties outward', i.e. 'beauties that are outward only', the phrase has much the same meaning.
158 **than blood decays** than passion

wanes (but with a literal meaning also, signifying physical decay and the drying of the blood owing to ageing)
161–2 'might be matched on your part with an equal quantity of love that is as pure as wheat winnowed from chaff'. *Affronted* means 'encountered, met face to face'.
163 **were I** would I be
　　**uplifted** exalted, elated, rendered proud (*OED* 3, citing this passage as its first instance and noting that the usage persists in modern times dialectally in the north of England and in Scotland)
164–5 'I am as true as the simple truth itself, and more innocent than truth in its pristine state before it encountered falsehood.' See LN.
167 **When right** when justice, correctness, righteousness, justifiable claim
　　**most right** most upright, true, good, just (playing on the noun)

154 presume] *QF;* presume 't *Ard*[1] *(Craig)* 155 aye] *F;* age *Q* flames] *QF;* flame *Cam*[1]
157 beauty's] *Capell;* beauties *QF*

Approve their truth by Troilus. When their rhymes,
Full of protest, of oath and big compare,                    170
Wants similes, truth tired with iteration –
'As true as steel, as plantage to the moon,
As sun to day, as turtle to her mate,
As iron to adamant, as earth to th' centre' –
Yet, after all comparisons of truth,                    175
As truth's authentic author to be cited,
'As true as Troilus' shall crown up the verse
And sanctify the numbers.
CRESSIDA                                    Prophet may you be!
If I be false, or swerve a hair from truth,
When time is old and hath forgot itself,                    180
When waterdrops have worn the stones of Troy,

169 **Approve** attest, confirm
  **by Troilus** with reference to Troilus
  as an ideal
170 **protest** protèst; protestations (of
  love) (*OED sb.* 1).
  **big compare** extravagant comparisons
171 'are in need of similes, having
  exhausted their vows with endlessly
  repeated clichés'. *Wants* may be a third
  person plural ending in *-s*, as is
  commonly found in Shakespeare
  (Abbott, 333), or may be drawn to the
  singular noun forms in 170. *Tired with*
  means 'weakened or exhausted by'.
172–4 A number of these frayed similes
  are of course proverbial: 'As true as
  steel' (Dent, S840), 'as turtle [turtle-
  dove] to her mate' (T624), 'As iron to
  adamant [i.e. magnet]' (A31.1).
  Fittingly and ironically, 'As true as
  Troilus' in 177 turns up as a proverb
  also (T527.1), despite Troilus' hope
  here that his name will bring freshness
  and authenticity to love poetry.
172 **plantage** vegetation (*OED* 2) – popularly supposed to increase in growth

at full moon and decay in the moon's
waning. See Scot's *Discovery of
Witchcraft*, 169, quoted by Richard
Farmer (in Var '78, 9.84) and subsequent editors.
173 **As sun to day** Cf. Corin's folk wisdom in *AYL* 3.2.26–7: 'a great cause of
  the night is lack of the sun'.
  **turtle** turtledove
174 **adamant** loadstone, magnet
  **th' centre** the centre of the earth
  itself, considered to be the point to
  which all things were attracted
175 **comparisons** illustrative similes
176 'when we want to cite as our authority
  the very fountainhead of truth itself'
177 **crown up** add the finishing touches
  to (*OED* crown *v.*[1] 9), add regal dignity to. Cf. 4.5.224, 'The end crowns all',
  and LN 4.5.224–6.
178 **numbers** verses
181 Cf. the proverb 'Constant dropping will
  wear the stone' (Dent, D618), Job, 14.19,
  'The water breaketh the stones', and
  Erasmus, *Adagia*, 2.782E (chil. 3, cent.
  3, prov. 3): *Assidua stilla saxum excavat.*

169 truth] *Q* (trueth*); truths *F*    171 Wants] *QF;* Want *F2*    simeles, truth] *F;* simele's truth *Q*
172–4] *inverted commas, Capell, subst.*    172 plantage] *QF;* planets *Pope;* floodage *Hudson*[2] *(Heath)*
175 Yet] *F; not in Q*    177] *inverted commas, Var '73, subst.*    180 and] *F;* or *Q*

And blind oblivion swallowed cities up,
And mighty states characterless are grated
To dusty nothing, yet let memory,
From false to false, among false maids in love,                    185
Upbraid my falsehood! When they've said 'As false
As air, as water, wind, or sandy earth,
As fox to lamb, or wolf to heifer's calf,
Pard to the hind, or stepdame to her son',
Yea, let them say, to stick the heart of falsehood,                190
'As false as Cressid'.

PANDARUS    Go to, a bargain made. Seal it, seal it; I'll be
the witness. Here I hold your hand, here my cousin's. If
ever you prove false one to another, since I have taken
such pains to bring you together, let all pitiful goers-           195
between be called to the world's end after my name: call

182 **blind** undiscriminating, heedless,
random, obscure (*OED* 3)
183 **characterless** unrecorded, leaving
not a trace. Probably accented on the
second syllable.
**grated** pulverized
185 'from one false one to another false
one among maids in love who are false'
(Ard¹)
186–9 **As . . . son** Cressida caps Troilus'
string of proverbial comparisons in
172–4 with a medley of her own: 'As
false as water' (Dent, W86.1), 'As
wavering as the wind' (W412), 'To
build on sand' (S88), 'As wily as a fox'
(F629), 'Give not the wolf (or fox) the
sheep to keep' (W602) and 'To be a
stepmother' (S848.1). Once again, history provides Shakespeare with the
irony that her own name has become
proverbial as well: 'As false as Cressid'.
Cf. Chaucer (*TC*, 5.1054–64), where,
after she has surrendered to Diomede,
Criseyde reflects in soliloquy that she

will be known forever as a betrayer of
her lover.
189 **Pard** leopard or panther
**hind** doe
**stepdame** stepmother
190 **stick the heart** pierce the centre of
the target
192–3 **Go . . . witness** See LN.
195 **pitiful** compassionate (with perhaps
unintended and ironically prognosticatory overtones of 'wretched', 'pitiable',
'contemptible')
196–7 ***call . . . panders** Pandarus offers
his name as a generic label as do
Troilus and Cressida, unaware of the
notorious meaning of 'panders, pimps,
procurers' that the audience, with its
knowledge of history subsequent to
the Trojan war and to Chaucer, will
bring to the name here. The word is
sometimes printed 'Pandars' in modern spelling editions here and at 199,
and 'Pandar' at 206, but the generic
use of the name seems underscored by

186 falsehood!] *Rowe, subst.* (Falsehood;); falsehood, *QF, subst.*    186–9] *inverted commas, Capell,
subst.*    187 wind, or] *Q*; as Winde, as *F*    188 or wolf] *Q*; as Wolfe *F*    191] *inverted commas, Staunton*
193 witness. Here] *Rowe*; witnesse here *QF, subst.*; witnesse, here *F2*    195 pains] *F*; paine *Q*
195–6 goers-between] *QF* (goers betweene)

them all panders. Let all constant men be Troiluses, all
false women Cressids, and all brokers-between
panders! Say 'Amen'.

TROILUS     Amen.                                                    200

CRESSIDA     Amen.

PANDARUS     Amen. Whereupon I will show you a chamber
with a bed; which bed, because it shall not speak of
your pretty encounters, press it to death. Away!

*Exeunt [Troilus and Cressida].*

And Cupid grant all tongue-tied maidens here          205
Bed, chamber, pander to provide this gear!                 *Exit.*

---

Q's shifting from the spelling 'Pandar'
at 1.1.91–9 and 3.2.12 to 'Panders',
'panders' and 'Pander' in the conclusion of this scene. (F generally follows
Q in these spellings, though it has
'*Pandarus*' at 3.2.12.) The detail epitomizes the tonal complexity of the play.

197 **constant** Although Pandarus asks
what will happen if the two lovers
prove 'false to one another' (194),
implying an inconstant rather than a
constant Troilus, he in fact supposes
that it is the woman who will prove
inconstant.

203 ***with a bed** This added phrase or
something close to it seems needed to
explain the antecedent of *which bed*,
and is a presumed error in transmission easily accounted for by eyeskip
and anticipation of the following *bed*,
especially if the MS read '*wᶦ a bed, wʰ
bed*' (Sisson, 2.114, subst.). If left un-
amended, the phrase *which bed* might
conceivably mean 'the bed in which'
(Seltzer).

**because** in order that

204 **press it to death** *Peine forte et dure*,
'severe and hard punishment', was a
punishment inflicted on those who
stood accused of felony but 'stood
mute and would not plead' (*OED* press
*v.*¹ 1b). The accused was subjected to
an increasing and finally crushing
weight, leading to an agonizing death.
Pandarus speaks of the lovers' sexual
encounter as one that will put their
bed under a harsh pressing in a
demand for silence.

204.1 *Exeunt* Cf. F's *Exeunt* at the scene's
end. Troilus and Cressida presumably
start to leave at 204.1, while Pandarus
remains behind to speak leeringly to
the audience as Troilus and Cressida
are disappearing from view.

205 **maidens here** i.e. virgins of either
sex here in the theatre, among the
audience

206 **gear** i.e. bed and chamber; but often
applied salaciously to the sexual organs
as well. See 1.1.6 and 14n. and G.
Williams, *Dictionary*, 587–8.

197, 199 panders] *QF (*Panders, panders*); *Pandars* / *Pope*    197 constant] *QF;* inconstant *Hanmer*
199] *inverted commas, Hanmer, subst.*    203 with a bed] *Hanmer; not in QF*    204.1 *Exeunt*] *Q; not in F*
*Troilus and Cressida*] *Capell*    206 pander] *Q (*Pander*);* and Pander *F*    SD] *Q; Exeunt. F*

[**3.3**]    *Flourish. Enter* ULYSSES, DIOMEDES, NESTOR,
          AGAMEMNON, [AJAX,] MENELAUS *and* CALCHAS.

CALCHAS

Now, princes, for the service I have done you,
Th'advantage of the time prompts me aloud
To call for recompense. Appear it to your mind
That, through the sight I bear in things to come,
I have abandoned Troy, left my possessions,                    5
Incurred a traitor's name, exposed myself,
From certain and possessed conveniences,
To doubtful fortunes, sequest'ring from me all
That time, acquaintance, custom and condition
Made tame and most familiar to my nature;                      10
And here, to do you service, am become
As new into the world, strange, unacquainted.
I do beseech you, as in way of taste,
To give me now a little benefit

**3.3** Location: the Greek camp. Before
Achilles' tent, as in 2.3.

2 **Th'advantage . . . time** favourable
opportunity (*OED* advantage 4)

3 **Appear it** let it appear

4 **sight I bear** 'foresight I am endowed
with, wield, have' (*OED sb.*[1] 8b, 12).
Calchas' prophetic knowledge of
Troy's future coexists ironically with
his (perhaps wilful) ignorance of his
daughter's prospects.
*****come** QF's 'loue' probably repre-
sents an easy misreading of *l* for the
Roman *c* that Shakespeare seems to
have preferred to the Secretary *c*, and
of *u* for *m* (Tannenbaum, 'Notes',
76–7).

5 *****possessions** *OED*'s citations (3) suggest that the plural form was the regu-

lar way of expressing the idea of
'belongings, property, wealth' as
opposed to 'possession' (the QF reading), 'a piece of property'. An easy
scribal or compositorial error.

7 **From** turning from, depriving myself
of

8 **sequest'ring** separating, removing

9 **condition** social rank and wealth, circumstances

10 **tame** familiar, customary (cited by
*OED* 3c)

11 **am become** have become

12 **strange** foreign, alien; unknown,
unfamiliar. The adjective describes
both Calchas and his new surround-
ings, since the word can modify *I* and
also *world*.

13 **as . . . taste** as a foretaste

**3.3**] *Capell, subst.*   0.1 *Flourish*] *F (at end of SD); not in Q*   DIOMEDES] *F; Diomed / Q*   0.2 AJAX]
*Capell; not in QF*   MENELAUS] *F; not in Q*   CALCHAS] *QF (Chalcas)*   1 done you] *F; done Q*   3
your mind] *F; mind Q;* your minds *Cam*[1]   4 come] *F4;* loue *QF*   5 possessions] *Capell;* possession
*QF;* profession *Oxf*   14 benefit] *F4 (*benefit,*);* benefit. *Q;* benefit: *F*

Out of those many registered in promise          15
Which, you say, live to come in my behalf.

AGAMEMNON

What wouldst thou of us, Trojan, make demand?

CALCHAS

You have a Trojan prisoner, called Antenor,
Yesterday took. Troy holds him very dear.
Oft have you – often have you thanks therefor –          20
Desired my Cressid in right great exchange,
Whom Troy hath still denied; but this Antenor,
I know, is such a wrest in their affairs
That their negotiations all must slack,
Wanting his manage; and they will almost          25
Give us a prince of blood, a son of Priam,
In change of him. Let him be sent, great princes,
And he shall buy my daughter; and her presence
Shall quite strike off all service I have done
In most accepted pain.

AGAMEMNON                    Let Diomedes bear him,          30

---

15 **many . . . promise** 'many benefits set down officially as promises'. Calchas insists that the Greek generals have signed on the dotted line, as it were.

16 **live to come** await fulfilment

17 *Most editors, following Rowe, repunctuate QF's line (' . . . Troian? make demand?') to read ' . . . Troian? Make demand.' The arrangement proposed here is at least as idiomatic in Elizabethan usage.

19 **took** taken. See Abbott, 344.

20 **therefor** in return for it

21 'offered to take Cressida in exchange for some prominent captive Trojan warrior whom you hold'

22 **still** continually

23 **wrest** tuning key, implement used to tune a spinet or harp, without which the strings might otherwise slacken. In this metaphor, Antenor is seen as essential to the harmonious working of the Trojan army. A *wrest* can also be a 'wrench'.

24 **slack** slacken; see previous n.

25 **Wanting his manage** lacking his management

26 **of blood** of the blood, of royal lineage

27 **change of** exchange for

30 **In . . . pain** 'in service that I have cheerfully endured as my lot, and which you, my lords, have found highly acceptable'. *Pain* means 'pains, trouble'. **Diomedes** perhaps to be pronounced 'Diomed' for reasons of scansion. See t.n. **bear him** take Antenor along, escort him (*OED* bear *v.*[1] 1e)

---

17 Trojan, make demand?] *this edn;* Troian? make demand? *QF;* Trojan? Make demand. *Rowe*
20 you thanks] *Q;* you, thankes *F*  29 off] *QF (*of, off*)*  30] *Cam; two lines (Proudfoot)* Diomedes]
*QF; Diomede / Hanmer*

And bring us Cressid hither; Calchas shall have
What he requests of us. Good Diomed,
Furnish you fairly for this interchange;
Withal, bring word if Hector will tomorrow
Be answered in his challenge. Ajax is ready.                    35

DIOMEDES

This shall I undertake, and 'tis a burden
Which I am proud to bear.                    *Exit [with Calchas].*

ACHILLES *and* PATROCLUS *stand in their tent.*

ULYSSES

Achilles stands i'th' entrance of his tent.
Please it our general pass strangely by him,
As if he were forgot; and, princes all,                    40
Lay negligent and loose regard upon him.
I will come last. 'Tis like he'll question me
Why such unplausive eyes are bent, why turned on him.
If so, I have derision medicinable

33 'outfit yourself with all things needed for this exchange of Cressida for Antenor'. *Interchange* also suggests a negotiation, an exchange of views; Diomedes is to help determine the conditions under which Hector and Ajax will fight.

34–5 'Moreover, bring answer back whether tomorrow is a suitable day for Hector to meet the answerer of his challenge, Ajax.' Diomedes cannot be asked to find out in Troy if Hector's challenge will be answered by the Greeks, as this passage might otherwise seem to suggest. The capital 'If' in Q and the comma before 'if' in F may suggest a pause here and a new phrase, emphasizing *tomorrow*, that could run on through *Ajax is ready*.

37.1 On staging possibilities, see LN.

39 **strangely** as though encountering a complete stranger; coldly and distantly; oddly, unaccountably

41 **loose** casual, slight

42 **like** likely

43 ***unplausive** disapproving (*OED*'s only citation and Shakespeare's only use). The metre and the repeated idea in *bent* and *turned* suggest the attractive possibility of emending the line (see t.n.), but the QF reading can perhaps be read with the first two stresses on *such* and *eyes*.

44 **derision medicinable** curative scorn. Ulysses does not plan to speak derisively himself; instead, he says that he can make use of the Greek generals' haughty aloofness, deriving from it a kind of harsh curative medicine for Achilles' pride.

34 bring word if] *QF, subst.;* bear word that *Oxf¹*   37 SD *with Calchas*] *Capell, subst.*   37.1 ACHILLES . . . *stand*] *Q, subst.;* Enter Achilles *and* Patroclus *F*   39 pass] *Q;* to passe *F*   43 unplausive] *F;* vnpaulsiue *Q*   bent . . . him.] *QF, subst.* (bent? why turnd on him,*);* bent on him? *Pope*

To use between your strangeness and his pride,                45
Which his own will shall have desire to drink.
It may do good. Pride hath no other glass
To show itself but pride; for supple knees
Feed arrogance, and are the proud man's fees.

AGAMEMNON

We'll execute your purpose, and put on                         50
A form of strangeness as we pass along.
So do each lord, and either greet him not
Or else disdainfully, which shall shake him more
Than if not looked on. I will lead the way.

[*They proceed in turn past Achilles' tent.*]

ACHILLES

What, comes the general to speak with me?                     55
You know my mind: I'll fight no more 'gainst Troy.

AGAMEMNON [*to Nestor*]

What says Achilles? Would he aught with us?

NESTOR [*to Achilles*]

Would you, my lord, aught with the general?

ACHILLES   No.

NESTOR [*to Agamemnon*]   Nothing, my lord.                   60

AGAMEMNON   The better.   [*Exeunt Agamemnon and Nestor.*]

ACHILLES [*to Menelaus*]   Good day, good day.

MENELAUS   How do you? How do you?               [*Exit.*]

---

45 **use** mediate, employ
46 'which medicine his own wilfulness will thirst for (since he will be so curious, out of wounded pride, to know why he is being snubbed and neglected)'
47–9 **Pride . . . fees** 'Only through the proud behaviour of his fellow Greek chieftains can Achilles be made to see an image of his own pride; submissive gestures on our part, which we too often pay proud persons as their due,

will only feed his arrogance.' For literary parallels, see LN.
50 **We'll** i.e. I, Agamemnon, will (the royal 'we'). The reference to *each lord* in 52 makes it clear that *We'll* here does not yet include the others.
51 **A form of strangeness** a false appearance, outward show
55 *****What, comes** For textual choices, see LN.
61 'So much the better.'

54.1] *Capell, subst.*   55 What, comes] *F4;* What comes *QF*   57 SD] *Oxf¹ (+ 62)*   58 SD] *Oxf (+ 60, 64, 70)*   61, 63 SD] *Capell, subst.*

ACHILLES [*to Patroclus*]   What, does the cuckold scorn me?

AJAX   How now, Patroclus?                                    65

ACHILLES   Good morrow, Ajax.

AJAX   Ha?

ACHILLES   Good morrow.

AJAX   Ay, and good next day too.                          *Exit.*

[*Ulysses remains behind, reading.*]

ACHILLES [*to Patroclus*]

    What mean these fellows? Know they not Achilles?      70

PATROCLUS

    They pass by strangely. They were used to bend,

    To send their smiles before them to Achilles,

    To come as humbly as they use to creep

    To holy altars.

ACHILLES                What, am I poor of late?

    'Tis certain, greatness, once fall'n out with fortune,   75

    Must fall out with men too. What the declined is

    He shall as soon read in the eyes of others

    As feel in his own fall; for men, like butterflies,

    Show not their mealy wings but to the summer,

    And not a man, for being simply man,                    80

---

71 **used** accustomed

72 **To . . . them** to send their smiles as harbingers, as if announcing their coming

73 **they** The pronoun ambiguously continues the sense of *They*, *their* and *them* in 71–2, referring to Agamemnon and his fellow generals, but now also broadened to include people generally. \***use** are accustomed. QF's 'vs'd' is an easy scribal or compositorial error brought about by reading *d* for *e* in Secretary hand or remembering the *used* of 71. 'Used' would imply that the Greeks no longer worship the gods (Cam¹).

73–4 **creep . . . altars** Patroclus refers to Greek religious practices, but with a

possible glance also at the Catholic custom of 'creeping' on knees to the cross on Good Friday (Milward, 26).

75–6 **greatness . . . too** i.e. 'greatness of reputation that suffers a decline in fortune soon leads to the desertion of erstwhile friends'

76 **the declined** the man brought low

79 **mealy** powdered as with cornmeal

80–2 \*'No one is honoured for himself, but rather for those dignities and gifts that are external to him – such as official position, wealth, and good looks or political influence.' A commonplace found in Seneca's *Epistulae Morales*, 'On Values', 42.1–10 and 76.8 (LCL,

---

69 SD] *Capell, subst.; Exeunt / QF*   69.1] *Bevington¹*   70 fellows?] *F*; fellowes *Q*   73–4 To come . . . altars] *Rowe¹; one line, QF*   73 use] *Dyce² (W. S. Walker);* vs'd *QF*

Hath any honour, but honour for those honours
That are without him – as place, riches and favour,
Prizes of accident as oft as merit;
Which when they fall, as being slippery standers,
The love that leaned on them as slippery too                    85
Doth one pluck down another and together
Die in the fall. But 'tis not so with me;
Fortune and I are friends. I do enjoy
At ample point all that I did possess,
Save these men's looks, who do, methinks, find out             90
Something not worth in me such rich beholding
As they have often given. Here is Ulysses;
I'll interrupt his reading. – How now, Ulysses?

ULYSSES    Now, great Thetis' son!

ACHILLES    What are you reading?                               95

ULYSSES    A strange fellow here
Writes me that man, how dearly ever parted,

1.278–85 and 2.150–3), and
Montaigne's *Essays*, trans. Florio, 1603
(pp. 139–40; Baldwin, Var). F's 'but
honour'd' in 81 in place of Q's 'but
honour' is a defensible reading, but
may be a sophistication. Proudfoot's
conj., 'but 's honour'd for', is attractive, and supposes that F represents an
incomplete correction.

84–7 **Which . . . fall** i.e. 'when men fall,
and when the *Prizes of accident* (83)
that often come to men in unmerited
ways collapse, the fawning attention
that unstable fortune always attracts
collapses also; they pull one another
down'. *Which* can refer ambivalently to
*men* (76) and to *Prizes of accident* (83).
For the classical background, see LN.

84 **being . . . standers** standing on slippery footing

89 **At ample point** in fullest measure;
also a metaphor (employed by Achilles
with presumably unintended irony) for
the highest point of Fortune's wheel,

from which one inevitably descends,
*point* here signifying 'the highest part
or degree, the height, summit, zenith,
acme' (*OED sb.*[1] 26)

91 'something in me not worthy of such
high regard or lavish contemplation'
(*OED* beholding *vbl. sb.* 1, 3)

94 Achilles' mother was the Nereid Thetis;
his father was a mortal, King Peleus. See
notes at 1.3.39, 169 and 211–12.
Chapman uses the epithet 'great Thetis'
son' in his 1598 translation, 'The Third
Book' (i.e. Bk 7), p. 52.

96ff. For the intellectual background, see
LN.

97–8 'writes that any individual, however
richly endowed by nature, however
much possessed with good qualities
both external and internal'. *Me* is an
emphatic idiom in the form of an ossi-
fied dative suggesting that the speaker
has benefited from the writing; cf.
1.3.165 and 170, and 2.1.19. See
Abbott, 220.

81 but honour for] *Q;* but honour'd for *F;* but 's honour'd for *(Proudfoot)*    86–7] *F; Q lines* fall, / mee, /

How much in having, or without or in,
Cannot make boast to have that which he hath,
Nor feels not what he owes, but by reflection; 100
As when his virtues, shining upon others,
Heat them, and they retort that heat again
To the first givers.

ACHILLES           This is not strange, Ulysses.
The beauty that is borne here in the face
The bearer knows not, but commends itself 105
To others' eyes; nor doth the eye itself,
That most pure spirit of sense, behold itself,
Not going from itself, but eye to eye opposed
Salutes each other with each other's form.
For speculation turns not to itself 110
Till it hath travelled and is mirrored there
Where it may see itself. This is not strange at all.

ULYSSES

I do not strain at the position –

100 **owes** owns
  **but by reflection** i.e. 'except in so far as his qualities are reflected in others' response to him'. Cf. Aquinas, *Summa Theologiae*, 2a–2ae, question 188, article 6.3: 'Better to illumine than merely to shine' (Ard²), and *JC* 1.2.51–70.
102 **retort** cast back, reflect (*OED v.*¹ 6, citing this passage as its first instance)
105 **but commends** 'unless it commends' (Abbott, 119); with a suggestion also of 'but instead it commends'
106–9 ***nor . . . form*** 'nor can the unaided eye, that most exquisite and spiritual of the five senses, see itself, since no eye can go out and look back on itself from an external vantage point; but when two persons gaze into each other's eyes, those eyes convey a sense of what each individual looks like from the other's point of view'. A proverbial idea (Dent, E231a and 232). Lines

106–7 appear in Q only, but the F excision may be an unintentional error at the bottom of a column of type.
110 **speculation** (1) power of sight; (2) contemplation, conjecture
111 **travelled** So Q ('trauel'd'). F's 'trauail'd' suggests also 'laboured'. The word often ambivalently contains both meanings in Renaissance usage.
  ***mirrored there*** i.e. 'reflected in another's eyes or some other mirror'. QF's 'married' is defended by some editors, who point out that *mirrored* is not used elsewhere, according to the *OED*, until Keats's *Lamia* in 1820. Both readings are plausible and find support elsewhere in the play; mirroring particularly is an important recurring motif.
113 **strain at** make a difficulty of accepting, scruple at (*OED v.*¹ 21)
  **position** thesis, assertion, proposition

101 shining] *F;* ayming *Q*   103 givers] *Q;* giuer *F*   106–7] *Q; not in F*   111 travelled] *Q (*trauel'd*);* trauail'd *F*   mirrored] *Singer (F2 ms. correction);* married *QF*   113 strain at] *Q;* straine it at *F*

It is familiar – but at the author's drift,
Who in his circumstance expressly proves                    115
That no man is the lord of anything,
Though in and of him there be much consisting,
Till he communicate his parts to others;
Nor doth he of himself know them for aught
Till he behold them formed in th'applause                    120
Where they're extended – who, like an arch,
    reverb'rate
The voice again, or, like a gate of steel
Fronting the sun, receives and renders back
His figure and his heat. I was much rapt in this,
And apprehended here immediately                    125
Th'unknown Ajax. Heavens, what a man is there!
A very horse, that has he knows not what.

114 **drift** i.e. tenor, purport, way of applying the general position
115 **circumstance** detailed exposition (*OED sb.* 9)
116–18 i.e. 'that however much a person is endowed with many fine qualities that cohere and harmonize in him, if he does not communicate them it is just as though he did not have them'. For the intellectual background, see LN.
119 **aught** anything of value
120–1 **formed . . . extended** given substance by the applause (1) of those by whom they are valued and assessed, (2) of those they reach, (3) where they are displayed or (4) where their significance is enlarged upon (*OED* extend *v.* 6, 9, 10)
121 **who** i.e. both the applause and those who applaud
    **arch** perhaps a city gate or arch of a bridge festively decorated for a royal entry, which is here imagined to *reverb'rate* or re-echo (*OED* 1b) the voice of the regal person passing through (Venezky, 183)
122 **gate of steel** perhaps a door plated in steel
123 **Fronting** facing
124 **His** its, the sun's (an image with royal associations; see 121n.)
    **rapt in** deeply engaged in, intent upon, transported by. (Indistinguishable in the theatre from 'wrapped', absorbed.)
125 **apprehended** perceived the significance of, recognized
126 **unknown** obscure. Ulysses also hints ironically that Ajax is about to become better known, through an undeserved fame thrust upon him by Achilles' standoffishness.
    **what . . . there!** ironically ambiguous: 'What a fine fellow!' and 'Is that what one calls a man?'
127 **A very horse** ambiguous again: 'He's strong as a horse' and 'He's more like a horse than a man'. The implied comparison returns at 307–8.
    **that . . . what** 'who doesn't even know his own strength'

116 man] *Q;* may *F*   117 be] *Q;* is *F*   120 th'applause] *F* (th'applause,*);* the applause. *Q*
121 they're] *Q* (th'are*);* they are *F*   126–8] *Q; F lines Aiax;* / Horse, / are. /

Nature, what things there are
Most abject in regard and dear in use!
What things again most dear in the esteem                    130
And poor in worth! Now shall we see tomorrow
An act that very chance doth throw upon him.
Ajax renowned? O heavens, what some men do,
While some men leave to do!
How some men creep in skittish Fortune's hall,              135
Whiles others play the idiots in her eyes!
How one man eats into another's pride,
While pride is fasting in his wantonness!
To see these Grecian lords! Why, even already
They clap the lubber Ajax on the shoulder,                  140
As if his foot were on brave Hector's breast,
And great Troy shrinking.

ACHILLES

  I do believe it; for they passed by me

---

129 'esteemed as worthless though valuable in practice'
130 **again** on the other hand
132 **very chance** 'pure happenstance'; but the image of throwing suggests the loaded dice we know Ulysses to be employing in this game of chance
133 **some men** i.e. men like Ajax
134 i.e. 'while others (like Achilles) leave undone the things they should do'
135–6 i.e. 'How some men sidle up to the Goddess Fortune in her palace while others foolishly squander her favour!' The rhetorical pattern of 133–8 suggests that Ajax is the first of these and Achilles the second, but the image is difficult, and could possibly signify instead that Achilles is one who refuses to seize the moment of Fortune's favour while Ajax puts himself flam-

boyantly on display.
137–8 i.e. 'How one man (like Ajax) eats into another's glory, while the pride of another man (like Achilles) perversely starves itself through arrogant self-satisfaction!' (*OED* wantonness 1e).
140 **lubber** lout, stupid fellow. Shakespeare uses the word twice elsewhere as a noun, and 'lubberly' once in adjectival use (*MW* 5.5.181). In the present instance the word could also be passing into the adjectival (clumsy, stupid, idle, loutish; *OED* 2).
142 *\*shrinking** shrinking under the approaching catastrophe. Q's 'shriking' is interpretable as the 'shrieking' of the Trojans in terror, but only a tilde over the *i* is required to turn 'shriking' into 'shri*n*king'.

---

129 abject] *F (*abiect*); obiect *Q*   131–2 tomorrow . . . him.] *Oxf*; to morrow, / . . . him *Q*; to morrow, / . . . him? *F*; to Morrow, / . . . him: *Rowe*; tomorrow, – . . . him, – *Delius*   133 renowned?] *QF*; renown'd! *F4*; renown'd. *Capell*   138 fasting] *Q*; feasting *F*   wantonness!] *Rowe*; wantonesse. *Q*; wantonnesse *F*   141 on] *F*; one *Q*   142 shrinking] *F*; shriking *Q*   143–5] *Capell*; *QF line* it: / beggars, / looke: / forgot? /

As misers do by beggars, neither gave to me
Good word nor look. What, are my deeds forgot?     145
ULYSSES
Time hath, my lord, a wallet at his back,
Wherein he puts alms for oblivion,
A great-sized monster of ingratitudes.
Those scraps are good deeds past, which are
Devoured as fast as they are made, forgot     150
As soon as done. Perseverance, dear my lord,
Keeps honour bright; to have done is to hang
Quite out of fashion, like a rusty mail
In monumental mock'ry. Take the instant way,
For honour travels in a strait so narrow     155
Where one but goes abreast. Keep then the path,
For emulation hath a thousand sons,
That one by one pursue. If you give way,

146–51 **Time . . . done** The proverb, 'We see not what is in the wallet behind' (Dent, W20), makes clear that this knapsack is worn over and behind the shoulder, where the carrier cannot see what it contains and where the contents are soon forgotten. Shakespeare's inventive reading sees the *wallet* as containing our few admirable deeds serving as *alms for oblivion*, i.e. gifts destined to be forgotten. For the intellectual background, see LN.
148 **monster** i.e. oblivion
    **ingratitudes** ungrateful acts
151 **Perseverance** Persèverance
152 **to have done** to have performed deeds only in the past
153 **mail** suit of armour
154 **In monumental mock'ry** serving as a mocking trophy of forgotten noble deeds, like fully armed figures

carved on tombs, or like armour hung up in churches at the tombs of dead knights (such as the Black Prince's armour in Canterbury Cathedral) (Oxf[1], Ard[2])
    **Take . . . way** 'march straight on without pause' (Ard[1])
155 **strait** narrow passage. A possible echo of Matthew, 7.14: 'the gate is streict [strait, A.V.], and the way narrow, that leadeth unto life' (Noble, 215). The QF spelling, 'straight', is probably an alternative form, though with overlapping meaning.
156 **one but** but one, only one (Abbott, 129). The figure is of walking single file.
    **Keep then the path** (1) keep moving forward; (2) don't leave the path
157 **emulation** envious rivalry
158 **That . . . pursue** that crowd after one another, vying for supremacy

148 ingratitudes] *QF*; ingratitude *Hanmer*   149–51] *this edn; QF line* past, / made, / Lord, / ; *Rowe lines* devour'd / soon / lord, /   153 mail] *QF (male)*   155 strait] *QF (straight)*   narrow] *F (narrow,)*; narrow: *Q*   156 one] *F*; on *Q*   abreast.] *Pope, subst. (*abreast;*)*; a breast, *QF*

Or hedge aside from the direct forthright,
Like to an entered tide they all rush by                                    160
And leave you hindmost;
Or, like a gallant horse fall'n in first rank,
Lie there for pavement to the abject rear,
O'er-run and trampled on. Then what they do in present,
Though less than yours in past, must o'ertop yours;         165
For Time is like a fashionable host
That slightly shakes his parting guest by th' hand,
And, with his arms outstretched as he would fly,
Grasps in the comer. Welcome ever smiles,
And Farewell goes out sighing. O, let not virtue seek      170
Remuneration for the thing it was;
For beauty, wit,
High birth, vigour of bone, desert in service,
Love, friendship, charity, are subjects all
. To envious and calumniating Time.                                         175

---

159 To *hedge* or go aside from the *direct forthright* or straight way carries the pejorative connotation of dodging, shuffling, leaving open a way of retreat (*OED* hedge *v.* 9). This line is *OED*'s first citation of *forthright* as a substantive.

160 **Like . . . tide** like a tide that has poured tumultuously in through a breakwater or other obstruction (such as the piers of London Bridge)

163 *(they leave you) lying there to be trampled on by the cowardly and mean-spirited troops bringing up the rear'. *Pavement* means a paved way, and perhaps also a paving stone (*OED* 1, 3). On ellipsis of the understood *you* at the start of this line, see Abbott, 401. Lines 162–4, 'Or . . . trampled on', are missing from Q, perhaps in

error, since F's 'hindmost' in 161 reads 'him, most' in Q, as part of a hypermetrical line making only difficult sense. See Nosworthy, 66–7.

167 **slightly** negligently, unceremoniously

168 **as he would** as if he wanted to or is about to

169 **Grasps in** embraces (*OED* *v.* 4; first citation)

170–1 **let . . . was** i.e. 'do not be so naive as to expect recognition and reward for virtuous past deeds'

170 **virtue** (1) noble excellence in character and action; (2) power, strength

173 **vigour of bone** bodily strength
**desert** meritoriousness

174 **charity** benevolence, fairness, love of fellow humans and of God

---

159 hedge] *F;* turne *Q*    161 hindmost;] *F* (hindmost:); him, most, *Q*    162–4 Or . . . trampled on]
*F; not in Q*    163 abject rear] *Hanmer;* abiect, neere *F*    165 past] *F;* passe *Q*    169 Welcome] *Pope;*
the welcome *QF*    170 Farewell] *Q* (farewell); farewels *F*    O, let] *F* (O let); Let *Q*    171–2] *Var '93;*
*one line, QF*    174 subjects] *QF;* subject *Cam¹*

One touch of nature makes the whole world kin,
That all with one consent praise new-born gauds,
Though they are made and moulded of things past,
And give to dust that is a little gilt
More laud than gilt o'er-dusted.                                    180
The present eye praises the present object.
Then marvel not, thou great and complete man,
That all the Greeks begin to worship Ajax,
Since things in motion sooner catch the eye
Than what not stirs. The cry went once on thee,          185
And still it might, and yet it may again,
If thou wouldst not entomb thyself alive
And case thy reputation in thy tent,
Whose glorious deeds but in these fields of late
Made emulous missions 'mongst the gods themselves     190
And drave great Mars to faction.

ACHILLES                                            Of this my privacy

176 **nature** natural human weakness –
here, the human propensity to praise
*new-born gauds* or frivolous novelties
(177); with a homophonic pun on
*gauds* and 'gods'
177 **with one consent** unanimously
178 i.e. 'even though their apparent novelty is just an illusion concealing their
derivative quality'
179–80 'and frail humans give more
praise to trivial things that glitter than
to things of true worth that have been
covered with the dust of oblivion'. An
example of antimetabole (cf. 3.2.68–9
and 164–5), playing on paradoxical
meanings of *gilt* as a thin veneer of
gold leaf and as true gold (*OED sb.*[1] 2,
3), and of *dust* as any insubstantial
thing and as pulverized earth, including decayed human flesh – an image of
the vanity of human wishes.
182 **complete** consummate, accom-
plished. Accented equally on both syl-

lables, as at 4.1.29.
185 **cry** acclaim
186 **still** even now; suggesting also
'despite your inaction'
**yet** (with a similar doubleness of
meaning)
188 **case** encase, enclose, shut up (*OED
v.*[2] 1d; first citation in a metaphorical
sense)
189 **but . . . late** only recently on this
field of battle (Abbott, 129)
190–1 **Made . . . faction** i.e. 'sparked
emulation among the gods themselves
(prompting them to join in the fighting
on opposing sides of the Trojan war),
and even drove the god of war to be
partisan'. A *mission* is 'the action or an
act of sending' (*OED sb.* 1; first citation), i.e. dispatching assistance, inter-
vening in mortal affairs. For the
Homeric background, see LN.
191 **Of** for (Abbott, 174)

179 give] *Theobald (Thirlby);* goe *QF* gilt] *QF* (guilt*);* + *180* 184 sooner] *Q;* begin to *F*
185 Than] *F (*Then*);* That *Q* not stirs] *F;* stirs not *Q* once] *Q;* out *F*

253

I have strong reasons.

ULYSSES                    But 'gainst your privacy
The reasons are more potent and heroical.
'Tis known, Achilles, that you are in love
With one of Priam's daughters.                              195

ACHILLES   Ha? Known?

ULYSSES   Is that a wonder?
The providence that's in a watchful state
Knows almost every grain of Pluto's gold,
Finds bottom in th'uncomprehensive deeps,                   200
Keeps place with thought, and almost, like the gods,
Do thoughts unveil in their dumb cradles.
There is a mystery – with whom relation
Durst never meddle – in the soul of state,

---

193 **heroical** appropriate to a hero
195 **one . . . daughters** Polyxena, who, in
post-Homeric tradition, was claimed
by Achilles' ghost as his prize at the
fall of Troy. For variations on this
story, see LN.
198 **providence** foresight, prudent management. For possible parallels in
Elizabethan politics, see LN.
199 **Pluto's** Pluto, equated with Hades,
the Greek god of the underworld, was
often conflated with Plutus, god of
riches. In fact, Pluto (*Plouton*, 'the
Rich'), was the wealth-giver in the
sense that the earth is the source of all
wealth, while Plutus (*Ploutos*), the
personification of wealth, seems originally to have symbolized agricultural
abundance. Since F has trouble with
italic *o* / *u* in names in *JC*, the error
here is possibly compositorial.
200 **uncomprehensive** unfathomable,
illimitable, incomprehensible (*OED*'s
only citation in these senses and
Shakespeare's only use). See Abbott,
445, and Hulme, 31.

201 **Keeps . . . thought** 'keeps up with
all that is being thought', 'moves as
rapidly as thought'
202 \*'uncovers thoughts as they are conceived and before they are put into
words'. For textual choices, see LN.
203 **mystery** secret of state (*OED* 5c);
but with distinct overtones of a religious truth known only from divine
revelation, something sacramental and
incomprehensible to mortals (203–6);
also suggesting a professional or trade
secret
203–4 **with . . . meddle** 'that must not be
talked about'. *Relation* means 'report,
narrative, account, statement' (*OED
sb.* 1, 2). This allusion to the sensitive
issue of discussing affairs of state is
ironically relevant to a play about
Ulysses, Achilles, Hector and other
great figures from Homeric legend
who were often implicitly compared to
Burghley, Cecil, Essex and other political leaders of Elizabeth's late years.
See Introduction, pp. 15–18.

---

199 grain of Pluto's gold] *F;* thing *Q*    200 th'uncomprehensive deeps] *F;* the vncomprehensiue
depth *Q*    201 place] *QF;* pace *Hanmer*    thought] *QF;* aught *Oxf*    202 Do] *QF (*Do, Doe*);* Does
*F2;* Doth *(anon. in Cam)*    thoughts] *QF;* infant thoughts *Oxf*    203 whom] *QF;* which *Pope*

Which hath an operation more divine                                    205
Than breath or pen can give expressure to.
All the commerce that you have had with Troy
As perfectly is ours as yours, my lord;
And better would it fit Achilles much
To throw down Hector than Polyxena.                                    210
But it must grieve young Pyrrhus now at home,
When Fame shall in our islands sound her trump
And all the Greekish girls shall tripping sing:
'Great Hector's sister did Achilles win,
But our great Ajax bravely beat down him'.                             215
Farewell, my lord. I as your lover speak;
The fool slides o'er the ice that you should break.        [*Exit.*]

PATROCLUS

To this effect, Achilles, have I moved you.
A woman impudent and mannish grown
Is not more loathed than an effeminate man                             220

206 **expressure** expression
207 **commerce** dealings (with Polyxena and her family); with a suggestion too of mercantile association
208 'is known as completely to us (of the Greek council) as to you, my lord'
211 **Pyrrhus** (i.e. 'yellow-haired'): Achilles' son, also called Neoptolemus, later the avenging son who comes to Troy after the death of his father and slays Priam. See LN 195.
212 *\*our islands* F's 'her Iland' may represent an anticipation of *her* in the same line and an easy error of singular for plural. Cf. Prologue 1, *isles of Greece*, and 3.1.148, *island kings*.
**her trump** Reputation's trumpet. Fame (Rumour) is often personified as winged and 'painted full of tongues', as in the Induction to *2H4* and in Virgil's *Aeneid*, 4.173–90 (LCL, 1.406–9).

213 **tripping** dancing and singing lightly and nimbly. Cf. 1 Samuel, 18.6–7: 'The women came out of all cities of Israel, singing and dancing . . . with timbrels', etc. (Shaheen, 121).
215 **him** Hector (but with a suggestion of besting Achilles as well)
216 **lover** well-wisher, friend
217 i.e. 'The fool easily escapes dangers that to a man of your dignity would be fatal' (Ard¹). Ajax is too much a buffoon to be injured in reputation as Achilles is likely to be. *Should* means 'would be sure to'. The association of ice with foolish risk is proverbial; cf. *MM* 2.1.39. *Speak* and *break* (216, 217) are perfect rhymes in Shakespearean English.
218 **moved** urged
219 **impudent** shameless
220 **effeminate** unmanly, feeble, self-indulgent (*OED* 1a)

212 our islands] *Q (*our Ilands*)*; her Iland *F;* his Island *Rowe³*   214–15] *inverted commas, Capell, subst.*   217 SD] *Pope*

In time of action. I stand condemned for this;
They think my little stomach to the war,
And your great love to me, restrains you thus.
Sweet, rouse yourself, and the weak wanton Cupid
Shall from your neck unloose his amorous fold                    225
And, like a dew-drop from the lion's mane,
Be shook to air.

ACHILLES                    Shall Ajax fight with Hector?

PATROCLUS

Ay, and perhaps receive much honour by him.

ACHILLES

I see my reputation is at stake.
My fame is shrewdly gored.

PATROCLUS                    O, then, beware!                    230

Those wounds heal ill that men do give themselves.
Omission to do what is necessary
Seals a commission to a blank of danger,
And danger, like an ague, subtly taints
Even then when we sit idly in the sun.                           235

---

222 **little stomach to** small appetite for
224–7 Patroclus appears to be urging
Achilles to conquer his enervating passion for the Trojan Polyxena and the
resulting conflict of loyalties that com-
promise him as a warrior, not to give
up his attachment to Patroclus. If only
Achilles will fight manfully, the speaker argues, his male friendship with
Patroclus will not be under suspicion.
225 **fold** embrace (*OED sb.*³ 4; first citation; the next and last is in 1885)
227 \***air** F's 'ayrie ayre' 'probably results
from simple dittography (ayre / ayre)
subsequently sophisticated into sense'
(*TxC*).
**Shall Ajax** must Ajax; is Ajax to
230 **shrewdly gored** severely stabbed.
To have one's reputation *at stake*
(229) is a common expression (Dent,

S813.2). In practice, the dogs were
more threatened with goring than was
the baited bull.
233 'gives unlimited licence to danger,
provides it with a warrant with blank
spaces (like a "blank cheque") to be
filled in as danger chooses'. The danger is thus unknown, indefinite. To
*seal a commission* is to affix an official
seal to a written warrant conferring
authority.
234 **ague** fever
**taints** touches with putrefaction, like
meat left to spoil in the sun. The image
of infection combines the ideas of
fever and putrefaction; the spring sun
was thought to engender chills and
fevers by drawing up vapours, as
Hotspur observes in *1H4* 4.1.111–12
(Oxf¹).

226 like a] *F;* like *Q*   227 air] *Q (*ayre*);* ayrie ayre *F*   235 we] *F;* they *Q*

ACHILLES

Go call Thersites hither, sweet Patroclus.
I'll send the fool to Ajax and desire him
T'invite the Trojan lords after the combat
To see us here unarmed. I have a woman's longing,
An appetite that I am sick withal,                    240
To see great Hector in his weeds of peace,

*Enter* THERSITES.

To talk with him, and to behold his visage
Even to my full of view. – A labour saved.

THERSITES   A wonder!

ACHILLES   What?                                      245

THERSITES   Ajax goes up and down the field, asking for
himself.

ACHILLES   How so?

THERSITES   He must fight singly tomorrow with Hector,
and is so prophetically proud of an heroical cudgelling    250
that he raves in saying nothing.

ACHILLES   How can that be?

THERSITES   Why, 'a stalks up and down like a peacock –
a stride and a stand; ruminates like an hostess that hath

---

239–41 Achilles appears to assume that
the *combat* (238) is not going to be
mortal (Proudfoot).

239 **a woman's longing** Women were
proverbially thought to experience
strong cravings in pregnancy and to be
generally ruled by appetite (Dent,
L421.1). On the homo-erotic possibilities of the speech, see Cook, 43.

240 **withal** with

241 **in . . . peace** out of armour. *Weeds*
are garments.

243 **Even . . . view** 'until I have completely satiated my craving to see all of him,

especially his face'. When he is fully
armed rather than in his *weeds of peace*
(241), Hector's face would be concealed
behind the closed beaver of his helmet
(Seltzer). *Full* carries forward the eating metaphor in 239–43 of a woman's
longing and a ravenous appetite.

247 **himself** i.e. 'Ajax' (possibly with a
quibble on 'a jakes', a latrine)

251 **raves . . . nothing** raves incoherent-
ly. For classical parallels, see LN.

253 **peacock** referring to the proverbial
comparison, 'as proud as a peacock'
(Dent, P157)

241.1] *F; after 243, Q*   246 asking] *QF; as asking Oxf*   253 'a] *Q (a); he F*

no arithmetic but her brain to set down her reckoning;      255
bites his lip with a politic regard, as who should say,
'There were wit in this head, an 'twould out' – and so
there is, but it lies as coldly in him as fire in a flint,
which will not show without knocking. The man's
undone for ever, for if Hector break not his neck i'th'     260
combat, he'll break't himself in vainglory. He knows
not me. I said, 'Good morrow, Ajax', and he replies,
'Thanks, Agamemnon'. What think you of this man,
that takes me for the general? He's grown a very land-
fish, languageless, a monster. A plague of opinion! A       265
man may wear it on both sides, like a leather jerkin.

ACHILLES   Thou must be my ambassador to him,
Thersites.

THERSITES   Who, I? Why, he'll answer nobody. He
professes not-answering; speaking is for beggars. He       270

254–5 **an hostess . . . reckoning** Tavern
hostesses and waiters were notoriously
slow in doing sums. Cf. 'a tapster's
arithmetic', 1.2.109 and n. *Arithmetic*
here means 'arithmetical knowledge' or
'method of computation' (*OED sb.*[1] 2).
256 **politic regard** sagacious look
**as who** as if one
258 **as coldly . . . flint** Thersites plays
with the proverb, 'in the coldest flint
there is hot fire' (Dent, F371), to stress
that fire is not easily extracted from
the flint, just as wit is extracted from
Ajax' head only with extreme difficulty. Hulme, 44, shows how Shakespeare
uses the proverb in various contexts to
suggest chastity, calmness, mechanical
skill and (as here and in *LLL* 4.2.86)
boneheadedness.
259 **knocking** more humorous analogy,
comparing a striking of the flint with a
cudgelling of Ajax' head

261 **he'll . . . vainglory** Ajax will break
his own neck, in a caricature of bravado, by his reckless showing off.
264–5 **a very . . . languageless** Cf. the
proverbial expressions, 'as mute
(dumb) as a fish' (Dent, F300) and 'a
fish out of water' (Dent, F318). A
*land-fish* is, according to *OED* (land *sb.*
12), 'a fish that lives on land; hence, an
unnatural creature'.
265–6 **A plague . . . jerkin** i.e. 'A curse
upon this wretched business of what
men think of themselves and what
people think of them! A man can turn
his fatuous arrogance inside out and
call it self-confidence, or turn a reputation for boorishness into a reputation
for intrepidity (as Ajax has done), just
as one can wear a close-fitting leather
jacket either side out.'
270 **professes not-answering** 'makes it
an article of faith not to answer'

257 this] *Q;* his *F    inverted commas, Dyce[1], subst.*    262–3] *inverted commas, Hanmer, subst.*    265 monster.]
*F (*monster:*);* monster, *Q*    267 to him] *F; not in Q*    270 not-answering] *F (*notanswering*);* not
answering *Q*

wears his tongue in's arms. I will put on his presence.
Let Patroclus make demands to me. You shall see the
pageant of Ajax.

ACHILLES   To him, Patroclus. Tell him I humbly desire
the valiant Ajax to invite the most valorous Hector to      275
come unarmed to my tent, and to procure safe-conduct
for his person of the magnanimous and most illustrious
six-or-seven-times-honoured captain-general of the
Grecian army, Agamemnon, *et cetera*. Do this.

PATROCLUS *[to Thersites, as though addressing Ajax]* Jove      280
bless great Ajax!

THERSITES *[Mimics Ajax' manner]* H'm!

PATROCLUS   I come from the worthy Achilles –

THERSITES   Ha?

PATROCLUS   Who most humbly desires you to invite      285
Hector to his tent –

THERSITES   H'm!

PATROCLUS   And to procure safe-conduct from Agamemnon.

THERSITES   Agamemnon?                                  290

PATROCLUS   Ay, my lord.

THERSITES   Ha!

PATROCLUS   What say you to't?

---

271 **arms** weapons. A common topos in
Shakespeare. See, e.g., *Mac* 5.8.7: 'My
voice is in my sword', and *JC* 3.1.77:
'Speak, hands, for me!'
   **put . . . presence** assume his demeanour (*OED* put *v.*¹ 47d)
272 **demands** requests, questions (*OED*
*sb.*¹ 6)
273 **pageant** theatrical representation.
Cf. 3.2.72.

279 *et cetera* and so forth. F's '*&c*' could
be a signal to the actor to improvise,
but it also makes sense as part of
Achilles' dialogue.
282, 287 **H'm** an inarticulate sound of
dissent, dissatisfaction, mild surprise,
bemusement or approval ('Hum'), or a
little cough of warning, doubt, etc.
('Hem')

---

272 demands] *Q;* his demands *F*   275 most valorous] *F;* valorous *Q*   277 magnanimous] *Q;*
magnanimious *F*   278 captain-general] *Hanmer;* Captaine Generall *Q;* Captaine, Generall *F*
279 Grecian] *F; not in Q   et cetera] F (&c); not in Q*   280 SD] *this edn; to Thersites / Oxf*   282 SD]
*this edn*   H'm] *QF (*Hum*); + 287*

THERSITES   God b'wi' you, with all my heart.

PATROCLUS   Your answer, sir.                                        295

THERSITES   If tomorrow be a fair day, by eleven o'clock it
  will go one way or other. Howsoever, he shall pay for
  me ere he has me.

PATROCLUS   Your answer, sir.

THERSITES   Fare ye well, with all my heart.                        300
                              [*A pretended exit. Achilles applauds
                                    their concluded pantomime.*]

ACHILLES   Why, but he is not in this tune, is he?

THERSITES   No, but he's out o' tune thus. What music
  will be in him when Hector has knocked out his brains,
  I know not; but I am sure, none, unless the fiddler
  Apollo get his sinews to make catlings on.               305

ACHILLES
  Come, thou shalt bear a letter to him straight.

THERSITES   Let me carry another to his horse, for that's
  the more capable creature.

ACHILLES
  My mind is troubled, like a fountain stirred,
  And I myself see not the bottom of it.                   310
                          [*Exeunt Achilles and Patroclus.*]

---

294 **God b'wi' you** QF's 'God buy you',
  commonly seen in Renaissance texts, is
  a corrupted form of this common salutation, confused with 'buy', redeem
  (Cercignani, 365).

297 **Howsoever** in any case (*OED* 3)

300.1–2 Staging opportunities are varied
  here, but presumably in some way (a
  bow, a wave to his audience on stage)
  Thersites brings his comic presentation to a close.

301 **tune** i.e. mood, disposition (*OED sb.*
  5), setting up Thersites' musical pun
  in 302

304 **the fiddler Apollo** Apollo was often
  associated with music, especially the
  lute.

305 **catlings** catgut, used for making
  strings for stringed instruments. *OED*
  2's earliest citations are from *RJ*
  4.5.130 ('Simon Catling') and here.

307 *****carry** Q's 'beare' is perfectly plausible, and can work as a comic iteration
  of Achilles' *bear* in the previous line,
  but the simplest textual explanation of
  F's *carry* is that it represents conscious
  revision.

308 **capable** able to comprehend

---

294 God b'wi' you] *QF (*God buy you*)*   296 eleven o'clock] *F (*eleuen a clocke*)*; a leuen of the clock
*Q*   300 ye] *Q*; you *F*   300.1–2] *this edn*   302 he's] *F; not in Q*   o'] *F (*a*)*; of *Q*   304 sure] *QF;*
feared *Oxf*   307 carry] *F;* beare *Q*   310.1] *Capell*

THERSITES  Would the fountain of your mind were clear
again, that I might water an ass at it! I had rather be a
tick in a sheep than such a valiant ignorance.          [*Exit.*]

[**4.1**]  *Enter, at one door,* AENEAS [*and a Torchbearer*] *with a torch;
at another,* PARIS, DEIPHOBUS, ANTENOR, DIOMEDES *the
Grecian* [*and others*] *with torches.*

PARIS  See, ho! Who is that there?
DEIPHOBUS  It is the Lord Aeneas.
AENEAS  Is the prince there in person?
Had I so good occasion to lie long
As you, Prince Paris, nothing but heavenly business          5
Should rob my bed-mate of my company.
DIOMEDES
That's my mind too. – Good morrow, Lord Aeneas.
PARIS
A valiant Greek, Aeneas; take his hand.
Witness the process of your speech, wherein
You told how Diomed, e'en a whole week by days,          10
Did haunt you in the field.

---

312 **that . . . it** 'that I might bring an ass,
the only animal that would care to do
so, to drink of it, for even he would not
taste it as it now is' (Ard¹)
313 **ignorance** ignoramus, ignorant fool
(*OED* provides no support for this
needed sense)
**4.1** Location: Troy, perhaps in a courtyard or antechamber of the palace; but
the sense of location is not specific.
See 38–42.
**1.0.1–3** *torch . . . torches* i.e. torch-
bearers with torches. The torches are
used not for stage illumination but as
visual signals indicating a night-time

scene, shortly before dawn.
3  **the prince** Paris
5  **heavenly business** worship of the
gods
7  **mind** opinion
9  **Witness . . . speech** i.e. 'The drift of
your own earlier remarks, Aeneas, can
bear witness to Diomedes' valour'.
*Process* here means 'drift, tenor, gist'
(*OED sb.* 3).
10  \***e'en . . . days** every day for a week.
F's 'in' can be interpreted, here as on
some other occasions, as *e'en*. The Q
reading, without this word, is also
entirely plausible.

313 SD] *Capell*  **4.1**] *Rowe, subst.*  0.1 *and a Torchbearer*] *Capell, subst.*  *with a torch*] *F; not in Q*
0.2 DEIPHOBUS] *QF (Deiphobus, Diephoebus)*  ANTENOR] *F (Anthenor); Autemor Q (+ 40, subst.)*
DIOMEDES] *Capell; Diomed QF*  0.3 *and others*] *Theobald, subst.*  5 you] *F;* your *Q*  9 speech, wherein]
*Q (*speech: wherein*);* speech within; *F*  10 e'en a] *Oxf;* a *Q;* in a *F*  11 haunt] *QF;* hunt *(Upton)*

AENEAS    Health to you, valiant sir,
    During all question of the gentle truce;
    But when I meet you armed, as black defiance
    As heart can think or courage execute.                    15
DIOMEDES
    The one and other Diomed embraces.
    Our bloods are now in calm; and, so long, health;
    But when contention and occasion meet,
    By Jove, I'll play the hunter for thy life
    With all my force, pursuit and policy.                    20
AENEAS
    And thou shalt hunt a lion that will fly
    With his face backward. – In human gentleness,
    Welcome to Troy! Now by Anchises' life,
    Welcome indeed! By Venus' hand I swear,
    No man alive can love in such a sort                    25
    The thing he means to kill more excellently.

13 'during all our discussions in this time of combat-free truce' (*OED* question *sb.* 4). On the truce, see 1.3.262, 2.3.223 and 256 and notes, and 3.1.142–3.
14 **as black defiance** i.e. 'I wish (or offer) you as black defiance'. There is a similar ellipsis before 'Health' (i.e. 'I wish you health') in 12; the two phrases are grammatically parallel.
16 **The one and other** i.e. Aeneas' offers of *health* and *defiance*
17 **so long** i.e. so long as the truce continues
18 'but when fighting resumes and opportunity arises'
20 **policy** cunning
22 **With . . . backward** i.e. facing the pursuing foe
    **human** The QF spellings ('humane', 'humaine') indifferently signify 'human' and 'humane'. The primary meaning here is close to our sense of 'humane', but *human* is the more embracing term, and finds a parallel in *Mac* 1.5.17: 'the milk of human kindness'.
23–4 **Anchises' . . . Venus' hand** Aeneas swears in his parents' names and by what he regards as most precious to them. Swearing by the parts of the body is a common formulation. See *RJ* 3.1.34–5: 'BENVOLIO By my head, here comes the Capulets. / MERCUTIO By my heel, I care not.' Cf. *MA* 4.1.331–2: 'By this hand, Claudio shall render me a dear account'; *TN* 1.3.34, etc.
25–6 'no man alive can love more excellently, and to such a degree, the thing he means to kill'

17 and, so long,] *Warburton;* and so long *QF;* and so long, *Rowe*   18 But] *F;* Lul'd *Q*   meet] *Q;* meetes *F*   22 backward. – ] *Theobald², subst.;* back-ward, *QF (*backward*)*   human] *QF (*humane, humaine*)*   gentleness,] *Theobald;* gentlenesse: *QF*

DIOMEDES

> We sympathize. Jove, let Aeneas live,
> If to my sword his fate be not the glory,
> A thousand complete courses of the sun!
> But in mine emulous honour let him die,                    30
> With every joint a wound, and that tomorrow!

AENEAS    We know each other well.

DIOMEDES

> We do, and long to know each other worse.

PARIS

> This is the most despiteful'st gentle greeting,
> The noblest hateful love, that e'er I heard of.           35
> [*to Aeneas*] What business, lord, so early?

AENEAS

> I was sent for to the King; but why, I know not.

PARIS

> His purpose meets you. 'Twas to bring this Greek
> To Calchas' house and there to render him,
> For the enfreed Antenor, the fair Cressid.                40
> Let's have your company, or, if you please,
> Haste there before us.
> [*aside to Aeneas*]          I constantly do think –

---

27 **sympathize** agree, are in accord
28 'if my sword is not to have the glory of slaying him' (Ard¹)
29 **complete** with equal accent on first and second syllables, as at 3.3.182
30 **in . . . honour** in the cause of my honour, actuated by the spirit of rivalry
32 **know** understand. (See next note for wordplay.)
33 **long . . . worse** 'long to encounter each other as enemies'; 'long to see the other reduced to misery'. Paris' oxymorons in 34–5 are an elaboration of the paradox of longing to know someone worse.

34 *****most despiteful'st** most contemptuous and malignant. F's 'despightful'st' could be an error for Q's 'despightfull' induced by the superlative form of *most*, but double superlatives of this sort are common in Shakespeare. See Abbott, 11, and 5.6.21 below.
38 **His . . . you** i.e. 'I bring you his meaning and his orders' (Johnson)
39 **To Calchas' house** i.e. where Cressida lives, in her father's absence. See 3.2.3 and n.
   **render him** give him in exchange
42 **constantly** assuredly

---

31 tomorrow!] *F (*to morrow.*);* to morrow – Q    34 despiteful'st] *F;* despightfull *Q*    36 SD] *Capell, subst.*    36] F; prose, *continuing from 35,* Q    38 'Twas] *Q;* it was *F*    39 Calchas'] *Pope; Calcho's Q; Calcha's F; Calchas's F4*    42, 47, 49 SD] *Cam¹, subst.*    42 do think] *F;* beleeue Q

Or rather, call my thought a certain knowledge –
My brother Troilus lodges there tonight.
Rouse him and give him note of our approach,                45
With the whole quality wherefore. I fear
We shall be much unwelcome.

AENEAS [*aside to Paris*]                That I assure you.
Troilus had rather Troy were borne to Greece
Than Cressid borne from Troy.

PARIS [*aside to Aeneas*]                There is no help.
The bitter disposition of the time                          50
Will have it so. – On, lord; we'll follow you.

AENEAS    Good morrow, all.          *Exit [with Torchbearer]*.

PARIS

And tell me, noble Diomed, faith, tell me true,
Even in the soul of sound good fellowship,
Who, in your thoughts, merits fair Helen most,             55
Myself or Menelaus?

DIOMEDES                Both alike.
He merits well to have her that doth seek her,
Not making any scruple of her soilure,
With such a hell of pain and world of charge;
And you as well to keep her that defend her,              60
Not palating the taste of her dishonour,

---

45 **note** notice (*OED sb.*[2] 20)

46 **With . . . wherefore** 'with full explanation of the cause or occasion of our coming' (*OED* quality *sb.* 8b, citing this passage and *Tim* 3.6.107–8, 'Know you the quality of Lord Timon's fury?', as its only instances). *Quality* means 'character, tenor' (Rolfe).

50 **disposition** inclination, mood; ordering; situation, circumstances

52 **morrow** morning

54 **soul** spirit, essence

57 **He** i.e. Menelaus, and any man in his situation, seeking to recover his wife

58–9 'not being troubled by her sexual defilement, and all the suffering and expense (of war) that have resulted'. Cf. Psalms, 18.4 and 116.3 (Shaheen, 121).

61 **Not palating** not tasting or experiencing, being insensible of (*OED*'s first citation, palate *v.*)

---

46 wherefore. I] *Q, subst.* (wherefore: I)*; whereof, I F*    46–7 With . . . unwelcome.] *F; Q lines* wherefore: / vnwelcome. /    47–9 That . . . Troy] *F; prose, Q*    50–1] *Pope; QF line* so: / you. /    52 SD] *Oxf[1]; not in Q; Exit Aeneas F; Exit with Servant. Dyce*    54 the] *F; not in Q*    55 merits fair Helen most] *F; deserues faire Helen best Q*    58 soilure] *F; soyle Q*

With such a costly loss of wealth and friends.
He, like a puling cuckold, would drink up
The lees and dregs of a flat 'tamed piece;
You, like a lecher, out of whorish loins      65
Are pleased to breed out your inheritors.
Both merits poised, each weighs nor less nor more,
But he as he. Which heavier for a whore?

PARIS

You are too bitter to your countrywoman.

DIOMEDES

She's bitter to her country. Hear me, Paris:      70
For every false drop in her bawdy veins
A Grecian's life hath sunk; for every scruple
Of her contaminated carrion weight
A Trojan hath been slain. Since she could speak,
She hath not given so many good words breath      75
As for her Greeks and Trojans suffered death.

63 **puling** whining, wailing
63–4 **would . . . piece** i.e. 'is prepared to settle for the leftover caresses of a used woman, like one who would drink the turbid sediment at the bottom of a wine cask that is broached and left open for so long that the wine has gone flat'. See LN.
65–6 **out . . . inheritors** 'are content to beget your heirs out of a whore's belly'; 'are content to exhaust and degenerate your line of descent through whoring' (*OED* breed *v*. III). Cf. *Tim* 1.1.262–3: 'The strain of man's bred out / Into baboon and monkey'.
67 **poised** weighed, balanced
  **nor less** neither less
68 *\**but are equal, man for man. Whichever of them is more burdened with guilt for having a whore?' (Whores are proverbially 'light', i.e. wanton.) Heath's conjectural emendation of

'each' for F's 'which' is plausible, and Q's 'the' also makes sense ('by so much the heavier for a whore'), but the F reading may be authorial and is intelligible.
69 Paris must feel that this is no time to pick a quarrel with one who is on a diplomatic mission. Paris has just been called a whoremaster in the most colourful terms. Instead of bridling, he chooses an indirect jibe: 'Don't forget, Greek, in your bitterness, that Helen is from your own country'.
72 **scruple** little bit – lit. one twenty-fourth of an ounce apothecaries' weight. The play on *scruple* in 58 suggests that men's scruples are often miniscule. The meaning in both senses derives from late Lat. *scrupulus*, little pebble.
73 **carrion** putrefied and rotten. Helen is a walking, infectious corpse. Cf. 'Most putrefied core, so fair without' (5.9.1).
76 **suffered** have suffered

67 nor less] *Q;* no lesse *F*    68 Which] *F (which); the Q; each Dyce (Johnson and Heath)*    whore?] *Knight;* whore. *QF*

PARIS

Fair Diomed, you do as chapmen do,
Dispraise the thing that you desire to buy.
But we in silence hold this virtue well:
We'll not commend what we intend to sell.                    80
Here lies our way.                                    *Exeunt.*

[**4.2**]                    *Enter* TROILUS *and* CRESSIDA.

TROILUS

Dear, trouble not yourself. The morn is cold.
CRESSIDA

Then, sweet my lord, I'll call mine uncle down.
He shall unbolt the gates.
TROILUS                    Trouble him not.
To bed, to bed! Sleep kill those pretty eyes
And give as soft attachment to thy senses        5
As infants' empty of all thought!
CRESSIDA

Good morrow, then.
TROILUS                    I prithee now, to bed.

---

77–80 *"Though you practise the buyer's
art, we will not practise the seller's. We
intend to sell Helen dear, yet we'll not
commend her' (Johnson, quoted in Var
'73). See LN.
77 **chapmen** merchants, traders. Cf.
Troilus' arguing by analogy that one
does not return used goods to the merchant (2.2.69–70).
79 'but we hold this merit to be in our
remaining silent (i.e. in declining to
praise Helen)'
**4.2** Location: Troy. The courtyard of
Calchas' house.

4 ***Sleep kill** may sleep overwhelm,
close. This QF reading, questioned by
some editors, is reinforced by *attachment* in 5; see next note.
5 **attachment** arrest, confinement
(*OED* 4, giving this line as its only citation in this metaphorical sense)
7 **Good morrow, then** Cressida accedes
reluctantly to Troilus' bidding her to
go back to bed while he goes about his
business. Perhaps she clings to him
even as she accepts his instruction.
Her reluctance may prompt the insistent repetition of his reply.

---

78 you] *F;* they *Q*    80 not commend] *QF;* but commend *Collier² (Z. Jackson)*    what we] *QF, subst.;*
that not *Ard² (Lettsom)*    intend to] *QF;* intend not to *Hanmer;* intend not *Warburton*    81] *F; prose,
continuing from 80, Q*    **4.2**] *Pope, subst.*    0.1 CRESSIDA] *QF (Cresseida, Cressida);* + *9 and 68*    4 kill]
*QF;* seal *Rowe³;* lull *Hudson² (Lettsom);* still *(Z. Jackson)*    6 As] *QF;* As to *Oxf (Keightley)*    infants']
*QF (*infants*);* infants' slumber(s) *(Proudfoot)*

CRESSIDA     Are you aweary of me?

TROILUS

O Cressida! But that the busy day,
Waked by the lark, hath roused the ribald crows,          10
And dreaming night will hide our joys no longer,
I would not from thee.

CRESSIDA                         Night hath been too brief.

TROILUS

Beshrew the witch! With venomous wights she stays
As tediously as hell, but flies the grasps of love
With wings more momentary-swift than thought.          15
You will catch cold and curse me.

CRESSIDA

Prithee, tarry. You men will never tarry.
O foolish Cressid, I might have still held off,
And then you would have tarried! – Hark, there's
   one up.

PANDARUS (*within*)   What's all the doors open here?          20

TROILUS     It is your uncle.

*Enter* PANDARUS.

CRESSIDA

A pestilence on him! Now will he be mocking.
I shall have such a life!

10 **ribald** offensively raucous, scurrilous
(*OED* B. *adj.* a, citing this line). See
LN.
12 **from** i.e. part from
13–14 **\*Beshrew . . . hell** 'My curses on
Night! She stays endlessly with
the evil-spirited and malignant.' F's
'hidiously' in 14, though well fitted
to the image of Night as a witch, is
also quite plausibly a copying error,
anticipating the 'h' of 'hell'. Q's
'tediously' is arguably the more persuasive reading, linked contrastingly
with 'momentary-swift' of 15. Cf.
Criseyde's complaint to Night for its
brevity in Chaucer, *TC* (3.1427–42).
15 Cf. the proverbial phrase, 'as swift as
thought' (Dent, T240).
20 **What's** why are (Abbott, 253)

11 joys] *Q;* eyes F   14 tediously] *Q;* hidiously F   15 momentary-swift] *Pope;* momentary swift *Q;*
momentary, swift *F*   18 Cressid] *QF (Cresseid, Cressid);* + 25   off] *QF (*of, off*)*   19 up.] *Q;* vp? *F*
20 SD] *F; not in Q*   21.1] *F; not in Q*

267

PANDARUS   How now, how now, how go maidenheads?
Here, you maid! Where's my cousin Cressid?                          25

CRESSIDA
Go hang yourself, you naughty mocking uncle!
You bring me to do – and then you flout me too.

PANDARUS   To do what, to do what? – Let her say what. –
What have I brought you to do?

CRESSIDA
Come, come, beshrew your heart! You'll ne'er be good,    30
Nor suffer others.

PANDARUS   Ha, ha! Alas, poor wretch! Ah, poor *capocchia*,
has 't not slept tonight? Would he not – ah, naughty
man – let it sleep? A bugbear take him!

CRESSIDA [*to Troilus*]
Did not I tell you? Would he were knocked i'th' head!    35

---

24 **how go** (1) what's the going price for; (2) how is it with

25 **Where's . . . Cressid?** Pandarus pretends to be unable to recognize his *cousin*, i.e. kinswoman, who was a virgin when he last saw her. This scene is based on Chaucer, *TC* (3.155–75), albeit Pandarus speaks more bawdily here.

26 **naughty** wicked (*OED* 2, 3). Whether the term anticipates the more modern sense of 'mischievous, wayward' is hard to say, given the bantering tone of the dialogue here, but the older meaning predominates. Cf. *naughty* at 33 and *naughtily* at 38.

27 **do** Cressida perhaps realizes too late that the verb she has chosen can be used obscenely by her uncle in order to tease her – as indeed he does. See G. Williams, *Dictionary*, 'do', 395–8.

30–1 **You'll . . . others** i.e. Your own mind is so dirty that you can't imagine others to be otherwise.

32 *capocchia* dolt, simpleton (It.); lit., according to Theobald, 'the thick head of a club', hence metaphorically 'a head of not much brain, a sot, dullard, heavy gull'. Florio defines it as 'the foreskin or prepuce' of a man's privy member (cited by Malone).

33 *****has 't** has it. The neuter pronoun is often used in speaking to or about children, as in German (e.g. *das Mädchen*, the little girl). Pandarus' tone is deliberately jocose and condescending. QF's 'hast' is defensible, since Pandarus is addressing Cressida directly, but it is also quite plausibly a way of representing 'has it', in anticipation of *let it* in 34.

34 **bugbear** hobgoblin

35 *****knocked i'th' head** i.e. killed (*OED* knock *v.* 3a). Some editors emend plausibly to 'o'th' head', i.e. 'on the head', but elsewhere Shakespeare variously uses 'over', 'about', etc.

---

25 Here] *Q* ; Heare *F*   30–1] *Capell; prose, QF*   32–3 Ah, . . . ah,] *Ard²;* a . . . a *QF;* Ah, . . . a *Dyce*
32 *capocchia] QF (chipochia, Chipochia)*   33 has 't] *Cam¹ (Tannenbaum, 'Notes');* hast *QF*   35 SD]
*Oxf*   35 i'th'] *QF (ith');* o'th' *Pope*   35–6] *Q; prose, F*

*One knocks.*

Who's that at door? Good uncle, go and see. –

My lord, come you again into my chamber.

You smile and mock me, as if I meant naughtily.

TROILUS    Ha, ha!                                                    39

CRESSIDA

Come, you are deceived. I think of no such thing.    *Knock.*

How earnestly they knock! Pray you, come in.

I would not for half Troy have you seen here.

*Exeunt [Troilus and Cressida].*

PANDARUS    Who's there? What's the matter? Will you

beat down the door? [*He opens the door.*] How now,

what's the matter?                                           45

[*Enter* AENEAS.]

AENEAS    Good morrow, lord, good morrow.

PANDARUS

Who's there? My Lord Aeneas? By my troth,

I knew you not. What news with you so early?

AENEAS    Is not Prince Troilus here?

PANDARUS    Here? What should he do here?                  50

AENEAS

Come, he is here, my lord. Do not deny him.

It doth import him much to speak with me.

PANDARUS    Is he here, say you? It's more than I know, I'll

be sworn. For my own part, I came in late. What should

he do here?                                                  55

---

38 **meant naughtily** implied a sexually immoral meaning; cf. 26 and n.

47–8 Pandarus normally speaks in prose, but seems here to use the more formal idiom of blank verse in his polite greeting of Aeneas. He immediately lapses back into prose under pressure of Aeneas' unexpected and uncomfortable questioning.

50 **should he do** would he be doing

52 **import** concern

35.1] *Capell, subst.; after 36, Q; after 34, F*    40 SD] *Capell, subst.; after 41, QF*    42.1 *Troilus and Cressida*] *Capell*    44 SD] *Capell, subst*    45.1] *Rowe*    53 It's] *Q (*its*);* 'tis *F*

AENEAS

> Ho, nay, then! Come, come, you'll do him wrong
> Ere you are ware. You'll be so true to him
> To be false to him. Do not you know of him,
> But yet go fetch him hither. Go.

*Enter* TROILUS.

TROILUS    How now, what's the matter?                    60
AENEAS

> My lord, I scarce have leisure to salute you,
> My matter is so rash. There is at hand
> Paris your brother and Deiphobus,
> The Grecian Diomed, and our Antenor
> Delivered to us; and for him forthwith,              65
> Ere the first sacrifice, within this hour,
> We must give up to Diomedes' hand
> The Lady Cressida.

TROILUS                            Is it concluded so?
AENEAS

> By Priam and the general state of Troy.
> They are at hand and ready to effect it.           70

TROILUS    How my achievements mock me! –

> I will go meet them. And, my Lord Aeneas,

---

56 ***Ho** expressing impatience. QF's
'Who' might also represent 'Whoa!'
57 **ware** not a contracted form, but from
OE *waer*, meaning 'aware, cognizant'
(*OED a.* 1). Shakespeare never uses
'aware' (Var). Cf. the imperative *Ware*
at 5.8.4.
57–9 **You'll . . . hither** i.e. 'In your loyalty
to Troilus and his secret, you'll harm
him by keeping from him a matter that
concerns him. Go ahead and pretend

you don't know he is here, but bring him
to me anyway.' *To be* means 'as to be'.
61 **salute** greet
62 **rash** urgent
66 **Ere . . . sacrifice** before the first early
morning sacrificial offering to the gods
68 **concluded** agreed, ordained
69 **general state** council, supreme ruling
body (*OED* state *sb.* 26)
70 **They** Paris, Diomedes, Antenor and
Deiphobus

---

56–9] *Oxf.; prose, QF; Capell lines* then: – / ware: / to him: / hither; / Go. /    56 Ho,] *Cam¹ (Tannenbaum, 'Notes');* Who, *QF;* Whoo! *Johnson;* Whoa! *Oxf*    57 you are] *Q;* y'are F    59.1] *F; not in Q*
63 Deiphobus] *QF (Deiphobus, Deiphoebus)*    64 Antenor] *QF (Anthenor); + 77, 78, 88, 92*    65 us] *F;* him
*Q*    for him] *F; not in Q*    67 Diomedes'] *Q (Diomedes);* Diomeds *F*    68 concluded so] *F;* so concluded *Q*

We met by chance; you did not find me here.

AENEAS

Good, good my lord, the secrets of nature
Have not more gift in taciturnity.                    75

*Exeunt* [*Troilus and Aeneas*].

PANDARUS   Is't possible? No sooner got but lost? The
devil take Antenor! The young prince will go mad. A
plague upon Antenor! I would they had broke 's neck!

*Enter* CRESSIDA.

CRESSIDA

How now? What's the matter? Who was here?

PANDARUS   Ah, ah!                    80

CRESSIDA

Why sigh you so profoundly? Where's my lord?
Gone? Tell me, sweet uncle, what's the matter?

PANDARUS   Would I were as deep under the earth as I am
above!

CRESSIDA   O the gods! What's the matter?                    85

PANDARUS   Pray thee, get thee in. Would thou hadst ne'er
been born! I knew thou wouldst be his death. O, poor
gentleman! A plague upon Antenor!

CRESSIDA   Good uncle, I beseech you, on my knees I
beseech you, what's the matter?                    90

---

73 i.e. remember to say that we met by
chance, and that you didn't find me
here. (A convenient fiction to which
Aeneas readily agrees.)

74 *the secrets of nature Nature is
proverbially slow to reveal her secrets.
F's reading thus makes perfect sense,

as Q's reference to the supposed secrecy of 'neighbor *Pandar*' does not.
Presumably Q's nonsense had its origin in an awkwardly placed SD in the
copy manuscript.

75.1 *For textual and staging options, see
LN.

74 good my] *some copies of Q;* good, my *some copies of QF*   secrets] *QF;* secret'st things *Theobald;*
secretest *Hanmer;* secrecies *Singer (Steevens)*   nature] *F;* neighbor *Pandar Q;* natures *Hanmer*
75.1 *Capell; Exeunt. Q; Exennt. / Enter Pandarus and Cressid. F*   76 lost?] *Hanmer;* lost, *Q;* lost: *F*
78.1] *Q (Enter Cress.) at start of 79 (see next note); not in F*   79 SP] *F (Cres.); SD, 78.1, serves also as
SP, Q*   80 Ah, ah!] *Q;* Ah, ha! *F*   81–2] *Malone; prose, QF*   86 Pray thee] *Q;* Prythee *F*
87 wouldst] *F (would'st);* wouldest *Q*   89–90 I beseech you] *F; not in Q*

PANDARUS  Thou must be gone, wench, thou must be
gone. Thou art changed for Antenor. Thou must to thy
father and be gone from Troilus. 'Twill be his death,
'twill be his bane; he cannot bear it.

CRESSIDA

O you immortal gods! I will not go.                                    95

PANDARUS  Thou must.

CRESSIDA

I will not, uncle. I have forgot my father.
I know no touch of consanguinity;
No kin, no love, no blood, no soul so near me
As the sweet Troilus. O you gods divine,                               100
Make Cressid's name the very crown of falsehood
If ever she leave Troilus! Time, force and death,
Do to this body what extremes you can;
But the strong base and building of my love
Is as the very centre of the earth,                                   105
Drawing all things to it. I'll go in and weep –

PANDARUS  Do, do.

CRESSIDA

Tear my bright hair and scratch my praised cheeks,
Crack my clear voice with sobs, and break my heart       109
With sounding 'Troilus'. I will not go from Troy.    *Exeunt.*

---

92 **changed** exchanged
94 **bane** poison, death, ruin
97–9 For biblical echoes, see LN.
98 **no . . . consanguinity** no feelings of
blood relationship; not even a trace of
attachment to kin (*OED* touch *sb.* 14,
19)
102 **force** violence, compulsion
103 ***extremes** F's 'extremitie' may have
been suggested erroneously to the

compositor by the similarly sounding
ending of *body* earlier in the line.
105–6 **the very . . . to it** Cf. *RJ* 2.1.2:
'Turn back, dull earth, and find thy
center out', and Marlowe's *Faustus*, A-
text, 2.3.36–7, for the commonplace
idea that the centre of the earth
attracts all things to it.
108 **praised** praisèd

101 Cressid's] *QF (Cresseids, Cressids)*    103 extremes] *Q*; extremitie *F*    106 I'll] *Q* (Ile); I will *F*
110] *inverted commas, Ard²*    SD] *F; not in Q*

**[4.3]** *Enter* PARIS, TROILUS, AENEAS, DEIPHOBUS,
       ANTENOR *and* DIOMEDES.

PARIS

It is great morning, and the hour prefixed
Of her delivery to this valiant Greek
Comes fast upon. Good my brother Troilus,
Tell you the lady what she is to do
And haste her to the purpose.

TROILUS                     Walk into her house.    5

I'll bring her to the Grecian presently;
And to his hand when I deliver her,
Think it an altar and thy brother Troilus
A priest, there off'ring to it his own heart.

PARIS   I know what 'tis to love;                 10

And would, as I shall pity, I could help!
Please you walk in, my lords.            *Exeunt.*

---

**4.3** Location: Troy. Before Calchas' house (where Cressida stays; see 4.1.39).

1 **great morning** broad day. Cf. Fr. *au grand jour*, in broad daylight.

1–2 **prefixed / Of** agreed upon beforehand for

3 **Comes fast upon** The expression is idiomatic in Shakespeare without adding 'us', as Pope does. Cf. *Ham* 1.2.179: 'Indeed, my lord, it followed hard upon', and Abbott, 192. Metrically, as well, Pope's emendation is too insistent on a regular iambic rhythm.

5 **haste . . . purpose** get herself ready. (See *OED* purpose *sb.* 12.) The remark could conceivably be instructing

Troilus to hasten her along, but Shakespeare rarely uses *haste* as a verb, and when he does so, it is in the reflexive sense: 'Haste you again', i.e. 'hurry up' (*AW* 2.2.68). The comma at the end of 4 in QF is probably rhythmic rather than an indication of a grammatical parallel between *Tell* and *haste* as imperatives.

6 **presently** at once

9 Troilus may exit at this point, in advance of the others. Line 12 may imply this, since it is addressed to the others, not to him.

11 'and I wish I could help as much as I shall pity!'

---

**4.3]** *Capell, subst.* 0.1 DEIPHOBUS] QF *(Deiphob, Deiphebus)* 0.2 ANTENOR *and*] *F (Anthenor and); Anth.* Q  2 Of] *F;* For *Q*  3 upon] *QF;* upon us *Pope*  9 own] *Q; not in F*  heart] *QF;* heart. *Exit* TROILUS. / *Capell*

[**4.4**]                    *Enter* PANDARUS *and* CRESSIDA.

PANDARUS    Be moderate, be moderate.
CRESSIDA
Why tell you me of moderation?
The grief is fine, full, perfect that I taste,
And violenteth in a sense as strong
As that which causeth it. How can I moderate it?          5
If I could temporize with my affection,
Or brew it to a weak and colder palate,
The like allayment could I give my grief.
My love admits no qualifying dross;
No more my grief, in such a precious loss.               10

*Enter* TROILUS.

PANDARUS    Here, here, here he comes. Ah, sweet ducks!
CRESSIDA [*Embraces Troilus*]    O Troilus! Troilus!

---

**4.4** Location: Calchas' house, where
Cressida is staying. In the absence of
scenic effects, the sense of location is
virtually continuous from the beginning of Act 4, in or in the vicinity of
the house. This present scene can be
imagined to take place in an interior.
**3 fine** refined, pure (*OED a.* 2)
  \*full, perfect F's omission of the
comma is suspect in view of that text's
longer stemma of transmission, even if
F's reading is defensible as meaning
'fully perfect'.
**4–5 And . . . it** 'and rages violently in
manner and degree proportionate to
the terrible event that caused it'. (*OED*
violent *v.* 5 gives this citation only for
an intransitive sense of the verb.)
**6 temporize . . . affection** negotiate
with my passion, trim it

**7** 'or dilute that passion to suit a weaker
and less ardent appetite'
**8 allayment** 'admixture of a modifying
element or agent; mitigation' (*OED*,
citing this and *Cym* 1.5.22 as its sole
instances; but see *Cor* 2.1.48–9: 'a cup
of hot wine with not a drop of allaying
Tiber in 't'). The image is one of literal or metaphorical dilution of com-
pounds; see next note.
**9 qualifying dross** foreign substance
ordinarily introduced to reduce a mixture to a more satisfactory condition
(*OED* qualify *v.* 8, dross *sb.* 2), but
with a suggestion here of impure scum
or residue that merely attenuates or
contaminates
**10 No . . . grief** no more does my grief
(admit such a qualifying substance), in
the loss of what is so precious

**4.4**] *Capell, subst.*  0.1 CRESSIDA] *Q (Cresseida); Cressid F*  3 full,] *Q;* full *F*  4 violenteth] *Q;* no
lesse *F*  6 affection] *F;* affections *Q*  9 dross] *Q;* crosse *F*  10.1] *Q; opp. 9, F*  11 Ah,] *Capell,
subst.;* a *QF*  ducks] *Q;* ducke *F*  12 SD] *Capell, subst.*

PANDARUS   What a pair of spectacles is here! Let me
embrace, too. 'O heart', as the goodly saying is,
> 'O heart, heavy heart,                                    15
> Why sigh'st thou without breaking?'

where he answers again:
> 'Because thou canst not ease thy smart
> By friendship nor by speaking.'

There was never a truer rhyme. Let us cast away      20
nothing, for we may live to have need of such a verse.
We see it, we see it. How now, lambs?

TROILUS

Cressid, I love thee in so strained a purity
That the blest gods, as angry with my fancy –
More bright in zeal than the devotion which           25
Cold lips blow to their deities – take thee from me.

---

13 **What . . . here!** 'What a spectacle you
two present!' The temptation to read this
as an apparent and rather pointless witticism comparing the lovers to eyeglasses
may be only an anachronistic hindsight;
nowhere else does Shakespeare speak of
spectacles as a pair. On the other hand, 'a
pair of spectacles' is a common
Renaissance usage (*OED* spectacle *sb.*[1]
6b), and Pandarus is certainly capable of
an inopportunely timed and feeble jest.

14 **the goodly saying** Pandarus seems to
refer to some versified rendition of the
proverb, 'Grief pent up will break the
heart' (Dent, G449).

15–19 Pandarus' verse takes up the theme
of sorrow at the parting of lovers; the
heart cannot be satisfied by friendship
or words alone. Cf. the Nurse's comment to Juliet that Romeo is as good as
dead to her, 'As living here and you no
use of him' (*RJ* 3.5.227).

17 **he** the heart. This verse fragment,
whether invented by Shakespeare or
from a lost popular ballad, is in the

form of a dialogue.

19 **friendship** i.e. mere friendship
**speaking** i.e. 'mere words, as opposed
to loving acts' (Rolfe)

22 **We see it** i.e. 'We see every day how
sentiments in verse can console'.

23 **strained** perfectly filtered, refined
(*OED* 7, citing this line)

24 **as** as if
**fancy** love, amorous inclination (*OED*
*sb.* 8b), but also suggesting 'invention',
and, to our ears at least, 'whim, inclination'. The gods, says Troilus, are resent-
ful of a profane amorous devotion
exceeding that bestowed on themselves.

25 **More bright** i.e. which fancy is more
bright

26 **Cold** chaste. Troilus boasts that his
love is more pure than that which tem-
ple virgins bestow upon the gods, *blow-
ing* or breathing out vows with chaste
lips. *Their deities* can mean 'the deities
the virgins worship' or can be an honorific title due to the gods; cf. *MND*
3.1.174: 'I cry your worships mercy'.

---

14–19] *Pope; prose, QF*   14] *inverted commas, Theobald, subst.*   15–19] *inverted commas, Pope, subst.*
15 heavy] *QF; O heavy / Pope*   16 sigh'st] *Q (sighst); sighest F*   23 strained] *Q; strange F*
purity] *Q (purity,); puritie; F*   26 deities –] *Q (dieties,); Deities: F*

CRESSIDA     Have the gods envy?
PANDARUS     Ay, ay, ay, ay, 'tis too plain a case.
CRESSIDA
    And is it true that I must go from Troy?
TROILUS
    A hateful truth.
CRESSIDA                         What, and from Troilus too?          30
TROILUS
    From Troy and Troilus.
CRESSIDA                         Is't possible?
TROILUS
    And suddenly, where injury of chance
    Puts back leave-taking, jostles roughly by
    All time of pause, rudely beguiles our lips
    Of all rejoindure, forcibly prevents          35
    Our locked embrasures, strangles our dear vows
    Even in the birth of our own labouring breath.
    We two, that with so many thousand sighs
    Did buy each other, must poorly sell ourselves
    With the rude brevity and discharge of one.          40
    Injurious Time now with a robber's haste

---

31 **Troilus** pronounced in three syllables (as opposed to two in the previous line)

32–3 **where . . . back** in a situation in which injurious Fortune repulses, rejects, prevents (*OED* put *v*.[1] 40a)

33 **by** (1) past; (2) aside

35 **Of all rejoindure** of the possibility of any reunion. *OED*'s only citation of *rejoindure*, and Shakespeare's only use. The nearly homophonic 'rejoinder', i.e. 'reply', might well suggest itself to a theatre audience.

36 **embrasures** embraces. *OED sb.*[1] gives this line as its only citation in this sense, coined presumably by Shakespeare from *embrace* + *ure*, a suffix denoting action or process.
**strangles** Unwanted babies were some-

times strangled, like the Third Witch's 'birth-strangled babe' in *Mac* 4.1.30.
**dear** precious; consequential; affectionate

37 **labouring** toiling; distressed; suffering the pain of giving birth (*OED* labour *v*. 11, 15, 16)

40 **discharge of one** 'exhalation of a single sigh'; with a suggestion too, in the commercial image, of discharging or paying a debt, of firing off a gun or pistol, and of a dismissal (*OED* discharge *v*. 1f, 5b, 10)

41–2 Time, like a thief hastily stowing his plunder in a bag, forces the lovers to 'cram into a moment the precious delight of leave-taking' (Ard[1]).

---

36 embrasures] *QF*; embraces *Pope*     40 one.] *F3, subst.*; one, *Q;* our *F*     41 Time] *Q (*time*);* time; *F*

Crams his rich thiev'ry up, he knows not how.
As many farewells as be stars in heaven,
With distinct breath and consigned kisses to them,
He fumbles up into a loose adieu                                45
And scants us with a single famished kiss,
Distasted with the salt of broken tears.

AENEAS (*within*)    My lord, is the lady ready?

TROILUS

Hark, you are called. Some say the Genius so
Cries 'Come!' to him that instantly must die. –              50
Bid them have patience. She shall come anon.

PANDARUS    Where are my tears? Rain, to lay this wind,

---

43 a proverbial comparison: 'as many as the stars' (Dent, S825.1)

44 'with the several utterances that should accompany those farewells, and with kisses that should ratify them' (Ard¹). *OED*'s first citation of *consigned*; here accented on the first syllable, as *distinct* may be also. *Consigned* signifies legal allotment and deliverance of a bond, ratified here by kisses.

45 **fumbles up** i.e. 'awkwardly huddles together (their vows and kisses of farewell)'; but also carrying forward the image of the robber in 41–2, clumsily gathering up what he has stolen (Ard²)
**loose** careless, slack, lax. Cf. 3.3.166–9, where Time is compared to 'a fashionable host / That slightly shakes his parting guest by th' hand' and quickly moves on to embrace the newcomer.

46 **scants us** furnishes us with an inadequate supply, stints us (*OED v.* 3; first citation). The culinary metaphor continues in *famished*, *Distasted* and *salt* (Whiter, 127 and 136, and Spurgeon, 321–4, cited by Oxf¹). See also 5.1.57 and n.

47 'robbed of all sweetness by the salt tears of broken sobs' (Ard¹). Cf. *distaste* at 2.2.123.
**broken** interrupted by sobs. The word may also have been suggested, in the sense of 'broken meats' or fragments of food, by the culinary metaphor of *scants*, *famished*, *Distasted* and *salt* in 46–7 (see Whiter, 127 and 136, and 46n. above).

48 SD *within* For staging options, see LN.

49 **Genius** in classical religious belief, 'the tutelary god or attendant spirit allotted to every person at his birth, to govern his fortunes and determine his character, and finally to conduct him out of the world' (*OED* 1)

52 **Rain . . . wind** i.e. 'I must shed tears, to allay my sighs', or, 'O, for a shower of tears . . .'. Pandarus thus bitterly applies the proverb, 'Small rain lays great winds' (Dent, R16), which expresses the popular superstition that the onset of rain causes the winds to decrease.

---

42 thiev'ry] *Q* (theeu'ry)*;* theeuerie *F*    47 Distasted] *Q;* Distasting *F*    tears.] *Q;* teares. *Enter Aeneus. F*    49–50 Genius so / Cries 'Come!'] *F, subst.; Genius / Cries so Q*    50] *inverted commas,* Hanmer, *subst.*

or my heart will be blown up by the root.                    [*Exit.*]

CRESSIDA

I must, then, to the Grecians?

TROILUS                                    No remedy.

CRESSIDA

A woeful Cressid 'mongst the merry Greeks!                    55
When shall we see again?

TROILUS

Hear me, my love. Be thou but true of heart –

CRESSIDA

I true? How now, what wicked deem is this?

TROILUS

Nay, we must use expostulation kindly,
For it is parting from us.                                    60
I speak not 'Be thou true' as fearing thee,
For I will throw my glove to Death himself
That there's no maculation in thy heart;
But 'Be thou true', say I, to fashion in
My sequent protestation: Be thou true,                       65
And I will see thee.

---

53 *blown . . . root* i.e. uprooted, like a
tree. (The Q reading, 'blowne vp by
my throate', is tempting in its grotes-
querie, and could mean that Pandarus'
cries of grief will burst his heart, but
the F reading continues the metaphor
of wind and rain, and may represent
an authorial choice.)

55 **merry Greeks** a proverbial phrase
(Dent, M901) for licentious hedonists,
dolefully recalling Cressida's more
sprightly use of the expression at
1.2.105 and n.

56 **see** see each other, meet

58 **deem** thought, surmise (*OED*'s first
citation and Shakespeare's only use of
the word as a substantive)

59–60 i.e. 'Take it easy, we must argue
and remonstrate gently, for soon even
this chance to speak will desert us'.

61 **as fearing thee** 'out of fear that you
will not be true'

62 **throw . . . Death** 'issue a formal challenge to Death (by throwing down my
glove)'

63 **maculation** stain of impurity or
inconstancy (Onions; *OED* 1 cites this
line). Shakespeare's only use of the
word.

64–5 **to fashion in . . . protestation** 'as
a way of working in and introducing
my own solemn affirmation of resolution, as follows:' (Onions, 'fashion', *v.*
5)

---

53 the root] *F*; my throate *Q*    SD] *Theobald, subst.*    56 When] *Q; Troy.* When *F*    57 my] *F; not in Q*
61] *inverted commas, Hanmer, subst. (+ 64, 73)*    63 there's] *F;* there is *Q*    65–6] *F;* one line, *Q*

CRESSIDA

O, you shall be exposed, my lord, to dangers
As infinite as imminent! But I'll be true.

TROILUS

And I'll grow friend with danger. Wear this sleeve.

CRESSIDA [*as they exchange favours*]

And you this glove. When shall I see you?                      70

TROILUS

I will corrupt the Grecian sentinels,
To give thee nightly visitation.
But yet, be true.

CRESSIDA                    O heavens! 'Be true' again?

TROILUS    Hear why I speak it, love.

The Grecian youths are full of quality;                        75
Their loving well composed with gifts of nature,
And flowing o'er with arts and exercise.
How novelty may move and parts with person,
Alas, a kind of godly jealousy –

---

69 **grow friend with** i.e. embrace, welcome
   **sleeve** The detachable sleeves or ornamental cuffs of Elizabethan garments both male and female were often given as favours or love tokens (Linthicum, 198). Chaucer's Criseyde gives such a token to Diomedes (*TC*, 5.1043). A *glove* (70) also made a suitable remembrance. More often in Elizabethan texts, a sleeve is given as a token by a woman to a man, but the exchanging of tokens is perfectly understandable here.
71 **corrupt** bribe
75 **quality** flair, good breeding, graceful manners, accomplishment (*OED* 2–4)
76 *\*'in courting ladies they are well endowed with natural gifts'. For textual choices, see LN.

77 **arts and exercise** skills sharpened by practice. An example of hendiadys; cf. 3.2.155 and Puttenham, 3.16 (177–8).
78 **parts with person** natural gifts and abilities combined with personal attractiveness (*OED* part *sb*. 12, person *sb*. 4b)
79 **godly jealousy** St Paul speaks of 'godly jealousy' in his fear that his wavering flock will be untrue to their divine husband Christ, much as Eve allowed herself to be beguiled by the serpent (2 Corinthians, 11.1–3, cited by Theobald in a letter to Warburton, 6 March 1730; Var). Paul's consciousness of his own 'folly' in being thus anxious is like Troilus' admission of a *virtuous sin* (80) in being both jealous (a sin) and wedded to constancy (a virtue).

---

69] *Q; F lines* danger. / Sleeue. /    danger. Wear] *F (*danger; / Weare*);* danger, were *Q*    70 SD] *Bevington², subst.*    70] *Q; F lines* Gloue. / you? /    72–3 To give . . . true] *F; one line, Q*    76] *F; not in Q*    gifts] *Theobald²;* guift *F*    77 And flowing o'er] *Staunton;* And swelling ore *Q;* Flawing and swelling ore *F*    78 novelty] *Q;* nouelties *F*    person] *F;* portion *Q*

Which, I beseech you, call a virtuous sin –      80
Makes me afeard.

CRESSIDA           O heavens, you love me not!

TROILUS    Die I a villain then!
In this I do not call your faith in question
So mainly as my merit. I cannot sing,
Nor heel the high lavolt, nor sweeten talk,      85
Nor play at subtle games – fair virtues all,
To which the Grecians are most prompt and
    pregnant.
But I can tell that in each grace of these
There lurks a still and dumb-discoursive devil
That tempts most cunningly. But be not tempted.      90

CRESSIDA    Do you think I will?

TROILUS    No.
But something may be done that we will not;
And sometimes we are devils to ourselves,
When we will tempt the frailty of our powers,      95
Presuming on their changeful potency.

AENEAS (*within*)
Nay, good my lord –

TROILUS           Come, kiss, and let us part.

---

**83–4 faith . . . merit** Troilus plays on the Protestant insistence on salvation through faith, not merit. His *merit* cannot make him worthy.

**84 mainly** much, strongly

**85** 'nor dance a fashionable and lively French dance requiring high leaps and fancy footwork, nor talk in a way that is sweet to the ear'

**86 subtle** clever; requiring skill; cunning, deceptive
**virtues** accomplishments (*OED* 5b)

**87 prompt and pregnant** readily inclined and resourceful (*OED* prompt *a*. 1b, citing this line as its first instance; pregnant *a*. 3a)

**89 dumb-discoursive** silently persuasive (Oxf[1])

**93 that we will not** that we do not intend or desire. Troilus transforms Cressida's 'Do you think I will?', i.e. 'Do you suppose I am likely to do that?' into the stronger sense of actively willing something. Cf. Romans, 7.18: 'For I know that in me (that is, in my flesh) dwelleth no good thing: for to will is present with me; but I find no means to perform that which is good' (Ard[2]).

**95 will tempt** deliberately make trial of

**96** i.e. 'trusting too readily in our power to control our wills, when in fact that wilfulness is all too changeable and unreliable'

---

81 afeard] *Q;* affraid *F*    92–3] *this edn; one line, QF*

PARIS (*within*)

   Brother Troilus!

TROILUS [*Calls out*]   Good brother, come you hither,

   And bring Aeneas and the Grecian with you.

CRESSIDA   My lord, will you be true?          100

TROILUS

   Who, I? Alas, it is my vice, my fault.

   Whiles others fish with craft for great opinion,

   I with great truth catch mere simplicity;

   Whilst some with cunning gild their copper crowns,

   With truth and plainness I do wear mine bare.          105

*Enter* [AENEAS, PARIS, ANTENOR,
         DEIPHOBUS *and* DIOMEDES].

   Fear not my truth. The moral of my wit

   Is 'plain and true'; there's all the reach of it. –

   Welcome, Sir Diomed. Here is the lady

   Which for Antenor we deliver you.

   At the port, lord, I'll give her to thy hand          110

   And by the way possess thee what she is.

---

102 **craft** cunning
   **opinion** reputation
103 'I, in my pursuit of truth, get a reputation for being plain and simple.' Cf.
   Sonnet 66.11: 'And simple truth mis-
   called simplicity' (Hillebrand, Var).
104 **crowns** coins; honorific headpieces.
   Both senses here suggest counterfeit
   show.
105 **wear mine bare** i.e. 'wear my head
   uncovered, showing myself to be
   exactly what I seem' (using *crown* in
   the sense of 'the top of the head'); but
   suggesting also the wearing bare of
   plain copper coins
106 **truth** fidelity
106–7 **The moral . . . Is** 'my wisdom

may be summed up in the maxim'
(Ard¹)
107 **all the reach** the full extent
110, 135 **port** gate of the city
110–36 **thy hand . . . thy head** In addressing Diomedes, Troilus consistently
   employs the second-person familiar
   form used in speaking to friends, children or servants. Increasingly in this
   passage his use of *thou* and *thee* may take
   on the character of a deliberate insult (as
   in *RJ* 3.1.44ff.: 'Mercutio, thou con-
   sortest with Romeo', etc.), especially
   since Diomedes insolently refuses to
   answer Troilus at first and then addresses him as *you* at 131 and 133.
111 **possess** inform (*OED v.* 10)

---

98 SD] *Ard²*, *subst.*   100 true?] *Q;* true? *Exit. F*   105 wear] *F (*weare*);* were *Q*   105.1–2] *Kittredge;*
*Malone, after 107; not in Q; Enter the Greekes. F*   107 *inverted commas, Capell, subst.*

Entreat her fair and, by my soul, fair Greek,
If e'er thou stand at mercy of my sword,
Name Cressid, and thy life shall be as safe
As Priam is in Ilium.

DIOMEDES                    Fair Lady Cressid,                    115
So please you, save the thanks this prince expects.
The lustre in your eye, heaven in your cheek,
Pleads your fair usage; and to Diomed
You shall be mistress and command him wholly.

TROILUS

Grecian, thou dost not use me courteously,                    120
To shame the zeal of my petition to thee
In praising her. I tell thee, lord of Greece,
She is as far high-soaring o'er thy praises
As thou unworthy to be called her servant.
I charge thee use her well, even for my charge;              125
For, by the dreadful Pluto, if thou dost not,
Though the great bulk Achilles be thy guard,
I'll cut thy throat.

DIOMEDES                    O, be not moved, Prince Troilus.
Let me be privileged by my place and message

---

112 **Entreat her fair** treat her well
116 i.e. 'Please save yourself the trouble
   of thanking Troilus for requesting that
   I treat you well; I will do so for your
   sake, not his'.
119 **mistress** woman whom a man devot-
   edly serves; see 124n. An actor is certainly entitled to insinuate something
   more intimate as well, since the illicit
   sense of the term was current (*OED*
   11).
   **him** i.e. 'me'. Diomedes speaks of
   himself in the third person.
121–2 **To . . . her** 'insulting me and my
   heartfelt request by praising her
   openly to my face'

121 **zeal** QF's spelling, 'seale', suggests
   wordplay on the idea of affixing a 'seal'
   to a *petition* (Heath). In the theatre,
   *zeal* and 'seal' would be close in sound.
124 **servant** one who is devoted to the
   service of his lady. See 119n.
125 **even for my charge** 'simply because
   I insist that you do'. The wordplay on
   *charge* involves a change in part of
   speech, from verb to noun.
127 **bulk** body of a huge frame (*OED sb.*[1]
   2c)
128 **moved** angry
129 **my place and message** i.e. as
   ambassador on a mission conferring
   diplomatic immunity

---

115 Ilium.] *Oxf*[1]; Illion? *QF*   118 usage] *Q* (vsage); visage *F*   121 zeal] *Theobald*; seale *QF*   to
thee] *Johnson;* to thee: *Q;* towards, *F;* towards thee *Rowe*   122 In] *Q;* I *F*

To be a speaker free. When I am hence,                    130
I'll answer to my lust. And know you, lord,
I'll nothing do on charge. To her own worth
She shall be prized; but that you say 'Be't so',
I'll speak it in my spirit and honour: 'No'.

TROILUS

Come, to the port. – I'll tell thee, Diomed,                    135
This brave shall oft make thee to hide thy head. –
Lady, give me your hand and, as we walk,
To our own selves bend we our needful talk.

> [*Exeunt Troilus, Cressida and Diomedes.*]
> *Sound trumpet* [*within*].

PARIS    Hark, Hector's trumpet!

AENEAS                    How have we spent this morning!
The prince must think me tardy and remiss,                    140
That swore to ride before him in the field.

PARIS

'Tis Troilus' fault. Come, come, to field with him.

DEIPHOBUS    Let us make ready straight.

---

131 **answer to my lust** 'do what I please'
– whether in response to carnal lust, or
to Troilus' request for honourable
treatment of Cressida, or to an opportunity to fight

132 **charge** command (throwing back at
Troilus his insistent use of the word in
125)

**To** commensurate with

133–4 **but that** . . . **'No'** various possible
meanings: 'but, by my honour, not
because you tell me to do so'; or, even
more insultingly, 'the mere fact of your
saying "Be't so" is enough to provoke
me, in the spirit of personal honour, to
say "No" to you'. In these two con-
structions, *but that* means 'but inas-

much as' or 'but in response to the fact
that'. If *but that* means 'were it not
that', Diomedes' sarcasm is even deep-
er: 'If you hadn't said "Treat Cressida
honourably", I might not have both-
ered about her'.

136 **brave** boast, defiance, bravado

138 **bend we** let us direct

139 **spent** consumed wastefully

141 **That** I who

*in Q's 'to' makes perfect sense, and
expresses the idea of a competition to
reach the battlefield first, but F also is
entirely defensible and could represent
an authorial choice.

142 **to** . . . **him** let us join Hector on the
battlefield

131 you, lord,] *Q (you Lord); my Lord; F*    133–4] *inverted commas, Hanmer, subst.*    134 I'll] *F*
*(Ile); I Q*    138.1] *Malone; Exeunt* TRO. *and* CRE. *Capell*    138.2] *Capell, subst. (Trumpet heard);*
*Sound Trumpet. F; not in Q*    141 in] *F; to Q*    142 him.] *Rowe; him. Exeu. Q; him. / Exeunt. F*
143–7] *F; not in Q*    143 SP] *Malone (Ritson); Dio. F*

AENEAS

Yea, with a bridegroom's fresh alacrity,
Let us address to tend on Hector's heels.                    145
The glory of our Troy doth this day lie
On his fair worth and single chivalry.                    *Exeunt.*


[**4.5**]     *Enter* AJAX, *armed,* ACHILLES, PATROCLUS,
            AGAMEMNON, MENELAUS, ULYSSES, NESTOR,
                    *etc.* [*and Trumpeter*].


AGAMEMNON [*to Ajax*]

Here art thou in appointment fresh and fair,
Anticipating time with starting courage.
Give with thy trumpet a loud note to Troy,
Thou dreadful Ajax, that the appalled air
May pierce the head of the great combatant                    5
And hale him hither.

AJAX [*Gives money*]          Thou, trumpet, there's my purse.
Now crack thy lungs and split thy brazen pipe.


144 Cf. the proverbial comparison, 'Fresh as a bridegroom' (Dent, B664.1), and Psalm 19.5 (Shaheen).
145 'let us make ready to follow closely behind Hector'
147 **single chivalry** individual feats of knightly valour (*OED* chivalry 4); single combat
**4.5** Location: midway between the Greek camp and the Trojan walls (see 1.3.278). Lists or barriers for combat are set out or are implicit in the stage arrangement.
0.2–3 *etc.* For staging options, see LN.
1 **appointment** equipment, accoutrement

**fresh and fair** spick and span (Oxf[1])
2 **starting** bounding, full of energy, eager to begin
4 **dreadful** awe-inspiring
**appalled** appallèd; terrified, dismayed (*OED* 3, citing this line as its first instance in this sense). The air, driven into disarray by the trumpet blast, will beat a hasty retreat to Troy, conveying the sound as it goes.
5 **head** i.e. ear
6 **hale** draw, pull
**trumpet** trumpeter
7 **brazen** brass; giving affront (*OED a.* 1, 3)


147 SD] *at 142 in QF (see 142n.)*   **4.5**] *Capell, subst.*   0.2 NESTOR] *Theobald; Nestor, Calcas QF*
0.3 *and Trumpeter*] *Oxf, subst.*   1 SD] *this edn*   2 time with . . . courage.] *Theobald;* time. With . . .
courage, *QF*   5–6 May . . . hither] *F; prose, Q*   6 SD] *Bevington[3], subst.*

Blow, villain, till thy sphered bias cheek
Outswell the colic of puffed Aquilon.
Come, stretch thy chest, and let thy eyes spout blood; 10
Thou blowest for Hector. [*Trumpet sounds.*]

ULYSSES No trumpet answers.

ACHILLES 'Tis but early days.

[*Enter* DIOMEDES *with* CRESSIDA.]

AGAMEMNON

Is not yond Diomed, with Calchas' daughter?

ULYSSES

'Tis he. I ken the manner of his gait; 15
He rises on the toe. That spirit of his
In aspiration lifts him from the earth.

AGAMEMNON

Is this the Lady Cressid?

DIOMEDES                    Even she.

AGAMEMNON

Most dearly welcome to the Greeks, sweet lady.
[*He kisses her.*]

NESTOR

Our general doth salute you with a kiss. 20

---

8 **villain** i.e. scoundrel, rogue, slave
   **sphered** spherèd
   **bias** puffed out like a weighted bowling ball on the biased side (*OED a.* A2,
   quoting Johnson and citing this as the
   only known instance in this sense).
   Bowling balls were weighted to one
   side to make possible a curved path of
   delivery. The image also conjures up
   Renaissance maps in which the winds
   were represented as heads with swollen
   cheeks puffing from the four corners
   of the earth (Steevens, Var '93). See

next note.
9 **colic . . . Aquilon** See LN.
10 hyperbole: 'blow so hard that you
   rupture the capillaries in your eye-
   balls'
11 **for Hector** to summon Hector
13 **early days** early in the day
14 **yond** yonder
15 **ken** recognize
19 **dearly** warmly; but with a suggestion
   of 'expensively' (Empson, *Pastoral*,
   41)

---

9 colic] *QF;* choler *(Delius, anon. conj.);* choller *Cam¹* 11 SD] *Hanmer* 13 days] *QF;* day *Pope*
13.1] *F2, subst.; after 17, Theobald* 14 yond] *Q;* yong *F* 15 gait] *QF (*gate*)* 16 toe] *F; Q (*too*)*
19.1] *Collier³, subst.* (+ 23, 26, 30, 34)

ULYSSES

> Yet is the kindness but particular;
> 'Twere better she were kissed in general.

NESTOR

> And very courtly counsel. I'll begin. [*He kisses her.*]
> So much for Nestor.

ACHILLES

> I'll take that winter from your lips, fair lady.                    25
> Achilles bids you welcome. [*He kisses her.*]

MENELAUS

> I had good argument for kissing once.

PATROCLUS

> But that's no argument for kissing now;
> For thus popped Paris in his hardiment,
> And parted thus you and your argument. [*He kisses her.*]   30

ULYSSES

> O deadly gall and theme of all our scorns,
> For which we lose our heads to gild his horns!

---

21 **Yet** and yet; as yet, until now
**particular** single; individual; private; special; intimate; familiar. Lines 21–2 develop a multiple antithesis between *particular* and *general*.

22 **in general** (1) by everyone (with a play on *Our general* in 20); (2) as a general practice; (3) indiscriminately; (4) universally, without exception

25 **that winter** alluding to Nestor's old age

27 **argument** theme, subject (i.e. Helen's beauty). See next note.

28 **argument** supporting reason (said as a riposte to Menelaus' use of the term in 27)

29 **popped** moved in suddenly, came on abruptly (with blatant sexual suggestion)
**hardiment** boldness, audacity; erect hardness

30 (1) 'and thus put an end to your claim'; (2) 'and thrust himself literally between you and the subject of your adoration, Helen'

31 'O deadly bitterness and subject both of our mockery and of the indignities to which we are subjected by this strife in which we are all involved'. The *theme* is thus both Helen individually and the tawdry business of her having been stolen away by Paris.

32 **lose our heads** risk our lives; but with a sense of 'lose our judgement or reason'
**to gild his horns** i.e. merely to put a specious appearance of decency on Menelaus' cuckold's horns. Cf. 3.3.179–80: 'And give to dust that is a little gilt / More laud than gilt o'er-dusted'.

21–4] *Pope; prose, QF*   30] *Q; not in F*   32 lose] *QF* (*loose*)

PATROCLUS

    The first was Menelaus' kiss; this, mine.

    Patroclus kisses you. [*He kisses her again.*]

MENELAUS               O, this is trim!

PATROCLUS

    Paris and I kiss evermore for him.          35

MENELAUS

    I'll have my kiss, sir. – Lady, by your leave.

CRESSIDA

    In kissing, do you render or receive?

MENELAUS

    Both take and give.

CRESSIDA            I'll make my match to live,

    The kiss you take is better than you give;

    Therefore no kiss.          40

MENELAUS

    I'll give you boot; I'll give you three for one.

CRESSIDA

    You are an odd man; give even, or give none.

MENELAUS

    An odd man, lady? Every man is odd.

CRESSIDA

    No, Paris is not, for you know 'tis true

    That you are odd, and he is even with you.    45

---

34 **trim** fine (said with bitter irony)

35 i.e. 'I kiss you in Menelaus' place, just as Paris always does when he kisses Helen'.

37 **render or receive** give or take (as 38–9 makes clear)

38 **I'll . . . live** I'll bet my life

41 **boot** odds, advantage

42 **odd** single and strange; the opposite of *even*. Cressida picks up satirically on Menelaus' *boot* ('odds') and *three . . . one* in 41, both odd numbers. The

wordplay continues in 43–5.

**even** in twos; steadily, evenly; in a just degree; fully. With wordplay of course on the opposition of *odd* and *even*, which is also the name of a game of chance. Cf. the phrase 'for even or odd', meaning 'for good and all'.

43 **is odd** is individual, unique

45 **odd** odd man out, lacking a sexual partner

**even** square or quits, having settled accounts tit for tat

38 SP MENELAUS] *White (Tyrwhitt, Var '73); Patr. QF*   39–40 The kiss . . . no kiss] *Pope; one line, Q; prose, F*   42 You are] *QF;* You're *Capell*   44 not] *F;* nor *Q*

MENELAUS

  You fillip me o'th' head.

CRESSIDA                       No, I'll be sworn.

ULYSSES

  It were no match, your nail against his horn.

  May I, sweet lady, beg a kiss of you?

CRESSIDA

  You may.

ULYSSES     I do desire it.

CRESSIDA                   Why, beg too.

ULYSSES

  Why then, for Venus' sake, give me a kiss,         50

  When Helen is a maid again, and his –

CRESSIDA

  I am your debtor; claim it when 'tis due.

ULYSSES

  Never's my day, and then a kiss of you.

DIOMEDES

  Lady, a word. I'll bring you to your father.  [*They talk apart.*]

---

46 **fillip . . . head** i.e. touch a sensitive spot, as though touching my cuckold's horns. To *fillip* is to tap smartly with the finger or deliver a smart blow.

47 i.e. 'You may well say so, for his horn is far too tough for your nail to make any impression upon it' (Ard¹).

48 **beg** entreat, ask for. Ulysses speaks with courtly politeness.

49 **desire** crave; ask for, request (*OED v.* 1, 5). Ulysses warily stops short of begging, even though he introduced the term *beg* in a polite sense.
    ***Why, beg too** i.e. 'Why, then, do more than just say you desire it: you must entreat by humbling yourself as a petitioner in love'. Cressida throws Ulysses' *beg* back at him as a put-down. For textual choices, see LN.

51 i.e. 'when Helen is chastely restored as Menelaus' wife –'. The long dash after *his* in *QF* can be questioned, since *his* rhymes with *kiss* and completes the sense, but the dash may be laden with innuendo. Ulysses sardonically stresses the impossibility of the condition he prescribes; *maid* normally means unmarried and virginal. Hence *Never's my day* in 53. He has no intention of kissing Cressida, even if he finds her attractive (see *desire* in 49).

52 Cressida seems to grant Ulysses' request for a kiss, but only on the conditional terms that he has prescribed: 'You may claim your kiss of me when Helen is a maid again'.

54 SD **They talk apart** For staging options, see LN.

---

49 too.] *Cam¹ (Ritson);* then. *Q;* then? *F;* then, too *(Kinnear);* two *Ard² (Johnson)*   50 kiss,] *Q;* kisse: *F*   51 his –] *QF;* his. *Capell*   54 SD] *Oxf;* Diomedes *leads out* Cressida, *then returns (after quick sense in 55)* / *Rowe*

NESTOR
  A woman of quick sense.

ULYSSES                    Fie, fie upon her!                    55
  There's language in her eye, her cheek, her lip,
  Nay, her foot speaks; her wanton spirits look out
  At every joint and motive of her body.
  O, these encounterers, so glib of tongue,
  That give accosting welcome ere it comes,                     60
  And wide unclasp the tables of their thoughts
  To every tickling reader! Set them down
  For sluttish spoils of opportunity
  And daughters of the game. *Exeunt [Diomedes and Cressida].*

*Flourish. Enter all of Troy:* HECTOR *[armed]*, PARIS, AENEAS,
    HELENUS, [TROILUS] *and Attendants.*

---

55 **quick sense** (1) lively wit; (2) vibrant sensuality
  **Fie** a strong expletive of disgust and disapproval
58 **motive** moving limb or organ (*OED sb*. 6, citing this passage and *R2* 1.1.193 as the only known examples)
59 **encounterers** 'forward' women, coquettes (*OED* b; sole instance). Cf. G. Williams, *Dictionary*, 'encounter', 437–8.
60 *\*'that sidle up to men aggressively, making advances with unseemly alacrity'. To *accost* is to approach, assail, make up to; QF's 'a coasting welcome' may mean much the same thing, though in a form unfamiliar today. There may be a pun on 'a costing welcome', one that will cost the male customer financially and in terms of health.
61 **tables** writing tablets, as in *Ham*

1.5.108: 'My tables – meet it is I set it down'. The image of *wide unclasping* conveys the primary sense of letting one's thoughts be seen. It is also blatantly sexual. Ulysses sees loose women as books spreading themselves suggestively before the gaze of fascinated men. See LN.
62 *\*tickling** For textual choices, see LN.
62–4 **Set . . . game** 'Write them down as sluttish women (like Helen and Cressida) who are easy sexual plunder on any occasion that offers itself – i.e. prostitutes.' (See Coleman, 215.) See LN.
64.2 **HELENUS, [TROILUS]** Helenus has no speaking part in this scene, and his name is omitted by some editors. Troilus, on the other hand, must enter here, or in any event by 96. See LN 94.1, LN 174 SD, and 277–93.

---

56 There's] *Q;* Ther's a *F*    60 accosting] *Hudson (Mason);* a coasting *QF*    62 tickling] *F;* ticklish *Q*    64 SD *Exeunt] F;* not in *Q    Diomedes and Cressida] Oxf; Calchas and Cressida / conj. G. W. Williams* 64.1 *Flourish] Q;* at end of SD, *F* HECTOR, PARIS, AENEAS] *F; not in Q* armed] *Capell* 64.2 HELENUS] *F; not in Q* TROILUS] *Rowe* and Attendants] *F; not in Q*

ALL

The Trojan's trumpet.

AGAMEMNON                    Yonder comes the troop.               65

AENEAS

Hail, all you state of Greece! What shall be done
To him that victory commands? Or do you purpose
A victor shall be known? Will you the knights
Shall to the edge of all extremity
Pursue each other, or shall they be divided               70
By any voice or order of the field?
Hector bade ask.

AGAMEMNON          Which way would Hector have it?

AENEAS

He cares not; he'll obey conditions.

AGAMEMNON

'Tis done like Hector.

ACHILLES                    But securely done,
A little proudly, and great deal disprizing               75

---

65 ***The Trojan's** Hector's. For textual
and staging choices, see LN.

66 *you state ruling body, noble lords
(*OED* state *sb.* 26). Conceivably, F's
'you' is an error deriving from manuscript 'yᵉ', 'the', as in Q; similarly, *state*
could be an error for 'states'. See t.n.
But F is intelligible as it stands.

66–7 What . . . commands? 'What honours will be awarded to the victor?' Cf.
David's question in 1 Samuel, 17.26:
'What shall be done to the man that
killeth this Philistine [i.e. Goliath]?'
(Steevens, Var '93). Aeneas undertakes
to negotiate the ground rules for the
fight between Hector and Ajax. See
also Esther, 6.6 (Shaheen, 123).

67–8 Or . . . known? 'Do you intend that
a victor will be adjudged and declared?'

68–71 Will . . . field? 'Do you prefer that
the combatants fight to the death, or that
they are to separate on order of the mar-
shals in accordance with the rules of
chivalry?' The conduct of this fight is
conceived in terms resembling those laid
down for medieval tournaments. If the
combatants were to be separated before a
fatal outcome, the contest would presumably be judged on 'points'.

73 conditions whatever conditions are
agreed upon

74 SP *ACHILLES For textual choices, see
LN.

74 securely overconfidently

75 *disprizing disparaging, devaluing.
Q's 'misprising' stresses the difficulty
of evaluation. Both readings are acceptable; F may represent authorial choice.

---

65 Trojan's] *Ard²* (*Delius*); Troyans *Q;* Troians *F; Trojans'* / *Theobald*   66 you] *F;* the *Q;* ye *Ard¹*
(*Dyce*)   state] *QF;* states *Hudson²* (*Dyce*)   70 they] *Q;* not in *F*   71–2 By . . . ask] *Rowe¹; one line,*
*QF*   74 SP AGAMEMNON] *QF; Achilles / Pope²* (*Theobald*)   SP ACHILLES] *Cam¹; not in QF*
75 disprizing] *F;* misprising: *Q*

The knight opposed.

AENEAS                    If not Achilles, sir,
What is your name?

ACHILLES                    If not Achilles, nothing.

AENEAS

Therefore Achilles. But whate'er, know this:
In the extremity of great and little,
Valour and pride excel themselves in Hector,                    80
The one almost as infinite as all,
The other blank as nothing. Weigh him well,
And that which looks like pride is courtesy.
This Ajax is half made of Hector's blood,
In love whereof half Hector stays at home;                    85
Half heart, half hand, half Hector comes to seek
This blended knight, half Trojan and half Greek.

ACHILLES

A maiden battle, then? O, I perceive you.


[*Enter* DIOMEDES.]


AGAMEMNON

Here is Sir Diomed. – Go, gentle knight;
Stand by our Ajax. As you and Lord Aeneas                    90
Consent upon the order of their fight,
So be it, either to the uttermost

77 **If . . . nothing** Cf. the well-known Borgia motto: *Aut Caesar, aut nihil*, 'Either Caesar or no one' (Var).

79–82 **In . . . nothing** 'Valour is extremely great in Hector, pride extremely little, his valour being virtually infinite and his pride non-existent.'

82 **Weigh** assess, consider

84 Ajax' mother is Hector's aunt, according to Caxton, 589–90, and Lydgate, 3.2045–8. Cf. 2.2.77 and n., and 121 below.

88 **maiden battle** combat without bloodshed. (For erotic possibilities, see G. Williams, *Dictionary*, 'maid, maiden', 839–42.)
**perceive** understand

89 **gentle** noble, well-born

91 **Consent** agree together
**order** procedure, disposition

92 **to the uttermost** from Fr. *à l'outrance*, 'to the edge of all extremity' (69)

76–7 If not . . . name?] *Pope² (Theobald); one line, QF*    78–9 this: . . . little,] *Pope, subst.;* this, . . . little: *QF*    88.1] *Theobald, subst.*    89 Sir] *Q;* sir, *F*    Diomed.] *F, subst. (Diomed:);* Diomed? *Q*

291

Or else a breath. The combatants being kin
Half stints their strife before their strokes begin.
[*Hector and Ajax enter the lists.*]
ULYSSES   They are opposed already.                                    95
AGAMEMNON [*to Ulysses*]
What Trojan is that same that looks so heavy?
ULYSSES
The youngest son of Priam, a true knight,
Not yet mature, yet matchless firm of word,
Speaking in deeds and deedless in his tongue;
Not soon provoked, nor being provoked soon calmed;     100
His heart and hand both open and both free.
For what he has he gives; what thinks, he shows;
Yet gives he not till judgement guide his bounty,
Nor dignifies an impair thought with breath;

93 **a breath** a friendly bout, for the exercise; cf. *Ham* 5.2.172: 'it is the breathing time of day with me'. *OED* 8
quotes this line and *TC* 2.3.110 to
illustrate the meaning, 'Opportunity
or time for breathing; exercise of the
respiratory organs'. To 'breathe' in
Shakespeare often has the sense of
pausing for breath in battle; see e.g.
*1H4* 5.4.15: 'We breathe too long'.
94 **stints** cuts short, checks (*OED v.* 7)
94.1 For alternative staging possibilities,
see LN.
95 **opposed** placed facing each other (in
the lists)
96 SP *AGAMEMNON Since Q's practice is
to abbreviate SPs, and since 97 in Q provides a normal '*Vlis*.' as SP, Q's '*Vlisses:*'
in 96 reads like an extrametrical direct
address to that person, who in F has just
spoken a line (95) missing in Q.
96 **heavy** sad
97–110 *Ulysses' description generally
resembles Chaucer's praise of Troilus

for youthful strength and bravery (*TC*,
5.827–40) and Lydgate's prolix elaboration (2.4861–95) of Chaucer. For
textual choices, see LN.
99 Cf. the proverb, 'Few words and many
deeds' (Dent, W797). The idea of
speaking through acts is a recurring
topos in Shakespeare; cf. 3.3.271 and
n., giving other citations.
   **deedless . . . tongue** i.e. never boastful
101 **free** open, generous, honourable
102 **what thinks** what he thinks
104 **impair** unconsidered (from Lat.
*imparatus*); unsuitable, unworthy (cf.
Fr. *impair*, unequal, and Lat. *impar*,
unworthy). Q's 'impare' and F's
'impaire' are spelling variants, though
the *OED* defines 'impar' or 'impare' as
'uneven, unequal' and *impair* as
'unsuitable'. As a nonce word in this
sense, *impair*'s meaning and derivation
are uncertain. Oxf[1] suggests as another possibility 'injurious' from the noun
*impair*, impairment or injury.

93 breath] *Q; * breach *F*   94.1] *Capell, subst.*   95] *F; not in Q*   96 SP] *F;* Vlisses: *Q*   SD] *Bevington[3]*
97 Priam, a true knight,] *Q; * Priam; / A true Knight; they call him *Troylus; F*   98 matchless firm] *Q;*
matchlesse, firme *F*   99 in deeds] *F;* deeds *Q*   104 impair] *QF (*impare, impaire*)*

Manly as Hector, but more dangerous,                    105
For Hector in his blaze of wrath subscribes
To tender objects, but he in heat of action
Is more vindicative than jealous love.
They call him Troilus, and on him erect
A second hope, as fairly built as Hector.               110
Thus says Aeneas, one that knows the youth
Even to his inches, and with private soul
Did in great Ilium thus translate him to me.

       *Alarum. [Hector and Ajax fight.]*

AGAMEMNON They are in action.

NESTOR Now, Ajax, hold thine own!                  115

TROILUS Hector, thou sleep'st. Awake thee!

AGAMEMNON

His blows are well disposed. – There, Ajax! *Trumpets cease.*

DIOMEDES

You must no more.

AENEAS     Princes, enough, so please you.

AJAX

I am not warm yet. Let us fight again.

DIOMEDES

As Hector pleases.

HECTOR     Why, then will I no more.    120
Thou art, great lord, my father's sister's son,

---

106–7 **subscribes . . . objects** 'grants merciful terms to the defenseless' (Seltzer). Cf. *TS* 1.1.81: 'Sir, to your pleasure humbly I subscribe', and *KL* 5.3.242: 'Seest thou this object, Kent?'

108 **vindicative** vindictive. Shakespeare's only use.

110 **as . . . Hector** 'as fair as that built on Hector' (Ard¹, comparing Chaucer, *TC*, 2.644: 'And, next his brother, holder up of Troye')

112 **Even . . . inches** every inch of him.

(The language is oddly amorous, as also in *erect*, 109, and *jealous love*, 108.) **with private soul** privately and from the heart

113 **translate** interpret, explain

117 **disposed** placed, directed

117 SD *Trumpets cease* Either the trumpets have sounded continuously during the fighting from 114 to 117, or someone now signals that the combatants are to cease: i.e. *Trumpets: 'cease'*.

121 See 84n.

---

113 Ilium] *Oxf¹;* Illion *QF*  113.1 *Hector . . . fight*] *Rowe*  117 disposed. – There,] *Rowe, subst.;* dispo'd, there *Q;* dispos'd there *F*

A cousin-german to great Priam's seed.
The obligation of our blood forbids
A gory emulation 'twixt us twain.
Were thy commixtion Greek and Trojan so                    125
That thou couldst say, 'This hand is Grecian all,
And this is Trojan; the sinews of this leg
All Greek, and this all Troy; my mother's blood
Runs on the dexter cheek, and this sinister
Bounds in my father's', by Jove multipotent,              130
Thou shouldst not bear from me a Greekish member
Wherein my sword had not impressure made
Of our rank feud. But the just gods gainsay
That any drop thou borrowed'st from thy mother,
My sacred aunt, should by my mortal sword                 135
Be drained. Let me embrace thee, Ajax.
By him that thunders, thou hast lusty arms!
Hector would have them fall upon him thus.
Cousin, all honour to thee! [*They embrace.*]

AJAX                          I thank thee, Hector.

---

122 **cousin-german** first cousin. *German* means closely akin. The phrase occurs in Caxton, 589–90, not in Lydgate. Hector's wishing he could separate the Trojan and Greek elements of Ajax is essentially similar in a comparable scene in T. Heywood's *The Iron Age*, Part 1, towards the end of Act 1 (p. 299).

123 **the obligation . . . blood** the sacred code of a blood tie and its consequential responsibilities

124 **gory emulation** bloody rivalry

125 **commixtion** commixture. Shakespeare's only use.

128–30 **my mother's . . . father's** For Renaissance medical theory, see LN.

130 **multipotent** very powerful (*OED*'s first citation and Shakespeare's only use)

132 **impressure** impression

133 **rank** high-minded, violent, hot, intemperate
**feud** i.e. the Trojan war. Hector has no personal animus against Ajax.
**gainsay** forbid

134 **thou borrowed'st** that you inherited

135 **sacred** 'The Greeks give to the aunt, the father's sister, the title of "sacred"' (Hudson, cited in Var).

136 **drained** probably but not certainly 'drainèd'. The spelling in QF ('drained', not 'drain'd') would normally point to a sounded syllable.

137 **By . . . thunders** by Jove
**lusty** strong. (But the language is also erotically suggestive, as at 112n.)

126–30] *inverted commas, Capell, subst.*    133 Of . . . feud] *F; not in Q*    134 drop] *F;* day *Q*    139 SD] *Bevington*[1]

Thou art too gentle and too free a man. 140
I came to kill thee, cousin, and bear hence
A great addition earned in thy death.

HECTOR

Not Neoptolcmus so mirable,
On whose bright crest Fame with her loud'st 'Oyez'
Cries, 'This is he', could promise to himsclf 145
A thought of added honour torn from Hector.

AENEAS

There is expectance here from both the sides
What further you will do.

HECTOR                    We'll answer it:
The issue is embracement. – Ajax, farewell.
[*They embrace again.*]

AJAX

If I might in entreaties find success – 150
As seld I have the chance – I would desire

140 **gentle** tender, noble, honourable.
Cf. 89.
**free** innocent, generous, honourable.
Cf. 101.
142 **addition** title, style of address;
something added to a coat of arms as a
mark of honour. *OED sb.* 5 gives this
line as its first citation, but Hulme,
292, cites John Ferne's *Blazon of
Gentry* (1586): 'For the crest, timber,
mantle, or word be no part of the coat-
armour; they be additions called
achievements' (185). Cf. 1.2.20.
**earned** earnèd. Possibly instead, *addition* should be sounded in four syllables, 'additïon', but the QF spelling of
'earned' rather than 'earn'd' normally
indicates a sounded syllable; see 136n.
143–6 'Not even the much-wondered-at
Achilles, on whose heraldic shield
Fame herself – like a public crier with
a loud shout of "Hear ye, hear ye!" –
proclaims "This is the very man",

could be confident of adding to his
honour by tearing it away from Hector.'
(*Neoptolemus* is actually the name of
Achilles' son, and conceivably this line
could refer to his future greatness; see
LN 3.3.195.) Cf. the proverbial phrase,
'You are *ipse*, he, the man' (Dent, I88).
147 **expectance** a state of waiting to
know and wishing an answer (*OED* 1b;
only citation in this sense)
149 **The issue is embracement** the
outcome (of this fight) is a mutual
embrace
150 **success** 'the attainment of my
desire'; but also 'a sequel to or termi-
nation of our affairs' (*OED sb.* 1), playing on *issue*, outcome, in 149
151 **As . . . chance** i.e. 'since I seldom
have the chance of inviting the great
Hector to my tent and thus getting to
know my famous cousin'
**desire** request the presence of, invite
(*OED v.* 8, citing this line)

144 'Oyez'] *QF* ((O yes)) *inverted commas, Staunton, subst.* 145] *inverted commas, Hanmer, subst.*
could] *Q;* could'st *F* 149.1] *Oxf¹, subst.*

My famous cousin to our Grecian tents.

DIOMEDES

'Tis Agamemnon's wish; and great Achilles

Doth long to see unarmed the valiant Hector.

HECTOR

Aeneas, call my brother Troilus to me,                    155

And signify this loving interview

To the expecters of our Trojan part;

Desire them home. [*to Ajax*] Give me thy hand, my
    cousin.

I will go eat with thee, and see your knights.

*Agamemnon and the rest* [*come forward*].

AJAX

Great Agamemnon comes to meet us here.                    160

HECTOR [*to Aeneas*]

The worthiest of them tell me name by name;

But for Achilles, mine own searching eyes

Shall find him by his large and portly size.

AGAMEMNON

Worthy of arms! As welcome as to one

That would be rid of such an enemy –                      165

---

153–4 Diomedes cautions that other invitations may take precedence.

155 Troilus would appear to be on stage, but standing moodily on the sidelines (as Agamemnon observes to Ulysses at 96) – unless the Oxford editors are right in having him leave with others at 117 and re-enter at 159.1; see LN 94.1. In any case he takes part in the greetings between the two sides; Agamemnon addresses him seemingly at 174.

156 **signify** announce

157 'to those awaiting news on our Trojan side'

158 **Desire them home** ask them to go home. Troilus evidently does not go home, however; see 155n. and LN 174 SD. He is certainly present at the scene's end (277–93) to ask Ulysses' help in finding Calchas' tent. Presumably Troilus evades Hector's request that he go home out of desire to see Cressida.

163 **portly** stately, dignified, imposing

164 *of arms** to bear arms in combat; to be embraced. Q's 'all arms' is an attractive reading, but F may represent authorial revision.

**As . . . one** 'you are as welcome as such a person can possibly be to one like myself'

158 SD] *this edn*   159.1] *Rowe, subst.; not in Q; Enter Agamemnon and the rest. F*   161, 177 SD] *Oxf*   162 mine] *F;* my *Q*   164 of] *F;* all *Q*

But that's no welcome. Understand more clear:
What's past and what's to come is strewed with husks
And formless ruin of oblivion;
But in this extant moment, faith and troth,
Strained purely from all hollow bias-drawing,                    170
Bids thee, with most divine integrity,
From heart of very heart, great Hector, welcome.

HECTOR

I thank thee, most imperious Agamemnon.

AGAMEMNON [*to Troilus*]

My well-famed lord of Troy, no less to you.

MENELAUS

Let me confirm my princely brother's greeting.                    175
You brace of warlike brothers, welcome hither.
[*He embraces Hector and Troilus.*]

HECTOR [*to Aeneas*]

Who must we answer?

AENEAS                    The noble Menelaus.

HECTOR

O, you, my lord? By Mars his gauntlet, thanks!

---

166 *'But what I've just said does not sound like a genuine welcome. Let me make myself clear.' Agamemnon goes on to say that, whatever the future may hold in the way of enmity and death, at this moment his welcome is heartily sincere. Lines 166–71, found in F only, could be material that Q omitted in error, or that was deliberately deleted from Q at some point, or that was added to F in revision. It is in any case relevant to the discussion of time; cf. 3.3.146–81.

167 husks i.e. mere shells or carcasses of once great achievements, the *formless ruin* (168) that is so characteristic of oblivion. The testimonials we see of a decayed past greatness assure us that the future will be strewed with such ruins as well.

169 extant present

169–70 faith . . . bias-drawing 'the obligations of trustworthiness and honesty, purified of all insincerities, all fruitless and tortuous dealings (like the bias given to the bowling ball in the game of bowls)'. See note on *bias* at 8, and cf. 4.4.23, 'so strained a purity'.

171 divine godlike

172 From . . . very heart from my inmost heart

173 imperious imperial

174 SD *to Troilus* For textual choices, see LN.

177 Who whom (Abbott, 274, as at 3.1.20)

178 By Mars his gauntlet by Mars' armoured leather glove

166–71] *F; not in Q*    166 clear:] *F4* (clear,); cleere *F*    171 Bids] *F;* Bid *Hanmer*    174 SD] *Rowe*
176.1] *Oxf*

Mock not that I affect th'untraded oath;
Your quondam wife swears still by Venus' glove.          180
She's well, but bade me not commend her to you.

MENELAUS

Name her not now, sir; she's a deadly theme.

HECTOR     O, pardon! I offend.

NESTOR

I have, thou gallant Trojan, seen thee oft,
Labouring for destiny, make cruel way          185
Through ranks of Greekish youth; and I have seen
   thee,
As hot as Perseus, spur thy Phrygian steed,
And seen thee scorning forfeits and subduements,
When thou hast hung thy advanced sword i'th' air,

---

179 **untraded** unhackneyed (*OED* 1b,
citing this as its only example;
Shakespeare's only use). Hector jests
that what might seem an affectation
for swearing ingenious new-minted
oaths (anticipating Sir Lucius
O'Trigger in Sheridan's *The Rivals*) is
in his case a militarily and satirically
appropriate riposte to Helen's swearing by Venus' glove. The antithesis of
Mars and Venus as representing war
and *amor* is conventional.

180 **quondam** former
    **by Venus' glove** In *LLL* 5.2.412,
Berowne swears 'By this white glove',
and characters often swear 'By this
hand' (as in *Cor* 4.5.154). Cf. 4.1.23–4
and n.

181 **bade me not** either (1) didn't ask me
to, or (2) asked me not to

182 **deadly theme** (1) occasion of mortal
combat (in the Trojan war); (2) gloomy
topic of discourse. *Deadly* can also be
used colloquially as an intensifier (J.
Wright, cited in Var).

185 **Labouring for destiny** doing the

work of Atropos, one of the three
Fates (by slaying those destined to
die). Atropos cut the thread of life.

187 **thy Phrygian steed** Nestor implicit-
ly compares Hector on horseback with
Perseus mounted on the winged
Pegasus. Although that famous horse
was Bellerophon's mount in the attack
on the Chimera, Perseus did ride
Pegasus to the rescue of Andromeda.
See LN 1.3.42. *Phrygian* means 'Trojan'.

188 **scorning ... subduements** refusing
easy prey; disdaining to subdue those
whose lives were forfeit (*OED*'s first
citation for *subduements*). *Forfeits and
subduements* uses the rhetorical figure of
hendiadys; see 3.2.155 and 4.4.77 and
notes, and Puttenham, 3.16 (177–8).

189 **hung** checked the swing of
    **advanced** raised aloft. Cf. Pyrrhus'
poised sword in *Ham* 2.2.477–82.
Probably pronounced 'advancèd'; cf.
*drained* and *earned*, 136 and 142 and
notes. Q's 'th'aduanced' tends to mili-
tate against pronouncing 'advanced' in
two syllables with the stress on the first.

---

179 that . . . oath] *F;* thy affect, the vntraded earth *Q*   188 And seen thee scorning] *F;* Despising
many *Q*   189 thy] *F;* th' *Q*

Not letting it decline on the declined,                    190
That I have said to some my standers-by:
'Lo, Jupiter is yonder, dealing life!'
And I have seen thee pause and take thy breath,
When that a ring of Greeks have hemmed thee in,
Like an Olympian, wrestling. This have I seen;                    195
But this thy countenance, still locked in steel,
I never saw till now. I knew thy grandsire,
And once fought with him. He was a soldier good,
But by great Mars, the captain of us all,
Never like thee. Let an old man embrace thee;                    200
And, worthy warrior, welcome to our tents. [*They embrace.*]
AENEAS [*to Hector*] 'Tis the old Nestor.
HECTOR
Let me embrace thee, good old chronicle,
That hast so long walked hand in hand with time.

---

190 **the declined** those already having fallen. Possibly pronounced 'declinèd', since the word in QF is printed 'declined' (see notes at 136, 142 and 189), but not necessarily for the metre of the line.

191 *****to some** Q's reading seems preferable on the principle of *difficilior lectio*, i.e. the more difficult reading, which is unlikely to have been arrived at without authorial design. The F reading may represent a smoothing out (though it is also possibly a product of authorial revision).

192 **dealing life** The expected phrase in war would be 'dealing life and death'. Hector, though fully capable of making 'cruel way / Through ranks of Greekish youth' (185–6), resembles here the chief of the gods in giving the gift of life, by his sparing of those unable to defend themselves.

194 **When that** when
*****hemmed** Q's 'shrupd', emended by

Sisson to 'shrap'd', yields plausible meanings of 'encircled, trapped, snared', but F's revision is sensible and could well be authorial.

195 **Olympian** (1) Olympian god (recalling *Jupiter* in 192); (2) wrestler in the Olympic games

196 **still** always, up till now

197 **grandsire** Laomedon. For the mythic background, see LN.

203 **chronicle** register of events, storehouse of memories. *OED* 1b cites this and *2H4* 4.4.126, 'The old folk, Time's doting chronicles', as its only examples in this sense prior to 1794. In Ovid, *Met.*, 12.178, Nestor, lauded by Achilles as *o facunde senex, aevi prudentia nostri*, 'eloquent old man, the sagacity of our age', delivers a lengthy chronicle of the Lapithae and Centaurs (178–576, LCL, 2.192–219). Cf. *R3* 4.4.28: 'Brief abstract and record of tedious days'.

---

191 to some] *Q;* vnto *F*    192] *inverted commas, Hanmer, subst.*    194 hemmed] *F (*hem'd*);* shrupd *Q;* shraped *Sisson*    200 Let] *F;* O let *Q*    201 SD] *Bevington¹*    202 SD] *Oxf*

Most reverend Nestor, I am glad to clasp thee.              205

NESTOR

I would my arms could match thee in contention

As they contend with thee in courtesy.

HECTOR     I would they could.

NESTOR

Ha! By this white beard, I'd fight with thee tomorrow.

Well, welcome, welcome. I have seen the time!              210

ULYSSES

I wonder now how yonder city stands

When we have here her base and pillar by us.

HECTOR

I know your favour, Lord Ulysses, well.

Ah, sir, there's many a Greek and Trojan dead

Since first I saw yourself and Diomed                      215

In Ilium, on your Greekish embassy.

ULYSSES

Sir, I foretold you then what would ensue.

My prophecy is but half his journey yet;

For yonder walls, that pertly front your town,

Yon towers, whose wanton tops do buss the clouds,          220

Must kiss their own feet.

HECTOR                          I must not believe you.

---

206 **arms** (1) upper limbs (with which to embrace); (2) weapons (with which to fight)

210 **I . . . time** i.e. 'There was a time when I would gladly have taken you on!' A proverbial truism appropriate to an aged and sometimes garrulous speaker; cf. Dent, D81.1: 'I have seen the day'. Cf. *2H4* 3.2.211–19 and *KL* 1.2.115.

212 **base** foundation. Ulysses' witticism is that if Hector is the pillar of his community, Troy should literally collapse when he is absent from the city.

213 **favour** countenance

215–16 For the mythic background, see LN.

219 **pertly front** audaciously stand in front of (*OED* front *v.*[1] 7a, citing this line)

220 **wanton** insolent, hedonistic, frolicsome (with a suggestion of amorousness in the metaphor of kissing)

**buss** kiss. Cf. Caxton (508) on the towers of Troy, 'so hyghe that hit semed to them that sawe hem fro ferre that they rought vnto the heuene'.

---

207] *F; not in Q*   209–10] *Q; prose, F; Capell lines* Ha? / to morrow. / time. /   210 time!] *QF (*time.*); time – F3*   216 Ilium] *Oxf*[1]*; Illion QF*   220 Yon] *Q; Yond F*

There they stand yet, and modestly I think
The fall of every Phrygian stone will cost
A drop of Grecian blood. The end crowns all,
And that old common arbitrator, Time,                          225
Will one day end it.
ULYSSES                    So to him we leave it.
Most gentle and most valiant Hector, welcome.
After the general, I beseech you next
To feast with me and see me at my tent.
ACHILLES
I shall forestall thee, Lord Ulysses, thou!                    230
Now, Hector, I have fed mine eyes on thee;
I have with exact view perused thee, Hector,
And quoted joint by joint.
HECTOR                         Is this Achilles?
ACHILLES    I am Achilles.
HECTOR
Stand fair, I pray thee. Let me look on thee.                  235
ACHILLES
Behold thy fill.
HECTOR                    Nay, I have done already.

222 **modestly** without exaggeration
224–6 **The end . . . end it** For the proverbial context, see LN.
226 **So . . . leave it** either indicative or hortatory: 'We leave everything up to Time' or 'Let us leave all to Time'. Probably the latter.
228–9 Perhaps Ulysses is once more manipulating Achilles into competition (Proudfoot).
230 **forestall** deprive; hinder, prevent by anticipation
230–1 **thee . . . thou . . . thee** a seemingly deliberate use of the familiar second-person singular to insult first Ulysses and then Hector, whom Achilles has

never met before; see LN.
232 **exact** pronounced with equal stress on the two syllables or with stress on the first
233 **quoted joint by joint** scrutinized limb by limb. Hector and Achilles similarly size each other up in Caxton (602–3) and Lydgate (3.3755–4038), though at an earlier point in the war. *Joint* could also mean a portion of meat served with the bone (*OED sb.* 8, dating from 1576); the grisly image of feasting continues from *fed* in 231.
235 **fair** in plain view (*OED a.* and *sb.*[2] 16, 17)

225–6 And . . . it] *F; one line, Q*   230 Ulysses, thou!] *QF, subst.;* Ulysses. [*To Hector*] Thou! *Oxf*
232–3 I . . . by joint] *F; one turned-over line, Q*   235 pray thee] *Q;* prythee *F*

ACHILLES

    Thou art too brief. I will the second time,

    As I would buy thee, view thee limb by limb.

HECTOR

    O, like a book of sport thou'lt read me o'er;

    But there's more in me than thou understand'st.     240

    Why dost thou so oppress me with thine eye?

ACHILLES

    Tell me, you heavens, in which part of his body

    Shall I destroy him? Whether there, or there, or there?

    That I may give the local wound a name

    And make distinct the very breach whereout     245

    Hector's great spirit flew. Answer me, heavens!

HECTOR

    It would discredit the blest gods, proud man,

    To answer such a question. Stand again.

    Think'st thou to catch my life so pleasantly

    As to prenominate in nice conjecture     250

    Where thou wilt hit me dead?

ACHILLES                 I tell thee, yea.

HECTOR

    Wert thou the oracle to tell me so,

    I'd not believe thee. Henceforth guard thee well;

    For I'll not kill thee there, nor there, nor there,

---

238 Achilles speaks ambiguously as though he would buy Hector in a slave market – or in a meat market. See 233n.

239 **book of sport** handbook for huntsmen. The notion of reading someone like a book is a commonplace; see Dent, B531.1, and 61n. above.

243 **Whether** metrically monosyllabic: *whe'er*

248 **Stand again** Perhaps Achilles has knelt while offering his fierce petition to the gods; or Hector may be simply repeating his admonition to Achilles to

'Stand fair' where he can be plainly seen, as in 235, or simply 'stand still', 'stop moving'.

249 **pleasantly** jocosely, by way of pleasantry

250 **prenominate** name beforehand (*OED v.*, citing this line)
**nice** precise

252–3 **Wert . . . thee** Mistrusting oracles is a dangerous sign in Shakespeare as in Greek tragedy. Cf. *WT* 3.2.131–47.

254 **there . . . nor there** Hector throws back at Achilles his taunt in 243.

252 the] *F;* an *Q*

| | |
|---|---|
| But, by the forge that stithied Mars his helm, | 255 |
| I'll kill thee everywhere, yea, o'er and o'er. – | |
| You wisest Grecians, pardon me this brag; | |
| His insolence draws folly from my lips. | |
| But I'll endeavour deeds to match these words, | |
| Or may I never – | |

AJAX                    Do not chafe thee, cousin.          260

And you, Achilles, let these threats alone,
Till accident or purpose bring you to't.
You may have every day enough of Hector,
If you have stomach. The general state, I fear,
Can scarce entreat you to be odd with him.          265

HECTOR [*to Achilles*]

I pray you, let us see you in the field.
We have had pelting wars since you refused
The Grecians' cause.

ACHILLES                    Dost thou entreat me, Hector?

Tomorrow do I meet thee, fell as death;
Tonight all friends.

HECTOR                    Thy hand upon that match.          270

AGAMEMNON

First, all you peers of Greece, go to my tent;

---

255 **stithied . . . helm** forged Mars' helmet (*OED* stithy *v.*, citing this line and one other passage from c. 1420). A *stithy* is an anvil or forge. The smith here is presumably Vulcan.

258 Hector is wise enough to fear the blind folly personified in Atē, the goddess of mischief through whose agency the Olympian gods could induce in a hero the self-deluded infatuation and *hubris* that would lead to rash destructive deeds and a fated downfall.

259 **endeavour deeds** exert myself in deeds. *OED* endeavour *v.* 1 notes that the verb is sometimes used transitively, as here.

260 **chafe thee** get angry

261–2 **let . . . to't** 'stop making these boastful threats until the fortunes of war or an intentional coming together bring you to fight with Hector'

264 **stomach** appetite (for fighting); hinting too at 'courage, haughtiness, spite' (*OED sb.* 5b, 8a, b, c)
    **general state** Greek commanders in council (cf. 66); the whole Grecian side and cause

265 **be odd** be at odds, at variance (*OED* odd *a.* and *adv.* 7c, citing this line as the second of two examples)

267 **pelting** paltry, insignificant

269 **fell** fierce, ruthless, deadly

255 stithied] *F (*stythied*); stithied *Q*    263 have] *Q; not in F*    266 SD] *Oxf*    267–8 We . . . cause] *F; one turned-over line, Q*    269–70 Tomorrow . . . friends] *F; one line, Q*

303

There in the full convive we. Afterwards,
As Hector's leisure and your bounties shall
Concur together, severally entreat him.
Beat loud the taborins, let the trumpets blow,                    275
That this great soldier may his welcome know.          [*Flourish.*]
                              *Exeunt [all but Troilus and Ulysses].*

TROILUS

My Lord Ulysses, tell me, I beseech you,
In what place of the field doth Calchas keep?

ULYSSES

At Menelaus' tent, most princely Troilus.
There Diomed doth feast with him tonight,                         280
Who neither looks on heaven nor on earth,
But gives all gaze and bent of amorous view
On the fair Cressid.

TROILUS

Shall I, sweet lord, be bound to you so much,
After we part from Agamemnon's tent,                              285
To bring me thither?

ULYSSES                              You shall command me, sir.
As gentle tell me, of what honour was
This Cressida in Troy? Had she no lover there
That wails her absence?

TROILUS

O sir, to such as boasting show their scars                       290

272 *\*in . . . convive we* let us feast together to the full. For textual choices, see LN.
274 **severally entreat** individually invite
and entertain
275 **taborins** drums. On the use of
drums and trumpets in a flourish
designed to greet honoured military
guests, cf. *AC* 2.7.133–6.
278 **keep** lodge (*OED v.* 37)
279 **Menelaus' tent** an apt setting for

Cressida's infidelity; not mentioned in
Shakespeare's sources. See 5.1.94–5n.
282 **bent** inclination, cast (of the eye)
(*OED sb.*² 6)
287 **As gentle** be so courteous as to, with
like courtesy
**honour** reputation
290–1 **O sir . . . due** Troilus tacitly
acknowledges that Ulysses has come to
the right man to ask about Cressida's

272 we] *Q;* you *F*  274–5 him. / Beat . . . taborins,] *F;* him / To taste your bounties, *Q*  276 SD
*Flourish*] *Capell*  276.1 *Exeunt . . . Ulysses*] *Rowe, subst. (Manent* Troilus *and* Ulysses*); Exeunt. QF*
281 on heaven nor on] *F;* vpon the heauen nor *Q*  284 you] *Q;* thee *F*  287 As] *F;* But *Q*

A mock is due. Will you walk on, my lord?
She was beloved, she loved; she is, and doth;
But still sweet love is food for Fortune's tooth. *Exeunt.*

**[5.1]** *Enter* ACHILLES *and* PATROCLUS.

ACHILLES
I'll heat his blood with Greekish wine tonight,
Which with my scimitar I'll cool tomorrow.
Patroclus, let us feast him to the height.

PATROCLUS
Here comes Thersites.

*Enter* THERSITES.

ACHILLES            How now, thou core of envy?
Thou crusty batch of nature, what's the news?      5
THERSITES    Why, thou picture of what thou seemest and

---

lover in Troy, but implies as well that
for him to boast of his being that lover
would subject him to deserved ridicule
– especially since, as they both appear
to understand or fear, Troilus' role
may now be that of the rejected lover.

290 **such as** those who

292 **is, and doth** is loved, and does love

293 Troilus plays wryly with the proverbial metaphor 'to have a sweet tooth'
(Dent, T420) to express his worry that
love will always prove the plaything of
fickle Fortune.

**5.1** Location and time: the Greek camp.
Before Achilles' tent, as evening comes
on (see 64.2, 69, etc.).

2 **Which** i.e. Hector's blood (not the
wine)
**scimitar** i.e. sword. Lit. a short,
curved, single-edged weapon associated with the Orient or Africa, notably in
the case of the Prince of Morocco

(*MV* 2.1.24) and Aaron the Moor (*TA*
4.2.92; Ard[2]).
**cool** 'by letting it out into the air' (Ard[1])

3 **to the height** to the utmost

4 *****core** hard mass of dead tissue at the
centre of a boil or tumour (anticipating
*crusty* in the next line); essence, centre,
'heart' (of envy); something dry and
horny that sticks in the throat, that one
cannot swallow or get over (*OED sb.*[1]
1a and b, 3, 14). See LN.

5 **crusty** scabby (as on a boil); crustlike
(as on a pie or loaf of bread); irascible,
cantankerous, cross-grained
*****batch of nature** quantity or lot of a
thoroughly depraved natural condition. For textual choices, see LN.

6 **picture** i.e. 'mere image or outward
representation, all show and no substance', and hence a suitable icon for
idiot-worshippers; or else 'true picture
of what you really are, a buffoon'

292 she loved] *F;* my Lord *Q*    **5.1**] *Rowe, subst.*    4 core] *F;* curre *Q*    5 batch] *QF;* botch *Theobald*
6–7] *F; Q lines* Idoll, / thee. /    6 seemest] *Q;* seem'st *F*

idol of idiot-worshippers, here's a letter for thee.

ACHILLES     From whence, fragment?

THERSITES     Why, thou full dish of fool, from Troy.

[*He gives a letter. Achilles stands aside to read it.*]

PATROCLUS     Who keeps the tent now?                              10

THERSITES     The surgeon's box, or the patient's wound.

PATROCLUS     Well said, adversity. And what need these
tricks?

THERSITES     Prithee, be silent, boy. I profit not by thy talk.
Thou art thought to be Achilles' male varlet.                       15

PATROCLUS     Male varlet, you rogue? What's that?

THERSITES     Why, his masculine whore. Now, the rotten
diseases of the south, guts-griping, ruptures, catarrhs,

8   **fragment** an unappetizing leftover
    from a meal; an unfinished creature;
    something detached and broken off
9   **dish of fool** shallow or hollow vessel
    filled with nonsense; big bowlful of
    folly (*OED* dish *sb.* 3c, citing this line);
    serving of 'a kind of clouted [i.e. clot-
    ted] cream called a fool or a trifle in
    English' (John Florio, *Mantiglia*, quot-
    ed by *OED* fool *sb.*² 1 and noted by
    Ard²)
10  Patroclus asks Thersites, 'Who is
    occupying or looking after Achilles'
    tent these days?'; or else poses his
    question rhetorically, saying in effect,
    'You see that Achilles can no longer be
    taunted with keeping his tent' (Ard¹).
    Evidently Achilles is preparing for
    combat with Hector and is less in evi-
    dence at the tent than he used to be. At
    44, Achilles orders Thersites to help
    *trim* or make ready the tent, suggesting
    that Thersites serves as a kind of
    attendant.
11  Thersites' witticism plays on *keeps* and
    *tent*: 'If by *tent* you mean a roll or
    probe of linen used to search and

cleanse a wound' (*OED sb.*³ 2), he wise-
cracks, 'it is *kept* in the doctor's kit or
thrust into the patient's wound'.
Achilles was well known for having
been instructed by Chiron in deeds of
arms and surgery (Baldwin, Var).
12  **adversity** perversity (in deliberately
    taking words in the sense not intend-
    ed), contrariety (*OED* 1, though giving
    no instances after c. 1450)
12–13  **what . . . tricks?** 'what's the point
    of these perverse word games?'
15  **varlet** manservant, groom (*OED* 1),
    but with derogatory meanings also of
    'knave, rascal, rogue' (*OED* 2), and, as
    Thersites goes on to specify, 'mascu-
    line whore' (see *OED* 2d, quoting this
    line). See LN.
18  **the south** For the medical back-
    ground, see LN.
18–19  **guts-griping . . . palsies** 'colic or
    other spasms of the abdomen, hernias,
    common colds or other infections of
    nose and throat, severe cases of kidney
    stones, illnesses like stroke that result
    in torpor or inertness, severe tremor
    and paralysis'

9.1] *Capell, subst.*   12  need these] *F;* needs this *Q;* needs these *Kittredge*   14–15] *F; Q lines* talke, /
varlot, /   14  boy] *F;* box *Q*   15  thought] *F;* said *Q*   15, 16  varlet] *QF (*varlot, Varlot*)*
18  guts-griping, ruptures,] *F4;* the guts griping ruptures: *Q;* guts-griping Ruptures, *F*   catarrhs] *F;
not in Q*

loads o' gravel i'th' back, lethargies, cold palsies, raw
eyes, dirt-rotten livers, wheezing lungs, bladders full of          20
imposthume, sciaticas, limekilns i'th' palm, incurable
bone-ache and the rivelled fee-simple of the tetter, take
and take again such preposterous discoveries!

PATROCLUS   Why, thou damnable box of envy, thou, what
mean'st thou to curse thus?                                         25

THERSITES   Do I curse thee?

PATROCLUS   Why, no, you ruinous butt, you whoreson
indistinguishable cur, no.

THERSITES   No? Why art thou then exasperate, thou idle
immaterial skein of sleave-silk, thou green sarsenet flap          30
for a sore eye, thou tassel of a prodigal's purse, thou?

---

19–22 *raw eyes . . . tetter For textual
choices and definitions of symptoms,
see LN.

20 wheezing Q's 'whissing' suggests a
whistling sound along with the wheezing.

22–3 take and take again strike or afflict
with disease many times over (*OED*
take *v.* 7). Cf. *Ham* 1.1.168–9: 'then no
planets strike, / No fairy takes'.

23 preposterous discoveries revelations
of practices that are 'arsy-versy', literally placing last that which should be
first, hence, perverted, unnatural,
backside foremost, sodomitical. For
the rhetorical figure of hysteron proteron, which Puttenham calls 'the cart
before the horse' or 'the preposterous',
see Puttenham, 3.13 and 3.22 (170,
255), and Parker, 20ff. 'Arsy-versy
love' was sometimes associated with
Rome and ancient classical practices of
homosexuality; see *OED* arsy-versy
*adv.* and *a.* B. Cf. 1.3.149 and n.

24 box large, empty container, like the
*dish* at 9

25 to curse by cursing (Abbott, 356)

27 ruinous butt dilapidated cask – a
large container for folly, like *box* and
*dish* (see 24n.); suggesting also one
who is a perniciously destructive butt
(lit. an archery target) of satirical
humour. And *butt* meaning 'buttock'
dates from c. 1450.

28 indistinguishable cur misshapen
mongrel, 'of indeterminable shape and
structure' (*OED* 1b, citing this line)

29 exasperate exasperated, angry

29–30 idle . . . sleave-silk useless, incon-
sequential loop of silk thread used in
embroidery. To *sleave* is to separate
silk into filaments. The image is of
something puny, flimsy. *OED v.* 2 cites
this line as an instance of 'sleaved silk',
quoting F's 'Sleyd silke'.

30–1 green . . . eye eye patch of fine, soft
green silk often used for dresses and
linings. *Sarsenet* often connotes soft
flimsiness and effeminacy, as in *1H4*
3.1.249: 'And givest such sarsenet
surety for thy oaths'.

31 tassel . . . purse fringed pendent
ornament on a spendthrift's purse –
more idle, frilly decoration

---

19 i'th'] *F;* in the *Q*   19–22 raw . . . tetter] *Q;* and the like *F*   20 wheezing] *Q* (whissing*)*
21 limekilns] *Q (*lime-kills*)*   25 mean'st] *F;* meanes *Q*   28 cur, no] *Q;* Curre *F*   30 sleave-silk] *Q*
*(*sleiue silke*);* Sleyd silke *F*   sarsenet] *F (*Sarcenet*);* sacenet *Q*   31 tassel] *F (*tassell*);* toslell *Q*

Ah, how the poor world is pestered with such
waterflies, diminutives of nature!

PATROCLUS    Out, gall!

THERSITES    Finch egg!                                                    35

ACHILLES

My sweet Patroclus, I am thwarted quite
From my great purpose in tomorrow's battle.
Here is a letter from Queen Hecuba,
A token from her daughter, my fair love,
Both taxing me and gaging me to keep                                       40
An oath that I have sworn. I will not break it.
Fall, Greeks; fail, fame; honour, or go or stay;
My major vow lies here; this I'll obey.
Come, come, Thersites, help to trim my tent;
This night in banqueting must all be spent.                                45
Away, Patroclus!                              *Exit [with Patroclus].*

THERSITES    With too much blood and too little brain,
these two may run mad; but if with too much brain and

---

33 **waterflies** flying insects that frequent
water, hence, tiny, annoying, buzzing
creatures that live on decaying flesh
like the waterflies that Cleopatra imagines causing her corpse to swell abhor-
rently with maggots (*AC* 5.2.58–9), or
the vapidly obsequious courtier Osric
in *Ham* (5.2.83)

34 **gall** one who harasses, distresses, irri-
tates, rails. Lit., a bitter secretion of
the gall bladder or liver (hence bilious);
or a painful pustule sometimes caused
by chafing, a place rubbed bare; or an
oak gall, an excrescence on trees.

35 **Finch egg** another hit at diminutive
size and inconsequentiality. Cf.
'pigeon egg' as a term of friendly
abuse applied to the tiny Mote or
Moth in *LLL* 5.1.71, and 'egg' in *Mac*
4.2.84 (for Macduff's son). *OED* finch
2 cites this line as an instance of use as
a contemptuous epithet.

40 **taxing** placing under a serious obligation (with suggestion also of 'reproving')
**gaging** binding by a pledge

41 **An oath** See LN 3.3.195.

42 **or go** either go

44 **trim** tidy, dress up (see 10n. above)

47 **blood** passion, 'humour', wilfulness.
Thersites' diagnosis of an inner conflict
in which the *blood* engenders an imbalance in the brain recalls what Ulysses
says about Achilles at 2.3.169–73; see
note there on faculty psychology.

48–9 **but if . . . madmen** It is totally
impossible, in Thersites' wry view, that
Achilles and Patroclus could ever go
mad from excess of brain power and not
enough wilful indulgence of their emotions, since they are inveterately stupid
and headstrong. Thersites can safely
boast of his ability to cure them of insan-
ity resulting from such an imbalance of
'humours', if only they had brains.

---

45–6] *F; one line, Q*   46 SD *Exit*] *F; not in Q   with Patroclus*] *Hanmer, subst.*

too little blood they do, I'll be a curer of madmen.
Here's Agamemnon, an honest fellow enough, and one          50
that loves quails, but he has not so much brain as ear-
wax. And the goodly transformation of Jupiter there,
his brother, the bull – the primitive statue and oblique
memorial of cuckolds, a thrifty shoeing-horn in a
chain, hanging at his brother's leg – to what form but          55
that he is should wit larded with malice and malice
farced with wit turn him to? To an ass were nothing; he

50 **honest fellow enough** with patroniz-
ing suggestion of Agamemnon's being
a 'good old boy' who is not averse to
wine, women and song. On *honest*, see
Empson, *Structure*, 185–249.

51 **quails** a cant term for 'prostitutes'; cf.
Fr. *caille coiffée* or *quoiffée* and see G.
Williams, *Dictionary*, 1123–4. *OED sb.* 4
cites this line as its first instance in
English. Nares gives citations to bolster
the contention that 'the quail was
thought to be a very amorous bird'. Cf.
the proverbial lecherousness of sparrows.

52–4 **goodly . . . cuckolds** Menelaus,
like the bull, is an original or archetypal representation of all cuckolded
husbands. As a horned creature, he is a
kind of absurd transformation of
Jupiter, who in turn transformed himself into a bull in order to seduce
Europa (Ovid, *Met.*, 2.833–75, LCL,
1.118–21), and yet the symbolic
resemblance or *memorial* is rudimen-
tary and perversely indirect (*primitive*
and *oblique*), since Menelaus cuts such
a ridiculous figure.

53–5 **\*brother . . . brother's** Tannenbaum, 'Critique' (205, n. 119), suggests that Q's 'be . . . bare' represents
the compositor's attempts to deal with
Shakespeare's MS abbreviations 'br'
and 'brs'.

54–5 **a thrifty . . . leg** i.e. 'a useful but

stingy and pedestrian tool always at the
beck and call of his brother, a hanger-
on not easily shaken off, like a shoe-
horn fastened by a little chain to
Agamemnon's leg'. See LN.

55–7 **to what form . . . turn him to?** 'to
what shape other than the ridiculous
appearance he now presents should my
malicious wit and witty malice turn
him into?' The idea of transformation
into various animals is comically
appropriate to Thersites' allusions to
Ovid's *Met.* and especially the story of
Jupiter's transformation into the shape
of a bull. Another arsy-versy figure;
see 23n.

57 **\*farced** stuffed, seasoned, spiced. Q's
'faced' is intelligible as meaning 'covered with another material, trimmed,
lined', but the Q compositor seems to
have found this speech difficult in his
MS (see t.n.), and in any event F's
'forced' seems intended for *farced*, an
apt cooking metaphor that matches
with *larded* (56), 'stuffed and smeared
with lard'. See also LN 1.2.22–3 and
2.3.219.

**turn him to** On the redundancy of *to*
(following *to what form* in 55), see
Abbott, 407.

**To . . . nothing** 'to change him into an
ass would accomplish nothing'.
Menelaus is 'beyond the reach of satirical exaggeration' (Ard²).

50 Here's] *QF* (her's, Heere's)   53 brother] *F*; be *Q*   55 hanging] *F*; *not in Q*   brother's] *F*;
bare *Q*   57 farced] *F* (forced); faced *Q*

is both ass and ox. To an ox were nothing; he is both ox
and ass. To be a dog, a mule, a cat, a fitchew, a toad, a
lizard, an owl, a puttock, or a herring without a roe, I　　60
would not care; but to be Menelaus! I would conspire
against destiny. Ask me not what I would be, if I were
not Thersites, for I care not to be the louse of a lazar so
I were not Menelaus. – Heyday! Sprites and fires!

*Enter* HECTOR, [TROILUS,] AJAX, AGAMEMNON, ULYSSES,
NESTOR, [MENELAUS] *and* DIOMEDES, *with lights.*

AGAMEMNON
　We go wrong, we go wrong.
AJAX　　　　　　　　　　　　No, yonder 'tis –　　　　　　65
　There, where we see the light.
HECTOR　　　　　　　　　　I trouble you.
AJAX
　No, not a whit.

*Enter* ACHILLES.

ULYSSES　　　　　Here comes himself to guide you.

58 **ass and ox** i.e. fool and cuckold (see
　examples of proverbial use in Dent,
　O105.1, O18.1 and A379.1). No one
　animal can capture all of Menelaus'
　ridiculousness.
59–61 **To be . . . care** See LN.
59 ***dog** *KL* 2.2.81 features a similar tex-
　tual variant: 'dayes' in Q and 'dogges'
　in F. See t.n.
61–2 **conspire against destiny** i.e. do
　anything to change my evil fate
63 **I care not to be** 'I wouldn't object
　strongly to being'. On this use of *to be*
　in the sense of 'to go about being', see

Abbott, 356.
　**lazar** leper, as at 2.3.31. For an associ-
　ation of 'lazars' with Cressida, see *H5*
　2.1.77: 'lazar kite of Cressid's kind'.
　**so** so long as
64 **Heyday! . . . fires!** Thersites, spying the
　approaching warriors with their torches
　in the dark of evening, jocosely imagines
　them to be supernatural beings like
　fairies creating the effect of *ignis fatuus*
　('foolish fire', will-o'-the-wisp) or wild-
　fire. *Heyday!* is an expression of wonder
　and surprise. Cf. *MW* 5.5.36–102.

58 he is] *F;* her's *Q*　59 dog] *F;* day *Q*　mule] *QF (*Moyle, Mule*)*　fitchew] *QF (*Fichooke,
Fitchew*)*　62 not what] *F;* what *Q*　64 Heyday! Sprites] *Q (*hey-day sprites*);* Hoyday, spirits *F*
64.1 HECTOR] *F; not in Q*　TROILUS] *Theobald*　AJAX] *F; not in Q*　64.2 MENELAUS] *Capell　and*]
*Q; not in F*　DIOMEDES] *QF (Diomed)*　65–6 No . . . light] *Capell; one line, QF*　66 light] *F;* lights
*Q*　67 SD] *F; not in Q*

ACHILLES

Welcome, brave Hector. Welcome, princes all.

AGAMEMNON

So now, fair prince of Troy, I bid good night.

Ajax commands the guard to tend on you.　　　　　　70

HECTOR

Thanks, and good night to the Greeks' general.

MENELAUS

Good night, my lord.

HECTOR　　　　　　Good night, sweet Lord Menelaus.

THERSITES [*aside*]　Sweet draught. 'Sweet', quoth 'a?
　Sweet sink, sweet sewer.

ACHILLES

Good night and welcome both at once to those　　　75
　That go or tarry.

AGAMEMNON　Good night.

*Exeunt Agamemnon [and] Menelaus.*

ACHILLES

Old Nestor tarries; and you too, Diomed,

Keep Hector company an hour or two.

DIOMEDES

I cannot, lord. I have important business,　　　　80

The tide whereof is now. – Good night, great Hector.

HECTOR　Give me your hand.

ULYSSES [*aside to Troilus*]

Follow his torch; he goes to Calchas' tent.

---

69 **fair** handsome
70 **to tend on you** assigned to escort you
and provide safe-conduct
73 **draught** privy, cesspool (because
Menelaus, as cuckold, is a thing of filth
to Thersites). *Sweet draught* is an oxymoron prompted by Hector's conven-

tional complimentary address, using the
term *sweet* to express affectionate regard.
74 **sink** cesspool
　**sewer** QF's 'sure' is essentially an
　older spelling of *sewer*.
81 **tide** time. Cf. Dent T323.
83 **his** Diomedes'

69 good night] *QF (*God night, goodnight*)*　73 SD] *Staunton*　73] *inverted commas, Staunton, subst.*
74 sewer] *Rowe;* sure *QF*　75–6] *Theobald; prose, QF*　75 at once] *F; not in Q*　77.1] *Q (Exeunt
Agam: Menelaus); not in F*　78 Nestor] *F; Nector Q*　83 SD] *Rowe, subst.*　83–4 Follow . . . com-
pany] *F; prose, Q*

I'll keep you company.

TROILUS [*aside to Ulysses*]    Sweet sir, you honour me.

HECTOR

And so, good night.

[*Exit Diomedes; Ulysses and Troilus following.*]

ACHILLES                    Come, come, enter my tent.           85

*Exeunt [Achilles, Hector, Ajax and Nestor].*

THERSITES    That same Diomed's a false-hearted rogue, a
most unjust knave. I will no more trust him when he
leers than I will a serpent when he hisses. He will spend
his mouth and promise, like Brabbler the hound, but
when he performs, astronomers foretell it; it is           90
prodigious, there will come some change. The sun
borrows of the moon when Diomed keeps his word. I
will rather leave to see Hector than not to dog him.
They say he keeps a Trojan drab, and uses the traitor

---

87 **unjust** dishonest, perfidious

88 **leers** casts side glances; gazes with a sly, immodest or malign expression; smiles disarmingly

88–9 **spend . . . promise** bay loudly as though assured of taking the game

89 **Brabbler** a quarrelsome person, brawler, boastful liar (*OED*). A 'bab-bler' is a hound that gives tongue too freely, even when off the scent (*OED* 3; first citation however in 1732). Shakespeare's name for this hound may combine these senses.

90–1 **astronomers . . . change** i.e. it foretells a rare and momentous happening. Diomedes seldom keeps his word. *Prodigious* captures various senses: portentous, astounding, marvellous, monstrous, huge.

92 **borrows of** reflects the light of (reversing the natural order of things, in a prodigy as unlikely as Diomedes' keeping his word)

93 **leave to see** forgo seeing

**dog him** dog Diomedes at his heels (playing on the repeated association of Thersites with a cur or dog at 2.1.7, 39, 49, 51, 83, 5.1.28, etc.). The word 'cynic' was thought to be derived from Gr. *kuon*, dog, and to signify a snarling contempt for complacent morality.

94–5 **uses . . . tent** 'makes it his practice to visit Calchas' tent' (where Cressida is staying, just as she lived in her father's house in Troy). We learn at 4.5.279 that Calchas and Diomedes are to be found 'At Menelaus' tent', suggesting that Calchas is staying with Menelaus. Calchas is a *traitor* not to Thersites' Greek nation but to Troy. The suggestion here of an affair that has been going on for some time (*They say . . . keeps . . . uses*) is logically impossible, since Cressida has only just arrived, but is the sort of theatrical telescoping of time that Shakespeare uses often.

---

84 SD] *Capell, subst.*   85 SD] *Capell*   85.1 *Achilles . . . Nestor*] *Hanmer, subst.*   90 it; it] *Q (*it, it*);* it, that it *F*

Calchas his tent. I'll after. Nothing but lechery! All        95
incontinent varlets!                                *Exit.*

[**5.2**]                    *Enter* DIOMEDES.

DIOMEDES    What, are you up here, ho? Speak.
CALCHAS [*within*]    Who calls?
DIOMEDES    Diomed. Calchas, I think? Where's your
daughter?
CALCHAS [*within*]    She comes to you.                        5

*Enter* TROILUS *and* ULYSSES [*at a distance,
and, separate from them,* THERSITES].

ULYSSES [*to Troilus, aside*]
Stand where the torch may not discover us.

*Enter* CRESSIDA.

TROILUS [*to Ulysses, aside*]
Cressid comes forth to him.
DIOMEDES [*to Cressida*]            How now, my charge?
CRESSIDA
Now, my sweet guardian. Hark, a word with you.
[*She whispers to him.*]

---

96 SD *Exit* See next note and LN, in
5.2, on the ambiguity of F's *Exeunt*
and the absence of any exit in Q.
**5.2** *Location and time: the Greek camp.
Outside Calchas' (and Menelaus')
tent, that same evening. See LN and
5.1.94–5 n. At 4.5.279–85, Troilus asks
Ulysses to guide him to 'Menelaus'
tent', so that 5.2 must be located there.
3 **Calchas, I think?** Is that Calchas'
voice I hear?

6 **torch** either a cresset light, in an iron
basket suspended from a pole or other
support, at the tent (Ard²), or an imaginary light of this sort invoked by the
dialogue. An actual light might be
hung out at a door in the tiring house,
suggesting an entry to Calchas' tent.
See headnote above.
**discover** reveal
7 **my charge** person entrusted to my
care

---

95 Calchas his] *F (Chalcas his); Calcas Q*   96 SD] *Hanmer; not in Q; Exeunt F*   **5.2**] *Rowe, subst.*
0.1 DIOMEDES] *QF (Diomed)*   2, 5 SD] *Hanmer*   3 your] *Q; you F*   5.1 *Enter . . . ULYSSES] F; not in
Q*   5.1–2 *at . . . THERSITES] Rowe, subst.*   6 SD] *Bevington², subst.*   6.1] *F (Enter Cressid); opp. 'to him',
7, Q (Enter Cressid)*   7 SD *to Ulysses, aside] Oxf, subst.    to Cressida] this edn*   8.1] *Rowe, subst.*

TROILUS [*aside*]   Yea, so familiar?

ULYSSES [*to Troilus, aside*]   She will sing any man at first     10
sight.

THERSITES [*aside*]   And any man may sing her, if he can
take her clef. She's noted.

DIOMEDES   Will you remember?

CRESSIDA   Remember? Yes.                                        15

DIOMEDES   Nay, but do, then,
And let your mind be coupled with your words.

TROILUS [*aside*]   What should she remember?

ULYSSES [*to Troilus, aside*]   List!

CRESSIDA

Sweet honey Greek, tempt me no more to folly.                   20

THERSITES [*aside*]   Roguery!

DIOMEDES   Nay then –

CRESSIDA   I'll tell you what –

DIOMEDES

Foh, foh, come, tell a pin! You are forsworn.

CRESSIDA

In faith, I cannot. What would you have me do?                  25

---

10–11 **sing . . . sight** (1) sing the Siren
song to any man she meets; (2) read
him quickly as though he were music
to be sightread

12 **sing her** (1) play her number; (2) celebrate her in song or verse

13 **take her clef** (1) figure out what key
she is in; (2) occupy her 'cleft', vulva
(G. Williams, *Dictionary*, 249–50)
**noted** (1) closely observed, pointed at,
branded with disgrace, notorious; (2)
set down in musical notation (*OED*
note *v.*² 1, 5b, 7ab, noted *ppl. a.* 1, 2).
Cf. *RJ* 4.5.119: 'Do you note me?'

17 i.e. 'and mean what you say, do as you
promised'

18 i.e. 'What did Cressida say to
Diomedes that he now bids her
remember having said?'

19 **List** listen (and be quiet)

20 **folly** wantonness; sin

24 **tell a pin** i.e. don't trifle with me,
don't talk to me of pins. Diomedes
picks up Cressida's *tell*, 'declare, say',
in 23. The word may also suggest
'count, enumerate'. A *pin* is something
of very slight value and is also a
derogatory sexual term; cf. the joke
about 'cleaving the pin', 'in', 'out',
'prick', etc., in *LLL* 4.1.132–7.

25 **I cannot** i.e. I cannot do what you
asked and I promised.

---

9 SD] *Oxf, subst.* (+ *10, 18, 19*)   12 SD] *Bevington³* (+ *21, 26*)   12 sing] *Q;* finde *F*   13 clef] *Q*
*(Cliff);* life *F*   15 SP] *F2; Cal. QF*   16–17] *Capell; prose, QF*   18 should] *F;* shall *Q*   24 pin!
You] *F (*pin, you*);* pin you *Q*   forsworn.] *Q;* a forsworne. – *F*

THERSITES [*aside*]    A juggling trick: to be secretly open.

DIOMEDES

What did you swear you would bestow on me?

CRESSIDA

I prithee, do not hold me to mine oath.

Bid me do anything but that, sweet Greek.

DIOMEDES    Good night. [*He starts to leave.*]                    30

TROILUS [*aside*]    Hold, patience!

ULYSSES [*to Troilus, aside*]    How now, Trojan?

CRESSIDA    Diomed –

DIOMEDES

No, no, good night. I'll be your fool no more.

TROILUS [*aside*]    Thy better must.                    35

CRESSIDA    Hark, one word in your ear. [*She whispers to him.*]

TROILUS [*aside*]    O plague and madness!

ULYSSES [*to Troilus, aside*]

You are moved, Prince. Let us depart, I pray you,

Lest your displeasure should enlarge itself

To wrathful terms. This place is dangerous,                    40

The time right deadly. I beseech you, go.

TROILUS [*to Ulysses, aside*]

Behold, I pray you.

ULYSSES [*to Troilus, aside*]    Nay, good my lord, go off.

---

26 **A juggling trick** a magic trick; a contradiction in terms, an impossibility. A
'juggler' is a magician or wizard, not
simply one who juggles objects in the
air. The *trick* here is to be sexually
available and yet seemingly modest.
Thersites implies that Cressida's reti-
cence is part of her act. *Trick* may also
suggest a 'turn' at sex with a prostitute; cf. Othello's bitter characterization of his brief stay with Desdemona:

'We have done our course' (*Oth*
4.2.97). *Secretly open* continues the
wordplay: (1) confidentially frank; (2)
sexually accessible.

34 **fool** dupe

35 Troilus bitterly suggests that he himself, a truer man than Diomedes, is
destined to be duped by Cressida. He
may hint too that other better men
might suffer the same fate.

40 **wrathful terms** i.e. an open quarrel

29 anything] *Q (*any thing*);* not any thing *F*    30 SD] *Bevington¹, subst.*    31 SD] *Oxf, subst. (+ 32, 35, 37, 38)*    36 one] *F;* a *Q*    SD] *Collier¹, subst. (They talk apart)*    38 pray you] *F;* pray *Q*    42 Nay,] *F;* Now *Q*    42–5 SD] *Oxf, subst. (+ 48, 49, 52–4)*

You flow to great distraction. Come, my lord.

TROILUS [*to Ulysses, aside*]

I prithee, stay.

ULYSSES [*to Troilus, aside*]    You have not patience. Come.

TROILUS [*to Ulysses, aside*]

I pray you, stay. By hell and all hell's torments,                    45

I will not speak a word.

DIOMEDES [*Starts to leave*]

And so, good night.

CRESSIDA                      Nay, but you part in anger.

TROILUS [*aside*]

Doth that grieve thee? O withered truth!

ULYSSES [*to Troilus, aside*]

Why, how now, lord?

TROILUS [*to Ulysses, aside*]    By Jove, I will be patient.

CRESSIDA

Guardian! Why, Greek!

DIOMEDES                      Foh, foh! Adieu. You palter.          50

CRESSIDA

In faith, I do not. Come hither once again.

ULYSSES [*to Troilus, aside*]

You shake, my lord, at something. Will you go?

You will break out.

TROILUS [*aside*]        She strokes his cheek!

ULYSSES [*to Troilus, aside*]                        Come, come.

TROILUS [*to Ulysses, aside*]

Nay, stay. By Jove, I will not speak a word.

---

43 **You . . . distraction** i.e. 'Your overfull heart will pour forth its distemper in distracted behaviour, like a rising tide'.
47 **you part** you are leaving
48 **grieve thee** distress you, Cressida
  **\*withered** For metrics and lineation, see LN.

**truth** fidelity (to Troilus)
50 **Adieu** goodbye (final!)
  **palter** play fast and loose, trifle; haggle in bargaining
53 **break out** i.e. (1) in anger; (2) from concealment

43 distraction] *F;* distruction *Q*   44 prithee] *Q* (prethee); pray thee *F*   45 all hell's] *Q;* hell *F*
47 SD] *this edn; after 49, Oxf, subst.*   49 Why, how now,] *F;* How now my *Q*   50 Adieu] *F* (adew);
*not in Q*   52–3 You shake . . . out] *F2; prose, QF*

There is between my will and all offences                55
A guard of patience. Stay a little while.

THERSITES [*aside*]   How the devil Luxury, with his fat
   rump and potato finger, tickles these together! Fry,
   lechery, fry.

DIOMEDES [*to Cressida*]   But will you, then?          60

CRESSIDA

In faith I will, la. Never trust me else.

DIOMEDES

Give me some token for the surety of it.

CRESSIDA   I'll fetch you one.                          *Exit.*

ULYSSES [*to Troilus, aside*]

You have sworn patience.

TROILUS [*to Ulysses, aside*]   Fear me not, sweet lord.

I will not be myself, nor have cognition              65
Of what I feel. I am all patience.

*Enter* CRESSIDA [*with Troilus' sleeve*].

55–6 **There** . . . **patience** i.e. 'My self-
control will guard me against translating my anger into offenceful
action'.   Troilus can barely control
with his reason the hot blood that, as
Ulysses observes at 43, threatens to
break out in irrational behaviour. *All
offences* could also mean 'anything
that might be done to offend me';
Troilus will not allow any insult to
break down his promise to remain
quiet.
57–8 **Luxury** . . . **rump** Thersites gives
Lechery a *fat rump* perhaps to signify
that Lechery is one of the three
Deadly Sins of the flesh, along with
Gluttony and Sloth. Feasting and
drinking proverbially incite lust, as in
*Mac* 2.3.27–35, where much drink

'provokes the desire' even if it 'takes
away the performance', making a man
'stand to' and then 'not stand to', and
so on. See G. Williams, *Dictionary*,
'rump', 1180.
58 **potato finger** Sweet potatoes were
thought to be aphrodisiac, and a finger
has a suggestive shape for tickling and
probing. See G. Williams, *Dictionary*,
1079–80.
   **Fry** (1) burn with passion; (2) fry in
hell
61 **la** an expression calling attention to an
emphatic statement
   **else** otherwise
65–6 **I will** . . . **I feel** i.e. 'I will not allow
my feelings to be translated into action
or even admit to myself that those violent passions exist'

57 SD] *Bevington³ (+ 67)*   58 these] *F; not in Q*   60 SD] *Oxf, subst. (+ 64, 69–71)*   60 But] *F; not
in Q*   61 la] *Theobald; lo QF*   64 sweet] *F; my Q*   66.1 *Enter* CRESSIDA] *QF (Enter Cress., Enter
Cressid.) with Troilus' sleeve] Bevington³*

THERSITES [*aside*]   Now the pledge; now, now, now!

CRESSIDA   Here, Diomed, keep this sleeve.

[*She gives him the sleeve.*]

TROILUS [*aside*]   O beauty, where is thy faith?

ULYSSES [*to Troilus, aside*]   My lord –                    70

TROILUS [*to Ulysses, aside*]

I will be patient; outwardly I will.

CRESSIDA

You look upon that sleeve? Behold it well.

He loved me – O false wench! – Give't me again.

[*She snatches the sleeve.*]

DIOMEDES   Whose was't?

CRESSIDA

It is no matter, now I have't again.                    75

I will not meet with you tomorrow night.

I prithee, Diomed, visit me no more.

THERSITES [*aside*]   Now   she   sharpens.   Well   said,
whetstone!

DIOMEDES   I shall have it.                    80

CRESSIDA   What, this?

DIOMEDES   Ay, that.

CRESSIDA

O all you gods! – O pretty, pretty pledge!

Thy master now lies thinking on his bed

Of thee and me, and sighs, and takes my glove,                    85

---

67 **the pledge** (1) the promise Cressida
has made (to Diomedes); (2) the token
she has brought (belonging to
Troilus)

68 **this sleeve** the detachable sleeve or
ornamental cuff that Troilus gave
Cressida as a token at 4.4.69

69 Cf. Luke, 8.25, 'Then he said unto
them, Where is your faith?', the

proverb, 'Beauty and chastity (honesty) seldom meet' (Dent, B163), and
*Ham* 3.1.104–16.

78 **sharpens** (1) whets Diomedes'
appetite as with a *whetstone* by playing the coquette; (2) sharpens her
attack

80 **shall** am determined to

68.1] *Cam¹, subst.*   71–2 I will be … I will. / CRESSIDA] *F; not in Q*   72 sleeve?] *F; sleeue Q;* Sleeve;
*F3*   73.1] *Cam¹, subst.*   75 have't] *QF (*ha't, haue't*)*   78 SD] *Bevington³*   84 on] *Q;* in *F*

And gives memorial dainty kisses to it –

As I kiss thee.     [*He grabs the sleeve; she tries to get it back.*]

DIOMEDES          Nay, do not snatch it from me.

CRESSIDA

He that takes that doth take my heart withal.

DIOMEDES

I had your heart before. This follows it.

TROILUS [*aside*]   I did swear patience.                    90

CRESSIDA

You shall not have it, Diomed, faith, you shall not.

I'll give you something else.

DIOMEDES   I will have this. Whose was it?

CRESSIDA   It is no matter.

DIOMEDES   Come, tell me whose it was.                    95

CRESSIDA

'Twas one's that loved me better than you will.

But now you have it, take it.

DIOMEDES                    Whose was it?

CRESSIDA

By all Diana's waiting-women yond,

And by herself, I will not tell you whose.

DIOMEDES

Tomorrow will I wear it on my helm                    100

And grieve his spirit that dares not challenge it.

---

86 **memorial** in loving remembrance
87 **thee** the sleeve, probably. Cressida
addresses the sleeve as 'thee' in 85, but
invariably addresses Diomedes as 'you'
throughout this interview; and see LN
87–8 on his reciprocation of this formal style of address.
87–8 *For textual choices, see LN.
91 SP *CRESSIDA omitted by Q,

probably in error, as Q does indent the
line.
**faith** in faith (a mild oath)
98 i.e. by all yonder stars. Diana
(Artemis), whose name Cressida
invokes in her moment of duress, was
goddess of the moon and of chastity.
101 **his spirit** 'the spirit of him, whoever
it may be, to whom it belonged' (Ard¹)

86–7 And . . . thee] *F; one line in Q*   87 As I kiss thee] *QF; assigned to Diomedes / Oxf*   SD] *this edn*
SP] *QF (*Dio.*); om. Theobald (Thirlby);* CRESSIDA / *Oxf*   88 SP] *QF; speech continued to Cressida /*
*Theobald*   88 doth take] *Q; rakes F*   90 SD] *Oxf, subst.*   91 SP] *F; not in Q*   96 one's] *Q (*on's*);*
one *F*   98 By] *F; And by Q*

TROILUS [*aside*]

> Wert thou the devil, and wor'st it on thy horn,
> It should be challenged.

CRESSIDA

> Well, well, 'tis done, 'tis past. And yet it is not;
> I will not keep my word.

DIOMEDES                    Why then, farewell.                    105

> Thou never shalt mock Diomed again. [*He starts to leave.*]

CRESSIDA

> You shall not go. One cannot speak a word
> But it straight starts you.

DIOMEDES                    I do not like this fooling.

TROILUS [*aside*]

> Nor I, by Pluto; but that that likes not you
> Pleases me best.

DIOMEDES                    What, shall I come? The hour?                    110

CRESSIDA

> Ay, come. – O Jove! – Do, come. – I shall be plagued.

DIOMEDES

> Farewell till then.                    *Exit.*

CRESSIDA                    Good night. I prithee, come. –

> Troilus, farewell! One eye yet looks on thee,
> But with my heart the other eye doth see.

---

108 **straight starts you** immediately makes you shy away and set off in some other direction
109–10 \***Nor . . . best** For textual choices, see LN.
109 **likes** pleases
111 **I . . . plagued** i.e. 'I shall have such a life'. *Plagued* also means 'afflicted as with divine punishment, tormented, vexed' (*OED* plague *v.* 1–2, noting that Lat. *plagare* means to strike).
112 SD \*The wish of most editors to

'correct' F's placement of this SD in order to allow Cressida to answer Diomedes before he leaves (see t.n.) does not take sufficient account of his brusqueness. The plaintiveness of her beseeching him to come again is all the more evident if he is disappearing while she speaks.
114 i.e. 'but my other eye, attuned to my heart, looks on Diomedes'. With a pun on 'eye / I'.

102 SD] *Oxf, subst.* (+ *109*)    105–8 Why . . . you] *F; prose, Q*    106 SD] *Bevington*[1]*, subst.*
109 SP] *Hanmer; Ther. QF*    109–10 Nor . . . best] *Hanmer; prose, QF*    109 you] *Q;* me *F*
110 What,] *Rowe;* What *QF*    hour?] *Pope;* houre – *Q;* houre. *F*    111 Do, come] *F;* do come *Q*    112
SD] *F; not in Q; opp. end of line, Capell, subst.*

Ah, poor our sex! This fault in us I find:                     115
The error of our eye directs our mind.
What error leads must err. O, then conclude:
Minds swayed by eyes are full of turpitude.                    *Exit.*
THERSITES [*aside*]

A proof of strength she could not publish more,
Unless she said, 'My mind is now turned whore'.                120
ULYSSES

All's done, my lord.
TROILUS                     It is.
ULYSSES                                 Why stay we, then?
TROILUS

To make a recordation to my soul
Of every syllable that here was spoke.
But if I tell how these two did co-act,
Shall I not lie in publishing a truth?                         125
Sith yet there is a credence in my heart,
An esperance so obstinately strong,
That doth invert th'attest of eyes and ears,
As if those organs had deceptious functions,

---

115 **poor our** our poor
116 **error** wandering – in both a physical and moral sense; extravagant passion; flaw, mistake (*OED* 1, 2, 4)
117 **What . . . err** Whatever is guided by error must err.
118 The quotation marks in the left margin at the commencement of this line in Q suggest the marking of a *sententia*. See 1.2.278n.
     **swayed** induced, caused to swerve
119 'she could not put the case in more forceful terms'. To *publish* is to announce, promulgate.
121 By 'All's done', Ulysses means that since Cressida and Diomedes have gone, there's no more to see and hear.

Troilus' 'It is' goes further to suggest that everything is finished and Troilus done for; cf. *Consummatum est*, 'It is finished' (John, 19.30).
     **Why stay we?** What are we waiting for?
122 **recordation** record, commemorative account (*OED* 3)
124 **co-act** act together (*OED v.* 5; the first of only two instances)
126 **Sith** since
     **credence** belief
127 **esperance** hope
128 **attest** testimony, witness (*OED*'s first intransitive occurrence)
129 **deceptious** deceiving, misleading (*OED*'s first occurrence and Shakespeare's only use)

---

118 Minds] *preceded by quotation marks in left margin, Q*  119 SD] *Bevington³*  120 said] *Q; say F inverted commas, Hammer, subst.*  124 co-act] *F (*coact*); Court Q*  128 th'attest] *Q; that test F*
129 had deceptious] *F; were deceptions Q*

Created only to calumniate.                                       130
Was Cressid here?
ULYSSES                    I cannot conjure, Trojan.
TROILUS
She was not, sure.
ULYSSES                    Most sure she was.
TROILUS
Why, my negation hath no taste of madness.
ULYSSES
Nor mine, my lord. Cressid was here but now.
TROILUS
Let it not be believed, for womanhood!                           135
Think, we had mothers. Do not give advantage
To stubborn critics, apt, without a theme
For depravation, to square the general sex
By Cressid's rule. Rather think this not Cressid.
ULYSSES
What hath she done, Prince, that can soil our mothers?           140
TROILUS
Nothing at all, unless that this were she.
THERSITES [*aside*]    Will 'a swagger himself out on's own
eyes?
TROILUS
This she? No, this is Diomed's Cressida.

130 **calumniate** slander, defame (*OED*'s first intransitive occurrence)
131 **conjure** i.e. 'raise spirits in the form of Cressida' (Johnson)
133 'My insistence that she was not here is not characteristic of mad talk.'
134 **but now** only a moment ago
135 **for** for the sake of
137–9 **To stubborn . . . rule** 'to inveterate misogynists who will be all too likely, even when they lack grounds for their vilification, to measure the female sex

generally by Cressida's example'. To *square* is literally to use a carpenter's square, hence, adjust, adapt, cause to correspond or harmonize (*OED v.* 4b). *Rule* continues the metaphor and wordplay.
140 ***soil** sully. On the variant between this F reading and Q's 'spoile', cf. 2.2.70, 'soild' (Q) and 'spoyl'd' (F).
141 **unless that** unless
142–3 'Is Troilus going to deny the evidence of his own eyes with his blustering talk?'
144–9 The rhetorical devices here include

130–1 Created . . . here?] *F; one line, Q*    131 Cressid] *QF (Cresseid, Cressed)*    134 Cressid] *QF (Cresseid, Cressid); + 139, 153, 161*    140 soil] *F (soyle);* spoile *Q*    142 SD] *Bevington*¹    142 'a] *Q (a);* he *F*    144 Diomed's Cressida] *QF (Diomeds Cresseida, Diomids Cressida)*

If beauty have a soul, this is not she;                                         145
If souls guide vows, if vows be sanctimonies,
If sanctimony be the gods' delight,
If there be rule in unity itself,
This is not she. O, madness of discourse,
That cause sets up with and against itself!                                     150
Bifold authority, where reason can revolt
Without perdition, and loss assume all reason
Without revolt! This is and is not Cressid.
Within my soul there doth conduce a fight

anaphora, or the repetition of the same word (*If*) at the start of succeeding clauses, and anadiplosis, a linking figure in which each clause starts with the last word of the previous: *beauty . . . soul, soul . . . vows, vows . . . sanctimonies, sanctimony . . . delight* (Vickers, *Appropriating*, 191). The device is also an example of climax, or 'ladder' (as Puttenham, 3.19, 207–8, calls it), a series of propositions in which each rises above the previous.

146 *be sanctimonies are sacred things (*OED* 2b). F's 'are sanctimonie' is also possible, but the substitution of 'are' for 'be' could be a sophistication, and *OED* records the meaning of 'things sacred' only as pertaining to the plural form, 'sanctimonies'. F's 'sanctimonie' could also be an anticipation of the word in the next line.

147 **sanctimony** holiness of life and character (*OED* 1)

148 'if unity is indivisible' (by which *rule*, or principle, Cressida cannot be two entities)

149–50 *O . . . itself! 'O mad and paradoxical reasoning, that sets up arguments for and against the very proposition being debated!' F's 'thy selfe' can perhaps be defended as an apostrophe to madness in discourse, but seems awkward, and can be explained as a

lapse on the part of the compositor.

151–3 **Bifold . . . revolt!** 'Inherent contradiction, when reasoning can rebelliously contradict its own argument (based on the evidence that Cressida was indeed here) without seeming to undo itself, and when unreasonableness can put on the appearance of rationality without seeming to contradict itself!' *Perdition* carries the sense of lapse from rationality, while *loss*, a less restricted term, can hardly fail to include the loss of Cressida. The rhetorical figure is chiasmus, or inverting the order of words in parallel phrases; cf. 3.2.68–9 and 164–5, and 5.1.23, on the similar figures of antimetabole and hysteron proteron.

153 **This . . . Cressid** Troilus puts the contradictions of his dilemma in the rhetorical form of oxymoron, a statement that appears absurd on its face because of inherent contradiction but that gropes at finding paradoxical truth. Cf. previous note.

154 **conduce** take place (*OED* 6b, giving this sole instance of an intransitive or reflexive usage). In a transitive sense, *conduce* (lit. 'lead or bring together') can mean 'bring about, bring to effect' (*OED* 3), which is intelligible here as constructed reflexively. Contending emotions assemble themselves tumultuously in Troilus' soul.

146 be sanctimonies] *Q;* are sanctimonie *F*   149 is] *F;* was *Q*   150 itself!] *Capell;* it selfe, *Q;* thy selfe *F*   151 Bifold] *Q (*By-fould*);* By foule *F*

Of this strange nature, that a thing inseparate          155
Divides more wider than the sky and earth,
And yet the spacious breadth of this division
Admits no orifex for a point as subtle
As Ariachne's broken woof to enter.
Instance, O instance, strong as Pluto's gates,          160
Cressid is mine, tied with the bonds of heaven;
Instance, O instance, strong as heaven itself,
The bonds of heaven are slipped, dissolved and
    loosed,
And with another knot, five-finger-tied,
The fractions of her faith, orts of her love,          165
The fragments, scraps, the bits and greasy relics
Of her o'ereaten faith, are bound to Diomed.
ULYSSES
  May worthy Troilus be half attached

155–9 **that . . . enter** 'that a supposedly
  indivisible entity (like Cressida) should
  turn out to be more widely divided
  than sky and earth, and yet the spacious
  breadth of this huge gap provides not
  even an orifice large enough for something as fine-spun as a spider's web to
  enter'. (*Subtilis* is 'fine-spun' in Latin.)
  On *Ariachne*, see LN.
156 **more wider** On the double comparative, see Abbott, 11; cf. 2.2.11 and
  5.6.21.
160 **Instance** illustrative example, proof
  **Pluto's gates** i.e. the gates of hell
164 **five-finger-tied** i.e. 'tied by giving
  her hand to Diomede' (Johnson);
  'impossible to untie' (Seltzer)
165 **fractions** fragments (*OED sb.* 4; first
  occurrence)
  **orts** leftover scraps (of food)
167 **o'ereaten** eaten away on all sides;
  surfeiting. 'The banquet of Cressida's

faith has been eaten over (as a dog or a
hog first eats over what is set before
him to get the best), and now only the
filthy scraps are left for Diomedes'
(Baldwin, Var).
\***bound** tied (continuing the
metaphor of *bonds* and *knot*, 163–4);
destined. Cam¹, preferring Q's
'giuen', argues that *bound* 'seems to
defeat the purpose of the distinction
between a "bond", which is a sacred
or legal obligation, and a mere
"knot"'. But even such a knot can
bind, and the F reading seems a conscious choice.
168 **half attached** half as much seized
with passion (as it appears).
Emendations have been proposed to
'improve' the metre of this line (see
t.n.), but if 'Troilus' is pronounced tri-
syllabically the line needs no emendation.

159 Ariachne's] *F (Ariachnes); Ariathna's Qu; Ariachna's Qc*   164 five-finger-tied] *Pope;* fiue finger
tied *F;* finde finger tied *Q*   167 bound] *F;* giuen *Q*   168 be] *QF;* be but *Dyce² (W.S. Walker);* e'en
be *Oxf*

With that which here his passion doth express?

TROILUS

Ay, Greek, and that shall be divulged well          170
In characters as red as Mars his heart
Inflamed with Venus. Never did young man fancy
With so eternal and so fixed a soul.
Hark, Greek: as much as I do Cressid love,
So much by weight hate I her Diomed.                175
That sleeve is mine that he'll bear in his helm.
Were it a casque composed by Vulcan's skill,
My sword should bite it. Not the dreadful spout
Which shipmen do the hurricano call,
Constringed in mass by the almighty sun,           180
Shall dizzy with more clamour Neptune's ear
In his descent than shall my prompted sword
Falling on Diomed.

THERSITES [*aside*]   He'll tickle it for his concupy.

---

170 **divulged** divulgèd
171 **as red . . . heart** i.e. as bloody as Mars' heart. Troilus will show the violence of his passion in warlike deeds.
172 **fancy** love
175 **So . . . weight** i.e. to the same extent
176 **in his helm** on his helmet. For *in* in place of 'on', cf. 4.2.35 and 5.4.4.
177 **casque** headpiece, helmet. Vulcan or Hephaestus is famed as an armourer and artificer (Homer, *Iliad*, 18.462–617, LCL, 2.322–35; Ovid, *Met.*, 2.5–7, 106–10, 4.175–81, LCL, 1.60–1, 66–9, 190–1, etc.).
178, 179 **spout, hurricano** waterspout. See LN.
180 **Constringed** compressed, drawn or squeezed together (*OED* constringe *v.* 1, first occurrence)
181 **dizzy** make dizzy (*OED v.* 2, citing this line)

182 **his descent** the waterspout's descent. See LN.
**prompted** incited to action, made prompt or ready to act
184 **He'll tickle it** i.e. Troilus is going to rain blows on Diomedes' helmet (*OED* tickle *v.* 6b), or merely annoy with feather-like strokes (4), or stir things up (7c). In any case, Thersites deflates Troilus' high passion of rage. 'He'll be well tickled for his concupiscence' (Hillebrand, Var). The phrase could apply to Diomedes, in the sense of 'fight it out'. On the erotic resonances of *tickle*, see G. Williams, *Dictionary*, 1388–90.
**concupy** concubine, whore; or, concupiscence (*OED*; sole occurrence); perhaps with a suggestion of 'occupy' in a sexual sense, as in *2H4* 2.4.147 (Partridge)

---

174 much as] *F2;* much *QF*   Cressid] *Q; Cressida F*   176 in] *F;* on *Q*   180 sun] *Q (*sunne*);* Fenne *F*   181–3] *F; Q lines* discent, / Diomed. /   184 SD] *Bevington³*

TROILUS

O Cressid! O false Cressid! False, false, false!          185
Let all untruths stand by thy stained name,
And they'll seem glorious.

ULYSSES                              O, contain yourself.
Your passion draws ears hither.

*Enter* AENEAS.

AENEAS [*to Troilus*]

I have been seeking you this hour, my lord.
Hector, by this, is arming him in Troy.                   190
Ajax, your guard, stays to conduct you home.

TROILUS

Have with you, Prince. – My courteous lord, adieu. –
Farewell, revolted fair! – And, Diomed,
Stand fast, and wear a castle on thy head!

ULYSSES     I'll bring you to the gates.                  195

TROILUS     Accept distracted thanks.

*Exeunt Troilus, Aeneas and Ulysses.*

THERSITES     Would I could meet that rogue Diomed! I
would croak like a raven; I would bode, I would bode.
Patroclus will give me anything for the intelligence of this
whore. The parrot will not do more for an almond than    200

---

186 **stained** stainèd
190 **by this** by this time
     **arming him** putting on armour, arm-
     ing himself
191 **guard** safeguard. See 5.1.70 and n.
     **stays** is waiting
192 **Have . . . Prince** I am ready to go
     with you, Aeneas
     **lord** Ulysses
193 **revolted fair** faithless beauty, who
     has cast off her allegiance
194 **castle** fortress, i.e. strong helmet

198 **bode** foretell (disaster). Cf. the pro-
     verb, 'The croaking raven bodes mis-
     fortune' (Dent, R33), as in *Mac*
     1.5.38–40.
199 **for the intelligence of** for informa-
     tion about
200–1 **The parrot . . . drab** Parrots were
     proverbially fond of almonds (Dent,
     A220). Thersites implies that
     Patroclus is always on the lookout for
     easily obtained sex.

189 SD] *Oxf*

he for a commodious drab. Lechery, lechery, still wars
and lechery; nothing else holds fashion. A burning
devil take them!                                          *Exit.*

[**5.3**]        *Enter* HECTOR *[armed] and* ANDROMACHE.

ANDROMACHE
When was my lord so much ungently tempered
To stop his ears against admonishment?
Unarm, unarm, and do not fight today.
HECTOR
You train me to offend you. Get you in.
By all the everlasting gods, I'll go!                          5
ANDROMACHE
My dreams will sure prove ominous to the day.
HECTOR
No more, I say.

*Enter* CASSANDRA.

CASSANDRA        Where is my brother Hector?
ANDROMACHE
Here, sister, armed, and bloody in intent.
Consort with me in loud and dear petition;
Pursue we him on knees. For I have dreamt              10
Of bloody turbulence, and this whole night
Hath nothing been but shapes and forms of slaughter.

---

201 **commodious drab** accommodating
whore. *Commodious* also suggests
'roomy' and 'convenient, useful' (*OED
a.* 1, 4, 5).
202–3 **A burning . . . them!** (1) 'May the
devil take them off to burning hell!';
(2) 'May venereal disease attack them!'
(*OED* take *v.* 7)

5.3 Location: Troy. The palace, morning.
1 **ungently tempered** discourteous,
moody, out of sorts
4 **train** induce, tempt
**offend** give pain to
6 **ominous to** prophetic regarding
9 **Consort with** join
**dear** ardent, consequential

203 SD] *Q; not in F*   **5.3**] *Rowe, subst.*   0.1 *armed] Capell*   4 in] *Q;* gone *F*   5 all] *Q; not in F*

327

CASSANDRA

O, 'tis true.

HECTOR [*Calls out*]   Ho! Bid my trumpet sound!

CASSANDRA

No notes of sally, for the heavens, sweet brother.

HECTOR

Begone, I say. The gods have heard me swear.                    15

CASSANDRA

The gods are deaf to hot and peevish vows.

They are polluted off'rings, more abhorred

Than spotted livers in the sacrifice.

ANDROMACHE [*to Hector*]

O, be persuaded! Do not count it holy

To hurt by being just. It is as lawful,                         20

For we would give much, to use violent thefts,

And rob in the behalf of charity.

CASSANDRA

It is the purpose that makes strong the vow,

But vows to every purpose must not hold.

Unarm, sweet Hector.

HECTOR                              Hold you still, I say.         25

---

14 **sally** sallying forth to battle; sortie
  **for the heavens** for heaven's sake
16 **peevish** headstrong, foolish. Cf. Dent,
  O7.
18 **spotted** tainted, diseased (and hence
  ill-omened)
20–2 *These lines, missing from Q,
  might be supposed to have been cut
  from F, if one were to assume for a
  moment the priority of F, but Q's ending 19 with a comma and then failing
  in the next line to provide a needed SP
  for Cassandra argue a defect in the Q
  version that F remedies. Even if there
  were a cut in production at some point,
  it might not be authorial.
20 **just** faithful to a vow

21–2 *'for us to rob in order to have
  money to give charitably'. Tyrwhitt's
  emendation (see t.n.), adopted by
  Malone and here, is based on the plausible assumption that the F compositor
  either repeated *count* from 19 or mis-
  takenly printed an inadequately deleted authorial first thought.
24 'but not every vow must be held sacred
  (since not all purposes are valid)'.
  Johnson sees in this utterance of a mad
  prophetess 'all the coolness and judg-
  ment of a skilful casuist'. Lines 23–4
  are in the rhetorical form of an
  antimetabole; see Puttenham, 3.19
  (208–9), and 3.2.68–9 and 164–5,
  5.2.151–3 and notes.

13 SD] *this edn*   14 SP] *F (Cass.); Cres. Q*   19 SD] *Oxf*   20–2] *F; not in Q*   21 give much, to use]
*Malone (Tyrwhitt); count giue much to as F*   23 SP] *F (Cass.); not in Q*

Mine honour keeps the weather of my fate.
Life every man holds dear, but the dear man
Holds honour far more precious-dear than life.

*Enter* TROILUS [*armed*].

How now, young man, mean'st thou to fight today?          29
ANDROMACHE
Cassandra, call my father to persuade.          *Exit Cassandra.*
HECTOR
No, faith, young Troilus, doff thy harness, youth.
I am today i'th' vein of chivalry.
Let grow thy sinews till their knots be strong,
And tempt not yet the brushes of the war.
Unarm thee, go, and doubt thou not, brave boy,          35
I'll stand today for thee and me and Troy.
TROILUS
Brother, you have a vice of mercy in you,
Which better fits a lion than a man.
HECTOR
What vice is that? Good Troilus, chide me for it.

---

26 **keeps the weather of** keeps to the
windward side of (for tactical advantage), i.e. gains advantage over, is superior to
27 'every man holds life to be precious,
but the esteemed man'. Cf. Dent,
L244.1: 'As dear as life'. Lines 27–8
again are in the form of antimetabole;
see 24n.
30 **father** father-in-law, Priam. Hector
may well not hear this speech; he is
talking with Troilus.
31 **doff thy harness** take off your
armour
32 **i'th'** . . . **chivalry** in a suitable mood

for chivalrous action, i.e. feats of
knightly valour (*OED* chivalry 4)
33 **knots** ligaments
34 'and do not adventure upon or risk the
perils of hostile encounters' (*OED*
tempt *v.* 2c)
38 Lions, as the kings of beasts, were
popularly supposed to spare the
defenceless, as Hector is famed for
doing; see, e.g., 4.5.106–7. Cf. the
proverbial commonplace: 'The lion
spares the suppliant' (Dent, L316),
and Pliny, *Natural History*, 8.19.48–52
(LCL, 3.36–41).

28 precious-dear] *Q (*precious deere*);* precious, deere *F*   28.1 *armed*] *Capell*   29 mean'st] *F;*
meanest *Q*   31 No, faith] *Theobald;* No faith *QF*

TROILUS

When many times the captive Grecian falls,                    40
Even in the fan and wind of your fair sword,
You bid them rise and live.

HECTOR

O, 'tis fair play.

TROILUS                    Fool's play, by heaven, Hector.

HECTOR

How now, how now?

TROILUS                    For th' love of all the gods,
Let's leave the hermit Pity with our mothers,                    45
And when we have our armours buckled on,
The venomed vengeance ride upon our swords,
Spur them to ruthful work, rein them from ruth.

HECTOR

Fie, savage, fie!

TROILUS                    Hector, then 'tis wars.

---

40 **captive** i.e. caitiff, 'wretched, miserable, base' (*OED* captive *a*. A4, caitiff *a*. B1–3). The more usual sense of *captive* also pertains to those who have been vanquished in battle.

41 i.e. 'felled simply by the whoosh of your even-handed sword', not even requiring an actual blow; also suggesting perhaps a gracious wave of Hector's sword as he spares the helpless enemy. *Fair*, a general epithet of praise, here suggests 'not taking undue advantage' (*OED a*. 10). Cf. *Ham* 2.2.473: 'But with the whiff and wind of his fell sword'.

42 **them** The plural follows the plural concept in 40 (though singular in form) of 'the captive Grecian falls', since that event happens 'many times'.

43 **Fool's play** a witty antithesis to *fair play* (using *fool* where we might expect 'foul'). Troilus objects that Hector is 'playing the fool', acting the part of a

fool or jester (*OED* fool *sb*. A2b), by throwing away perfectly fair opportunities to prevail over his opponents.

45 *\*mothers This F reading could be a corruption of Q's 'Mother', by attraction from *gods*, *armours* and *swords* (Ard²), but both readings make good sense. F may represent an intentional generalizing to include the Trojan warriors generally, not just the sons of Hecuba.

47 **The venomed vengeance** 'may the poisonous spirit of vengeance'. *Venomed* means both 'envenomed', impregnated with venom, and 'venomous', noxious.

48 **ruthful** lamentable, piteous, exciting compassion (*OED a*. 2)
**ruth** pity, mercy

49 **then 'tis wars** i.e. 'then (when we leave pity behind) we will have war in earnest'; 'that's what war is'

45 mothers] *F;* Mother *Q*

330

HECTOR

　Troilus, I would not have you fight today.　　　50

TROILUS　Who should withhold me?

　Not fate, obedience, nor the hand of Mars

　Beck'ning with fiery truncheon my retire;

　Not Priamus and Hecuba on knees,

　Their eyes o'ergalled with recourse of tears;　　　55

　Nor you, my brother, with your true sword drawn

　Opposed to hinder me, should stop my way,

　But by my ruin.

*Enter* PRIAM *and* CASSANDRA.

CASSANDRA

　Lay hold upon him, Priam, hold him fast;

　He is thy crutch. Now if thou loose thy stay,　　　60

　Thou on him leaning, and all Troy on thee,

　Fall all together.

PRIAM　　　　　　Come, Hector, come. Go back.

　Thy wife hath dreamt, thy mother hath had visions,

　Cassandra doth foresee, and I myself

　Am like a prophet suddenly enrapt　　　65

　To tell thee that this day is ominous.

---

52–3 **nor . . . retire** 'nor Mars himself, with fiery staff in hand, beckoning me to withdraw'. A *truncheon* could be a marshal's baton or staff of authority, a cudgel, or a spear shaft. 'In combats between two champions, the arbiter of the proceedings directed their course by a truncheon, or "warder," which was thrown down when the combat was to cease' (Ard[1], citing *R2* 1.3.118–20).

55 'their eyes completely chafed with tears coursing down their cheeks'; or, 'even if their distressed eyes were to resort to (have recourse to) tears'. *O'ergalled* = o'ergallèd.

58 'except by killing me'

60 **loose thy stay** let go your prop or support. *Loose*, the QF spelling, can also signify 'lose'.

63 Caxton, 610, tells of Andrometha's (i.e. Andromache's) 'meruayllous vysion' and 'dremes'. Cf. Joel, 2.28: 'your old men shall dream dreams, and your young men shall see visions', and Acts, 2.17.

65 **enrapt** 'carried away' by prophetic ecstasy (*OED*'s first occurrence)

58] *F; not in Q*

Therefore, come back.

HECTOR                              Aeneas is afield,
And I do stand engaged to many Greeks,
Even in the faith of valour, to appear
This morning to them.

PRIAM                              Ay, but thou shalt not go.              70

HECTOR    I must not break my faith.
You know me dutiful; therefore, dear sir,
Let me not shame respect, but give me leave
To take that course by your consent and voice
Which you do here forbid me, royal Priam.              75

CASSANDRA
O Priam, yield not to him!

ANDROMACHE                      Do not, dear father.

HECTOR
Andromache, I am offended with you.
Upon the love you bear me, get you in.     *Exit Andromache.*

TROILUS
This foolish, dreaming, superstitious girl
Makes all these bodements.

CASSANDRA                      O, farewell, dear Hector!              80
Look how thou diest! Look how thy eye turns pale!
Look how thy wounds do bleed at many vents!
Hark, how Troy roars, how Hecuba cries out,
How poor Andromache shrills her dolour forth!

---

69 **faith** assurance, pledge (as also in 71)
70 **shalt** must
73 **shame respect** violate my filial duty
to you
78 **Upon . . . me** 'I command you, in the
name of your wifely love and obedience to me'
79 **This** (gesturing to indicate Cassandra)
80 **bodements** omens that bode ill.

(Presumably this is earlier than *OED*'s
first citation, *Mac* 4.1.96: 'Sweet bodements, good!')
84 **shrills** wails shrilly
\***dolour** Q's 'dolours' is certainly pos-
sible, and F could represent a sophistication of it, but may also reflect a
deliberate choice.

---

72 sir] *QF;* sire *Oxf*   81 thy] *QF;* thine *(Collier MS)*   82 do] *Q;* doth *F*   84 dolour] *F;*
dolours *Q*

Behold, distraction, frenzy and amazement,     85
Like witless antics, one another meet,
And all cry, 'Hector! Hector's dead! O, Hector!'
TROILUS     Away! Away!
CASSANDRA
Farewell. Yet soft! Hector, I take my leave.     89
Thou dost thyself and all our Troy deceive.     *Exit.*
HECTOR [*to Priam*]
You are amazed, my liege, at her exclaim.
Go in and cheer the town. We'll forth and fight,
Do deeds of praise, and tell you them at night.
PRIAM
Farewell. The gods with safety stand about thee!
     [*Exeunt Priam and Hector at different doors.*]
     *Alarum.*

TROILUS
They are at it, hark! – Proud Diomed, believe,     95
I come to lose my arm or win my sleeve.

*Enter* PANDARUS [*with a letter*].

PANDARUS     Do you hear, my lord? Do you hear?
TROILUS     What now?

---

85 **amazement** bewilderment, alarm
86 **antics** performers who play grotesque or ludicrous parts, such as the clown or mountebank (*OED* B4). Cassandra imagines the fall of Troy as like a weird pageant or a scene in a lunatic asylum.
89 **soft** i.e. stay, wait a moment (short for 'go soft'; Onions). 'Take my leave' may suggest that Cassandra gives Hector a parting kiss.
90 'You are deluding yourself and betraying Troy' (with a bitter pun on two

meanings of *deceive*; *OED* 1, 2).
91 **amazed** perplexed, dumbstruck. Cf. *amazement*, 85.
**exclaim** outcry. This singular form as in QF is plausible, though the three examples given by *OED sb.* from 1489 to 1633 of this rare nominative form (not including this present instance) are all plural.
93 **of** worthy of
94 **with . . . thee** protect you
96 For rhetorical figures, see LN.

---

85 distraction] *F;* destruction *Q*     86 antics] *QF (*antiques, Antickes*)*     87] *inverted commas, Hanmer, subst.*     89 Yet] *Q;* yes, *F*     90 SD] *F; not in Q*     91 SD] *Oxf* exclaim] *QF;* exclaims *Cam¹*     92] *F; Q lines* towne, / fight, /     93 of] *F;* worth *Q*     94.1] *Malone, subst.*     96 lose] *QF (*loose*)*     96.1 PANDARUS] *QF (Pandar)*     with a letter] *this edn*

PANDARUS  Here's a letter come from yond poor girl.

TROILUS  Let me read.  [*Troilus reads.*]  100

PANDARUS  A whoreson phthisic, a whoreson rascally
phthisic so troubles me, and the foolish fortune of this girl,
and what one thing, what another, that I shall leave you
one o'these days. And I have rheum in mine eyes too, and
such an ache in my bones that, unless a man were cursed,  105
I cannot tell what to think on't. – What says she there?

TROILUS

Words, words, mere words, no matter from the heart;
Th'effect doth operate another way.
[*He tears the letter and tosses it away.*]
Go, wind, to wind! There turn and change together.
My love with words and errors still she feeds,  110
But edifies another with her deeds.  *Exeunt* [*severally*].

<hr>

101 **phthisic** consumptive cough or
other afflictions of lung and throat
104 **rheum** watery discharge
105 **ache in my bones** sometimes caused
by syphilis, the 'Neapolitan bone-ache'
(2.3.17–18), or by arthritis.
**cursed** under a spell or curse
107 Cf. 'Words, words, words' (*Ham*
2.2.193).
108 'Her words are belied by her actions';
but also suggesting that the effect
on Troilus of her words, not coming
from the heart, is quite other than
what they were intended to produce.
109 'Go, empty words, to the air, where
(like the perfidious writer of these

words) you can whirl and mingle as
scraps of paper.' Troilus' bitter irony
plays on multiple meanings of *turn*
(revolve, reverse position, mislead,
beguile, desert) and *change* (exchange,
alter, change countenance, quit one
thing for another, remove to another
place). Cf. Dent, W833: 'Words are but
wind', and W412: 'As wavering as the
wind'.
110 **errors** deceits; vexation (*OED* 2, 3c)
111 **edifies** raises up (to the preferred
position of lover, perhaps with erotic
suggestion); but with an ironic suggestion of 'improves morally'
\***deeds** For textual choices, see LN.

100 SD] *Oxf, subst.* 101 phthisic] *QF* (tisick, tisicke) 104 o'these] *Rowe;* ath's *Q;* o'th's *F*
108.1] *Rowe, subst.* 111 deeds.] *Q;* deedes. / *Pand.* Why, but heare you? / *Troy.* Hence brother lackie;
ignomie and shame / Pursue thy life, and liue aye with thy name. *F* 111 SD *severally*] *Malone*

**[5.4]** *Alarum; excursions. Enter* THERSITES.

THERSITES Now they are clapper-clawing one another.
I'll go look on. That dissembling abominable varlet,
Diomed, has got that same scurvy doting foolish young
knave's sleeve of Troy there in his helm. I would fain see
them meet, that that same young Trojan ass that loves          5
the whore there might send that Greekish whoremasterly
villain with the sleeve back to the dissembling luxurious
drab, of a sleeveless errand. O'th' t'other side, the policy
of those crafty swearing rascals – that stale old mouse-
eaten dry cheese, Nestor, and that same dog-fox,          10
Ulysses – is proved not worth a blackberry. They set me

---

**5.4** The battlefield between Troy and the
Greek camp serves as the location for
the remainder of the play.

**0.1** *excursions* sorties or issuings forth of
soldiers. A standard shorthand for battle on the Elizabethan stage, usually
accompanied by the sound of *alarums*
or calls to arms played ordinarily on
drum and trumpet.

**1** **clapper-clawing** clawing, scratching,
mauling, thrashing. In the publisher's
preface, *clapper-clawed* (borrowed perhaps from this passage) seems to mean
'applauded raucously' (playing on the
verb 'to clap'). A *clapper* can be a
device for making a continuous noise,
used as a child's toy or as a means to
scare off birds or demand attention.

**2** **abominable** QF's 'abhominable' is
the spelling invariably used in eighteen
occurrences in the First Folio (see,
e.g., *LLL* 5.1.24 and *MM* 3.2.25), and
represents a supposed derivation from
*ab homine*, 'away from mankind, inhuman', whereas the truer derivation is
from *abominari*, 'to deprecate as an ill
omen' (*OED*).

**3–4** **young . . . Troy** young knave of

Troy's sleeve

**4** **fain** gladly

**7–8** **luxurious drab** lecherous slut

**8** **of a sleeveless errand** on a profitless
errand; with wordplay on *sleeve*. If
Troilus takes away the sleeve from
Diomedes and sends him back to
Cressida, Diomedes will arrive literally
sleeveless. A common expression; see
Dent, E180.

**policy** cunning stratagem (also in 12 and
16), with Machiavellian connotations

**9** **crafty swearing** craftily uttering
solemn vows and promises

**10** **dog-fox** male fox (*OED*'s only occurrence as applied to a man). The crafti-
ness of foxes is legendary; see Dent,
F629, 'As wily (subtle, crafty) as a fox',
and Tilley, F647 and 648.

**11** **not . . . blackberry** a proverbial comparison. Cf. *1H4* 2.4.237 ('If reasons
were as plentiful as blackberries'), *2H4*
1.2.172 ('not worth a gooseberry') and
Dent, B441.1 and 442.

**11–12** **set . . . policy** set up, to suit their
own crafty purposes. (*Me* is used colloquially to present the speaker's satirical
point of view. See Abbott, 220.)

---

**5.4**] *Rowe, subst.* 0.1 *Alarum*] *not in Q; before 'Exeunt', 5.3.111, F* excursions. Enter THERSITES]
*Capell; Enter Thersites: excursions. Q; Enter Thersites in excursion. F* 2 abominable] *QF (*abhominable*)*
3 Diomed] *QF (Diomede)* young] *F; not in Q* 9 stale] *Q; stole F* 11 proved not] *Cam¹ (anon. in
Cam); not proou'd QF*

up, in policy, that mongrel cur, Ajax, against that dog of
as bad a kind, Achilles. And now is the cur Ajax prouder
than the cur Achilles, and will not arm today,
whereupon the Grecians began to proclaim barbarism,          15
and policy grows into an ill opinion.

*Enter* DIOMEDES [*wearing Cressida's sleeve on his helmet*]
*and* TROILUS [*following*].

Soft! Here comes sleeve and t'other. [*He stands aside.*]

TROILUS [*to Diomedes*]
Fly not, for shouldst thou take the river Styx
I would swim after.

DIOMEDES                    Thou dost miscall retire.
I do not fly, but advantageous care                          20
Withdrew me from the odds of multitude.
Have at thee! [*They fight.*]

---

12 **mongrel . . . dog** The doglike
qualities of Ajax (mongrel, because
half-Greek and half-Trojan) are set off
against the dog-in-the-manger propen-
sities of Achilles. Both have become
currish in their rivalry.

15 ***began** Rowe's 'begin' is tidy and logical, and may be right, but the sequence of
events is intelligible in the QF reading.
See Abbott, 347, for examples of Shakespeare's use of the simple past where we
would use the perfect or present.
**proclaim barbarism** 'declare in
favour of uncivilized ignorance'
(instead of the discredited *policy* or
cunning statecraft of their current
leaders, which they will tolerate no
longer). For Greeks to choose barbarism would amount to denial of
their very identity as a people, since

the word 'barbarian' originally meant
one who was not a Greek and did not
speak the Greek language.

18 **shouldst . . . Styx** 'even if you were to
attempt escape by swimming across
the river Styx to the underworld'.
Dead souls had to pay the ferryman
Charon for passage across this fear-
some river; no one swam. *Take* means
'take to, jump into'.

19 **miscall retire** misname my tactical
withdrawal (by calling it 'flight')

20–1 **advantageous . . . multitude**
'opportune prudence prompted me to
withdraw from where I faced heavily
uneven odds'. (See *OED* advantageous
*a.* 1, citing Florio's definition of '*avan-
taggioso*, advantageous, having odds'
and this passage as its earliest occurrences.)

---

15 began] *QF*; begin *Rowe³*  16.1–2 *Enter . . .* TROILUS] *this edn; Enter Diomed and Troylus. F; not
in Q*  16.2 *following*] *Capell*  17 t'other] *Q* (tother); th'other *F*  SD] *this edn*  18 SD] *Oxf*
18–19 Fly . . . after] *F; prose, Q*  21–2] *F; one line, Q*  22 SD] *Rowe, subst. (They go off fighting);
see 24.1*

THERSITES   Hold thy whore, Grecian! Now for thy
whore, Trojan! Now the sleeve, now the sleeve!
[*Exeunt Troilus and Diomedes, fighting.*]

*Enter* HECTOR.

HECTOR

What art thou, Greek? Art thou for Hector's match?        25
Art thou of blood and honour?

THERSITES   No, no, I am a rascal, a scurvy railing knave,
a very filthy rogue.

HECTOR   I do believe thee. Live.                          [*Exit.*]

THERSITES   God-a-mercy, that thou wilt believe me; but    30
a plague break thy neck for frighting me! What's
become of the wenching rogues? I think they have
swallowed one another. I would laugh at that miracle –
yet, in a sort, lechery eats itself. I'll seek them.       *Exit.*

23 **Hold** uphold your right to keep
23–4 **for thy whore** i.e. fight bravely in
the name of your right to Cressida
25–6 **Art . . . honour?** 'Are you of sufficiently noble rank and honour to fight
with Hector?' Persons of noble rank
might not be challenged in battle by
one of lower rank, and, if so challenged, could refuse to fight (Siegel,
42, quoting Sir William Segar, *The
Book of Honor and Arms* (1590), Bk 3,
chap. 4, and *Vincentio Saviolo, His
Practice* (1595), Bk 2, sig. Gg2).
29 i.e. (delivered with the urbanity of a
perfect gentleman) 'Yes, I can see that
you're everything you say you are. Go
and enjoy your pitiable existence.'
30 **God-a-mercy** thank you (*OED* 2),
playing also on 'thank God' and 'God
have mercy!'

31 **a plague . . . neck** The original meaning of *plague* (see 5.2.111n.) is a stroke
or blow. In late Latin the nominative
form was applied to outbreaks of pestilence because of the terrifying way in
which the infection strikes; cf. the
disease-bearing arrows of Apollo in Bk
1 of the *Iliad*.
34 **in a sort** in a way
**lechery eats itself** Cf. Sonnet 129,
where lust is 'Enjoyed no sooner but
despisèd straight' and is 'a swallowed
bait / On purpose laid to make the
taker mad', etc. As this sonnet also
suggests in its final image of 'the heav-
en that leads men to this hell', one frequent consequence of uncontrolled
lust is wasting venereal disease. At
1.3.121–4, appetite (greed) eats up
itself.

23–4] *F; Q lines* Troian, / sleeue. /   24.1] *see* 22 SD *n.*   25 thou, Greek?] *F, subst.;* Greeke, *Q*
29 SD] *Rowe*

**[5.5]**                 *Enter* DIOMEDES *and* Servant.

DIOMEDES

  Go, go, my servant, take thou Troilus' horse;
  Present the fair steed to my Lady Cressid.
  Fellow, commend my service to her beauty;
  Tell her I have chastised the amorous Trojan                                4
  And am her knight by proof.
SERVANT                                    I go, my lord.                    [*Exit.*]

*Enter* AGAMEMNON.

AGAMEMNON

  Renew, renew! The fierce Polydamas
  Hath beat down Menon; bastard Margareton
  Hath Doreus prisoner,
  And stands colossus-wise, waving his beam
  Upon the pashed corpses of the kings                                        10

---

**5.5.0.1** \*On the inconsistency of Q's '*Seruant*' and F's '*Seruants*', and of Q's '*Man*' and F's '*Ser.*' at 5, see n. on LIST OF ROLES (SERVANT *attending on Diomedes*).

**2–5** Caxton (608) reports that Diomedes 'fought with troillous at his comyng and smote hym doun and toke hys horse / and sente hit to breseyda', instructing his servant to say 'that hit was troyollus horse her loue / that he had beten hym by his prowesse / and prayd her fro than forth on that she wold holde hym for her loue and frende &c'.

**4** **amorous** perhaps to be pronounced 'am'rous'

**5** **by proof** by trial (of arms) and by the result (*OED sb.* 6, 7)

**6** **Renew!** To it again!

**6–15** On the warriors' names, see LN.

**7** \***Margareton** Q and F both consistently give the name as '*Margarelon*', but Caxton ('margareton', 612, etc.) and Lydgate ('Margariton' or 'Margarytone', 3.5204) essentially agree on the spelling of Benoît's *Roman de Troie*, and a *t:l* error would be easy (Ard²). See n. on LIST OF ROLES. Pronounced 'Màrgaréton'.

**9** **colossus-wise** like the great bronze statue of Apollo standing astride the harbour at Rhodes, one of the seven wonders of the ancient world
  **beam** large timber, here serving as lance or spear-shaft for the colossus. Goliath's spear is 'like a weaver's beam' in 1 Samuel, 17.7 (Shaheen, 124).

**10** **pashed** pashèd; battered, crushed by blows. Cf. 2.3.200.

---

**5.5]** *Capell, subst.*  **0.1** DIOMEDES] *QF (Diomed)*  Servant] *Q; Seruants F*  **5** SP] *F (Ser.); Man. Q*  SD] *Hanmer, subst.*  **5.1]** *F; after* proofe, *Q*  **6** Polydamas] *Q (Polidamas); Polidamus F*  **7** Margareton] *Oxf; Margarelon QF*  **9** colossus-wise] *QF (Colossus* wise, Colossus-wise*)*  **10** corpses] *QF (*corses, courses*)*  kings] *F3, subst.;* Kings: *QF*

Epistrophus and Cedius. Polyxenes is slain,
Amphimachus and Thoas deadly hurt,
Patroclus ta'en or slain, and Palamedes
Sore hurt and bruised. The dreadful Sagittary
Appals our numbers. Haste we, Diomed,                    15
To reinforcement, or we perish all.

*Enter* NESTOR [*with soldiers bearing Patroclus' body*].

NESTOR [*to his soldiers*]
Go, bear Patroclus' body to Achilles,
And bid the snail-paced Ajax arm for shame.
                    [*Exeunt some soldiers with the body.*]
There is a thousand Hectors in the field.
Now here he fights on Galathe his horse,                  20
And there lacks work; anon he's there afoot,
And there they fly or die, like scaled schools
Before the belching whale; then is he yonder,
And there the strawy Greeks, ripe for his edge,

11 A hypermetric line, perhaps with five main stresses ('Cédius' in two syllables): 'Epístrophus and Cédius. Polýxenès is sláin'.
13 ta'en taken (monosyllabic)
14 Sagittary See LN 6–15.
15 Appals our numbers dismays (lit. 'makes pale') our troops
16 To reinforcement to add to our strength, to reinforce our hard-pressed comrades
16.1 The bringing of Patroclus' dead body on stage briefly here is not certain, in that Nestor could be directing some action off stage, but the action seems likely.
18 snail-paced Cf. 1.2.21 and Dent, S579: 'As slow as a snail'. On the rousing of Ajax to anger, and the

parallelism of this action to Achilles' wrath over the death of Patroclus, see LN 43.
20 Galathe mentioned as Hector's horse in Caxton, 600, and Lydgate, 3.3518. Pronounced *Gálathè*.
21 And there For textual choices, see LN.
22 scaled schools scattering schools of scaly fish. QF's 'sculls', 'sculs', is a variant spelling of *schools*. The image of *scaled* (scalèd) is appropriate not only to fish but to warriors in armour (*OED ppl. a.*[1] 2a; cf. 'scale-armour').
23 belching spouting
24 strawy strawlike, ready for mowing his edge the edge of his scythelike sword

11 Epistrophus] *Var '73; Epistropus QF* Cedius] *Capell; Cedus QF* Polyxenes] *QF (Polixenes)*
12 Amphimachus] *QF (Amphimacus)* Thoas] *Pope; Thous QF* 16.1 *with . . . body*] *this edn; with Patroclus' body Oxf* 17 SD] *Capell, subst.* 18.1] *Oxf, subst.* 21 And there] *QF; And here Ard*[2]
22 scaled] *F; scaling Q* schools] *Oxf*[1] *(anon. in Cam);* sculls *Q;* sculs *F* 24 strawy] *Q;* straying *F*

Fall down before him, like the mower's swath.          25
Here, there and everywhere he leaves and takes,
Dexterity so obeying appetite
That what he will he does, and does so much
That proof is called impossibility.

*Enter* ULYSSES.

ULYSSES

O, courage, courage, princes! Great Achilles          30
Is arming, weeping, cursing, vowing vengeance.
Patroclus' wounds have roused his drowsy blood,
Together with his mangled Myrmidons,
That noseless, handless, hacked and chipped, come to
      him,
Crying on Hector. Ajax hath lost a friend          35
And foams at mouth, and he is armed and at it,
Roaring for Troilus, who hath done today
Mad and fantastic execution,
Engaging and redeeming of himself

---

25 **swath** row of grain as it falls or lies
when mown or reaped. See next note.
26 **leaves and takes** 'In perfect rhythm,
the skilled mower drops or "leaves"
the grain of one cut as he "takes" that
of another' (Baldwin, Var).
27 **appetite** inclination, desire
28 ***will** Capell's conjectural emendation
to 'wills' makes explicit the active
meaning of volition, but *will* can be
used non-modally without another
verb (Abbott, 316); cf. 49 ('I will none
but Hector') and *Ham* 5.2.245 ('I stand
aloof and will no reconcilement'). *Will*
in the present passage could thus mean
'will do'.
29 **proof** visible evidence, accomplishment. Even when it is done it seems
impossible. Cf. 5.2.122–67.

33 **Myrmidons** a people created by Zeus
out of ants (Gr. *murmekes*) to replace
the plague-stricken people of Aegina.
They have come to Troy as followers
of Achilles. Cf. 1.3.379.
35 **Crying on** exclaiming against
38 **execution** accomplishment; carrying
out of a (battle) plan; effective action;
slaughter (*OED* 1, 2, 5). Pronounced
in five syllables.
39–42 'fighting at close quarters and res-
cuing himself from danger with such
nonchalant use of strength and effort-
less self-defence that it was as if
Fortune herself, in defiance of his enemies' skill in arms, directed him to win
all'. On metaphors and rhetorical figures, see LN.

---

25 the] *F;* a *Q*   28 will] *QF;* wills *(Capell)*

With such a careless force and forceless care          40
As if that luck, in very spite of cunning,
Bade him win all.

*Enter* AJAX.

AJAX    Troilus! Thou coward Troilus!                   *Exit.*
DIOMEDES    Ay, there, there!                           *Exit.*
NESTOR    So, so, we draw together.                     45

*Enter* ACHILLES.

ACHILLES    Where is this Hector?
Come, come, thou boy-queller, show thy face!
Know what it is to meet Achilles angry.
Hector! Where's Hector? I will none but Hector.

*Exit [with others].*

**[5.6]**                    *Enter* AJAX.

AJAX

Troilus, thou coward Troilus, show thy head!

*Enter* DIOMEDES.

DIOMEDES    Troilus, I say! Where's Troilus?

---

43 On Ajax' fury, see LN.
44 On Diomedes' role in the battle, see
    LN.
45 **we draw together** i.e. at last we
    Greeks are pulling together (since Ajax
    and Achilles have entered the battle).
47 **boy-queller** boy-killer, slayer of
    Patroclus. To kill a 'boy' would be a

cowardly act; cf. *2H4* 2.1.51–2 and *H5*
4.7.1–2. Yet even though Thersites
calls Patroclus 'boy' (5.1.14), he is a
warrior in Homer and not at all like the
boys guarding the luggage who are
defencelessly slaughtered in *H5*.
Achilles, in his anger, is looking for an
excuse to call Hector a coward.

41–2] *Rowe¹; one line, QF*    41 luck] *F; lust Q*    42.1] *F; before 43, serving also as SP, Q*    43 SP] *F;
not in Q*    44 SD] *Cam¹, subst.; opp. 45, QF*    49.1 *with others*] *Capell, subst.   (Exeunt)*
**5.6**] *Capell, subst.*    0.1] *F; before 1 in Q, serving also as SP*    1.1] *F (Enter Diomed.); before 2 in Q,
serving also as SP*    2 SP] *F; not in Q*

AJAX    What wouldst thou?

DIOMEDES    I would correct him.

AJAX

> Were I the general, thou shouldst have my office          5
> Ere that correction. – Troilus, I say! What, Troilus!

*Enter* TROILUS.

TROILUS

> O traitor Diomed! Turn thy false face, thou traitor,
> And pay the life thou owest me for my horse!

DIOMEDES    Ha, art thou there?

AJAX

> I'll fight with him alone. Stand, Diomed.          10

DIOMEDES

> He is my prize. I will not look upon.

TROILUS

> Come, both you cogging Greeks. Have at you both!

*Enter* HECTOR.

---

**5.6.5 Were I** even if I were

6    **Ere that correction** i.e. 'sooner than deprive me of the right to "correct" Troilus'. On Ajax' unspecified motive for pursuing Troilus, see LN 5.5.43. Troilus seems unconcerned; he pays no attention to Ajax at first.

8    **horse** See 5.5.2–5n. for the relevant passage in Caxton; see also Lydgate, 3.4620–41. The abrupt mention here of this horse is more sardonic in effect; it is so unprepared for that the audience might wonder if Troilus meant to say, 'And pay the life thou owest me for my whore'.

10    **Stand** stand aside

11    **prize** trophy, symbol of victory, for whom the victor could demand ransom

**look upon** stand aside as a mere onlooker

12    **cogging** deceitful. See 1.3.246n. for the implications of 'cunning or wily person' or 'cheater at cards' that are commonly associated with the term *Greek*.

12.1–2 The action is continuous here. Q provides no stage directions at all. F indicates an exit for Troilus, followed immediately by an entrance for Hector, but Hector's first speech makes clear that the action of Troilus' fighting with Ajax and Achilles as they exit overlaps with Hector's entrance. Hence this edn reverses the order of the SDs in F.

5] *Q; F lines* Generall, / office, /    7] *Q; F lines* Diomed! / traytor, /    8 the] *Capell;* thy *QF*
12.1 *Enter* HECTOR] *F, below* 'Exit Troylus'; *not in Q*

> *Exit Troilus [ fighting with Ajax and Diomedes].*

HECTOR

Yea, Troilus? O, well fought, my youngest brother!

*Enter* ACHILLES.

ACHILLES

Now do I see thee. Ha! Have at thee, Hector!     [*They fight.*]

HECTOR     Pause, if thou wilt.                                                15

ACHILLES

I do disdain thy courtesy, proud Trojan.

Be happy that my arms are out of use.

My rest and negligence befriends thee now,

But thou anon shalt hear of me again;

Till when, go seek thy fortune.                                    *Exit.*

HECTOR                                    Fare thee well.          20

I would have been much more a fresher man,

Had I expected thee.

*Enter* TROILUS.

How now, my brother!

TROILUS

Ajax hath ta'en Aeneas. Shall it be?

14 SD As various editors have suggested (see t.n.), Achilles tires or is bested, or drops his sword, or slips.

18 **befriends** The singular form of the verb follows an implied single subject: Achilles' condition of being inactive and neglectful of the war.

19 **anon** said with urgency: very soon

21 **much more a fresher** On the double comparative, see Abbott, 11, citing this line among others; on the transposed article *a*, which would normally pre-

cede *much*, see Abbott, 422.

22 **Had . . . thee** But of course Hector did expect Achilles; that is why he resisted the fears of his family. Shakespeare has credited Hector with knowledge shared by the audience but known (in the act) by only Achilles and Patroclus.

23 **ta'en** taken captive
**Shall it be?** Are we going to allow this to happen?

12.2 *Exit Troilus] F, preceding 'Enter* HECTOR*'; not in Q* 13.1] *F; before 14 in Q, serving also as SP* 14 SP] *F; not in Q* 14 Ha] *Q (*ha,*); not in F* SD] *Rowe, subst.; dropping his sword / Capell; Achilles is bested / Oxf* 19 hear] *QF (*here, heare*)* 22 SD] *Cam; after* brother, *QF*

No, by the flame of yonder glorious heaven,
He shall not carry him. I'll be ta'en too,                    25
Or bring him off. Fate, hear me what I say!
I reck not though thou end my life today.                    *Exit.*

*Enter one in [Greek] armour.*

HECTOR

Stand, stand, thou Greek! Thou art a goodly mark.
No? Wilt thou not? I like thy armour well;
I'll frush it and unlock the rivets all,                     30
But I'll be master of it.              *[Exit one in armour.]*
                          Wilt thou not, beast, abide?
Why then, fly on. I'll hunt thee for thy hide.
                                         *Exit [in pursuit].*

24 **flame . . . heaven** i.e. sun
25 **carry** win by military assault, prevail
   over (*OED v.* 15–17)
25–6 **I'll . . . off** The expected sequence
   of events is inverted in a kind of hysteron proteron, as at 5.3.96 (Ard²).
26 **bring him off** rescue him
27 **reck** care
27.1 [*Greek*] *armour* Caxton describes
   how Hector 'had taken a moche noble
   baron of grece moche queyntly and
   rychely armed' (613). Lydgate is more
   detailed about 'ful many riche stoon' in
   the coat of armour, pearls, emeralds,
   sapphires of India, etc. (3.5332–45).
28 **mark** target. The Grecian's goodly
   armour (see 29) persuades Hector that
   he now faces a worthy opponent

(unlike Thersites, whom he spares at
5.4.29), one whose armour will prove
a noble trophy of war. As is conventional in Homer, Hector will strip his
defeated opponent of his armour.
30–1 **I'll . . . of it** 'I'll win it, if I have to
   batter it and knock out its rivets to do
   so.' *Frush* means 'bruise, smash'.
   Shakespeare could have found the
   word ('all to frusshid') in Caxton's
   account of Hector assailing Achilles,
   595.
32 **hide** i.e. outer garment, armour. Such
   armour taken from a defeated opponent is *spolia opima*, rich spoils of war,
   from *spolium*, animal hide. The
   metaphor derives from the *hunt* after a
   *beast* (31–2). See Edelman, 136–7.

27 reck] *Pope;* wreake *QF*   thou] *F;* I *Q*   27.1   *Greek*] *this edn; goodly / Capell; sumptuous / Malone*
28] *Q; F lines* Greeke, / marke: /   31 SD] *Cam¹, subst.; see next note*   32.1] *Cam¹, subst.; Exit. QF;*
*Exeunt. / Malone*

**[5.7]**     *Enter* ACHILLES, *with* Myrmidons.

ACHILLES

Come here about me, you my Myrmidons;
Mark what I say. Attend me where I wheel.
Strike not a stroke, but keep yourselves in breath,
And when I have the bloody Hector found,
Empale him with your weapons round about;     5
In fellest manner execute your arms.
Follow me, sirs, and my proceedings eye.
It is decreed Hector the great must die.     *Exeunt.*

**[5.8]**   *Enter* THERSITES; MENELAUS *and* PARIS [*fighting*].

THERSITES    The cuckold and the cuckold-maker are at it.
Now, bull! Now, dog! 'Loo, Paris, 'loo! Now, my

---

**5.7.2 Attend me where** (1) follow me wherever; (2) pay attention to where. Line 7 seems to reiterate both meanings.
**wheel** move in a circling manoeuvre. In Caxton (638–9) and Lydgate (4.2647–67), Achilles orders his Myrmidons (pronounced Mýrmidòns) to manoeuvre in this fashion not when he kills Hector but at a later date when he kills Troilus.

5 **Empale** fence, enclose. *OED* defines as 'make pale', which may be a resonance here; to threaten a person with death can cause him to turn pale. Yet *OED* is surely wrong to ignore the meaning derived from pale, *sb.*, 'fence made of stakes'. The sense of 'impale' plays about this locution as well, since the Myrmidons are to impale Hector with their weapons, and the words are virtually indistinguishable to the ear in the theatre. QF's spelling, 'Empale', allows any of these meanings.

6 **fellest** fiercest, cruellest
**execute your arms** carry out the purpose of your weapons, bring them into

operation (*OED* execute *v.* 1b, 2)

7 **sirs** form of address to social and military inferiors
**my proceedings eye** watch what I do

8 **It is decreed** (1) the fates have decreed; (2) I, godlike Achilles, hereby decree

**5.8** The battle continues. On scene numbering, see LN.

2 **bull** a horned creature; hence the cuckold, Menelaus. Cf. note at 5.1.52–4.
**dog** Dogs were used to 'bait' (bite, worry, attack) the chained bull in bull-baiting, esp. in the appropriately named 'Paris Garden' on the south bank of the Thames near the Globe theatre (Baldwin, Var). Thersites directs his mocking cry of *'Loo!* (a shout of encouragement to the hounds) to Paris because Paris is the cuckolder 'worrying' the horned Menelaus. *Dog* may also suggest currishness and other unsavoury qualities associated with dogs in this play and with Thersites; see LN 5.1.4.

---

**5.7]** *Capell, subst.*   1 SP] *F; not in Q*   6 arms] *Q;* arme *F*   8 SD] *Pope; Exit.* QF   **5.8]** *Capell, subst.*   0.1 *and*] *F; not in Q*   fighting] *Capell*   2, 3 'Loo, 'loo] QF *(*lowe, lowe*)*

double-horned Spartan! 'Loo, Paris, 'loo! – The bull
has the game. Ware horns, ho!     *Exeunt Paris and Menelaus.*

*Enter Bastard* [MARGARETON].

MARGARETON    Turn, slave, and fight.                                    5
THERSITES    What art thou?
MARGARETON    A bastard son of Priam's.
THERSITES    I am a bastard too; I love bastards. I am
bastard begot, bastard instructed, bastard in mind,
bastard in valour, in everything illegitimate. One bear    10
will not bite another, and wherefore should one
bastard? Take heed, the quarrel's most ominous to us.
If the son of a whore fight for a whore, he tempts
judgement. Farewell, bastard.                              [*Exit.*]
MARGARETON    The devil take thee, coward!                      *Exit.*

---

3 ***Spartan** Menelaus was ruler of
Sparta. The well-known attributes of
the Spartans, frugality and laconic
speech, may also be invoked here to
mock one who says little in this play
and leads perforce a spare life.
Menelaus is *double-horned* as a cuckold
and with a bull's two horns. For textual
choices, see LN.

4 **has the game** wins
**Ware horns** beware of horns – perhaps a wry general observation, for the
audience, that cuckolds may turn on
their tormentors. On *Ware* as an
uncontracted form, see 4.2.57n.

9 **instructed** educated

10–11 **One . . . another** a bit of erroneous proverbial folklore going back at
least to Juvenal (*Saevis inter se convenit
ursis,* 'savage bears live in harmony

with one another', Satire 15.164, LCL,
300–1) and applied to various large
beasts: 'One wolf (etc.) will not eat
another' (Dent, W606). Cf. *MA*
3.2.72–3: 'And then the two bears [i.e.
Benedick and Beatrice] will not bite
one another when they meet' (Anders,
284, cited in Var).

13–14 **he tempts judgement** he tempts
divine wrath. A war fought over a
whore like Helen puts bastards in particular jeopardy, since bastards are sons
of whores who nevertheless do not
know their own parentage and may not
even recognize their own siblings.

14, 15 SD [*Exit*] . . . *Exit* Margareton and
Thersites may exit simultaneously,
perhaps by separate doors (or with
Margareton pursuing Thersites). Q
has only an *Exit* at 15, F an *Exeunt*.

---

3 double-horned Spartan] *Alexander (Kellner);* double hen'd spartan *Q;* double hen'd sparrow *F*
4 SD *Exeunt*] *Pope (Ex.), Hanmer (Exeunt); Exit QF*   4.1 MARGARETON] *Bevington¹; Margarelon /
Capell*   5, 7, 15 SP] *Bevington¹; Bast. QF;* MAR[GARELON] *Capell*   8–9 am bastard] *Q;* am a
Bastard *F*   14 SD] *Capell*   15 SD] *Q; Exeunt. F*

**[5.9]**      *Enter* HECTOR [*dragging the Greek in armour*].

HECTOR

Most putrefied core, so fair without,
Thy goodly armour thus hath cost thy life.
Now is my day's work done. I'll take good breath.
Rest, sword; thou hast thy fill of blood and death.
[*He starts to disarm.*]

*Enter* ACHILLES *and his* Myrmidons.

ACHILLES

Look, Hector, how the sun begins to set,                    5
How ugly night comes breathing at his heels.
Even with the vail and dark'ning of the sun
To close the day up, Hector's life is done.

HECTOR

I am unarmed. Forgo this vantage, Greek.

ACHILLES

Strike, fellows, strike! This is the man I seek.            10

---

**5.9.1 putrefied core** Hector contrasts
the goodly armour with its now dead
and decaying former owner by appeal-
ing to a familiar antithesis: 'Fair without but foul within' (Dent, F29). Cf.
the prevailing image in this play of a
boil with a hard mass at its centre, as at
5.1.4: 'How now, thou core of envy!'
*Core* may also suggest 'corpse' or
'corse' (Ard²); in Fr. *corps*, the *p* is not
sounded.
**4.1** Hector may simply lay down his
sword, or may start to disarm; see 'I
am unarmed' in 9.
**5** *how Rowe's emendation to 'now'
(meaning 'now that') is attractive,
especially since QF's 'how' could be an

anticipation of *How* in 6, but the repetition yields an intelligible meaning.
**6  breathing** panting
**7  vail** going down; the sole occurrence
(*OED sb.²*) as a noun in this sense. The
basic signification of the more common verb (*OED v.²*) is to lower a flag,
weapon, eyes, hat, sail, etc., in token of
submission. A theatre audience might
also hear 'veil', since it accords with
darkening and closing from view. 'Veil'
is often spelled 'vail' or 'vaile', and *vail*
can be spelled 'veil'.
**9  Greek** For connotations of devious-
ness and cunning, see 1.3.246n. and
5.6.12n.

---

5.9] Capell, subst.   0.1 dragging . . . armour] Oxf, subst.; bearing the armor he has taken / Bevington¹
3 good] F; my Q   4.1] Malone, subst.; putting off his helmet / Capell, after 3   4.2 his] F; not in Q
5 how] QF; now Rowe¹   6–7 heels. . . . sun] Rowe, subst.; heeles . . . Sunne, Q; heeles, . . . Sunne. F
7 dark'ning] Q (darkning); darking F

[*They fall upon Hector and kill him.*]
So, Ilium, fall thou! Now, Troy, sink down!
Here lies thy heart, thy sinews and thy bone. –
On, Myrmidons, and cry you all amain,
'Achilles hath the mighty Hector slain'.

                *Retreat* [*sounded from both sides*].

Hark! A retire upon our Grecian part.       15

A MYRMIDON

The Trojan trumpets sound the like, my lord.

ACHILLES

The dragon wing of night o'erspreads the earth
And, stickler-like, the armies separates.
My half-supped sword, that frankly would have fed,
Pleased with this dainty bait, thus goes to bed.    20
[*He sheathes his sword.*]
Come, tie his body to my horse's tail;
Along the field I will the Trojan trail.

                *Exeunt* [*with the bodies*].

---

13 **amain** with might and main (see *OED* main *sb.*[1] 2)

14.1 The *Retreat* or signal to retire from combat is sounded from both camps. The two sides may have been represented visually throughout the battle sequences by two doors in the tiring-house façade. Cf. 1.2.171 SD and n.

15 **retire** call to withdraw from battle at day's end; not a falling back under pressure.

18 'and, like a referee, [the dragon wing of night] separates the armies'. A *stickler* is an umpire at a tournament, wrestling-match, etc., who ensures fair play and parts the combatants 'when they have fought enough' (*OED* 1).

19 **frankly** freely, bountifully; possibly, too, with a resonance of feeding abundantly and greedily, 'like a hog in a *frank* or sty' (Collier[3]), since a *frank* is both a sty in which to feed hogs and the process of fattening them (*OED* *sb.*[2]).

20 **dainty bait** tasty snack

21 Hector's deplorable fate is like that described in Homer (22.395–405, LCL, 2.484–5), who tells how Hector's body is fastened to Achilles' chariot. The wording is closer to the account of Achilles' slaying of Troilus, rather than Hector, in Caxton (639) and Lydgate (4.2737–79); both report that Troilus' body is tied to the horse's tail.

10.1] *Hanmer; after 8, Rowe*   11 Ilium] *Oxf*[1]; Illion *QF*   thou! Now] *F (*thou: now*);* thou next, come *Q*   13 and] *Q; not in F*   14] *inverted commas, Hanmer, subst.*   14.1 *sounded . . . sides*] *Capell, subst. (Retreat heard)*   15 retire] *Q;* retreat *F*   part] *F;* prat *Q*   16 SP] *Rowe (Myr.);* One: *Q; Gree. F*   16 Trojan trumpets] *F;* Troyans trumpet *Q*   sound] *Q;* sounds *F*   20 bait] *Q;* bed *F*
20.1] *Capell, subst.*   22.1 *with the bodies*] *Oxf, subst.;* dragging out the Body / *Capell*

[**5.10**] *Sound retreat. Enter* AGAMEMNON, AJAX, MENELAUS,
NESTOR, DIOMEDES *and the rest, marching* [*to the sound of
drums*]. *Shout* [*within*].

AGAMEMNON    Hark, hark, what shout is that?
NESTOR    Peace, drums!                                      [*Drums cease.*]
SOLDIERS (*within*)
    Achilles! Achilles! Hector's slain! Achilles!
DIOMEDES
    The bruit is, Hector's slain, and by Achilles.
AJAX
    If it be so, yet bragless let it be;                          5
    Great Hector was as good a man as he.
AGAMEMNON
    March patiently along. Let one be sent
    To pray Achilles see us at our tent.
    If in his death the gods have us befriended,
    Great Troy is ours, and our sharp wars are ended.          10
                                                    *Exeunt* [*marching*].

[**5.11**] *Enter* AENEAS, PARIS, ANTENOR *and* DEIPHOBUS.

AENEAS
    Stand, ho! Yet are we masters of the field.

---

**5.10.4 The bruit is** i.e. they are shouting.
*Bruit* can suggest noise, clamour, tidings, rumour.
5 **bragless** 'without brag or vain boast'
(*OED*; sole occurrence)
6 *****as good a man** F's 'a man as good' is
perfectly intelligible, and might be a
deliberate revision, but a metathesis
here would be an easy error in transmission.

7 **patiently** calmly and expectantly,
quietly awaiting the outcome of events
(*OED* patient *a.* 1c)
9 **his** Hector's
10 **sharp** harsh, painful, merciless
**wars** frequently used in a singular
sense, as in *AW* 2.1.25–6 and
2.3.278–86, where 'To the wars' and
'to th' war' appear close together.
**5.11.1 Yet** still

---

**5.10**] *Capell, subst.*   0.1 *Sound retreat*] F *(after 'Exeunt' at 5.9.22.1); not in Q*   0.2 DIOMEDES] *QF
(Diom:, Diomed)*   0.2–3 *to . . . drums*] *Oxf*¹   0.3 *Shout within*] F, *subst. (Sound Retreat. Shout.) after
'Exeunt', 5.9.22.1; not in Q; Shouts within / Capell*   1 shout is that] *F; is this Q*   2 SD] *Ard*²   3 SP,
SD SOLDIERS (*within*)] *Q (Sould: within); Sold. F*   3 slain! Achilles!] *F (slaine, Achilles.); slaine
Achilles. Q*   6 as good a man] *Q; a man as good F*   10.1 *marching*] *Capell*   **5.11**] *Capell, subst.*
0.1 ANTENOR] *QF (Antenor, Anthenor)   and*] *F; not in Q*   DEIPHOBUS] *QF (Diephobus, Diephoebus)*

Never go home; here starve we out the night.

*Enter* TROILUS.

TROILUS
Hector is slain.

ALL                              Hector! The gods forbid!

TROILUS
He's dead, and at the murderer's horse's tail,
In beastly sort, dragged through the shameful field.          5
Frown on, you heavens, effect your rage with speed!
Sit, gods, upon your thrones and smite at Troy!
I say at once: let your brief plagues be mercy,
And linger not our sure destructions on!

AENEAS
My lord, you do discomfort all the host.                      10

TROILUS
You understand me not that tell me so.
I do not speak of flight, of fear, of death,
But dare all imminence that gods and men

2  *For textual choices, see LN.
5  **In beastly sort** in brutish fashion
7  *smite  Some editors defend QF's
   'smile', suggesting that Troilus is
   imploring the gods to smile in scorn,
   like the God of Psalms, 2.4 and 37.13
   who has the heathen 'in derision' and
   laughs at the wicked (Upton, 1748,
   223, cited in Var), but Hanmer's emendation assumes an easy *t:l* error and
   anticipates the thought of the next two
   lines, whereas 'smile' is at odds with
   *Frown on* (6). 'Smile' is arguably more
   compatible with the image of the seat-
   ed gods, and with Troilus' celestial
   laughter at the end of Chaucer's *TC*.
8  **at once** (1) once for all; (2) immediately
   **let . . . mercy** 'be mercifully brief; let

your plagues put us quickly out of our
misery'
9  'and do not protract your inevitable
   destruction of each one of us'
10  **discomfort . . . host** dishearten the
    army
13–14  **But . . . in** 'but dare to face all the
    impending evils that gods and mortals
    alike can prepare to endanger me
    with'. Troilus insists that his is not a
    counsel of cowardice; to the contrary,
    the despairing thought of Hector's
    death makes him all the more reckless,
    as having lost everything. He will court
    Death by fighting remorselessly.
    (*Imminence* is *OED*'s first occurrence
    in this sense of 'threats of imminent
    disaster', definition 2.)

2 Never] *F; Troy.* Neuer *Q*   2.1] *F; after 1, Q*   3 SP TROILUS] *F (Troy.); not in Q*   7 smite]
*Hanmer;* smile *QF*   12 fear,] *F;* feare *Q*

Address their dangers in. Hector is gone.
Who shall tell Priam so, or Hecuba?                              15
Let him that will a screech-owl aye be called
Go into Troy, and say their Hector's dead.
There is a word will Priam turn to stone,
Make wells and Niobes of the maids and wives,
Cold statues of the youth, and, in a word,                       20
Scare Troy out of itself. But march away.
Hector is dead. There is no more to say.
Stay yet. – You vile abominable tents,
Thus proudly pitched upon our Phrygian plains,
Let Titan rise as early as he dare,                              25
I'll through and through you! And, thou great-sized
     coward,
No space of earth shall sunder our two hates.
I'll haunt thee like a wicked conscience still,

16 **screech-owl** i.e. a bearer of evil omen
   **aye** forever (also at 34)
17 ***their** Both Q ('their') and F ('there')
   make good sense, and F could be an
   authoritative reading, but it might
   instead be a sophistication, a copying
   error in anticipation of 'There' in 18,
   or ambiguity in the copy (such as
   'ther').
18 **will Priam turn** that will turn Priam
19 **wells** flowing springs of water, i.e.
   tears
   **Niobes** When Niobe boasted that her
   six sons and six daughters (seven each
   in some accounts) made her superior
   to Latona, the mother of only two
   children, Apollo and Diana, Niobe was
   obliged for her blasphemy to witness
   her children put to death by the arrows
   of the two deities. She was then turned
   into a stone, from which her tears continued to flow (Ovid, *Met.* 6.273–312,
   LCL, 1.306–9).

20 **Cold . . . youth** The young men of
   Troy will appear frozen in the stony
   silence of their grief.
21–2 ***The apparent finality of this
   couplet might support the theory that
   the play, in some versions, ended at
   this point.
25 **Titan** i.e. Helios, the sun god, or his
   father Hyperion, one of the Titans,
   also identified with the sun
26 **coward** i.e. Achilles, a coward in
   Troilus' eyes for the way in which he
   abused Hector's corpse – or for the
   manner in which Achilles killed
   Hector, if Troilus is apprised of this
   information
27 **sunder** keep apart (*OED v.* 3; first
   occurrence)
   **two hates** mutual hatred
28 **haunt** (1) pursue with malign intent;
   (2) visit eerily as a ghost would do
   **still** continually

16 screech-owl] *F (screechoule);* scrich-ould *Q*   17 their] *Q;* there, *F*   20 Cold] *Q (*Could*);* Coole
*F*   21 Scare] *QF (*Scarre*)*   21–2 But . . . dead] *F; not in Q*   23 yet. –] *F (*yet:*);* yet *Q*   vile] *F;*
proud *Q*   abominable] *QF (abhominable)*   24 pitched] *QF (*pitcht, pight*)*

That mouldeth goblins swift as frenzy's thoughts.
Strike a free march to Troy! With comfort go.                    30
Hope of revenge shall hide our inward woe.

*Enter* PANDARUS.

PANDARUS   But hear you, hear you!

TROILUS

Hence, broker-lackey! Ignomy and shame
Pursue thy life, and live aye with thy name!

*Exeunt all but Pandarus.*

PANDARUS   A goodly medicine for my aching bones! O      35
world, world, world! Thus is the poor agent despised.
O traitors and bawds, how earnestly are you set a-work
and how ill requited! Why should our endeavour be so
desired and the performance so loathed? What verse for
it? What instance for it? Let me see:                          40

---

29 **mouldeth goblins** creates malicious demons, conjures up hobgoblins in the guilty conscience

30 **a free march** a quick march that is not in formal marching order

31 **shall** must

32–4 *These three lines, modified in one word only, are duplicated in F at the end of 5.3. The remainder of the text, in effect an epilogue spoken by Pandarus, is printed at the end of both Q and F, but may have been cut from some theatrical productions of the play. See LN 5.3.111 and pp. 416–22 for the rationale for including Pandarus' epilogue in this edition.

33 **broker-lackey** pander
**Ignomy** ignominy. An example of syncope, the omission of a letter or syllable from the interior of a word.

34 *and . . . name** (1) and may ignominy and shame always attend you in your infamy; (2) and may you have the

deserved misfortune to be forever associated with your name of 'pander'. The comma after 'life' in QF tends to support the latter reading, but may be only rhetorical.

35 **aching bones** with a suggestion of syphilis, the 'Neapolitan bone-ache' at 2.3.17–18; see also Pandarus' 'ache in my bones' at 5.3.105.

37 *traitors** Sometimes emended to 'traders', following Craig's conjecture (see t.n.), but QF's reading makes good sense. Pandarus' analogy is a witty one, comparing traitors and pimps as persons whose services are indispensable and yet whose efforts are hypocritically scorned and insufficiently rewarded.

39 **verse** (1) rhymed composition or song, like the one Pandarus produces in 41–4; (2) text for a (mock) sermon, as in 'chapter and verse'

40 **instance** illustrative example

---

30 march to Troy!] *F (*march to Troy,*); march, to Troy *Q*   33 broker-lackey] *Dyce;* broker, lacky *QF;* broker lacquey *Johnson, Var '73*   Ignomy and] *F;* ignomyny, *Q*   34.1] *Q; Exeunt. F*   35 my] *Q;* mine *F*   36 world, world, world!] *F;* world, world – *Q*   37 traitors] *QF;* traders *Ard¹ (Craig)*   39 desired] *F;* lou'd *Q*

Full merrily the humble-bee doth sing,
Till he hath lost his honey and his sting;
And being once subdued in armed tail,
Sweet honey and sweet notes together fail.
Good traders in the flesh, set this in your painted     45
cloths:
As many as be here of Panders' hall,
Your eyes, half out, weep out at Pandar's fall;
Or if you cannot weep, yet give some groans,
Though not for me, yet for your aching bones.           50
Brethren and sisters of the hold-door trade,
Some two months hence my will shall here be made.
It should be now, but that my fear is this:
Some galled goose of Winchester would hiss.

41 **humble-bee** bumblebee
43 'and having lost its sting' (with suggestion of ejaculation and perhaps of sexual infection). The point of the song
appears to be that lovers are content
(with the pander who brought them
together, and in other ways) until sexual fulfilment ends the euphoria and
leads to unfortunate consequences. Cf.
Sonnet 129.
   **armèd** armèd
45–6 **painted cloths** inexpensive wall
hangings decorated with scenes and
morally improving commonplaces. Cf.
*AYL* 3.2.270: 'I answer you right
painted cloth'.
47 \***Panders'** Q's *Pandars* can be read as
singular or plural (see t.n.). Either can
be defended. In favour of the singular
is the linking to what appears to be a
singular form in the next line (spelled
*Pandar's* in F, 48); in favour of *Panders'*
in 47 is the potential of a witty analogy
comparing *Panders' hall* to other livery
companies. F distin-
guishes *-er* and *-ar* forms, as though
pointing towards the generic in 47 (cf.
3.2.197–206), and then returning in 48
to the individual name. F also shifts

from roman type in 47 (Panders hall) to
italic in 48 (*Pandar's hall*). This
edition follows the F shift in spelling.
   **hall** guild, i.e. profession or livery
company
48 **half out** half blind with weeping and
with venereal disease
50 **aching bones** Cf. 35 above, 2.3.17–18
and 5.3.105 on the 'Neapolitan bone-
ache' as a symptom of syphilis.
51 'You pimps and bawds who attend the
doors of brothels' (said mockingly to
the audience)
52 See p. 65 on the possible promise here
of a sequel play that appears not to
have materialized. It would appear as
though there was not enough material
left in any case.
54 **galled . . . Winchester** i.e. a prostitute, or her client being *galled* with
venereal disease. The brothels of
Southwark, where the Globe and other
theatres stood, were under the jurisdiction of the Bishop of Winchester.
(See Dent, G366.) Pandarus fears that
any such Winchester geese in the theatre audience, being *galled* (*gallèd*) or
vexed, might *hiss* him for his sardonic
remarks.

46 cloths] *QF (cloathes)*    47 Panders'] *Kittredge; Pandars Q;* Panders *F; Pandar's / Rowe*
48 Pandar's] *F (Pandar's); Pandars Q*    50 your] *F;* my    51 hold-door] *F (*hold-dore*);* hold-ore *Q*

Till then I'll sweat and seek about for eases,                               55
And at that time bequeath you my diseases.                                 *Exit.*

55 **sweat** a standard treatment for venereal disease that involved medica-
tion, diet and the use of heat to induce
sweating
**eases** means of relieving pain or discomfort (*OED sb.* 10)

56 SD] *Rowe³; Exeunt. F; not in Q*

# LONGER NOTES

*A Never Writer*, 1–3 **never staled . . . vulgar** *Staled* can mean 'cheapened', 'lowered in dignity by excessive familiarity' (*OED v.*² 2b; cf. 2.3.188); it also suggests both urination (*OED v.*¹) and prostitution (*OED sb.*³ 4 and G. Williams, *Dictionary*, 1303–4). *Clapper-clawed* literally means 'clawed or scratched with the open hand and nails; beaten, thrashed, drubbed' and, later, 'reviled, abused'. (*OED* cites this present passage, along with *MW* 2.3.59–63, but does not provide a suitable definition for this present instance.) Cf. Thersites' *clapper-clawing* in 5.4.1 and n. The plebs are seen as rapacious; the tone is insistently antitheatrical.

29 **Inquisition** Oxf¹ sees a possible allusion here to Archbishop Whitgift's appeal to Queen Elizabeth to establish a new ecclesiastical commission charged with the responsibility of searching out unlawfully printed books, especially of a Puritanical persuasion. Lord Burghley, distressed by this extreme of anti-Puritanism, complained in 1584 that Whitgift's document was written in a florid and circumstantial style outdoing the manner in which 'the Inquisitors of Spain' attempted to 'trap their prey' (quoted in Read, 295).

PROLOGUE 23 **armed** In Jonson's *Poetaster* (1601), an armed Prologue (6.205, 6) speaks defensively in the behalf of the play and its author; see Introduction, pp. 7–10. Jonson and Shakespeare seem to have been anticipated by the 'armed Epilogue' of Marston's *Antonio and Mellida*, 1599–1600, who, like Shakespeare's Prologue, declines to be 'a peremptory challenger of desert, either for him that composed the comedy or for us that acted it' (quoted by Ard¹).

28 **Beginning . . . middle** Homer's *Iliad* and *Odyssey* and Virgil's *Aeneid* provide models for beginning epic poems *in medias res*, in the midst of things (usually towards the close of the action), and narrating earlier events as past action, presumably to provide a kind of unity of time. Horace's *Ars Poetica*, 146–8 (LCL, 462–3), commends the rule as especially suited to a play on the Trojan war; the skilful poet does not begin his story with the 'twin eggs' that represent the births of Helen and Clytemnestra, but 'hastens to the issue, and hurries his hearer into the story's midst' (*in medias res*) (Ard²). For all the changes of tone and circumstance, Shakespeare starts his play pretty much where the *Iliad* does. A. and J. Thompson (13–16) demonstrate that the action of the play, from 1.3 onwards, is limited to just three days. See also Daniel, 'Time-Analysis', 180–3, and Stříbrný, 105–21, on the play's 'double-time structure' invoking both swiftness and long duration.

1.1.2–3 **The war in the body's members** is a commonplace of medieval allegorizing, notably in Prudentius' *Psychomachia* (fourth century AD), derived in part from Romans, 7.23: 'But I see another law in my members, rebelling against the law of my mind, and leading me captive unto the law of sin which is in my members' (Ard²). Such themes of religious conflict were often applied to erotic love situations in medieval romance and song, and would moreover find precedent in classical poetry, as in Ode 13 ('I want to love') of the *Anacreontea*: 'My shield (and spears and corslet) are useless: why hurl weapons from me when the fight is within me?' The ode was translated by both Ronsard and Belleau (*Les Odes d'Anacreon*, 1556), and in Henry Stephens's translation of Pindar, widely available in the Renaissance (Baldwin, Var). Cf. 'Kingdomed Achilles' at 2.3.172 and n. Var cites *JC* 2.1.67–9 and other parallels.

1.2  Location: The location of this scene is fluid. Cressida, her man and then Pandarus could be conversing at her house or in a public location; Pandarus is summoned to his own house at 263–5. At 172ff., Cressida and Pandarus find a place where they can look down, as though from a window or raised location, on the troops returning from battle. In the scene's opening line it is noted that Queen Hecuba and Helen have passed by; wherever the location or locations, Cressida is in a position to observe the comings and goings of the town. The scene is based in part on Chaucer, *TC*, 2.610ff., though in that passage Criseyde is by herself when she watches Troilus alone return from the fighting. Later, in 2.1247–60, Pandarus invites her to look at Troilus as the young man rides beneath her window. More indirectly, the scene recalls the so-called *teichoscopia* in 3.161–258 of Homer's *Iliad* (LCL, 1.128–37), when Helen and Priam view the Greek chieftains from the walls of Troy. Both accounts are subjected to satiric deflation in the present scene.

1.2.19–21  **many beasts . . . elephant** Alexander appeals to the traditional attributes of beasts in bestiary lore and proverbs. See Dent, L308, 308.11 and 323, and Seager, 30–1, 100–4 and 182–6, quoting Bartholomew, Bk 18, cap. 42–5, 65 and 112–13. Pliny is another popular source, as well as Topsell's *History of Four-Footed Beasts* (bear, 28–34; elephant, 149–65; lion, 355–79) and *Hortus Sanitatis* (elephant, p. 41, cap. 55; bear, p. 76, cap. 148; lion, p. 5, cap. 80). Cf. *KL* 3.4.92–3.

1.2.22–3  **\*his valour . . . discretion** Ajax is a paradox: his natural valour is *crushed into* or mixed with foolish recklessness, and yet that recklessness is also *sauced* or flavoured with discretion. If true valour is to be seen as a temperate, Aristotelean mean between folly and Falstaff-like *discretion*, between foolish excess of bravery and an excess of caution, then Ajax is an imperfect model erring on the side of recklessness. Homer depicts Ajax as obstinately intrepid to the point of stupidity. The well-known story of Ajax' madly venting his wrath on a flock of sheep that he mistakes for the enemy, though not mentioned in the play, may inform Alexander's wry estimate of the man. The image of humours crowded together suggests that *crushed into* means 'forcibly squeezed into' (*OED* crush *v*. 3), though it may also suggest 'squeezed, as by a cook, adding flavour to the dish' (Ard²), in light of the culinary metaphor in *sauced*. Theobald's suggestion of emending QF's 'sauced' to 'farced' (see t.n.) is orthographically plausible and attractive as a reading; it would mean 'stuffed, crammed', in a continuation of the culinary image.

1.2.27–30  **he hath . . . sight** i.e. Ajax is the distillation of all qualities in other men, being 'joined' or fitted together out of many parts. But, paradoxically, he is also *out of joint* or disordered, and is thus like *Briareus*, one of three giant, hundred-handed sons of Uranus and Ge, here imagined to have gouty inflammation of the joints in all of his hands and hence to be unable to use them; or like *Argus*, the watchman over Io with a hundred eyes all over his body (as described in Ovid's *Met*., 1.713–21, LCL, 1.52–3; 1.775ff. in Golding's translation), here imagined to be *purblind* or dim-sighted in each of his many eyes. *Purblind* can range in meaning from totally blind to near-sighted. Briareus, as Ard² notes, is called Aegaeon in Virgil (*Aeneid*, 10.565, LCL, 1.208–9; he is called 'Briareus' at 6.287, LCL, 1.526–7) and Ovid (*Met*., 2.10, LCL, 1.60–1); Homer notes in the *Iliad* (1.403, LCL, 1.32–3) that he is called Aegaeon by men but Briareus by the gods. Shakespeare could then have found the name in Chapman's *Seven Books* (1.406), though the name Briareus may well have been current elsewhere in the Renaissance. The many eyes of Argus were proverbial (Dent, E254).

1.2.53  **he** Some editors remove Alexander at this point so that he will not be present to hear the intimate talk and soliloquizing that follow. No exit is marked in Q or F, however, nor does Cressida make any signal that would authorize Alexander's departure. A suitable moment is hard to identify. The actor doing this bit part will have no trouble discreetly standing to one side, out of earshot, and departing when his mistress indicates it is time for them to go. If the scene is public, he is presumably needed to attend on Cressida. If the scene is private, his departure would be fitting. In production, his continued presence can be distracting. A director's choice.

1.2.173 **stand up here** Pandarus seems to suggest that they find some elevated position – conceivably the 'window' position in the gallery, if the entry of the warriors is staged in such a way as to cover their ascent to it (cf. *Tit* 1.1.63.1–2), though the dialogue in this present scene (172–8) seems continuous in a way that would make ascent difficult. Perhaps Pandarus and Cressida simply move down stage to be near the audience, as in *AW* 3.5, *H8* 2.1 and *AC* 1.1. The placing of the overhearers in 5.2 of *TC* raises similar questions. Staging conventions in the Elizabethan theatre offer few precedents for a raised platform.

1.2.251 **Upon my back** Cressida blends metaphors of fencing and siege warfare to express her wariness of sexual encounter. *Lie* is Pandarus' fencing term; to Cressida, the word invites consideration of a woman's expected posture. Lying on her back seems an odd way for a woman to resist penetration of her *belly* or womb, but in siege warfare a city's gates face the ever present enemy and must resist assault. Cressida may regard sexuality itself as a defence, as Adelman, 'Cressid', argues (121). Cf. *WT* 1.2.204–6: 'No barricado for a belly. Know 't, / It will let in and out the enemy / With bag and baggage'. Upon her back, Cressida can kick; with her back to something firm, she can fight back and resist penetration (as D. Hooker argues, 911). Alternatively, Cressida may mean that she will use her back to 'support' or 'uphold' her belly (*OED* defend 5); see notes on *honesty* (1.2.253) and on *and you to defend all these* (253–4). She may also speak ironically, for it is clear that she does not really expect Pandarus to defend her chastity; see 257–61. See G. Williams, *Dictionary*, 'ward', 1501, and 'back', 51–4.

1.3.5–9 **Checks . . . growth** *Disasters* in its root sense (*dis*, reversing the action, + *aster*, planet, star) suggests malign planetary influence (*OED* 1). Knots either inhibit the flowing of sap and thereby stunt growth, or are caused by the damming up of sap. *Conflux*, 'confluence, flowing together', and *Tortive* occur only once in Shakespeare and may be his coinage. *Tortive and errant* means 'twisted and straying'. Implicit in the metaphor is the proverbial idea that the mightiest enterprises court failure by the greatness of their daring.

1.3.8 *****Infects** The singular form of the verb in *infects* and *diverts* agrees with the single concept of the action of the knots. Some editors adopt the F reading ('infect') and emend *diverts* to 'divert', but the Q form is perfectly acceptable in Elizabethan English, and F may well be a sophistication. 'Though F might have overlooked the Q error in the second word, it seems less likely that Q made the same error twice in the line than that F made it once' (*TxC*).

1.3.13–15 **Sith . . . thwart** The image of movement athwart the grain expands Agamemnon's metaphor of distorted tree growth in 5–9. In a parallel metaphor, taken from the game of bowls, every attempt at successful execution (every *trial*) moves obliquely and at cross purposes, so as to obstruct movement in the right direction. Both *bias* and *thwart* are adverbial. *Trial* appears to be the subject of this clause, *action* its object. *Record* is here accented on the second syllable.

1.3.22 **metal** As Ard² notes, images of refining and purgation are to be found in the Bible, as in Job, 23.10, and Zachariah, 13.9; more broadly, the idea of being tested in adversity by divine will is widespread in Holy Writ.

1.3.42 **Perseus' horse** In the usual mythological account, Bellerophon, not Perseus, rode the winged horse Pegasus when together they destroyed the Chimera. But Shakespeare may be following Caxton, 198, who reports that Perseus 'took hys hors volant' on the expedition. Ovid (*Met.*, 4.785–6, LCL, 1.232–3) relates how Pegasus sprang from the blood of Medusa, beheaded by Perseus when Medusa was with child by Poseidon, god of the sea. Hesiod (*Theogony*, 281–3, LCL, 100–1) reports that

Pegasus was born near the sources of the ocean; later, Jupiter placed him among the constellations, where he remains prominently visible. Pegasus might thus be imagined to be at home in the two elements of water and air.

1.3.50 **knees** Knee-timber is timber that has grown naturally or artificially into an angular bend and is thus well suited to making the angular pieces (known as *knees*) used in shipbuilding to connect the beams and the timbers (*OED* knee *sb*. 7). The image here, as in Hakluyt and elsewhere, is concretely nautical; a ship is groaning and stretching apart under the force of the wind and the sea. The image also suggests oak trees bending at their knotty joints as the wind buffets them; trees do not normally have knees or joints, but are given such properties here. Oaks and other mighty trees have been part of the discourse since 5–9.

1.3.54 **\*Retorts** The QF reading, 'Retires', is perhaps defensible as meaning 'returns, retreats, retracts, reverts', but the idiom is strained. *OED* retire *v*. 4 cites Lyly's *Euphues*: 'Though the falcon be reclaimed to the fist, she retireth to her haggardness' (1.191), i.e. goes back to her wildness. In *VA*, Venus, having decided to run no further from the wild boar, 'back retires to rate the boar for murder' (906). See Onions, intransitive definition 1. None of these is wholly convincing as a parallel. Pope's emendation to 'Returns' seems unnecessary in view of the *OED*'s now obsolete meaning of 'retire' as 'return' (*v*. 4). Hulme, 261–2, suggests a meaning of 'rant, bluster, "go on"', relating the root *-tire* to 'tear' (*OED* tear *v*.[1] 8), but the construction with *to* makes this awkward and improbable. Dyce's conj., *Retorts*, is the most satisfactory.

1.3.66–7 **the axletree . . . ride** As Mephistopheles explains to Doctor Faustus, the earth and the heavenly spheres 'all move upon one axletree, / Whose terminine is termed the world's wide pole' – that is, the poles of the earth and of the Ptolemaic universe are co-extensive (Marlowe, *Faustus*, A-text, 2.3.40–1; see also 'the axletree of heaven' in *1 Tamburlaine* 4.2.50, and *2 Tamburlaine* 1.1.90). *Axletree* was commonly contracted to 'ax-tree', in two syllables (*OED* ax-tree).

1.3.73 **rank** The striking image is from Chapman's translation in 1598 of Homer's *Seven Books of the Iliads* (2.207). Similarly, Agamemnon's ironic reference to 'music, wit and oracle' in 74 recalls Chapman's description of Thersites' 'ravenlike voice' and 'tuneless jarring' (2.206), thus freely translating *crocitabat*, from *crocito*, 'to croak loudly', from the Latin verse translation that Chapman used; Homer's text (2.217–20, LCL, 1.66–7) has no suggestion of a raven (Baldwin, Var). Chapman's 1611 edition of *The Iliads of Homer* (2.181ff.) words these passages quite differently.

1.3.78–108 Ulysses' speech echoes two homilies, 'Concerning Order, and Obedience to Rulers and Magistrates' and 'Against Disobedience and Wilful Rebellion', that were often heard in English churches. The second of these was added to the second volume of *Homilies* (originally published in 1563) after the failure of the Northern Rebellion of 1569. Both pay particular attention to the virtues of obedience to authority. The first reads, in part: 'Take away kings, princes, rulers, magistrates, judges and such estates of God's order . . . there must needs follow all mischief and utter destruction both of soul, bodies, goods, and commonwealths' (quoted in Milward, 119). Parallel passages can be found in Euripides' *The Phoenician Maidens*, 538–85 (LCL, 386–9); Ovid, *Met.*, 1.1–88 (LCL, 1.2–9); Elyot's *The Governor*, Bk 1, chap. 1 (fols 1–6) and *passim*; Spenser's *The Faerie Queene*, Bk 5, stanzas 4–7; and R. Hooker's *Ecclesiastical Polity*, Bk I, chap. 3.2 and *passim*, esp. pp. 65–6. See LN 109ff. below. The conception of an ordered cosmos interconnected with physical and moral order in life on earth goes back to Pythagoras, the Platonists and the Stoics. Seminal texts for Renaissance Europe include Plato's *Timaeus*, Cicero's *Somnium Scipionis* with the Commentary of Macrobius, and Bk 2 of Pliny. Cf. the scene of Thomas More calming a rebellion in *STM* (a scene probably added to the play by Shakespeare).

1.3.81 **like the hive** The analogy of the political kingdom to a hive of bees ruled by a king bee is a familiar one, as in *H5* 1.2.187–204. It goes back at least to Pliny (11.17.53, LCL, 3.464–5), and is reiterated by, among others, Bartholomew, Bk 18, cap. 12. Cf. Lyly's *Midas*, 3.1.58–60.

1.3.87 **Insisture** Cf. the Latin *insisto*, press upon, follow, persevere, continue, persist in. The suggestion of stasis, as when a planet (as seen from the earth's perspective) appears to pause and even reverse course, might appeal to Shakespeare's interest in the complexities of retrograde astronomical motion (see, e.g., *1H6* 1.2.1–2), and is thus used by Cicero in his *Tusculan Disputations* (cited by Var, 402). Cooper's *Thesaurus* defines *insisto* as 'to rest, stop, or stand still'.

1.3.92 **\*aspects** Strictly speaking in astrological terms, the word signifies the way the planets, from their relative positions, look on each other, but more popularly is conceived to be the way they jointly look on the earth (*OED* 4). In certain *aspects*, a planet's influence may be malign. The sun can correct the *ill aspects* or malign influence of the planets, much as a good king can hold in check the sometimes baleful disaffections and rivalries of his nobles and subjects. Q's 'influence' is also an astrological term meaning 'the supposed flowing or streaming from the stars or heavens of an ethereal fluid acting upon the character and destiny of men, and affecting sublunary things generally' (*OED* 2). Q's reading is perfectly defensible, but F appears to represent an authorial choice. *Aspects* is accented on the second syllable.

1.3.106 **\*primogeneity** It is possible that Q's 'primogenitie', not found elsewhere and not recognized as a separate word by the *OED*, is a misreading of 'primogeniture' and that F's 'primogenitiue' is affected by 'Prerogatiue' in the next line, but it may be also that Shakespeare coined his own form in a scene with numerous coinages (*conflux*, *tortive*, *protractive*, *persistive*, *deracinate*, 7, 9, 20, 21, 99). He does not use the term in any form elsewhere.

1.3.109ff. See LN 78–108 and R. Hooker, *Ecclesiastical Polity*, Bk I, 3.2: 'If Nature should intermit her course, and leave altogether, though it were but for a while, the observation of her own laws; . . . if the frame of that heavenly arch erected over our heads should loosen and dissolve itself; . . . if the moon should wander from her beaten way . . . what would become of man himself, whom these things now do all serve?' (65–6). The analogy to musical harmony is a Renaissance commonplace much used by Shakespeare. See, e.g., *Oth* 2.1.200–1: 'O, you are well tuned now! / But I'll set down the pegs that make this music.' The Pythagorean concept of the music of the spheres is integral to the analogy; see *MV* 5.1.55–65, John Davies's *Orchestra*, etc.

1.3.110–11 **\*meets . . . oppugnancy** F's *meets*, followed here, is persuasive and may well be authorial, but could also represent a sophistication or misreading of the more difficult metaphor in Q's 'melts'. Melting and its synonyms (such as 'discandy' and 'dislimn', *AC* 4.12.22 and 4.14.10) are, as Ard[2] and others note, recurrent metaphors in Shakespeare for dissolution of identity, as in *AC* 2.5.79, 'Melt Egypt into Nile!', and 4.15.65, 'The crown o'th' earth doth melt'. In the storm at sea in *Oth* 2.1.8, mountainous seas 'melt' on the ships.

1.3.117 Aristotle's definition of justice as a middle state between the opposite vices of excess and deficiency (*Nicomachean Ethics*, 5.4.1–14, LCL, 272–7) was well known in the Renaissance; the idea of *discordia concors*, describing a harmony that arises out of discord, was associated with the name of Boethius (see 111n.) and others including John Davies (*Orchestra*, 1596).

1.3.127–9 **\*And . . . climb** The image of climbing and stepping down a ladder invokes the root meaning of *degree*; see 102 and n. The image also points to the following lines, in which each greedy aspirant looks over his shoulder at the rival immediately below him (and, by stepping backwards, makes even more difficult and ludicrous the art of competitive climbing). F's 'is it' for Q's *it is* in 127 is likely to be a printer's error of metathesis, but F's *in* for Q's 'with' in 128 is more likely to be intentional.

1.3.134 **emulation** Envy is often portrayed in allegory as *pale and bloodless* (i.e. with the blood drained away from the complexion as a physiological response to the emotion, leading to a lack of vigour and a failure to accomplish noble deeds). Var and Ard² give citations from Ovid (*Met.*, 2.775, LCL, 1.114–15), Alciati (Emblem 71), and *Piers Plowman* (Envy 'was as pale as a pelet – in the palsye he semed', B-text, Passus V.78). Envy in Marlowe's *Faustus* is 'lean with seeing others eat' (A-text, 2.3.134).

1.3.137 *****lives** Although editors have often preferred Q's 'stands', the substantive change in F is not easy to explain other than as having been authorial. Either word makes sense: 'stands' recapitulates Ulysses' opening image of 'Troy, yet upon his basis' (75) and of Troy 'on foot' (135), whereas *lives* follows the line of imagery about choking and cannibalism in 121–6, as well as sickness and fever (91–2, 103, 132), which the following dialogue in 139–41 will pursue.

1.3.155–6 The hendiadys of *wooden dialogue and sound* may suggest that the sound being heard is that of the actor's tread on the stage; *wooden dialogue* connotes a lifeless sound produced by real wood that is being trodden upon. At the same time, the phrase plays on the idea of inert spoken dialogue. *Stretched* suggests both something that is physically extended (cf. *thy stretched-out life*, 61) and something that is 'strained, affected' (Rolfe). *Scaffoldage* is a rare form in English, used here for the first time, according to *OED*.

1.3.200 **The . . . parts** Ulysses alludes to what John Davies, in *Nosce Teipsum*, 1599, calls the '*passive*' or *mental* part of the higher brain that receives the form of things observed by the senses and co-operates with the *active* function in perceiving the true form of things (1073ff., esp. 1161–8; cited by Var, 416). In Ulysses' analogy, the Greek army needs to work like the human body, allowing the *mental* function of the strategic high command to operate in tandem with the *active* function of warriors.

1.3.245 *****Sir, you** With the omission of the comma, as in Q, the phrase could be constructed as an open insult (Cam¹, Ard²), but such an omission is common, and the F reading with a comma may be correct. Aeneas has backed away adroitly from his implied slighting of Agamemnon (see 1.3.224n.), and the Greek leader probably observes decorum, though barely so.

1.3.293 *****in our Grecian mould** Q's reading ('hoste') plausibly refers to the Greek army assembled before Troy, and it is possible that the F compositor echoed 'old' in 292 or anticipated 'gould' in 296 (Ard²), but the F reading is probably authoritative. Proudfoot conjectures that F's correction was incomplete and should have changed 'in' to 'of'. In any event, F's 'mould' anticipates a Promethean 'one spark of fire' in 294.

1.3.352–4 *****who miscarrying . . . themselves!** The Q reading (see t.n. 353) seems to say instead, interrogatively: 'If our champion fails, what Greek heart can hope to find a share of encouragement to strengthen self-esteem?' The F revision seems deliberate and authorial; moreover, it encourages the wordplay on *steel* and 'steal' noted by Oxf¹. A theatre audience might well hear 'steal'.

1.3.355–7 *****Honigmann** (*Stability*, 98) argues that lines so 'involved' and stylistically infelicitous, missing from Q, may have been cut for performance, and are arguably dispensable from the modern director's point of view. But F may reflect Shakespeare's choice.

2.1 The location is understood to be the Greek camp, at Achilles' tent. Perhaps no stage setting is required, although an effect like the two tents in *R3* 5.3, pitched evidently at two stage doors, is entirely possible. In any case, one door here must represent the entrance to Achilles' tent, as in 2.3.20.1ff., through which Achilles and Patroclus presumably enter at 52.1 in the present scene. Thersites and Ajax probably come on stage at 1 by another door, as though from elsewhere in the Greek camp.

2.1.13 *****vinewed'st leaven** Cf. St Paul's preaching that salvation can come 'not with old leaven, neither in the leaven of maliciousness and wickedness' (1 Corinthians, 5.8, cited by Cam¹). Q's 'vnsalted' makes sense biblically also – 'Ye are the salt of the earth', etc. (Matthew, 5.13) – but the F reading is too remarkable not to represent some authorial intent. The image here occurs only this once in Shakespeare, and *leaven* only one other time (*Cym* 3.4.62), though also 'leavening' in *TC* 1.1.19 and 'leavened' in *MM* 1.1.52.

2.1.41 *stool *Stool for a witch* also suggests a cucking-stool or ducking-stool, sometimes in the form of a close-stool, in which offending scolds, those suspected of witchcraft, etc., were fastened and ducked in a pond or otherwise publicly humiliated. Since the SP at 36 was mistaken by the Q compositor for a part of Thersites' speech (see t.n.), Cam¹ speculates that 41 should be addressed to Ajax, exploiting the common pun of *Ajax* – *a jakes* or latrine (see 62), but many of the insults traded in this passage apply equally to the speaker and to his intended target.

2.1.108 *much Many editors follow Capell in reading 'much wit' (see t.n.), arguing that something is needed to supply QF, since Ajax is not literally dumb, and that *wit* is a recurring word of Thersites at 96, 101 and 115; but if *matter* is the implied noun here, wittily playing on '*Tis no matter* in two senses of 'it doesn't matter' and 'there is no substance', the speech in QF is intelligible. Cf. 8–9, where *matter* is similarly an implied subject in Thersites' second sentence.

2.2.17 Let Helen go Whether the Trojans should keep Helen or not was a favourite topic for argumentative discourse in the Renaissance, as in Erasmus's *De conscribindis epistolis*, a handbook Shakespeare could have known in grammar school. Baldwin (*Small Latine*, 1.89, 2.239–40) shows that debates on the subject were standard exercises in the Elizabethan schoolroom. And as Soellner ('Prudence', 256) observes, 'The orthodoxy of Hector's and the heresy of Troilus' positions become transparent when they are set off against the standard work on moral duty for the Renaissance, Cicero's *De officiis*'.

2.2.50 *Make livers pale The liver was regarded as the seat of violent passions like love and courage. In a fearful response to danger, the blood was thought to desert the liver, showing the person to be 'white-livered' or cowardly (see Dent, F180). Cf. *2H4* 4.3.103–4: 'the liver white and pale, which is the badge of pusillanimity and cowardice', and *Mac* 5.3.15: 'Thou lily-livered boy'. F's 'Makes' is also defensible as a reading, since *reason and respect* could be considered as a singular concept; but Q is presumably closer to Shakespeare's papers in such a case where misreading may have occurred.

2.2.58–60 *Infectiously, for which *OED* gives this passage as its earliest example, can mean both 'so as to infect' and 'as if infected'. The image is of a circular reciprocity. The wordplay on 'infect / affect' (*infectiously, affected*) recalls *LLL* 5.2.407–24, with its similar worrying about external v. internal worth. The Q text, reading 'attributiue' in place of F's 'inclinable', suggests that the will is besotted when it attributes to the desired object certain qualities which it then morbidly admires and wishes to have. Both versions are plausibly authorial; the F version may be the revised reading.

2.2.70 *soiled The F reading, 'spoyl'd', is plausible and often adopted, but it could be a vulgarization of Q. *Soiled* is perfectly apt, especially because it incorporates the idea of contaminating use rather than damage (as in 'spoiled'). See Adelman, 'Union', 41. At 2.2.148, Paris refers to 'the soil of her fair rape'. Both words suggest by analogy that sexual union is unclean; the F reading stresses that it 'spoils' the woman for any other mate. Cf. 5.2.140.

2.2.77 an old aunt In Shakespeare's sources, Hesione is mother of Ajax, saved from Poseidon's sea monster by Hercules and bestowed by him on the Greek chieftain Telamon as his prize for assisting Hercules' successful overthrow of Hesione's father, Laomedon, who had cheated first Poseidon and then Hercules. See 2.1.12 and n. *Aunt* is often a derogatory term for a loose woman, as in *WT* 4.3.11. *Queen* in 78 is similarly suggestive of 'quean', harlot (see G. Williams, *Dictionary*, 48–9, 1127).

2.2.81–3 **a pearl . . . merchants** The image of kings behaving like merchants in quest of a pearl recalls Matthew, 13.45–6: 'the kingdom of heaven is like to a merchant man, that seeketh good pearls; who, having found a pearl of great price, went and sold all that he had, and bought it' (Noble, 214). Line 82 may also echo Marlowe's *Faustus* (A-text, 5.1.107): 'Was this the face that launched a thousand ships?' The image was a familiar one, reaching back to Lucian's *Dialogues of the Dead*, 18 (LCL, 7.22–3), Virgil's *Aeneid*, 2.198 (LCL, 1.308–9), and Ovid's *Met.*, 12.7 (LCL, 2.180–1; Var, and Cam¹). The image has inspired a modern, tongue-in-cheek definition among scientists: one milli-Helen = the quantity of beauty needed to launch one ship. Ulysses, in Robert Greene's *Euphues His Censure to Philautus*, speaks of Helen as a 'pearl' (Shaheen, 118). Cf. 1.1.96 and n.

2.2.96.1 In QF, Cassandra enters ('*rauing*' in Q) at this point. Virtually all other editors, beginning with Theobald, move the entrance to 100.1, to provide verisimilitude for Priam's 'What noise?', etc., and Troilus' 'I do know her voice' in 97–8. Admittedly, casual placement of SDs is common enough in Renaissance dramatic texts. Still, characters often enter 'unseen' by persons on stage. Dessen, 72–3, defends the QF arrangement as a calculated effect underscoring the faulty 'seeing' of the Trojan council. Cassandra would be unlikely to go entirely unnoticed by the Trojan leaders, of course, especially since they are seeking to identify the source of the outcry, but she is distraught and strikingly changed in appearance. Her entry with her hair about her ears betokens, in a conventional stage signal of the Elizabethan theatre, both an unmarried virgin and, as in this instance, one who is distracted. Cf. Ophelia in *Ham*, who enters (according to Q1) '*playing on a Lute, and her haire downe singing*' (4.5.20.1). Cassandra enters in a similar Trojan scene in Heywood's *The Iron Age* '*with her hair about her ears*' (Part I, 1.1, p. 269). Cf. also *KJ* 3.4.16–75.

2.2.166–7 **Aristotle . . . philosophy** In his *Nicomachean Ethics*, 1.3.5 (LCL, 8–9), Aristotle says that young men are not fitted to hear *political* philosophy; since he is discussing the ethics of civil society, the terms come to much the same thing. Shakespeare could have encountered Aristotle's view in Erasmus's *Colloquia*, '*De colloquiorum utilitate*', *Opera Omnia*, 1.901: *quos recte scripsit Aristoteles inidoneos auditores Ethicae Philosophiae dumtaxit ejus, quae feriis praeceptis traditur*, translated by Nathan Bailey in his *Familiar Colloquies* (3rd edn, 1733, pp. 575–6): 'young persons, whom Aristotle accounted not to be fit auditors of moral philosophy, *viz.*, such as is delivered in serious precepts'; or in Richard Mulcaster's *Position wherein those primitive circumstances be examined, which are necessary for the training up of children* (1581), Nicholas Grimald's preface to *Marcus Tullius Cicero's Three Books of Duties* (1556–1600), and still others (Var; Soellner, 'Prudence', 261–2). Aristotle (384–322 BC) lived long after the Trojan war (c. early twelfth century BC) and Homer (probably ninth century BC), and the anachronism offended some early editors of Shakespeare like Rowe, but these dates were imperfectly understood in the Renaissance. For indications that Shakespeare may have had the *Nicomachean Ethics* in mind as background for the rest of this speech and other parts of this scene, see Ard², App. 3, and Elton, 'Nicomachean'.

2.3.76 ***shent** Theobald's emendation, adopted here with hesitation, is hard to explain as a word that, if misinterpreted by a copyist or compositor, might produce Q's 'sate'. But Taylor's (Oxf) 'faced' ('facd'), i.e. 'braved, bullied', lacks convincing parallels in the Shakespeare canon for a construction like the present one taking *messengers* or a comparable term as a direct object; so does Hulme's defence of 'sate' as 'ignored, set aside' (260); and Sisson's 'fobbed' ('fobd', 2.111) is not very close to 'sate' or 'sent'. Perhaps F's 'sent' is a typographical error, omitting one letter, for Shakespeare's revised reading, *shent*, whatever the Q original may have been. Proudfoot offers the best alternative, requiring only that we suppose a word inadvertently dropped and mislineation: 'He sent our messengers back, and we / Lay by our appertainments . . .'.

2.3.103 *Hortus Sanitatis* (1490–1521) expresses the proverbial misconception that the elephant 'hath no joints in his legs, wherefore he can neither bow nor kneel' (p. 41, chap. 55). The idea is refuted by Aristotle (*Historia Animalium*, Bk 2.1, 498a 8–13, LCL, 78–9, and *Movement and Progression of Animals*, 9.10, 709a, LCL, 510–11), Sir Thomas Browne (*Pseudodoxia Epidemica*, Bk 3, chap. 1), Thomas Topsell (*The History of Four-Footed Beasts*, pp. 149–65, esp. p. 154), and others. Bartholomew holds to the view that the elephant 'sleepeth standing' and cannot bend all four legs at once, though it 'bendeth the hinder legs right as a man' (Bk 18, cap 43). Ulysses picks his way through this clash of opinions by allowing joints while at the same time characterizing Achilles as unbending in his pride.

2.3.169–73 **Imagined . . . himself** Shakespeare uses the technical language of the faculty psychology of his day. Achilles' hot blood engenders in his imagination such an inflated sense of self-worth that the proper balance between the *mental* (i.e. passive) and the *active* functions of his reason is upset, destroying his judgement. John Davies, in *Nosce Teipsum*, 1599, describes how common sense (*imagination*) transmits sense impressions to the higher brain, where *phantasie* and *wit* discern the form of things, receiving shapes with the '*passive* part' and perceiving their form by 'that part which *acts*' (1085–164; cited by Var, 416). See 1.3.200 and LN. Alternatively, 'his mental and his active parts' may simply mean 'his mind and body'.

2.3.172 **Kingdomed** The idea of the human body as a microcosm or epitome of the 'great world' or universe is a commonplace; e.g. King James I refers in 1604 to 'the divers parts of our microcosm or little world within ourselves' (*A Counterblast to Tobacco*, ed. Edmund Goldsmid, Edinburgh, 1883, 15–16). See *OED* microcosm 1. In *JC* 2.1.67–9, Brutus reflects how in a time of conspiracy 'the state of man, / Like to a little kingdom, suffers then / The nature of an insurrection'; see also Menenius' fable of the belly, *Cor* 1.1.94ff.

2.3.235ff. This hyperbolic paean blasphemously echoes Luke, 11.27, in which a woman says to Christ: 'Blessed is the womb that bare thee, and the paps which thou hast sucked'. The language is especially close, as Ard² notes, to the version in the Book of Common Prayer (1559), which Shakespeare would have heard often: 'the paps which gave thee suck'. Baldwin (Var, citing Warburton in Theobald, and Steevens, Var '93) proposes that the passage also may recall Ovid, *Met.*, 4.322–6 (LCL, 1.200–1), *qui te genuere, beati . . . dignabere taeda*, translated by Golding as 'right happy folk are they / By whom thou cam'st into this world; right happy is, I say, / Thy mother and thy sister too, if any be; good hap / That woman had that was thy nurse, and gave thy mouth her pap. / But far above all other, far more blest than these is she / Whom thou vouchsafest for thy wife and bedfellow for to be' (4.391–7). The idea is ultimately derived from Homer's *Odyssey*, 6.154–63 (LCL, 1.216–19). Cf. *TS* 4.5.38: 'Happy the parents of so fair a child!'

2.3.241 Milo, an athlete of Crotona during the sixth century BC, was famous for many feats, the most notable of which was to carry a bull on his shoulders for 40 yards, kill it with one blow of his fist, and consume it in a single day. (See, e.g., Pliny, 7.20.83, LCL, 2.558–61.) An *addition* in heraldry is something added as a mark of honour to a coat of arms. Cf. 4.5.142.

2.3.250–1 *In Q, Ajax appears to address Nestor at this point, since it is Nestor in Q who answers, 'Ay, my good son'. This may well have been Shakespeare's first choice. Whether F represents an authorial revision in changing '*Nest.*' to '*Vlis.*' (see t.n.) is a difficult question. Either can be made to work. In the Q version, Ajax now turns to Nestor, whom Ulysses has just called 'father Nestor' and whose elderly role throughout the play entitles him to be appealed to as a fatherly protector. In the F version, Ulysses' fulsome praise of Ajax, and his dominant role in this scene as giver of advice, earn for him the role of Ajax' wise counsellor. Plausibly, but not certainly, the change is authorial, reflecting perhaps experience in rehearsal and production.

2.3.260 *greater . . . deep* F's 'bulkes' could easily be a misprint for Q's 'hulkes', which perhaps fits the passage somewhat better: a 'hulk' is a ship, usually large (*OED sb.²*), whereas a 'bulk' is any large mass, including a ship's cargo, and by transference the hull or hold of a ship. Both are possible.

3.1.14 Cf. 2 Corinthians, 9.8: 'And God is able to make all grace to abound toward you, that ye, always having all sufficiency in all things, may abound in every good work'. For other similar passages in Paul's epistles, see Ephesians, 2.5–8, Romans, 5.15, etc.; see Shaheen, 119–20. The Servant plays sardonically on a cant phrase of the reformers to suggest that Pandarus, being in a state of grace in this Pauline sense, would be enabled to give to the poor, not as a good work meriting salvation but as a manifestation of being one of the Elect (Noble, 214–15). But Pandarus, taking 'Grace' as a title suited to a duke or prince, answers that he is only a member of the gentry class.

3.1.83 The word *disposer* is difficult. In the sense of 'one who arranges, controls, directs' (*OED* 1, 2) it might mean 'mistress', i.e. a lady whom one serves in the dutiful office of lover. Or the word may mean 'dispenser', one who gives a dispensation or pardon (*OED* dispenser 4). Perhaps Paris speaks of Cressida as one who can relieve Troilus' suffering by dispensing mercy to him; Paris calls her '*my* disposer' in the sense that she will act with Paris' blessing. Or Paris may simply speak in amused courtly compliment: as a beautiful woman, Cressida may dispose him to mirth and dispense favour as she wishes. Since *OED* gives 'dispenser' as one definition (*OED* disposer 5), citing this present passage but with later instances as well, there would seem to be little advantage in emending to 'dispenser'.

3.1.107 *Love . . . but love* Delius (see t.n.) is probably right in proposing quotation marks to suggest that Paris here recites the first line of the song called 'This love will undo us all', since Helen has named the song, and it appears to be a favourite that they both would like to hear. Paris prompts Pandarus, as it were. Pandarus replies (108) by allowing that Paris has it right. Another reading is, however, possible: Paris simply says, 'Let your song be about love and nothing but love', to which Pandarus responds that Paris has intuitively hit upon the very first line of the song he is about to sing. Line 108 appears in F only, providing an exchange that Q might have omitted in error or that was added at some point in revision.

3.2.8–9 *Stygian . . . Charon* In classical mythology (see Aristophanes' *Frogs*, 179–268, LCL, 312–21, and Virgil's *Aeneid* 6.384–417, LCL, 1.532–5), the souls of the dead had to be conveyed across the river Styx ('the abhorrent'), the principal river of Hades, by the ferryman Charon. Those favoured by the gods were granted abode in Elysium or the islands of the blest, sometimes located far from Hades in the west but, in later myth, often assumed to be part of the nether world. Troilus hopes, as a meritorious lover, to *wallow* with Cressida in *those fields . . . / Proposed for the deserver* (10–12), as do Antony with Cleopatra and Aeneas with Dido in *AC* 4.14.51–4.

3.2.11 *wallow* Various critics (Ard², Oxf¹) have undertaken to exculpate Troilus from bestial sensuality in this image, pointing out that the verb originally means simply to roll or toss about (*OED v.* 1–2), as in Chaucer's description of Troilus not in bed with Cressida but in agony: 'To bedde he goth, and walwith ther and torneth' (*TC* 5.211). Even so, Troilus' moment of ecstatic anticipation here is, at a minimum, morbidly self-indulgent in its preoccupation with death and sexuality. If the *lily-beds* are from the Song of Solomon (2.16, 4.5, 6.1–2, 7.2), as Baldwin (Var) proposes, rather than from the *Aeneid*, 6.637–59 (LCL, 1.550–1) and its description of the abode of the blessed, that biblical resonance adds to the erotic dimension and to the sense of religious devotion transformed into worship of a woman: 'I am my well-beloved's, and my well-beloved is mine, who feedeth among the lilies' (6.2).

3.2.164–5 Troilus equates a prelapsarian innocence with childhood, as in *WT* 1.2.68–71: 'What we changed / Was innocence for innocence; we knew not / The doctrine of ill-doing, nor dreamed / That any did'. Troilus' deft antimetabole (see 68–9 and n. and

Puttenham, 3.19, 208–9) makes use of two proverbs: 'It is as true as truth itself' and 'Truth's tale is simple' (Dent, T565 and 593). The wordplay focuses on *simple* in the multiple senses of 'pure', 'innocent', 'unaffected', 'unspoiled', 'unschooled', etc., and on *truth* in the various senses explored in 93–4.

3.2.192–3 **Go . . . witness** Joining hands in the presence of a witness (and sealing the *bargain* with a kiss; cf. *RJ* 5.3.114–15 and *VA* 511) was the means to formalize a betrothal and marriage *de praesenti*, as in *Tem* 3.1.81–91. Such a union was inviolable and irrevocable in the eyes of the Church. The seriousness of such a ceremony in English law and custom deepens the seriousness for a Renaissance English audience of the vows these lovers pronounce. It also presumably accentuates the transgressive nature of their relationship for a Renaissance audience in that the lovers do not appear to commit themselves to matrimony.

3.3.37.1 The Q stage direction, given here, derives its literary and presumably authorial flavour from Ulysses' description in 38; the F reading is in the theatrical idiom of the prompt-book (Ard²). The action required is the same in both: Achilles and Patroclus appear at a stage door understood to represent the entrance to Achilles' tent (as in 2.3), or possibly stand in some stage structure or curtain hanging erected at a door.

3.3.47–9 **Pride . . . fees** Pride is allegorized in Spenser's *The Faerie Queene* (1.4.10) as holding in her hand a mirror with which to view her own face. Hulme (85–6) compares an epigram by Dekker: 'Knees / Are made for kings, they are the subjects' fees', and *Tim* 3.6.79–80: 'The rest of your fees, O gods – the senators of Athens, together with the common leg [F: 'legge'] of people'.

3.3.55 *****What, comes** 'What' can sometimes mean 'why' or 'for what reason', as in Cleopatra's last utterance, 'What should I stay–' (*AC* 5.2.313), or *TC* 4.2.20, 'What's all the doors open here?', and F4's insertion of a comma into QF's 'What comes' might be an erroneous guess; but the idiom of this present instance differs from those offered in Abbott, 253, and the sense of this passage seems to require that Achilles proudly triumph in the fact that Agamemnon has come to speak with him ('Well, well, do you mean to tell me', etc.) rather than inquiring why Agamemnon might be thus coming. But the latter is possible in the sense of 'Why does Agamemnon choose to waste his time and mine, coming to talk when he knows it's useless!'

3.3.84–7 **Which . . . fall** The sentiment is recognizably Senecan; see *Thyestes*, 391–403 (LCL, 122–5), and Wyatt's translation of that passage in his Epigram 49: 'Stand whoso list upon the slipper top / Of court's estates' (94). Cf. the portrait of Fortune's slippery slope in *Tim* 1.1.68–99 and generally in that play.

3.3.96ff. Ulysses' (and Shakespeare's) reading could have included, anachronistically, Sir John Davies's *Nosce Teipsum* (1594 edn, pp. 5, 9), Plato's *Alcibiades* 1 'On the Nature of Man' (esp. LCL, 172–3), Cicero's *Tusculan Disputations* (trans. by John Dolman as *Those Five Questions which Mark Tully Cicero disputed in his manor of Tusculanum*, London, 1561, sig. E4–5ʳ), and Montaigne, 'Of Vanity' (which quotes Seneca and Cicero's *De Amicitia*), but the ideas discussed in the present passage were commonplaces of the era (Cam¹). Soellner, *Patterns* (198–9), plausibly proposes T. Wright's *The Passions of the Mind*, 261. Since Plato was available to Shakespeare only in Latin and Greek, his dialogues seem an unlikely direct source. Shakespeare had already made use of these ideas in *JC* 1.2.52–3.

3.3.116–18 Erasmus's *Adagia*, 2.295B (chil. 1, cent. 7, prov. 84), *Occultae musices nullus respectus*, 'no heed is paid to unheard song', captures the essence of Ulysses' argument. Cf. *MM* 1.1.28–41, and Persius, *O mores, usque adeone / scire tuum nihil est, nisi te scire hoc sciat alter?*, 'O strange ways of men, is all your knowledge to go for nothing unless others are aware that you have it?' (Satire 1.26–7, LCL, 318–19, cited by Cam¹). The idea is also found in T. Wright, 261; see LN 96ff.

3.3.146–51 **Time . . . done** Time's ingratitude and forgetfulness are so proverbially monstrous (Dent, I66.1) that our few worthy achievements in Time's pack are all too soon lost to memory. The proverb is to be found in Catullus, 22.21, LCL, 26–7 (*sed non videmus manticae quod in tergo est*), in Persius' *Satires*, 4.23–4 (LCL, 360–1), in Erasmus's *Adagia*, 2.256B (chil. 1, cent. 7, prov. 90), in John Withals's *A Short Dictionary in Latin and English* (1602, cited in Var), and in T. Wright (261) as a marginal gloss to ideas like those expressed in this passage. See Baldwin, *Small Latine*, 2.544–5, Soellner, *Patterns*, 198 and 3.3.96ff., and LN 116–18 above. To Hulme, 173–5, the proverb and Ulysses' speech contain a serious warning to Achilles not to be like Ajax at 2.3.234–50, who can see and reprehend other mens' faults but not his own.

3.3.190–1 **Made . . . faction** In 5.455–595 of Homer's *Iliad* (LCL, 1.228–37), Ares (Mars) intervenes on the Trojan side. Neither this episode nor the general *mêlée* of the gods in Bk 20 of the *Iliad* had yet appeared in Chapman's translation when the play was written, but were available in other translations and were probably generally known as part of the story of Achilles' belated entry into battle. So too with Ares' fighting with Athene in 21.402–17. The conflicts in Bks 20 and 21 are occasioned by Achilles' entry into the war.

3.3.195 **one . . . daughters** To honour the claim of Achilles' ghost to Polyxena, Achilles' son Neoptolemus sacrificed Polyxena on his dead father's tomb (Ovid, *Met.*, 13.448ff., LCL, 2.260–1; cf. Seneca, *Troades*, 938–44, LCL, 202–3). Caxton (621ff.) and Lydgate (4.609ff.) elaborate the story, reporting that Achilles met and fell in love with Polyxena on the anniversary of his having slain Hector, whereupon Achilles secretly offered to induce the Greeks to leave Troy in peace if Queen Hecuba would give him Polyxena. When the Greeks refused to raise their siege, Achilles withdrew from the fighting.

3.3.198 **providence** The canniness of watchful ministers of state in knowing as much as possible about the private lives and political persuasions of important personages, as described by Ulysses in this speech, may well have reminded audiences of the things that were said about Elizabeth's ministers like Cecil (Lord Burghley) and Walsingham; see Introduction, pp. 15–8. *A Treatise of Treasons* (1572), probably by John Leslie, offered in its 'Preface to the English Reader' an extended parallel between the famous story of the Trojan horse and the alleged treason of Elizabeth's Catholic enemies, along with a comparison of Cecil to Ulysses (see Milward, 189–90).

3.3.202 **Do** is defensible as a plural by attraction to *gods* in 201, though 'Doth' is a plausible emendation, as Proudfoot observes, in that it presupposes haplography: a copyist or compositor could have produced *th* only once instead of twice in 'Do*th th*oughts'. Malone's conjectural reading, 'Do infant thoughts unveil . . .', clarifies the image and improves the metre, as T×C points out.

3.3.251 **raves . . . nothing** Perhaps Shakespeare (or Thersites) is thinking of a later incident in the saga of Ajax Telamonian, the 'Greater' Ajax, whom Homer portrays as obstinately and mindlessly brave and whom Ulysses in this play calls 'blockish Ajax' (1.3.376). As dramatized by Sophocles in his tragedy of *Ajax* (14–65, LCL, 30–7), the protagonist becomes demented with envious resentment when the arms of the slain Achilles are awarded not to him but to Odysseus (Ulysses), and takes out his wrath on a flock of sheep as though they were the enemy. Shakespeare may well not have known the Sophoclean play, but with the story of Ajax' raving he was surely familiar, especially in Ovid (*Met.*, 13.1–398, LCL, 2.228–57).

4.1.63–4 **would . . . piece** *Dregs* can suggest sediment that is fetid and fecal (*OED sb.* 1–2). *'Tamed* ('tamèd) is an abbreviated form of 'attamed', i.e. 'pierced or broached so as to let the liquor run out' (*OED* attame *v.* 2), with a pun on the idea of a woman who has been 'tamed' or sexually dominated. A *piece* is both a wine cask (from Fr. *pièce*) and a degrading term for a woman, viewing her as a sexual object (*OED sb.* 3d, 5, and G. Williams, *Dictionary*, 1025). *Flat* may also contain a sexual slur by assigning the woman to a prone position (G. Williams, *Dictionary*, 500–1); the equivalent word, 'stale', is another derogatory term for a promiscuous woman. Cf. *A Never Writer*, LN 1–3.

4.1.77–80 *Paris seems to say that he and the Trojans will not engage in the commercial hyperbole and pitchman's exaggerations of the Greeks; even if the Trojans were disposed to sell something (and Paris does not concede that they are), they would not overpraise their wares. He has in mind the proverbs, 'He that blames would buy' and 'He praises who wishes to sell' (Dent, B445 and P546, and Proverbs, 20.14). The passage is often emended by editors. Conceivably, a second 'not' has been skipped or misunderstood in 80; Sonnet 21.14, 'I will not praise that purpose not to sell', might seem to offer support for Warburton's emendation. The emendation of Ard² (see t.n.) makes good sense but is not easy to explain as an original reading that would have produced QF's version. Oxf's emendation (see *TxC*) is possible but loses the force of the negative. This present edition prefers to make sense of QF.

4.2.10 **ribald** For a suggestion of sexual meaning ('whorish', 'filthy', etc.), see G. Williams, *Dictionary*, 1153–4. The antithesis of larks and crows to night seems deliberately deflationary, as contrasted with Romeo and Juliet's discourse about larks and nightingales in *RJ* 3.5.1–7. *Crows* may suggest the carrion crow, 'a large black bird that feeds upon the carcasses of beasts' (Johnson, cited in *OED sb.*¹ 1), appropriate in this play to the battlefield and to images of devouring.

4.2.75.1 *F reads '*Exennt*' [*sic*] at this point and follows with an SD not in Q: '*Enter Pandarus and Cressid*'. Conceivably this represents a change of staging for F, in which Pandarus exits at 59 in response to Aeneas' bidding and then re-enters here at 75.1. This possible arrangement is awkward, however, for it fails to explain how Pandarus learns the bad news of the order for Cressida's return to her father; Cressida clearly still knows nothing, and could not have told him. The Q entry for Cressida alone at 78.1 is substantially more persuasive. If F is in error at that point, it is presumably in error in implying Pandarus' absence during 60–75. Perhaps an annotator decided to bring on Pandarus at 75.1 as a way of making up for Q's general deficiency in SDs.

4.2.97–9 An echo of Matthew, 19.5: 'For this cause [marriage] shall a man leave father and mother, and shall cleave unto his wife, and they twain shall be one flesh' (Noble, 215–16), made all the more bitter by the fact that Cressida has no marital claims on Troilus. The apocryphal book of 1 Esdras, 4.20, expresses a similar idea: 'A man leaveth his own father which hath nourished him, and his own country, and is joined with his wife' (Baldwin, Var). See also Psalms, 45.10 (Shaheen, 122), and *AW* 1.1.79–85.

4.4.48 SD *within F provides an SD here: '*Enter AEneus*' [*sic*], even though F also repeats Q's '*AEneas (within)*' as an SP for 48. Probably the staging is much the same: in F, Aeneas may appear briefly at the stage door and then steps back out of sight. The fact that Aeneas and Paris speak *within* in both Q and F at 97 and 98 tends to suggest that F's *Enter* at 48 is essentially an interpretation of the Q staging.

4.4.76 *The omission of this line in Q is remedied in F, but in the process of correction, Q's 'And swelling' in 77 was changed to 'Flawing and swelling' in F (further emended to 'Flowing and swelling' in F2). Perhaps the author's intent was to change 'swelling' to 'flowing', but was misinterpreted by the compositor, who retained both (Staunton). The resulting F reading, inefficiently corrected, is both hypermetrical and redundant.

4.5.0.2–3 *etc.* Both Q and F list Calchas as entering also at this point. G. W. Williams ('Entrance') has argued forcefully that Calchas does indeed come on here, silent and standing to one side; that Diomedes takes Cressida over to Calchas at 54; that father and daughter (not Diomedes) exit at 64; and that Diomedes does not re-enter at 88.1, but instead comes forward as Agamemnon introduces him to Aeneas. Against this scenario is the awkwardness of Calchas' not greeting his own daughter while she is being kissed by all the Greek generals, and the lack of any dialogue or SD indicating

that we are then to imagine the meeting of father and daughter while Ulysses speaks
dispraisingly of her at 55–64. Agamemnon's words at 89 sound as though Diomedes
has just arrived. The chief virtue of Williams's hypothetical reconstruction is that it
does preserve the QF SD at 0.2–3, and it has the potential benefit of establishing a
connection between Diomedes and Calchas this early in the play. Ian Judge's production for the RSC in 1996 followed the QF staging by having Cressida silently
reject her father's approaches when she arrived on stage (see Jackson, 213). The textual hypothesis of this present edition is that Shakespeare may simply have brought
Calchas on here with the Greek generals as he did at the beginning of 3.3, but without conceptualizing a role for Calchas in this scene and without then bothering to
delete him from the scene, whereupon F may have copied the misleading entry SD
from Q. The imprecise *Exeunt* at 64 in F alone may suggest that Shakespeare was not
especially concerned with who might leave the stage at this point.

4.5.9 **colic . . . Aquilon** Cf. Hotspur's description of the 'teeming earth' as 'with a kind
of colic pinched and vexed / By the imprisoning of unruly wind / Within her
womb', resulting in earthquake (*1H4* 3.1.26–9). Here it is Aquilon, the North wind,
that is evidently distended by what was known as wind colic, *tormina ventris* or *flatus
hypochondriacus* (Ard²).

4.5.49 **\*Why, beg too** F's 'Why begge then?' is entirely plausible as meaning 'Why, then,
if you want it, go ahead and beg', but 'then' interrupts the pattern of couplet rhymes
that prevails from 44 to 53 (and, with some irregularities, from 29 to 53) and could well
be a miscopying in anticipation of *Why then* in the next line. The exceptions to the couplet pattern from 29 to 53 do not involve single word choices that could complete a couplet, as here, but are inserted phrases or non-rhyming discrete lines (at 33, 40 and 43).

4.5.54 SD **\*They talk apart** Many editors have Diomedes and Cressida exit at this point,
and such an arrangement is quite possible; but the otherwise unexplained '*Exeunt*' in
F at 64 may well be intended to indicate their departure there, as provided in this present edition. Having them remain on stage and conversing intimately until Ulysses
finishes what he has to say disapprovingly about Cressida (55–64) would make for an
effective visual juxtaposition. Similar moments occur in *Oth* 2.1.165–78 and *WT*
1.2.177ff. See also LN 0.2–3 above, and G. W. Williams ('Entrance') on the possibility that Calchas has been on stage since the beginning of the scene and that Diomedes
here brings Cressida to her father.

4.5.61 **tables** Capulet's wife, in *RJ* 1.3.82–95, elaborates an extensive conceit in which
Paris is a book to be locked in Juliet's 'gold clasps'. Hulme, 137, cites J. Heywood's
epigram 'Of Table-Play' ('The First Hundred of Epigrams', no. 53): 'Wife, I will no
more play at tables with thee', as illustrating a common double sense of 'tables' in a
figurative and obscene sense.

4.5.62 **\*tickling** This F reading is close in meaning to Q's 'ticklish', i.e. easily aroused
and tittilated (*OED ppl. a.*). F offers the more active verb, and one that recalls the
image of catching trout by tickling (*TN* 2.5.21–2). Shakespeare uses 'tickling' seven
times, 'ticklish' only in this one uncertain instance. 'Ticklish' is arguably an anticipation of *sluttish* in the next line, with which it jingles. F could represent an error in
transmission, but may be an authorial choice. In any event, the burden of Ulysses'
complaint here is directed at vamping women, and portrays the men as more susceptible than aggressive.

4.5.62–4 **Set . . . game** Cf. the proverb, 'Opportunity (night, midnight) is whoredom's
bawd' (Dent, O70), and *RL* 869–1036. Perhaps *opportunity* carries also the sense
(which *OED* 6 calls erroneous) of 'importunity', as in Anne Page's exhortation to
Fenton: 'If opportunity and humblest suit / Cannot obtain it [my father's love], why,
then – hark you hither' (*MW* 3.4.20–1).

4.5.65 **The Trojan's** The QF spellings ('Troyans', 'Troians') are ambiguously singular
or plural; see t.n. *The Trojan's trumpet* punningly suggests 'The Trojan strumpet'

(Rossiter, 133), in response to Cressida's exit at this point. Hector's trumpet first sounded at 4.4.138.2, but is not heard by the Greeks at the start of 4.5, when instead Ajax' trumpet challenge to Hector is sounded at 11. The seeming discrepancy is not perceived as such in the theatre; logically Hector's trumpet call at 4.4.138.2 might well be identified with the trumpet signal heard here at 4.5.65, but it is also possible to imagine that Hector signals twice, first summoning his own forces to assemble and now signalling a challenge to the Greeks. In any case, the sequence of dramatic action allows a portrayal of simultaneous events on both sides of the conflict and an integration of the war plot with the story of the exchange of Cressida. See A. and J. Thompson, 14–15. In this present situation, the entry of *all of Troy* plainly can continue while ALL exclaim and AGAMEMNON speaks at 65.

4.5.74 SP *ACHILLES The SP is missing in QF. Aeneas' addressing Achilles at 76 seems to require that Achilles speak at least part of what is assigned in QF to Agamemnon (' 'Tis done . . . opposed', 74–6). Theobald (following Dryden) assigns all to Achilles, as does Oxf, arguing that both Q and F would more likely misread than overlook a SP; but SPs are indeed sometimes overlooked, and the shift in 74–6 from magnanimity to carping is well suited to a shift of speakers.

4.5.94.1 *The Oxford Shakespeare has an alternative arrangement of the following action, in which Ajax and Hector, accompanied by Diomedes and Aeneas, exit at 93 in order to fight off stage. Agamemnon and the rest, hearing the sounds of combat, exeunt at 117 to join them, thus ending a scene. Hector and Ajax enter again fighting, with Aeneas and Diomedes interposing. Aeneas exits at 158 to summon the Trojans, whereupon, at 159.1, Agamemnon and all the rest re-enter. The presumed advantage of this arrangement is to read F's direction at 159.1, '*Enter Agamemnon and the rest*', literally and as a revised staging, an authentic SD reflecting theatrical practice, and to explain Troilus' seeming absence at 155, but it involves a number of newly provided entrances and exits, and has to assume at 114–17 that the shouts of encouragement to the fighters are directed to action off stage. The more efficient arrangement, in the view of this edition, is to interpret the SD at 159.1 as meaning that Agamemnon and the rest come forward, having seen the fighting on stage. *Enter* can sometimes mean 'come forward'.

4.5.97–110 *F's addition after *knight* of 'They call him *Troylus*' in 97 seems to be a duplication of the phrase as it appears metrically in Q and F at 109. See pp. 414–16 for an argument that Q must be essentially correct, and that F's duplication of the phrase and its metrical irregularity at 97 suggest an *ad hoc* revision perhaps introduced by an actor or annotator. Or, if F does represent revision, its significance might be that cutting Ulysses' speech from 98 to 109 was contemplated, then rejected, in which case Q offers the better reading.

4.5.128–30 **my mother's** . . . **father's** The idea that certain parts of the body were derived from the father and others from the mother was acceptable medicine in Shakespeare's day. *Dexter* and *sinister* also invoke conventions of heraldry in which the husband's arms were displayed on one side (usually the *dexter* or right side) of a heraldic display and the wife's, if she was so entitled by inheritance, on the *sinister* or left side (Ard²). Cf. Marston, *AR* 3.3.20–1, where the avenger longs to know 'which joint, which side, which limb, / Were father all, and had no mother in't' (Boyle, 54, Var). *AR*, produced in the winter of 1600–1, is very likely earlier than *TC* (late 1601).

4.5.174 SD *to Troilus* Agamemnon seems to be addressing Troilus as a 'well-famed lord of Troy', since he has already greeted Hector, and since Aeneas is already well known to the Grecian general. Helenus, another son of Priam, also entered at 64.2, but has said nothing. Similarly, Menelaus must embrace Hector and Troilus as 'You brace of warlike brothers' at 176. Troilus is not listed in F among those entering at 64.1–2 (Q does not specify who enters), but must appear then or at some point; see 64.2n., LN 94.1 and 155n.

4.5.197 **grandsire** When Hector's grandfather Laomedon, builder of the walls of Troy, defrauded Hercules, that hero raised a victorious Greek army against Troy and gave Laomedon's daughter Hesione to Telamon as a prize – leading (in Shakespeare's sources) to the birth of Ajax, the rape of Helen and all that followed; see 2.1.12n. and LN 2.2.77. Laomedon also treated Jason inhospitably on his way to the Golden Fleece. On their return, the Argonauts attacked and conquered Troy. Nestor, one of the allies, fought with Laomedon (Lydgate, 1.4147–97).

4.5.215–16 Hector refers to the diplomatic mission of Ulysses and Diomedes, early in the Trojan war, offering peace on the condition that Helen be returned to the Greeks. The episode, absent in Homer, is described in Lydgate (2.6720–7105) and in Caxton (556–62); Lydgate alone includes in Ulysses' prophecy a specific reference to Troy's walls and towers, as here in 220–1 (Ard²). In Homer's *Iliad*, Bk 10 (the so-called *Doloneia*), Odysseus and Diomedes surreptitiously visit Troy in a daring night-time raid, killing the spy Dolon and capturing Rhesus' horses.

4.5.224–6 **The end . . . end it** Hector appeals to proverbial wisdom – 'The end crowns all (the work)', or *Finis coronat opus* in the familiar Latin formulation (Dent, E116), 'The end tries (proves, etc.) all' (E116.1), and 'Time tries all things' (T336) – to bolster his assertion that Troy will survive the Grecian siege even though it will decay eventually. An audience's historical consciousness of Troy as an ancient ruin adds ironic perspective to this observation that Time will end all things. Shakespeare uses this proverb in *2H6* 5.2.28, *2H4* 2.2.44 and *AW* 4.4.35.

4.5.230–1 **thee . . . thou . . . thee** Hector replies in the same terms at 239ff. The power semantic of these pronouns has been in play throughout the scene. Hector and Ajax address each other as *thee* since they are cousins, even if enemies; other generals on both sides use the familiar form with one another as they embrace; Nestor especially, as an old man, enjoys the privilege of this familiarity. Ulysses and Hector are more correct and restrained in their greetings. See Abbott, 232–5.

4.5.272 ***in . . . convive we** This is *OED*'s sole instance of *convive* as a verb, though Steevens observes in Var '78 that the word is used several times in *The History of the Noble Helyas* by Chevalier au Cygne. F's emendation of *we* to 'you' may be a simple error of confusing pronouns; Q's reading seems preferable, in that Agamemnon would have no reason to exclude himself. The optative use of the subjunctive, dispensing with 'let', also favours *we* as arguably more idiomatic; see Abbott, 365.

5.1.4 ***core** Q's 'curre' may well represent the dramatist's first thought, since the word 'cynic' is derived from Gr. *kunikos*, 'dog-like, snarling, currish'. Diogenes, a kind of model for Thersites, was known in the Renaissance as a snarling, doglike railer; see Lyly's *Campaspe*. Patroclus calls Thersites a *cur* at 28. 'Curre' also suggests Fr. *coeur*, heart. Cf. *core* at 2.1.6 and 5.9.1.

5.1.5 ***batch of nature** This QF reading nicely fits the culinary imagery of *crusty, fragment, dish of fool*, etc. (5, 8–9); *nature* can also suggest innate disposition, particular quality or character, or semen (*OED sb.* 2, 3, 7). Theobald's 'botch' is plausible in the sense of 'hump, swelling, tumour, wen; boil, ulcer, pimple; blemished piece of workmanship' (*OED sb.*¹·²), and is often adopted by editors, since it could be the correction of an easy error; but *batch* works as it stands. Shakespeare could have taken some of the unsavoury details about Thersites from Homer's portrayal of Hephaestus (Vulcan) as well as of Thersites (e.g. *Iliad*, 1.599–600, 2.216–19, 21.331; LCL, 1.48–9 and 66–7, 2.432–3).

5.1.15 **varlet** An erotic relationship between Achilles and Patroclus is assumed in Aeschylus, Sophocles, Plato, Theocritus, Martial, Lucian and other classical authors; writers in the sixteeenth century were more likely to characterize the two as intimate friends (Baldwin, Var). QF's spelling, 'varlot' (cf. Q 'varlots', F 'Varlets' at 96), may underscore an implied rhyme with 'harlot'.

5.1.18 **the south** Italy and especially Naples were notorious in England as the source of the 'Neapolitan bone-ache', syphilis, and generally had a bad reputation for contagious diseases (see 2.3.17–18n. and Ard²). The south wind was also regarded as infectious. Many of the symptoms in Thersites' list of complaints were associated with venereal disease, as in Robert Greene's *Planetomachia*, 5.103–4, and *Epistle* to *A Disputation between a He Coney-Catcher and a She Coney-Catcher*: 'sores incurable, ulcers brusting out of their joints', etc. (10.198, cited by Baldwin, Var, and Cam¹).

5.1.19–22 **\*raw eyes . . . tetter** This continuation of Thersites' catalogue of illnesses, spelled out in full in Q, is reduced in F to 'and the like'. Probably this cut reflects theatrical practice. It is less certain that the cut gives us Shakespeare's preferred version. Revision here is of a different kind from the short substitutions of word and phrase that characterize most of F's departures from Q. Hence the Q passage is included here. The list comprises: chronic eye inflammation, liver ailments like hepatitis, asthma, bladder infections caused by cysts or abscesses (*impostumes*), lower back pain (*sciaticas*), gout (which can produce white lumps in the joints and knuckles) or else psoriasis (causing dry, reddish itchy patches on the skin of the hand), bone-ache (including the 'Neapolitan bone-ache' or syphilis; cf. 2.3.17–18), and pustular outbreaks of the skin caused by herpes, impetigo, ringworm, etc. This last, the *tetter*, produces a *rivelled fee-simple* or irreversible wrinkling; *fee-simple* is absolute and permanent ownership, as when an estate belongs to an owner and his heirs for ever, hence 'chronic'.

5.1.54–5 **a thrifty . . . leg** Shoehorns share with cuckolds and bulls the property of horn; shoehorns and cuckolds are dependent, subservient tools. In Dekker's *Match Me in London* (4.2.17), one character says contemptuously to another: 'You are held but as shoeing-horns to wait on great lords' heels' (cited by Ard¹). Nares cautiously speculates of this passage: 'Whether it was ever the practice of thrifty persons so to carry their shoeing-horns, as seems to be implied, I cannot undertake to say'.

5.1.59–61 **To be . . . care** These animals are paraded here for their negative associations: currishness (*dog*), stubbornness (*mule*), craven spitefulness and wantonness (*cat*; cf. Bertram's contemptuous dismissal of Parolles as a 'cat' in *AW* 4.3.241), stench and lecherousness (*fitchew* or polecat), loathsomeness to the touch (*toad*; cf. *Oth* 3.3.286: 'I had rather be a toad', etc.), slothfulness (*lizard*; *OED* 2), dullness with the appearance of wisdom (*owl*), ignobleness and greedy feeding on carrion (*puttock* or kite, a pout-hawk or pullet-hawk, i.e. chicken-hawk), and being sexually emaciated (a herring that has 'spent' its roe, like the 'shotten herring' in *1H4* 2.4.127–8; see Dent, H447).

5.2 **\*The scene break** may be illusory. F calls for a clear stage (*Exeunt*) at the end of 5.1 but then does not specify the re-entrance of Thersites at the beginning of 5.2, leaving open the possibility that Thersites never exits. Q provides no exit at all for Thersites. Perhaps his intent to go in search of Diomedes and Cressida is prevented by the return of Diomedes. Q also provides no re-entry for Ulysses and Troilus, suggesting the possibility that in some staging version they hover quietly about and do not take leave with the others in the vague *Exeunt* (QF) at 5.1.85.1. Whatever the sequence of entrances or remaining on stage, Thersites may 'hide' himself down stage in front of a stage pillar, fully in view of the audience, while Troilus and Ulysses perhaps similarly 'conceal' themselves at the other pillar. Thersites must be so placed as to see and hear both other pairs while he himself is understood to remain unseen and unheard by them. Other staging solutions are possible. See 5.2.6n.

5.2.48 **\*withered** possibly pronounced 'witherèd', given the spelling in QF ('withered') and the metrical shortness of the line, but the metre is irregular and the lineation of 47–8 uncertain. Perhaps the stresses are to fall on *Doth / grieve / O / with– / truth*, though this leaves unresolved the question of reading *withered* as trisyllabic or not. Given the metrical uncertainties of this passage, it seems best to keep lines and speeches intact as in the QF lineation, and thus not divide 48 ('Doth . . . truth!') into

two halves, pairing each half with preceding and following short lines as some editors
do. This edn pairs half-lines in this passage only when the speakers are addressing
each other, in 47, 49 and 50.

5.2.87–8 *Most editors follow Theobald's deletion of two seemingly problematic SPs in
QF at 87–8 (see t.n.). *TxC* (436), arguing that 'Q is most unlikely to have interpolat-
ed two prefixes out of the blue, and F unlikely to have overlooked such a double
error', hypothesizes that Q erroneously misread the SP '*Dio.*' as being intended to
precede 'Nay . . . from me' instead of 'As I kiss thee', and thereupon also had to move
the SP '*Cres.*' down one line from its proper place; and that the F annotator simply
failed to correct this double error. This emendation is ingenious, but runs up against
the difficulty that Diomedes regularly addresses Cressida in this scene as 'you' rather
than 'thou' or 'thee' until the very end of their interview (106), by which time he is
fed up with her. This edition proposes that QF is perfectly intelligible if at 87
Diomedes grabs the sleeve and then plays keep-away, saying mockingly, 'Nay, do not
snatch it from me', as she tries in vain to get it back.

5.2.109–10 *Nor . . . best QF's assignment of this speech to '*Ther.*' instead of '*Troy.*' is
an error easily made by a compositor or copyist. The iambic pentameter cadence
(though QF set the speech as prose) is something Thersites uses only in satirical couplets (as at 119–20), whereas the personal animus here is perfectly suited to Troilus as
an angry rival, and the reference to Pluto accords with allusions to Pluto and the underworld in Troilus' speeches elsewhere (see 3.2.8–12, 4.4.126, 5.2.160 and 5.4.18, cited by
Ard²). The QF assignment to Thersites is nonetheless possible, and could be made to
work in the theatre.

5.2.155–9 that . . . enter Ovid (*Met.*, 6.1–145, LCL, 1.288–99) tells how Arachne challenged Pallas or Minerva to a weaving contest, whereupon the angry goddess tore up
Arachne's weaving (hence the *broken woof*) and turned her into a spider. The form
*Ariachne* also seems to suggest 'Ariadne', who gave Theseus a thread with which to
make his way out of the Cretan Labyrinth (*Met.*, 8.152–83, LCL, 1.416–19), but this
story provides no equivalent of the *broken woof*. Perhaps Troilus plays bitterly with
the paradox that sky and earth, though they meet with no gap in between, are as dif-
ferentiated as the elements of air and earth.

5.2.178, 179 spout, hurricano Cf. *KL* 3.2.2–3 ('You cataracts and hurricanoes, spout /
Till you have drenched our steeples') and Michael Drayton, 'The Moone-Calf' in
*The Battle of Agincourt*, 1627 (Menston, Eng., 1972), 168 (cited by *OED* spout *sb.* 6
along with the present instance as its only examples in this sense). Hillebrand, Var,
argues that the waterspout is a cloudburst here, as it would appear to be in *KL*, even
though the *OED* (waterspout 3b) does not allow such a meaning before 1779; but see
LN 182.

5.2.182 his descent Waterspouts pull water from the sea's surface up into the whirling
vortex in an upward spiral, but also appear, like tornadoes, to descend from the roil-
ing clouds above. The action of hovering and then violent descent fits the action that
Troilus plans against Diomedes. Cf. the First Player's description of Pyrrhus' sword
hanging in the air over Priam at the fall of Troy, with its similar image of a terrible
storm (*Ham* 2.2.471–92).

5.3.96 The wit of this line plays on the antithesis of *lose / win* and the close relationship
of *arm* and *sleeve*. *Arm* signifies both an upper limb and arms, weapons. *Arm* is also a
metonymy for the whole body. Troilus will risk his life to win back the token he gave
Cressida, since Diomedes' wearing it is for Troilus a badge of a kind of cuckoldry.
Rhetorically, the line also inverts the expected sequence of events in a kind of hysteron proteron; Troilus means that he will either win back the sleeve or suffer in the
attempt (Ard²). Cf. 5.6.25–6 and n.

5.3.111 *deeds F follows at this point with a three-line version of 5.11.32–4, suggesting
that at some point in *TC*'s early performance history, Pandarus was to have made his

departure from the play here, at the end of 5.3, rather than returning in 5.11 for the epilogue. See essay on 'The text of *TC*', pp. 416–22, for the rationale in this edition of deleting F's three lines here and retaining the ending as it appears in 5.11 of both Q and F.

5.5.6–15 The names of the warriors engaged in the combat here are from Caxton (esp. 579 and 599–600). Polídamàs (approximate pronunciations of names are indicated here by strong and weak accent marks) is an illegitimate son of Priam, Ménon and Thóas cousins of Achilles, Dóreus (two syllables) and Amphímachùs (the latter slain by Hector) dukes or earls who came to Troy with Ajax, Epístrophùs and Cédius ('Epistropus' and 'Cedeus' or 'Cedus', pronounced in two syllables) brother kings slain by Hector, Polyxenes (Políxenès) a noble duke slain by Hector, Pàlamédes an important warrior who later succeeds Agamemnon as Greek leader, and the Ságittàry (lit. 'the archer') a centaur, half-man and half-horse, who is slain by Diomedes. Shakespeare selects and rearranges to suit his dramatic verse.

5.5.21 **And there** Ard²'s emendation, 'And here' (see t.n.), helps to lighten the repetition of *there* in 21–6, and offers an attractive symmetry (here / here, there / there, yonder / there), but the antithetical pattern of 'Here, there and everywhere' (26) might work itself out in various patterns (such as here / there, here / there, yonder / there). Ard² could be correcting an easy error, but the purported error might be elsewhere in these lines.

5.5.39–42 *Engaging and redeeming* (39) carries the financial metaphor of committing and then freeing oneself from an obligation to pay (Ard²). *Careless* further suggests 'reckless'. *Careless force and forceless care* (40) is a fine example of antimetabole and chiasmus, figures of symmetrical repetition in inverted order, and of hysteron proteron, placing the last first. The phrases also play with the oxymorons 'careless care' and 'forceless force', since *forceless* can mean 'careless'; cf. 'I force not', 'I don't care' (*OED* force *v.*¹ 14). See 5.1.23n.

5.5.43 We learned at 5.4.14 that Ajax 'will not arm today'; at 5.5.18 he is 'snail-paced'. Yet here he enters, furious at Troilus. Plainly he has suffered a personal loss like Achilles' loss of Patroclus. Ajax has 'lost a friend', possibly Doreus or Amphimachus, and is 'Roaring for Troilus' (35–7), who is presumably the slayer of the friend. This sequence of events, original with Shakespeare, prepares us for the brief contest between Diomedes and Ajax in 5.6.1–12 as to which of them will get to claim Troilus as his prize.

5.5.44 *Diomedes, who has not spoken since the beginning of the scene, is seemingly aroused to action by Ajax' cry of pursuit after Troilus. Diomedes has already taken Troilus' horse from him, but still wishes to teach him a further lesson. Hence the *Exit* opposite Nestor's speech at 45 in QF seems more likely to have been intended for Diomedes. The small misplacement would have been an easy error for the Q compositor. Nestor is more likely to stay with Agamemnon and the rest, who seemingly move off at the end of the scene, though the exact movement is uncertain (Ard²).

5.8 Most editors omit Pope's and Capell's marking of a scene here, and in a sense the matter is arbitrary since the action is virtually continuous in a battle sequence, but there is as much reason for marking a new scene here as at 5.5, 6 and 7. Cf. *AC* 3.8 and 3.9 for what are conventionally marked as separate scenes in a battle sequence, though they are only six and four lines long respectively.

5.8.3 *Spartan The textual choice of this edition here concurs with Kellner's conjectural emendation (p. 55, § 77c) of the seemingly corrupted readings of QF; see t.n. Hulme (109–10) argues for F's 'double hen'd sparrow', commenting that in Shakespeare's day sparrows were noted for their lecherousness, and that 'double-henned' could apply to Paris as a cock who has kept two hens, i.e. Oenone and Helen.

5.11.2 *In Q, this is Troilus' opening line as he enters; F treats the line as a continuation of Aeneas' speech beginning in 1, and brings Troilus on only after 1–2 are spoken.

The difference may reflect authorial revision, though both versions are defensible. In Q, Aeneas announces success on the Trojan part in 1, and, since retreat has already been sounded (5.10.0.1), seems on the verge of returning to Troy as the Trojan army normally did after the day's fighting. Troilus enters, forestalling the expected order to return to camp with the bitter news that Hector is slain. F conversely interprets 2 as a continuation of Aeneas' thought: 'Since we have won the field, let us stay in anticipation of tomorrow's fight, putting up with the cold'. Troilus then enters with a devastatingly laconic utterance, appalling in its declarative simplicity: 'Hector is slain'. In either text, *starve me out* means 'let us endure in perishing cold' (*OED v.* 5b, giving this line as its sole example in this sense).

# 'INSTRUCTED BY THE ANTIQUARY TIMES': SHAKESPEARE'S SOURCES

We cannot know for certain all that Shakespeare read about the Trojan war and about Troilus and Cressida, for both stories were widely disseminated in the Renaissance and had long been linked to each other. Several lost plays on various aspects of these stories seem to have preceded Shakespeare, including an anonymous *Troilus and Pander*, a romantic interlude acted at court by the Chapel Children on 6 January 1516–17; Nicolas Grimald's *Troilus ex Chaucero* (*Troilus, from Chaucer*), a comedy in Latin acted at Oxford c. 1540–7; a play referred to in the Stationers' Register for 6 April 1601 as 'The old *destruction of Troye*', of which 'one Impression onely thereof' is to be printed 'for the Company', perhaps to be identified with the *Troy* recorded by Philip Henslowe as having been acted at his Rose Theatre in June and July 1596 (but probably not an early abbreviated version of Thomas Heywood's *The Iron Age*, acted in two parts in 1612–13); Henry Chettle and Thomas Dekker's *Troilus and Cressida*, performed by the Admiral's men in April of 1599, of which a 'plot' fragment survives; and still others on related topics, such as Nicholas Udall's *Thersites* in 1537, an *Ajax Flagellifer* in Latin at Cambridge in 1564, another Latin play called *Ajax and Ulysses* at court in 1572 and a 'tragedie of Agamemnon' by Dekker and Chettle, 1599. Non-dramatic treatments of the Troy material are to be found in George Peele's 500–line *Tale of Troy*, first published in 1589, in Robert Greene's *Euphues His Censure to Philautus*, 1587, and more briefly in other works.[1] Even if the stories were widely known and often repeated, however, we can perhaps still recover some sense of how Shakespeare may have worked with some major sources.

Shakespeare must have known George Chapman's translation (in fourteeners) of *Seven Books of the Iliads of Homer, Prince of Poets*, published in 1598. The 'seven books' were 1, 2 and 7 through 11. A translation of *Achilles' Shield*, excerpted from Book 18, appeared later that same year in rhymed decasyllabic verse. Chapman's *Twelve Books* were published in 1608 and the complete twenty-four in 1611, too late for consideration when Shakespeare wrote *Troilus and Cressida*. For Books 1 through 10, Arthur Hall's *Ten Books of Homer's Iliads*, an English translation in fourteeners from the French of Hugues Salel, 1581, was available. In French, Shakespeare could have read Jehan Samxon's complete prose translation from the Latin, 1530, and Salel's verse translation published in various stages, 1545–99, completed by Amadis Jamyn. Lorenzo Valla's prose Latin translation, originally published in 1474, was the first of several; H. Eobanus Hessus, the author of a Greek and literal Latin version, V. Obsopoeus, and Spondanus all published partial or complete translations before the end of the sixteenth century.[2]

From one or more of these earlier translations, Shakespeare may well have gained some information, since Homeric episodes not covered in Chapman's *Seven Books* are put to use. When

1  S.R., 3.69b, 6 April 1601; Greg, *Documents*, for the 'plot' of *TC;* Foakes & Rickert, 47–8, for *Henslowe's Diary* entries; Chambers, *Elizabethan*, 2.144 and 3.345; Harbage, *Annals*; Tatlock, esp. 676–83. Henslowe, 320, notes in the inventory of properties owned by the Admiral's men in March 1598 a 'great horse with his leages [legs]', well suited for one or more plays on the siege of Troy. Henslowe authorized a loan of £3 to Chettle and Dekker on 7 April 1599 'in earneste of ther boocke called Troyeles & creasse daye', and paid them 20 shillings on 16 April 'in parte of payment of ther boocke called Troyelles & cressada' (Foakes & Rickert, 106–7). See also 118 for an entry seemingly by Thomas Brise acknowledging payment of £4 10s. on 29 January 1594 in connection with 'Troyeles & creasseday'. See Rollins, esp. 417. On Shakespeare's possible use of Greene's *Euphues His Censure to Philautus*, see Whitaker.

2  Tatlock, 742.

Cressida and Pandarus view the Trojan soldiers as they return from the day's fighting in 1.2, Shakespeare combines a detail from Chaucer (in which Cressida alone sees Troilus returning from the field of battle) with a passage from the *Iliad* (3.161–258) in which Helen and Priam view the Greek chieftains from the walls of Troy. Ulysses' recollection of how Achilles has 'Made emulous missions 'mongst the gods themselves / And drave great Mars to faction' (3.3.190–1) sounds like an echo of a *mêlée* among the gods in the *Iliad*, Book 20, though moved from its Homeric position after the entry of Achilles into the war to an earlier conversation in which Ulysses urges Achilles to look to his reputation for honour. Achilles' perusing of Hector's body 'joint by joint' in order to determine where to destroy him (4.5.231–46) may be an echo of the *Iliad*'s 'He was eyeing Hector's splendid body, to see where it might best / give way' (22.321–2), though again moved from the fatal encounter of the two warriors to an earlier scene. Achilles' motive for entering the fighting in Shakespeare, as in Homer, is to avenge the death of Patroclus (5.5.30–5, 18.80–93) – not, as reported in William Caxton's *Recuyell of the Historyes of Troye*, Achilles' own danger and especially the slaughter of his Myrmidons (637). Achilles' resolve to tie Hector's body 'to my horse's tail' and drag it through the field (5.9.21–2) recalls the *Iliad*'s account of the 'shameful treatment' accorded the dead Trojan hero (22.395–405).[1] (Shakespeare borrows verbal details here from Caxton's description, 639, of Achilles' slaying of Troilus.)[2]

Shakespeare's use of Chapman's *Seven Books* seems most

---

1 Some of these examples, citing Richmond Lattimore's translation of Homer's *Iliad* (Chicago, 1951) for passages not in Chapman's *Seven Books*, are from Tatlock, 740–1. Cf. Tillyard, 33–5, who argues that, though Shakespeare is very likely to have read Chapmen's Homer, he had no need of it to write this play.

2 Ard[2], 34–5. G. K. Hunter (esp. 8) argues forcefully that the Homeric view of a universe of discontinuity and flux, in which 'there was no order there to be destroyed' and in which 'animal violence was the rule of life and not the exception' (strikingly different from what Keats found in Homer), came to Shakespeare as a 'profoundly unliberating shock' and thereby enabled him to relate Homer to the medieval tradition that was so widely available to him.

evident in his characterization of Thersites. Verbal echoes suggest a direct acquaintance. Chapman's description of a 'rank
mind', a 'ravenlike voice' and the 'tuneless jarring' of 'unre-
garded words' (2.206–7) appears to have inspired Agamemnon's
sardonic remarking on the unlikelihood that 'When rank
Thersites opes his mastic jaws, / We shall hear music, wit and
oracle' (1.3.73–4). Compare also Thersites' rumination at
5.2.197–8: 'I would croak like a raven; I would bode, I would
bode'. Other physical characteristics in Chapman – 'a goggle eye',
'Stark-lame . . . of either foot', shoulders that are stooped and
drawn together over his breast, a pointed and balding head
(2.210–13) – prepare us for the 'porcupine' whom Ajax threatens
to 'beat . . . into handsomeness' (2.1.13–24). Ajax' epithet for
Thersites, 'Cobloaf' (2.1.36), a small roundish or lumpy loaf,
nicely captures the sneer in Chapman at Thersites' misshapen
dome. Shakespeare's Thersites seems to confirm Chapman's
description as 'the filthiest Greek that came to Troy' (2.210)
when he protests to Hector, 'No, no, I am a rascal, a scurvy railing knave, a very filthy rogue' (5.4.27–8). More broadly,
Shakespeare found in his source a railer who 'rashly and beyond
all rule used to oppugne the lords' (2.208), and whose role as
obscene critic of the war could be greatly expanded past his sole
appearance in Book 2 of the *Iliad*. Perhaps Shakespeare also knew
Nicholas Udall's *Thersites* (1537). (Thomas Heywood's *The Iron
Age* may point to an enlarged role for Thersites in other late
Renaissance treatments of the story that Shakespeare might have
known; see pp. 394–7 below.)[1]

Books 1, 2 and 7–11 in Chapman's *Seven Books* could have
provided Shakespeare with much of the material he needed to
describe the war situation in Acts 1 through 4: the commencement of the story *in medias res* after many years of fighting
(Prologue 27–8), the debate in the Greek camp (1.3.1–212;

---

1  See Ard², 35. Ovid mentions Thersites in a single line only (*Met.*, 13.233, LCL,
2.244–5).

*Seven Books,* pp. 22ff.), the 'faint defects of age' and 'palsy fumbling' that are attributed to Nestor (1.3.172–4; cf. 'the defects that fail best minds in age / Or find the palsy', in 'The Fourth Book', i.e. Bk 8, p. 62), Hector's challenge to the Greeks (1.3.216–83; 'Third Book', i.e. Bk 7, p. 48), the debate among the Trojan leaders, albeit briefly told in Homer (2.2; 'Third Book', pp. 54–5), the device of a lottery to choose Hector's opponent (1.3.375ff.; 'Third Book', p. 51), the Homeric epithet for Achilles, 'great Thetis' son' (3.3.94; 'Third Book', p. 52), the encounter of Hector and Ajax (4.5.114–49; 'Third Book', pp. 52–3), Achilles' disaffection and his friendship with Patroclus, and still more.[1]

Book 2 especially gave Shakespeare material for the debate in the Greek camp in 1.3, including Ulysses' speech on order and degree. In Chapman's *Seven Books,* Ulysses insists that 'The rule of many is absurd; one lord must lead the ring / Of far-resounding government' (2.198–9). At the same time, one can find many parallels to Shakespeare's debate in famous texts of classical antiquity and the Renaissance: Aristotle's *Nicomachean Ethics,* Books 1 and 11–13 of Ovid's *Metamorphoses,* Boethius' *The Consolation of Philosophy,* Richard Hooker's *Of the Laws of Ecclesiastical Polity,* Sir Thomas Elyot's *The Book of the Governor,* Edmund Spenser's *The Faerie Queene* (Bk 5, stanzas 4–7), Sir John Davies's *Orchestra,* official homilies 'Of Obedience' and 'Against Disobedience and Rebellion', and perhaps Euripides' *The Phoenician Women* and Sophocles' *Ajax* (see commentary notes to 1.3.78–120). Homer was thus a starting point rather than a single source, even in those places where Shakespeare seems to have known the *Iliad.* Other translations than Chapman's may have played a part.

Shakespeare's many departures from Homer are certainly as significant as his borrowings. For example, we see him making

---

1  J. S. Palmer. Ard[2] provides some possible verbal parallels (36–7). See also Thomas, 26–35, and Presson, 3–103.

light of Menelaus' wounding of Paris (1.1.105–8, 1.2.205–7), whereas Homer describes the encounter as so violent that Aphrodite is obliged to rescue Paris (3.324–82). Hector's challenge to the Greeks is a much more serious matter in the *Iliad* than it is in Shakespeare's play, and Ajax the son of Telamon is chosen by an honest lottery in Homer (Book 7).[1] When Hector refers in 4.5 to a diplomatic mission that Ulysses and Diomedes undertook early in the war to negotiate a peaceful return of Helen to the Greeks (215–16), he reports an incident missing in Homer but described in Caxton's *Recuyell* (556–62) and in Lydgate's *Troy Book* (2.6720–7105). Achilles' reputation is severely deglamorized in Shakespeare. Ajax is much more a buffoon than in Homer – partly because Ajax Telamon and Ajax the son of Oileus were often conflated in the Renaissance, as in Shakespeare's play, to the detriment of Ajax Telamon (see Lydgate, 2.457ff., and Golding's translation of Ovid's *Metamorphoses*). Ulysses is more wily than in Homer – again partly through the destabilizing of the epic idiom in Ovid, who calls him 'sly Ulysses . . . who doth all his matters in the dark' (Golding's Ovid, 13.115 and 129).[2] Nestor is more senile, Agamemnon more pompous and ineffectual. Homer's pro-Greek perspective gives way to a matter-of-fact view of war in which the few real heroes like Hector are victimized by an all-engulfing conflict.

The love plot of Troilus and Cressida plays no part in the *Iliad*. Troilus is mentioned only briefly in that poem, as a lover of horses and a son of Priam who falls in battle some time before Hector (24.257). The name 'Chriseyda' appears only as an accusative form (1.182) of Chryseis, the captive mistress of Agamemnon whom that Greek chieftain unwillingly releases to her father Chryses in order to appease Apollo's anger at the insult given to his priest (1.111–84). Calchas appears in Homer

1  Thomas, 29–30.
2  Bate, 109; Brower, 123; and J. A. K. Thomson, 213–14.

as augur to the Greeks, warning that Chryseis must be returned to her father, but Calchas is not the father of Chryseis (1.92–100). Pandarus in Homer is a warrior who treacherously breaks the truce by wounding Menelaus (4.85–140) and is eventually killed by Diomedes (5.280–96).

For the story of Troilus and Cressida in the context of the Trojan war, Shakespeare turned to post-Homeric medieval accounts by Chaucer, Caxton and (perhaps) Lydgate. Those authors in turn were retelling and elaborating on an extensive tradition. Dictys the Cretan's *Ephemeris Belli Troiani* is a lengthy fourth-century Latin work taken from a Greek original and purporting to be an eyewitness account. Dictys tells the whole narrative of the Trojan war from the rape of Helen to the return of the Greek heroes to their homes, reflecting a mistrust of Homer as insufficiently historical and as having lived too long after the event. Next came Dares Phrygius' *De Excidio Troiae Historiae*, from the sixth century, once again claiming eyewitness authority, this time from the Trojan side. Dares widens his history to extend all the way from the expedition of the Argonauts to the destruction of Troy. He often mentions Troilus and Diomedes as warriors, and Briseida as a beautiful woman, but does not introduce them to one another. Dares' history was translated by Joseph of Exeter into Latin hexameters in the twelfth century.[1]

Benoît de Sainte-Maure, relying more on Dares than on Dictys, expanded the narrative to include, in his *Roman de Troie*, the sad love story of Troilus and Briseida. By beginning this episode with Briseida's being sent from Troy to her father Calchas in the Greek camp, where she soon meets Diomedes and quickly forgets Troilus, Benoît focuses on her faithlessness; he does not tell of the wooing. The account takes up some 1,349 lines (not including the death of Troilus at the hands of Achilles and Hecuba's lament for him), interspersed midway through a

---

1   Chaucer, *TC*, xxi–xxii and *passim*.

poem of 30,316 lines in octosyllabic couplets. It was written in the latter half of the twelfth century and was followed by a Latin paraphrase (1287) by Guido delle Colonne, of Messina, called *Historia Trojana*. Guido claimed as his authorities Dictys and Dares, without even mentioning Benoît, but in fact his redaction of Benoît is so nearly identical that one cannot always be certain which work became the basis for further redactions.

Probably relying more on Benoît than on Guido, Giovanni Boccaccio took the story of the faithless Breseida and made of it a central plot for his *Il Filostrato* (c. 1338). He renamed the heroine Criseida, in part presumably because he perceived that 'Briseis' meant 'daughter of Brises', and because Ovid's third epistle of his *Heroides*, 'Briseis to Achilles', makes clear that Briseis was the slave girl whom Achilles had taken away from Agamemnon. (Boccaccio probably did not know Homer directly.) Ovid's *Remedia Amoris* (ll. 467–84), on the other hand, could be read in such a way as to suggest that Chryseis, whom Agamemnon had had to give up in order to appease Apollo, was the daughter of the seer Calchas. In his poem, Boccaccio relates the wooing of Criseida by Troilo with passionate intensity, and introduces Pandaro as a gallant encourager of the lovers.

Shakespeare almost surely knew and used Geoffrey Chaucer's elegant recasting of Boccaccio in *Troilus and Criseyde* (1385–7), though the bare essentials of the story also appear in Lydgate and Caxton.[1] In Chaucer, Shakespeare would have found a loving psychological study of the main characters and a delicately humorous perspective on their joys and tribulations. He would have found a jocular, witty and urbane Pandarus who counsels

---

1 Small, 154–67, was the first to amass a detailed argument on Shakespeare's use of Chaucer. For a more recent step-by-step comparison of the love stories in Chaucer and Shakespeare, see Presson, 107–33. Muir, *Sources*, 1.78, calls Chaucer's poem 'the main source of *T&C*'. Those who deny such indebtedness include Sommer, Introduction to Caxton, *Recuyell*, xlv, and Jusserand, 3.254. Bradbrook points out that each of Chaucer's five books is represented by one or two scenes in Shakespeare, 'the division between Chaucer's books corresponding roughly to the division between Shakespeare's acts' (313). On Pandarus, see Dyer.

Troilus and speaks praisingly to him of Criseyde (1.547–1061, especially 880–9 and 981–7; cf. 1.1.1–84 of Shakespeare's play); calls upon Criseyde, inquiring what she is reading and endeavouring to impress her with a detailed comparison of Troilus and Hector (2.155–210, *TC* 1.2.38–88); points out Troilus to her when the young man comes riding beneath her window (2.1247–60, *TC* 1.2.219–31); bundles the lovers off to bed after much ado (3.512ff., *TC* 3.2.38–206); and joshes his niece about her having enjoyed little sleep during her first night with Troilus (3.1555–75, *TC* 4.2.24–34).

In still other linked passages, Criseyde witnesses the return of Troilus from battle, reflecting privately on his excellence (2.610–86, *TC* 1.2.218–86); joins with Troilus in cursing the coming of the day that ends their night of bliss (3.1422–70, *TC* 4.2.1–15); immoderately weeps and faints at the news of her impending return to Troy, tearing her hair (4.666–72, 736–99, 1128–414, *TC* 4.2.95–110, 4.4.1–56); and rebukes her lover for doubting her fidelity to him, binding herself by solemn oaths to remain true (4.1485–596, *TC* 4.4.57–105). In both Chaucer and Shakespeare, the consummation of the love relationship is immediately followed by a scene in which Calchas successfully pleads with the Greeks to exchange his daughter Criseyde for Antenor (4.50–140, *TC* 3.3.1–33); and in both Chaucer and Shakespeare, Calchas plays a more dominant role than in Lydgate or Caxton. Troilus' warning to Criseyde that she is likely to see 'many a lusty knyght / Amonge the Grekis' (4.1485–6) may well anticipate Shakespeare's Troilus: 'The Grecian youths are full of quality', etc. (4.4.75–90). Diomedes' importunity and quick success with Criseyde are vividly evoked in Chaucer (5.841–1050), and the 'sleeve' given Cressida by Troilus which she then gives to Diomedes is bestowed upon him in Chaucer as well (5.1043). Diomedes also acquires a glove from Criseyde (5.1013), as does Troilus in the play (4.4.70), but such a glove is also mentioned in Caxton (604), as the sleeve is not. Criseyde's regretful concern for her imperiled reputation, her evasive letters, Troilus' bitterness at being betrayed and Pandarus' dismay (5.1051–631, *TC* 5.2.121–87, 5.3.97–111) make up the substance of the failed love relationship in Act 5 of Shakespeare's play.[1]

Talbot Donaldson makes a strong case for the proposition that 'Shakespeare understood Chaucer's poem for what it is'. Shakespeare did not need the tradition of a Cressida thoroughly degenerated since Chaucer's time, especially in Robert Henryson's *The Testament of Cresseid*, to know that her literary character had been that of the prototypical unfaithful woman; such a heroine was just what Shakespeare needed for a play in which all the men who profess any ideals go about subverting everything that they claim to believe. Chaucer's Cressida, as Shakespeare must have perceived, is ultimately indefensible in her conduct and yet is daringly made sympathetic by the Chaucerian narrator. She is, like Shakespeare's reincarnation of her, paradoxical and ambiguous, at once modestly timid and calculatingly erotic, controlling the timing of her surrender and yet susceptible to the importunity of men. This is not to deny important differences as well: Cressida is much taken with Troilus at the start of Shakespeare's play, and is also at once more brazen and more vulnerable, so that the affair hurries on in a way suited to a play about the pressures of war without the exquisite leisure of Chaucer's psychological exploration of nuance. Cressida is more alone than Chaucer's Criseyde: she has no confidante like Celia or Nerissa, no Nurse, no attendant women to give us the impression of a stable, large household. Even so, argues Donaldson, Chaucer's insights into his heroine served Shakespeare well.[2]

---

1 Some of these examples are pointed out by Ard², 24–5, and by A. Thompson, 111–65.

2 Donaldson, *Swan*, 74–94. See also Stiller, 21–38. D. Wilson sees Shakespeare's Cressida as less successful in coping with a dominant narcissism than Chaucer's Criseyde, in whom narcissism gives way to a discovery of mature love.

Troilus too, described in Lydgate and Caxton simply as a martial hero, may well owe something to the Chaucerian original – allowing always that we do not know about a lost play that Shakespeare could have revamped, or other untraceable potential sources. Shakespeare's Troilus, like Chaucer's, is enervated by love, self-pitying, dependent on Pandarus and prone to think of Cressida in physical terms. Pandarus, on the other hand, is a more degraded figure than in Chaucer: the genteel and well-meaning friend has become a seedy, voyeuristic, dirty old man whose vapidity serves as the occasion for wit even in ordinary servants (see 3.1.1–41). Troilus' closeness to Pandarus helps bring down the tone of love by all the participants. Yet even here Shakespeare appears to be responding to the Chaucerian model, if only because no other literary model presents itself. To the perhaps large extent that Shakespeare is turning to contemporary satire and to observations from his own experience, he seems to be doing so as a meaningfully disillusioning way of rewriting Chaucer.[1]

Shakespeare telescopes events, as he so often does in working with his sources. The events of two nights in the final surrender of Chaucer's Criseyde to Troilus are collapsed into one. Things generally happen faster: the giving in to Diomedes is more rapid. Shakespeare's recollection of Chaucer is more general than detailed; verbal parallels are not common. Shakespeare creates episodes not found in any medieval treatment of the love story, such as Diomedes' and Troilus' open quarrelling even before Diomedes has left Troy with Cressida (4.4.108–36); the scene in which Troilus, accompanied by Ulysses, witnesses Cressida's betrayal of him (5.2); and Troilus' curt dismissal of Pandarus for attempting to bring him a letter (5.3.97–111). Most significantly, Shakespeare deflates his narrative of love. All in all, however, it seems clear that Chaucer has made a significant contribution to the play – not least of all,

---

1   A. Thompson, 116–48.

perhaps, because it is a serious philosophical poem deeply concerned with issues of order, will versus reason, mutability and value.[1]

For the narrative of the Trojan war, Shakespeare relied more on Caxton and Lydgate than on Homer or Chaucer, and especially (perhaps entirely) on Caxton. William Caxton translated and printed *The Recuyell of the Historyes of Troye* in about 1471–5, from Raoul Lefèvre's *Recueil des Histoires de Troie*, the best known of the French translations of Guido's *Historia Trojana*. Caxton's work, the first book to be printed in English, was reprinted in 1502 and 1503 (by Winkyn de Worde), in 1553 (by William Copland), and in 1596 and 1607, in a 'newly corrected' version, 'much amended' by William Fiston (by the printer Thomas Creede). It was consulted by many writers in the English Renaissance, including George Peele, Robert Greene and Thomas Heywood. Subsequent editions appeared in 1617, 1636, 1663, 1670, 1676, 1680 and still later. The book was a classic – more for the interest of its narrative than for any genuine literary merit on Caxton's part. Shakespeare may have consulted an edition prior to that of 1596, since the word 'orgulous' (Prologue 2), found in earlier editions of Caxton, was changed to 'proud' in 1596, but it is also likely that he knew the 1596 edition.[2]

Following his model in Lefèvre (and hence in Guido), Caxton tells an expansive tale, beginning with the genealogies of the Olympian gods and the early encounters between Greece and Troy that led to the most famous Trojan war: Hercules' two military expeditions against King Laomedon of Troy in revenge for Laomedon's treachery, with the awarding of Laomedon's daughter Exione (Hesione) to the Greek Telamon. Much time is devoted to Hercules' well-known labours, his troubles with Deianira and Nessus, and the like, all of which is relevant to the book's titular subject only in that we learn of the first two destructions of Troy.

1   A. Thompson, 154ff.
2   Caxton, lxxxii–cxii, and Ard², 27–8. On 'orgulous', see Bullough, *Sources*, 6.94.

Not until Book 3, at p. 505 out of a total of 703, do we come to Priam's summoning a council of leaders in Troy, from which emerges Paris' resolution to bring home from Greece some noble lady in reprisal for the Greeks' having taken Priam's sister Hesione (520). Thence the story proceeds to the war itself, concluding with such post-*Iliad* episodes as the opening of Troy to the Trojan Horse (660ff.), Agamemnon's fateful homecoming, the revenge of Orestes on Clytemnestra, and Thelagonus' (i.e. Telemachus') journey in quest of his father Ulysses.

Shakespeare's debt to Caxton is demonstrable not only in outlines of narrative events but in details. The play repeatedly alludes to the earlier episodes of the taking of Hesione and the 'rape' of Helen in reprisal (see 2.1.11–12, 2.2.77–80, 4.5.84 and 121–2 and notes). The Prologue speaks of 'Sixty and nine' Greek leaders (5), following Caxton's exact wording (545–6). The six gates of Troy, resonantly named by the Prologue (16–17), are from Caxton (507), and Lydgate, too (2.596–205), but in spellings closer to those of Caxton. Troy's towers in Caxton reach 'vnto the heuene' (508); cf. 'Yon towers, whose wanton tops do buss the clouds' (4.5.220). Agamemnon speaks of a 'seven years' siege' (1.3.12), following Caxton's chronology, whereas in Homer the war is in its tenth year (*Iliad*, 2.134 and 295). The debate in Troy (2.2) owes much to Caxton's account (517–24), albeit moved in Shakespeare from its original position in Caxton, prior to Paris' voyage in quest of Helen, to a time late in the war. Hector's is the voice of reason, urging consideration of the long-range consequences of violent action; Paris urges a chivalrous response to the Greeks' insult of a Trojan woman; Helenus warns against 'coveteise of vengeance' that is sure to invite the gods' anger; and Troilus contemptuously replies to 'this Coward preste here' (524; cf. 2.2.37–50), accusing him of 'pusillanymytie' and sybaritic delight in his own creature comforts (cf. 38: 'You fur your gloves with reason'). Ulysses' later description of Troilus as 'A second hope, as fairly built as Hector' (4.5.110) recalls Caxton's observation that

Troilus 'resamblid moche to hector And was the seconde after hym of prowesse' (543) – a sentiment also expressed by Chaucer (2.644).

The military action in the latter part of the play is especially rich in echoes of the *Recueil*. Hector, when he meets Ulysses (4.5.213–16), recalls their encounter early in the war when Diomedes and Ulysses came to Troy on a diplomatic mission that failed to achieve peace; the episode is reported in Caxton (556–62) and Lydgate (2.6702–7105), not in Homer. When in the same scene Hector and Achilles meet and size each other up (4.5.230–60), Shakespeare makes use of an earlier event in Caxton of Hector's visit to the Greek camp during a truce and his challenge of Achilles to one-to-one combat (602–3). Ajax, 'cousin-german' and Hector's 'father's sister's son' in Shakespeare (4.5.121–2), is 'cosyn germayn of hector' and 'sone of his aunte' in Caxton (589). In the ensuing fighting, Caxton (600) and Lydgate (3.3518) both name Achilles' horse, Galathe (cf. 5.5.20). Several warriors whom Shakespeare names only once in the *mêlée* (5.5.6–13), presumably for the high-sounding effect of so many princely titles – Polydamas (Polidamas in Caxton), Doreus (Doreus or Dorius), Epistrophus (Epistropus), Cedius (Cedeus or Cedus), Polyxenes (Polixenes), Amphimachus (Amphymacus), Thoas, etc. – are mentioned together in Caxton (579, 599–600). The Sagittary (5.5.14), a centaur fighting on the Greek side though unnamed by Homer, turns up in Caxton (600) and in Lydgate (3.3433–506). Hector's great and sometimes misplaced generosity contributes to his death and the defeat of his cause, in Caxton (590) as in Shakespeare (5.6.14–22), though it is shown in different ways.

The differences too are great. By staging the council of Trojan leaders late in the war, rather than before Paris has gone in quest of Helen, Shakespeare compresses time and puts the emphasis on the Trojans' inability to deal rationally with an impossible situation that has gone on for years. Shakespeare trims and selects: he does not, for example, include in that council meeting Deiphobus' speech in favour of cynical expediency (Caxton, 522–3), nor does he permit Paris to recount his judging the rivalry of Venus, Athene and Juno (Caxton, 520–2). Shakespeare presents us with a Hector who reverses his position, as he does not in Caxton. The cynicism with which Ulysses arranges a corrupt lottery so that Ajax will answer Hector's challenge (1.3.375–81) is Shakespeare's (there is a lottery in Homer, 7.171, but not thus abused). He follows his sources (Caxton, 589, Lydgate, 3.2046–8) in conflating Ajax, the son of Telamon and Periboea, with his half-brother Teucer, the son of Telamon and Hesione (see 2.1.11–12, 2.2.77–80 and notes), but ignores the distinction offered earlier in Lydgate (2.4571–96) between the noble Ajax Telamon and the cowardly, ill-spoken Ajax who was the son of Oileus. (Homer distinguishes the two, though less censoriously.) The decision to move the meeting of Hector and Achilles to a date towards the end of the war (4.5.231–61; cf. Caxton, 602, and Lydgate, 3.3755–4036) intensifies the dramatic focus of their duel, so that the deplorable outcome follows soon after the first encounter and underscores the desperation of Achilles' search for fame.

Cassandra's prophetic warnings similarly function as a comment on the paralysis of many years of conflict (2.2.101–12, 5.3.13–90), and do not, as in Caxton, immediately follow the marriage of Paris and Helen (537). Shakespeare substantially expands the roles of Thersites as satiric observer and of Aeneas as tactful ambassador. He mentions briefly the secret love of Achilles for Polyxena, daughter of Priam, showing us how Ulysses uses his knowledge of this compromising difficulty to put pressure on Achilles to join in battle (3.3.194–217) and how Achilles has been negotiating privately with Hecuba (5.1.36–41), but rearranges the chronology and abbreviates the accounts in Caxton (621ff.) and Lydgate (4.1524ff.), where Achilles falls in love with Polyxena on the anniversary of his having slain Hector and then, without Ulysses knowing of it, enters into extensive negotiations to obtain her. Achilles' resolve to set aside his love for Polyxena and enter the battle thus occurs far later in Shakespeare's sources than in the play, and indeed long after the deaths of Patroclus and Hector.

Many battles, separated by periods of truce, are compressed into the play's final action. The death of Patroclus at the hands of Hector, vividly described in Caxton (580) and Lydgate (3.757–811), is mentioned only in passing in the play as an uncertain report, and with no indication as to who may have done the slaying (5.5.13); moreover, in both sources this death occurs earlier in the war than in the play. The bastard Margareton, whose death at the hands of Achilles is reported in Caxton (612) and Lydgate (3.5204–20), turns up in the play (5.5.7, 5.8.5–15), albeit in a variant spelling (Margarelon) that may be an error of transmission, and performing deeds of valour not credited to him by Shakespeare's sources – perhaps because Shakespeare wanted a valorous bastard to juxtapose with Thersites ('I am a bastard too; I love bastards', etc., 5.8.8). For his disillusioning account of the death of Hector (5.9.5–22), Shakespeare turns to Caxton's (638–9) and perhaps Lydgate's (4.2647–779) versions of the death of Troilus, where Achilles instructs his Myrmidons to close Troilus round about so that Achilles can dispatch his victim unfairly, and then brutally ties his victim's body to the tail of his horse and drags it through the army. (In Homer, 22.395–400, after a heroic fight, Hector is dragged behind Achilles' chariot; and since Chapman had not translated this book in 1598, the probable sources are Caxton and Lydgate.)

Virtually all of the episodes Shakespeare could have found in Lydgate were also in Caxton, as indicated above, so that it is not always easy to be sure that Shakespeare knew Lydgate's *Troy Book* (begun in 1412, printed in 1513 and, revised, in 1555) as well. Spellings of some proper names, like Polyxena ('Polixena', 'Polixene' and 'Polyxena' in Caxton, always 'Pollicene' in Lydgate), suggest a strong dependence on Caxton, though conceivably Shakespeare could have learned how to spell Polyxena's name from Thomas Cooper's *Dictionarium historicam & poeticum*, attached to his *Thesaurus* of 1565.[1] Some episodes, in addition to those mentioned already, appear in Caxton alone, such as the Greek chieftains' greeting of Breseyda and bestowing gifts on her (605–6; cf. 4.5.14–54); Lydgate reports merely that Calchas 'Received hir, logged ther he lay', 3.4428–9, while Chaucer, too, 5.190–4, focuses on the father's receiving her. Still other episodes used by Shakespeare are found in both works: Hector's overcoming a Trojan warrior in goodly armour (5.6.28–32, 5.9.1–4; cf. Caxton, 613, and Lydgate, 3.5332–83); Diomedes' taking of Troilus' horse and dispatching a servant to present it to Cressida (5.5.1–5; cf. Caxton, 608, Lydgate 3.4620–41); and still more.

A few details may possibly suggest indebtedness to the *Troy Book*. The scene in which Hector's family unsuccessfully attempts to dissuade him from fighting on the fatal day of his death (5.3) is presented more graphically by Lydgate (3.5021–143) than by Caxton (610–11): Andromache's dream and her eloquent pleas are followed in turn by the urgings of Cassandra, Hecuba, Polyxena and Helen, at which point Andromache enlists Priam's assistance. Even in this scene, however, we find Caxton-like touches not found in Lydgate, as when Hector says to his wife, 'You train me to offend you. Get you in' (5.3.4); cf. Caxton's observation that 'hector was angry and sayd to his wyf many wordes reprochable' (611). Elsewhere, Shakespeare may have gathered impressions of characterization from Lydgate's tendency to describe and editorialize, such as his denunciation of Achilles' barbarity (4.2780–854), or his rebuking of Guido for abusing women (3.4264–417). Lydgate's description of Troilus (2.4861–95) is fuller than Caxton's (543), and closer on the whole to Ulysses' admiring portrait in 4.5.97–110, but a similar appraisal was available in Chaucer (5.827–40), to whom Lydgate was indeed closely indebted. Lydgate's description of the

1  Var, 425.

warrior in goodly armour killed by Hector is more graphic than Caxton's in describing that armour (3.5334–43), but none of the details makes its way into 5.6 or 5.9 of the play. To the contrary, the vivid word 'frush' at 5.6.30 may instead have come from an earlier account in Caxton of Hector's assault on Achilles (595), and Lydgate's sermonizing about Hector's covetousness (3.5354–74) is certainly not something that Shakespeare was about to adopt. On the whole, Caxton is so comprehensive, and Shakespeare's imagination so capable of supplying any deficiencies, that we cannot be sure that Shakespeare had any real need for Lydgate.[1]

The disillusionment in Shakespeare's play, so often directly contrary to the chivalric tone of Caxton and Lydgate, may well owe something to Robert Henryson's *The Testament of Cresseid*, a narrative poem by a Scottish schoolmaster that was published in Thynne's edition of Chaucer in 1532 and in all subsequent editions until 1721, though it was also separately published in Edinburgh in 1593. It purports to be a continuation of Chaucer's *Troilus and Criseyde*, and was regarded as Chaucer's composition by Thomas Speght in his edition of 1598. Henryson's moralistic spin-off tells how Cresseid is deserted by a bored Diomed, lives reputedly for a time 'in the courte as commune' (76–7), returns to her father, dreams that she is to be punished by Venus and the other gods for her infidelity by contracting leprosy, awakens to find that she is indeed diseased, and is placed by her father (with her consent) in a 'spittaill hous' (391), where she becomes a begging leper. In this pitiful plight she encounters Troilus, who, not recognizing her but somehow

---

1   The few verbal parallels suggested by Ard², 29–30, seem to me too general to be convincing. The same is true of Hillebrand's proposed links (Var, 425ff.) and those of Thomas, 35–40, and Muir, *Sources*, 181–5. Some of the details Thomas attributes to an indebtedness to Lydgate are also to be found in Caxton or Chaucer. Tillyard (40–4) and Henderson argue for indebtedness to Lydgate, but put forward no tangible evidence. On Shakespeare's sources for the Hector–Andromache scene (5.3), see Arnold. G. K. Hunter (1) concludes that Caxton is the likelier source, citing E. Stein.

stirred by remembrances of his lost love, gives her alms. She dies, having sent her ruby ring to Troilus, who mournfully erects a monument in her memory.[1]

Henryson's tale made a vivid impression on Elizabethan poets like George Gascoigne and George Whetstone, as Hyder Rollins has chronicled.[2] Indeed, Shakespeare echoes the infamous story in Pistol's reference to 'the lazar kite of Cressid's kind' (*H5* 2.1.77) and in Feste's observation that 'Cressid was a beggar' (*TN* 3.1.55). Although Shakespeare includes none of Henryson's narrative in *Troilus and Cressida*, and avoids the pious judgements of Henryson's poem ('O fals Cresseid, and trew Knicht Troilus', 553), his play consciously reflects and analyses the diminished ethical stature of Cressida and other major characters as they were perceived in the culture of his era. At the same time, we must heed Talbot Donaldson's warning against supposing that such an intelligent reader as Shakespeare would really have supposed *The Testament of Cresseid* to be by Chaucer (since, even in Thynne's combined editions, the narrator plainly speaks of Chaucer as the author of the earlier book, 57–60), or that Shakespeare would have been in any way restricted by a kind of historical determinism into conforming to his sources. Shakespeare made imaginative use of Henryson and the rest, adapting them to his own needs as a dramatist.[3]

Whether Shakespeare garnered much from some contemporary play, such as Chettle and Dekker's lost *Troilus and Cressida*, performed at the Rose by the Admiral's men in April of 1599, or another play on the '*destruction of Troye*' (Stationers' Register, 6 April 1601) that may be Henslowe's *Troy* acted at the Rose in 1596, is a difficult matter to assess. A damaged 'plot' seemingly prepared for the Chettle–Dekker play (or possibly for the *Troy*

---

1   Citations of Henryson are from the 1593 edition. Excerpts are printed by Bullough, *Sources*, 6.215–19. See also Stiller, 43–53.

2   Rollins, *passim*.

3   Donaldson, *Swan*, 75–9, warns against critics like Lawrence, *Problem* ('No other course was open to him [Shakespeare] than to treat Cressida realistically', 167), Phillips, 113–14, and Campbell, 195. See also Sacharoff, 125.

produced by Henslowe in 1596) survives, giving for thirteen scenes the entrances, exits, and names of the characters and of some actors as an outline used to direct performances from behind the scenes. Even this skeletal outline makes clear that the play had a council scene in Troy with ambassadors (Ulysses and Diomed) from the Greeks, evidently dramatizing the episode in Caxton (556–62) or Lydgate (2.6725ff.) in which the Greeks come to negotiate the return of Helen. Other scenes show Troilus with Cressida and Pandarus and 'a waiting maid with a light', Achilles at his tent being wooed unsuccessfully by Ulysses and others until the dead body of Patroclus is brought in by Ajax, Cressida 'with beggars' encountering Troilus (from Henryson's *The Testament of Cresseid*), and various scenes of fighting, including an encounter between Troilus and Diomed and another (presumably fatal) between Achilles and Hector. A dozen or so scenes may be lost. Various actors' names in the 'plot' tend to confirm a date of 1599.[1] The presumption is strong that Shakespeare knew this play and may indeed have been responding to it, in the spirit of rivalry between the Admiral's men and the Lord Chamberlain's men that had encouraged Shakespeare to write *The Merchant of Venice*, *1* and *2 Henry IV* and still more.

Heywood's *The Iron Age*, once tentatively identified with the *Troy* produced by Henslowe in 1596, was probably not written until 1609–10, at least in the version performed in 1612–13, so that it cannot be shown to have influenced Shakespeare.[2] Even so, the resemblances and differences of the two plays give some insight into the seeming vogue of plays on the subject around 1596–1601 and afterwards, and into varying strategies for dramatization on the public stage of classical Greek sources. Conceivably, *The Iron Age* made some use of the lost *Troy* play of 1596 and that of Chettle and Dekker performed in 1599.

---

1    Tatlock, 697–703, and Bullough, 'Lost *TC*'. For reproductions of the 'plot', see 376 n. 1 above (Greg, *Documents*) and Var, 459–61.

2    Var, 462ff.

Heywood's two-part play is the conclusion of a larger project dramatizing ancient mythology and history, beginning with *The Golden Age* (published 1611), *The Silver Age* (1613) and *The Brazen Age* (1613). Subjects range from the lives of Jupiter, Saturn and Hercules to the tragic stories of Proserpine, Meleager, Jason and Medea, and thence to the Trojan war, following the expansive scheme of Caxton and Lydgate, Heywood's main sources.[1]

*The Iron Age, Part I* resembles Shakespeare's play in its combining of material from Caxton with details out of other authors (though not always the same authorities), especially Ovid's *Metamorphoses,* Book 13, for Ajax' madness and suicide, and Greene's *Euphues His Censure to Philautus.* (*Part II*, based in part on Virgil, is not relevant to Shakespeare's play, since it goes on to narrate the fall of Troy, the deaths of Agamemnon and Clytemnestra, and still more.) Various scenes create effects not unlike those in Shakespeare, as when, in *Part I*, Act 1, Cassandra enters the Trojan council meeting '*with her hair about her ears*' (see the same direction at 2.2.96.1 in Shakespeare's play), asking what Troy has deserved that Paris should kindle flames to destroy it. As in Caxton, this scene occurs before the rape of Helen, not during the ensuing war. The action proceeds with Paris' desertion of Oenone, his expedition to Greece, his wooing of the flirtatious Helen, and her consent to an elopement, much to the displeasure of Diomed. Hector disapproves of Paris' expedition, but accepts the result. Thersites is there from the start to leer at the sordid business of war and lechery.

The love story of Troilus and Cressida is interwoven with the war plot. Ajax is something of a comic figure, though tragic in his suicide. At Ajax' encounter with Hector, the latter wishes he could divide the Trojan blood in Ajax' veins from the Greek, so that he could kill the one and not the other (Act 2, p. 299; compare Shakespeare, 4.5.125–36, and Marston's *Antonio's Revenge,*

1  Tatlock, 705–9.

3.3.20–1ff.). Heywood invents a number of scenes, as when Helen is given a chance again to choose between Paris and Menelaus, saying, 'But I'll this way, for Paris kisses sweeter' (Act 3, p. 309). The plays revel in military skirmishing throughout. As in Caxton, Heywood brings on Andromache with her young son, Astyanax, to sway Hector's mind against fighting. Achilles bids his Myrmidons surround Hector and attack him so that Achilles can administer an easy *coup de grâce*.

Thersites' characterization offers the most intriguing resemblances between Heywood's play and Shakespeare's. Thersites' presence on the field of battle in Heywood's play enables him to 'laugh at madmen'. To Troilus, the 'base Thersites' is no more than a coward; to Achilles, whom Thersites rails at, he is 'Dogged Thersites' (Act 4, pp. 325–7). Thersites inveighs comically against 'the crafty fox Ulysses' and 'mad bull Ajax' (Act 5, p. 334); cf. Thersites' reflections on Ulysses as 'that same dog-fox' in Shakespeare, 5.4.10, and on Menelaus as 'the bull', 5.1.53, 5.8.2–4. Heywood's Thersites boasts that he can 'rail . . . better than fight', and 'curse . . . better than either' (p. 342). He calls Ajax 'fool' and 'ass' (p. 342); cf. Shakespeare, 2.1.25–85, 2.3.52–65, 5.1.9 and 57–9. (In Chapman's *Iliads*, 11.485, Ajax is similarly likened to a 'dull mill ass'.) Most suggestively, perhaps, Heywood's Thersites is catechized by Ajax in a wry appraisal of the Grecian high command: 'What's Agamemnon, our great general? . . . Well, and what's Menelaus? . . . Amen. What's Diomed? . . . Amen. Amongst these, what's Thersites?' etc., with opportunities at each question for a witty and censorious sketch (p. 343); cf. Thersites' catechizing in Shakespeare that begins with Achilles' 'Come, what's Agamemnon?', 2.3.40–65. Thersites sums himself up as 'A rogue, a railing rogue, a cur, a barking dog'. In a gloating epilogue, Thersites sums up for the audience the absurdity of tragic action and invites the spectators to rail on him as he has railed at others (p. 345). The characterization exploits the possibilities of satire on the public stage in the late 1590s and afterwards. More broadly, Heywood's and

Shakespeare's free dramatizations of their sources indicate how public dramatists could deal in varying ways with Greek history, much as Shakespeare, Heywood and others had learned to explore English history.

# 'WORDS, WORDS, MERE WORDS': THE TEXT OF *TROILUS AND CRESSIDA*

Two substantive texts of *Troilus and Cressida* survive: the Quarto of 1609 (Q), whose preliminary pages exist in two states, and the Folio of 1623 (F). The play is first mentioned in the Stationers' Register, 7 February 1602/3, in the following entry[1]:

> Ent$^r$ed for his copie in Full Court holden this
> mr day. to print when he hath gotten sufficient
> Robertes. aucthority for yt. The booke of Troilus and
> Cresseda as yt is acted by my lo: Chamb*er*lens
> Men vj$^{:d}$

Once regarded as a 'blocking' entry designed to protect the Lord Chamberlain's men against unauthorized printing of a play they owned, or as a first step towards publication once the company gave its authorization to Roberts as publisher, or possibly both, this entry is instead (as Peter Blayney has shown) one of a large number of such items in the Stationers' Register referring to the necessity of obtaining permission to print from the ecclesiastical authorities. Almost surely the play is Shakespeare's.[2]

---

1 Stationers' Hall, Register C, fol. 91$^v$. See Greg, *Bibliography*, 1.18. The 1608/9 SR entry is in Greg, 1.25.
2 Greg, *TC*, introductory note. The unfounded myths perpetuated by Pollard and others, hypothesizing that stationers who failed to register a play were probably dealing in piratical goods and that registered plays not then published were probably registered to forestall piracy, have been effectively exploded by P. Blayney, 'Publication'.

Despite this Stationers' Register entry in 1603, no copy of an edition prior to 1609 is known to exist. On 28 January 1608/9, a subsequent entry in the Stationers' Register indicates that the play had been reassigned:

Ri.Bonion      Entred for their Copy vnder thandes of
Henry Walleys  m$^r$ Segar deputy to S$^r$ Geo. Bucke and
               m$^r$ war$^d$. Lownes a booke called. The
               history of Troylus and Cressida      vj$^d$
                              (Register C, fol. 178$^v$)

Whether Roberts ever received the 'sufficient aucthority' that was pending in 1603 we do not know, though it is surely significant, as Blayney observes, that Roberts never in fact published a play on his own; he occasionally printed plays for some other stationer, but seems to have been uninterested in taking the commercial risks of publication. His entry may have been designed instead to enable him to resell the property he had acquired. Richard Bonion or Bonian and Henry Walleys or Walley presumably bought Shakespeare's play from Roberts, possibly after they had been unsuccessful in obtaining a copy from the 'grand possessors' whom the dedicatory epistle of the first edition (in its second state) blames for the delay in publication.[1] George Eld printed it for Bonian and Walley in 1609 with the following title-page:

THE / Historie of / Troylus and Cresseida. / *As it was acted* by *the Kings Maiesties* / seruants at the Globe. / *Written by* William Shakespeare. / [ornament] / LON- DON / Imprinted by *G. Eld* for *R. Bonian and H. Walley*, and / are to be sold at the spred Eagle in Paules / Church-yeard, ouer against the / great North doore. / 1609.

This is the so-called first state (Qa). The only difference

---

1 Blayney, 'Publication', and in private communication with the present editor.

between Qa and Qb is in the first two leaves. Qb, published also in 1609, contains a new title-page and a blurb from the publishers to the reader entitled 'A neuer writer, to an euer reader. Newes.' The title-page of the second state reads as follows:

> THE / Famous Historie of / Troylus *and* Cresseid. / *Excellently expressing the beginning* / of their loues, with the conceited wooing / of *Pandarus* Prince of *Licia*. / *Written by* William Shakespeare.

The attribution to Shakespeare and the remainder of the title-page do not differ from that of the first state, and indeed employ the same standing type.

The differences between the two states are striking. The first, using the play title found also in the Stationers' Register entry of 1608/9, proclaims that the play has been acted by the King's men at the Globe Theatre. The second makes no mention of the acting company, and instead offers itself to the reader in literary terms, featuring eloquent expression, a love story and a humorous character (Pandarus) who appears, from this evidence, to have gained the kind of notoriety (not unlike that of Falstaff) that might attract buyers wishing to add the book to their library; compare also Edgar, whose 'sullen and assumed humor of Tom of Bedlam' is offered on the title-page of the 1608 Quarto of *King Lear* as an enticement. The advertisement to the reader in Qb of *Troilus* employs this same vein of literary appeal. Addressed to 'an ever reader' and an 'Eternal reader', this text audaciously insists that the reader is being offered 'a new play, never staled with the stage, never clapper-clawed with the palms of the vulgar'. (See pp. 1–3 for further evidence of the anti-theatrical thrust of this publishers' advertisement.)

Quite possibly, as Richard Dutton has recently argued, the seemingly irreconcilable differences between Qa and Qb reflect diverse impulses in Shakespeare himself. He was a man of the theatre, vitally concerned with producing scripts that his company could mount successfully; at the same time, he must have cared about his plays as works of poetic art to be read and remembered. *Troilus* is the third longest of Shakespeare's plays, and his other long plays, especially *Hamlet* and *King Lear*, exist in far greater length than would have been feasible for public performance. Arguably, Shakespeare wrote them thus because he had something remarkable to say, and may have cared to have them preserved in their entirety for discriminating readers – the sorts of readers appealed to in the Qb advertisement as distinguished from a theatrical audience, of whom Shakespeare sometimes speaks condescendingly (e.g. Hamlet's remark about 'caviare to the general', 2.2.436ff). Perhaps Shakespeare's contractual arrangements with his own company hindered or delayed publication, but we need not assume that he was indifferent to the survival of *Troilus* as he wrote it. Hence, possibly, the duality of Qa and Qb.[1]

The changeover from state one to state two seems to have occurred before the play left Eld's printing shop. Copies survive in which the first version had been printed off before the change took place, giving us the original title-page and no publishers' preface; others give us state two. Paper was sufficiently dear that the cancelled pages would have been sold, especially since the second state was almost certainly printed with the final half-sheet of the play ($M^2$) as a single sheet.[2]

The history of publication of the Folio text of *Troilus and Cressida* is no less unusual and perplexing than that of the Quarto. The play presumably still belonged in 1622–3 to Walley; Bonian was now dead. Perhaps Walley, with unsold copies still on hand of a Quarto that may not have sold particularly well, refused to co-operate with Heminges and Condell in their large task of assembling permission to print the plays that were under copyright.[3] At any rate, this play alone among the thirty-six is

---

1   Dutton, esp. 84.
2   P. Williams, 'Second Issue'; Bowers, 'Evidence'.
3   Blayney, *First Folio*, 17; Greg, *First Folio*, 445.

not even listed in the 'Catalogue' of the Folio. It made its way into the volume belatedly, inserted anomalously between the last of the histories (*Henry VIII*) and the first of the tragedies (*Coriolanus*). This positioning happens to express quite wonderfully the play's ambiguous genre (see p. 3), but cannot have been planned that way. The text of *Troilus and Cressida* begins by numbering its second and third pages as '79' and '80', but then drops any further attempt at this. The play is the only one in the Folio not paginated throughout.

*Troilus and Cressida* was originally to have followed *Romeo and Juliet*. In the published F text, *Romeo and Juliet* ends with the sequence of pages gg1, gg1$^v$, gg2, gg2$^v$, and then gg1 (repeated) with the first page of *Timon of Athens* on gg1$^v$. Yet a surviving single cancelled printed leaf, paged '77' and signed 'gg3', makes clear that in its original setting *Romeo and Juliet* ended on gg3, with *Troilus and Cressida* beginning on the verso side without Prologue and paginated as '78'. The printing of this play got no further at this stage than the next leaf, numbered 79 on its recto side and 80 on its verso. Difficulties then intervened, probably having to do with copyright. The printer, William Jaggard, abandoned *Troilus and Cressida*, and apparently sold a few copies of F with the play simply omitted.[1] Subsequently, once the copyright difficulties had been worked out, he returned to *Troilus and Cressida*, saving intact the leaf that had been paginated as 79–80. He reset the first page of the play from gg3$^v$ (with a few changes in the accidentals) and inserted before it, in an anomalous position, a new Prologue, setting it in large type in order that it might fill the recto side of a new leaf; he needed to begin Act 1 on the verso side in order to save pp. 79–80 intact as the next leaf. As a result, the first two leaves of the play are separate or non-conjugate, having been printed at different

---

1   The unique cancelled leaf is reproduced in Hinman, *Norton Folio*, 916–19. See Dawson, and Greg, 'Printing'. On the copies sold with *Timon* in place of *Troilus*, see Blayney, *First Folio*, 17, 21–4.

# THE TRAGEDIE OF
## Troylus and Cressida.

### *Actus Primus. Scœna Prima.*

*Enter Pandarus and Troylus.*

*Troylus.*

ALl heere my Varlet, Ile vnarme againe.
Why should I warre without the wals of Troy
That finde such cruell Battell heere within?
Each Troian that is master of his heart
Let him to Field, *Troylus* alas hath none.

*Pan.* Will this geere ne're be mended?

*Tro.* The Greeks are strong & skilful to their strength
Fierce to their skill, and to their fiercenesse Valiant ;
But I am weaker then a Womans teare;
Tamer then sleepe, fonder then Ignorance,
Lesse valiant then the Virgin in the night,
And skillesse as vnpractis'd Infancie.

*Pan.* Well, I haue told you enough of this : For my
part, Ile not meddle nor make no farther. Hee that will
haue a Cake out of the Wheate, must needes tarrie the
grinding.

*Troy.* Haue I not tarried?

*Pan.* I the grinding; but you must tarry the boulting.

*Troy.* Haue I not tarried?

*Pan.* I the boulting, but you must tarry the leau'ning.

*Troy.* Still haue I tarried.

*Pan.* I, to the Leauening: but heeres yet in the word
heereafter, the Kneading, the making of the Cake, the
heating the Ouen, and the Baking ; nay, you must stay
the cooling too, or you may chaunce to burne your lips.

*Troy.* Patience her selfe, what Goddesse ere she be,
Doth lesser blench at sufferance, then I do :
At *Priams* Royall Table do I sit,
And when faire *Cressid* comes into my thoughts,
So'(Traitor) then she comes, when she is thence.

*Pan.* Well,
She look'd yesternight fairer, then euer I saw her looke,
Or any woman else.

*Troy.* I was about to tell thee, when my heart,
As wedged with a sigh, would riue in twaine,
Least *Hector*, or my Father should perceiue me :
I haue (as when the Sunne doth light a-scorne)
Buried this sighe, in wrinkle of a Smile :
But sorrow, that is couch'd in seeming Gladnesse,
Is like that myrth, Fate turnes to sodaine Sadnesse.

*Pan.* And her haire were not somewhat darker then
*Helens*, well go too, there were no more comparison betweene the Women. But for my part she is my Kinswoman, I would not (as they terme it) praise it, but I wold

some-body had heard her talke yesterday as I did : I will
not dispraise your sister *Cassandra's* wit, but——

*Troy.* Oh *Pandarus* ! I tell thee *Pandarus*;
When I do tell thee, there my Hopes lye drown'd:
Reply not in how many Fadomes deepe
They lye indrench'd. I tell thee, I am mad
In *Cressids* loue. Thou answer'st she is Faire,
Powr'st in the open Vlcer of my heart,
Her Eyes, her Haire, her Cheeke, her Gate, her Voice,
Handlest in thy discourse. O that her Hand
(In whose comparison, all whites are Inke)
Writing their owne reproach; to whose soft seyzure,
The Cignets Downe is harsh, and spirit of Sense
Hard as the palme of Plough-man. This thou tel'st me,
As true thou tel'st me, when I say I loue her :
But saying thus insteed of Oyle and Balme,
Thou lay'st in euery gash that Loue hath giuen me
The Knife that made it.

*Pan.* I speake no more then truth.

*Troy.* Thou dost not speake so much.

*Pan.* Faith, Ile not meddle in't : Let her be as shee is,
if she be faire, 'tis the better for her : and she be not, she
ha's the mends in her owne hands.

*Troy.* Good *Pandarus* : How now *Pandarus*?

*Pan.* I haue had my Labour for my trauell, ill thought
on of her, and ill thought on of you : Gone betweene &
betweene, but small thankes for my Labor.

*Troy.* What art thou angry *Pandarus*? what with me?

*Pan.* Because she's Kinne to mee, therefore she's not
so faire as *Helen*, and she were Kinne to me, shee would
bee as faire on Friday, as *Helen* is on Sunday. But what
care I? I care not and she were a Black-a-Moore, 'tis all
one to me.

*Troy.* Say I she is not faire.

*Pan.* I do not care whether you doe or no. Shee's a
Foole to stay behinde her Father : Let her to the Greeks,
and so Ile tell her the next time I see her : for my part, Ile
meddle nor make no more i'th'matter.

*Troy. Pandarus.*      *Pan.* Not I.

*Troy.* Sweet *Pandarus*.

*Pan.* Pray you speake no more to me, I will leaue all
as I found it, and there an end.       *Exit Pandar.*

*Sound Alarum.*

*Tr.* Peace you vngracious Clamors, peace rude sounds,
Fooles on both sides, *Helen* must needs be faire,
When with your blood you dayly paint her thus.
I cannot fight vpon this Argument :

It

# THE TRAGEDIE OF
## Troylus and Cressida.

### *Actus Primus.*  *Scœna Prima.*

*Enter Pandarus and Troylus.*

*Troylus.*

Call here my Varlet, Ile vnarme againe.
Why should I warre without the wals of Troy
That finde such cruell batteil here within?
Each Troian that is master of his heart,
Let him to field, *Troylus* alas hath none.

*Pan.* Will this geere nere be mended?

*Troy.* The Greeks are strong,& skilful to their strength,
Fierce to their skill,and to their fiercenesse Valiant:
But I am weaker then a womans teare;
Tamer then sleepe,fonder then ignorance;
Lesse valiant then the Virgin in the night,
And skillesse as vnpractis'd Infancie.

*Pan.* Well, I haue told you enough of this: For my
part, Ile not meddle nor make no farther. Hee that will
haue a Cake out of the Wheate, must needes tarry the
grinding.

*Troy.* Haue I not tarried?

*Pan.* I the grinding; but you must tarry the bolting.

*Troy.* Haue I not tarried?

*Pan.* I the boulting; but you must tarry the leau'ing.

*Troy.* Still haue I tarried.

*Pan.* I, to the leauening: but heeres yet in the word
hereafter, the Kneading, the making of the Cake, the
heating of the Ouen, and the Baking; nay, you must stay
the cooling too,or you may chance to burne your lips.

*Troy.* Patience her selfe, what Goddesse ere she be,
Doth lesser blench at sufferance,then I doe:
At *Priams* Royall Table doe I sit;
And when faire *Cressid* comes into my thoughts,
So (Traitor) then she comes,when she is thence.

*Pan.* Well?
She look'd yesternight fairer,then euer I saw her looke,
Or any woman else.

*Troy.* I was about to tell thee,when my heart,
As wedged with a sigh, would riue in twaine,
Least *Hector,*or my Father should perceiue me:
I haue (as when the Sunne doth light a-scorne)
Buried this sigh,in wrinkle of a smile:
But sorrow,that is couch'd in seeming gladnesse,
Is like that mirth,Fate turnes to sudden sadnesse.

*Pan.* And her haire were not somewhat darker then
*Helens,*well go too, there were no more comparison betweene the Women. But for my part she is my Kinswoman, I would not (as they tearme it) praise it,but I wold

some-body had heard her talke yesterday as I did; I will
not dispraise your sister *Cassandra's* wit, but——

*Troy.* Oh *Pandarus*! I tell thee *Pandarus*;
When I doe tell thee,there my hopes lye drown'd:
Reply not in how many Fadomes deepe
They lye indrench'd. I tell thee, I am mad
In *Cressids* loue. Thou answer'st she is Faire,
Powr'st in the open Vlcer of my heart,
Her Eyes, her Haire,her Cheeke,her Gate,her Voice,
Handlest in thy discourse. O that her Hand
(In whose comparison,all whites are Inke)
Writing their owne reproach; to whose soft seizure,
The Cignets Downe is harsh,and spirit of Sense
Hard as the palme of Plough-man. This thou tel'st me;
As true thou tel'st me, when I say I loue her:
But saying thus,insteadof Oyle and Balme,
Thou lai'st in euery gash that loue hath giuen me,
The Knife that made it.

*Pan.* I speake no more then truth.

*Troy.* Thou do'st not speake so much.

*Pan.* Faith, Ile not meddle in't: Let her be as shee is,
if she be faire, 'tis the better for her ; and she be not, she
ha's the mends in her owne hands.

*Troy.* Good *Pandarus* : How now *Pandarus*?

*Pan.* I haue had my Labour for my trauell,ill though-
on of her, and ill thought on of you : Gone betweene and
betweene,but small thankes for my labour.

*Troy.* What art thou angry *Pandarus*? what with me?

*Pan.* Because she's Kinne to me, therefore shee's not
so faire as *Helen,* and she were not kin to me, she would
be as faire on Friday, as *Helen* is on Sunday. But what
care I? I care not and she were a Black-a-Moore, 'tis all
one to me.

*Troy.* Say I she is not faire?

*Troy.* I doe not care whether you doe or no. She's a
Foole to stay behinde her Father : Let her to the Greeks,
and so Ile tell her the next time I see her : for my part,Ile
meddle nor make no more i'ch'matter.

*Troy.* Pandarus?   *Pan.* Not I.

*Troy.* Sweete *Pandarus.*

*Pan.* Pray you speake no more to me, I will leaue all
as I found it,and there an end.   *Exit Pand.*

*Sound Alarum.*

*Tro.* Peace you vngracious Clamors,peace rude sounds,
Fooles on both sides, *Helen* must needs be faire,
When with your bloud you daily paint her thus.
I cannot fight vpon this Argument:

16   The reset and enlarged version of the Folio first page of *Troilus and Cressida*,
backing a 'Prologue' to *Troilus and Cressida*

404

times. Neither bears a signature; for purposes of reference they are designated as χ1 and χ2.[1] The remainder of *Troilus and Cressida*, set without pagination, is signed with the anomalous signatures ¶ 1–6, ¶¶ 1–6, and ¶¶¶.

Jaggard's first three pages of *Troilus and Cressida*, completed at an early stage before he ran into difficulties, simply reprint the Quarto text with minor variants in the accidentals and correction of a few 'obvious' errors. When he returned to his task shortly before F was published, on the other hand, he had acquired new material. Already in possession of a copy of Q, he now had access to a manuscript that could be used to mark up a copy of Q for the compositors, or a marked copy of Q already annotated with reference to such a manuscript by Hemings or Condell or some other person serving in an editorial function.[2] Printers like to follow printed copy. The annotation supplied only a few additions of two to five lines, and even fewer deletions, which did not significantly augment or cut the Q text. At the same time, the annotation made for a lot of smaller changes, freely substituting words and phrases throughout.[3]

The Q text seems to have been set by formes, with casting off of printer's copy – that is, the dividing of the copy into stints estimated to suffice for each page of type. Three compositors

1  Ard², 4; Hinman, *Printing*, 1.27–8, 2.261–4 and 335.
2  Alexander, '*TC*', confirmed with further documentation by P. Williams, '*TC*'. Williams's proofs are instances where the F reading reproduces peculiarities in Q that must have originated in Eld's printing shop: idiosyncratic uses of roman or italic type, anomalous speech-heading forms, and spellings that appear to override the compositors' own preferences. See Cam¹, 123ff.
3  Palmer's speculation (Ard², 4) that since Jaggard had acquired Roberts's publishing business some time around 1608, he might have acquired manuscript material that would enable him to claim independent title to *TC* on the basis of the SR entry of 1602/3 and thus evade the difficulties presumably imposed by Walley, has been refuted by Blayney, 'Publication'; see p. 399 n. 1 above. Palmer's hypothesis does not explain why Jaggard would have begun work on the F text in 1622–3 with an unaltered Q text rather than with this purported Roberts manuscript; nor is it clear that the company of Stationers would have awarded title to Bonian and Walley in 1608/9 unless Roberts's claim was seen to have lapsed or been superseded, in which case the emergence in 1622 of a somewhat altered text would have provided a flimsy justification at best for a reclaiming of copyright.

appear to have shared the work. The stints of Eld A and B have been identified on the basis of spellings like Cressid/Cresseid, Cressida/Cresseida, Hellen/Helen, shalbe/shall be, wilbe/will be, ritch/rich and els/else, together with Eld A's preference for colons in place of full stops and his predilection for question marks. Eld A's share is as follows: 1.1 and all of 1.2 except for the last ten lines, 1.3.296 through 2.2.103, 2.3.204–3.1.98, 3.3.51–4.1.46 ('wherefore'), 4.3.4–4.5.137, 4.5.290–5.2.128, 5.2.167 to end of scene and 5.4.24 to the end of the play.[1] The rest belongs to Eld B except for sheet F, where an inexperienced compositor, Eld C, appears to have set type for 3.1.97 through 3.3.50. These divisions correspond to pages in Q: Eld A set from the play's beginning through B2$^v$, C3–D2$^v$, E3–E4$^v$, all of G, H3–I2$^v$, K–K3$^v$, K4$^v$, and L3 to the end of the play.[2]

The Q text bears many features of what Greg and others in the tradition of the 'new bibliography' call a 'foul paper' text – that is, a play presumably based on an authorial manuscript containing handwritten cancellations and interpolations (of which the degree of readability might vary considerably) and not yet regularized by the acting company for theatrical production. The label itself is suspect, since, as Paul Werstine has shown, no extant play manuscript of the era consistently demonstrates the features of so-called 'foul papers' throughout, whereas, conversely, vague, misplaced or missing stage directions are fairly

---

1  Cam$^1$, 129–31. See MacD. Jackson, confirming the spelling habits of Eld A and B by an examination of their work on the *Sonnets*, also in 1609. Jackson adds other spelling differences, such as Oh/O and dost/doost. Ard$^2$ provides evidence for casting off of copy (crowding, wasting of space, shortage of sorts, etc.) in App. 1, 304–6.
2  See Ard$^2$, 304–6, for the evidence establishing Eld C's identity, adding the spellings ticle / tickle, bucle / buckle, himself / him-self, -y / -ie, -'d / -d, Cress. / Cres, and *Vlyss. / Vlys.* as ways of discriminating this compositor. The evidence does not, however, lend any real support to Palmer's hypothesis that sheet F incorporates some newly introduced fresh copy. The simpler and more consistent hypothesis is that a third, less experienced worker was given the job of setting sheet F. The contention of Bowers ('Evidence') and Hinman (*Printing*, 1.40ff.) that a schedule of composition and presswork was established for each book going through a printing house has been effectively dismantled by McKenzie and by Blayney, *Texts of 'Lear'*, 53–7.

common in play-texts that show other signs of having been put to theatrical use. Playwrights and players often collaborated in the complex process by which a theatrical text came into being, so that the very notion of an original script that was the author's alone may be seriously misleading. The difficulty is compounded in the case of *Troilus and Cressida* by uncertainties as to whether Q shows signs of having been printed from a scribal transcript.[1] Even so, we need to take account of certain characteristics in Q that may have originated with the author as he worked on his play.

Stage directions essential to the management of stage action are frequently missing.[2] Most but not all of these omissions are remedied in F. The Q stage direction at 3.3.37.1, 'Achilles *and* Patro *stand in their Tent*', is clear enough in intent, but is less theatrically couched than F's '*Enter* Achilles *and* Patroclus *in their Tent*'. Important exits are missing in Q on at least twenty-two occasions. The Q text seems only sporadically interested in specifying sound effects.[3] Q is not without some indications of this

1  Walker's thesis (*Textual*, 76ff.) that Q was based on a transcript of Shakespeare's papers rather than on those papers themselves depends in good part on mistaken assumptions of error in Q's assignment of speech prefixes; see especially the textual and commentary notes of this present edition at 3.1.82 and 5.2.87–8, where Q's speech prefixes make better sense than Walker supposed. Even those in error are ascribable to a compositor dealing with a difficult manuscript rather than requiring the thesis of a scribal copy. Nosworthy (65ff.) argues that at least one Q compositor was capable of sophistications that would account for some features that Walker regards as evidence of transcription. Taylor, '*TC*', argues that many Q misreadings are perfectly normal if we assume that the compositor was working directly from an authorial manuscript (107). On the other hand, extant scribal transcripts display some of the features of Q *TC* that are often explained with the hypothesis of 'foul' papers. On this matter and on the uncertainties of Chambers's and Greg's labels for manuscript copy (Chambers, *Shakespeare*, 1.126–204, Greg, *Editorial Problem*, and Greg, *First Folio*), see Werstine, 'Foul Papers', 'Narratives' and 'Plays in Manuscript'; and Long, 'Stage-Directions' and 'A bed'. Paul Werstine has read a draft of this textual introduction and has given me invaluable criticism on it.
2  Entrances are lacking in Q for Pandarus at 1.2.35.1, 3.2.27.1 and 95.1; for common soldiers at 1.2.231.1; for Aeneas at 1.3.214.1; for Achilles and Patroclus at 2.1.52.1; for five Grecian lords at 4.4.105.1–2; for Diomedes at 4.5.88.1; for Diomedes and Troilus at 5.4.16.1–2; and for Hector at 5.6.12.1.
3  A sennet is missing in Q at 1.3.0.1, a tucket at 1.3.212, music sounding within at 3.1.0.1, a trumpet signal at 4.4.138.2 and an alarum at 5.4.0.1, all of which are provided in F.

sort, as at 1.1.84.1 and 100.1, and 1.3.259.1, but their deploy-
ment is sparse.

Q contains occasional vaguenesses as to who is to come on
stage and who is to speak. For example, the Greek generals enter
at 1.3.0 '*with others*'; at 4.5.0.1–3, their names are followed by
'*&c.*' and at 5.10.0.1–2 by '*the rest, marching*'. '*All of Troy*' enter
at 4.5.64.1, without indication as to who is to be included in this
roster. *Exits* and *Exeunts* in Q are sometimes imprecise about
which persons among a group of characters on stage are to leave.
Against this evidence, however, we must note that F too is occasionally vague in its stage directions. Perhaps Nosworthy is right
in supposing that Shakespeare had a major hand in supplying
the amended stage action featured in F.[1]

Imprecisely placed stage directions are common in Q.[2] On the
other hand, stage directions in all sorts of extant manuscripts
can be found in the margins, sometimes in the hands of book-
keepers, without care as to their precise locations in relation to
the dialogue they govern, so that the appearance of misplaced
stage directions in Q of *Troilus and Cressida* is not conclusive evidence of so-called 'foul papers'. Several misplaced stage
directions in Q remain unaltered in F.

Speech prefixes in Q are at times vague and imprecise. '*One*'
must stand for a Myrmidon at 5.9.16. Q often omits speech prefixes, as at 2.1.37 ff., where several omissions of speech prefixes
for Thersites and Ajax make jibberish of their exchange of
insults; or at 1.3.304–9, where a speech of Agamemnon's is

1 Other imprecise SDs in Q include 4.5.64.1, 3.3.0.1–2, 4.1.0.1, 5.1.46 and 64.3 and
 5.1.85.1; vaguenesses occur in F at 4.4.104.1–2 and 4.5.159.1. The lack of a clear
 distinction between Q and F in regard to imprecise stage directions illustrates the
 sorts of problems that Paul Werstine finds with Greg's labels of 'foul papers' and
 'prompt-books'; see p. 407 n. 1 and Werstine, 'Plays in Manuscript'. Walker contrasts the occasional vaguenesses in F SDs with those of *Lear* as part of her
 argument that the manuscript used to annotate Q in order to produce copy for F was
 'Shakespeare's foul papers' (*Textual*, 73ff.). Nosworthy, while stressing the revision-
 ary nature of F resulting from changing theatrical circumstances, believes that many
 F stage directions may be authorial (79–80). See also Bjelland, 'Analytical'.
2 See, e.g., 3.3.241.1, 4.5.35.1 and 40, 5.5.45 and 5.6.22, and Honigmann, 'Re-enter',
 117–18.

printed as a continuation of what Ulysses has just been saying. Q often deploys an entry stage direction as though it were also a speech prefix: for example, '*Enter Cress.* How now?' (4.2.79), '*Enter Aiax. Troylus*, thou coward *Troylus*' (5.5.43) and similarly at 5.6.1–2 and 14 and at 5.7.1. F provides both entry direction and speech prefix; whatever the motive that lay behind this consistent pattern of alteration, it does make the F script more immediately clear for actors as well as readers. Paul Werstine, to be sure, shows that omitted speech prefixes can be a result of theatrical annotation, but his cited example from the playbook of *Charlemagne* shows that the theatrical annotator omitted a speech prefix by mistake, whereas the pattern in *Troilus and Cressida* is repeated fairly consistently.[1] Genuine errors in speech prefixes are not infrequent, as when Q's '*Vlysses*' at 4.5.96 is an error (corrected in F) resulting from the inadvertent omission of a line of dialogue in Q. (See also 2.3.250–1n. and 5.3.23.)

Lineation in Q often suggests reliance on a manuscript that crowded its material and was hard to interpret metrically. Verse is sometimes turned into prose and prose into verse.[2] Quite frequently, dialogue that seems intended for division into pentameter lengths and half-lines is run on in a single line in Q, turned over if necessary but in such a way as to save space.[3] Inset verse is sometimes doubled up in its lineation, as in Pandarus' love song at 3.1.110–13. At 5.2.181–3, Q crowds two and a half lines of pentameter verse into two hypermetric lines.

Q is not always deficient in matters that, in Greg's hypothesis differentiating 'prompt copy' from 'foul paper' text, the bookkeeper would presumably care about. Its speech prefixes are quite regular and consistent. The minor variations we find in the abbreviations are simply a matter of the extent of

---

1 Werstine, 'Foul Papers', 246 n.15.
2 See 1.3.1–2, 2.3.190–1, 4.1.35–6, 4.4.14–19 and 5.1.75–6; and 3.1.64–7.
3 E.g., 2.2.51–2, 2.3.190–1, 3.3.171–2, 4.4.65–6, 4.5.39–40, 225–6, 232–3 and 267–70, 5.1.45–6, 5.2.130–1 and 5.5.41–2.

abbreviation.[1] Generic names are not used except for Priam's illegitimate son Margareton, who is called 'Bastard' in stage directions and speech prefixes at 5.8.5–15. We are a far distance from the 1599 (second) Quarto of *Romeo and Juliet*, with its *La.*, *Wife*, and *Mo.* for Capulet's Wife, or the 1598 Quarto of *Love's Labour's Lost*, with its shifting back and forth between proper names like *Armado*, *Nathaniel* and *Holofernes* and generic names like *Braggart*, *Curate* and *Pedant*. Such features, often cited as evidence of 'foul papers', are missing in Q of *Troilus and Cressida*, and would seem to confirm once again Werstine's wariness of sharp distinctions between 'foul papers' and 'prompt-book copy'. Similarly obscuring the presumed difference in types of copy is the fact that Q is not without practical stage directions and adept lineation. All seems well within the capabilities of the author, however, and we find very little if anything that needs to be explained by the hypothesis of a bookkeeper's ministrations. Some Shakespearean spellings and punctuation may have survived the compositors' imposition of their own spelling predilections, such as *shrike* (F: 'shreeke') at 2.2.97.[2] Occasional apparent misreadings that suggest authorial errors that have made their way into Q (and in some instances into F as well) additionally confirm the case for an authorial manuscript or transcript of such a manuscript as printer's copy for Q.

The F text contains many characteristics suggesting that it was based upon an exemplar of Q annotated with reference to a manuscript that had been put to use in the theatre, as we have already seen in comparing Q with F, assuming too that Shakespeare himself may have provided some of the augmented F stage

---

1   *Tro. Troy. Troyl.*; *Cres. Cress.*; *Pand. Pan.*; *AEne. Aeneas. Eneas.*; *Ulisses. Vlysses. Uliss. Vliss. Vlis. Uli.*; *Nestor. Nest.*; *Agamem. Agam. Aga.*; *Aiax. Aia.*; *Diom. Dio. Diomed.*; *Achil. Achill. Ach.*; *Patro. Patrocl. Patr.*; *Hec. Hect.*; *Priam. Pria.*; *Paris. Par.*; *Cass. Cas.*; *Hel. Hell.*

2   Honigmann, *Stability*, esp. 88–9, pointing also to 'shrike' at 2.2.210 (F: 'strike') and 'shriking' at 3.3.142 (F: 'shrinking'). The spelling also occurs, as Honigmann points out, in Q2 and F of *RJ*, at 4.3.47 ('shrikes') and 5.3.190 ('shrike'), and Q and F of *MND*, 1.2.70 ('shrike').

directions.[1] Many substantive differences in wording between F and Q can best be explained as authorial revision. No editor, scribe, annotator or compositor would undertake to exchange 'shew our fowlest Wares' (the F reading) for 'First shew foule wares' (Q), nor 'yet to shew, / Shal shew the better' for 'shall exceed, / By shewing the worse first', in a rewritten passage at 1.3.358–63. Can we tell, however, which is the earlier version and which is the revision? The passages follow a speech by Nestor in which Q fails to give the final three lines found in F (355–7). Conceivably Q's version could represent a cut, but it is no less probable that F provides new material omitted by Q in error or added as revision in F. The argument of priority is reversible when we consider these lines by themselves. Herein lies the greatest difficulty in understanding the textual history of *Troilus and Cressida*, and it is one on which textual scholars continue to disagree.

Whatever the nature of priority in the rival claims of Q and F, the revision throughout *Troilus and Cressida* is notable for its limited scale. As in the example cited above, it generally keeps its material to the same number of lines. It substitutes, rearranges and shifts emphasis, but does so in the same allotted space. Often single words are substituted on a basis of one for one or nearly so: suchlike / so forth (1.2.245–6), silly / awkward (1.3.149), worthy / noble (2.2.86) and many more.[2] Longer substitutions preserve not only metre but sentence structure and grammatical relationship: influence of euill Planets / ill Aspects of Planets

---

1 The differences in speech prefixes between F and Q are so minor, and attributable to compositors' work, that they do not bear on the question of F's theatrical provenance. See P. Williams, '*TC*', 139–40. Godshalk argues that the F compositors were working not with an annotated exemplar of Q but with a manuscript and an unannotated exemplar of Q, or with a scribal fair copy prepared in the same manner.

2 See also broad / lowd (1.3.27), right / just (1.3.164), eyes / ears (1.3.219), couple / compass (1.3.276), hoste / mould (1.3.293), for-fend / forbid (1.3.302) keeping / holding (2.2.52), attributiue / inclinable (2.2.58), notable / noble (3.1.6), ayming / shining (3.3.101), turne / hedge (3.3.159), Lul'd / But (4.1.18), soyle / soilure (4.1.58), tediously / hideously (4.2.14), shrupd / hem'd (4.5.194), we / you (4.5.272), sing / finde (5.2.12), Cliff / life (5.2.13), giuen / bound (5.2.167), proud / vile (5.11.23), lou'd / desir'd (5.11.39), etc. (These examples all give the Q reading followed by the F reading.)

euill (1.3.92), and so on.[1] The pattern of revision is not unlike that in *Othello*, a play that is increasingly viewed as one in which Shakespeare changed some words and phrases when he made a copy of his own earlier draft.[2]

It is as though Shakespeare, having occasion to write out a new script for his acting company, or perhaps for an influential patron, was not content merely to copy what he had written before; his active poetic intelligence led him to substitute what seemed to him more felicitous phrases. The situation is generally not, however, like that of *Hamlet* or *Lear*, where Quarto and Folio differ in the addition or deletion of lengthy passages that could have been variously caused by shortening for performance, censorship or authorial reimagining of his play and its characters.[3] Even the longest passages occurring in F alone – five lines each at 1.3.70–4, 2.3.53–7 and 4.4.143–7 – can be taken to be the result of Q's having inadvertently or deliberately omitted some material or of F's containing dialogue added in revision, since both texts make sense as they stand; the second of these comes at a scene end that terminates plausibly in both Q and F. Two 3-line passages in F alone, at 3.3.162–4 and 5.3.20–2, are similarly explicable either as F additions or as Q cuts, though the latter of these significantly omits a speech prefix for Cassandra in the Q version, thus misassigning a speech and suggesting that the omission here in Q is not felicitous or deliberate. Here and in other instances, we need to remember that subjective grounds for comparison of variant readings are notoriously untrustworthy.

---

1  See also: my withered brawnes / this wither'd brawne (1.3.297), for the better / as the worthier (1.3.378), of the Prouer / to the creator (2.3.64), course, and time / pettish lines (2.3.128), streame of his commencement / carriage of this action (2.3.129), My very soul of councell / My soule of counsell from me (3.2.129), deserues faire *Helen* best / merits fair *Helen* most (4.1.55), etc.

2  Honigmann, ed., *Oth*, Ard[3], 354ff., and *Texts*. Stanley Wells places more stress on authorial revision (*TxC*, 476–7) than does Honigmann, but common ground is discernible that allows Shakespeare to have done some rewriting as he copied.

3  See Urkowitz, Taylor & Warren, Honigmann, *Texts* and *Oth*, Ard[3], and Weis. On the speculation that Shakespeare may have chosen on some occasions to present a manuscript copy to some wealthy patron, and that such a copy could serve as the basis for a printed edition, see Love, 67–8, and Werstine, 'Plays in Manuscript'.

In most of their many differences, Q and F seem more or less equally satisfactory and plausible.

Only two 2-line passages occur in Q and not in F, at 2.1.27–8 and 3.3.106–7. The first of these is a single sentence at the end of Thersites' speech, easily overlooked by the F compositor. The second instance occurs only one line from the bottom of the right-hand column of sig. ¶6ᵛ in F, and truncates the sense of Achilles' speech about the eye's inability to behold itself, strongly suggesting an omission of casting off or other oversight; this was the last forme of gathering ¶ to be set. Other omissions in F are few in number and generally involve single words or short phrases (1.2.265, 1.3.250, 2.1.6, 3.1.83, 4.3.9, 4.5.263). We can say with some assurance, then, that F is slightly the fuller text, and that its relatively few omissions of material found in Q alone are sometimes explicable as errors in transmission. At the same time, the possibility remains that Q's omissions represent cutting and that the many verbal differences between Q and F are the result of a revision that reveals its latter state in Q. We need to review editorial conjectures about the nature of the copy lying behind Q and F in order to define as clearly as we can the issues of debate.

Our narrative begins with E. K. Chambers's hypothesis, promulgated in 1930 and widely accepted until recently (and anticipated in part by Peter Alexander in 1928–9), that most of F was set from a copy of Q that had been annotated by reference to Shakespeare's original manuscript and that Q was printed from a transcript of author's papers containing some later thoughts by the dramatist. Chambers thus saw no reason to accept F. J. Furnivall's hypothesis that F incorporates some alterations by Shakespeare that postdate the Q text.[1] Chambers

---

1 Chambers, *Shakespeare,* 1.438–49, taking issue with Furnivall and Munro. Alexander, '*TC*', 274, anticipates one of Chambers's main points in 1929 by arguing that Q gives us a later draft of the play than that used to correct a copy of Q for the F text, using the example from the end of 5.3 and 5.11.32–4 to argue that the first version is Shakespeare's first thought. Walker, *Textual,* agrees with Chambers's position, as do Honigmann, *Stability,* Nosworthy and some others.

based his argument especially on two passages. The first is at 4.5.97–109, where F twice gives to Ulysses' speech in praise of Troilus the phrase, 'They call him *Troylus*'. Q gives the phrase only once, at 109. Chambers argued that the duplication in F provides evidence of F's having been set from an original authorial manuscript, giving us a first shot and second thought. Yet such a theory does not well explain the metrical anomalies of line 97 in F. Q's version is metrically regular:

*Vlis*. The yongest sonne of *Priam*, a true knight,

whereas F's version is printed in two lines:

*Vlis*. The yongest Sonne of *Priam*;
A true Knight; they call him *Troylus*.

In both texts, the line at 109 is well integrated into the blank verse: 'They call him *Troylus*; and on him erect, / A second hope', etc. Q's text is the more consistent in metrical terms and in resolving or avoiding duplication. F's arrangement might then be an imperfect attempt at revision, since it is hard to imagine why, if it were the earlier version, it would begin so irregularly. Conceivably, as Chambers hypothesizes, Shakespeare wrote 'The youngest son of Priam; they call him Troilus' and then decided to reserve the second phrase for later in the speech, inserting 'A true knight' instead at line 97 and marking 'they call him Troilus' with a mark of deletion that the printer later failed to observe, but the hypothesis is a very speculative one on which to base a whole theory of Q's being the later version. Why would the supposed scribe of the copy to be used in printing Q observe correctly a deletion mark that was then missed by the F annotator?[1]

Q shows us a reading so complete in itself as to suggest that the original rhetorical strategy of the speech might have been to

---

1 Honigmann, *Stability*, 95. Honigmann's thesis ('Date and Revision', 46) that the eleven lines between the repeated 'they call him Troilus' were an insertion at some point after original composition would account for the duplication and would encourage an editor to select only one, plausibly the second.

delay 'They call him *Troylus*' until line 109. Perhaps we should regard the use of the phrase at 97 as an insertion introduced by some corrector or copier, or a player, acting hastily in error or else wishing to identify Troilus by name early in the speech.[1] Even if that were the case, we have the awkwardnesses of F suggesting that the change was *ad hoc* and that Q might well represent a more coherent form of what Shakespeare wrote. In any event, the duplication in F need not be read as evidence that the first 'They call him *Troylus*' was the author's first thought and that accordingly F's variants generally precede those of Q. The point here is not to insist on the priority of either Q or F but rather to argue that Chambers's case of first shots and second

---

1  W. G. Clark and W. A. Wright, in Cam, argue that the insertion in F of a second 'They call him *Troylus*' was probably the work of a hasty corrector. Most editors have found Q's version the more satisfactory.

Vlyfses : what Troyan is that fome that lookes fo heauy?
  Vlif. The yongeft fonne of *Priam*, a true knight,
Not yet mature, yet match'effe firme of word,
Speaking deeds, and deedleffe in his tongue,
Not foone prouok t nor beeing prouok't foone calm'd,
His heart and hand both open and both free.

          I 2                  For

For what he has he giues, what thinkes he fhewes,
  Yet giues hee not till iudgement guide his bounty,
Nor dignifies an impare thought with breath;
Manly as *Hettor*, but more dangerous,
For *Hettor* in his blaze of wrath fubfcribes
To tender obiects, but he in heate of action,
Is more vindicatiue then iealous loue.
They call him *Troylus*, and on him erect,
A fecond hope as fairely built as *Hettor*:
Thus faies *Æneas* one that knowes the youth,
Euen to his ynches : and with priuate foule
Did in great Illion thus tranflate him to me.      *Alarum*,

---

17  4.5.97–109, as printed in the 1609 Quarto

thoughts is not a strong instance upon which to generalize about the prior composition of F throughout.

Chambers's second instance is at the end of 5.3, where F completes the scene with a three-line passage that also appears, slightly altered, at 5.11.32–4. The F version in 5.3 reads as follows:

> *Pand.* Why, but heare you?
> *Troy.* Hence brother lackie; ignomie and shame
>       Pursue thy life, and liue aye with thy name.

The version found in 5.11 in F and Q differs chiefly in its superior reading of 'broker' for 'brother' in line 2 of the passage ('brother', the commoner word, probably representing an error of

> *Aga.* What Troian is that fame that lookes fo heauy?
>  *Vlif.* The yongeft Sonne of *Priam* ;
> A true Knight; they call him *Troylus* ;
> Not yet mature, yet matchleffe,firme of word,
> Speaking in deedes, and deedeleffe in his tongue ;
> Not foone prouok'c, nor being prouok't,foone calm'd ;
> His heart and hand both open,and both free :
> For what he has, he giues ; what thinkes,he fhewes ;
> Yet giues he not till iudgement guide his bounty,
> Nor dignifies an impaire thought with breath :
> Manly as *Hector*, but more dangerous ;
> For *Hector* in his blaze of wrath fubfcribes
> To tender obiects ; but he,in heate of action,
> Is more vindecatiue then iealous loue.
> They call him *Troylus* ; and on him erect,
> A fecond hope, as fairely built as *Hector*.
> Thus faies *Æneas*, one that knowes the youth,
> Euen to his inches : and with priuate foule,

18   4.5.97–109, as printed in the 1623 Folio

416

transmission). Both F and Q then complete the play with a wry comic epilogue delivered by Pandarus alone on stage.

Chambers again saw this disparity between Q and F as evidence that F was based on an original authorial manuscript giving us Shakespeare's first shot at the end of 5.3, whereas the version found in Q as well as in F at 5.11.32–4 is the author's second thought. Alice Walker agreed with him in 1957,[1] and for some decades the Q text was regarded as the more authoritative throughout. More recently (1982), Gary Taylor has countered with a demonstration that Chambers's key evidence is reversible. While conceding that his own explanation is 'as subjective and literary as Chambers's' (102), Taylor does indeed show that the first appearance of the duplicate ending for Pandarus (at the end of 5.3) can plausibly be read not as Shakespeare's first shot but as a revision designed to conclude Pandarus' deteriorating

---

1 Cam[1], 206 n. 96. Godshalk hypothesizes that the double rejection may have been intentional and dramatically effective.

---

*The history*

*Pand.* Do you heere my Lord, do you heere.
*Troyl.* What now ?
*Pand;* Heer's a letter come from yond poore girle,
*Troy.* Let me read,
*Pand.* A whorſon tiſick , a whorſon raſcally tiſick , ſo troubles me, and the fooliſh fortune of this girle, and what one thing, what another ; that I ſhall leaue you one ath's dayes : and I haue a rheume in mine eyes too , a d ſuch an ache in my bones, that vnleſſe a man were curſt I cannot tell what to thinke on't. What ſayes ſhe there ?
*Troy.* Words, words, meere words, no matter fró the heart, Th'effect doth operate another way.
Go winde to winde, there turne and change together :
My loue with words and errors ſtill ſhe feedes,
But edifies another with her deedes.          *Exeunt.*

---

19 5.3.107ff. as printed in the 1609 Quarto, lacking the three lines that appear in 5.3 of the Folio (see Fig. 20); both Q and F print essentially the same lines at 5.11.32–4

relationship with Troilus at this point and subsequently allow
the play to end on Troilus' bitter note of revenge and inward woe
for the death of Hector (5.11.4–31). The argument is useful to
the important extent of showing that the repeated phrases, upon
which Chambers bases his theory of Q as the later version, can
be read in an opposite way. Chambers's hypothesis 'has no claim
to bibliographical objectivity' (102).[1]

The main vulnerability of Taylor's argument, as he concedes,
is that his counterclaim that F gives us Shakespeare's revision
depends in good part on literary judgements. As Phebe Jensen
sees it, Taylor's championing of F serves 'a larger interpretive
end', one that views *Troilus and Cressida* as a play originally

1   Taylor, '*TC*'; *TxC*, 425, 437–8.

---

*Pand.* A whorſon tiſicke, a whorſon raſcally tiſicke,
ſo troubles me; and the fooliſh fortune of this girle, and
what one thing, what another, that I ſhall leaue you one
o'th's dayes : and I haue a rheume in mine eyes too; and
ſuch an ache in my bones ; that vnleſſe a man were curſt,
I cannot tell what to thinke on't.   What ſayes ſhee
there ?
   *Troy.*   Words, words, meere words , no matter from
    the hart ;
Th'effect doth operate another way.
Goe winde to winde, there turne and change together :
My loue with words and errors ſtill ſhe feedes ;
But edifies another with her deedes.
   *Pand.* Why, but heare you ?
   *Troy.* Hence brother lackie ; ignomie and ſhame
Purſue thy life, and liue aye with thy name.
        *A Larum.*                    *Exeunt.*

20   5.3.107ff. as printed in the 1623 Folio, containing three lines (the last three
     lines in this excerpt) that do not appear in 5.3 of the Quarto (see Fig. 19)

written for the Inns of Court and then revised for a more public audience at the Globe, thereby turning a play that was essentially satiric and comic into a tragic vision. Q represents the author's 'original intention', F his 'final thoughts'. In relegating to an appendix of 'Additional Passages' the ending that is printed in both Q and F, Taylor is obliged to rely on a hypothesis of deletion marks that went unobserved and (in Jensen's view) on circular reasoning, using the theory of Inns of Court performance to explain the presence of the ending and justifying its removal largely on the grounds of a supposed public performance.[1] Taylor's thesis motivates him to imagine how the F stage directions can be made to work at virtually all points, even when they are highly problematic; see, for example, 4.4.48 and 4.5.89ff.

Taylor is not the first scholar to view the epilogue as an interpolation and to suppose that Pandarus was originally dismissed at the end of 5.3 so that the play could end without him; W. S. Walker made this point in 1860, H. N. Hudson agreed with him in 1881, and J. M. Nosworthy skilfully argued in 1965 that the apparent duplication in F 'merely provides for an alternative ending to the play'.[2] Conceivably, Shakespeare might have written the play originally with the dismissal of Pandarus in 5.3,

---

1   Jensen criticizes Taylor, '*TC*', but generally accepts his argument that the MS used to correct Q for the F copy was a theatrical script, and quite possibly the playbook itself, in which circumstance the authority of F must be given serious consideration.

2   W. S. Walker, 3.203–4; Hudson[2], 16.358; Nosworthy, 81. Walker reports that George Steevens also believed that the play should end without Pandarus' epilogue. Honigmann, who is sceptical of Taylor's argument overall, argues that the three lines in which Troilus angrily dismisses Pandarus were apparently 'first written for act 5, scene 3' ('Date and Revision', 45). For a retraction by the Oxford editors regarding their decision to print Pandarus' final soliloquy as Additional Passage B, see Wells & Taylor, 'Re-viewed', 14–15. Their proposal, following a suggestion made to them by Wilbur Sanders (and in fact made earlier by Hudson[2], 16.358), that the passage be printed at the end of 5.3 rather than as Additional Passage B, avoids the embarrassment of omitting entirely from the play text a passage present in both substantive texts, but it has the serious flaw of locating the passage – which clearly reads as an epilogue – in a place sanctioned by neither Q nor F. Surely the passage is more suitably regarded as something intended to conclude the play in one version, but which may then not have been used on some other occasion.

after which he undertook to provide an epilogue for an Inns of Court production when that opportunity arose, splicing in the epilogue with three lines from the conclusion of 5.3 and cancelling the first passage (hence its non-appearance in Q). Subsequently, in this hypothesized scenario, he might then have gone back to his original intention with a view to public performance, making revisions that were entered in a subsequent manuscript (hence the appearance in F of the three-line passage at the end of 5.3). We can explain the F inclusion of the Q ending if we suppose that the preparer of copy for the F compositors, annotating a copy of Q with reference to the later manuscript, either neglected to delete the Q ending or decided that the Q ending was genuine – something that Shakespeare wrote and that provided a suitable ending for the play as the author had envisaged it at one point.

Interestingly, none of these hypotheses can explain the fact that an unusually large company of fourteen men and four boys plus extras is needed for production in both Q and F (see commentary notes on the List of Roles, p. 127). Whatever the nature of the revision between Q and F, curtailing the text for more efficient production (as might perhaps be expected in moving the play from the Inns of Court to a public theatre) seems not to have been a criterion. The unusually large cast is also of course consistent with a hypothesis that the play was never acted, although, as we have seen, some of F's stage directions do seem to suggest playhouse experience.

One thing seems clear from the debate over the epilogue: the Q ending and the hypothesized F ending without epilogue both work well, but in very different ways. Q ends with the sardonic epilogue of Pandarus, implicating the audience in his world of pimps, whores and sexually transmitted diseases; F, if we delete the epilogue, ends on a note of heroic and tragic failure. One can well imagine Shakespeare envisaging his play with different endings at different times. The hypothesized F ending may well represent a revised theatrical production, one in which the company no longer wished to hint at the sequel that Pandarus seems to promise 'Some two months hence' (5.11.52). And if one text is to be seen as a theatrical revision of the other, on the basis of the three lines repeated at 5.3.111ff. and 5.11.32–4, then F must be that theatrical revision, since the repeated lines do not occur in Q at 5.3.111ff. Alternatively Q could contain a 'theatrical' revision of the dramatist's original intention, occasioned perhaps by the opportunity to put the play on at the Inns of Court. Whatever the scenario, Q and F show us a play in evolution to meet changing circumstances; neither text is 'final' in any definitive sense.

The Oxford Shakespeare relegates the entire ending of 5.11.32–56, with its epilogue, to an appendix, arguing that the revision was intentional and that a printer probably missed the cancellation marks for this passage in his copy. Such oversight of cancellation marks is not unknown; *Love's Labour's Lost*, 4.3.292ff., offers a seemingly clear example. At the same time, we cannot be sure that the F editors wished to see the epilogue of *Troilus and Cressida* excised. There it stands, in F as in Q, and it makes a perfectly good ending. Quite possibly, the F editors had some reason to conclude that the epilogue should stay. They should have cancelled one version or the other of the three-line repetition, clearly, but we cannot be sure which ending they would have preferred. If we credit them with knowing what they were doing when they turned to an authoritative manuscript as a way of updating the Q printed text, we should also consider that the inclusion of the ending common to Q and F was their choice. For this reason the present edition includes the epilogue and deletes the repeated three-line passage at the end of 5.3.

Taylor's championship of F as Shakespeare's revised version has not remained uncontested. E. A. J. Honigmann continues to argue with force and wit, albeit with appeals to subjective standards of literary taste, that some F readings are abandoned first shots.[1] Phebe Jensen argues the theatrical viability of both endings,

---

1 Honigmann, 'Date and Revision'.

one comic and one tragic, thereby underscoring the play's generic indeterminacy – comic, satirical, historical and tragic all at the same time.[1] Arguably, she concedes, the manuscript used in compiling F 'could have equal or greater authority than Q'. Taylor's arguments for an increased authority of F 'allows editors a reasonable basis either for using F as the control text or for correcting corrupt passages in Q with the help of F if the former is used as control'.[2]

While endorsing the spirit of Jensen's indeterminate and inclusive position regarding the rival claims of Q and F, this present edition would like to suggest the following ways in which the F text (including the epilogue that it prints at the end) may enjoy a significant edge as the later and revised version.

1   The F text is marginally fuller than Q. The hypothesis that its passages not found in Q were intentionally cut rests, as we have seen, on literary judgements, against which there is no substantial doubt that they are genuinely Shakespearean. The shorter and less numerous passages found only in Q can usually be explained on bibliographical grounds of eye-skip and the like. A sensible way out of reliance on subjective literary criteria is to include what is found in F.

2   F stage directions are often more plentiful, informative, accurately placed and precise than their equivalents in Q. Added indications of sound effects are not outside the capacity of the author, but their new appearance in F could point to theatrical use of the manuscript employed to annotate an examplar of Q in order to provide copy for the F printers. Faulty lineation in Q suggests a manuscript that was sometimes hard to decipher.

3   Heminges and Condell apparently decided that an unannotated exemplar of Q was not sufficiently representative of the play they wanted to print. They turned to a manuscript

---

1   Jensen, esp. 421.
2   Jensen, 415 and 417, discussing Taylor, '*TC*'.

that evidently bore some signs of theatrical use. Confronting two versions that differed in many word choices and short passages, they chose to go to the trouble of substituting the readings we find in F.

Chiefly for these reasons, the present edition chooses F as its control text except for the first three pages of F (down through 1.2.226 'how he'), which are essentially a reprint of Q and hence without independent authority.[1] At the same time, we must consider certain factors that urge caution in choosing between individual Q and F readings.

1  The manuscript used to annotate an exemplar of Q in order to provide printer's copy for F must have stood at some remove from Shakespeare's original manuscript. Presumably Shakespeare provided his acting company with a fair copy, no doubt incorporating some revisions as he copied. The playbook then produced may or may not have been a scribal copy, and it may or may not be identical with the manuscript used in the preparation of copy for F. Whatever manuscript was used, it seems to have been involved in theatrical performance and therefore might have come to incorporate features of production designed for stage presentation and derived in some cases from the trial and error of rehearsal and performance. Revival for a subsequent production or productions might well have led to further 'improvements' in the playbook, including the new ending without epilogue hypothesized by Taylor and others. A prologue came along at some point and became part of the copy for F. All of this means that Q offers better authority for the accidentals in an old-spelling edition, including some Shakespearean spellings and punctuation.[2] Such considerations are, to be sure, of limited relevance in a

1   Walker, *Textual*, 71.
2   See Greg, 'Rationale', and Tanselle, 19–21, 48–50 and 300–5 on the complexities of choosing a 'copy-text' or 'control-text' and the dangers of assuming that the editor can safely identify a single such text.

modern-spelling edition like the present one, but they do mean that F's readings must be regarded with caution.

2   Some F readings show signs of being errors of transmission, including typographical errors that are generally easy to identify as such. Many of F's 'corrections' of the numerous mechanical errors that occur in Q seem sensible, but their authority may be nothing more than the common sense of the F 'editors' or compositors. Sometimes F follows Q in what appears to be an error, though here again each instance demands separate consideration and decision on its merits.[1] Evaluation of such cruxes must depend in good part on Elizabethan standards of usage, Shakespearean habits, likeliness of error made in copying Secretary hand and the like, since there is no inherent reason why F should not occasionally follow Q in error. Emendations proposed in the subsequent Folios of the seventeenth century deserve consideration, but only in the same way that emendations proposed by Hanmer, Theobald, Pope and others may or may not have the merit of logical guesswork.

3   Given F's comparatively greater distance from Shakespeare's papers than Q's, we must be careful to watch out for sophistications. An editor, scribe or compositor is certainly capable of changing 'in it' to 'in't' (1.1.63), for example. Granted that Pandarus is speaking here in a prose passage, and that he frequently uses contractions, an editor might well choose (as does this edition) to follow Q, preserving contractions like 'Ile' and ' 'tis' when they appear in Q while eschewing a consistency in F that may have been editorially superimposed. Similarly, when F substitutes 'Ere y'are ware' at 4.2.57 for Q's 'Ere you are ware', F may be striving for consistency, noting that Aeneas uses contractions like 'youle' elsewhere in this speech. Dittography can perhaps

---

1   For examples of variants between Q and F and discussion of their relative bibliographical merits, see the textual and commentary notes *passim*.

explain some of F's contractions, as when Q's 'mans date is out' becomes 'mans dates out' in F (1.2.248). Compositors, setting with a view to getting a neatly justified line, were often tempted to introduce such 'minor' adjustments of this sort.[1] For these reasons, an editor needs to be cautious about F's expanded contractions, 'improvements' in agreement between subject and verb, regularizing of pronouns like 'ye / you' and 'thou / you', and inverting of word order, even though F's alterations of Q in these respects cannot be taken as uniformly unpersuasive. Generally, we need to be wary that F's alterations may sometimes be the result of error or sophistication, and mindful that F's more complex line of transmission renders it capable of new error, while at the same time being sensitive to the likelihood in many individual cases that F's version is authentic.

In view of the complex relationship of Q and F, a modern critical edition like the present one must be 'eclectic' in the sense of preserving many readings from both texts, checking one against the other in every instance. Such a critical edition must not be eclectic, however, in the sense too often illustrated in previous editions, of selecting from Q or from F on the basis of the editor's aesthetic preference. Such a procedure is destined to be arbitrary and to rest on that editor's sense of what sounds 'right' because of how the reading has been traditionally received. Instead, the editor's first responsibility is to justify the chosen readings on textual grounds. For reasons already explained, this edition inclines towards the F reading in the case of indeterminate claims, other than in the first three pages of F set from an unannotated Q and presenting no independent authority. F is in this limited sense the 'control' text of this present edition, but

---

1   See Prosser, 51–121, on the F compositors' penchant for tinkering with their copy when faced with the difficulties of cast-off copy, the narrow width of the F column, strict demands of page layout, etc. But F is not always manifestly in error when it introduces contractions in place of Q's fuller forms or the reverse; see, for example, t.n. at 1.2.227, 1.2.234, 2.3.212, 3.3.121, 4.4.63.

philosophically the commitment here is to a text that represents as well as can be done the play's own indeterminate nature.

Serious students of the play need to consult the original texts or photographic copies of them, and certainly a case can be made for a parallel-text edition offering the reader Q and F side by side for detailed comparison. At the same time, more than one editorial strategy can be appropriate to a play that seems to have been modified at various times during its early textual and theatrical history in ways that can perhaps never be recovered with certainty. The hope of this present edition is to respect both early texts and the indeterminacies they represent. As Nosworthy puts it, the editor 'will at least have the comfort of knowing that he is right if he interprets *Troilus and Cressida* as comedy, and equally right if he takes it for tragedy'.[1] Given the play's generic and textual uncertainties, and the problems involved in regarding Q and F as discrete and independent, editing *Troilus and Cressida* remains in one sense an impossible job. The present edition, making no claim to be definitive, attempts to present Shakespeare's remarkable and controversial play in something approaching its full complexity.

---

The text of the present edition is in modernized spelling, providing modern orthography when the change is essentially one of variation in spelling: freightage (frautage), struck (stroke), marvellous (maruel's), lose (loose), scaffoldage (scaffolage), fifth (fift), clodpolls (clotpoles), refractory (refracturie), serpigo (suppeago), lest (least), too (to), truth (troth, trueth), an (and, meaning 'if'), off (of), they're (th'are), strait (straight), than (then), o'clock (a clocke), Oyez (O yes), varlet (varlot), wheezing (whissing), prithee (prethee), antics (antiques, antickes), pitched (pight), cloths (cloathes), etc. Even when the spelling variants are more marked and might seem to indicate different words, tempting some modern

---

1 Nosworthy, 85. See also Kastan.

editors to preserve the older form, this present edition modernizes when the linguistic evidence indicates a historical continuity that can account for the spelling variants as essentially those of dialect and pronunciation: porcupine (porpentine), shriek (shrike, shreeke), corpse (course, coarse), swooning (sounding), thills (filles, fils), cherubims (cherubins), God b' wi' you (God buy you), farced (forced) and the like. Sometimes spelling variants indicate a misconception of the word's etymological meaning, as in the common Elizabethan spelling of 'abominable' as 'abhominable', as though it means 'away from mankind' instead of 'deprecating as an ill omen' (see 5.4.2n.)

This edition does not, on the other hand, modernize strong forms of conjugation and declension. Nor does it smooth out matters of agreement between subject and verb, especially when Elizabethan usage provides instances of a plural subject followed by a singular verb, such as 'knots . . . Infects . . . and diverts' at 1.3.7–8. *Troilus* is remarkable for the number of words appearing only once in Shakespeare and sometimes only once in the English language (tortive, mastic, insisture, primogeneity, o'erwrested, propension, roisting, assubjugate, unplausive); these coinages are preserved.

This edition represents the colloquial 'a', meaning 'he', with an apostrophe to characterize the ellipsis: ''a were' for the original 'a were'. Possessives with apostrophes are often modern in form: Diomedes' (Diomedes), enemy's (enemies), etc. Apostrophes in aphetic forms are sometimes supplied: i'faith (yfaith). Words are sometimes joined together or unlinked in accord with modern practice: whosomever (who some euer).

Proper names can present a problem in modern spelling. This edition standardizes in accord with classical practice, since *Troilus* is set in ancient times: Ilium (Ilion), Trojan (Troyan or Troian), Margareton (Margarelon), Polydamas (Polidamus), Epistrophus (Epistropus), Cedius (Cedus), Thoas (Thous), Antenor (Anthenor), Calchas (Calcas), Calchas' (Calcho's, Calcha's), etc. Where proper names are given in variant forms in the original texts, the more common form does not necessarily dictate the choice of this edition: Cressida, for example, is called 'Cressid' more often than 'Cressida' in the play's dialogue, and yet the stage directions and indeed the history of her appearance in Chaucer, Lydgate, Caxton and others suggest that her formal name is 'Cressida'. (In the original texts, the spelling is sometimes 'Cresseida'.) So too with Diomedes, more often called 'Diomed', and Helen, also called 'Helena'. Priam is sometimes referred to as 'Priamus', chiefly for reasons of metre, and Pandarus is called 'Pandar', in reference to his generic role. (See commentary notes on the List of Roles, pp. 127–8).

There are times when any modernized spelling edition obfuscates a fruitful ambiguity of older spelling. A good example is to be found in Pandarus' 'I have had my labour for my travail', 1.1.67, where QF's 'trauell' nicely catches the dual meaning of travelling and labouring. 'Trojan' instead of 'Troyan' misses something of the import of the original, with its suggestion of 'inhabitant of Troy' (see 1.3.240n.). 'Mettle' in place of 'mettell' loses the ambiguity of the modern 'metal' as well as 'mettle' (1.3.258). Faced with difficulties like this, a modern spelling edition can only choose a single modern form and explain the ambiguity in a commentary note.

Lineation presents no great difficulties in this text, but the reader should be aware that the pairing of half-lines into a single line of blank verse is a modern editorial imposition, since in Q and F all speeches, no matter how brief, begin at the left margin following the speech prefix. Q and F also sometimes line prose as verse or the reverse, and occasionally break verse into lines that seem metrically implausible. All emendations to the original text are recorded in the textual notes.

Stage directions in the original are printed here without brackets, whereas editorially added stage directions, or portions of stage directions, are in square brackets. The textual notes record the name of the editor who first proposed any such addition or emendation. Latin phrases are translated and, when necessary, rephrased with the use of square brackets, as at 1.3.309.1, where F's *Exeunt. Manet Vlysses, and Nestor* becomes [*As all are leaving, Ulysses detains Nestor*]. All such departures from the original text are recorded in the textual notes. Those notes also record all verbal emendations, emendations in punctuation that materially affect meaning, and regularization of speech headings. The textual notes do not bother to record obvious typographical errors, such as wrong letters or turned letters.

# ABBREVIATIONS AND
# REFERENCES

Quotations and references relating to *Troilus and Cressida* are keyed to the present edition. Other references to Shakespeare are to *The Complete Works of Shakespeare*, ed. David Bevington, 4th edn, updated (New York, 1997). Biblical quotations are taken from *The Geneva Bible*, a facsimile of the 1560 edn, intro. Lloyd E. Berry (Madison: University of Wisconsin Press, 1969), unless otherwise stated. Abbreviations of the parts of speech (*sb.*, *v.*, *a.*, *ppl. a.*, *adv.*, etc.) are those used in the *OED*, second edition. Titles of collected editions of Shakespeare other than the Folios are simplified as *Works* if they include the poems and as *Plays* if they do not; titles of editions of the play alone, including the Quartos, are given as *Troilus and Cressida* or *TC*; and variations in the spelling of the name Shakespeare are not recorded in citing these editions.

In all references, place of publication is London unless otherwise stated. 'Cambridge' means Cambridge, England, unless specified as 'Cambridge, Mass.'.

## ABBREVIATIONS

### ABBREVIATIONS USED IN NOTES

| | |
|---|---|
| A.V. | Authorized Version: the so-called King James Bible of 1611 |
| cent. | century (i.e. 100, in Erasmus citations) |
| chil. | chiliad (i.e. 1,000, in Erasmus citations) |
| conj. | conjecture |
| Fr. | French |
| It. | Italian |
| Gr. | Greek |
| Lat. | Latin |
| lit. | literally |
| LN | longer note |
| n.s. | new series |

| | |
|---|---|
| om. | omitted |
| opp. | opposite |
| SD | stage direction |
| ser. | series |
| SP | speech prefix |
| Sp. | Spanish |
| subst. | substantively |
| this edn | a reading adopted for the first time in this edition |
| t.n. | textual note |
| * | indicates discussion of textual choices from early editions |

## SHAKESPEARE'S WORKS AND WORKS PARTLY BY SHAKESPEARE

| | |
|---|---|
| *AC* | *Antony and Cleopatra* |
| *AW* | *All's Well That Ends Well* |
| *AYL* | *As You Like It* |
| *CE* | *The Comedy of Errors* |
| *Cor* | *Coriolanus* |
| *Cym* | *Cymbeline* |
| *Ham* | *Hamlet* |
| *1H4* | *King Henry IV, Part 1* |
| *2H4* | *King Henry IV, Part 2* |
| *H5* | *King Henry V* |
| *1H6* | *King Henry VI, Part 1* |
| *2H6* | *King Henry VI, Part 2* |
| *3H6* | *King Henry VI, Part 3* |
| *H8* | *King Henry VIII* |
| *JC* | *Julius Caesar* |
| *KJ* | *King John* |
| *KL* | *King Lear* |
| *LC* | *A Lover's Complaint* |
| *LLL* | *Love's Labour's Lost* |
| *MA* | *Much Ado About Nothing* |
| *Mac* | *Macbeth* |
| *MM* | *Measure for Measure* |
| *MND* | *A Midsummer Night's Dream* |
| *MV* | *The Merchant of Venice* |
| *MW* | *The Merry Wives of Windsor* |
| *Oth* | *Othello* |
| *Per* | *Pericles* |
| *PP* | *The Passionate Pilgrim* |

| PT  | *The Phoenix and Turtle* |
| R2  | *King Richard II* |
| R3  | *King Richard III* |
| RJ  | *Romeo and Juliet* |
| RL  | *The Rape of Lucrece* |
| Son | *The Sonnets* |
| STM | *The Book of Sir Thomas More* |
| TC  | *Troilus and Cressida* |
| Tem | *The Tempest* |
| TGV | *The Two Gentlemen of Verona* |
| Tim | *Timon of Athens* |
| Tit | *Titus Andronicus* |
| TN  | *Twelfth Night* |
| TNK | *The Two Noble Kinsmen* |
| TS  | *The Taming of the Shrew* |
| VA  | *Venus and Adonis* |
| WT  | *The Winter's Tale* |

# REFERENCES

## EDITIONS OF SHAKESPEARE COLLATED

| Alexander | *Works*, ed. Peter Alexander, 4 vols (London and Glasgow, 1951) |
| Ard[1] | *Troilus and Cressida*, ed. K. Deighton, Arden Shakespeare, 1st ser. (1906) |
| Ard[2] | *Troilus and Cressida*, ed. Kenneth Palmer, Arden Shakespeare, 2nd ser. (1982) |
| Ard[3] | Refers to the volumes thus far having appeared in the Arden Shakespeare, 3rd ser., i.e. *Antony and Cleopatra*, *Henry V*, *Julius Caesar*, *King Lear*, *Love's Labour's Lost*, *Othello*, *Shakespeare's Sonnets*, *Titus Andronicus* and *The Two Noble Kinsmen* |
| Baldwin | See Var |
| Bevington[3] | *Works*, ed. David Bevington, 3rd edn (Glenview, Il., 1980) |
| Bevington[4] | *Works*, ed. David Bevington, 4th edn (New York, 1992, updated, 1997) |
| Boswell | See Var '21 |
| Cam | *Works*, ed. William George Clark and William Aldis Wright, The Cambridge Shakespeare, 9 vols (Cambridge and London, 1863–6) |
| Cam[1] | *Troilus and Cressida*, ed. Alice Walker, The Cambridge New Shakespeare (Cambridge, 1957) |
| Capell | *Plays*, ed. Edward Capell, 10 vols (1767–8) |
| Collier | *Works*, ed. John Payne Collier, 8 vols (1842–4) |

| | |
|---|---|
| Collier[2] | *Works*, ed. John Payne Collier, 6 vols (1853) |
| Collier[3] | *Works*, ed. John Payne Collier, 6 vols (1858) |
| Cowden Clarke | *Works*, ed. Charles and Mary Cowden Clarke (1864, 1868) |
| Craig | *Works*, ed. W. J. Craig (1905) |
| Deighton | See Ard[1] |
| Delius | *Works* (*Werke*), ed. Nicolaus Delius, 7 vols (Elberfeld, 1854–61) |
| Dyce | *Works*, ed. Alexander Dyce, 6 vols (1857) |
| Dyce[2] | *Works*, ed. Alexander Dyce, 9 vols (1864–7) |
| Dyce[3] | *Works*, ed. Alexander Dyce, 9 vols (1875–6) |
| F | *Mr William Shakespeares Comedies, Histories, and Tragedies* (1623) (First Folio) |
| Fa | first printing of opening pages of F |
| Fb | second printing of opening pages of F |
| Fc | F corrected state |
| Fu | F uncorrected state |
| F2 | *Mr William Shakespeares Comedies, Histories, and Tragedies* (1632) (Second Folio) |
| F3 | *Mr William Shakespeares Comedies, Histories, and Tragedies* (1663) (Third Folio) |
| F4 | *Mr William Shakespeares Comedies, Histories, and Tragedies* (1685) (Fourth Folio) |
| Foakes, *TC* | *Troilus and Cressida*, ed. R. A. Foakes, New Penguin Shakespeare (Harmondsworth, 1987) |
| Furnivall & Munro | F. J. Furnivall and John Munro, *Life and Work of Shakespeare* (1908) |
| Globe | *Works*, ed. William George Clark and William Aldis Wright (1864) |
| Greg, *TC* | *Troilus and Cressida*, ed. W. W. Greg, First Quarto, 1609, in collotype facsimile (1952) |
| Hanmer | *Works*, ed. Thomas Hanmer, 6 vols (Oxford, 1743–4) |
| Hillebrand | See Var |
| Hudson | *Works*, ed. Henry N. Hudson, 11 vols (1851–6) |
| Hudson[2] | *Works*, ed. Henry N. Hudson, 20 vols (Boston and Cambridge, Mass., 1880–1) |
| Johnson | *Plays*, ed. Samuel Johnson, 8 vols (1765) |
| Keightley | *Plays*, ed. Thomas Keightley, 6 vols (1864) |
| Kittredge | *Works*, ed. George Lyman Kittredge (Boston, 1936) |
| Knight | *Works*, ed. Charles Knight, 8 vols (1838–43) |
| Malone | *Works*, ed. Edmond Malone, 10 vols (1790) |
| Muir | See Oxf[1] |
| New Var | See Var |
| Oxf | *Works*, ed. Stanley Wells and Gary Taylor, with John Jowett and William Montgomery (Oxford, 1986) |
| Oxf[1] | *Troilus and Cressida*, ed. Kenneth Muir, Oxford Shakespeare (Oxford, 1982) |

| | |
|---|---|
| Palmer | See Ard² |
| Pope | *Works*, ed. Alexander Pope, 6 vols (1723–5) |
| Pope² | *Works*, ed. Alexander Pope, 8 vols (1728) |
| Porter & Clarke | *The Tragedie of Troylus and Cressida*, ed. Charlotte Porter and Helen A. Clarke (New York, 1903) |
| Q | *Troilus and Cressida* (1609) |
| Qa | (first state) *The Historie of Troylus and Cresseida. As it was acted by the King's Maiesties seruants at the Globe* (London: printed by G. Eld for R. Bonian and H. Walley, 1609) |
| Qb | (second state) *The Famous Historie of Troylus and Cresseid. Excellently expressing the beginning of their loues, with the conceited wooing of Pandarus Prince of Licia* (London: printed by G. Eld for R. Bonian and H. Walley, 1609) |
| Qc | Q corrected state |
| Qu | Q uncorrected state |
| Rann | *Plays*, ed. Joseph Rann, 6 vols (Oxford, 1786–94) |
| Riv | *Works*, textual editor, G. Blakemore Evans, The Riverside Shakespeare (Boston, 1974, 2nd edn, 1997) |
| Rolfe | *TC*, ed. W. J. Rolfe (New York, 1882, rpt. 1898) |
| Rowe | *Works*, ed. Nicholas Rowe, 6 vols (1709) |
| Rowe² | *Works*, ed. Nicholas Rowe, 6 vols (1709) |
| Rowe³ | *Works*, ed. Nicholas Rowe, 8 vols (1714) |
| Singer | *Works*, ed. S. W. Singer, 10 vols (1856) |
| Singer² | *Works*, ed. S. W. Singer, 8 vols (1875) |
| Sisson | *Works*, ed. C. J. Sisson (1954) |
| Staunton | *Works*, ed. Howard Staunton, 15 vols (1858) |
| Steevens | See Var '73, '78, '85, '93, '03 |
| Taylor | See Oxf |
| Theobald | *Works*, ed. Lewis Theobald, 7 vols (1733) |
| Theobald² | *Works*, ed. Lewis Theobald, 8 vols (1740) |
| Var | *Troilus and Cressida*, ed. Harold N. Hillebrand, supplemental editor, T. W. Baldwin, a New Variorum Edition (Philadelphia, 1953) |
| Var '73 | *Plays*, notes by Samuel Johnson and George Steevens, 10 vols (1773) (Johnson–Steevens Variorum) |
| Var '78 | Johnson–Steevens Variorum (1778) |
| Var '85 | Johnson–Steevens Variorum (1785) |
| Var '93 | Johnson–Steevens Variorum (1793) |
| Var '03 | Johnson–Steevens Variorum, rev. Isaac Reed (1803) |
| Var '21 | Boswell–Malone Variorum (1821) |
| Verity & Marshall | *Troilus and Cressida*, ed. A. W. Verity and F. A. Marshall, in the Henry Irving edn (1889) |
| Walker | See Cam¹ |
| Warburton | *Works*, ed. William Warburton, 8 vols (1747) |
| Wells | See Oxf |
| White | *Works*, ed. Richard Grant White (1857–65) |

## ANCIENT TEXTS

Wherever possible, Graeco-Roman texts are cited by the standard reference to book, chapter and paragraph for prose texts, and by book and line (for Homer and Virgil) or by book, poem and line number (for Horace, Ovid, etc.). The Loeb Classical Library (LCL) offers a convenient edition for many of the following classical authors.

| | |
|---|---|
| Aeschylus | *The Seven Against Thebes* and *Agamemnon*, vol. 1, LCL, trans. Herbert Weir Smyth (1922) |
| Anacreon | *Greek Lyrics*, vol. 2, LCL, trans. David A. Campbell (1988) |
| Aristophanes | *Frogs*, vol. 2, LCL, trans. Benjamin Bickley Rogers (1924) |
| Aristotle | *Historia Animalium*, 3 vols, LCL, trans. A. L. Peck (1965) |
| Aristotle | *Nicomachean Ethics*, LCL, trans. H. Rackham (1926) |
| Aristotle | *Parts of Animals; Movement and Progression of Animals*, LCL, trans. A. L. Peck (1937) |
| Catullus | *Catullus, Tibullus, Pervigilium Veneris*, LCL, trans. J. W. Mackail (1913) |
| Cicero | *Cicero's Three Books of Duties*, with Preface by Nicholas Grimald (1556–1600) |
| Cicero | *Tusculan Disputations*, LCL, trans. J. E. King (1927) |
| Euripides | *The Phoenician Maidens, Iphigeneia at Aulis* and *The Trojan Women*, vols 1 and 3, LCL, trans. Arthur S. Way (1912) |
| Hesiod | *Theogony*, in *Hesiod, The Homeric Hymns and Homerica*, LCL, trans. Hugh G. Evelyn-White, rev. ed. (1936) |
| Homer | *Iliad*, 2 vols, LCL, trans. A. T. Murray (1924); also trans. Richard Lattimore (Chicago, 1951) |
| Homer | *Odyssey*, 2 vols, LCL, trans. A. T. Murray, rev. George E. Dimock (1995) |
| Homeric Hymns | *Hesiod, The Homeric Hymns and Homerica*, LCL, trans. Hugh G. Evelyn-White, rev. edn (1936) |
| Horace | *The Odes and Epodes*, LCL, trans. C. E. Bennett (1914) |
| Horace | *Ars Poetica*, in *Satires, Epistles, and Ars Poetica*, LCL, trans. H. Rushton Fairclough (1926) |
| Juvenal | *Juvenal and Persius*, LCL, rev. edn, trans. G. G. Ramsay (1940) |
| Lucian | *Works* (*Dialogues of the Dead* and *Dialogues of the Gods*), vol. 7, LCL, trans. M. D. Macleod (1961) |
| Ovid | *Fasti*, LCL, trans. James George Frazer, rev. G. P. Goold (1989) |
| Ovid | *Heroides and Amores*, LCL, 2nd edn, trans. Grant Showerman (1977) |
| Ovid | *Metamorphoses*, 2 vols, LCL, 3rd edn, trans. Frank Justus Miller (1977) |
| Ovid | *Remedia Amoris*, LCL, in *The Art of Love and Other Poems*, trans. J. H. Mozley, rev. G. P. Goold (1979) |

| Persius | *Satires*, see Juvenal |
|---|---|
| Petronius | *Petronius, Seneca (Apocolocyntosis)*, LCL, trans. Michael Heseltine, rev. E. H. Warmington (1987) |
| Plato | *Alcibiades*, LCL, trans. W. R. M. Lamb (1927) |
| Pliny | Gaius Plinius Secundus, *Natural History*, LCL, rev. edn, trans. H. Rackham (1949); references are to book and paragraph |
| Publilius Syrus | *Sententiae*, in *Minor Latin Poets*, LCL, trans. J. Wight Duff and Arnold M. Duff (1934) |
| Seneca | *Epistulae Morales*, 3 vols, LCL, trans. Richard M. Gummere (1918) |
| Seneca | *Troades* and *Thyestes*, vols 1 and 2, LCL, trans. Frank Justus Miller (1917) |
| Sophocles | *Ajax*, vol. 1, LCL, trans. Hugh Lloyd-Jones (1994) |
| Terence | *Andria* and *Eunuchus*, vol. 1, LCL, trans. John Sargeaunt (1912) |
| Virgil | *Aeneid*, 2 vols, LCL, rev. edn, trans. H. Rushton Fairclough (1965) |

## OTHER WORKS

| Abbott | E. A. Abbott, *A Shakespearian Grammar*, new edn (1886) (references are to numbered entries) |
|---|---|
| Adams | Howard C. Adams, ' "What Cressid Is" ', in *Sexuality and Politics in Renaissance Drama*, ed. Carole Levin and Karen Robertson (Lewiston, N.Y., 1991), 75–93 |
| Adamson | Jane Adamson, '*Troilus and Cressida*', Harvester New Critical Introductions to Shakespeare (Brighton, 1987) |
| Adelman, 'Cressid' | Janet Adelman, ' "This Is and Is Not Cressid": The Characterization of Cressida', in *The (M)other Tongue: Essays in Feminist Psychoanalytic Interpretation*, ed. Shirley Nelson Garner, Claire Kehane and Madelon Sprengnether (Ithaca, N.Y., 1985), 119–41 |
| Adelman, 'Union' | Janet Adelman, ' "Is Thy Union Here?": Union and Its Discontents in *Troilus and Cressida* and *Othello*', in *Suffocating Mothers: Fantasies of Maternal Origin in Shakespeare's Plays, 'Hamlet' to 'The Tempest'* (New York and London, 1992), 38–75 |
| Alciati | Andreas Alciati, *Emblemata cum Commentarii* (Padua, 1621, rpt. New York and London, 1976) |
| Alexander, *Life* | Peter Alexander, *Shakespeare's Life and Art* (New York, 1961) |
| Alexander, '*TC*' | Peter Alexander, '*Troilus and Cressida*, 1609', *The Library*, 4th ser., 9 (1928–9), 267–86 |
| Anders | H. R. D. Anders, *Shakespeare's Books: A Dissertation on Shakespeare's Reading and the Immediate Sources of His Works* (Berlin, 1904) |

| | |
|---|---|
| Aquinas | Saint Thomas Aquinas, *Summa Theologiae*, 2a2ae, vol. 47, ed. Jordan Aumann (1973) |
| Arnold | Aerol Arnold, 'The Hector–Andromache Scene in Shakespeare's *Troilus and Cressida*', *MLQ*, 14 (1953), 335–40 |
| Aronson | Alex Aronson, 'Appetite', in *Psyche and Symbol in Shakespeare* (Bloomington, Ind., 1972), 64–93 |
| Asp, 'Expense' | Carolyn Asp, 'Th' Expense of Spirit in a Waste of Shame', *SQ*, 22 (1971), 345–57 |
| Asp, 'Defense' | Carolyn Asp, 'In Defense of Cressida', *SP*, 74 (1977), 406–17 |
| Atkins & Bergeron | G. Douglas Atkins and David M. Bergeron, eds, *Shakespeare and Deconstruction* (New York, 1988) |
| A.V. | 'Authorized Version', the so-called King James version of the Bible, 1611 |
| Bache & Loggins | William B. Bache and Vernon P. Loggins, *Shakespeare's Deliberate Art* (Lanham, Md., 1996), 215–31 |
| Bakhtin | M. M. Bakhtin, *The Dialogic Imagination, Four Essays*, ed. Michael Holquist, trans. Caryl Emerson and Michael Holquist (Austin, Tex., 1986) |
| Bald | R. C. Bald, 'Shakespeare on the Stage in Restoration Dublin', *PMLA*, 56 (1941), 369–78 |
| Baldwin, *Small Latine* | T. W. Baldwin, *William Shakspere's 'Small Latine & Less Greeke'*, 2 vols (Urbana, Ill., 1944) |
| Barfoot | C. C. Barfoot, '*Troilus and Cressida*: "Praise us as we are tasted"', *SQ*, 39 (1988), 45–57 |
| Bartholomew | *Bartholomaeus de Proprietatibus Rerum* (Thomas Berthelet, 1535). Later editions in English, having Stephen Bateman's commentary, are often referred to as *Batman upon Bartholome.* |
| Bate | Jonathan Bate, *Shakespeare and Ovid* (Oxford, 1993) |
| Bayley, 'Time' | John Bayley, 'Time and the Trojans', *EIC*, 25 (1975), 55–73 |
| Bayley, *Tragedy* | John Bayley, *Shakespeare and Tragedy* (1981), 96–117 |
| Becket | Andrew Becket, *Shakespeare's Himself Again*, 2 vols (1815) |
| Bednarz | James P. Bednarz, 'Shakespeare's Purge of Jonson: The Literary Context of *Troilus and Cressida*', *SSt*, 21 (1993), 175–212 |
| Belleau | Remy Belleau, *Les Odes d'Anacreon Teien traduites de Grec en François* (Paris, 1556) |
| Belsey | Catherine Belsey, 'Desire's Excess and the English Renaissance Theatre', in Zimmerman, ed., *Erotic Politics*, 84–102 |
| Bentley | Greg W. Bentley, '"The poor agent depised": Commercialism and Syphilis in *Troilus and Cressida*', in *Shakespeare and the New Disease: The Dramatic Function of Syphilis in 'Troilus and Cressida', 'Measure for Measure', and 'Timon of Athens'* (New York and Bern, 1989), 41–99 |

Berger                  Harry Berger, Jr, '*Troilus and Cressida*: The Observer as
                        Basilisk', *CompD*, 2 (1968), 122–36
Bernhardt               W. W. Bernhardt, 'Shakespeare's *Troilus and Cressida* and
                        Dryden's *Truth Found Too Late*', *SQ*, 20 (1969), 129–41
Berry                   Ralph Berry, *Changing Styles in Shakespeare* (1981)
Bethell                 S. L. Bethell, *Shakespeare and the Popular Dramatic
                        Tradition* (Durham, N.C., 1944)
Bevington, *AC*         David Bevington, ed., *Antony and Cleopatra* (Cambridge,
                        1990)
Bevington,              David Bevington, *From 'Mankind' to Marlowe* (Cambridge,
   *Mankind*            Mass., 1962)
Bevington, *Politics*   David Bevington, *Tudor Drama and Politics* (Cambridge,
                        Mass., 1968)
Bevington, 'Satire'     David Bevington, 'Shakespeare vs. Jonson on Satire', in
                        *Shakespeare 1971: Proceedings of the World Shakespeare
                        Congress, Vancouver, August, 1971*, ed. Clifford Leech and
                        J. M. R. Margeson (Toronto, 1972), 107–22
Bevington               See Marlowe, *Faustus*
   & Rasmussen
Bible                   See headnote to 'Abbreviations and References', p. 430
Bjelland,               Karen Bjelland, 'The Cultural Value of Analytical
   'Analytical'         Bibliography and Textual Criticism: The Case of *Troilus
                        and Cressida*', in *Text: Transactions of the Society for
                        Textual Scholarship*, ed. D. C. Greetham and W. Speed
                        Hill (Ann Arbor, Mich., 1994), 273–95
Bjelland, 'Cressida'    Karen Bjelland, 'Cressida and the Renaissance
                        "Marketplace"–The Role of Binarism and Amphibology
                        in Shakespeare's Articulation of the Troy Legend', in
                        *Ideological Approaches to Shakespeare: The Practice of
                        Theory*, ed. Robert P. Merrix and Nicholas Ranson
                        (Lewiston, N.Y., 1992), 165–85
Blayney, *First Folio*  Peter W. M. Blayney, *The First Folio of Shakespeare*
                        (Washington, D.C., 1991)
Blayney,                Peter W. M. Blayney, 'The Publication of Playbooks', in
   'Publication'        Cox & Kastan, ed., *New History*, 383–422
Blayney,                Peter W. M. Blayney, *The Texts of 'King Lear' and Their
   *Texts of 'Lear'*    Origins*, vol. 1, *Nicholas Okes and the First Quarto*
                        (Cambridge, 1982)
Boas                    Frederick S. Boas, *Shakspere and His Predecessors* (1896,
                        rpt. New York, 1968)
Boethius                Boethius, *The Consolation of Philosophy*, trans. W. V. Cooper
                        (1940)
Bowden                  William R. Bowden, 'The Human Shakespeare and
                        *Troilus and Cressida*', *SQ*, 8 (1957), 167–77
Bowen, *Gender*         Barbara E. Bowen, *Gender in the Theater of War:*

*Shakespeare's 'Troilus and Cressida'* (New York and London, 1993)

Bowen, 'Stage History'
Barbara E. Bowen, '*Troilus and Cressida* on the Stage', in *Troilus and Cressida*, ed. Daniel Seltzer, The Signet Classic Shakespeare (New York, 1963, rev. 1988), 265–87

Bowers
Fredson Bowers, 'Running-Title Evidence for Determining Half Sheet Imposition', *Papers of the Bibliographical Society, University of Virginia*, 1 (1948–9), 199–202

Boyle
Robert Boyle, '*Troilus and Cressida*', *Englische Studien*, 30 (1902), 21–59

Bradbrook
M. C. Bradbrook, 'What Shakespeare Did to Chaucer's *Troilus and Criseyde*', *SQ*, 9 (1958), 311–19

Bredbeck
Gregory W. Bredbeck, *Sodomy and Interpretation: Marlowe to Milton* (Ithaca, N.Y., 1991)

Briggs
John Channing Briggs, 'Chapman's *Seaven Bookes of the Iliades*: Mirror for Essex', *SEL*, 21 (1981), 59–73

Brooke
C. F. Tucker Brooke, 'Shakespeare's Study in Culture and Anarchy', in *Essays on Shakespeare and Other Elizabethans* (New Haven, 1948), 71–7

Brooks
Harold Brooks, '*Troilus and Cressida*: Its Dramatic Unity and Genre', in *'Fanned and Winnowed Opinions': Shakespearean Essays Presented to Harold Jenkins*, ed. John W. Mahon and Thomas A. Pendleton (1987), 6–25

Brower
Reuben A. Brower, *Hero and Saint: Shakespeare and the Graeco-Roman Heroic Tradition* (Oxford, 1971), 239–76

Browne
*Pseudoxia Epidemica*, in *The Works of Sir Thomas Browne*, ed. Geoffrey Keynes, 4 vols (1928), vol. 2

Bruster
Douglas Bruster, '"The Alteration of Men": *Troilus and Cressida*, Troynovant, and Trade', in *Drama and the Market in the Age of Shakespeare* (Cambridge, 1992), 97–117

Bullough, 'Lost *TC*'
Geoffrey Bullough, 'The Lost *Troilus and Cressida*', *Essays and Studies*, n.s. 17 (1964), 24–40

Bullough, *Sources*
Geoffrey Bullough, ed., *Narrative and Dramatic Sources of Shakespeare*, 8 vols (1957–75)

Burns
M. M. Burns, '*Troilus and Cressida*: The Worst of Both Worlds', *SSt*, 13 (1980), 105–30

Burton
Robert Burton, *The Anatomy of Melancholy*, ed. Thomas C. Faulkner, Nicolas K. Kiessling and Rhonda L. Blair, 3 vols (Oxford, 1994)

Bush
Douglas Bush, *Mythology and the Renaissance Tradition in English Poetry* (Minneapolis, 1932)

*CahiersE*
*Cahiers Élisabéthains*

Campbell
Oscar James Campbell, *Comicall Satyre and Shakespeare's 'Troilus and Cressida'* (San Marino, Cal., 1938)

| | |
|---|---|
| Cartelli | Thomas Cartelli, 'Ideology and Subversion in the Shakespearean Set Speech', *ELH*, 53 (1986), 1–25 |
| Carter | Thomas Carter, *Shakespeare and Holy Scripture* (New York, 1905, rpt. 1970) |
| Caxton | *The Recuyell of the Historyes of Troye*, written in French by Raoul Lefèvre, trans. and printed by William Caxton (c. 1474), ed. H. Oskar Sommer (1894) |
| Cercignani | Fausto Cercignani, *Shakespeare's Works and Elizabethan Pronunciation* (Oxford, 1981) |
| Chambers, *Elizabethan* | E. K. Chambers, *The Elizabethan Stage*, 4 vols (Oxford, 1923) |
| Chambers, 'Epilogue' | E. K. Chambers, 'William Shakespeare: An Epilogue', *Review of English Studies*, 16 (1940), 385–401 |
| Chambers, *Lee* | E. K. Chambers, *Sir Henry Lee: An Elizabethan Portrait* (Oxford, 1936) |
| Chambers, *Shakespeare* | E. K. Chambers, *William Shakespeare: A Study of Facts and Problems*, 2 vols (Oxford, 1930) |
| Chambers, *Survey* | E. K. Chambers, *Shakespeare: A Survey* (1925, rpt. New York, 1958) |
| Chapman's *Iliads* | *The Iliads of Homer* (1611), in *Chapman's Homer*, ed. Allardyce Nicoll, 2 vols (New York, 1956), 1.3–499 |
| Chapman's *Seven Books* | *Seven Books of the Iliades* (1598), in *Chapman's Homer*, ed. Allardyce Nicoll, 2 vols (New York, 1956), 1.503–39 (first two books only); citations to Books 7–11 refer to the 1598 edn |
| Charnes | Linda Charnes, ' "So Unsecret to Ourselves": Notorious Identity and the Material Subject in *Troilus and Cressida*', in *Notorious Identity: Materializing the Subject in Shakespeare* (Cambridge, Mass., 1993), 70–102, rpt. from *SQ*, 40 (1989), 413–40 |
| Charney | Maurice Charney, *Shakespeare's Roman Plays: The Function of Imagery in the Drama* (Cambridge, Mass., 1961) |
| Chaucer, *CT* | *The Canterbury Tales*, in *The Riverside Chaucer*, gen. ed. Larry D. Benson (Boston, 1987) |
| Chaucer, *TC* | *The Book of Troilus and Criseyde*, ed. Robert Kilburn Root (Princeton, 1926) |
| Clarke | Larry R. Clarke, ' "Mars His Heart Inflam'd with Venus": Ideology and Eros in Shakespeare's *Troilus and Cressida*', *MLQ*, 50 (1989), 209–26 |
| Coghill | Nevill Coghill, *Shakespeare's Professional Skills* (Cambridge, 1964), 78–127 |
| Cohn | Ruby Cohn, *Modern Shakespeare Offshoots* (Princeton, 1976) |
| Cole | Douglas Cole, 'Myth and Anti-Myth: The Case of *Troilus and Cressida*', *SQ*, 31 (1980), 76–84 |
| Coleman | E. A. M. Coleman, *The Dramatic Use of Bawdy in Shakespeare* (1974) |

| | |
|---|---|
| Coleridge | S. T. Coleridge, *Lectures and Notes on Shakspere and Other English Poets*, collected by T. Ashe (1902) |
| Colie | Rosalie L. Colie, *Shakespeare's Living Art* (Princeton, 1974) |
| *CompD* | *Comparative Drama* |
| Concordance | Martin Spevack, *The Harvard Concordance to Shakespeare* (Cambridge, Mass., 1973) |
| Conti | Natale Conti, *Natalis Comitis Mythologiae* (Frankfort, 1581) |
| Cook | Carol Cook, 'Unbodied Figures of Desire', *ETJ*, 38 (1986), 34–52; rpt. in *Performing Feminism: Feminist Critical Theory and Theatre*, ed. Sue-Ellen Case (Baltimore, 1990), 177–95 |
| Cooper | Thomas Cooper, *Thesaurus, Linguae Romanae & Britanicae* (1565) |
| Cotgrave | Randle Cotgrave, *A Dictionarie of the French and English Tongues* (1611, rpt. Menston, Eng., 1968) |
| Cox | John D. Cox, 'The Error of Our Eye in *Troilus and Cressida*', *CompD*, 10 (1976), 147–71 |
| Cox & Kastan | John D. Cox and David Scott Kastan, eds, *A New History of Early English Drama* (New York, 1997) |
| *CritQ* | *Critical Quarterly* |
| Crosse | Gordon Crosse, *Fifty Years of Shakespearean Playing* (1941) |
| Daniel, *Notes* | P. A. Daniel, *Notes and Conjectural Emendations of Certain Doubtful Passages in Shakespeare's Plays* (1870) |
| Daniel, 'Time-Analysis' | P. A. Daniel, 'Time-Analysis of the Plots of Shakespeare's Plays', *New Shakspere Society Transactions* (1877–9), Part 2, 'The Tragedies', 117–316 |
| Daniels | F. Quinland Daniels, 'Order and Confusion in *Troilus and Cressida* I.iii', *SQ*, 12 (1961), 285–91 |
| Danson | Lawrence Danson, *Tragic Alphabet: Shakespeare's Drama of Language* (New Haven, 1974), 68–96 |
| Davies | *The Poems of Sir John Davies*, ed. Robert Krueger (Oxford, 1975) |
| Dawson | Giles E. Dawson, 'A Bibliographical Problem in the First Folio of Shakespeare', *The Library*, 4th ser., 22 (1941–2), 25–33 |
| de Beauvoir | Simone de Beauvoir, *The Second Sex*, trans. and ed. H. M. Parshley (New York, 1974) |
| de Rougemont | Denis de Rougemont, *Love in the Western World* (New York, 1940, rev. 1956) |
| Dekker | *The Dramatic Works of Thomas Dekker*, ed. Fredson Bowers, 4 vols (Cambridge, 1953–61) |
| Dent | R. W. Dent, *Shakespeare's Proverbial Language: An Index* (Berkeley, 1981) |
| Dessen | Alan C. Dessen, *Recovering Shakespeare's Theatrical Vocabulary* (Cambridge, 1995) |

441

| | |
|---|---|
| *DNB* | *The Dictionary of National Biography* (Oxford, 1903) |
| Dodd | Mark Robert Dodd, 'The History of *Troilus and Cressida*', *Upstart Crow*, 11 (1991), 39–51 |
| Dollimore | Jonathan Dollimore, *Radical Tragedy: Religion, Ideology and Power in the Drama of Shakespeare and His Contemporaries* (1984), chap. 2 |
| Donaldson, 'Cressid' | E. Talbot Donaldson, 'Cressid False, Criseyde Untrue: An Ambiguity Revisited', in *Poetic Traditions of the English Renaissance*, ed. Maynard Mack and George deForest Ford (New Haven, 1982), 67–83 |
| Donaldson, *Swan* | E. Talbot Donaldson, *The Swan at the Well: Shakespeare Reading Chaucer* (New Haven, 1985) |
| Donne | *The Poems of John Donne*, ed. Herbert J. C. Grierson, 2 vols (Oxford, 1912) |
| Dryden, *Essays* | *Essays of John Dryden*, ed. W. P. Ker, 2 vols (Oxford, 1926) |
| Dryden, *Works* | *The Works of John Dryden*, ed. George Saintsbury, with a life by Sir Walter Scott (1882–93) |
| Dusinberre | Juliet Dusinberre, '*Troilus and Cressida* and the Definition of Beauty', *SS*, 36 (1983), 85–95 |
| Dutton | Richard Dutton, 'The Birth of the Author', in *Elizabethan Theater: Essays in Honor of S. Schoenbaum*, ed. R. B. Parker and S. P. Zitner (Newark, Del., and London, 1996), 71–92 |
| Dyer | Frederick B. Dyer, Jr, 'The Destruction of Pandare', in *Shakespeare Encomium*, ed. Anne Paolucci (New York, 1964), 123–33 |
| Eagleton | Terry Eagleton, *Shakespeare and Society: Critical Essays in Shakespearean Drama* (1967) |
| Edelman | Charles Edelman, *Brawl Ridiculous: Swordfighting in Shakespeare's Plays* (Manchester, 1992) |
| Edwards | Philip Edwards, *Shakespeare and the Confines of Art* (1968) |
| EETS | Early English Text Society |
| *EIC* | *Essays in Criticism* |
| Eldridge | Elaine Eldridge, 'Moral Order in Shakespeare's *Troilus and Cressida*: The Case of the Trojans', *Anglia*, 104 (1986), 33–44 |
| *ELH* | *ELH (Journal of English Literary History)* |
| Elliott | Robert C. Elliott, *The Power of Satire: Magic, Ritual, Art* (Princeton, 1960) |
| Ellis-Fermor | Una Ellis-Fermor, ' "Discord in the Spheres": The Universe of *Troilus and Cressida*', in *The Frontiers of Drama*, 2nd edn (1946), 56–76 |
| *ELR* | *English Literary Renaissance* |
| Elton, 'Ajax' | William Elton, 'Shakespeare's Portrait of Ajax in *Troilus and Cressida*', *PMLA*, 63 (1948), 744–8 |

| | |
|---|---|
| Elton, *Inns of Court* | William Elton, *Shakespeare's 'Troilus and Cressida' and the Inns of Court Revels* (Aldershot, 1997) |
| Elton, *'Nicomachean'* | William Elton, 'Aristotle's *Nicomachean Ethics* and Shakespeare's *Troilus and Cressida*', *Journal of the History of Ideas*, 58 (1997), 331–7 |
| Elton, 'Textual Transmission' | William Elton, 'Textual Transmission and Genre of Shakespeare's *Troilus*', in *Literatur als Kritik des Lebens*, ed. Rudolf Haas, Heinz-Joachim Müllenbrock and Claus Uhlig (Heidelberg, 1975), 63–82 |
| Elton, 'Ulysses' | William Elton, 'Shakespeare's Ulysses and the Problem of Value', *SSt*, 2 (1966), 95–111 |
| Elyot | Sir Thomas Elyot, *The Book of the Governor* (1531) |
| Empson, *Pastoral* | William Empson, *Some Versions of Pastoral* (New York, 1974) |
| Empson, *Structure* | William Empson, *The Structure of Complex Words* (1951), 185–249 |
| Enck | John J. Enck, 'The Peace of the Poetomachia', *PMLA*, 77 (1962), 386–96 |
| Engle | Lars Engle, *Shakespeare and Pragmatism: Market of His Time* (Chicago, 1993), 147–63 |
| Erasmus | Desiderius Erasmus, *Adagia* and *Colloquia*, in the *Opera Omnia*, ed. J. Leclerc, 10 vols (Leiden, 1703–6) |
| *ES* | *English Studies* (Amsterdam) |
| *ETJ* | *Educational Theatre Journal* |
| Evans | Bertrand Evans, *Shakespeare's Comedies* (Oxford, 1960), 167–85 |
| Everett | Barbara Everett, 'The Inaction of *Troilus and Cressida*', *EIC*, 32 (1982), 119–39 |
| Farnham | Willard Farnham, 'Troilus in Shapes of Infinite Desire', *SQ*, 15.2 (1964), 257–64 |
| Ferne | John Ferne, *The Blazon of Gentry* (1586) |
| Fiedler | Leslie A. Fiedler, 'Shakespeare's Commodity-Comedy: A Meditation on the Preface to the 1609 Quarto of *Troilus and Cressida*', in *Shakespeare's 'Rough Magic': Renaissance Essays in Honor of C. L. Barber*, ed. Peter Erickson and Coppélia Kahn (Newark, Del., 1985), 50–60 |
| Findlay | Alison Findlay, *Bastards in Renaissance Drama* (Manchester, 1994) |
| Fineman | Joel Fineman, 'Fratricide and Cuckoldry: Shakespeare's Doubles', in Schwartz & Kahn, eds, *Representing Shakespeare*, 70–109 |
| Finkelpearl | Philip J. Finkelpearl, 'Henry Walley of the Stationers' Company and John Marston', *PBSA*, 56 (1962), 366–8 |
| Fischer | Sandra K. Fischer, *Econolingua: A Glossary of Coins and Economic Language in Renaissance Drama* (Newark, Del., 1985) |

| | |
|---|---|
| Flannery | Christopher Flannery, '*Troilus and Cressida*: Poetry or Philosophy?', in *Shakespeare as Political Thinker*, ed. John Alvis and Thomas G. West (Durham, N.C., 1981), 145–56 |
| Fleay | Frederick Gard Fleay, *A Biographical Chronicle of the English Drama, 1559–1642*, 2 vols (1891) |
| Florio | John Florio, *A World of Words* (1598) |
| Fluchère | Henri Fluchère, *Shakespeare* (1953) |
| Fly, 'I Cannot' | Richard D. Fly, '"I cannot come to Cressid but by Pandar": Mediation in the Theme and Structure of *Troilus and Cressida*', *ELR*, 3 (1973), 145–65 |
| Fly, 'Suited' | Richard D. Fly, '"Suited in Like Conditions as Our Argument": Imitative Form in Shakespeare's *Troilus and Cressida*', *SEL*, 15 (1975), 273–92 |
| Foakes, *Dark Comedies* | R. A. Foakes, *Shakespeare: The Dark Comedies to the Last Plays: From Satire to Celebration* (1971) |
| Foakes, 'Reconsidered' | R. A. Foakes, '*Troilus and Cressida* Reconsidered', *UTQ*, 32 (1962–3), 142–54 |
| Foakes & Rickert | R. A. Foakes and R. T. Rickert, eds, *Henslowe's Diary* (Cambridge, 1961) |
| Freedman | Barbara Freedman, 'Misrecognizing Shakespeare', in Holland *et al.*, eds, *Shakespeare's Personality*, 244–60 |
| French | Marilyn French, *Shakespeare's Division of Experience* (New York, 1981) |
| Freud | Sigmund Freud, 'Über die Allgemeinste Erniedrigung des Liebeslebens' (1912), *Gesammelte Werke*, ed. Anna Freud *et al.*, 18 vols (Frankfurt am Main, 1940–68), 8.78–91, in *The Standard Edition of the Complete Psychological Works of Sigmund Freud*, trans. James Strachey, in collaboration with Anna Freud, assisted by Alix Strachey and Alan Tyson, 14 vols (1953–74), 11.179–90, and in *Sexuality and the Psychology of Love*, ed. Philip Rieff (New York, 1963), 58–70 |
| Freund | Elizabeth Freund, '"Ariachne's broken woof": the Rhetoric of Citation in *Troilus and Cressida*', in Parker & Hartman, eds, *Shakespeare and the Question of Theory*, 19–36 |
| Frye, *Fools* | Northrop Frye, *Fools of Time: Studies in Shakespearean Tragedy* (Toronto, 1967) |
| Frye, *Myth* | Northrop Frye, *The Myth of Deliverance: Reflections on Shakespeare's Problem Comedies* (Toronto, 1983) |
| Furnivall & Munro | F. J. Furnivall and John Munro, eds, *Life and Work of Shakespeare* (1908) |
| Gagen | Jean Gagen, 'Hector's Honor', *SQ*, 19 (1968), 129–37 |
| Garber | Marjorie Garber, *Coming of Age in Shakespeare* (1981) |
| Garner | Shirley Nelson Garner, 'Male Bonding and the Myth of Women's Deception in Shakespeare's Plays', in Holland *et al.*, eds, *Shakespeare's Personality*, 135–50 |

| | |
|---|---|
| Gaudet | Paul Gaudet, ' "As True as Troilus," "As False as Cressid": Tradition, Text, and the Implicated Reader', *English Studies in Canada*, 16 (1990), 125–48 |
| Gérard | Albert Gérard, 'Meaning and Structure in *Troilus and Cressida*', *ES*, 40 (1959), 144–57 |
| Girard | René Girard, 'The Politics of Desire in *Troilus and Cressida*', in Parker & Hartman, eds, *Shakespeare and the Question of Theory*, 188–209 |
| Glasser | Marvin Glasser, 'Baroque Formal Elements in Shakespeare's *Troilus and Cressida*', *Upstart Crow*, 6 (1986), 54–70 |
| Goddard | Harold C. Goddard, *The Meaning of Shakespeare*, 2 vols (Chicago, 1951, rpt. 1968), 2.1–37 |
| Godshalk | W. L. Godshalk, 'The Texts of *Troilus and Cressida*', *Early Modern Literary Studies*, 1.2 (1995), 1–54 |
| Gohlke | Madelon Gohlke, ' "I wooed thee with my sword": Shakespeare's Tragic Paradigms', in Schwartz & Kahn, eds, *Representing Shakespeare*, 170–87; first published in Lenz *et al.*, eds, *The Woman's Part*, 150–70 |
| Golding's Ovid | *The XV Books of P. Ovidius Naso, Entitled Metamorphosis*, trans. Arthur Golding (1567, rpt. 1904 and 1961) |
| Gosson | Stephen Gosson, *The School of Abuse* (1579), in English Reprints, ed. Edward Arber (1869) |
| Green | Lawrence D. Green, ' "We'll Dress Him Up in Voices": The Rhetoric of Disjunction in *Troilus and Cressida*', *Quarterly Journal of Speech*, 70 (1984), 23–40 |
| Greene, 'Cressida' | Gayle Greene, 'Shakespeare's Cressida: "A kind of self" ', in Lenz *et al.*, eds, *The Woman's Part*, 133–49 |
| Greene, *Works* | *The Life and Complete Works of Robert Greene*, ed. Alexander B. Grosart (1881–3) |
| Greg, *Bibliography* | W. W. Greg, *A Bibliography of the English Printed Drama to the Restoration*, 2 vols (1939) |
| Greg, *Documents* | W. W. Greg, ed., *Dramatic Documents from the Elizabethan Playhouses: Stage Plots; Actors' Parts; Prompt Books*, 2 vols (Oxford, 1931) |
| Greg, *Editorial Problem* | W. W. Greg, *The Editorial Problem in Shakespeare*, 3rd edn (Oxford, 1954) |
| Greg, *First Folio* | W. W. Greg, *The Shakespeare First Folio: Its Bibliographical and Textual History* (Oxford, 1955) |
| Greg, 'Printing' | W. W. Greg, 'The Printing of Shakespeare's *Troilus and Cressida* in the First Folio', *PBSA*, 45 (1951), 273–82 |
| Greg, 'Rationale' | W. W. Greg, 'The Rationale of Copy-Text', *SB*, 3 (1950–1), 19–36 |
| Grey | Zachary Grey, *Critical, Historical and Explanatory Notes on Shakespeare*, 2 vols (1754) |

445

| | |
|---|---|
| Grudin | Robert Grudin, 'The Soul of State: Ulyssean Irony in *Troilus and Cressida*', *Anglia*, 93 (1975), 55–69 |
| Hakluyt | Richard Hakluyt, *Divers Voyages Touching the Discovery of America* (1582) |
| Hale | David Hale, '"Madness of Discourse": Language and Ideology in *Troilus and Cressida*', paper delivered at a conference on Seventeenth-Century Literature, Orlando, Fla., March 1991 |
| Hall | Joseph Hall, *Satires*, ed. Thomas Warton (1824) |
| Hammer | Paul Hammer, 'Upstaging the Queen: The Earl of Essex, Francis Bacon and the Accession Day Celebrations of 1595', in *The Politics of the Stuart Court Masque*, ed. Peter Holbrook and David Bevington (Cambridge, 1998) |
| Harbage, *Annals* | Alfred Harbage, *Annals of English Drama, 975–1700*, 2nd edn rev. S. Schoenbaum (Philadelphia, 1964); 3rd edn rev. Sylvia Stoler Wagonheim (1989) |
| Harbage, *Rival Traditions* | Alfred Harbage, *Shakespeare and the Rival Traditions* (New York, 1952) |
| Hargreaves | H. A. Hargreaves, 'An Essentially Tragic *Troilus and Cressida*', *Humanities Association Bulletin*, 18.2 (1967), 49–60 |
| Harrier | Richard C. Harrier, 'Troilus Divided', in *Studies in the English Renaissance Drama*, ed. Josephine W. Bennett, Oscar Cargill and Vernon Hall, Jr (New York, 1959), 142–56 |
| Harris | Sharon M. Harris, 'Feminism and Shakespeare's Cressida: "*If* I be false . . ."', *Women's Studies*, 18 (1990), 65–82 |
| Harrison, *Elizabethan* | G. B. Harrison, ed., *The Elizabethan Journals*, 3 vols (1955) |
| Harrison, *Essex* | G. B. Harrison, *The Life and Death of Robert Devereux, Earl of Essex* (1937) |
| Harrison, 'Essex' | G. B. Harrison, 'The Earl of Essex', *TLS*, 29 (20 Nov. 1930), 974 |
| Haydn | Hiram Haydn, *The Counter-Renaissance* (New York, 1950) |
| Hazlitt | *The Collected Works of William Hazlitt*, ed. A. R. Waller and Arnold Glover, 12 vols (1902) |
| Heath | Benjamin Heath, *A Revisal of Shakespear's Text* (1765) |
| Hegel | *Introduction to the Reading of Hegel: Lectures on the Phenomenology of Spirit*, assembled by Raymond Queneau, trans. James H. Nichols, Jr, ed. Allan Bloom (New York, 1969) |
| Heine | *Heine on Shakespeare*, trans. Ida Barecke (1895), 42–5 |
| Helms | Lorraine Helms, '"Still Wars and Lechery": Shakespeare and the Last Trojan Woman', in *Arms and the Woman:* |

|  | *War, Gender, and Literary Representation*, ed. Helen M. Cooper, Adrienne Auslander Munich and Susan Merrill Squier (Chapel Hill, N.C., 1989), 25–42 |
| Helton | Tinsley Helton, 'Paradox and Hypothesis in *Troilus and Cressida*', *SSt*, 10 (1977), 115–31 |
| *Helyas* | Chevalier du Cygne, *The History of Helyas, Knight of the Swan*, trans. Robert Copland from the French version published in Paris in 1504. A literal reprint of the edition of Wynkin de Worde, 1512 (New York, 1901) |
| Henderson | W. B. Drayton Henderson, 'Shakespeare's *Troilus and Cressida* Yet Deeper in Its Tradition', in *Essays in Dramatic Literature: The Parrott Presentation Volume*, ed. Hardin Craig (Princeton, 1935), 127–56 |
| Henslowe | See Foakes & Rickert |
| Heywood, J. | *The Proverbs, Epigrams, and Miscellanies of John Heywood*, ed. John S. Farmer, EETS (1906, rpt. New York, 1966) |
| Heywood, T. | Thomas Heywood, *The Iron Age, Parts 1 & 2*, in *The Dramatic Works of Thomas Heywood*, 6 vols (1874), vol. 3 |
| Hinman, *Norton Folio* | Charlton Hinman, ed., *The First Folio of Shakespeare*, The Norton Facsimile (New York, 1968) |
| Hinman, *Printing* | Charlton Hinman, *The Printing and Proof-Reading of the First Folio of Shakespeare*, 2 vols (Oxford, 1963) |
| Hjort | Mette Hjort, *The Strategy of Letters* (Cambridge, Mass., 1993) |
| Hobbes | *The English Works of Thomas Hobbes of Malmesbury*, ed. William Molesworth, 11 vols (1839) |
| Hodgdon | Barbara Hodgdon, 'He Do Cressida in Different Voices', *ELR*, 20 (1990), 254–86 |
| Hogan | Charles B. Hogan, *Shakespeare in the Theatre, 1701–1800*, 2 vols (Oxford, 1952–7) |
| Holland *et al.* | Norman N. Holland, Sidney Homan and Bernard J. Paris, eds, *Shakespeare's Personality* (Berkeley, 1989) |
| *Homilies* | *The Book of Homilies*, vol. 1 (1547), vol. 2 (1563) |
| Honigmann, 'Date and Revision' | E. A. J. Honigmann, 'The Date and Revision of *Troilus and Cressida*', in *Textual Criticism and Literary Interpretation*, ed. Jerome J. McGann (Chicago, 1985), 38–54 |
| Honigmann, 'Re-enter' | E. A. J. Honigmann, 'Re-enter the Stage Direction: Shakespeare and Some Contemporaries', *SS*, 29 (1976), 117–25 |
| Honigmann, 'Shakespeare Suppressed' | E. A. J. Honigmann, 'Shakespeare Suppressed: The Unfortunate History of *Troilus and Cressida*', in *Myriad-Minded Shakespeare: Essays, Chiefly on the Tragedies and Problem Comedies* (New York, 1989), 112–29 |
| Honigmann, *Stability* | E. A. J. Honigmann, *The Stability of Shakespeare's Text* (1965) |

| | |
|---|---|
| Honigmann, *Texts* | E. A. J. Honigmann, *The Texts of 'Othello' and Shakespearian Revision* (1996) |
| Hooker, D. | Deborah A. Hooker, 'Coming to Cressida Through Irigaray', *South Atlantic Quarterly*, 88 (1989), 899–932 |
| Hooker, R. | Richard Hooker, *Of the Laws of Ecclesiastical Polity*, 1594, in *The Folger Library Edition of the Works of Richard Hooker*, gen. ed. W. Speed Hill (Cambridge, Mass., 1977–), vol. 1: Preface, Bks 1 to 4, ed. Georges Edelen (1977) |
| *Hortus Sanitatis* | *The Noble Lyfe and Nature of Man of Bestes Serpentys Fowles & Fisshes* (Antwerp, c. 1521). At least five editions were published between 1490 and 1521. Rpt. 1954. |
| Houser | David J. Houser, 'Armor and Motive in *Troilus and Cressida*', *Renaissance Drama*, n.s. 4 (1971), 121–34 |
| Hulme | Hilda M. Hulme, *Explorations in Shakespeare's Language: Some Problems of Lexical Meaning in the Dramatic Text* (1962) |
| Hunt | Maurice Hunt, 'Shakespeare's *Troilus and Cressida* and Christian Epistemology', *Christianity and Literature*, 42.2 (1993), 243–60 |
| Hunter, G. K. | G. K. Hunter, '*Troilus and Cressida*: A Tragic Satire', *Shakespeare Studies* (Tokyo), 13 (1977), 1–23 |
| Hunter, R. G. | Robert Grams Hunter, *Shakespeare and the Comedy of Forgiveness* (New York, 1965) |
| Hyland, 'Legitimacy' | Peter Hyland, 'Legitimacy in Interpretation: The Bastard Voice in *Troilus and Cressida*', *Mosaic*, 26 (1993), 1–13 |
| Hyland, *TC* | Peter Hyland, '*Troilus and Cressida*', Penguin Critical Studies (Harmondsworth, 1989) |
| Irigaray | Luce Irigaray, *Ce sexe qui n'en est pas un* (Paris, 1977), originally published as 'Le marché des femmes' in *Sessualità e politica* (Milan, 1978) |
| Jackson, MacD. | MacD. P. Jackson, 'Punctuation and the Compositors of Shakespeare's *Sonnets*, 1609', *The Library*, 5th ser., 30.1 (1975), 1–24 |
| Jackson, R. | Russell Jackson, 'Shakespeare in Stratford-upon-Avon: The Royal Shakespeare Company's "Half-Season", April–September 1996', *SQ*, 48 (1997), 208–15 |
| Jackson, Z. | Zachariah Jackson, *Shakespeare's Genius Justified* (1819) |
| Jagendorf | Zvi Jagendorf, 'All against One in *Troilus and Cressida*', *English*, 31 (1982), 199–210 |
| James | Heather James, '"Tricks we play on the dead": Making History in *Troilus and Cressida*', in *Shakespeare's Troy: Drama, Politics and the Translation of Empire* (Cambridge, 1997), 85–118 |
| Jamieson | Michael Jamieson, 'The Problem Plays, 1920–1970: A Retrospect', *SS*, 25 (1972), 1–10 |

448

| | |
|---|---|
| Jardine | Lisa Jardine, 'Twins and Travesties: Gender Dependency and Sexual Availability in *Twelfth Night*', in Zimmerman, ed., *Erotic Politics*, 27–38 |
| *JEGP* | *Journal of English and Germanic Philology* |
| Jensen | Phebe Jensen, 'The Textual Politics of *Troilus and Cressida*', *SQ*, 46 (1995), 414–23 |
| *JMRS* | *Journal of Medieval and Renaissance Studies* |
| Jones-Davies | M. T. Jones-Davies, 'Discord in Shakespeare's *Troilus and Cressida*; or, The Conflict between "Angry Mars and Venus Queen of Love"', *SQ*, 25 (1974), 33–41 |
| Jonson | *Ben Jonson*, ed. C. H. Herford and Percy and Evelyn Simpson, 11 vols (Oxford, 1925–52) |
| Jusserand | J. J. Jusserand, *A Literary History of the English People*, 3 vols (New York, 1906–7) |
| *JWCI* | *Journal of the Warburg and Courtauld Institutes* |
| Kahn | Coppélia Kahn, *Man's Estate: Masculine Identity in Shakespeare* (Berkeley, 1981) |
| Kastan | David Kastan, 'The Mechanics of Culture: Editing Shakespeare Today', *SSt*, 24 (1996), 30–7 |
| Kaufmann, 'Ceremonies' | R. J. Kaufmann, 'Ceremonies for Chaos: The Status of *Troilus and Cressida*', *ELH*, 32.2 (1965), 139–59 |
| Kaufmann, 'Poetics' | R. J. Kaufmann, 'On the Poetics of Terminal Tragedy: Dryden's *All for Love*', in *John Dryden: Twentieth Century Views* (Englewood Cliffs, N.J., 1963) |
| Kaula | David Kaula, 'Will and Reason in *Troilus and Cressida*', *SQ*, 12 (1961), 270–83 |
| Keightley | Thomas Keightley, *The Shakespeare-Expositor: An Aid to the Perfect Understanding of Shakespeare's Plays* (1867) |
| Kellner | Leon Kellner, *Restoring Shakespeare: A Critical Analysis of the Misreadings in Shakespeare's Works* (1925) |
| Kendall | Paul M. Kendall, 'Inaction and Ambivalence in *Troilus and Cressida*', in *English Studies in Honor of James Southall Wilson*, ed. Fredson Bowers (Charlottesville, Va., 1951), 131–45 |
| Kermode | Frank Kermode, 'Opinion, Truth and Value', *EIC*, 5 (1955), 181–7 |
| Kernan | Alvin Kernan, *The Cankered Muse: Satire of the English Renaissance* (New Haven, 1959) |
| Kimbrough | Robert Kimbrough, *Shakespeare's 'Troilus and Cressida' and Its Setting* (Cambridge, Mass., 1964) |
| King | T. J. King, *Casting Shakespeare's Plays: London Actors and Their Roles, 1590–1642* (Cambridge, 1992) |
| Kinnear | Benjamin Gott Kinnear, *Cruces Shakespearianae: Difficult Passages in the Works of Shakespeare* (1883) |
| Knight | G. Wilson Knight, *The Wheel of Fire* (Oxford, 1930) |

| | |
|---|---|
| Knights, '*TC*' | L. C. Knights, '*Troilus and Cressida*', *TLS*, 2 June 1932, 408 |
| Knights, 'Theme' | L. C. Knights, 'The Theme of Appearance and Reality in *Troilus and Cressida*', in *Some Shakespearean Themes* (1959), 65–83; rpt. from *Scrutiny*, 18 (1951–2), 144–57 |
| Knowland | A. S. Knowland, '*Troilus and Cressida*', *SQ*, 10 (1959), 353–65 |
| Knutson | Roslyn L. Knutson, 'Falconer to the Little Eyases: A New Date and Commercial Agenda for the "Little Eyases" Passage in *Hamlet*', *SQ*, 46 (1995), 1–31 |
| Kopper | John M. Kopper, 'Troilus at Pluto's Gates: Subjectivity and the Duplicity of Discourse in Shakespeare's *Troilus and Cressida*', in Atkins & Bergeron, eds, *Shakespeare and Deconstruction*, 149–71 |
| Kott | Jan Kott, '*Troilus and Cressida* – Amazing and Modern', in *Shakespeare Our Contemporary*, trans. Boleslaw Taborski (1964), 75–83 |
| Kristeva | Julia Kristeva, *Tales of Love*, trans. S. Roudiez (New York, 1987) |
| Kyd | Thomas Kyd, *The Spanish Tragedy*, ed. David Bevington (Manchester, 1996) |
| LaBranche | Linda LaBranche, 'Visual Patterns and Linking Analogues in *Troilus and Cressida*', *SQ*, 37 (1986), 440–50 |
| Lacan | Jacques Lacan, *Écrits*, 2 vols (Paris, 1966) |
| Langland | See *Piers Plowman* |
| Langman | F. H. Langman, '*Troilus and Cressida*', in *Jonson and Shakespeare*, ed. Ian Donaldson (Atlantic Highlands, N.J., 1983), 57–73 |
| Lawrence, *Problem* | William Witherle Lawrence, *Shakespeare's Problem Comedies*, 2nd edn (New York, 1960) |
| Lawrence, 'Troilus' | William Witherle Lawrence, 'Troilus, Cressida and Thersites', *MLR*, 37 (1942), 422–37 |
| LCL | Loeb Classical Library |
| Leech | Clifford Leech, 'Shakespeare's Greeks', *Stratford Papers on Shakespeare 1963*, ed. B. W. Jackson (Toronto, 1964), 1–20 |
| Leiter | *Shakespeare Around the Globe: A Guide to Notable Postwar Revivals*, ed. Samuel L. Leiter (New York, 1986) |
| Lenz, J. | Joseph Lenz, 'Base Trade: Theater as Prostitution', *ELH*, 60 (1993), 833–55 |
| Lenz *et al.* | Carolyn Ruth Swift Lenz, Gayle Greene and Carol Thomas Neely, eds, *The Woman's Part: Feminist Criticism of Shakespeare* (Urbana, Ill., 1980) |
| Lettsom | W. N. Lettsom, 'New Readings in Shakespeare', *Blackwood's Edinburgh Magazine*, 74 (August 1853), 181–202 |

| | |
|---|---|
| Lévi-Strauss | Claude Lévi-Strauss, *Les Structures élémentaires de la Parenté* (*The Elementary Structures of Kinship*), trans. James Harle Bell, John Richard von Sturmer and Rodney Needham (Boston, 1969) |
| Levine | Laura Levine, '*Troilus and Cressida* and the Politics of Rage', in *Men in Women's Clothing: Anti-theatricality and Effeminization* (Cambridge, 1994), 26–43 |
| Linthicum | Marie Channing Linthicum, *Costume in the Drama of Shakespeare and His Contemporaries* (Oxford, 1936) |
| Lodge | *The Complete Works of Thomas Lodge*, Hunterian Club (1883) |
| Loggins | Vernon P. Loggins, *The Life of Our Design: Organization and Related Strategies in 'Troilus and Cressida'* (Lanham, Md., 1992) |
| Long, Michael | Michael Long, *The Unnatural Scene: A Study in Shakespearean Tragedy* (1976), 102–22 |
| Long, 'A bed' | William B. Long, ' "A bed / for woodstock": A Warning for the Unwary', *MRDE*, 2 (1985), 91–118 |
| Long, 'Stage-Directions' | William B. Long, 'Stage-Directions: A Misinterpreted Factor in Determining Textual Provenance', *Text*, 2 (1985), 121–37 |
| Love | Harold Love, *Scribal Publication in Seventeenth-Century England* (Oxford, 1993) |
| Lydgate | *Lydgate's Troy Book*, A.D. 1412–20, ed. Henry Bergen, EETS, extra series 97, 103, 106 (1906, 1908, 1910) |
| Lyly, *Campaspe* | John Lyly, *Campaspe* and *Sappho and Phao*, ed. George Hunter and David Bevington (Manchester, 1991) |
| Lyly, *Euphues* | John Lyly, *Euphues*, in *The Complete Works of John Lyly*, ed. R. Warwick Bond, 3 vols (Oxford, 1902) |
| Lyly, *Midas* | John Lyly, *Midas*, in *The Complete Works of John Lyly*, ed. R. Warwick Bond, 3 vols (Oxford, 1902) |
| Lynch, 'Cressida' | Stephen J. Lynch, 'Shakespeare's Cressida: "A Woman of Quick Sense" ', *PQ*, 63 (1984), 357–68 |
| Lynch, 'Hector' | Stephen J. Lynch, 'Hector and the Theme of Honor in *Troilus and Cressida*', *Upstart Crow*, 7 (1987), 68–79 |
| Lyons, Charles | Charles Lyons, 'Cressida, Achilles, and the Finite Deed', *Études Anglaises*, 20 (1967), 233–42 |
| Lyons, Clifford | Clifford P. Lyons, 'The Trysting Scenes in *Troilus and Cressida*', *Shakespearean Studies*, ed. Alvin Thaler and Norman Sanders (Knoxville, Tenn., 1964), 105–20 |
| McAlindon | T. McAlindon, 'Language, Style, and Meaning in *Troilus and Cressida*', *PMLA*, 84 (1969), 29–43 |
| McCoy | Richard McCoy, ' "A Dangerous Image": The Earl of Essex and Elizabethan Chivalry', *JMRS*, 13 (1983), 313–29 |
| McKenzie | D. F. McKenzie, 'Printers of the Mind: Some Notes on Bibliographical Theories and Printing-House Practices', *SB*, 22 (1969), 1–75 |

Main                William W. Main, 'Character Amalgams in Shakespeare's *Troilus and Cressida*', *SP*, 58 (1961), 170–8

Mallin            Eric S. Mallin, 'Emulous Factions and the Collapse of Chivalry: *Troilus and Cressida*', *Representations*, 29 (1990), 145–79; rpt. in *Inscribing the Time: Shakespeare and the End of Elizabethan England* (Berkeley, 1995), 25–61

Mann               Jill Mann, 'Shakespeare and Chaucer: "What is Criseyde Worth?"', *Cambridge Quarterly*, 18 (1989), 109–28

Marcuse          Herbert Marcuse, *Eros and Civilization: A Philosophical Inquiry into Freud* (New York, 1962, Boston, 1966)

Marlowe, *Faustus*    Christopher Marlowe, *Doctor Faustus, A- and B- Texts*, ed. David Bevington and Eric Rasmussen (Manchester, 1993)

Marlowe,         Christopher Marlowe, *Tamburlaine the Great*, ed. J. S.
   *Tamburlaine*    Cunningham (Manchester, 1981)

Marsh              Derick R. C. Marsh, 'Interpretation and Misinterpretation: the Problem of *Troilus and Cressida*', *SSt*, 1 (1965), 182–98

Marston, *AM*       John Marston, *Antonio and Mellida*, ed. W. Reavley Gair (Manchester, 1991)

Marston, *AR*       John Marston, *Antonio's Revenge*, ed. W. Reavley Gair (Manchester, 1978)

Martin             Priscilla Martin, ed., *Shakespeare's 'Troilus and Cressida': A Casebook* (1976)

Mason             John Monck Mason, *Comments on the Last Edition of Shakespeare's Plays* [Var '78] (1785, with subsequent volumes in 1797 and 1807)

Mead              Stephen X. Mead, '"Thou art chang'd": Public Value and Personal Identity in *Troilus and Cressida*', *JMRS*, 22 (1992), 237–59

Meyer             George Wilbur Meyer, 'Order out of Chaos in Shakespeare's *Troilus and Cressida*', *Tulane Studies in English*, 4 (1954), 45–56

Miller, J. H.       J. Hillis Miller, 'Ariachne's Broken Woof', *Georgia Review*, 31 (1977), 44–60

Miller, R.         Robert P. Miller, 'The Myth of Mars's Hot Minion in *Venus and Adonis*', *ELH*, 26 (1959), 470–81

Milward          Peter Milward, *Shakespeare's Religious Background* (1973)

Minsheu         John Minsheu, *Ductor in Linguas (Guide into the Tongues)* (1617, rpt. Delmar, N.Y., 1978)

*MLN*              *Modern Language Notes*

*MLQ*              *Modern Language Quarterly*

*MLR*              *Modern Language Review*

Montaigne       Michel de Montaigne, *Essays*, trans. John Florio (1603)

Montrose        Louis Adrian Montrose, '"Shaping Fantasies": Figurations of Gender and Power in Elizabethan Culture', *Representations*, 2 (Spring 1983), 61–94

| | |
|---|---|
| Morris | Brian Morris, 'The Tragic Structure of *Troilus and Cressida*', *SQ*, 10 (1959), 481–91 |
| Mowat | Barbara A. Mowat, 'Shakespearean Tragicomedy', in *Renaissance Tragicomedy: Explorations in Genre and Politics*, ed. Nancy Klein Maguire (New York, 1987), 80–96 |
| *MRDE* | *Medieval and Renaissance Drama in England* |
| Muir, *Sources* | Kenneth Muir, *Shakespeare's Sources*, 2 vols (1917, rpt. 1961, 1965) |
| Muir, '*TC*' | Kenneth Muir, '*Troilus and Cressida*', *SS*, 8 (1955), 28–39 |
| Muir, 'Adaptations' | Kenneth Muir, 'Three Shakespeare Adaptations', *Proceedings of the Leeds Philosophical and Literary Society*, 8 (1958), 233–40 |
| *N&Q* | *Notes and Queries* |
| Nares | Robert Nares, *A Glossary of Words, Places, Names, and Allusions*, new edn (1905) |
| Nass | Barry Nass, '"Yet in the trial much opinion dwells": The Combat between Hector and Ajax in *Troilus and Cressida*', *ES*, 65 (1984), 1–10 |
| Naylor | Edward W. Naylor, *Shakespeare and Music* (1931) |
| Neely | Carol Thomas Neely, *Broken Nuptials in Shakespeare's Plays* (New Haven, 1985) |
| Newlin, 'Darkened Stage' | Jeanne T. Newlin, 'The Darkened Stage: J. P. Kemble and *Troilus and Cressida*', in *The Triple Bond: Plays, Mainly Shakespearean in Performance*, ed. Joseph G. Price (University Park, Penn., 1975) |
| Newlin, 'Modernity' | Jeanne T. Newlin, 'The Modernity of *Troilus and Cressida*: The Case for Theatrical Criticism', *Harvard Library Bulletin*, 17 (1967), 353–73 |
| Nicoll | Allardyce Nicoll, '"Passing over the Stage"', *SS*, 12 (1959), 47–55 |
| Noble | Richmond Noble, *Shakespeare's Biblical Knowledge and Use of The Book of Common Prayer* (1935) |
| Norbrook | David Norbrook, 'Rhetoric, Ideology and the Elizabethan World Picture', in *Renaissance Rhetoric*, ed. Peter Mack (1994), 140–64 |
| Nosworthy | J. M. Nosworthy, *Shakespeare's Occasional Plays: Their Origin and Transmission* (1965) |
| Novy | Marianne L. Novy, *Love's Argument: Gender Relations in Shakespeare* (Chapel Hill, N.C., 1984), 99–124 |
| Nowottny | Winifred M. T. Nowottny, '"Opinion" and "Value" in *Troilus and Cressida*', *EIC*, 4 (1954), 282–96 |
| Oates | Joyce Carol Oates, 'The Ambiguity of *Troilus and Cressida*', *SQ*, 17 (1966), 141–50 |

| Odell | George C. D. Odell, *Shakespeare from Betterton to Irving*, 2 vols (New York, 1920, rpt. 1966) |
| --- | --- |
| *OED* | *Oxford English Dictionary*, 2nd edn |
| Offenbach | Jacques Offenbach, *La Belle Hélène, opéra bouffe en 3 actes*, performed in Paris, 1864, *arrangée par Léon Rogues* (Paris, no date) |
| Onions | C. T. Onions, *A Shakespeare Glossary*, enlarged and revised by Robert D. Eagleson (Oxford, 1986) |
| Orger | John G. Orger, *Critical Notes on Shakspere's Histories and Tragedies* (1890) |
| Ornstein | Robert Ornstein, *The Moral Vision of Jacobean Tragedy* (Madison, Wis., 1960) |
| O'Rourke | James O'Rourke, '"Rule in Unity" and Otherwise: Love and Sex in *Troilus and Cressida*', *SQ*, 43 (1992), 139–58 |
| Palmer, J. S. | J. S. Palmer, in *Transactions of the Royal Society of Literature*, 2nd ser., 15 (1893), 64ff. |
| Palmer, K. | See Ard[2] |
| Panofsky | Erwin Panofsky, *Studies in Iconology* (New York, 1962) |
| Parker | Patricia Parker, *Shakespeare from the Margins: Language, Culture, Context* (Chicago, 1996) |
| Parker & Hartman | Patricia Parker and Geoffrey Hartman, eds, *Shakespeare and the Question of Theory* (1985) |
| Parnassus Plays | *The Three Parnassus Plays (1598–1601)*, ed. J. B. Leishman (1949) |
| Partridge | Eric Partridge, *Shakespeare's Bawdy* (New York, 1960) |
| Patke | Rajeev S. Patke, '*Troilus* and the Divisiveness of Experience', in *Shakespeare in India*, ed. S. Nagarajan and S. Viswanathan (Delhi, 1987), 1–17 |
| *PBSA* | *Papers of the Bibliographical Society of America* |
| Penniman | Josiah H. Penniman, *The War of the Theatres* (Boston, 1897) |
| Phillips | James Emerson Phillips, Jr, *The State in Shakespeare's Greek and Roman Plays* (New York, 1940) |
| Pico | G. Pico della Mirandola, *De Hominis Dignitate, Heptaplus, De Ente et Uno*, etc., with Commentary, ed. Eugenio Garin (Florence, 1942) |
| *Piers Plowman* | *The Vision of William Concerning Piers the Plowman, in Three Parallel Texts*, by William Langland, ed. Walter W. Skeat, 2 vols (Oxford, 1886) |
| *PMLA* | *Publications of the Modern Language Association of America* |
| Poel | William Poel, *Shakespeare in the Theatre* (1913) |
| Pollard | A. W. Pollard, *Shakespeare's Fight with the Pirates and the Problems of the Transmission of His Text*, 2nd edn (1917) |
| Potter | A. M. Potter, '*Troilus and Cressida*: Deconstructing the Middle Ages?' *Theoria*, 72 (1988), 23–35 |

Potts    Abbie Findlay Potts, '*Cynthia's Revels, Poetaster*, and *Troilus and Cressida*', *SQ*, 5 (1954), 297–302

Powell   Neil Powell, 'Hero and Human: The Problem of Achilles', *CritQ*, 21 (1979), 17–28

*PQ*     *Philological Quarterly*

Presson   Robert K. Presson, *Shakespeare's 'Troilus and Cressida' and the Legends of Troy* (Madison, Wis., 1953)

Prosser   Eleanor Prosser, *Shakespeare's Anonymous Editors: Scribe and Compositor in the Folio Text of '2 Henry IV'* (Stanford, 1981)

Proudfoot  Richard Proudfoot, in private correspondence as general editor of this edition

Puttenham  George Puttenham, *The Arte of English Poesie*, ed. Gladys Doidge Willcock and Alice Walker (Cambridge, 1936)

Rabkin   Norman Rabkin, *Shakespeare and the Common Understanding* (New York, 1967), 30–79

Ramsey   Jarold W. Ramsey, 'The Provenance of *Troilus and Cressida*', *SQ*, 21 (1970), 223–40

Read    Conyers Read, *Lord Burghley and Queen Elizabeth* (1960)

Reid    Stephen A. Reid, 'A Psychoanalytic Reading of *Troilus and Cressida* and *Measure for Measure*', *Psychoanalytic Review*, 57 (1970–1), 263–73

Reynolds  George F. Reynolds, '*Troilus and Cressida* on the Elizabethan Stage', in *Joseph Quincy Adams Memorial Studies*, ed. James G. McManaway, Giles E. Dawson and Edwin E. Willoughby (Washington, D.C., 1948), 229–38

Richards   I. A. Richards, '*Troilus and Cressida* and Plato', *Hudson Review*, 1 (1948), 362–76; rpt. in *Speculative Instruments* (Chicago, 1955)

Rickey   Mary Ellen Rickey, ' 'Twixt the Dangerous Shores: *Troilus and Cressida* Again', *SQ*, 15.1 (1964), 3–13

Ritson   Joseph Ritson, *Remarks, Critical and Illustrative, on the Text and Notes of the Last Edition of Shakespeare* (1783)

Roberts   Jeanne Addison Roberts, *The Shakespearean Wild: Geography, Genus, and Gender* (Lincoln, Nebr., 1991)

Rodway   Norman Rodway, '*Troilus and Cressida*', in *Shakespeare in Perspective*, ed. Roger Sales, 2 vols (1985), 41–50

Rollins   Hyder E. Rollins, 'The Troilus–Cressida Story from Chaucer to Shakespeare', *PMLA*, 34 (1917), 383–429

Rossiter   A. P. Rossiter, *Angel with Horns and Other Shakespeare Lectures*, ed. Graham Storey (1961), 129–51

Roy    Emil Roy, 'War and Manliness in Shakespeare's *Troilus and Cressida*', *CompD*, 7 (1973), 107–20

Rubin   Gayle Rubin, 'The Traffic in Women: Notes on the "Political Economy" of Sex', in *Toward an Anthropology of Women*, ed. Rayna P. Reiter (New York, 1975), 157–210

| | |
|---|---|
| Rutter, 'Cressida's Glove' | Carol Rutter, 'Shakespeare, His Designers, and the Politics of Costume: Handing Over Cressida's Glove', *Essays in Theatre / Études Théâtrales*, 12.2 (1994), 106–28 |
| Rutter, *Voices* | Carol Rutter, *Clamorous Voices: Shakespeare's Women Today* (1989) |
| Sacharoff | Mark Sacharoff, 'The Traditions of the Troy-Story Heroes and the Problem of Satire in *Troilus and Cressida*', *SSt*, 6 (1972 for 1970), 125–35 |
| Savage | James E. Savage, '*Troilus and Cressida* and Elizabeth [*sic*] Court Factions', *University of Mississippi Studies in English*, 5 (1964), 43–66 |
| *SB* | *Studies in Bibliography* |
| Schanzer | Ernest Schanzer, *The Problem Plays of Shakespeare: A Study of 'Julius Caesar', 'Measure for Measure', 'Antony and Cleopatra'* (1963) |
| Schlegel | August Wilhelm von Schlegel, *Lectures on Dramatic Art and Literature* (1808; trans. into English by John Black, 1815; 2nd edn, rev. A. J. W. Morrison, 1889) |
| Schmidt | Alexander Schmidt, *Shakespeare-Lexicon*, 3rd edn (New York, 1971) |
| Schmidt di Simoni | Karen Schmidt di Simoni, *Shakespeare's 'Troilus and Cressida'. Eine sprachlich-stilistische Untersuching* (Heidelberg, 1960) |
| Schwartz | Elias Schwartz, 'Tonal Equivocation and the Meaning of *Troilus and Cressida*', *SP*, 69 (1972), 304–19 |
| Schwartz & Kahn | Murray M. Schwartz and Coppélia Kahn, eds, *Representing Shakespeare: New Psychoanalytic Essays* (Baltimore, 1980) |
| Scot | Reginald Scot, *The Discovery of Witchcraft* (1584) |
| Scott | William O. Scott, 'Self-Difference in *Troilus and Cressida*', in Atkins & Bergeron, eds, *Shakespeare and Deconstruction*, 129–47 |
| Seager | H. W. Seager, *Natural History in Shakespeare's Time* (1896, rpt. New York, 1971) |
| Sedgwick | Eve Kosofsky Sedgwick, *Between Men: English Literature and Male Homosocial Desire* (New York, 1985) |
| *SEL* | *Studies in English Literature* |
| Seltzer | Daniel Seltzer, ed., *Troilus and Cressida*, The Signet Classic Shakespeare (New York, 1963, rev. 1988) |
| *ShAB* | *Shakespeare Association Bulletin* |
| Shaheen | Naseeb Shaheen, *Biblical References in Shakespeare's Tragedies* (Newark, Del., 1987) |
| Shakespeare | See headnote to 'Abbreviations and References', p. 430 |
| Shalvi | Alice Shalvi, '"Honor" in *Troilus and Cressida*', *SEL*, 5 (1965), 283–302 |

| | |
|---|---|
| Sharpe | Robert B. Sharpe, *The Real War of the Theatres: Shakespeare's Fellows in Rivalry with the Admiral's Men, 1594–1603, Repertories, Devices, and Types* (Boston, 1935) |
| Shattuck | Charles H. Shattuck, *The Shakespeare Promptbooks* (Urbana, Ill., 1965) |
| Shaw | William P. Shaw, '*Troilus and Cressida*, V, iv–V, x: Giving Chaos a Name and a Local Habitation', abstract of a conference paper, *ShN*, 26 (1976), 24 |
| Sheppard | Angela Sheppard, 'Soiled Mother or Soul of Woman?: A Response to *Troilus and Cressida*', in *The Undiscover'd Country: New Essays on Psychoanalysis and Shakespeare*, ed. B. J. Sokol (1993), 130–49 |
| *ShN* | *Shakespeare Newsletter* |
| Shrimpton | Nicholas Shrimpton, 'Shakespeare's Performances in London and Stratford-upon-Avon, 1984–5', *SS*, 39 (1987), 191–205 |
| Siegel | Paul N. Siegel, 'Shakespeare and the Neo-Chivalric Cult of Honor', *Centennial Review*, 8 (1964), 39–70 |
| Simmons | J. L. Simmons, *Shakespeare's Pagan World: The Roman Tragedies* (Charlottesville, Va., 1973) |
| Sisson, *New Readings* | C. J. Sisson, *New Readings in Shakespeare*, 2 vols (Cambridge, 1956) |
| *SJ(E)* | *Shakespeare Jahrbuch* (*East*) |
| Skura | Meredith Anne Skura, *Shakespeare the Actor and the Purposes of Playing* (Chicago, 1993) |
| Slater | Ann Pasternak Slater, *Shakespeare the Director* (Brighton, 1982) |
| Slights | Camille Slights, 'The Parallel Structure of *Troilus and Cressida*', *SQ*, 25 (1974), 42–51 |
| Small | R. A. Small, *The Stage-Quarrel between Ben Jonson and the So-called Poetasters* (Breslau, 1899) |
| Smith, A. J. | A. J. Smith, 'Time's Fools', in *Literary Love: The Role of Passion in English Poems and Plays of the Seventeenth Century* (1983), 10–34 |
| Smith, B., *Desire* | Bruce R. Smith, *Homosexual Desire in Shakespeare's England: A Cultural Poetics* (Chicago, 1991) |
| Smith, B., 'Rape' | Bruce R. Smith, 'Rape, rap, rupture, rapture: R-rated Futures on the Global Market', *Textual Practice*, 9.3 (1995), 421–43 |
| Smith, J. O. | J. Oates Smith, 'Essence and Existence in Shakespeare's *Troilus and Cressida*', *PQ*, 46 (1967), 167–85 |
| Smith, W. | Warren D. Smith, 'The *Henry V* Choruses in the First Folio', *JEGP*, 53 (1954), 38–57 |
| Snyder | Susan Snyder, *The Comic Matrix of Shakespeare's Tragedies* (Princeton, 1979) |

| | |
|---|---|
| Soellner, *Patterns* | Rolf Soellner, '*Troilus and Cressida*: Fragmenting a Divided Self', in *Shakespeare's Patterns of Self-Knowledge* (Columbus, Oh., 1972), 195–214 |
| Soellner, 'Prudence' | Rolf Soellner, 'Prudence and the Price of Helen: The Debate of the Trojans in *Troilus and Cressida*', *SQ*, 20 (1969), 255–63 |
| Southall | Raymond Southall, '*Troilus and Cressida* and the Spirit of Capitalism', in *Shakespeare in a Changing World*, ed. Arnold Kettle (1964), 217–32 |
| *SP* | *Studies in Philology* |
| *SPD* | *Calendar of State Papers, Domestic Series, of the Reign of Elizabeth, 1595–1597*, ed. Mary Anne Everett, ser. 1, vol. 4 (1869) |
| Speaight, *Poel* | Robert Speaight, *William Poel and the Elizabethan Revival* (1954) |
| Speaight, *Shakespeare on Stage* | Robert Speaight, *Shakespeare on the Stage: An Illustrated History of Shakespearean Performance* (1973) |
| Speaight, '1960' | Robert Speaight, 'The 1960 Season at Stratford-upon-Avon', *SQ*, 11 (1960), 445–53 |
| Speaight, '1970' | Robert Speaight, 'Shakespeare in Britain', *SQ*, 21 (1970), 444–5 |
| Spear | Gary Spear, 'Shakespeare's "Manly" Parts: Masculinity and Effeminacy in *Troilus and Cressida*', *SQ*, 44 (1993), 409–22 |
| Speed | John Speed, *History of Great Britain* (1611) |
| Spencer, H. | Hazelton Spencer, *Shakespeare Improved: The Restoration Versions in Quarto and on the Stage* (Cambridge, Mass., 1927) |
| Spencer, T. | Theodore Spencer, *Shakespeare and the Nature of Man* (New York and Cambridge, 1943) |
| Spencer, T. J. B. | T. J. B. Spencer, '"Greeks" and "Merrygreeks": A Background to *Timon of Athens* and *Troilus and Cressida*', in *Essays on Shakespeare and Elizabethan Drama in Honor of Hardin Craig*, ed. Richard Hosley (Columbia, Mo., 1962), 223–33 |
| Spurgeon | Caroline Spurgeon, *Shakespeare's Imagery and What It Tells Us* (Cambridge, 1935) |
| *SQ* | *Shakespeare Quarterly* |
| S.R. | *A Transcript of the Registers of the Company of Stationers of London, 1554–1640 A.D.*, ed. Edward Arber, 5 vols (1876) |
| *SS* | *Shakespeare Survey* |
| *SSt* | *Shakespeare Studies* |
| Stamm | Rudolf Stamm, 'The Glass of Pandar's Praise: The Word-Scenery, Mirror Passages, and Reported Scenes in |

Shakespeare's *Troilus and Cressida*', *Essays and Studies*, n.s. 17 (1964), 55–77

Stein, A.     Arnold Stein, '*Troilus and Cressida*: The Disjunctive Imagination', *ELH*, 36 (1969), 145–67

Stein, E.     Elizabeth Stein, 'Caxton's *Recuyell* and Shakespeare's *Troilus*', *MLN*, 45 (1930), 144–6

Sternfeld     F. W. Sternfeld, *Music in Shakespearean Tragedy* (1963)

Stiller     Nikki Stiller, *The Figure of Cressida in British and American Literature: Transformations of a Literary Type* (Lewiston, N.Y., 1990)

Stockholder     Katherine Stockholder, 'Power and Pleasure in *Troilus and Cressida*, or Rhetoric and Structure of the Anti-Tragic', *College English*, 30 (1968–9), 539–54

Stříbrný     Zdenek Stříbrný, 'Time in *Troilus and Cressida*', *SJ(E)*, 112 (1976), 105–21

Strong     Roy Strong, *The Cult of Elizabeth: Elizabethan Portraiture and Pageantry* (1977)

Styan, *Comedy*     John Styan, *The Dark Comedy: The Development of Modern Comic Tragedy*, 2nd edn (Cambridge, 1968)

Styan, *Revolution*     John Styan, *The Shakespeare Revolution: Criticism and Performance in the Twentieth Century* (Cambridge, 1977)

Swanston     Hamish F. G. Swanston, 'The Baroque Element in *Troilus and Cressida*', *Durham University Journal*, n.s. 19 (1957), 14–23

Swinburne     Algernon C. Swinburne, *A Study of Shakespeare* (1880, rpt. New York, 1965)

Tannenbaum, 'Notes'     Samuel A. Tannenbaum, 'Notes on *Troilus and Cressida*', *ShAB*, 7 (1932), 72–81

Tannenbaum, 'Critique'     Samuel A. Tannenbaum, 'A Critique of the Text of *Troilus and Cressida*', *ShAB*, 9 (1934), 55–74, 125–44, 198–214

Tanselle     G. Thomas Tanselle, *Textual Criticism and Scholarly Editing* (Charlottesville, Va., 1990)

Tatlock     John S. P. Tatlock, 'The Siege of Troy in Elizabethan Literature, Especially in Shakespeare and Heywood', *PMLA*, 30 (1915), 673–770

Taylor, 'Copy-Text'     Gary Taylor, 'Copy-Text and Collation (with Special Reference to *Richard III*)', *The Library*, 6th ser., 3 (1981), 33–42

Taylor, *Reinventing*     Gary Taylor, *Reinventing Shakespeare: A Cultural History, from the Restoration to the Present* (New York, 1989)

Taylor, '*TC*'     Gary Taylor, '*Troilus and Cressida*: Bibliography, Performance, and Interpretation', *SSt*, 15 (1982), 99–136

| Taylor & Warren | Gary Taylor and Michael Warren, eds, *The Division of the Kingdoms: Shakespeare's Two Versions of 'King Lear'* (Oxford, 1983) |
| Taylor, 'Attitude' | George Coffin Taylor, 'Shakespeare's Attitude towards Love and Honor in *Troilus and Cressida*', *PMLA*, 45 (1930), 781–6 |
| Taylor, *Montaigne* | George Coffin Taylor, *Shakspere's Debt to Montaigne* (Cambridge, Mass., 1925) |
| *TES* | *Times Educational Supplement* |
| Thirlby | Styan Thirlby's conjectures, unpublished, chiefly in the form of manuscript annotations in his copies of eighteenth-century editions and in letters to editors including Theobald; contributor to Theobald's 1733 edition |
| Thiselton | Alfred E. Thiselton, *Notulae Criticae* (1907) |
| Thomas | Vivian Thomas, *The Moral Universe of Shakespeare's Problem Plays* (Totowa, N.J., 1987), 81–139 |
| Thompson, A. | Ann Thompson, *Shakespeare's Chaucer: A Study in Literary Origins* (Liverpool, 1978) |
| Thompson, A. & J. | Ann and John O. Thompson, *Shakespeare: Meaning and Metaphor* (Iowa City, 1987) |
| Thomson, J. A. K. | J. A. K. Thomson, *Shakespeare and the Classics* (1952) |
| Thomson, P. | Patricia Thomson, 'Rant and Cant in *Troilus and Cressida*', *Essays and Studies*, n.s. 22 (1969), 33–56 |
| Tiffany | Grace Tiffany, 'Not Saying No: Female Self-erasure in *Troilus and Cressida*', *TSLL*, 35 (1993), 44–56 |
| Tilley | Morris Palmer Tilley, *A Dictionary of the Proverbs in England in the Sixteenth and Seventeenth Centuries* (Ann Arbor, Mich., 1950) |
| Tillyard | E. M. W. Tillyard, *Shakespeare's Problem Plays* (1971), 33–88 |
| *TLS* | *Times Literary Supplement* (London) |
| Toole | William B. Toole, *Shakespeare's Problem Plays: Studies in Form and Meaning* (The Hague, 1966), 198–230 |
| Topsell | Edward Topsell, *The History of Four-Footed Beasts*, collected out of the writings of Conrad Gesner (1607–8, printed with Thomas Mouffet's *The Theatre of Insects*, 1658; rpt. New York, 1967) |
| Traversi | Derek Traversi, *An Approach to Shakespeare: 'Troilus and Cressida' to 'The Tempest'*, 3rd edn (1969), 26–42 |
| *TSLL* | *Texas Studies in Literature and Language* |
| *TxC* | Stanley Wells and Gary Taylor, *William Shakespeare: A Textual Companion* (Oxford, 1987) |
| Tylee | Claire M. Tylee, 'The Text of Cressida and Every Ticklish Reader: *Troilus and Cressida*, The Greek Camp Scene', *SS*, 41 (1989), 63–76 |

| | |
|---|---|
| Tyrwhitt | Thomas Tyrwhitt, *Observations and Conjectures upon Some Passages of Shakespeare* (Oxford, 1766) |
| Upton | John Upton, *Critical Observations on Shakespeare* (1746) |
| Ure | Peter Ure, *William Shakespeare: The Problem Plays* (1964) |
| Urkowitz | Steven Urkowitz, *Shakespeare's Revision of 'King Lear'* (Princeton, 1980) |
| *UTQ* | *University of Toronto Quarterly* |
| Van Doren | Mark Van Doren, *Shakespeare* (New York, 1939), 172–8 |
| Venezky | Alice S. Venezky, *Pageantry on the Shakespearean Stage* (New York, 1951) |
| Vickers, *Appropriating* | Brian Vickers, *Appropriating Shakespeare: Contemporary Critical Quarrels* (New Haven, 1993) |
| Vickers, *Artistry* | Brian Vickers, *The Artistry of Shakespeare's Prose* (1968) |
| Voth & Evans | Grant L. Voth and Oliver H. Evans, 'Cressida and the World of the Play', *SSt*, 8 (1975), 231–9 |
| Waddington | Raymond B. Waddington, 'Antony and Cleopatra: "What Venus did with Mars"', *SSt*, 2 (1966), 210–26 |
| Walker, *Textual* | Alice Walker, *Textual Problems of the First Folio: Richard III, King Lear, Troilus and Cressida, 2 Henry IV, Hamlet, Othello* (Cambridge, 1953) |
| Walker, W. S. | William Sidney Walker, *A Critical Examination of the Text of Shakespeare*, 3 vols (1860) |
| Walter | J. H. Walter, in private communication to the editor of Ard[2] |
| Warren | Roger Warren, 'Shakespeare in Britain, 1985', *SQ*, 37 (1986), 114–20 |
| Watson | Curtis Brown Watson, *Shakespeare and the Renaissance Concept of Honor* (Princeton, 1960) |
| Weimann | Robert Weimann, *Shakespeare and the Popular Tradition in the Theater* (Baltimore, 1978) |
| Weis | René Weis, ed., *King Lear: A Parallel Text Edition* (1993) |
| Wells & Taylor, 'Re-viewed' | Stanley Wells and Gary Taylor, 'The Oxford Shakespeare Re-viewed by the General Editors', *AEB: Analytical and Enumerative Bibliography*, n.s. 4 (1990), 6–20 |
| Werstine, 'Foul Papers' | Paul Werstine, '"Foul Papers" and "Prompt-books": Printer's Copy for Shakespeare's *Comedy of Errors*', *SB*, 41 (1988), 232–46 |
| Werstine, 'Narratives' | Paul Werstine, 'Narratives about Printed Shakespeare Texts: "Foul Papers" and "Bad" Quartos', *SQ*, 41 (1990), 65–86 |
| Werstine, 'Plays in Manuscript' | Paul Werstine, 'Plays in Manuscript', in Cox & Kastan, eds, *New History*, 481–97 |
| Wheeler | Richard P. Wheeler, *Shakespeare's Development and the Problem Comedies: Turn and Counter-Turn* (Berkeley, 1981) |

| | |
|---|---|
| Whitaker | Virgil K. Whitaker, 'Still Another Source for *Troilus and Cressida*', in *English Renaissance Drama, Essays in Honor of Madeleine Doran and Mark Eccles*, ed. Standish Henning, Robert Kimbrough and Richard Knowles (Carbondale, Ill., 1976), 100–7 |
| Whiter | Walter Whiter, *A Specimen of a Commentary on Shakspeare* (1794) |
| Willbern | David Willbern, 'What Is Shakespeare?' in Holland *et al.*, eds, *Shakespeare's Personality*, 226–43 |
| Williams, G., *Dictionary* | Gordon Williams, *A Dictionary of Sexual Language and Imagery in Shakespearean and Stuart Literature*, 3 vols (1994) |
| Williams, G., *Sex* | Gordon Williams, *Shakespeare, Sex and the Print Revolution* (1996) |
| Williams, G. W., 'Entrance' | George Walton Williams, 'The Entrance of Calchas and the Exit of Cressida', *ShN*, 44.2 (Spring 1994), 5, 18 |
| Williams, P., 'Second Issue' | Philip Williams, Jr, 'The "Second Issue" of Shakespeare's *Troilus and Cressida*, 1609', *SB*, 2 (1949–50), 25–33 |
| Williams, P., '*TC*' | Philip Williams, Jr, 'Shakespeare's *Troilus and Cressida*: The Relationship of Quarto and Folio', *SB*, 3 (1950–1), 131–43 |
| Wilson, D. | Douglas B. Wilson, 'The Commerce of Desire: Freudian Narcissism in Chaucer's *Troilus and Criseyde* and Shakespeare's *Troilus and Cressida*', *English Language Notes*, 21 (1983) 11–22 |
| Wilson, J. D. | J. Dover Wilson, *The Essential Shakespeare* (Cambridge, 1935) |
| Wind | Edgar Wind, *Pagan Mysteries in the Renaissance*, new and enlarged edn (New York, 1958) |
| Wright, G. | George T. Wright, *Shakespeare's Metrical Art* (Berkeley, 1988) |
| Wright, J. | Joseph Wright, *The English Dialect Dictionary* (1898–1905) |
| Wright, T. | Thomas Wright, *The Passions of the Mind* (1601) |
| Wyatt | *Sir Thomas Wyatt: The Complete Poems*, ed. R. A. Rebholz (New Haven, 1978) |
| Yates | Frances A. Yates, 'Elizabethan Chivalry: The Romance of the Accession Day Tilts', *JWCI*, 20 (1957), 4–25 |
| Yeats, *Autobiography* | William Butler Yeats, *Autobiography* (New York, 1953) |
| Yeats, *Essays* | William Butler Yeats, *Essays and Introductions* (1961) |
| Yoder, A. | Audrey Yoder, *Animal Analogy in Shakespeare's Character Portrayal* (New York, 1947) |
| Yoder, R. A. | R. A. Yoder, '"Sons and Daughters of the Game": An Essay on Shakespeare's *Troilus and Cressida*', *SS*, 25 (1972), 11–25 |
| Zimmerman | Susan Zimmerman, ed., *Erotic Politics: Desire on the Renaissance Stage* (New York and London, 1992) |

# INDEX

Adams, Howard 73
Adelman, Janet xx, 68
Admiral's men 375, 393–4
Adrian, Max, actor 96–7, 101
Aeschylus 127n. 129n., 196n., 370n.
Agrippa, Cornelius 186n.
Ajax, son of Oileus 389
Alciati, Andreas 160n., 360n.
Alexander, Bill, director 117n.
Alexander, Peter 88, 413
Anacreon 355n.
Andromeda 298n.
Annis, Francesca, actress 103
Apollo 137n., 192, 195n, 196n., 337n.
Aquinas, Thomas 69, 248n.
Arachne 82, 324n., 372n.
Argus 356n.
Ariadne 82, 372n.
Aristophanes 364n.
Aristotle 200n., 201n., 356n., 359n.,
    362n., 363n., 379
Armstrong, Alun, actor 111–12
Athene 366n., 389
Atkins, Robert, director 39, 94, 98
Atreus 35
Aurora (Eos) 171n., 195n.

Baker, Sean, actor 110
Bakhtin, M. 80
Bartholomew (Bartholomaeus de
    Proprietatibus Rerum) 356n., 359n.,
    363n.
Barfoot, C. C. 72
Baroque, the 79
Barry, Richard Jones, actor 27, 102
Barton, John, director 27–8, 36, 39, 51,
    59, 66, 101–5, 108
Bayley, John 77
Baylis, Lilian, director 94–5
Beale, Simon Russell, actor 113–15
Bednarz, James 10
Belleau, Rémy 355n.
Bellerophon 298n., 357n.
Benoît de Sainte-Maure 338n., 381–2
Benson, F. R., director 94

Berger, Jr., Harry 74
Betterton, Thomas, actor 92
Betterton, Mary Saunderson, actress 92
Bible, The: 1 Samuel 255n., 290n.,
    338n.; Job 157n., 217n., 239n., 357n.;
    Psalms 200n., 264n., 284n., 350n.,
    367n.; Proverbs 187n., 189n., 367n.;
    Ecclesiastes 188n.; Song of Solomon
    39, 364n.; Joel 331n.; Zachariah
    157n., 357n.; 1 Esdras 367n.; Esther
    290n.; Matthew 149n., 157n., 158n.,
    186n., 187n., 193n., 224n., 226n.,
    251n., 361n., 362n., 367n.; Luke
    157n., 186n., 226n., 318n., 363n.;
    John 321n.; Romans 200n., 280n.,
    355n., 364n.; 1 Corinthians 360–1n.;
    2 Corinthians 279n., 364n.; Ephesians
    364n.; Hebrews 157n.; 1 John 190n.
Billington, Michael, reviewer 111, 115
Birch, Frank, director 94
Blayney, Peter 398–9
Boccaccio, Giovanni 382
Boethius, Anicius Manlius Severinus
    164n., 359n., 379
Bonian, Richard, stationer 399, 401
Boreas 158n.
Bowen, Barbara 75, 103, 117
Brecht, Bertolt 79, 112
Briarius 356n.
Bridges-Adams, W., director 94
Browne, Thomas 363n.
Bryden, Ronald, reviewer 102
Burbage, Richard, actor 7
Burden, Suzanne, actress 105–7
Burghley, William Cecil, Lord 15, 18,
    254n., 355n., 366n.
Burke, David, actor 111
Burton, Robert, Anatomy of Melancholy
    186n.

Caballero, Katia, actress 114
Calderon, Paul, actor 116
Camp, Bill, actor 116
Catullus 366n.
Caxton, William, Recuyell 37, 65, 78,

128n., 129n., 130n., 136n., 137n., 149n., 156n., 174n., 182n., 291n., 294n., 300n., 301n., 331n., 338n., 339n., 342n., 344n., 345n., 348n., 357n., 366n., 370n., 373n., 377, 380, 381, 383, 386–92, 394–6
Cecil, Robert 15, 18, 254n., 366n.
Cerberus 184n.
Chamberlain's men 11, 16–17, 394, 398
Chambers, E. K. 413–18
Chapel Children 375
Chapman, George 10, 12, 15, 21, 129n., 137n., 161n., 228n., 247n., 356n., 358n., 366n., 376–80, 396
*Charlemagne* (a play) 409
Charnes, Linda 22
Charon 336n., 364n.
Chaucer, Geoffrey, *Troilus and Criseyde* 29, 37, 49, 59, 72, 89n., 118n., 127n., 136n., 143n., 231n., 232n., 240n., 267n., 268n., 279n., 292n., 293n., 350n., 356n., 364n., 381–5, 388, 391–3
*Canterbury Tales, The* 146n., 148n.
Chettle, Henry 375, 393–4
Chevalier au Cygne 370n.
Chimera, the 298n., 357n.
Chiron 306n.
Church, Tony, actor 103–7
Cicero 72, 358n., 359n., 361n., 362n., 365n.
Clarke, Larry 70
Coghill, Nevill 89
Coleridge, Samuel Taylor 4
Common Prayer, The Book of 232n., 363n.
Condell, Henry 401, 405, 422
Conti, Natale 184n.
Cook, Carol 72
Copland, William, stationer 386
Counter-Renaissance 79
Coveney, Michael, reviewer 108
Covent Garden, Theatre Royal in 92–3
Creede, Thomas, stationer 386
Cuffe, Henry, secretary to Essex, 15n.
Cushman, Robert, reviewer 104

Daphne 137n.
Dardanus, founder of Troy 130n.
Dares Phrygius 381
Davies, Howard, director 25, 28, 54, 59, 66, 108–11
Davies, Sir John 359n., 360n., 363n., 365n., 379

de Rougemont, Denis 76–7
Dekker, Thomas 6–7, 9, 365n., 371n., 375, 393–4
Denison, Michael, actor 96
Devereux, *see* Essex
Dexter, Sally, actress 113
Diana (Artemis) 319n.
Dictys the Cretan 381
Dillane, Richard, actor 114
Diogenes the Cynic 370n.
Donaldson, Talbot 384, 393
Dolman, John, translator of Cicero 365n.
Donne, John 78, 153n.
Dorset Garden Theatre 90
Drayton, Michael 372n.
Drury Lane, Theatre Royal in 92
Dryden, John 90–2, 118n., 369n.
Duncan, Lindsay, actress 111
Dusinberre, Juliet 74
Dutton, Richard 400

Eagleton, Terry 68
Edwards, Philip 79
Eld, George, printer 399, 401
Elizabeth I, Queen of England 6, 11–12, 14–17, 254n., 355n., 366n.
Elizabethan Stage Society 93
Elliot, Denholm, actor 101
Ellis, Robin, actor 103
Ellis-Fermor, Una 68, 79
Elton, William 68–9
Elyot, Sir Thomas 358n., 379
Engle, Lars 71
Erasmus, Desiderius 158n., 177n., 208n., 233n., 237n., 239n., 361n., 362n., 365n., 366n.
Essex, Robert Devereux, second Earl of 6, 11–18, 94, 254n.
Euripides 32n., 127n., 129n., 358n., 379
Europa 309n.
Evans, Edith, actress 93
Everett, Barbara 79

Fates, the three 298n.
Fearon, Ray, actor 114
Field, Nathan, 225n.
Finkelpearl, Philip 88
Fiston, William, reviser of Caxton 386
Florio, John 247n., 306n., 336n.
Fly, Richard 79
Francis, Clive, actor 60, 114
Freud, Sigmund 42n., 46n.
Freund, Elizabeth 81
Fry, Charles, director 93

Frye, Northrop 4
Furnivall, F. J. 413

Gaines, Barbara, director 117n.
Gascoigne, George 393
Gingold, Hermione, actress 93
Globe Theatre xvii, 3, 89, 353n., 400
Godfrey, Derek, actor 102
Godfrey, Michael, actor 98
Golding, Arthur, translator of Ovid
    137n., 167n., 356n., 363n., 380
Gosson, Philip 145n.
Grant, Steve, reviewer 114
Gray's Inn 89
Great Queen Street Theatre 93
Greene, Gayle 72
Greene, Robert 362n., 371n., 375, 386,
    395
Greg, W. W. 409
Grimald, Nicholas 362n., 375
Guido delle Colonne 382, 386, 391
Guthrie, Tyrone, director 59, 66, 100,
    110

Hack, Keith, director 36, 103n.
Hades, god of underworld 39, 364n.
Hakluyt, Richard 358n.
Hall, Adrian, director 103n.
Hall, Arthur, translator of the *Iliad* 376
Hall, Joseph 10, 183n.
Hall, Peter, director 51, 59, 101–2
Hamilton, Victoria, actress 60, 114
Hands, Terry, director 21, 24, 51, 59,
    104–7, 110
Hanmer, Thomas 424
Harbage, Alfred 6
Harfouch, Corinna, actress 112
Harington, John 9
Harris, Rosemary, actress 100
Harvey, Laurence, actor 99
Haydn, Hiram 78–9
Hazlitt, William 4
Hecuba, wife of Priam 366n., 381
Helios 214n., 351n.
Heminges, John 401, 405, 422
Henryson, Robert, *The Testament of
    Cresseid* 384, 392–4
Henslowe, Philip 375, 393–4
Hercules 35, 85, 128n., 361n., 370n., 386
Hesiod 357n.
Hesione, Priam's sister 21, 31, 35, 38,
    72, 128n., 182n., 194n., 195n., 291n.,
    294n., 361n., 386–7, 389

Heywood, John 368n.
Heywood, Thomas, *The Iron Age* 294n.,
    362n., 375, 378, 386, 394–7
Hiller, Wendy, actress 100
Hinds, Ciaran, actor 113
*Histriomastix* 161n.
Hobbes, Thomas 68–9
Hodgdon, Barbara 99, 104
Homer, *Iliad* 12, 21, 23, 26, 28–9, 65,
    127n., 129n., 138n., 139n., 156n.,
    167n., 180n., 182n., 325n., 337n.,
    348n., 355n., 356n., 358n., 366n.,
    370n., 375–80, 387, 389–91
    *Odyssey* 85n., 169n., 357n., 365n.
Homilies 162n., 358n., 379
Honigmann, E. A. J. 17–18, 421
Hooker, Richard 164n., 201n., 358n.,
    359n., 379
Horace 192n., 355n.
*Hortus Sanitatis* 356n., 363n.
Howard, Alan, actor 27, 102
Hoyle, Martin, reviewer 114
Hudson, H. N. 419
Huff, Neal, actor 116
humours theory 140n., 180n., 198n.,
    201n., 210n., 308n., 361n.
Hunter, Chris, actor 104
Hurry, Leslie, set designer 101
Hyland, Peter 75
Hyperion 214n., 351n.

Ibsen and Ibsenism 92
Inns of Court 5, 88–9, 419–21
Iris 181n.

Jaggard, William, printer 402, 405
James I, King of England 363n.
Jamyn, Amadis, translator 376
Jeffrey, Peter, actor 110
Jensen, Phebe 418–19, 421–2
Jongh, Nicholas, reviewer 114
Jonson, Ben 6–11, 42n., 121n., 161n.,
    355n.
Jorgensen, Paul xix
Joseph of Exeter 381
Judge, Ian, director 36, 59–60, 114–15,
    368n.
Juno 181n., 389
Juvenal 346n.

Kastan, David Scott xx
Kaula, David 76–7
Keats, John 248n.
Kellner, Catherine, actress 116
Kemble, John Philip, actor 90n.
Kempe, Will, actor 10–11
Keown, Eric, reviewer, 100, 101
King, T. J. 89, 127n.
King's men 3, 18, 88, 400
Knight, G. Wilson 77
Knights, L. C. 4, 77
Kohler, Estelle, actress 108
Kott, Ian 4
Kyd, Thomas 154n.
Kyle, Barry, director 103–4

Langham, Michael, director 103n.
Laomedon 31, 35, 128n., 299n., 361n.,
  370n., 386
Lawrence, W. W. 88
Lee, Mary, actress 92
Lefèvre, Raoul 156n., 386
Leslie, John, *A Treatise of Treasons* 366n.
Lesser, Anton, actor 106
Levin, Bernard, reviewer 101
Levine, Laura 75
Llewellyn, Raymond, actor 105
Lodge, Thomas 174n.
Lucian 362n., 370n.
Lydgate, John, *Troy Book* 78, 129n.,
  130n., 174n., 182n., 291n., 292n.,
  301n., 338n., 339n., 342n., 344n.,
  345n., 348n., 366n., 370n., 380–1, 383,
  386–92, 394–5
Lyly, John *Euphues* 358n.
  *Midas* 359n.
  *Campaspe* 370n.
  *Sappho and Phao* 228n.

Machiavelli, Niccolò 69
Macowan, Michael, director 36, 59, 66,
  96–7, 100
Maddermarket Theatre 95
Mallin, Eric 16–17
Malone, Edmond 88
Mann, Jill 72
Mannerism 79n.
Manning, Hugh, actor 98
Marcuse, Herbert 42n.
Marlowe, Christopher, *Doctor Faustus*
  xvi, 149n., 272n., 358n.
  *Tamburlaine Parts I and II* 358n.,
  360n., 362n.

Marlowe Society, of Cambridge
  University 94, 98
Mars (Ares) 84–5, 184n., 297n., 303n.,
  325n., 366n.
Marston, John 6–7, 9–20, 87–8, 355n.,
  369n., 395–6
Martial 370n.
Marx, Karl 72
Marvel, Elizabeth, actress 116
Mask Theatre Company, London 96–7
McAlindon, T. 80
McCabe, Richard, actor 114
Mead, Stephen 71
Medusa 357n.
Medwall, Henry 68n.
Mendes, Sam, director 36, 58–9, 66,
  113–14
Mercury (Hermes) 192n., 203n.
Meres, Francis, *Palladis Tamia* 121n.
Merrison, Clive, actor 111
Michell, Keith, actor 99
Miller, J. Hillis 81
Miller, Jonathan, director 28–9, 105–8
Milton, John 236n.
Mirren, Helen, actress 102
Monck, Nugent, director 95
Montaigne, Michel de 69, 247n., 365n.
Morand, Sylvester, actor 113
More, Thomas 358n.
Mountjoy, Charles Blount, Lord 14
Mowat, Barbara xvi
Mulcaster, Richard 362n.
Murray, Stephen, actor 96

Nelson, Tim Blake, actor 116
Neoptolemus, son of Achilles 255n.,
  294n., 366n.
Newlin, Jeanne 96
Nightingale, Benedict, reviewer 116
Nokes, David, reviewer 104–5
Nosworthy, J. M. 419, 426

O'Connor, Joseph, actor 110
Oenone, deserted by Paris 395
Old Vic Theatre 100
Omphale 85
Open Air Theatre, Regent's Park 98
Orestes 35, 387
Ornstein, Robert 46
O'Toole, Peter, actor 101
Ovid, *Metamorphoses* 85n., 137n., 167n.,
  169n., 192n., 299n., 309n., 325n., 351n.,
  356n., 357n., 358n., 360n., 362n., 363n.,
  366n., 372n., 378n., 379–81, 395

*Fasti* 167n.
*Heroides* 229n.
*Remedia Amoris* 382
Palmer, Kenneth xxi, 86
Papp, Joseph, director 104
Parker, Patricia 71
Parnassus trilogy 7, 11
Pavlov, Muriel, actress 99
Payne, B. Iden, director 94–5
Pearce, G. M. 105
Peele, George 375, 386
Pegasus 298n., 357–8n.
Peleus, Achilles' father 247n.
Perseus 158n., 298n., 357n.
Persius 365n., 366n.
Petronius 42n.
Pico della Mirandola 85
*Piers Plowman* 360n.
Plato 358n., 365n., 370n.
Platt, Hugh 12
Plautus 1, 3, 121n.
Pliny, *Natural History* 329n., 356n.,
    358n., 359n., 363n.
Plutarch 85
Pluto 254n., 372n.
Plutus, god of riches 254n.
Poel, William, director 39, 93–5
Polyxena, daughter of Priam and Hecuba
    254n., 255n., 256n., 366n., 389–91
Pope, Alexander 424
Poseidon 357n., 361n.
Potter, A. M. 78
Proserpina 184n.
Proudfoot, Richard xx
Prudentius, *Psychomachia* 355n.
Ptolemaic universe 162–3n.
Publilius Syrus, *Sententia* 237n.
Purchase, Bruce, actor 104
Puttenham George, *Arte of English Poesie*
    80, 166n., 232n., 238n., 279n., 298n.,
    307n., 323n., 328n.
Pyrrhus, Achilles's son 255n., 298n.,
    372n.; see also Neoptolemus
Pythagoras 358n., 359n.

Quayle, Anthony, director and actor 36,
    98–9

Rasmussen, Eric xvii
Read, David, actor 98
Richards, I. A. 81
Rickman, Alan, actor 111
Roberts, James, stationer 18, 398

Roberts, Jeanne Addison 81–2
Rodway, Norman, actor 102, 113
Rogers, Paul, actor 100
Rollins, Hyder 393
Romano, Giulio 34
Ronsard, Pierre de 355n.
Root, Amanda, actress 113
Rose Theatre 375, 393
Ross, Oriel, actress 96–7
Rossiter, A. P. 78
Roy, Emil 30
Royal Shakespeare Company 60, 103–5,
    107–15, 368n.
Royle, Carol, actress 104
Rutter, Carol, actress and theatre critic
    102, 105
Rylands, George, director 98, 99n.

Salel, Hugues, translator 376
Samxon, Jehan, translator 376
Saviolo, Vincent 12, 337n.
Scofield, Paul, actor 98
Scot, Reginald, *Discovery of Witchcraft*
    239n.
Sedgwick, Eve Kosovsky 26
Segar, William, *Book of Honor and Arms*
    337n.
Seneca 158n. 246n., 365n., 366n.
Shakespeare, William
    *All's Well That Ends Well* 5, 92, 128n.,
        188n., 194n., 198n., 273n., 349n.,
        357n., 367n., 370n., 371n.
    *Antony and Cleopatra* xx, 32n., 47,
        64n., 85, 91, 304n., 308n., 357n.,
        359n., 364n., 365n., 373n.
    *As You Like It* 11, 131n., 184n.,
        192n., 209n., 231n., 239n., 353n.
    *Comedy of Errors, The* 89, 93
    *Coriolanus* 4, 32, 183n., 184n., 233n.,
        236n., 274n., 298n., 363n., 402
    *Cymbeline* 31, 274n., 361n.
    *Hamlet* xvi, xvii, 5, 19, 32, 75, 82, 84,
        87–9, 147n., 159n., 213n., 214n.,
        275n., 289n., 292n., 298n., 307n.,
        308n., 318n., 330n., 334n., 340n.,
        362n., 372n., 401, 412
    *Henry IV, Part I* 48–9, 64n., 65n., 66,
        144n., 152n., 153n., 162n., 192n.,
        256n., 292n., 307n., 335n., 356n.,
        368n., 371n., 394, 400
    *Henry IV, Part II* xvi, 255n., 299n.,
        300n., 325n., 335n., 341n., 361n.,
        370n., 394

*Henry V* xvi, xvii, 5, 14–16, 138n.,
  162n., 163n., 182n., 187n., 188n.,
  222n., 310n., 341n., 359n., 393
*Henry VI, Part I* 359n.
*Henry VI, Part II* xvi, 57–8, 370n.
*Henry VI, Part III* xvi
*Henry VIII* 357n. 402
*Julius Caesar* 4–5, 32, 248n., 254n.,
  259n., 363n.
*King John* 4
*King Lear* xvi, xviii, 81, 188n., 229n.,
  293n., 300n., 310n., 356n., 372n.,
  400–1, 412
*Love's Labour's Lost* 144n., 147n.,
  153n., 213n., 258n., 298n., 308n.,
  314n., 335n., 361n., 410, 421
*Macbeth* xix, 139n., 145n., 259n.,
  262n., 276n., 317n., 326n., 332n.,
  361n.
*Measure for Measure* 5, 92–3, 108,
  184n., 198n., 255n., 335n., 361n.,
  365n.
*Merchant of Venice, The* 40n., 57,
  182n., 305n., 308n., 359n., 394
*Merry Wives of Windsor, The* xvi,
  187n., 250n., 310n., 368n.
*Midsummer Night's Dream, A* xvii, 58,
  128n., 195n., 232n., 275n.
*Much Ado about Nothing* 57, 226n.,
  236n., 262n., 346n.
*Othello* xvi, xviii, 45n., 99, 142–3n.,
  169n., 183n., 184n., 224n., 315n.,
  359n., 368n., 371n., 412
*Rape of Lucrece, The* 31–2, 89n.,
  160n., 368n.
*Richard II* 4, 16, 18, 187n., 188n., 331n.
*Richard III* 56n., 75n., 146n., 299n.
*Romeo and Juliet* 40, 43, 53, 59, 64,
  74n., 93, 120n., 147n., 150n., 152n.,
  183n., 228n., 260n., 262n., 272n.,
  275n., 281n., 314n., 365n., 367n.,
  368n., 402–3, 410
*Sonnets* 5, 42n., 49n., 57–8, 134n.,
  233n., 281n., 337n., 367n.
*Taming of the Shrew, The* 49–50,
  215n., 224n., 293n.
*Tempest, The* 183n., 365n.
*Timon of Athens* 5, 264n., 265n.,
  365n., 402
*Titus Andronicus* 305n., 357n.
*Troilus and Cressida*
  date 11, 17–18
  epilogue, function of 59, 64–5,
    417–22

Essex rebellion, context for 11–19
genre and experimentalism 3–6
Greek generals, deglamourization
  of 22–9
imagery and recurring motifs: animal
  imagery 81–2; appearance and
  reality 77; capitalism, early
  modern, the shift to 70; chivalry,
  decline of 15–16, 70; commercial
  valuation 37–8, 67–72; decon-
  struction of language 80–1;
  disease, metaphors of 84; eating,
  cooking, appetite, metaphors of
  82–3; feudalism, decline of 16–17,
  70; fragmentation, disjunction,
  discontinuity 45–6, 76–81;
  homosocial interactions,
  bisexuality 21, 26–9, 59–64;
  inflation, commercial and
  linguistic 71–2; Mars-Venus-
  Vulcan 84–5; mercantile voyaging,
  images of 67–8; metatheatricality
  19–20, 75–6; mirroring and
  reflected images, specular images
  73, 75; performance and
  expectation, the gap between 40,
  76–7; relativity of worth,
  subjectivity 68–9, 94; scepticism
  69–70, 75; self-knowing, failures of
  74, 186n.; time as renewer and
  destroyer 85–7
male nightmares about women
  57–8
male obsessions with honour and
  chivalry 37–46, 70
notoriety of reputation 20, 22ff.,
  41, 59
performance history 3, 87–117
publisher's preface 1–3, 400–1
sources 375–97
text, publishing history 3, 17–19,
  398–429
Thersites as satirist and choric
  figure 65–7
Trojan warriors, deflation of 29–37
War of the Theatres, context for
  6–11
women as objects of desire 47–59
*Twelfth Night* 49n., 144n., 182n.,
  205n., 219n., 231n., 262n., 368n.,
  393
*Two Gentlemen of Verona, The* 49n.
*Venus and Adonis* 85, 232n., 358n.,
  365n.

*Winter's Tale, The* 152n., 231n., 302n., 357n., 361n., 364–5n., 368n.
Shakespeare Memorial Theatre, Stratford-upon-Avon 99
Shaw, George Bernard 92
Shaw, Glen Byam, director 59, 99
Sheridan, Richard Brinsley 298n.
Sidney, Sir Philip 15
Siegel, Paul 79
Skybell, Stephen, actor 116
Smith, Bruce 28
Smock Alley, Dublin 90
Soellner, Rolf 69–70
Sophocles 162n., 366n., 370n., 379
Southall, Raymond 70, 83
Southampton, Henry Wriothesley, third Earl of 15–16
Speaight, Robert, actor and theatre critic 93, 96, 101
Speght, Thomas 392
Spenser, Edmund, *The Faerie Queene*, 14, 129n., 358n., 365n., 379
Spinella, Stephen, actor 116
Spurgeon, Caroline 82
Squire, William, actor 98
Staff, Ivan, actor 98
Stannard, Heather, actress 98
Stein, Arnold 78
Stevenson, Juliet, actress 108–110
Suchet, David, actor 104–5
Swanston, Hamish F. G. 79
Swinburne, Algernon Charles 4
Swinley, Ion, actor 95

Tandy, Jessica, actress 101
Taylor, Gary xviii, 111–13, 417–19, 421–3
Telamon, father of Ajax and Teucer 35, 128, 361n., 370n., 386, 389
Terence 1, 3, 121n., 187n.
Tethys, wife of Oceanus 158n.
Teucer, son of Telamon and Hesione 389
Theobald, Lewis 424
Theocritus 370n.
Theseus 372n.
Thetis, mother of Achilles 158n., 170n., 247n.
Thomas, Vivian 80–1, 110
Thompson, Ann xx
Thorndike, Russell, actor 98
Thynne, Francis, ed. Chaucer 392
Topsell, Thomas 356n., 363n.
Tunie, Tamara, actress 116
Turner, Jerry, director 103n.

Tutin, Dorothy, actress 101
Tylee, Claire 72, 109
Typhon or Typhoeus 167n.
Tyrone, Hugh O'Neill, second Earl of 14

Udall, Nicholas 375, 378

Valla, Lorenzo, translator 376
Van Griethuysen, Ted, actor 101
Venus (Aphrodite) 84–5, 121n., 167n., 220n., 298n., 358n., 389
Virgil, *Aeneid* 32, 39, 197n., 255n., 355n., 356n., 362n., 364n.
Visconti, Luchino, director 100n.
Voss, Philip, actor 115
Vulcan (Hephaestus) 84–5, 167n., 325n., 370n.

Walker, Alice xvi, 417
Walker, W. S. 419
Walley, Henry, stationer 88, 399, 401
Walsingham, Francis 366n.
Walton, William, 117n.
War of the Theatres 6–7, 11
Wardle, Irving, reviewer 105, 108, 113
Warren, Michael xviii
Warren, Roger 109
Wekwerth, Manfred, director 111–2
Wells, Stanley 108
Werstine, Paul xvi, 406, 409
Wheeler, Richard 57–8
Whetstone, George 393
Whitgift, John, Archbishop of Canterbury 355n.
Wilcher, Robert, reviewer 109
Wilders, John 106
William, David, director 117n.
Williams, Clifford, actor 100
Williams, George Walton 367–8n.
Williams, Michael, actor 102
Wing-Davey, Mark, director 36, 59, 116
Withals, John 366n.
Wood, Terry, actor 105
Worde, Winkyn de, early printer 386
Wright, Thomas, *Passions of the Mind* 365n., 366n.
Wyatt, Sir Thomas 365n.

Yeats, William Butler 4

Zeffirelli, Franco, director and set designer 100n.
Zeus (Jove, Jupiter) 130n., 172n., 192n., 206n., 299n., 309n., 340n., 358n.